SOCIAL PSYCHOI

MW01108379

Editor
Mark H. Davis
Eckerd College

Mark H. Davis received a doctorate in psychology from the University of Texas at Austin and is currently an associate professor at Eckerd College, in St. Petersburg, Florida. He is a member of the American Psychological Association and serves as a consulting editor for the *Journal of Personality and Social Psychology*. His primary research interest is the study of empathy. He is the author of a number of articles on this topic, as well as the book *Empathy: A Social Psychological Approach* (Westview Press, 1996).

Annual Editions
A Library of Information from the Public Press
Dushkin Publishing Group/Brown & Benchmark Publishers
Sluice Dock, Guilford, Connecticut 06437

The Annual Editions Series

ANNUAL EDITIONS is a series of over 65 volumes designed to provide the reader with convenient, low-cost access to a wide range of current, carefully selected articles from some of the most important magazines, newspapers, and journals published today. ANNUAL EDITIONS are updated on an annual basis through a continuous monitoring of over 300 periodical sources. All ANNUAL EDITIONS have a number of features that are designed to make them particularly useful, including topic guides, annotated tables of contents, unit overviews, and indexes. For the teacher using ANNUAL EDITIONS in the classroom, an Instructor's Resource Guide with test questions is available for each volume.

VOLUMES AVAILABLE

Abnormal Psychology
Adolescent Psychology
Africa
Aging
American Foreign Policy
American Government
American History, Pre-Civil War
American History, Post-Civil War
American Public Policy
Anthropology
Archaeology
Biopsychology
Business Ethics
Child Growth and Development
China
Comparative Politics
Computers in Education
Computers in Society
Criminal Justice
Criminology
Developing World
Deviant Behavior
Drugs, Society, and Behavior
Dying, Death, and Bereavement

Early Childhood Education
Economics
Educating Exceptional Children
Education
Educational Psychology
Environment
Geography
Global Issues
Health
Human Development
Human Resources
Human Sexuality
India and South Asia
International Business
Japan and the Pacific Rim
Latin America
Life Management
Macroeconomics
Management
Marketing
Marriage and Family
Mass Media
Microeconomics

Middle East and the
  Islamic World
Multicultural Education
Nutrition
Personal Growth and Behavior
Physical Anthropology
Psychology
Public Administration
Race and Ethnic Relations
Russia, the Eurasian Republics,
  and Central/Eastern Europe
Social Problems
Social Psychology
Sociology
State and Local Government
Urban Society
Western Civilization,
  Pre-Reformation
Western Civilization,
  Post-Reformation
Western Europe
World History, Pre-Modern
World History, Modern
World Politics

Cataloging in Publication Data
Main entry under title: Annual Editions: Social psychology. 1997/98.
    1. Psychology—Periodicals. I. Davis, Mark, comp. II. Title: Social psychology.
302'.05   ISBN 0–697–35425–3

© 1997 by Dushkin Publishing Group/Brown & Benchmark Publishers, Guilford, CT 06437

Copyright law prohibits the reproduction, storage, or transmission in any form by any means of any portion of this publication without the express written permission of Dushkin Publishing Group/Brown & Benchmark Publishers, and of the copyright holder (if different) of the part of the publication to be reproduced. The Guidelines for Classroom Copying endorsed by Congress explicitly state that unauthorized copying may not be used to create, to replace, or to substitute for anthologies, compilations, or collective works.

Annual Editions® is a Registered Trademark of Dushkin Publishing Group/
Brown & Benchmark Publishers, a Times Mirror Higher Education Group company.

First Edition

Printed in the United States of America

Printed on Recycled Paper

Editors/Advisory Board

Members of the Advisory Board are instrumental in the final selection of articles for each edition of ANNUAL EDITIONS. Their review of articles for content, level, currentness, and appropriateness provides critical direction to the editor and staff. We think that you will find their careful consideration well reflected in this volume.

EDITOR

Mark H. Davis
Eckerd College

ADVISORY BOARD

Anita P. Barbee
University of Louisville

Bernardo J. Carducci
Indiana University Southeast

Susan E. Cross
Iowa State University

Stephen L. Franzoi
Marquette University

Karen Freiberg
*University of Maryland
Baltimore*

Curtis Haugtvedt
Ohio State University

Martin Heesacker
University of Florida - Gainesville

Don Riggio
*California State University
Fullerton*

Mark Schaller
University of British Columbia

James Sheppard
University of Florida

Jonathan Springer
Kean College of New Jersey

Charles Stangor
*University of Maryland
College Park*

Michael R. Stevenson
Ball State University

Shelly A. Theno
*University of Alaska
Anchorage*

Fred W. Whitford
Montana State University

Staff

Ian A. Nielsen, Publisher

EDITORIAL STAFF

Roberta Monaco, Developmental Editor
Addie Raucci, Administrative Editor
Cheryl Greenleaf, Permissions Editor
Deanna Herrschaft, Permissions Assistant
Diane Barker, Proofreader
Lisa Holmes-Doebrick, Program Coordinator

PRODUCTION STAFF

Brenda S. Filley, Production Manager
Charles Vitelli, Designer
Shawn Callahan, Graphics
Lara M. Johnson, Graphics
Laura Levine, Graphics
Mike Campbell, Graphics
Libra A. Cusack, Typesetting Supervisor
Juliana Arbo, Typesetter
Jane Jaegersen, Typesetter
Marie Lazauskas, Word Processor
Larry Killian, Copier Coordinator

To the Reader

In publishing ANNUAL EDITIONS we recognize the enormous role played by the magazines, newspapers, and journals of the *public press* in providing current, first-rate educational information in a broad spectrum of interest areas. Many of these articles are appropriate for students, researchers, and professionals seeking accurate, current material to help bridge the gap between principles and theories and the real world. These articles, however, become more useful for study when those of lasting value are carefully *collected, organized, indexed,* and *reproduced* in a *low-cost format,* which provides easy and permanent access when the material is needed. That is the role played by ANNUAL EDITIONS. Under the direction of each volume's *academic editor,* who is an expert in the subject area, and with the guidance of an *Advisory Board,* each year we seek to provide in each ANNUAL EDITION a current, well-balanced, carefully selected collection of the best of the public press for your study and enjoyment. We think that you will find this volume useful, and we hope that you will take a moment to let us know what you think.

The field of contemporary social psychology is a little difficult to define. Historically, of course, it was easier. Initially, social psychology was the study of groups (or crowds, or mobs), and, in particular, the effect that groups had on individual behavior. As the years have gone by, however, social psychology has steadily expanded its focus to encompass phenomena that are less clearly "social" in nature. Social psychologists today now study a wide variety of topics, some of which necessarily involve groups (even if the group is only two people), but many of which deal with internal cognitive processes that can occur when a person is completely alone.

In fact, one way to define contemporary social psychology is this: it scientifically examines the thoughts, feelings, and actions of normal humans. As you may notice, this is an incredibly broad definition. While it eliminates persons with psychological disorders, it keeps for itself the study of virtually anything that the average person might think, feel, or do. The good news, for those about to read this book, is that many of the most interesting kinds of human activity will be represented here.

The form in which social psychological research is usually summarized and communicated is the research article, written by scientists for scientists. The goal in such writing is precision and, although it is sometimes hard to believe, clarity. Unfortunately, such writing is often impossible for a nonprofessional audience to understand or enjoy. The purpose of this volume is to provide interesting, highly readable examples of some of the ideas and insights that social psychology can offer about the human experience. The selections come primarily from magazines and newspapers in the popular press, a medium that sacrifices some detail and precision in exchange for a much livelier style of writing. My hope is that by reading these articles in conjunction with your textbook, you can have greater appreciation for just how fascinating and important the topics of social psychology can be.

This volume is divided into ten units, each of which deals with issues falling into one of contemporary social psychology's areas of concern. Although social psychology textbooks differ somewhat in how they "carve up" these topics, you will probably find that each of the units in this volume corresponds, at least roughly, to one of the chapters in your text. The articles generally fall into one of two categories. Some of them describe, in an interesting and readable way, social psychological research in a particular topic area. Other selections take a different approach, and explicitly try to apply social psychological findings to real-world problems and events. Some articles, of course, do both.

Although the units are organized so as to mirror the content usually found in social psychology textbook chapters, you might also find it useful to consult the *Topic Guide* that appears after the Table of Contents. This guide indicates how each article in the volume is related to a number of different topics that have traditionally been of concern to social psychology. Thus, no matter how your own textbook is organized, it should be possible to find articles in this volume that are relevant to any subject.

Finally, I hope that you will take the time to provide some feedback to guide the annual revision of this anthology. You can do this by completing and returning the article rating form in the back of the book; by doing so you will help us understand which articles are effective and which are not. Because you hold in your hand the very *first* edition of *Annual Editions: Social Psychology,* your help in the revision process would be very much appreciated. Thank you.

Mark H. Davis
Editor

Contents

UNIT 1

Self and Personality

Seven articles in this section examine the evolution of an individual's personality and sense of self.

The concepts in bold italics are developed in the article. For further expansion please refer to the Topic Guide and the Index.

UNIT 2

Social Perception

Five selections in this section consider the process of how an individual develops social perception.

UNIT 3

Attitudes

Four articles in this section discuss how an individual's attitude can be influenced by memory, other people's opinion of them, and propaganda.

UNIT 4

Social Cognition

Five articles in this section discuss how an individual gains a sense of reality and social understanding.

UNIT 5

Social Influence

Four selections in this section look at what social dynamics influence an individual.

UNIT 6

Social Relationships

Five articles in this section consider how social affiliation and love establish personal relationships.

UNIT 7

Prejudice, Discrimination, and Stereotyping

Six articles in this section look at what influences an individual's sense of prejudice, discrimination, and stereotyping.

The concepts in bold italics are developed in the article. For further expansion please refer to the Topic Guide and the Index.

UNIT 8

Aggression

Six selections in this section consider how biology, early social experiences, and the mass media impact on the level of an individual's aggression.

UNIT 9

Helping

Four articles in this section examine how an individual develops a sense of social support and personal commitment.

The concepts in bold italics are developed in the article. For further expansion please refer to the Topic Guide and the Index.

Topic Guide

This topic guide suggests how the selections in this book relate to topics of traditional concern to psychology students and professionals. It is useful for locating articles that relate to each other for reading and research. The guide is arranged alphabetically according to topic. Articles may, of course, treat topics that do not appear in the topic guide. In turn, entries in the topic guide do not necessarily constitute a comprehensive listing of all the contents of each selection.

TOPIC AREA	TREATED IN	TOPIC AREA	TREATED IN
Accuracy	8. Spotting Lies 9. EQ Factor 10. EQ	Compliance	23. Committed Heart 24. What Is the Influence of One Flower Given? 25. Suspect Confessions
Advertising	15. What's in a Brand? 16. Mindless Propaganda, Thoughtful Persuasion	Conflict	30. What Makes Love Last? 40. In an Angry World 43. Roots of Good and Evil
Affiliation	26. Nation of Hermits	Conformity	22. Making Sense of the Nonsensical 48. Blowup 49. '90s Style Brainstorming
Aggression	33. Psychologists Examine Attacks on Homosexuals 37. Biology of Violence 38. Violence in the Blood 39. Big. Bad. Bully. 40. In an Angry World 41. Televised Violence and Kids 42. Frankenstein Must Be Destroyed	Cooperation	43. Roots of Good and Evil 50. New Post-Heroic Leadership
		Deception	8. Spotting Lies
Attachment	29. Lessons of Love	Decision Making	13. Attitude Affects Memory, Decisions, and Performance 18. Road to Reward Is Rutted with Psychological Peril 47. Group Decision Fiascoes Continue 48. Blowup
Attribution	11. Inferential Hopscotch		
Automatic and Controlled Processes	11. Inferential Hopscotch 19. Mindfulness and Mindlessness 20. Influences from the Mind's Inner Layers 31. Prejudice Is a Habit That Can Be Broken 32. Breaking the Prejudice Habit	Discrimination	33. Psychologists Examine Attacks on Homosexuals 34. Crimes against Humanity 35. Whites' Myths about Blacks
Biology	7. Are You Shy? 37. Biology of Violence 38. Violence in the Blood 40. In an Angry World 43. Roots of Good and Evil	Education	2. Race and the Schooling of Black Americans
		Elaboration Likelihood Model	16. Mindless Propaganda, Thoughtful Persuasion
Brainstorming	49. '90s Style Brainstorming	Emotions	3. Who Is Happy? 4. At Last, a Rejection Detector!
Childhood and Adolescence	2. Race and the Schooling of Black Americans 7. Are You Shy? 39. Big. Bad. Bully. 40. In an Angry World 41. Televised Violence and Kids 42. Frankenstein Must Be Destroyed 45. Getting By with a Little Help	Empathy	9. EQ Factor 10. EQ 45. Getting By with a Little Help
		Evolutionary Psychology	28. Up from Gorilla Land 29. Lessons of Love 37. Biology of Violence
Cognitive Biases	18. Road to Reward Is Rutted with Psychological Peril 19. Mindfulness and Mindlessness 47. Group Decision Fiascoes Continue	Gender	28. Up from Gorilla Land 36. Gendered Media
Cognitive Dissonance	22. Making Sense of the Nonsensical	Group Productivity	49. '90s Style Brainstorming
		Groupthink	47. Group Decision Fiascoes Continue 48. Blowup
Community	26. Nation of Hermits 27. Laughs		

TOPIC AREA	TREATED IN	TOPIC AREA	TREATED IN
Helping	43. Roots of Good and Evil 44. Volunteerism and Society's Response to the HIV Epidemic 45. Getting By with a Little Help 46. Mobilization and Deterioration of Social Support Following Natural Disasters	Prejudice	31. Prejudice Is a Habit That Can Be Broken 32. Breaking the Prejudice Habit 34. Crimes against Humanity
		Self-Concept	1. Body Mania 2. Race and the Schooling of Black Americans 6. Decline and Fall of Personality 39. Big. Bad. Bully.
Leadership	22. Making Sense of the Nonsensical 50. New Post-Heroic Leadership		
Legal System	25. Suspect Confessions	Self-Esteem	2. Race and the Schooling of Black Americans 3. Who Is Happy? 4. At Last, a Rejection Detector!
Love	28. Up from Gorilla Land 29. Lessons of Love 30. What Makes Love Last?		
		Self-Fulfilling Prophecy	12. Motivational Approaches to Expectancy Confirmation
Mass Media	36. Gendered Media 41. Televised Violence and Kids 42. Frankenstein Must Be Destroyed	Social Inference	11. Inferential Hopscotch 12. Motivational Approaches to Expectancy Confirmation
Memory	13. Attitude Affects Memory, Decisions, and Performance		
		Social Support	3. Who Is Happy? 26. Nation of Hermits 33. Psychologists Examine Attacks on Homosexuals 46. Mobilization and Deterioration of Social Support Following Natural Disasters
Motivations	12. Motivational Approaches to Expectancy Confirmation 13. Attitude Affects Memory, Decisions, and Performance 15. What's in a Brand? 44. Volunteerism and Society's Response to the HIV Epidemic		
		Stereotyping	2. Race and the Schooling of Black Americans 20. Influences from the Mind's Inner Layers 21. In Japan, Blood Type Can Be Key to Success—or Failure 31. Prejudice Is a Habit That Can Be Broken 35. Whites' Myths about Blacks 36. Gendered Media
Personality	3. Who Is Happy? 6. Decline and Fall of Personality 7. Are You Shy? 9. EQ Factor 10. EQ		
		Stress	46. Mobilization and Deterioration of Social Support Following Natural Disasters
Persuasion	14. How Do You Persuade? 15. What's in a Brand? 16. Mindless Propaganda, Thoughtful Persuasion 22. Making Sense of the Nonsensical 23. Committed Heart		
		Subjective Well-Being	3. Who Is Happy? 7. Are You Shy? 26. Nation of Hermits
Physical Attractiveness	1. Body Mania	Thought Suppression	17. Forbidden Thinking

Self and Personality

- Self-Concept (Articles 1–3)
- Self-Esteem (Articles 4 and 5)
- Personality (Articles 6 and 7)

What are you *really* like? Are you extraverted or introverted? Are you optimistic or pessimistic? The kind of person who is spontaneous and impulsive, or the kind who is organized and orderly?

How do you define yourself? That is, if called upon to describe yourself to others, which characteristics would you mention first? Would it be personality characteristics, such as extraversion, shyness, impulsivity, and so on? Would it be physical characteristics such as your height, weight, speed, strength, or physical attractiveness? Would you mention social categories such as your sex, race, religion, or nationality? Finally, no matter which of these characteristics you focus on, what is your overall evaluation of yourself—that is, do you generally see yourself in a positive or negative light?

As you can see from these questions, there are many ways in which people can define themselves, and an issue of considerable interest to contemporary social psychologists is where these different views of the self come from, and what implications they have for how we act. This interest in the individual self, however, is of relatively recent vintage; traditionally the field of social psychology placed more emphasis on the ways in which individuals are influenced by situations. That is, the traditional approach was to manipulate features of the situation and see what effect it had on behavior. Essentially, in this approach people were thought to be similar and interchangeable; the focus was on the role of environmental factors.

More recently, contemporary social psychology has recognized the important role played by stable characteristics of the individual. That is, not only do certain situations tend to make all people act alike, but some people act in consistent ways no matter what the situation. Thus, one feature of modern social psychology is the realization that personality variables—shyness, self-esteem, and many more—can be important influences on human behavior. This growing emphasis on the self has also coincided with modern social psychology devoting considerable attention to understanding the notion of self-concept: that is, how people go about acquiring self-knowledge, organizing and integrating such knowledge, and how self-information then influences our thoughts, feelings, and actions.

The three sections of this unit address the issues of self and personality in several ways. The first subsection deals with the notion of self-concept. In "Body Mania," Judith Rodin describes the growing obsession in our culture with body image. Increasingly, she argues, we have come to define ourselves in terms of such physical characteristics as attractiveness. In large part this is the result of the declining importance of other characteristics (income, education, family ties) that traditionally defined us and our role in society. The second selection, "Race and the Schooling of Black Americans," argues that the components of self-concept frequently differ between white Americans and African Americans. Author Claude Steele contends that while performance in school is typically a significant influence on the self-esteem of white children, it frequently is not for African American children. In essence, Steele believes, these children learn that there are few rewards for them in educational settings, and so they come to define their self-worth in nonacademic ways. The final selection in this section, "Who Is Happy?" takes a different approach to the issue of self-concept and examines the factors that contribute to a generally happy and satisfied outlook on the world.

The second subsection addresses the issue of self-esteem. The first article, "At Last, A Rejection Detector!" describes recent work by Mark Leary that indicates that self-esteem levels can be thought of as a gauge by which we measure our social standing: rejection by others leads to lower self-esteem and acceptance by others to higher esteem. The value of such a gauge is that it can signal us when it is necessary to do repair work to increase our social standing. In "Is Self-Esteem Really All That Important?" author Randall Edwards reports on the controversy surrounding the issue of whether self-esteem leads to personal success, or whether personal success leads to self-esteem.

The final subsection deals with the general issue of personality. In his article "The Decline and Fall of Personality," Kenneth Gergen makes the provocative claim that the rapid evolution of modern technology has had powerful repercussions for the notion of personality and self-concept. In his view, the traditional idea of a genuine, "real" self has become increasingly irrelevant. The final

selection in this unit, "Are You Shy?" reviews research on this very common trait, arguing that shyness is determined both by inherited temperament and by experiences during early childhood.

Looking Ahead: Challenge Questions

Of what does a person's self-concept consist? Which characteristics are the most important in determining how a person views the self? Why would people differ in the kind of characteristics they use to define the self? In particular, what differences in self-concept would you expect to find between men and women? People of different ethnic groups? People of different socioeconomic status?

What determines a person's level of self-esteem? How important is self-esteem for influencing that person's behavior? Does low self-esteem lead to violence, drug addiction, teenage pregnancy, and so on? Defend your answer. How successful are programs designed to increase self-esteem?

Is there such a thing as a "true self," or are we all social chameleons, changing our behaviors to fit whatever situation we are in? How could you tell what your "true" self is? What would make it the "true" one?

Body Mania

After a lifetime of work on the body-image front, one of the country's leading experts reveals her insights into the dilemma—and offers a way out

Judith Rodin, Ph.D.

Judith Rodin, a professor of psychology, medicine, and psychiatry at Yale University, is the author of more than 200 articles and papers as well as Breaking the Body Traps *(William Morrow, 1992). She is codirector of the Yale Center for Eating and Weight Disorders and past president of the Society for Behavioral Medicine.*

If *Pygmalion* were written today it would not be a story about changing Eliza Doolittle's speech, clothing, or manners, but rather about changing her face and body. Using methods from face-lifts to miracle diets to liposuction, women in increasing numbers are striving—with a degree of panic and, more often than not, to their own detriment—to match the ultimate template of beauty.

Has the situation worsened in the past few decades? The answer is undeniably yes. Since beginning this research 20 years ago, I have witnessed growing concern with appearance, body, and weight among women of all ages. Men, too, no longer seem immune.

In 1987, PSYCHOLOGY TODAY published the results of a survey of readers' feelings about appearance and weight. Only 12 percent of those polled indicated little concern about their appearance and said they didn't do much to improve it. The results of this survey are similar to those of many studies where the participants are selected at random: People feel intense pressure to look good.

An earlier survey on body image was published in PSYCHOLOGY TODAY in 1972. The 1970s respondents were considerably more satisfied with their bodies than were the 1980s respondents. The pressure to look good has intensified for both sexes in the last two decades. As the table below shows, our dissatisfaction has grown for every area of our bodies.

Unhappy Bodies

THE SURVEY ALSO SHOWS HOW IMPORTANT weight has become to body image; it is the focus of dissatisfaction in both studies and the area showing the greatest increase. I recently evaluated a survey for *USA Today* which also showed identical results. People today are far more critical of themselves for not attaining the right weight and look.

Body preoccupation has become a societal mania. We've become a nation of appearance junkies and fitness zealots, pioneers driven to think, talk, strategize, and worry about our bodies with the same fanatical devotion we applied to putting a man on the moon. Abroad, we strive for global peace. At home, we have declared war on our bodies.

It is a mistake to think that concern with appearance and weight is simply an aberration of contemporary Western culture. Generations of ancient Chinese women hobbled themselves by binding their feet in order to match the beauty ideal of the time. And we all remember Scarlett O'Hara in search of the 17-inch waist. What *Gone With The Wind* did not show us was that tight corseting induced shortness of breath, constipation, and, occasionally, uterine prolapse. But if we moderns are following a tradition hallowed by our forebears, the industrialization of fitness and beauty is conspiring with other trends to raise the stakes to their highest point in history.

Of all the industrial achievements of the 20th century that influence how we feel about our bodies, none has had a more profound effect than the rise of the mass media. Through movies, magazines, and TV, we see beautiful people as often as we see our own family members; the net effect is

People Dissatisfied With Body Areas or Dimensions

1972	MEN	WOMEN	1987	MEN	WOMEN
Height	13%	13%	Height	20%	17%
Weight	35	48	Weight	41	55
Muscle Tone	25	30	Muscle Tone	32	45
Overall Face	8	11	Face	20	20
Breast/Chest	18	26	Upper Torso	28	32
Abdomen	36	50	Mid Torso	50	57
Hips and Upper Thighs	12	49	Lower Torso	21	50
Overall	15	25	"Looks As They Are"	34	38

From *Psychology Today*, January/February 1992, pp. 56-60. Excerpted from *Breaking the Body Traps* by Judith Rodin. © 1992 by Judith Rodin. Reprinted by permission of William Morrow and Company, Inc.

to make exceptional beauty appear real and attainable. Narcissus was lucky: He had only to find a lake. The modern woman has television, in which she doesn't see herself reflected.

In my experience as a researcher and clinician, I have found that many women avoid the mirror altogether; those who do look may scrutinize, yet still fail to see themselves objectively. Most of us see only painful flaws in exquisite detail. Others still see the fat and blemishes that used to be there in the teenage years, even if they're no longer there.

Like a perverse Narcissus, a woman today looks at her reflection in a mirror and finds it wanting—and then is consumed by a quest to make herself fit the reflection the media has conditioned her to expect is possible. She works harder and harder to attain what is, as I will explain, most likely impossible. Ignoring the hours movie stars spend on makeup and hair, forgetting how easily and well the camera can lie, she aspires to a synthetic composite of what she thinks her reflection should be.

It is also likely that she is unaware of what other research shows: Such detailed attention has a negative influence on self-esteem. It makes us feel that many features of ourself are flawed, even those having little to do with weight or appearance.

Many of us have traveled through the looking glass with Alice into a world where what is and what might be blur and confuse us. We may be thin and think we are not. We may be heavy and think that life isn't worth living because we do not match our culture's physical ideal. Our self-image has become far too plastic, too malleable. It depends too much on transitory moods, on what we feel is expected of us and how we feel we are lacking. It is not dependent enough upon a stable internal sense of ourself. We grow larger or smaller, in our mind's eye, in response to the image of woman modern society has encouraged us to idealize.

Unlike Alice, however, we have not returned. We are stuck there in a world of obsessional self-criticism, where what we see is not at all what we really are. The mirror is woman's modern nemesis.

Some call such obsession with appearance vanity—but that misses the point. We are responding to the deep psychological significance of the body. Appearance does indeed affect our sense of self and how people respond to us; it always has, always will. What's different today is that the body and how it looks has become a significant component of our self-worth.

Why Now?

WHY DO WEIGHT AND APPEARANCE MATTER so much? And why now? What is occurring at this particular moment in time?

Our society has changed dramatically in this century. There are few remaining hierarchies or social structures based on religion, parentage, money, or education. Society has become more egalitarian, but intrinsic to human nature is the desire to judge, evaluate, and compare ourselves to others. If class and lineage no longer provide the tools for measuring ourselves against our neighbors, what are the new social standards? It is my premise that they are the more visible, tangible, observable aspects—first among these, the physical self.

Our bodies have become the premier coin of the realm. Appearance, good looks, and fitness are now the measure of one's social worth. How closely we can approximate a perfect body has also unfortunately become a sign of how well we're doing in life.

Not only is how we look suddenly of the utmost importance, but we have also come to accept and idealize a single image of beauty—slim but fit. The media now expose us to this single "right" look, and the beauty industry promises it is attainable by all. When the prescription for how we should look is so well-defined, deviations are all the more noticeable.

What's more, our culture holds out the lure of an easy fix for all corporeal dissatisfactions. The goal of looking good is attainable by anyone, as long as he or she works out hard enough, exercises long enough, and eats little enough.

Beauty, health, diet, and fitness have become very big businesses. But they weren't always. During the late l950s and early '60s—when models and Miss Americas wore girdles, did a little exercise just for their thighs and hips, and wore a size l0—only overweight women dieted. A survey of *Ladies Home Journal* issues from the 1960s showed an average of only one diet article every six months. But by the mid-'70s almost every woman in America had tried some kind of diet, and losing weight was a national obsession.

Because we sincerely believe that the perfect body is attainable by anyone, Americans spend more on beauty and fitness aids than they do on social services or education. Such distribution of a primary resource is a shocking revelation of our true priorities.

Yet another reason appearance is everything today hinges on the blurring of traditional definitions of female and male. Our view of the differences between the sexes is in flux, as women move into such traditionally male domains as the office and men become more involved in the household. In many ways our bodies remain our most visible means of expressing the differences between the sexes. Having the right body may be a way for women who have moved into male occupations to declare their feminine identity without compromising their professional persona.

Asked to make it in a man's world, they are, like the rest of society, still confused about women's roles. Internalizing society's ambivalence, they succeed in one domain and fall back in the other, reverting to the traditionally feminine arena of competition over thinness and beauty.

In addition, the fitness movement, taken to extremes, has fostered the notion that a "good" physique not only equals a healthy body but a healthy soul. Getting in shape has become the new moral imperative—an alluring substitute for altruism and good work, the desire to look good replacing the desire to do good. In this new secular morality, values and ideals of beauty and appearance supplement moral and religious standards.

Today's moral transgressions involve eating something we feel we shouldn't have or feeling we don't look good enough or haven't tried hard enough to look good.

If our current self-absorption has its reasons, it also has its comforts. The quest for physical perfection is the up-to-date way we barter with the uncertainty of life. Like a set of worry beads, we always have our calories to count, our minutes of aerobics to execute. If everything else in our lives seems out of control, we at least have our diet and exercise regimens. In the chaos called modern life, ordering the body to do what we want it to may give us a much-needed illusion of control.

Where we differ, too, from our forebears is that the body today is no longer considered a finished product, a fait accompli. It is strictly a work in progress. And we devote ourselves to perfecting it with the dedication of the true artist. According to the American Society of Plastic and Reconstructive Surgeons, "aesthetic" surgeries are up 6l percent over the past decade. A marketing research firm in New York calculates that Americans spent $33 billion on diets and diet-related services in 1990, up from $29 billion in 1989. By the turn of the century we will be spending $77 billion to lose weight—just slightly less than the entire gross national product of Belgium.

The Limits of the Body

THERE IS AN OVERRIDING FALLACY IN THIS view of ourselves. The body is not infinitely malleable in the way that advertisers with a product to sell would have us believe. Despite wide dissemination of news about great advances in science and medicine, the individual American remains virtually unaware of the role that physiology plays in body weight, in determining how quickly we lose or gain weight and in how our general health and appearance respond to exercise and diet. Most of us are exposed to and accept a staggering amount of misinformation.

Genes play a major role in setting metabolism as well as body shape and size; they determine how much fat we burn, how much we can store easily, and where it's distributed on our bodies. One of our clinic patients came from a family where everyone had thick, solid legs and big thighs. For years she tried every diet that became popular. No matter how much she lost, no matter how thin she became, she couldn't change the size of her legs and thighs nearly as much as the rest of her body. "My greatest goal in life," she admitted, "is to have thin legs....I know why women have liposuction. It's the ultimate solution. I used to dream about a big vacuum cleaner sucking out the fat—it was my constant childhood wish—but I just can't afford it yet."

The Pursuit Is Costly

THE QUEST FOR THE PERFECT BODY IS, LIKE most wars, a costly one—emotionally and physically, to say nothing of financially. It leaves most of us feeling frustrated, ashamed, and defeated. Yet we keep at it, wearing down our bodies and our optimism while narrowing the focus of our lives.

In addition, as a society obsessed with a set standard of beauty, we have become intolerant of and sometimes cruel to those who do not meet it, especially the overweight. We learn early in life that there is something shameful about obesity. And the obese are painfully stigmatized. Even children with a life-threatening chronic illness would rather be sick than fat.

We learn these antifat attitudes in childhood, and they figure strongly into

Social Attitudes Scale

Please read the following statements and indicate how strongly you agree or disagree with each.

1. A man would always prefer to go out with a thin woman than one who is heavy.

Strongly Agree	Agree Somewhat	Agree	Neither Agree nor Disagree	Disagree	Disagree Somewhat	Strongly Disagree
☐	☐	☐	☐	☐	☐	☐

2. Clothes are made today so that only thin people can look good.

Strongly Agree	Agree Somewhat	Agree	Neither Agree nor Disagree	Disagree	Disagree Somewhat	Strongly Disagree
☐	☐	☐	☐	☐	☐	☐

3. Fat people are often unhappy.

Strongly Agree	Agree Somewhat	Agree	Neither Agree nor Disagree	Disagree	Disagree Somewhat	Strongly Disagree
☐	☐	☐	☐	☐	☐	☐

4. It is not true that attractive people are more interesting, poised, and socially outgoing than unattractive people.

Strongly Agree	Agree Somewhat	Agree	Neither Agree nor Disagree	Disagree	Disagree Somewhat	Strongly Disagree
☐	☐	☐	☐	☐	☐	☐

5. A pretty face will not get you very far without a slim body.

Strongly Agree	Agree Somewhat	Agree	Neither Agree nor Disagree	Disagree	Disagree Somewhat	Strongly Disagree
☐	☐	☐	☐	☐	☐	☐

6. It is more important that a woman be attractive than a man.

Strongly Agree	Agree Somewhat	Agree	Neither Agree nor Disagree	Disagree	Disagree Somewhat	Strongly Disagree
☐	☐	☐	☐	☐	☐	☐

7. Attractive people lead more fulfilling lives than unattractive people.

Strongly Agree	Agree Somewhat	Agree	Neither Agree nor Disagree	Disagree	Disagree Somewhat	Strongly Disagree
☐	☐	☐	☐	☐	☐	☐

8. The thinner a woman is, the more attractive she is.

Strongly Agree	Agree Somewhat	Agree	Neither Agree nor Disagree	Disagree	Disagree Somewhat	Strongly Disagree
☐	☐	☐	☐	☐	☐	☐

9. Attractiveness decreases the likelihood of professional success.

Strongly Agree	Agree Somewhat	Agree	Neither Agree nor Disagree	Disagree	Disagree Somewhat	Strongly Disagree
☐	☐	☐	☐	☐	☐	☐

These items test how much you believe that appearance matters. Score your responses as follows:

For items 1, 2, 3, 5, 7, and 8, give yourself a zero if you said "strongly disagree"; a 2 for "disagree"; up to a 6 for "strongly agree."

Items 4, 6, and 9 are scored in reverse. In other words, give yourself a zero for "strongly agree" and a 6 for "strongly disagree."

Add together your points for all nine questions. A score of 46 or higher means that you are vulnerable to being influenced by the great importance that current society places on appearance.

why normal-weight people greatly fear becoming overweight. In our research, we hear many people state that they would kill themselves if they were fat. While this is just a figure of speech, some overweight people are so unhappy about their appearance that they *do* contemplate suicide. A few follow through.

The accompanying test will give you an idea of how much you subscribe to society's standards of beauty.

The vast majority of American women have accepted at face value the message we have been continually exposed to: that beauty and physical perfection are merely a matter of personal effort and that failure to attain those goals is the result of not doing enough. Consequently, we are now subjecting ourselves and even our children to an ever more complicated regimen of diet, exercise, and beauty. We have come to believe in what I see as the "techno-body," shaped by dieting and surgical techniques.

Humans appear to be the only animals who decline to eat when hungry, who willingly starve the body. Occasionally they do it to feed the soul. Many religions have institutionalized fasting as a way of asking for redemption. But in the more modern version of these self-denial rituals, people fast and starve, purge and renew in search of a better self.

It has become fashionable, even politically correct, to worry about the environment. We rally to plant trees to save the Earth without even realizing that at the very same moment in history we are defacing and dehumanizing our bodies by using chemical peels, dermabrasion, hair dye, synthetic diet foods, and fake fats and sweeteners. Where is our concern for the human part of our environment?

What Is the Problem?

MY STUDIES SHOW THAT SURGERY, DIET, and exercise are only symptoms of the real problem: body preoccupation and an obsessive concern with body image. In accepting the quick fix as a solution, we are overlooking the depth and complexity of the problem we are facing. Shedding pounds, counting calories, and pumping iron—manifestations of body preoccupation—are only a reflection of the fact that we now believe the body is the window to the self, perhaps even the soul.

The psychological self is fundamental to our preoccupation with the physical self. Of all the ways we experience ourselves, none is so primal as the sense of our own bodies. Our body image is at the very core of our identity. Our feelings about our bodies are woven into practically every aspect of our behavior. Our bodies shape our identity because they are the form and substance of our persona to the outside world. Appearance will always be important because we are social beings. How we look sends messages, whether we want it to or not, and people respond to us accordingly.

The old saw cites death and taxes, but in fact we have one other nonnegotiable contract in life: to live in and with our bodies for the duration. People must learn to treat the issue of body image seriously and validate their concerns about their bodies. In my clinical experience, people find that hard to do because admitting how deeply we anguish about our bodies often leads to a profound sense of shame.

In an era of acid rain, AIDS, nuclear disaster, and poverty, we are embarrassed by our body preoccupation—but that, of course, does not stop it.

Getting Out of the Body Trap

RECOGNIZING THE PROBLEM IS THE FIRST step to solving it. Our work has shown that people do better when they are nonjudgmental about their concerns with body, diet, and exercise patterns. These are not trivial worries and complaints, but painful experiences and issues deserving attention. It is crucial to acknowledge the scope and depth of what you are feeling. No one is alone in their body concerns. All women share them to some extent—as do many men these days, as well.

If you treat your body with more respect, you will like it better. What your body really needs is moderate exercise, healthy foods, sensual pleasures, and relaxation. Give it those, and it will respond by treating you better. Not everyone can afford expensive trinkets or clothes, but everyone can afford small indulgences—a long, warm bath, a half-hour of time off, a new haircut. Some of you will be amazed at how hard it is to do something nice for yourself. But treating your body better will make you feel better about yourself.

To break the body-image barrier, we must bring self-image into focus. When people worry about how they look, they are worrying about who they are. That's not necessarily good, but we need to acknowledge that there is a deep connection between the two. In my work with patients, I strive to help them overcome the feeling that their happiness rises or falls depending on what the scale said that morning.

We must also look at what we really want and need from our lives and pursue those goals; it is not wise to continue expending so much of our creative energy on thinness and appearance. Since our bodies are not infinitely plastic, it may be easier to add other joys to life than to subtract pounds. Increasing and nurturing self-complexity by expanding the number of roles we value may boost health in many ways. Current research suggests that multiple roles are typically health enhancing. Varying our routines and adding new interests to our lives will help broaden our horizons so that how we look is not the sum of what we are.

As a character in Henry Jaglom's movie *Eating* says, "Twenty or thirty years ago, sex was the secret subject of women. Now it's food." In fact, sex and food have become interchangeable. "I like the feel of food. I don't like knives and forks because I like to touch it all over," says one woman. Another: "I think it is erotic. It's the safest sex you can have, eating." Food. It is comfort, balm for a trying day in a trying world, sometimes even more. Moderation is the best advice. It is the key to body sanity.

Whether we want to value, accept, or change our bodies, we need first to change our minds. We have to relearn how we observe ourselves. Instead of searching for flaws, we must attempt to see ourselves objectively. We must scrutinize our appearance less.

Caring about our bodies is normal, but how we look has become far too significant. Women have become martyrs to their appearance, slaves of that impossible master, perfection. Men go through life judged mostly on their achievements; women bear the burden of society's image. Although the effort is exhausting and painful, the deep, psychological significance of the body has made it seem worthwhile.

The burden of maintaining a perfect body image is far too costly. Women are crippled by a tragic degree of self-consciousness that limits other aspects of their lives—friendships, careers, even families.

One of the most important steps toward changing your body image is to have compassion for the millions of women struggling with their own body-image problems—especially for yourself. It is time to face the person you see in the mirror with profound new insight: She hasn't been worrying about nothing. In fact, she hasn't been taking the real problem, body preoccupation, seriously enough. Neither has society. It's time to understand the price she has been paying and help her shed that burden.

Race and the Schooling of Black Americans

*Claude Steele's article from the **Atlantic Monthly** is a perceptive and troubling analysis of why black children are more likely than their white counterparts to fail in school. Steele notes the subtle and not-so-subtle ways that lead young blacks to "disidentify" with school, to resist measuring themselves against the values and goals of the classroom. He advocates the concept of "wise schooling," in which teachers and classmates see value and promise in black children rather than the opposite. Although he does not refer directly to them, note how Steele's analysis fits very well with modern social psychological theories about the development and maintenance of self-esteem.*

Claude M. Steele

My former university offered minority students a faculty mentor to help shepherd them into college life. As soon as I learned of the program, I volunteered to be a mentor, but by then the school year was nearly over. Undaunted, the program's eager staff matched me with a student on their waiting list—an appealing nineteen-year-old black woman from Detroit, the same age as my daughter. We met finally in a campus lunch spot just about two weeks before the close of her freshman year. I realized quickly that I was too late. I have heard that the best way to diagnose someone's depression is to note how depressed you feel when you leave the person. When our lunch was over, I felt as gray as the snowbanks that often lined the path back to my office. My lunchtime companion was a statistic brought to life, a living example of one of the most disturbing facts of racial life in America today: the failure of so many black Americans to thrive in school. Before I could lift a hand to help this student, she had decided to do what 70 percent of all black Americans at four-year colleges do at some point in their academic careers—drop out.

I sense a certain caving-in hope of America that problems of race can be solved. Since the sixties, when race relations held promise for the dawning of a new era, the issue has become one whose persistence causes "problem fatigue"—resignation to an unwanted condition of life.

This fatigue, I suspect, deadens us to the deepening crisis in the education of black Americans. One can enter any de-segregated school in America, from grammar school to high school to graduate or professional school, and meet a persistent reality: blacks and whites in largely separate worlds. And if one asks a few questions or looks at a few records, another reality emerges: these worlds are not equal, either in the education taking place there or in the achievement of the students who occupy them.

As a social scientist, I know that the crisis has enough possible causes to give anyone problem fatigue. But at a personal level, perhaps because of my experience as a black in American schools, or perhaps just as the hunch of a myopic psychologist, I have long suspected a particular culprit—a culprit that can undermine black achievement as effectively as a lock on a schoolhouse door. The culprit I see is *stigma*, the endemic devaluation many blacks face in our society and schools. This status is its own condition of life, different from class, money, culture. It is capable, in the words of the late sociologist Erving Goffman, of "breaking the claim" that one's human attributes have on people. I believe that its connection to school achievement among black Americans has been vastly underappreciated.

This is a troublesome argument, touching as it does on a still unhealed part of American race relations. But it leads us to a heartening principle: if blacks are made less racially vulnerable in school, they can overcome even substantial obstacles. Before the good news, though, I must at least sketch in the bad: the worsening crisis in the education of black Americans.

Despite their socioeconomic disadvantages as a group, blacks begin school with test scores that are fairly close to the test scores

From *Psychology Is Social: Readings and Conversations in Social Psychology*, 3/E by Edward Krupat, 1994, pp. 54–66. Originally from *The Atlantic Monthly*, April 1992, pp. 68–78. © 1992 by Claude Steele. Reprinted by permission.

of whites their age. The longer they stay in school, however, the more they fall behind; for example, by the sixth grade blacks in many school districts are two full grade levels behind whites in achievement. This pattern holds true in the middle class nearly as much as in the lower class. The record does not improve in high school. In 1980, for example, 25,500 minority students, largely black and Hispanic, entered high school in Chicago. Four years later only 9,500 graduated, and of those only 2,000 could read at grade level. The situation in other cities is comparable.

Even for blacks who make it to college, the problem doesn't go away. As I noted, 70 percent of all black students who enroll in four-year colleges drop out at some point, as compared with 45 percent of whites. At any given time nearly as many black males are incarcerated as are in college in this country. And the grades of black college students average half a letter below those of their white classmates. At one prestigious university I recently studied, only 18 percent of the graduating black students had grade averages of B or above, as compared with 64 percent of the whites. This pattern is the rule, not the exception, in even the most elite American colleges. Tragically, low grades can render a degree essentially "terminal" in the sense that they preclude further schooling.

Blacks in graduate and professional schools face a similarly worsening or stagnating fate. For example, from 1977 to 1990, though the number of Ph.D.s awarded to other minorities increased and the number awarded to whites stayed roughly the same, the number awarded to American blacks dropped from 1,116 to 828. And blacks needed more time to get those degrees.

Standing ready is a familiar set of explanations. First is societal disadvantage. Black Americans have had, and continue to have, more than their share: a history of slavery, segregation, and job ceilings; continued lack of economic opportunity; poor schools; and the related problems of broken families, drug-infested communities, and social isolation. Any of these factors—alone, in combination, or through accumulated effects—can undermine school achievement. Some analysts point also to black American culture, suggesting that, hampered by disadvantage, it doesn't sustain the values and expectations critical to education, or that it fosters learning orientations ill suited to school achievement, or that it even "opposes" mainstream achievement. These are the chestnuts, and I had always thought them adequate. Then several facts emerged that just didn't seem to fit.

For one thing, the achievement deficits occur even when black students suffer no major financial disadvantage—among middle-class students on wealthy college campuses and in graduate school among black students receiving substantial financial aid. For another thing, survey after survey shows that even poor black Americans value education highly, often more than whites. Also, as I will demonstrate, several programs have improved black school achievement without addressing culturally specific learning orientations or doing anything to remedy socioeconomic disadvantage.

Neither is the problem fully explained, as one might assume, by deficits in skill or preparation which blacks might suffer because of background disadvantages. I first doubted that such a connection existed when I saw flunk-out rates for black and white students at a large, prestigious university. Two observations surprised me. First, for both blacks and whites the level of preparation, as measured by Scholastic Aptitude Test scores, didn't make much difference in who flunked out; low scorers (with combined verbal and quantitative SATs of 800) were no more likely to flunk out than high scorers (with combined SATs of 1,200 to 1,500). The second observation was racial: whereas only two percent to 11 percent of the whites flunked out, 18 percent to 33 percent of the blacks flunked out, even at the highest levels of preparation (combined SATs of 1,400). Dinesh D'Souza has argued recently that college affirmative-action programs cause failure and high dropout rates among black students by recruiting them to levels of college work for which they are inadequately prepared. That was clearly not the case at this school; black students flunked out in large numbers even with preparation well above average.

And, sadly, this proved the rule, not the exception. From elementary school to graduate school, something depresses black achievement *at every level of preparation, even the highest.* Generally, of course, the better prepared achieve better than the less prepared, and this is about as true for blacks as for whites. But given any level of school preparation (as measured by tests and earlier grades), blacks somehow achieve less in subsequent schooling than whites (that is, have poorer grades, have lower graduation rates, and take longer to graduate), no matter how strong that preparation is. Put differently, the same achievement level requires better preparation for blacks than for whites—far better: among students with a C+ average at the university I just described, the mean American College Testing Program (ACT) score for blacks was at the 98th percentile, while for whites it was at only the 34th percentile. This pattern has been documented so broadly across so many regions of the country, and by so many investigations (literally hundreds), that it is virtually a social law in this society—as well as a racial tragedy.

Clearly, something is missing from our understanding of black underachievement. Disadvantage contributes, yet blacks underachieve even when they have ample resources, strongly value education, and are prepared better than adequately in terms of knowledge and skills. Something else has to be involved. That something else could be of just modest importance—a barrier that simply adds its effect to that of other disadvantages—or it could be pivotal, such that were it corrected, other disadvantages would lose their effect.

That something else, I believe, has to do with the process of identifying with school. I offer a personal example:

I remember conducting experiments with my research adviser early in graduate school and awaiting the results with only modest interest. I struggled to meet deadlines. The research enterprise—the core of what one does as a social psychologist—just wasn't *me* yet. I was in school for other reasons—I wanted an advanced degree, I was vaguely ambitious for intellectual work, and being in graduate school made my parents proud of me. But as time passed, I began to like the work. I also began to grasp the value system that gave it meaning, and the faculty treated me as if they thought I might even be able to do it. Gradually I began to think of myself as a social psychologist. With this change in self-concept came a new accountability; my self-esteem was affected now by what I did as a social psychologist, something that hadn't been true before. This added a new motivation to my work; self-respect, not just parental respect, was on the line. I noticed changes in myself. I worked without deadlines. I bored friends with applications of arcane theory to their daily lives. I went to conventions. I lived and died over how experiments came out.

Before this transition one might have said that I was handicapped by my black working-class background and lack of motivation. After the transition the same observer might say that even though my background was working-class, I had special advantages: achievement oriented parents, a small and attentive college. But these facts alone would miss the importance of the identification process I had experienced: the change in self-definition and in the activities on which I based my self-esteem. They would also miss a simple condition necessary for me to make this identification: treatment as a valued person with good prospects.

I believe that the "something else" at the root of black achievement problems is the failure of American schooling to meet this simple condition for many of its black students. Doing well in school requires a belief that school achievement can be a promising basis of self-esteem, and that belief needs constant reaffirmation even for advantaged students. Tragically, I believe, the lives of black Americans are still haunted by a specter that threatens this belief and the identification that derived from it at every level of schooling.

The Specter of Stigma and Racial Vulnerability

I have a good friend, the mother of three, who spends considerable time in the public school classrooms of Seattle, where she lives. In her son's third-grade room, managed by a teacher of unimpeachable good will and competence, she noticed over many visits that the extraordinary art work of a small black boy named Jerome was ignored—or, more accurately perhaps, its significance was ignored. As a genuine art talent has a way of doing—even in the third grade—his stood out. Yet the teacher seemed hardly to notice. Moreover, Jerome's reputation, as it was passed along from one grade to the next, included only the slightest mention of his talent. Now, of course, being ignored like this could happen to anyone—such is the overload in our public schools. But my friend couldn't help wondering how the school would have responded to this talent had the artist been one of her own, middle-class white children.

Terms like "prejudice" and "racism" often miss the full scope of racial devaluation in our society, implying as they do that racial devaluation comes primarily from the strongly prejudiced, not from "good people" like Jerome's teacher. But the prevalence of racists—deplorable though racism is—misses the full extent of Jerome's burden, perhaps even the most profound part.

He faces a devaluation that grows out of our images of society and the way those images catalogue people. The catalogue need never be taught. It is implied by all we see around us: the kinds of people revered in advertising (consider the unrelenting racial advocacy of Ralph Lauren ads) and movies (black women are rarely seen as romantic partners, for example); media discussions of whether a black can be President; invitation lists to junior high school birthday parties; school curricula; literary and musical canons. These details create an image of society in which black Americans simply do not fare well. When I was a kid, we captured it with the saying "If you're white you're right, if you're yellow you're mellow, if you're brown stick around, but if you're black get back."

In ways that require no fueling from strong prejudice or stereotypes, these images expand the devaluation of black Americans. They act as mental standards against which information about blacks is evaluated: that which fits these images we accept; that which contradicts them we suspect. Had Jerome had a reading problem, which fits these images, it might have been accepted as characteristic more readily than his extraordinary art work, which contradicts them.

These images do something else as well, something especially pernicious in the classroom. They set up a jeopardy of double devaluation for blacks, a jeopardy that does not apply to whites. Like anyone, blacks risk devaluation for a particular incompetence, such as a failed test or a flubbed pronunciation. But they further risk that such performances will confirm the broader, racial inferiority they are suspected of. Thus, from the first grade through graduate school, blacks have the extra fear that in the eyes of those around them their full humanity could fall with a poor answer or a mistaken stroke of the pen.

Moreover, because these images are conditioned in all of us, collectively held, they can spawn racial devaluation in all of us, not just in the strongly prejudiced. They can do this even in blacks themselves: a majority of black children recently tested said they like and prefer to play with white rather than black dolls—almost fifty years after Kenneth and Mamie Clark, conducting similar experiments, documented identical findings and so paved the way for *Brown v. Topeka Board of Education*. Thus Jerome's devaluation can come from a circle of people in his world far greater than the expressly prejudiced—a circle that apparently includes his teacher.

In ways often too subtle to be conscious but sometimes overt, I believe, blacks remain devalued in American schools, where, for example, a recent national survey shows that through high school they are still more than twice as likely as white children to receive corporal punishment, be suspended from school, or be labeled mentally retarded.

Tragically, such devaluation can seem inescapable. Sooner or later it forces on its victims two painful realizations. The first is that society is preconditioned to see the worst in them. Black students quickly learn that acceptance, if it is to be won at all, will be hard-won. The second is that even if a black student achieves exoneration in one setting—with the teacher and fellow students in one classroom, or at one level of schooling, for example—this approval will have to be rewon in the next classroom, at the next level of schooling. Of course, individual characteristics that enhance one's value in society—skills, class status, appearance, and success—can diminish the racial devaluation one faces. And sometimes the effort to prove oneself fuels achievement. But few from any group could hope to sustain so daunting and everlasting a struggle. Thus, I am afraid, too many black students are left hopeless and deeply vulnerable in America's classrooms.

"Disidentifying" with School

I believe that in significant part the crisis in black Americans' education stems from the power of this vulnerability to undercut identification with schooling, either before it happens or after it has bloomed.

Jerome is an example of the first kind. At precisely the time when he would need to see school as a viable source of self-esteem, his teachers fail to appreciate his best work. The devalued status of his race devalues him and his work in the classroom. Unable to entrust his sense of himself to this place, he resists measuring himself against its values and goals. He languishes there, held by the law, perhaps even by his parents, but not allowing achievement to affect his view of himself. This psychic alienation—the act of not caring—makes him less vulnerable to the specter of devaluation that haunts him. Bruce Hare, an educational researcher, has documented this process among fifth-grade boys in several schools in Champaign, Illinois. He found that although the black boys had considerably lower achievement-test scores than their white classmates, their overall self-esteem was just as high. This stunning imperviousness to poor academic performance was accomplished, he found, by their deemphasizing school achievement as a basis of self-esteem and giving preference to peer-group relations—a domain in which their esteem prospects were better. They went where they had to go to feel good about themselves.

But recall the young reader whose mentor I was. She had already identified with school, and wanted to be a doctor. How can racial vulnerability break so developed an achievement identity? To see, let us follow her steps onto campus: Her recruitment and admission stress her minority status perhaps more strongly than it has been stressed at any other time in her life. She is offered academic and social support services, further implying that she is "at risk" (even though, contrary to common belief, the vast majority of black college students are admitted with qualifications well above the threshold for whites). Once on campus, she enters a socially circumscribed world in which blacks—still largely separate from whites—have lower status; this is reinforced by a sidelining of minority material and interests in the curriculum and in university life. And she can sense that everywhere in this new world her skin color places her under suspicion of intellectual inferiority. All of this gives her the double vulnerability I spoke of: she risks confirming a particular incompetence, at chemistry or a foreign language, for example; but she also risks confirming the racial inferiority she is suspect of—a judgment that can feel as close at hand as a mispronounced word or an ungrammatical sentence. In reaction, usually to some modest setback, she withdraws, hiding her troubles from instructors, counselors, even other students. Quickly, I believe, a psychic defense takes over. She *disidentifies* with achievement; she changes her self-con-

ception, her outlook and values, so that achievement is no longer so important to her self-esteem. She may continue to feel pressure to stay in school from her parents, even from the potential advantages of a college degree. But now she is psychologically insulated from her academic life, like a disinterested visitor. Cool, unperturbed. But, like a pain-killing drug, disidentification undoes her future as it relieves her vulnerability.

The prevalence of this syndrome among black college students has been documented extensively, especially on predominantly white campuses. Summarizing this work, Jacqueline Fleming, a psychologist, writes, "The fact that black students must matriculate in an atmosphere that feels hostile arouses defensive reactions that interfere with intellectual performance. . . . They display academic demotivation and think less of their abilities. They profess losses of energy." Among a sample of blacks on one predominantly white campus, Richard Nisbett and Andrew Reaves, both psychologists, and I found that attitudes related to disidentification were more strongly predictive of grades than even academic preparation (that is, SATs and high school grades).

To make matters worse, once disidentification occurs in a school, it can spread like the common cold. Blacks who identify and try to achieve embarrass the strategy by valuing the very thing the strategy denies the value of. Thus pressure to make it a group norm can evolve quickly and become fierce. Defectors are called "oreos" or "incognegroes." One's identity as an authentic black is held hostage, made incompatible with school identification. For black students, then, pressure to disidentify with school can come from the already demoralized as well as from racial vulnerability in the setting.

Stimatization of the sort suffered by black Americans is probably also a barrier to the school achievement of other groups in our society, such as lower-class whites, Hispanics, and women in male-dominated fields. For example, at a large midwestern university I studied women match men's achievement in the liberal arts, where they suffer no marked stigma, but underachieve compared with men (get lower grades than men with the same ACT scores) in engineering and premedical programs, where they, like blacks across the board, are more vulnerable to suspicions of inferiority.

"Wise" Schooling

"When they approach me they see . . . everything and anything except me. . . . [This] invisibility occurs because of a peculiar disposition of the eyes. . . ."

Ralph Ellison, *Invisible Man*

Erving Goffman, borrowing from gays of the 1950s, used the term "wise" to describe people who don't themselves bear the stigma of a given group but who are accepted by the group. These are people in whose eyes the full humanity of the stigmatized is visible, people in whose eyes they feel less vulnerable. If racial vulnerability undermines black school achievement, as I have argued, then this achievement should improve significantly if schooling is made "wise"—that is, made to see value and promise in black students and to act accordingly.

And yet, although racial vulnerability at school may undermine black achievement, so many other factors seem to contribute—from the debilitations of poverty to the alleged dysfunctions of black American culture—that one might expect "wiseness" in the classroom to be of little help. Fortunately, we have considerable evidence to the contrary. Wise schooling may indeed be the missing key to the schoolhouse door.

In the mid-seventies black students in Philip Uri Treisman's early calculus courses at the University of California at Berkeley consistently fell to the bottom of every class. To help, Treisman developed the Mathematics Workshop Program, which, in a surprisingly short time, reversed their fortunes, causing them to outperform their white and Asian counterparts. And although it is only a freshman program, black students who take it graduate at a rate comparable to the Berkeley average. Its central technique is group study of calculus concepts. But it is also wise; it does things that allay the racial vulnerabilities of these students. Stressing their potential to learn, it recruits them to a challenging "honors" workshop tied to their first calculus course. Building on their skills, the workshop gives difficult work, often beyond course content, to students with even modest preparation (some of their math SATs dip to the 300s). Working together, students soon understand that everyone knows something and nobody knows everything, and learning is speeded through shared understanding. The wisdom of these tactics is their subtext message: "You are valued in this program because of your academic potential—regardless of your current skill level. You have no more to fear than the next person, and since the work is difficult, success is a credit to your ability, and a setback is a reflection only of the challenge." The black students' double vulnerability around failure—the fear that they lack ability, and the dread that they will be devalued—is thus reduced. They can relax and achieve. The movie *Stand and Deliver* depicts Jaime Escalante using the same techniques of assurance and challenge to inspire advanced calculus performance in East Los Angeles Chicano high schoolers. And, explaining Xavier University's extraordinary success in producing black medical students, a spokesman said recently, "What doesn't work is saying, 'You need remedial work.' What does work is saying, 'You may be somewhat behind at this time but you're a talented person. We're going to help you advance at an accelerated rate.'"

The work of James Comer, a child psychiatrist at Yale, suggests that wiseness can minimize even the barriers of poverty. Over a fifteen-year period he transformed the two worst elementary schools in New Haven, Connecticut, into the third and fifth best in the city's thirty-three-school system without any change in the type of students—largely poor and black. His guiding belief is that learning requires a strongly accepting relationship between teacher and student. "After all," he notes, "what is the difference between scribble and a letter of the alphabet to a child? The only reason the letter is meaningful, and worth learning and remembering, is because a *meaningful* other wants him or her to learn and remember it." To build these relationships Comer focuses on the over-all school climate, shaping it not so much to transmit specific skills, or to achieve order per se, or even to improve achievement, as to establish a valuing and optimistic atmosphere in which a child can—to use his term—"identify" with learning. Responsibility for this lies with a team of ten to fifteen members, headed by the principal and made up of teachers, parents, school staff, and child-development experts (for example, psychologists or special-education teachers). The team develops a plan of specifics: teacher training, parent workshops, coordination of information about students. But at base I believe it tries to ensure that the students—vulnerable on so many counts—get treated essentially like middle-class students, with conviction about their value and promise. As this happens, their vulnerability diminishes, and with it the companion defenses of disidentification and misconduct. They achieve, and apparently identify, as their achievement gains persist into high school. Comer's genius, I believe, is to have recognized the importance of these vulnerabilities as barriers to *intellectual* development, and the corollary that schools hoping to educate such students must learn first how to make them feel valued.

These are not isolated successes. Comparable results were observed, for example, in a Comer-type program in Maryland's Prince Georges County, in the Stanford economist Henry Levin's accelerated-schools program, and in Harlem's Central Park East Elementary School, under the principalship of Deborah Meier. And research involving hundreds of programs and schools points to the same conclusion: black achievement is consistently linked to conditions of schooling that reduce racial vulnerability. These include relatively harmonious race relations among students; a commitment by teachers and schools to seeing minority-group members achieve; the instructional goal that students at all levels of preparation achieve; desegregation at the classroom as well as the school level; and a de-emphasis on ability tracking.

That erasing stigma improves black achievement is perhaps the strongest evidence that stigma is what depresses it in the first place. This is no happy realization. But it lets in a ray of hope: whatever other factors also depress black achievement—poverty, social isolation, poor preparation—they may be substantially overcome in a schooling atmosphere that reduces racial and other vulnerabilities, not through unrelenting niceness or ferocious regimentation but by wiseness, by *seeing* value and acting on it.

What Makes Schooling Unwise

But if wise schooling is so attainable, why is racial vulnerability the rule, not the exception, in American schooling?

One factor is the basic assimilationist offer that schools make to blacks: You can be valued and rewarded in school (and society), the schools say to these students, but you must first master the culture and ways of the American mainstream, and since that mainstream (as it is represented) is essentially white, this means you must give up many particulars of being black—styles of speech and appearance, value priorities, preferences—at least in mainstream settings. This is asking a lot.

But it has been the "color-blind" offer to every immigrant and minority group in our nation's history, the core of the melting-pot ideal, and so I think it strikes most of us as fair. Yet non-immigrant minorities like blacks and Native Americans have always been here, and thus are entitled, more than new immigrants, to participate in the defining images of the society projected in school. More important, their exclusion from these images denies their contributive history and presence in society. Thus, whereas immigrants can tilt toward assimilation in pursuit of the opportunities for which they came, American blacks may find it harder to assimilate. For them, the offer of acceptance in return for assimilation carries a primal insult: it asks them to join in something that has made them invisible.

Now, I must be clear. This is not a criticism of Western civilization. My concern is an omission of image-work. In his incisive essay "What America Would Be Like Without Blacks," Ralph Ellison showed black influence on American speech and language, the themes of our finest literature, and our most defining ideals of personal freedom and democracy. In *The World They Made Together,* Mechal Sobel described how African and European influences shaped the early American South in everything from housing design and land use to religious expression. The fact is that blacks are not outside the American mainstream but, in Ellison's words, have always been "one of its major tributaries." Yet if one relied on what is taught in America's schools, one would never know this. There blacks have fallen victim to a collective self-deception, a society's allowing itself to assimilate like mad from its constituent groups while representing itself to itself as if the assimilation had never happened, as if progress and good were almost exclusively Western and white. A prime influence of American society on world culture is the music of black Americans, shaping art forms from rock-and-roll to modern dance. Yet in American schools, from kindergarten through graduate school, these essentially black influences have barely peripheral status, are largely outside the canon. Thus it is not what is taught but what is *not* taught, what teachers and professors have never learned the value of, that reinforces a fundamental unwiseness in American schooling, and keeps black disidentification on full boil.

Deep in the psyche of American educators is a presumption that black students need academic remediation, or extra time with elemental curricula to overcome background deficits. This orientation guides many efforts to close the achievement gap—from grammar school tutoring to college academic-support programs—but I fear it can be unwise. Bruno Bettelheim and Karen Zelan's article "Why Children Don't Like to Read" comes to mind: apparently to satisfy the changing sensibilities of local school boards over this century, many books that children like were dropped from school reading lists; when children's reading scores also dropped, the approved texts were replaced by simpler books; and when reading scores dropped again, these were replaced by even simpler books, until eventually the children could hardly read at all, not because the material was too difficult but because they were bored stiff. So it goes, I suspect, with a great many of these remediation efforts. Moreover, because so many such programs target blacks primarily, they virtually equate black identity with substandard intellectual status, amplifying racial vulnerability. They can even undermine students' ability to gain confidence from their achievement, by sharing credit for their successes while implying that their failures stem from inadequacies beyond the reach of remediation.

The psychologist Lisa Brown and I recently uncovered evidence of just how damaging this orientation may be. At a large, prestigious university we found that whereas the grades of black graduates of the 1950s improved during the students' college years until they virtually matched the school average, those of blacks who graduated in the 1980s (we chose only those with above-average entry credentials, to correct for more-liberal admissions policies in that decade) worsened, ending up considerably below the school average. The 1950s graduates faced outward discrimination in everything from housing to the classroom, whereas the 1980s graduates were supported by a phalanx of help programs. Many things may contribute to this pattern. The Jackie Robinson, "pioneer spirit of the 1950s blacks surely helped them endure. And in a pre-affirmative-action era, they may have been seen as intellectually more deserving. But one cannot ignore the distinctive fate of the 1980s blacks: a remedial orientation put their abilities under suspicion, deflected their ambitions, distanced them from their successes, and painted them with their failures. Black students on today's campuses may experience far less overt prejudice than their 1950s counterparts but, ironically, may be more racially vulnerable.

The Elements of Wiseness

For too many black students school is simply the place where, more concertedly, persistently, and authoritatively than anywhere else in society, they learn how little valued they are.

Clearly, no simple recipe can fix this, but I believe we now understand the basics of a corrective approach. Schooling must focus more on reducing the vulnerabilities that block identification with achievement. I believe that four conditions, like the legs of a stool, are fundamental.

- If what is meaningful and important to a teacher is to become meaningful and important to a student, the student must feel valued by the teacher for his or her potential and as a person. Among the more fortunate in society, this relationship is often taken for granted. But it is precisely the relationship that race can still undermine in American society. As Comer, Escalante, and Treisman have shown, when one's students bear race and class vulnerabilities, building this relationship is the first order of business—at all levels of schooling. No tactic of instruction, no matter how ingenious, can succeed without it.
- The challenge and the promise of personal fulfillment, not remediation (under whatever guise), should guide the education of these students. Their present skills should be taken into account, and they should be moved along at a pace that is demanding but doesn't defeat them. Their

ambitions should never be scaled down but should instead be guided to inspiring goals even when extraordinary dedication is called for. Frustration will be less crippling than alienation. Here psychology is everything: remediation defeats, challenge strengthens—affirming their potential, crediting them with their achievements, inspiring them.

But the first condition, I believe, cannot work without the second, and vice versa. A valuing teacher-student relationship goes nowhere without challenge, and challenge will always be resisted outside a valuing relationship. (Again, I must be careful about something: in criticizing remediation I am not opposing affirmative-action recruitment in the schools. The success of this policy, like that of school integration before it, depends, I believe, on the tactics of implementation. Where students are valued and challenged, they generally succeed.)

- Racial integration is a generally useful element in this design, if not a necessity. Segregation, whatever its purpose, draws out group differences and makes people feel more vulnerable when they inevitably cross group lines to compete in the larger society. This vulnerability, I fear, can override confidence gained in segregated schooling unless that confidence is based on strongly competitive skills and knowledge—something that segregated school-

ing, plagued by shortages of resources and access, has difficulty producing.

- The particulars of black life and culture—art, literature, political and social perspective, music—must be presented in the mainstream curriculum of American schooling, not consigned to special days, weeks, or even months of the year, or to special-topic courses and programs aimed essentially at blacks. Such channeling carries the disturbing message that the material is not of general value. And this does two terrible things: it wastes the power of this material to alter our images of the American mainstream—continuing to frustrate black identification with it—and it excuses in whites and others a huge ignorance of their own society. The true test of democracy, Ralph Ellison has said, is "the inclusion—not assimilation—of the black man."

Finally, if I might be allowed a word specifically to black parents, one issue is even more immediate: our children may drop out of school before the first committee meets to accelerate the curriculum. Thus, although we, along with all Americans, must strive constantly for wise schooling, I believe we cannot wait for it. We cannot yet forget our essentially heroic challenge: to foster in our children a sense of hope and entitlement to mainstream American life and schooling, even when it devalues them.

WHO IS HAPPY?

David G. Myers and Ed Diener
Hope College and University of Illinois

Address correspondence to David G. Myers, Hope College, Holland, MI 49422-9000, e-mail: myers@hope.edu, or Ed Diener, University of Illinois, Department of Psychology, 603 East Daniel St., Champaign, IL 61820, e-mail: ediener@s.psych.uiuc.edu.

A flood of new studies explores people's subjective well-being (SWB). Frequent positive affect, infrequent negative affect, and a global sense of satisfaction with life define high SWB. These studies reveal that happiness and life satisfaction are similarly available to the young and the old, women and men, blacks and whites, the rich and the working-class. Better clues to well-being come from knowing about a person's traits, close relationships, work experiences, culture, and religiosity. We present the elements of an appraisal-based theory of happiness that recognizes the importance of adaptation, cultural worldview, and personal goals.

Books, books, and more books have analyzed human misery. During its first century, psychology focused far more on negative emotions, such as depression and anxiety, than on positive emotions, such as happiness and satisfaction. Even today, our texts say more about suffering than about joy. That is now changing. During the 1980s, the number of *Psychological Abstract* citations of "well-being," "happiness," and "life satisfaction" quintupled, to 780 articles annually. Social scientists, policymakers, and laypeople express increasing interest in the conditions, traits, and attitudes that define quality of life.

Studies (see Diener & Diener, 1994) reveal that happiness is more abundant than believed by writers from Samuel Johnson ("That man is never happy for the present is so true"; Boswell, 1776/1973, Vol. 2, p. 37) to John Powell ("Professionals estimate that only 10 to 15 percent of Americans think of themselves as truly happy"; Powell, 1989, p. 4). Thomas Szasz (quoted by Winokur, 1987) summed up the assumption of many people: "Happiness is an imaginary condition, formerly attributed by the living to the dead, now usually attributed by adults to children, and by children to adults" (p. 133).

Recognizing that most people are reasonably happy, but that some people are happier than others, researchers are offering a fresh perspective on an old puzzle: Who are the happy people? Does happiness favor those of a particular age, sex, or race? Does wealth enhance well-being? Does happiness come with having certain traits? a particular job? close friends? an active faith?

The scientific study of emotional well-being is new, but theories about happiness are ages old. The philosophers of ancient Greece believed that happiness accompanies a life of intelligent reflection. "There is no fool who is happy, and no wise man who is not," echoed the Roman philosopher Cicero (in *De Finibus*). The Epicurean and Stoic philosophers offered variations on this song of happy wisdom. Aristotle regarded happiness as the *summum bonum*, the supreme good. Virtue, he believed, is synonymous with happiness. In the centuries since, sages have offered contrasting ideas about the roots of happiness. They have told us that happiness comes from knowing the truth, and from preserving healthy illusions; that it comes from restraint, and from purging ourselves of pent-up emotions; that it comes from being with other people, and from living in contemplative solitude. The list goes on, but the implication is clear: Discerning the actual roots of subjective well-being requires rigorous scientific inquiry.

MEASURING SUBJECTIVE WELL-BEING

Psychological investigations of well-being complement long-standing measures of physical and material well-being with assessments of subjective well-being (SWB). Researchers have, for example, asked people across the industrialized world to reflect on their happiness and life satisfaction. Measures range from multi-item scales to single questions, such as "How satisfied are you with your life as a whole these days? Are you very satisfied? satisfied? not very satisfied? not at all satisfied?"

Self-reports of global well-being have temporal stability in the 0.5 to 0.7 range over periods from 6 months to 6 years (Diener, 1994; Magnus & Diener, 1991). But can we believe people's answers? Or are "happy" people often "in denial" of their actual misery? It is reassuring, first, that response artifacts, such as the effects of social desirability and current mood, do not invalidate the SWB measures (Diener, Sandvik, Pavot, & Gallagher, 1991; Diener, Suh, Smith, & Shao, in press). For example, social desirability scores do correlate modestly with self-reported SWB scores, but they predict non-self-report SWB measures (such as peer reports) equally well, suggesting that social desirability is a substantive characteristic that enhances well-being.

Second, people's self-reported well-being converges with other measures (e.g., Pavot, Diener, Colvin, &

From *Psychological Science*, January 1995, pp. 10-19. © 1995 by the American Psychological Society. Reprinted by permission of Cambridge University Press.

Sandvik, 1991; Sandvik, Diener, & Seidlitz, 1993). Those who describe themselves as happy and satisfied with life seem happy to their friends and to their family members. Their daily mood ratings reveal mostly positive emotions. They recall more positive events and fewer negative events (Seidlitz & Diener, 1993). And ratings derived from clinical interviews converge well with their SWB scores.

Third, SWB measures exhibit construct validity. They are responsive to recent good and bad events and to therapy (e.g., Headey & Wearing, 1992; Sandvik et al., 1993). They correlate inversely with feeling ill (Sandvik et al., 1993). And they predict other indicators of psychological well-being. Compared with depressed people, happy people are less self-focused, less hostile and abusive, and less vulnerable to disease. They also are more loving, forgiving, trusting, energetic, decisive, creative, helpful, and sociable (Myers, 1993a; Veenhoven, 1988).

Finally, the research concerns *subjective* well-being, for which the final judge is whoever lives inside a person's skin. For all these reasons, researchers take seriously people's reports of their subjective unhappiness (or happiness), especially when supported by converging reports from informants and by observations of accompanying dysfunction (or social competence).

THE COMPONENTS OF WELL-BEING

High SWB reflects a preponderance of positive thoughts and feelings about one's life. At the cognitive level, SWB includes a global sense of satisfaction with life, fed by specific satisfactions with one's work, marriage, and other domains. At the affective level, people with high SWB feel primarily pleasant emotions, thanks largely to their positive appraisal of ongoing events. People with low SWB appraise their life circumstances and events as undesirable, and therefore feel unpleasant emotions such as anxiety, depression, and anger.

Surprisingly, positive and negative emotions correlate with different predictor variables (e.g., Costa & McCrae, 1980; Magnus & Diener, 1991). Moreover, positive and negative emotions are only weakly correlated with each other (Bradburn, 1969; Diener & Emmons, 1985). Knowing the global amount of good feeling a person experiences over time does not indicate the global amount of bad feeling the person experiences. How could this be? If good feelings exclude bad feelings at the same moment in time, then the more time one spends up the less time one can spend down. Thus, the frequencies of good and bad moods are inversely related. People who experience their good moods intensely, however, tend similarly to experience intense bad moods. For some people, high highs alternate with low lows. Others are characteristically happy, or melancholy, or unemotional.

Thus, positive and negative affect seem not to be bipolar opposites. Positive well-being is not just the absence of negative emotions. Rather, SWB is defined by

three correlated but distinct factors: the relative presence of positive affect, absence of negative affect, and satisfaction with life.

MYTHS OF HAPPINESS

So, who are the happy people? By identifying predictors of happiness and life satisfaction, psychologists and sociologists have exploded some myths.

Is Happiness Being Young? Middle-Aged? Newly Retired?

Many people believe there are notably unhappy times of life—typically the stress-filled teen years, the "midlife crisis" years, or the declining years of old age. But interviews with representative samples of people of all ages reveal that no time of life is notably happier or unhappier than others (Latten, 1989; Stock, Okun, Haring, & Witter, 1983). This conclusion is reinforced by a 1980s survey of 169,776 people representatively sampled in 16 nations (Inglehart, 1990; see Fig. 1). The predictors of happiness do change with age (e.g., satisfaction with social relations and health become more important in later life; Herzog, Rogers, & Woodworth, 1982). And the emotional terrain varies with age (teens, unlike adults, usually come up from gloom or down from elation within an hour's time; Csikszentmihalyi & Larson, 1984). Yet knowing someone's age gives no clue to the person's average sense of well-being.

Nor does one find in rates of depression, suicide, ca-

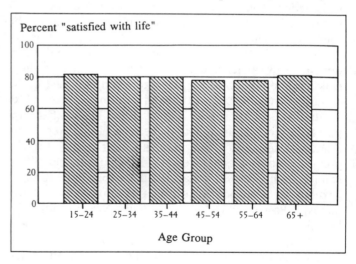

Fig. 1. Age and well-being in 16 nations. Data from 169,776 people, representatively sampled from 1980 to 1986, and reported by Inglehart (1990).

reer change, or divorce any evidence of increased personal upheaval during the supposed early 40s "midlife crisis" years. People do face crisis times, but not at any predictable age (Hunter & Sundel, 1989; McCrae &

Costa, 1990). The "empty nest syndrome"—a sense of despondency and lost meaning when children leave home—also turns out to be rare (Adelmann, Antonucci, Crohan, & Coleman, 1989; Glenn, 1975). For most couples, the empty nest is a happy place—often a place where marital happiness rebounds after the stresses of child rearing.

Does Happiness Have a Favorite Sex?

There are striking gender gaps in misery: Women are twice as vulnerable as men to disabling depression and anxiety, and men are five times as vulnerable as women to alcoholism and antisocial personality disorder (Robins & Regier, 1991). Women's more intense sadness, given bad circumstances, must be considered in light of their greater capacity for joy under good circumstances (Diener, Sandvik, & Larsen, 1985; Fujita, Diener, & Sandvik, 1991). Although women report slightly greater happiness than men when only positive emotions are assessed (Wood, Rhodes, & Whelan, 1989), the net result is roughly equal hedonic balance for women and men. In a meta-analysis of 146 studies, gender therefore accounted for less than 1% of people's global well-being (Haring, Stock, & Okun, 1984). The finding generalizes worldwide. In the 1980s collaborative survey of 16 nations, 80% of men and 80% of women said that they were at least "fairly satisfied" with life (Inglehart, 1990; see Fig. 2). A similar result appeared in a study of 18,032 university students surveyed in 39 countries (Michalos, 1991).

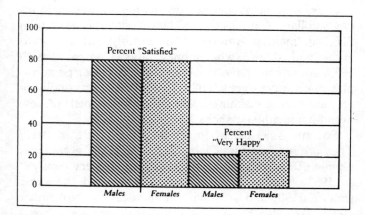

Fig. 2. Gender and well-being in 16 nations. Data from 169,776 people, representatively sampled from 1980 to 1986, and reported by Inglehart (1990).

Does Happiness Vary by Race?

Knowing someone's race or ethnic group also gives little clue to the person's psychological well-being. African-Americans, for example, report nearly as much happiness as European-Americans and are actually slightly

less vulnerable to depression (Diener, Sandvik, Seidlitz, & Diener, 1993; Robins & Regier, 1991; Stock, Okun, Haring, & Witter, 1985). Blacks and whites, like women and men, and people with and without disabilities, also score similarly on tests of self-esteem (Crocker & Major, 1989). Despite discrimination, noted Crocker and Major, people in disadvantaged groups maintain self-esteem by valuing the things at which they excel, by making comparisons within their own groups, and by attributing problems to external sources such as prejudice.

Does Happiness Vary by Culture?

Interestingly, nations differ strikingly in happiness, ranging from Portugal, where about 10% of people say they are very happy, to the Netherlands, where about 40% of people say the same (Inglehart, 1990). Nations differ markedly in happiness even when income differences are controlled for (Diener, Diener, & Diener, 1994). Although national levels of SWB covary with whether basic physical needs are met, countries such as Japan have much lower SWB than one would expect based only on material considerations. In general, collectivist cultures report lower SWB than do individualistic cultures, where norms more strongly support experiencing and expressing positive emotions (Diener, Suh, Smith, & Shao, in press).

National differences appear not to reflect mere differences in the connotations of the translated questions. For example, regardless of whether they are German-, French-, or Italian-speaking, the Swiss rank high on self-reported life satisfaction—significantly higher than their German, French, and Italian neighbors (Inglehart, 1990).

Does Money Buy Happiness?

The American dream seems to have become life, liberty, and the purchase of happiness. In 1993, 75% of America's entering collegians declared that an "essential" or "very important" life goal was "being very well off financially"—nearly double the 39% who said the same in 1970 (Astin, Green, & Korn, 1987; Astin, Korn, & Riggs, 1993). This goal topped a list of 19 possible life objectives, exceeding the rated importance even of "raising a family" and "helping others in difficulty." Most adults share this materialism, believing that increased income would make them happier (Strumpel, 1976). Few agree that money can buy happiness, but many agree that a little more money would make them a little happier.

Are wealth and well-being indeed connected? We can make the question more specific: First, are people in rich countries more satisfied than those in not-so-rich countries? As Figure 3 illustrates, the correlation between national wealth and well-being is positive (+.67, despite curious reversals, such as the Irish reporting greater life satisfaction than the wealthier West Germans). But national wealth is confounded with other variables, such as number of continuous years of democracy, which correlates + .85 with average life satisfaction (Inglehart, 1990).

Second, within any country, are rich individuals happiest? Having food, shelter, and safety is basic to well-being. Thus, in poor countries, such as Bangladesh and India, satisfaction with finances is a moderate predictor of SWB (Diener & Diener, in press). But once people are able to afford life's necessities, increasing levels of affluence matter surprisingly little. Although the correlation between income and happiness is not negative, it is modest. In the United States, one study (Diener et al., 1993) found a mere + .12 correlation between income and happiness; increases or decreases in income had no long-term influence on SWB. And Inglehart (1990) noted that in Europe, income "has a surprisingly weak (indeed, virtually negligible) effect on happiness" (p. 242). Although satisfaction with income predicts SWB better than actual income, there is only a slight tendency for people who

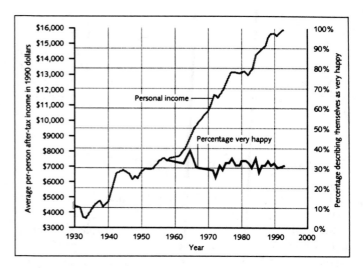

Fig. 4. Inflation-adjusted income and happiness in the United States. National Opinion Research Center happiness data from Niemi, Mueller, and Smith (1989) and T. Smith (personal communication, November 1993). Income data from Bureau of the Census (1975) and *Economic Indicators*.

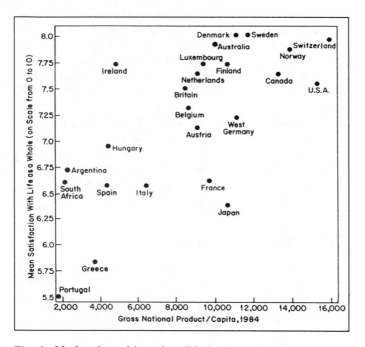

Fig. 3. National wealth and well-being in a 24-nation collaborative survey. Euro-Barometer and World Values Survey data reported by Inglehart (1990).

make a great deal of money to be more satisfied with what they make (Campbell, 1981).

Wealth, it seems, is like health: Its absence can breed misery, yet having it is no guarantee of happiness. In one survey, people on *Forbes*'s list of wealthiest Americans reported only slightly greater happiness than other Americans; 37% were less happy than the average American (Diener, Horwitz, & Emmons, 1985). Even lottery winners gain only a temporary jolt of joy (Argyle, 1986; Brickman, Coates, & Janoff-Bulman, 1978). The emo-

tional effects of some tragedies are likewise temporary: After a period of adaptation, people with disabilities usually report a near-normal level of well-being (Diener, 1994). Thus, concluded Kammann (1983), "Objective life circumstances have a negligible role to play in a theory of happiness" (p. 18). Satisfaction is less a matter of getting what you want than wanting what you have.

Third, over time, as cultures become more affluent, do their people become happier? In 1957, as economist John Galbraith was about to describe America as *The Affluent Society*, Americans' per person income, expressed in today's dollars, was less than $8,000. Today it is more than $16,000, making America "the doubly affluent society"—with double what money buys. Compared with 1957, Americans have twice as many cars per person—plus microwave ovens, color TVs, VCRs, air conditioners, answering machines, and $12 billion worth of new brand-name athletic shoes a year.

So, are Americans happier than they were in 1957? They are not (see Fig. 4). In 1957, 35% told the National Opinion Research Center that they were "very happy." In 1993, with doubled affluence, 32% said the same (Smith, 1979, and personal communication, November 1993). To judge by soaring rates of depression (Cross-National Collaborative Group, 1992), a quintupled rate of reported violent crime since 1960, a doubled divorce rate, a slight decline in marital happiness among the marital survivors (Glenn, 1990), and a tripled teen suicide rate, Americans are richer and no happier. Easterlin (in press) has reported the same for European countries and Japan. Thus, although policymakers and economists are wedded to the assumption that SWB rises with income (Easterlin, in press), the data indicate that economic growth in affluent countries gives little boost to human morale.

HAPPY PEOPLE

If happiness is similarly available to people of any age, sex, or race, and to those of most income levels, who is happiest? Through life's ups and downs, some people's capacity for joy persists undiminished. In one National Institute of Aging study of 5,000 adults, the happiest of people in 1973 were still relatively happy a decade later, despite changes in their work, their residence, and their family status (Costa, McCrae, & Zonderman, 1987). Who are these chronically happy people?

The Traits of Happy People

In study after study, four inner traits mark happy people: self-esteem, a sense of personal control, optimism, and extraversion.

First, happy people like themselves (Campbell, 1981). On tests of self-esteem, they agree with such statements as "I'm a lot of fun to be with" and "I have good ideas." Indeed, happy people often exhibit a self-serving bias by believing themselves more ethical, more intelligent, less prejudiced, better able to get along with others, and healthier than average (Janoff & Bulman, 1989; Myers, 1993b; Taylor & Brown, 1988). (The findings bring to mind Freud's joke about the man who said to his wife, "If one of us should die, I think I would go live in Paris.") Most people do express positive self-esteem. This helps explain why, contrary to those who would have us believe that happy people are rare, 9 in 10 North Americans describe themselves as at least "pretty happy." The strong link between self-esteem and SWB so often found in individualistic Western cultures is, however, weaker in collectivist cultures, where the group is given priority over the self (Diener & Diener, in press).

Second, happy people typically feel personal control (Campbell, 1981; Larson, 1989). Those who feel empowered rather than helpless typically do better in school, cope better with stress, and live more happily. When deprived of control over their own lives—an experience studied in prisoners, nursing home patients, and people living under totalitarian regimes—people suffer lower morale and worse health. Severe poverty demoralizes when it erodes people's sense of control over their life circumstances (Dumont, 1989).

Third, happy people are usually optimistic. Optimists—those who agree, for example, that "when I undertake something new, I expect to succeed"—tend to be more successful, healthier, and happier than are pessimists (Dember & Brooks, 1989; Seligman, 1991).

Fourth, happy people tend to be extraverted (Costa & McCrae, 1980; Diener, Sandvik, Pavot, & Fujita, 1992; Emmons & Diener, 1986a, 1986b; Headey & Wearing, 1992). Compared with introverts, extraverts are happier both when alone and with other people (Pavot, Diener, & Fujita, 1990), whether they live alone or with others, whether they live in rural or metropolitan areas, and whether they work in solitary or social occupations (Diener et al., 1992).

Reasons for the trait-happiness correlations are not yet fully understood. The causal arrow may go from traits to SWB, or the reverse. Extraversion, for example, may predispose happiness, perhaps because of the social contacts extraversion entails. Or happiness may produce outgoing behavior. Outgoing people, for example, usually appear temperamentally high-spirited and relaxed about reaching out to others, which may explain why they marry sooner, get better jobs, and make more friends (Magnus & Diener, 1991). Twin studies indicate genetic influences on SWB (Tellegen et al., 1988).

The Relationships of Happy People

One could easily imagine why close relationships might exacerbate illness and misery. Close relationships are fraught with stress. "Hell is other people," mused Jean-Paul Sartre (1944/1973, p. 47). Fortunately, the benefits of close relationships with friends and family usually outweigh the strains. People who can name several intimate friends with whom they share their intimate concerns freely are healthier, less likely to die prematurely, and happier than people who have few or no such friends (Burt, 1986; Cohen, 1988; House, Landis, & Umberson, 1988). People report higher positive affect when they are with others (Pavot et al., 1990). In experiments, people relax as they confide painful experiences. In one study, 33 Holocaust survivors spent 2 hr recalling their experiences, often revealing intimate details never before disclosed. Fourteen months later, those who were most self-disclosing had the most improved health (Pennebaker, 1990).

Seligman (1991) contended that today's epidemic levels of depression stem partly from impoverished social connections in increasingly individualistic Western societies. Individualistic societies offer personal control, harmony between the inner and outer person, and opportunity to express one's feelings and talents, though with the risks of a less embedded, more detached self. Today, 25% of Americans live alone, up from 8% half a century ago.

For more than 9 in 10 people, the most significant alternative to aloneness is marriage. As with other close social bonds, broken marital relationships are a source of much self-reported unhappiness, whereas a supportive, intimate relationship is among life's greatest joys (Glenn, 1990). To paraphrase Henry Ward Beecher, "Well-married a person is winged; ill-matched, shackled." Three out of 4 married people say that their spouse is their best friend, and 4 out of 5 say they would marry the same person again (Greeley, 1991). Such feelings help explain why over the 1970s and 1980s, 24% of never-married adults, but 39% of married adults, told the National Opinion Research Center that they were "very happy" (Lee, Seccombe, & Shehan, 1991; see Fig. 5).

1. SELF AND PERSONALITY: Self-Concept

The traffic between marriage and happiness, however, appears to be two-way: Happy people are more appealing as potential marriage partners and more likely to marry (Mastekaasa, 1992; Scott, 1992).

Is marriage, as is so often supposed, more strongly associated with men's happiness than women's? The happiness gap between married and never-married people (Fig. 5) was slightly greater among men (37.7% vs. 20.1%, for a 17.6% difference) than women (41.6% vs. 25.7%, for a 15.9% difference). In European surveys, and in a meta-analysis of 93 other studies, the happiness gap between the married and never-married was virtually identical for men and women (Inglehart, 1990; Wood et al., 1989). Although a bad marriage may indeed be more depressing to a woman than a man, the myth that "single

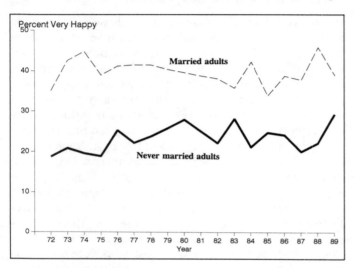

Fig. 5. Percentage of people who reported they were "very happy" among married and never-married U.S. adults. Derived from National Opinion Research Center data reported by Lee, Seccombe, and Shehan (1991).

women report greater life satisfaction than married women" can be laid to rest. Throughout the Western world, married people of both sexes report more happiness than those never married, divorced, or separated.

The "Flow" of Happy People

Turn-of-the-century Russian writer Maksim Gorky anticipated recent studies of work satisfaction: "When work is a pleasure, life is a joy! When work is a duty, life is slavery." Work satisfaction affects life satisfaction (Crohan, Antonucci, Adelmann, & Coleman, 1989; Freedman, 1978; Michalos, 1986). Why? And why are out-of-work people less likely to feel satisfied with life than those productively engaged?

For many people, work provides personal identity: It helps people define who they are. Work also adds to a sense of community: It offers people a network of supportive relationships and a "we feeling." This sense of pride and belonging to a group helps people construct

their social identity. And work can add focus and purpose—a sense that one's life matters. Studs Terkel (1972) described "the Chicago piano tuner, who seeks and finds the sound that delights; the bookbinder, who saves a piece of history; the Brooklyn fireman, who saves a piece of life. . . . There is a common attribute here: a meaning to their work well over and beyond the reward of the paycheck" (p. xi).

Work is, however, sometimes unsatisfying, for two reasons. We can be overwhelmed: When challenges exceed our available time and skills, we feel anxious, stressed. Or we can be underwhelmed: When challenges do not engage our time and skills, we feel bored. Between anxiety and boredom lies a middle ground where challenges engage and match skills. In this zone, we enter an optimal state that Csikszentmihalyi (1990) termed "flow" (Fig. 6).

To be in flow is to be un-self-consciously absorbed. In such times, one gets so caught up in an activity that the mind does not wander, one becomes oblivious to surroundings, and time flies. Csikszentmihalyi formulated the flow concept after studying artists who would spend hour after hour painting or sculpting with enormous concentration. Immersed in a project, they worked as if nothing else mattered. The artists seemed driven less by the external rewards of doing art—money, praise, promotion—than by the intrinsic rewards of creating the work.

Csikszentmihalyi conducted studies in which people reported on their activities and feelings when paged with electronic beepers. He discovered that happiness comes not from mindless passivity but from engagement in mindful challenge. Whether at work or at leisure, people enjoyed themselves more when absorbed in the flow of an activity than when doing nothing meaningful. Thus,

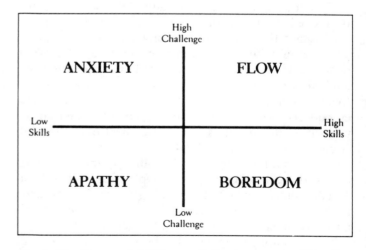

Fig. 6. The flow model. When a challenge engages skills, people often become so absorbed in the flow of an activity that they lose consciousness of self and time. Adapted from Csikszentmihalyi and Csikszentmihalyi (1988, p. 251).

involvement in interesting activities, including engaging work, is a major source of well-being. As playwright Noel

Coward observed, interesting work "is more fun than fun."

The Faith of Happy People

The links between religion and mental health are impressive. Religious people (often defined as those who attend church regularly) are much less likely than irreligious people to become delinquent, to abuse drugs and alcohol, to divorce or be unhappily married, and to commit suicide (Batson, Schoenrade, & Ventis, 1993; Colasanto & Shriver, 1989). Religiously active people even tend to be physically healthier and to live longer, in part because of their healthier smoking, eating, and drinking habits (Koenig, Smiley, & Gonzales, 1988; Levin & Schiller, 1987; McIntosh & Spilka, 1990).

Across North America and Europe, religious people also report higher levels of happiness and satisfaction with life (e.g., Poloma & Pendleton, 1990). Religious people are slightly less vulnerable to depression (Brown, 1993; Gartner, Larson, Allen, & Gartner, 1991). The most striking finding, however, comes from the Gallup Organization (Gallup, 1984), which compared people low in "spiritual commitment" with highly spiritual people (who consistently agree with statements such as "My religious faith is the most important influence in my life."). The highly spiritual were twice as likely to say they were "very happy." Other surveys, in the United States and across 14 Western nations, found that happiness and life satisfaction rise with strength of religious affiliation and frequency of worship attendance (Inglehart, 1990; Witter, Stock, Okun, & Haring, 1985). One meta-analysis among the elderly revealed that the two best predictors of well-being among older persons were health and religiousness (Okun & Stock, 1987).

Other studies have probed the connection between faith and coping with a crisis. Compared with religiously inactive widows, recently widowed women who worshipped regularly reported more joy in their lives (Harvey, Barnes, & Greenwood, 1987; McGloshen & O'Bryant, 1988; Siegel & Kuykendall, 1990). Among mothers of disabled children, those with a deep religious faith were less vulnerable to depression than were those who were irreligious (Friedrich, Cohen, & Wilturner, 1988). People with a strong faith also retained greater happiness after suffering divorce, unemployment, serious illness, or bereavement (Ellison, 1991; McIntosh, Silver, & Wortman, 1993).

What explains these positive links between faith and well-being? Is it the supportive close relationships often enjoyed by people who are active in local congregations (of which there are 258,000 in the United States)? Is it the sense of meaning and purpose that many people derive from their faith? Is it a religious worldview that offers answers to life's deepest questions and an optimistic appraisal of life events? Is it the hope that faith affords when people suffer or face what social psychologists Sol-

omon, Greenberg, and Pyszczynski (1991) called "the terror resulting from our awareness of vulnerability and death" (p. 97)? Such proposed explanations await more rigorous exploration.

Elements of a Theory of Happiness

A viable theory of happiness must, first, recognize the importance of adaptation. Over time, the immediate affective response to significant life events inevitably fades. Thus, variables such as income (Diener et al., 1993), physical attractiveness (Diener, Wolsic, & Fujita, in press), and health (Okun & George, 1984) have minimal long-term influence on SWB despite having powerful effects on people's lives. Although lottery winners are initially elated, their euphoria soon wanes. "Continued pleasures wear off," noted Frijda (1988, p. 353). "Pleasure is always contingent upon change and disappears with continuous satisfaction."

Likewise, the agony of most bad events gradually subsides. Even the initial psychological trauma of paralyzing car accidents typically gives way to a return of normal happiness (Wortman & Silver, 1987). Reflecting on the successes and mental health of American Jews who survived horrific Holocaust experiences, Helmreich (1992) noted that "the story of the survivors is one of courage and strength, of people who are living proof of the indomitable will of human beings to survive and of their tremendous capacity for hope. It is not a story of remarkable people. It is a story of just how remarkable people can be" (p. 276).

In a recent longitudinal study, only life events within the last 3 months influenced SWB (Suh, Diener, & Fujita, in press). The more recent an event, the greater its emotional effect. Studies of daily moods (e.g., Clark & Watson, 1988; Stone & Neale, 1984) confirm Benjamin Franklin's surmise that happiness "is produced not so much by great pieces of good fortune that seldom happen as by little advantages that occur every day." Thanks to our human capacity for adaptation, the affect system is most attuned to the information value of new events.

In addition to adaptation, a second component of a theory of happiness is cultural worldview. Some cultures construe the world as benevolent and controllable. Other cultures emphasize the normality of negative emotions, such as anxiety, anger, and guilt (Diener, Suh, Smith, & Shao, in press). Cultural templates for interpreting life events predispose varying SWB in the absence of differing objective life circumstances. Likewise, some individuals appear habitually to interpret many of life's events negatively, whereas others tend to interpret events positively.

A third component of a theory of happiness is values and goals. Emmons (1986) found that having goals, making progress toward goals, and freedom from conflict among one's goals were all predictors of SWB. Diener and Fujita (in press) discovered that resources such as money, social skills, and intelligence were predictive of SWB only if they were relevant to a person's goals. This finding helps explain why income predicts SWB in very poor nations and why self-esteem predicts SWB in wealthy, individualistic nations. Happiness grows less from the passive experience of desirable circumstances than from involvement in valued activities and progress toward one's goals (Diener & Larsen, 1993).

CONCLUSION

Who is happy? Knowing a person's age, sex, race, and income (assuming the person has enough to afford life's necessities) hardly gives a clue. Better clues come from knowing a person's traits, whether the person enjoys a supportive network of close relationships, whether the person's culture offers positive interpretations for most daily events, whether the person is engaged by work and leisure, and whether the person has a faith that entails social support, purpose, and hope.

This new research on psychological well-being is a welcome complement to long-standing studies of depression and anxiety, and of physical and material well-being. By asking who is happy, and why, we can help people rethink their priorities and better understand how to build a world that enhances human well-being.

REFERENCES

Adelmann, P.K., Antonucci, T.C., Crohan, S.F., & Coleman, L.M. (1989). Empty nest, cohort, and employment in the well-being of midlife women. *Sex Roles, 20*, 173–189.
Argyle, M. (1986). *The psychology of happiness.* London: Methuen.
Astin, A.W., Green, K.C., & Korn, W.S. (1987). *The American freshman: Twenty year trends.* Los Angeles: University of California at Los Angeles, Graduate School of Education, Higher Education Research Institute.
Astin, A.W., Korn, W.S., & Riggs, E.R. (1993). *The American freshman: National norms for fall 1993.* Los Angeles: University of California at Los Angeles, Graduate School of Education, Higher Education Research Institute.
Batson, C.D., Schoenrade, P.A., & Ventis, W.L. (1993). *Religion and the individual: A social-psychological perspective.* New York: Oxford.
Boswell, J. (1973). *The life of Samuel Johnson.* London: Dent. (Original work published 1776)
Bradburn, N. (1969). *The structure of psychological well-being.* Chicago: Aldine.
Brickman, P., Coates, D., & Janoff-Bulman, R.J. (1978). Lottery winners and accident victims: Is happiness relative? *Journal of Personality and Social Psychology, 36*, 917–927.
Brown, L.B. (Ed.). (1993). *Religion, personality and mental health.* New York: Springer-Verlag.
Bureau of the Census. (1975). *Historical statistics of the United States, colonial times to 1970.* Washington, DC: Superintendent of Documents.
Burt, R.S. (1986). *Strangers, friends and happiness* (GSS Technical Report No. 72). Chicago: University of Chicago, National Opinion Research Center.
Campbell, A. (1981). *The sense of well-being in America.* New York: McGraw-Hill.
Clark, L.A., & Watson, D. (1988). Mood and the mundane: Relations between daily life events and self-reported mood. *Journal of Personality and Social Psychology, 54*, 296–308.
Cohen, S. (1988). Psychosocial models of the role of social support in the etiology of physical disease. *Health Psychology, 7*, 269–297.
Colasanto, D., & Shriver, J. (1989, May). Mirror of America: Middle-aged face marital crisis. *Gallup Report*, pp. 34–38.
Costa, P.T., Jr., & McCrae, R.R. (1980). Influence of extraversion and neuroticism on subjective well-being: Happy and unhappy people. *Journal of Personality and Social Psychology, 38*, 668–678.
Costa, P.T., Jr., McCrae, R.R., & Zonderman, A.B. (1987). Environmental and dispositional influences on well-being: Longitudinal follow-up of an American national sample. *British Journal of Psychology, 78*, 299–306.
Crocker, J., & Major, B. (1989). Social stigma and self-esteem: The self-protective properties of stigma. *Psychological Review, 96*, 608–630.

Crohan, S.E., Antonucci, T.C., Adelmann, P.K., & Coleman, L.M. (1989). Job characteristics and well-being at midlife. *Psychology of Women Quarterly, 13*, 223–235.
Cross-National Collaborative Group. (1992). The changing rate of major depression. *Journal of the American Medical Association, 268*, 3098–3105.
Csikszentmihalyi, M. (1990). *Flow: The psychology of optimal experience.* New York: Harper & Row.
Csikszentmihalyi, M., & Csikszentmihalyi, I.S. (1988). *Optimal experience: Psychological studies of flow in consciousness.* New York: Cambridge University Press.
Csikszentmihalyi, M., & Larson, R. (1984). *Being adolescent: Conflict and growth in the teenage years.* New York: Basic Books.
Dember, W.N., & Brooks, J. (1989). A new instrument for measuring optimism and pessimism: Test-retest reliability and relations with happiness and religious commitment. *Bulletin of the Psychonomic Society, 27*, 365–366.
Diener, E. (1994). Assessing subjective well-being: Progress and opportunities. *Social Indicators Research, 31*, 103–157.
Diener, E., & Diener, C. (1994). *Most people in the United States experience positive subjective well-being.* Unpublished manuscript, University of Illinois, Champaign.
Diener, E., & Diener, M. (in press). Cross-cultural correlates of life satisfaction and self-esteem. *Journal of Personality and Social Psychology.*
Diener, E., Diener, M., & Diener, C. (1994). *Factors predicting the subjective well-being of nations.* Manuscript submitted for publication.
Diener, E., & Emmons, R.A. (1985). The independence of positive and negative affect. *Journal of Personality and Social Psychology, 47*, 71–75.
Diener, E., & Fujita, F. (in press). Resources, personal strivings, and subjective well-being: A nomothetic and ideographic approach. *Journal of Personality and Social Psychology.*
Diener, E., Horwitz, J., & Emmons, R.A. (1985). Happiness of the very wealthy. *Social Indicators, 16*, 263–274.
Diener, E., & Larsen, R.J. (1993). The experience of emotional well-being. In M. Lewis & J.M. Haviland (Eds.), *Handbook of emotions* (pp. 404–415). New York: Guilford Press.
Diener, E., Sandvik, E., & Larsen, R.J. (1985). Age and sex effects for emotional intensity. *Developmental Psychology, 21*, 542–548.
Diener, E., Sandvik, E., Pavot, W., & Fujita, F. (1992). Extraversion and subjective well-being in a U.S. national probability sample. *Journal of Research in Personality, 26*, 205–215.
Diener, E., Sandvik, E., Pavot, W., & Gallagher, D. (1991). Response artifacts in the measurement of subjective well-being. *Social Indicators Research, 24*, 35–56.
Diener, E., Sandvik, E., Seidlitz, L., & Diener, M. (1993). The relationship between income and subjective well-being: Relative or absolute? *Social Indicators Research, 28*, 195–223.
Diener, E., Suh, E., Smith, H., & Shao, L. (in press). National and cultural differences in reported well-being: Why do they occur? *Social Indicators Research.*
Diener, E., Wolsic, B., & Fujita, F. (in press). Physical attractiveness and subjective well-being. *Journal of Personality and Social Psychology.*
Dumont, M.P. (1989, September). An unfolding memoir of community mental health. *Readings: A Journal of Reviews and Commentary in Mental Health*, pp. 4–7.
Easterlin, R.A. (in press). Will raising the incomes of all increase the happiness of all? *Journal of Economic Behavior and Organization.*
Ellison, C.G. (1991). Religious involvement and subjective well-being. *Journal of Health and Social Behavior, 32*, 80–99.
Emmons, R.A. (1986). Personal strivings: An approach to personality and subjective well-being. *Journal of Personality and Social Psychology, 51*, 1058–1068.
Emmons, R.A., & Diener, E. (1986a). Influence of impulsivity and sociability on subjective well-being. *Journal of Personality and Social Psychology, 50*, 1211–1215.
Emmons, R.A., & Diener, E. (1986b). An interactional approach to the study of personality and emotion. *Journal of Personality, 54*, 371–384.
Freedman, J. (1978). *Happy people.* New York: Harcourt, Brace, Jovanovich.
Friedrich, W.N., Cohen, D.S., & Wilturner, L.T. (1988). Specific beliefs as moderator variables in maternal coping with mental retardation. *Children's Health Care, 17*, 40–44.
Frijda, N. (1988). The laws of emotion. *American Psychologist, 43*, 349–358.
Fujita, F., Diener, E., & Sandvik, E. (1991). Gender differences in dysphoria and well-being: The case for emotional intensity. *Journal of Personality and Social Psychology, 61*, 427–434.
Gallup, G., Jr. (1984, March). *Religion in America. Gallup Report.*
Gartner, J., Larson, D.B., Allen, G.D., & Gartner, A.F. (1991). Religious commitment and mental health: A review of the empirical literature. *Journal of Psychology and Theology, 19*, 6–25.
Glenn, N.D. (1975). Psychological well-being in the postparental stage: Some evidence from national surveys. *Journal of Marriage and the Family, 37*, 105–110.
Glenn, N.D. (1990). The social and cultural meaning of contemporary marriage. In B. Christensen (Ed.), *The retreat from marriage* (pp. 33–54). Rockford, IL: Rockford Institute.
Greeley, A.M. (1991). *Faithful attraction.* New York: Tor Books.
Haring, M.J., Stock, W.A., & Okun, M.A. (1984). A research synthesis of gender

and social class as correlates of subjective well-being. *Human Relations, 37,* 645–657.

Harvey, C.D., Barnes, G.E., & Greenwood, L. (1987). Correlates of morale among Canadian widowed persons. *Social Psychiatry, 22,* 65–72.

Headey, B., & Wearing, A. (1992). *Understanding happiness: A theory of well-being.* Melbourne: Longman Cheshire.

Helmreich, W.B. (1992). *Against all odds: Holocaust survivors and the successful lives they made in America.* New York: Simon & Schuster.

Herzog, A.R., Rogers, W.L., & Woodworth, J. (1982). *Subjective well-being among different age groups.* Ann Arbor: University of Michigan, Survey Research Center.

House, J.S., Landis, K.R., & Umberson, D. (1988). Social relationships and health. *Science, 241,* 540–545.

Hunter, S., & Sundel, M. (Eds.). (1989). *Midlife myths: Issues, findings, and practice implications.* Newbury Park, CA: Sage.

Inglehart, R. (1990). *Culture shift in advanced industrial society.* Princeton, NJ: Princeton University Press.

Janoff-Bulman, R. (1989). The benefits of illusions, the threat of disillusionment, and the limitations of inaccuracy. *Journal of Social and Clinical Psychology, 8,* 158–175.

Kammann, R. (1983). Objective circumstances, life satisfactions, and sense of well-being: Consistencies across time and place. *New Zealand Journal of Psychology, 12,* 14–22.

Koenig, H.G., Smiley, M., & Gonzales, J.A.P. (1988). *Religion, health, and aging: A review and theoretical integration.* Westport, CT: Greenwood Press.

Larson, R. (1989). Is feeling "in control" related to happiness in daily life? *Psychological Reports, 64,* 775–784.

Latten, J.J. (1989). Life-course and satisfaction, equal for every-one? *Social Indicators Research, 21,* 599–610.

Lee, G.R., Seccombe, K., & Shehan, C.L. (1991). Marital status and personal happiness: An analysis of trend data. *Journal of Marriage and the Family, 53,* 839–844.

Levin, J.S., & Schiller, P.L. (1987). Is there a religious factor in health? *Journal of Religion and Health, 26,* 9–36.

Magnus, K., & Diener, E. (1991, May). *A longitudinal analysis of personality, life events, and well-being.* Paper presented at the annual meeting of the Midwestern Psychological Association, Chicago.

Mastekaasa, A. (1992). Marriage and psychological well-being: Some evidence on selection into marriage. *Journal of Marriage and the Family, 54,* 901–911.

McCrae, R.R., & Costa, P.T., Jr. (1990). *Personality in adulthood.* New York: Guilford Press.

McGloshen, T.H., & O'Bryant, S.L. (1988). The psychological well-being of older, recent widows. *Psychology of Women Quarterly, 12,* 99–116.

McIntosh, D.N., Silver, R.C., & Wortman, C.B. (1993). Religion's role in adjustment to a negative life event: Coping with the loss of a child. *Journal of Personality and Social Psychology, 65,* 812–821.

McIntosh, D.N., & Spilka, B.B. (1990). Religion and physical health: The role of personal faith and control beliefs. In M.L. Lynn & D.O. Moberg (Eds.), *Research on the social scientific study of religion* (Vol. 2, pp. 167–194). Greenwich, CT: JAI Press.

Michalos, A.C. (1986). Job satisfaction, marital satisfaction, and the quality of life: A review and a preview. In F.M. Andrews (Ed.), *Research on the quality of life* (pp. 57–83). Ann Arbor: University of Michigan, Survey Research Center.

Michalos, A.C. (1991). *Global report on student well-being: Vol. 1. Life satisfaction and happiness.* New York: Springer-Verlag.

Myers, D.G. (1993a). *The pursuit of happiness.* New York: Avon Books.

Myers, D.G. (1993b). *Social psychology* (4th ed.). New York: McGraw-Hill.

Niemi, R.G., Mueller, J., & Smith, T.W. (1989). *Trends in public opinion: A compendium of survey data.* New York: Greenwood Press.

Okun, M.A., & George, L.K. (1984). Physician- and self-ratings of health, neuroticism and subjective well-being among men and women. *Personality and Individual Differences, 5,* 533–539.

Okun, M.A., & Stock, W.A. (1987). Correlates and components of subjective well-being among the elderly. *Journal of Applied Gerontology, 6,* 95–112.

Pavot, W., Diener, E., Colvin, C.R., & Sandvik, E. (1991). Further validation of the Satisfaction With Life Scale: Evidence for the cross-method convergence of well-being measures. *Journal of Personality Assessment, 57,* 149–161.

Pavot, W., Diener, E., & Fujita, F. (1990). Extraversion and happiness. *Personality and Individual Differences, 11,* 1299–1306.

Pennebaker, J. (1990). *Opening up: The healing power of confiding in others.* New York: William Morrow.

Poloma, M.M., & Pendleton, B.F. (1990). Religious domains and general well-being. *Social Indicators Research, 22,* 255–276.

Powell, J. (1989). *Happiness is an inside job.* Valencia, CA: Tabor.

Robins, L., & Regier, D. (Eds.). (1991). *Psychiatric disorders in America.* New York: Free Press.

Sandvik, E., Diener, E., & Seidlitz, L. (1993). Subjective well-being: The convergence and stability of self-report and non-self-report measures. *Journal of Personality, 61,* 317–342.

Sartre, J.-P. (1973). *No exit.* New York: Vintage Books. (Original work published 1944)

Scott, C. (1992). *Personality versus the situational effect in the relation between marriage and subjective well-being.* Unpublished doctoral dissertation, University of Illinois, Champaign.

Seidlitz, L., & Diener, E. (1993). Memory for positive versus negative life events: Theories for the differences between happy and unhappy persons. *Journal of Personality and Social Psychology, 64,* 654–664.

Seligman, M.E.P. (1991). *Learned optimism.* New York: Random House.

Siegel, J.M., & Kuykendall, D.H. (1990). Loss, widowhood, and psychological distress among the elderly. *Journal of Consulting and Clinical Psychology, 58,* 519–524.

Smith, T.W. (1979). Happiness: Time trends, seasonal variations, intersurvey differences, and other mysteries. *Social Psychology Quarterly, 42,* 18–30.

Solomon, S., Greenberg, J., & Pyszczynski, T. (1991). A terror management theory of social behavior: The psychological functions of self-esteem and cultural world-views. *Advances in Experimental Social Psychology, 24,* 93–159.

Stock, W.A., Okun, M.A., Haring, M.J., & Witter, R.A. (1983). Age and subjective well-being: A meta-analysis. In R.J. Light (Ed.), *Evaluation studies: Review annual* (Vol. 8, pp. 279–302). Beverly Hills, CA: Sage.

Stock, W.A., Okun, M.A., Haring, M.J., & Witter, R.A. (1985). Race and subjective well-being in adulthood. *Human Development, 28,* 192–197.

Stone, A.A., & Neale, J.M. (1984). Effects of severe daily events on mood. *Journal of Personality and Social Psychology, 46,* 137–144.

Strumpel, B. (1976). Economic lifestyles, values, and subjective welfare. In B. Strumpel (Ed.), *Economic means for human needs* (pp. 19–65). Ann Arbor: University of Michigan, Survey Research Center.

Suh, E., Diener, E., & Fujita, F. (in press). Events and subjective well-being: Only recent events matter. *Journal of Personality and Social Psychology.*

Taylor, S.E., & Brown, J.D. (1988). Illusion and well-being: A social psychological perspective on mental health. *Journal of Personality and Social Psychology, 103,* 193–210.

Tellegen, A., Lykken, D.T., Bouchard, T.J., Wilcox, K.J., Segal, N.C., & Rich, S. (1988). Personality similarity in twins reared apart and together. *Journal of Personality and Social Psychology, 54,* 1031–1039.

Terkel, S. (1972). *Working: People talk about what they do all day and how they feel about what they do.* New York: Pantheon Books.

Veenhoven, R. (1988). The utility of happiness. *Social Indicators Research, 20,* 333–354.

Winokur, J. (1987). *The portable curmudgeon.* New York: New American Library.

Witter, R.A., Stock, W.A., Okun, M.A., & Haring, M.J. (1985). Religion and subjective well-being in adulthood: A quantitative synthesis. *Review of Religious Research, 26,* 332–342.

Wood, W., Rhodes, N., & Whelan, M. (1989). Sex differences in positive well-being: A consideration of emotional style and marital status. *Psychological Bulletin, 106,* 249–264.

Wortman, C.B., & Silver, R.C. (1987). Coping with irrevocable loss. In G.R. VandenBos & B.K. Bryant (Eds.), *Cataclysms, crises, and catastrophes: Psychology in action* (pp. 185–235). Washington, DC: American Psychological Association.

(RECEIVED 2/1/94; REVISION ACCEPTED 9/9/94)

At Last—a Rejection Detector!

What to do when you find yourself running low on self-esteem.

Self-esteem, it turns out, is a lot like love. We often go looking for it in all the wrong places.

We attempt to bolster our sense of self from within. We may even resort to repeating simplistic self-affirmations.

But in fact, self-esteem is more a reflection of our relationship to others. In a bold new theory that turns conventional wisdom inside out, psychologist Mark R. Leary, Ph.D., proposes that self-esteem is a kind of a meter built into us to detect—and to prompt us to avert—the threat of social rejection.

After all, when asked about happiness, people usually focus on the quality of their relationships to others. A happy marriage, a good family life, good friends—all rank above occupational success, financial security, and possessions. "Clearly, potent affective reactions are tied to the degree to which people are included in meaningful interpersonal relationships," says Leary, a professor at Wake Forest University in Winston-Salem, North Carolina.

When self-esteem is low, the appropriate response is not to fix our inner selves but to repair our standing in the eyes of others.

Think of self-esteem as the fuel gauge on a car. Most of us are busy driving around trying to keep the indicator from registering "empty." The whole time, we're focused on the alerting system—instead of on its true function: keeping fuel in the tank. "In the same way, in focusing on the psychological gauge, many psychologists have erred by concluding that people are motivated to maintain self-esteem for its own sake," Leary says. Instead, we should be using self-esteem as a gauge "to keep our 'interpersonal gas tanks' from running low."

Call it a "sociometer." When self-esteem sinks to the danger zone, the appropriate response is not to fix some inner sense of self, but to repair your standing *in the eyes of others,* to behave in ways that maintain connections with other people.

Like, check your own behavior for things that could be turning people off. "It's a primitive emotional warning system to get you to analyze the situation you're in," says Leary. "Say you're talking to someone and notice the person's suddenly frowning; a sign of social disapproval. You think to yourself, 'I said something they don't like. I've got to let them know I was just kidding.'"

Happiness: From the Praise of Others

The sociometer is built into us not just because we are happiest when basking in the acceptance and praise of others—but because without them we wouldn't have survived in the first place. "Early humans who struck out on their own, who had no 'need to belong,' were less likely to pass on their genes to successive generations," Leary observes. So the self-esteem system evolved to monitor the degree to which we are being accepted and included—versus rejected and excluded.

Although the self-esteem system is strongly tied to maintenance of supportive social relationships, you could be forgiven if a negative read-out hasn't sent you flying into the arms of others. "Western culture has taught us to march to our own drummer—in effect, to override the sociometer," Leary insists.

"Our ideology of individualism forces us to buck this internal monitor," he points out. "So when we are feeling low, we don't attempt to do what we need to do to fit in."

Although self-esteem is tied to supportive social relationships, Western culture forces us to override this sociometer we carry within.

As psychological systems go, self-esteem is nearly perfectly designed to help you avoid rejection and promote affiliation: It's highly sensitive to indications your social status is in jeopardy; it operates constantly with or without your awareness, so threats to your inclusionary status are detected no matter

Reprinted with permission from *Psychology Today,* November/December 1995, pp. 46-52, 62. © 1995 by Sussex Publishers, Inc.

what else you're doing; and it makes you feel awfully uncomfortable when it spots such cues.

Leary has carried out a variety of clever studies in which subjects are led to believe that others are rejecting them. Even *imagining* social rejection lowers people's self-esteem. When subjects rate how others might react to them in various situations, actions that pose the possibility of rejection—talking too loud, saying rude things—consistently lower their sense of self-esteem.

Studies show that just imagining social rejection lowers people's self-esteem. So do actions that pose a possibility of rejection.

In fact, experimentally manipulating an individual's rejection status produced the strongest effects Leary's seen in 15 years of research. In one study, he invited subjects to enter into a situation in groups of five. He told them that three would need to form a working group and two would work by themselves. All were asked to rate and rank one another before selecting.

"There were huge differences in how people feel about themselves when told they were not selected," Leary reports. Self-esteem plummeted. Anxiety levels skyrocketed.

Outsize Attempts at Repair

Interestingly, those who were rejected went on to engage in outsize attempts to repair their standing with others.

Even though deep down they felt less positive about themselves, they described themselves to newcomers in even more positive terms than did those who had not been rejected. The reason is that loss of self-esteem increases your motivation to be liked by all others, not just those who rejected you.

The connection between perceived rejection and self-esteem, Leary finds, also helps explain why people who are physically abused or assaulted often show significant drops in self-esteem. "Not only does physical violence connote rejection of one's worth as a person, but in many cases victims of assault worry that their victimization will lead others to reject them."

That the self-esteem system processes information at a preconscious level can be seen in the speed of our ability to pick up signs of disapproval. Studies by other researchers demonstrate that people are particularly fast at detecting angry faces in a picture of a crowd.

Actually, the whole monitoring mechanism is weighted towards the negative. Even neutral feedback registers almost as low as rejection, Leary finds.

When someone tells us, "I don't care if you stay or go," the statement may be perfectly neutral—but it doesn't do us much good. We need clear demonstrations of acceptance for self-esteem to hit positive.

And when it doesn't, we suffer a plethora of ill effects. Many studies show that low self-esteem is associated with depression, anxiety, and every other negative emotion, as well as with maladjustment and even ill health. Leary does not dispute those findings; he just thinks they've been misattributed to the wrong cause.

"The reason low self-esteem is associated with all manner of ill effects is that they are really a consequence of long-term perceived rejection. Or they may be a consequence of dysfunctional attempts to connect with others."

We need clear demonstrations of acceptance for self-esteem to be positive. Neutral feedback registers almost as low as rejection.

Count among them joining gangs or other groups that pose a danger to oneself. And people who engage in substance abuse or extreme risk-taking usually suffer from some deficit in belongingness, the North Carolina psychologist points out.

For over 200 years, Western culture has been marked by a rise in emphasis on the individual and on individuality. Now at its zenith, such thinking has also been accompanied by a deepening psychospiritual malaise.

Perhaps recognizing the real meaning of self-esteem will allow us to see that some group-centeredness, some attempt to fit in with others, is a badly needed corrective.

Is Self-Esteem Really All That Important?

Psychologists differ on the need for educators and parents to continuously applaud a child's efforts.

Randall Edwards

Randall Edwards is a freelance writer and reporter with The Columbus Dispatch.

Bill Damon, PhD, believes society is damning its children with false praise.

Damon, a developmental psychologist and director of Brown University's Center for the Study of Human Development, is one of growing number of psychologists who question the human-potential movement and say its emphasis on fostering children's self-esteem is misguided.

Champions of self-esteem promise better academic performance, superior social skills and the ability to resist evil temptations like drug abuse and suicide. Countless books say building a child's self-esteem leads to better grades and enables children to build healthy relationships with others. Parents are exhorted to heap praise and rewards on youngsters in hopes of inspiring confidence and a better sense of self.

White Lies?

But psychologists like Damon disagree. They assert that research shows no causal relationship between self-esteem and positive developments in a child's personal or academic life.

Basing an educational system around self-esteem concepts, they say, is a dangerous distraction from teaching skills, building knowledge and letting students experience the thrill of real accomplishment.

The self-esteem movement dates back to the 1970s, but its present incarnation was born in California in 1987 when the state government set up a commission to boost self-esteem among citizens as a way to reduce welfare dependency and teen-age pregnancy.

The concept caught on across the country. Now, especially in kindergarten through sixth grade, teachers constantly praise students for any effort put forth.

"Self-esteem is the armor that protects kids from the dragons of life: drugs, alcohol, unhealthy relationships and delinquency," a parenting manual promised. Damon quoted from this manual in his recently released book, *Greater Expectations,* to show the extent to which some psychologists and educators rely on self-esteem enhancement.

But this faith in self-esteem has no factual basis to support it, Damon said. Psychologists, teachers and others who push for self-esteem enhancement have been misled by studies that show a correlation between high self-esteem and positive accomplishments, such as better grades, he said.

"Research psychologists, who ought to know better, have confused correlation with causality, and . . . blown weak correlation data out of proportion," Damon said in a recent interview. "Psychologists have allowed themselves to be driven more by their biases than by standards of evidence."

In his book, Damon asserts that "no matter how many correlations are found between self-esteem and anything else, self-esteem is just as likely to be the result of the positive developments as it is to be the cause of them."

Martin Seligman, PhD, spoke on the self-esteem movement at the American Psychological Association's convention last summer. Seligman, president of APA's Div. 12 (Clinical), argues that "self-esteem is caused by a whole panoply of successes and failures. . . . What needs improving is not self-esteem, but improvement of our skills [for dealing] with the world."

In his book, *What You Can Change and What You Can't,* Seligman says low self-esteem is the least of the problems he sees in seriously depressed people.

"Bolstering self-esteem without changing hopelessness or passivity . . . accomplishes nothing," Seligman argues.

"To put it exactly, I believe that low self-esteem is an epiphenomenon, a mere reflection that your commerce with the world is going badly. It has no power in itself."

Accurate Appraisal

Children try to weigh their own skills and their performance on specific

From *APA Monitor*, May 1995, pp. 43-44. © 1995 by Randall Edwards. Reprinted by permission.

tasks, Damon said. They may believe they are good readers, but poor in math. And they become suspicious when their parents or teachers invariably praise them, but never acknowledge their weaknesses, Damon said.

"The key to development is teaching a child to accurately appraise the quality of his or her own efforts," Damon said. "To praise a child willy-nilly is very disingenuous and the child begins to distrust the lines of communication."

The indiscriminate praise can make the child distrustful and selfish, Damon suggests. It is leading to a culture that respects no legitimate authority and accepts no responsibility.

Harold Stevenson, PhD, a professor in the department of psychology at the University of Michigan and head of the university's Center for Human Growth and Development, agrees that the human-potential movement and packaged self-esteem programs used by educators can be meaningless.

"So many of these programs are insincere and not reality-based," Stevenson said. When the praise isn't meaningful, he said, "it just sloughs off [the students]."

Stevenson also asserts that research has shown that on average, American children have more than enough self-esteem when compared to children in other parts of the world. "Surely there are kids who need to develop self-esteem," said Stevenson, "but most American kids don't lack positive self-evaluation."

Damon acknowledged that the self-esteem movement may be a response to the shame-based parenting of previous generations.

"This may well be a reaction against the heavy, guilt-inducing parenting style of the past, but now we've gone too far in the other direction," he said. "I've read parenting manuals that have suggested, 'Don't make your child feel bad if they've lied or stolen something.' [But I believe] if they do something wrong, they should feel guilty for a while."

Recognizing the Merits

Damon and other critics make important points but go too far, said Bill Pfohl, PsyD, a professor in Western Kentucky University's school psychology program. Although some parenting manuals rely too heavily on enhancing self-esteem, it should not be abandoned as a goal, he said.

Building self-esteem must be done in the context of striving for success, Pfohl said. Aimless flattery is useless, but he blames that problem on the "whim of the most recent best-selling parenting book," not on contemporary psychological theory.

In his work with severely abused, hyperactive and emotionally disturbed children, Pfohl said he blames factors such as poverty, single-parent families and television violence more than the self-esteem movement for the problems youth are facing.

Susan Harter, PhD, a professor of psychology at the University of Denver and director of the graduate program in developmental psychology there, said self-esteem is an important part of a child's development.

Harter rejects the argument that teachers need to focus only on skill development. "Skill training isn't enough," she said. "You've got to influence the values of these kids to make them think, [for example, that] math is important." Her research and that of others shows a "very robust" connection between low self-esteem and indicators of depression and suicide. In her work, about half of children who suffer from depression indicate that their feelings of inadequacy preceded the depression. Children who are depressed over their feelings of inadequacy about their appearance, Harter said are not going to be helped by studying math.

She believes a productive self-esteem program should help children minimize the importance of attributes they don't have and maximize the importance of skills they can achieve. No one intervention program can do this, she said. Instead, self-esteem de-velopment must be tailored to the individual.

"THIS MAY WELL BE A REACTION AGAINST THE HEAVY, GUILT-INDUCING PARENTING STYLE OF THE PAST, BUT NOW WE'VE GONE TOO FAR. . . . I'VE READ PARENTING MANUALS THAT HAVE SUGGESTED, 'DON'T MAKE YOUR CHILD FEEL BAD IF THEY'VE LIED OR STOLEN SOMETHING.' [BUT I BELIEVE] IF THEY DO SOMETHING WRONG, THEY SHOULD FEEL GUILTY FOR A WHILE."
BILL DAMON, PHD
BROWN UNIVERSITY

Kevin P. Dwyer, assistant executive director of the National Association of School Psychologists, suggests that while there may be no proven causal connection between self-esteem and achievement, "we do know that kids seem to learn better in a cooperative learning situation, and for that kids need to feel good about what they can contribute."

Stevenson offers this advice for parents and teachers: "Be sincere and honest with your kids. Don't be devastating with your criticism, but tell them in a positive way what they are doing wrong and offer to help them."

The Decline and Fall of Personality

How the fax, the phone, and the VCR are taking us beyond ourselves

Kenneth J. Gergen, Ph.D.

We listen to George Bush's speech, but know it was produced by a team of experts. We watch the presidential hopefuls, so earnest and well poised, but we are aware of the hours of coaching necessary to produce these images. We wonder about their private lives and how long it will take before startling revelations hit the press. On the talk shows we hear the stars "telling all"; yet we are conscious that even their sorriest secrets are calculated for career advancement. When we listen to the executive officer address the annual meeting, we know that every garment is geared for impact, every syllable designed to sell. As we observe the professor give a lecture, we are aware that even the casual dress and informal manner are carefully crafted.

Many of us believe that somewhere behind these masks lies the real person, that all this role playing is so much sham. We may also believe that for the sake of society and ourselves we should drop the roles and be what we truly are. Yet if by chance you are beginning to doubt that there *is* a factual self beneath the fake, and feel the mask *may* just be the genuine article, that "image is

everything," you are entering the new world of postmodern consciousness.

Twenty years ago I was privileged enough to write a cover story for *Psychology Today*, in which I described the multiple masks we must wear in meeting the demands of everyday life. Rather than finding inconsistency and incoherence in personality a cause for alarm—possibly a reason to seek therapy—I championed its positive possibilities. Rather than admonishing people to seek a firm and fixed identity, I saw such identities as limiting and in many ways incapacitating. It seemed to me that people who demonstrated a protean elasticity were healthier and more fulfilled.

The article was provocative; it was reprinted numerous times both in the United States and abroad, and was even the topic of a television special. Clearly I was touching sensitive issues, questioning the traditional value of a firm sense of identity, of knowing where one stands and to whom one is committed. At the same time, many readers were curious or relieved; many felt the limitations of the old virtues of coherence and authenticity.

Because the implications of these issues for our ways of life are broad and significant, I have continued to

ponder them. On the one hand, by favoring the fixed identity, one also opts for orderly and predictable ways of life, trustworthiness, long-term commitments, and a sense of security and tranquility. One shudders to think of their disappearance. Yet we no longer live in the world that imparted such high value to these ways of life, and, even if painful, we must continuously question the adequacy of past traditions for the demands of the present. It is now, with the benefit of hind-sight, that I see my concerns of 20 years ago as part of a broader cultural story—a single chapter of a tale in which we all participate.

That tale is one of cultural change, now reaching staggering proportions, and from which there is little chance of escape. It is also a tale in which we are all losing our identities and the coherent and committed lives that go with it. But just possibly, if we are wise and fortunate, we can still create a story with a happy ending. In it, we gain the security that comes from discovering our essential relatedness with others.

To begin, let us consider the ingredients required for a centered identity. What is it that holds the personality together, giving it determined direction? It is difficult to understand such a question in a vacuum—cut away

Reprinted with permission from *Psychology Today*, November/December 1992, pp. 59-63. © 1992 by Sussex Publishers, Inc.

from a cultural language of self understanding. Rather, we have little choice but to rely for answers on the accumulated wisdom of the past. Here, it seems to me, we stand today as the beneficiaries of two primary traditions. Both are highly respected, both give us a sense of strong and stable identity, and both are now in jeopardy.

The first is the *romantic* tradition, which reached its pinnacle in the last century. It is largely from the romantic tradition that we derive our beliefs in a profound and stable center of identity—a center which harbored the vital spirit of life itself. Poets such as Shelley, Keats, and Byron; composers such as Beethoven, Brahms, and Chopin; and a host of philosophers, painters, architects, theologians, and the like, all created a vivid portrait of the romantic self. It was a compelling account of powerful forces buried beneath the surface of consciousness, in the deep interior of one's being.

These forces once defined the individual, furnishing the essential reason for being. For some, the forces were identified as the soul; others saw them as fiery passions; and still others felt they were dark and dangerous. Invariably, however, the forces were wondrous, and their expression (in committed love, loyalty, and friendships) was fulfilling if not heroic. Because of the power of these passions, one could experience profound grief at the loss of a loved one, and a sense of longing or remorse so intense that suicide could be an attractive option. The deep interior was also held to be the source of inspiration, creativity, genius, moral courage—even madness.

Romanticism continues to be a pervasive cultural presence. It is alive in everyday life—in our popular songs, television "soaps," and epic films. The romantic vocabulary is essential to most courtships, weddings, and funerals. And if ever asked what makes our lives worth living, most of us will talk about these deep and vital forces.

Romantic views also remain robust in psychotherapeutic groups. The theories of Freud and Jung, for example, are the children of the romantic tradition. Without their poetic and artistic forebearers, Freud's belief in unconscious dynamics and Jung's search for primordial archetypes would seem nonsensical. And when contemporary therapists speak of self-actualizing tendencies, primal screams, catharsis, defense mechanisms, and rebirthing, they are keeping romanticist flames alive. They are making real the self's deep interior.

Yet for most people the romance with romanticism has cooled. For, as most cultural commentators agree, romanticism has been replaced by perspectives, ways of life, and a conception of the self that we now call *modernist*. As a cultural movement, modernism can be traced largely to industrialization, the world wars, and major advances into science.

In each case, fascination turned from the deep interior of the individual to the demands and opportunities made possible by technology. It was time to "get down to business" and "enter the fast track of progress." It also appeared that scientists were beginning to master the fundamental order of the universe—harnessing energies, mastering flight, curing illnesses, and filling homes with marvelous conveniences. With such mastery, one could truly begin to imagine creating a utopian world.

Fired by such optimism, philosophers set about to generate the rules of procedure by which such progress could be achieved across the cultural spectrum. A rational search for fundamentals enabled composers to cast aside popular conventions in favor of tonal experimentation, invited choreographers to abandon ballet in search of elemental movements (now termed modern dance), and stimulated poets to emphasize formal properties over sentiment in their verse. Modern architecture was preoccupied with reducing design to its most functional elements, while modern art abandoned the decorative in search for the essentials of form and color.

Through modernism, the self was slowly being redefined. The emphasis shifted from deep and mysterious processes to human consciousness in the here and now. The deep interior of the romanticist no longer seemed so important; indeed talk of souls, passions, moral courage, and inspiration began to seem quaint, ill-suited to life in the material world. To survive in a complex world, the modernist needed conscious capability for keen observation and careful reason. Such capacities allow us to make progress.

Where the romanticists placed drama, passion, and intensity at the center of existence, modernists valued efficacy of action, smooth and stable functioning, and progress toward a goal. The difference in attitude toward love is emblematic. For romanticists, love could be all-consuming; it was a reason to live (or to die), it was unpredictable, and for its sake one might pledge a lifetime—or an eternity—of commitment. The modernist attempts to develop a technology of mate selection through the use of computerized software. Questionnaire compatibility replaced love by thunderbolt.

Modernist views of the self now dominate the profession of psychology. Most research is lodged in the assumption that psychologists can use their powers of observation and reason to master the fundamentals of human functioning. There are, by definition, no mysterious reservoirs, souls, inspirations, and evil forces deep within the individual.

Rather, for contemporary psychologists, people are much like input/output machines—what they do depends on what goes into them. The critical psychological ingredient of the self is thought, or cognition. And cognition, too, is machine-like, functioning much as a computer. With increased abilities to predict and control human behavior, it is believed, programs can be developed to change and repair the individual. Good personalities, like motor cars, can be properly manufactured through social engineering. Should individuals go

astray, therapists, like mechanics, can put them right. Both behavior modification and cognitive therapy—primary technologies for repair—define the self in the modernist idiom.

Slowly we are losing confidence that there is a coherent, identifiable substance behind the mask. The harder we look, the more difficult it is to find "anyone at home."

Yet there is good reason to believe that modernism, while dominant, is now slowly crumbling as a cultural movement. New cultural conditions have emerged which many characterize as post-modern. Not only do soul, passion, and creativity become suspicious as centers of human existence, but so does rational thought and the efficient control of one's own actions. Slowly we are losing confidence that there is a coherent, identifiable substance behind the mask. The harder we look, the more difficult it is to find "anyone at home."

What is the driving force behind this shift to postmodernism? In view, the central ingredient is technology, more specifically a range of technologies that shower us with social relationships both direct and vicarious. The telephone, automobile, radio, television, motion pictures, mass publication, Xerox, cassette recordings, urban mass transportation, the national highway system, jet transportation, satellite transmission, VCR, the computer, fax, and the mobile telephone—all have emerged within the past century, most within the past 50 years. All have grown by leaps and bounds, becoming standard equipment for a normal life.

And all expand the range of our social life. No longer is our social existence tied to a small town, a suburban community, or an urban neighborhood. Rather, was we wake to *Good Morning America*, read the papers, listen to radio talk shows, travel miles to work, meet people from around the globe, answer faxes and electronic mail, drive children to cross-town games, check the answering machine, phone long distance, visit with old friends from out of town, order air tickets to the Caribbean, and take a late evening graze through cable-TV channels, we consume and are consumed by a social world of unbounded proportion. We are exposed to more opinions, values, personalities, and ways of life than was any previous generation in history; the number of our relationships soars, the variations are enormous: past relationships remain (only a phone call apart) and new faces are only a channel away. There is in short, an explosion in social connection.

What does this explosion have to do with our sense of selves, who we are, and what we stand for? How does it undermine beliefs in a romantic interior or in a rational center of the self?

First, there is a *populating of the self*, that is, an absorption of others into ourselves. Through countless exposure to others, we rapidly increase the range of appreciations, understandings, and action possibilities available to us. Through friends, acquaintances, family members, the media and so on, we come to see and to feel myriad possibilities for being—along with their opposites.

We come to appreciate the possibility of homosexuality, and yet to understand reasons against it; we are encouraged to feel heterosexual longings, and yet to consider ourselves capable of homosexual urges, along with homophobic reactions. Standing alongside these multiple tendencies we also come to see the rationality of androgyny—expressing characteristics of both genders—and the many arguments against any gender

differences in the first place. Each of us becomes populated with dozens of potentials, all reasonable and good by some criterion, in some relationship, in some context. Where in the mix is the genuine self, the true feelings, or the rational core? To paraphrase the poet Walt Whitman, "We contain multitudes."

The sense of a centered self also begins to collapse under the *demands of multiple audiences*. In one of the most rousing scenes from the film *Bugsy*, the infamous gangster (played by Warren Beatty) races desperately from one room of his mansion to another. Breathlessly he plays the affable host for his daughter's birthday party, abandons her to plead for the affection of his doubting wife, reappears with swagger and gusto to impress his gangster cronies in the adjoining room, only to race away again to his daughter's failing party. As we laugh, pity, and loathe this poor figure, we are simultaneously reacting to our own lives. For the socializing technologies are constructing an enormous mansion of conflicting demands for each one of us.

Consider the poor man of today, who must simultaneously demonstrate professional responsibility, soft and romantic sensitivity, macho toughness, and family dedication; he must have expertise in sports, politics, software, the stock market, mechanics, food, and wine; he must have a circle of friends, a fitness program, the right CDs, interesting vacation plans, and an impressive car—that is, if he is to survive in an increasingly complex world. So, like Bugsy Seigel, he races from one situation to another, shifting demeanors, clothing, intensities, views, and values. Where in the chaos of competing personas is he to locate the true and the real man behind the masks?

The third way in which the socializing technologies undermine confidence in deep or essential selves is through the *repetition of images*. The countless reproductions of our ways of life slowly sap them of authenticity. Consider the case of romance. By traditional standards, expressions of

love, passion, and desire should be spontaneous eruptions of one's basic self—energetic impulses that suddenly burst into the open. Now consider the number of times you have been exposed to such expressions— on television from your fourth year to the present, in film, books and magazines, in friends' accounts, and indeed in your own life. You know all the words, all the movements of eyes and mouth, all the gestures and postures.

Where am I? Hollywood? The Soaps? A teenage novel? With countless repetition of images, reality becomes rhetoric. Substance slowly becomes style.

And with these countless repetitions, authenticity begins to wear thin. Substance slowly becomes style. One loses trust in romantic expressions; the words are stifled in the throat. "Where am I? Hollywood? The soaps? A teenage novel?" And so it is with all our cherished expressions—religious devotion, grief, happy enthusiasm, political remonstrance. With continued repetition, reality becomes rhetoric.

Is this just another disgruntled commentary on the sorry state of contemporary life? Not entirely. Yes, there is room for lament, as we cease to believe in inner mysteries, passions, or inspiration; when we no longer seem to be the authors of our lives, knowing who we are, what we stand for, or where we are going; when reason no longer leads in any particular direction; when expanding relationships turn quiet days into chaos; when intimacy turns into ritual, and commitment becomes a relic of yesteryear.

Yet, when we complain, we are revealing our own roots in the past. If we did not still retain a romanticist belief in the deep interior, would we care whether passion and inspiration were vanished ideas? And if we didn't cling to the modernist idea of a rationally organized life, would chaos be a problem?

Our children will scarcely feel the pinch as we do; they will scarcely understand why anyone would make such a fuss over real, true, or inner selves. And for we who do feel the pinch, there are good reasons for expanding our horizons as well. For the technologies that saturate us with others will hardly be abandoned. There is no reversing the cultural clock. As many scientists proclaim, the socializing technologies are only in their infancy.

As we troop toward the future, let us consider some of the positive possibilities of a postmodern life. For there is in these expanding technologies an enormous increase in the possibilities for human development. Each new relationship is simultaneously an opportunity, an open door to growth of expression, appreciation, and skill.

This is especially noticeable in the lives of young women. A half century ago, there was only one strong model against which women could measure the value of their lives: that of devoted wife and mother. The limitations on expression, exploration, and development were numbingly oppressive. Today that image is simply one of many. And even though daily life may bring a torrent of competing demands, each new wrinkle in personality is also a new dimension. The best of moments may even bring an enormous sense of exhilaration, an awed sense of "look at all that I can do, be, see, feel, and know!" During these moments one scarcely worries about inconsistency and incoherence; one does not question what lies behind the many performances. The games are on, and they are everything.

We experience the satisfaction of continuous and sometimes rapturous engagement. Such engagement not only welcomes new facets of self, but opens the way to recapturing the past. In romanticist and modernist times, one had always to be concerned with the true and the genuine. Is this really what I feel, what I think, who I am? If the answer was "no," certain actions were ruled out for plans abandoned. But if we cease to ask such questions, then nothing is prevented in principle. If we cease to believe that there is any deep and essential criterion, any rule of logic, or any internal essence against which actions must be compared, then we are liberated to play the many games offered by this culture, as well as by others.

In the example of romanticism, talk of souls, passions, and inspirations has lost much of its vitality during the modernist age; for the rational and objective mind, such talk is so much folklore. The socializing technologies have further reduced our beliefs in these dimensions of self. Romantic passions are as quaint as old movies. Yet, from the postmodern standpoint, such actions are also essential parts of some of our most valued traditions. We can be romantic not because it is a true reflection of our inner core, not as a life-or-death matter, but because it is one way for us to participate in a special form of relationship our culture offers to us. We can sing in a chorus or play touch football on Sundays not because these actions "reveal the true self." Rather the actions are themselves part of relationships, and gain their value in just this way.

If postmodern life is more richly expressive, it is also less self-centered. Beliefs in a singular, coherent and stable self can be closely linked with greed, egotism, and selfishness. "If I am a separate self from you," the logic goes, "then better my welfare than yours." But as the socializing technologies expand, beliefs in separate self-directing individuals decline. We become increasingly aware that all our expressions, beliefs, values, thoughts, and desires are lega-

cies from other persons, little gifts they leave with us in passing.

We may indeed be unique, never repeating these expressions in just the same way. But this uniqueness is not self-determined; rather, it reflects the particular patterns of our relationships. "I am you within me," one realizes, "and you are me within you. We are united." With the dawning of this consciousness, selfishness becomes unrewarding. To stuff one's own face, seek one's own riches, be exclusively concerned with one's own image, cuts one away from the very wellsprings of one's potentials. If it is I *against* you, then I am removed from the sources that fire my enthusiasm, enrich my potentials, and furnish life with value. Left to feed upon the residues of past relationships, the "I" would slowly wither.

If our concerns move away from the interior of the self and outward toward relationships, a new sense of optimism is born. We exist in a society where conflict abounds—between racial and ethnic groups, religions, unions and management, men and women, the rich and the poor, prochoicers and pro-lifers, and more. Much the same picture can be painted at the global level, where Arabs and Jews, Muslims and Hindus, blacks and whites, the haves and the have-nots, are pitted against each other. These conflicts follow a familiar logic: each group believes itself to be singular, bounded, and independent, and that it must stick up for its rights, privileges, and well-being in the face of an opposing group. In effect, conflicts among groups are based on much the same thinking that has traditionally colored our perceptions of self.

If the socializing technologies can break down the sense of independent selves, can we look forward to a time when the same can occur at the national and international level? As the technologies increase our contact with those from other walks of life, other value systems, and other cultures, we may continue to expand our range of understanding and appreciation. As we form relationships in business, government, education, the arts, and so on, we may further our sense of interdependence. Have Americans not already absorbed many Japanese points of view, tastes, and appreciations, and vice versa? And is our economy not dependent on theirs and vice versa? To this extent, there is no distinctly American identity. America exists as it does because of the relationships of which it is a part.

So in the end, as the socializing technologies continue their expansion, we can move from a self-centered system of beliefs to consciousness of an inseparable relatedness with others. Perhaps then our postmodern selves will contribute to making the globe a better place for living.

ARE YOU SHY?

*You have lots of company. Nearly one of two Americans claims to be shy.
What's more, the incidence is rising, and technology may be turning ours into
a culture of shyness.*

**Bernardo J. Carducci,
Ph.D., with Philip G.
Zimbardo, Ph.D.**

In sharp contrast to the flamboyant lifestyle getting under way at dance clubs across the country, another, quieter, picture of Americans was emerging from psychological research. Its focus: those on the sidelines of the dance floor. In 1975 *Psychology Today* published a ground-breaking article by Stanford University psychologist Philip Zimbardo, Ph.D., entitled "The Social Disease Called Shyness." The article revealed what Zimbardo had found in a survey conducted at several American colleges: An astonishing 40 percent of the 800 questioned currently considered themselves to be shy.

In addition to documenting the pervasiveness of shyness, the article presented a surprising portrait of those with the condition. Their mild-mannered exterior conceals roiling turmoil inside. The shy disclosed that they are excessively self-conscious, constantly sizing themselves up negatively, and overwhelmingly preoccupied with what others think of them. While everyone else is meeting and greeting, they are developing plans to manage their public impression (*If I stand at the far end of the room and pretend to be examining the painting on the wall, I'll look like I'm interested in art but won't have to talk to anybody*). They

are consumed by the misery of the social setting (*I'm having a horrible time at this party because I don't know what to say and everyone seems to be staring at me*). All the while their hearts are pounding, their pulses are speeding, and butterflies are swarming in their stomach—physiological symptoms of genuine distress.

The article catalogued the painful consequences of shyness. There are social problems, such as difficulty meeting people and making new friends, which may leave the shy woefully isolated and subject to loneliness and depression. There are cognitive problems; unable to think clearly in the presence of others, the shy tend to freeze up in conversation, confusing others who are trying to respond to them. They can appear snobbish or disinterested in others, when they are in fact just plain nervous. Excessively egocentric, they are relentlessly preoccupied with every aspect of their own appearance and behavior. They live trapped between two fears: being invisible and insignificant to others, and being visible but worthless.

The response to the article was overwhelming. A record number of letters to the editor screamed HELP ME!, surprising considering that then, as now, PT readers were generally well-educated, self-aware, and open-minded—not a recipe for shyness.

The article launched a whole new field of study. In the past 20 years, a variety of researchers and clinicians, including myself, have been scrutinizing shyness. To celebrate the 20th anniversary of PT's epochal report, we decided to spotlight recent advances in understanding this social disease:

• Research in my laboratory and elsewhere suggests that, courtesy of changing cultural conditions, the incidence of shyness

in the U.S. may now be as high as 48 percent—and rising.

• Most shyness is hidden. Only a small percentage of the shy appear to be obviously ill at ease. But all suffer internally.

• Some people are born with a temperamental tilt to shyness. But even that inheritance doesn't doom one to a life of averting others' eyes. A lot depends on parenting.

• Most shyness is acquired through life experiences.

• There is a neurobiology of shyness. At least three brain centers that mediate fear and anxiety orchestrate the whole-body response we recognize as shyness. Think of it as an over-generalized fear response.

• The incidence of shyness varies among countries. Israelis seem to be the least shy inhabitants of the world. A major contributing factor: cultural styles of assigning praise and blame to kids.

• Shyness has huge costs to individuals at all ages, especially in Western cultures.

• Shyness does have survival value.

• Despite the biological hold of shyness, there are now specific and well-documented ways to overcome its crippling effects.

Shy on the Sly

How is it possible that 40 to 50 percent of Americans—some of your friends, no doubt—are shy? Because while some people are obviously, publicly shy, a much larger percentage are privately shy. Their shyness, and its pain, is invisible to everyone but themselves.

Only 15 to 20 percent of shy people actually fit the stereotype of the ill-at-ease person. They use every excuse in the book to avoid social events. If they are unlucky enough to find themselves in casual conversation, they can't quite manage to make eye

Reprinted with permission from *Psychology Today*, November/December 1995, pp. 34-40, 64, 66, 68, 70, 78, 82. © 1995 by Sussex Publishers, Inc.

contact, to reply to questions without stumbling over their words, or to keep up their end of the conversation; they seldom smile. They are easy to pick out of a crowd because their shyness is expressed behaviorally.

The other 80 to 85 percent are privately shy, according to University of Pittsburgh psychologist Paul Pilkonis, Ph.D. Though their shyness leaves no behavioral traces—it's felt subjectively—it wreaks personal havoc. They feel their shyness in a pounding heart and pouring sweat. While they may seem at ease and confident in conversation, they are actually engaging in a self-deprecating inner dialogue, chiding themselves for being inept and questioning whether the person they are talking to really likes them. "Even though these people do fairly well socially, they have a lot of negative self-thought going on in their heads," explains Pilkonis. Their shyness has emotional components as well. When the conversation is over, they feel upset or defeated.

The Natural History of Shyness

Shyness has not always been a source of pain. Being shy or inhibited serves a very protective function: It breeds caution. No doubt shyness has pulled *H. sapiens* out of some pretty tight spots over the eons.

Originally, shyness served as protective armor around the physical self. After all, only after an animal has fully acquainted itself with a new environment is it safe to behave in a more natural, relaxed manner and explore around. The process of habituation is one of the most fundamental characteristics of all organisms.

As conscious awareness has increased, the primary threat is now to the psychological self—embarrassment. Most people show some degree of social inhibition; they think about what they are going to say or do beforehand, as well as the consequences of saying or doing it. It keeps us from making fools of ourselves or hurting the feelings of others.

According to Wellesley psychologist Jonathan Cheek, Ph.D., situational shyness "can help to facilitate cooperative living; it inhibits behaviors that are socially unacceptable." So, a little bit of shyness may be good for you and society. But too much benefits no one.

"There are a lot of people who have private aspects of shyness who are willing to say they are shy but don't quite gibe with the people we can see trembling or blushing," notes Pilkonis.

Shyness can lurk in unlikely hosts—even those of the talk show variety. Take David Letterman, king of late-night TV. Although his performance in front of a live studio audience and countless viewers seems relaxed and spontaneous, Letterman is known to be relentless in the planning and orchestration of each nightly performance down to the last detail. Like Johnny Carson, he spends little time socializing outside a very small circle of friends and rarely attends social functions.

Letterman is the perfect example of what Zimbardo calls the shy extrovert: the cool, calm, and collected type whose insides are in fact churning. A subset of the privately shy, shy extroverts may be politicians, entertainers, and teachers. They have learned to act outgoing—as long as they are in a controlled environment. A politician who can speak from a prepared script at a mass political rally really may get tongue-tied during a question-and-answer period. A professor may be comfortable as long as she is talking about her area of expertise; put in a social gathering where she may have to make small talk, she clams up.

Zimbardo's short list of notable shy extroverts: funny lady Carol Burnett, singer Johnny Mathis, television reporter Barbara Walters, and international opera star Joan Sutherland. These stars are not introverts, a term often confused with shyness. Introverts have the conversational skills and self esteem necessary for interacting successfully with others but prefer to be alone. Shy people want very much to be with others but lack the social skills and self-esteem.

What unites the shy of any type is acute self-consciousness. The shy are even self-conscious about their self-consciousness. Theirs is a twisted egocentricity. They spend so much time focusing on themselves and their weaknesses, they have little time or inclination to look outward.

Wired for Shyness?

According to developmental psychologist Jerome Kagan, Ph.D., and colleagues at Harvard University, up to a third of shy adults were born with a temperament that inclined them to it. The team has been able to identify shyness in young infants before environmental conditions make an impact.

In his longitudinal studies, 400 four-month-old infants were brought into the lab and subjected to such stimuli as moving mobiles, a whiff of a Q-Tip dipped in alcohol, and a tape recording of the human voice. Then they were brought back at a later age for further study. From countless hours of observation, rerun on videotapes, Kagan, along with Harvard psychologists Nancy Snidman, Ph.D, and Doreen Arcus, Ph.D., have nailed down the behavioral manifestations of shyness in infants.

About 20 percent of infants display a pattern of extreme nervous-system reactivity to such common stimuli. These infants grow distressed when faced with unfamiliar people, objects, and events. They momentarily extend their arms and legs spastically, they vigorously wave their arms and kick their legs, and, on occasion, arch their backs. They also show signs of distress in the form of excessive fretting and crying, usually at a high pitch and sustained tension that communicates urgency. Later on, they cling to their parents in a new new play situation.

In contrast, 40 percent of all infants exposed to the same stimuli occasionally move an arm or leg but do not show the motor outbursts or fretting and crying typical of their highly reactive brethren. When the low-reactive infants do muster up a crying spell, it is nothing out of the ordinary.

Lab studies indicate that highly reactive infants have an easily excitable sympathetic nervous system. This neural network regulates not only many vital organs, including the heart, but the brain response of fear. With their high-strung, hair-trigger temperament, even the suggestion of danger—a stranger, a new environment—launches the psychological and physiologic arousal of fear and anxiety.

One of the first components of this reaction is an increased heart rate. Remarkably, studies show that high-reactive infants have a higher-than-normal heart rate—and it can be detected even before birth, while the infant is still *in utero*. At 14 months, such infants have over-large heart rate acceleration in response to a neutral stimulus such as a sour taste.

Four years later, the same kids show another sign of sympathetic arousal—a cooler temperature reading in their right ring finger than in their left ring finger while watching emotionally evocative film clips. Too, as children they show more brain wave activity in the right frontal lobe; by contrast, normally reactive children display more brain wave activity in the left frontal area. From other studies it is known that the right side of the brain is more involved in the expression of anxiety and distress.

The infant patterns point to an inborn variation in the response threshold of the

amygdala, an almond-shaped brain structure linked to the expression of fear and anxiety (see page 39). This neural hypersensitivity eventually inclines such children to avoid situations that give rise to anxiety and fear—meeting new people or being thrown into new environments. In such circumstances they are behaviorally inhibited.

Though it might sound strange, there may even be a season for shyness—specifically early fall. Kagan and Harvard sociologist Stephen Gortmaker, Ph.D., have found that women who conceive in August or September are particularly likely to bear shy children. During these months, light is waning and the body is producing increasing amounts of melatonin, a hormone known to be neurally active; for example, it helps set our biological clocks. As it passes through the placenta to the developing fetal brain, Kagan surmises, the melatonin may act on cells to create the hyperaroused, easily agitated temperament of the shy.

Further evidence of a biological contribution to shyness is a pattern of inheritance suggesting direct genetic transmission from one generation to the next. Parents and grandparents of inhibited infants are more likely to report being shy as children than the relatives of uninhibited children, Snidman found in one study. Kagan and company are looking for stronger proof—such as, say, an elevated incidence of panic disorder (acute episodes of severe anxiety) and depression in the parents of inhibited children. So far he has found that among preschool children whose parents were diagnosed with panic attack or depression, one-third showed inhibited behavior. By contrast, among children whose parents experience neither panic disorder nor depression, only about five percent displayed the inhibited reactive profile.

Are inhibited infants preordained to become shy adults? Not necessarily, Doreen Arcus finds. A lot has to do with how such children are handled by their parents. Those who are overprotected, she found from in-home interviews she conducted, never get a chance to find some comfortable level of accommodation to the world; they grow up anxious and shy. Those whose parents do not shield them from stressful situations overcome their inhibition.

Snidman, along with Harvard psychiatrist Carl Schwartz, M.D., examined the staying power of shyness into adolescence. They observed 13- and 14-year-olds who were identified as inhibited at two or three years of age. During the laboratory interview, the adolescents with a history of inhibition tended to smile less, made fewer spontaneous comments, and reported being more shy than those who were identified as uninhibited infants.

Taken over a lifetime, gender doesn't figure much into shyness. Girls are more apt to be shy from infancy through adolescence, perhaps because parents are more protective of them than boys, who are encouraged to be more explorative. Yet in adolescence, boys report that shyness is more painful than do girls. This discomfort is likely related to sex-role expectations that boys must be bold and outgoing, especially with girls, to gear up for their role as head of family and breadwinner. But once into adulthood, gender differences in shyness disappear.

Bringing Biology Home

If only 15 to 20 percent of infants are born shy and nearly 50 percent of us are shy in adulthood, where do all the shy adults come from? The only logical answer is that shyness is acquired along the way.

One powerful source is the nature of the emotional bond parents forge with their children in the earliest years of life. According to Paul Pilkonis, children whose parenting was such that it gave rise to an insecure attachment are more likely to end up shy. Children form attachments to their caregivers from the routine experiences of care, feeding, and caressing. When caretaking is inconsistent and unreliable, parents fail to satisfy the child's need for security, affection, and comfort, resulting in insecure bonds. As the first relationship, attachment becomes the blueprint for all later relationships. Although there are no longitudinal studies spotlighting the development of shyness from toddlerhood to adulthood, there is research showing that insecure early attachment can predict shyness later on.

"The most damnable part of it is that this insecure attachment seems to become self-fulfilling," observes Pilkonis. Because of a difficult relationship to their parents, children internalize a sense of themselves as having problems with all relationships. They generalize the experience—and come to expect that teachers, coaches, and peers won't like them very much.

These are the narcissistically vulnerable—the wound to the self is early and deep, and easily evoked. They are quick to become disappointed in relationships, quick to feel rejection, shame, ridicule. They are relentlessly self-defeating, interpreting even success as failure. "They have negative perceptions of themselves and of themselves in relation to others that they hold onto at all costs," says Pilkonis. The narcissistically vulnerable are among the privately shy—they are seemingly at ease socially but torture themselves beneath the surface. Theirs is a shyness that is difficult to ameliorate, even with psychotherapy.

Shyness can also be acquired later on, instigated at times of developmental transition when children face new challenges in their relationships with their peers. For instance, entering the academic and social whirl of elementary school may leave them feeling awkward or inept with their peers. Teachers label them as shy and it sticks; they begin to see themselves that way—and act it.

Adolescence is another hurdle that can kick off shyness. Not only are adolescents' bodies changing but their social and emotional playing fields are redefining them. Their challenge is to integrate sexuality and intimacy into a world of relationships that used to be defined only by friendship and relatives. A complicated task!

Nor are adults immune. Shyness may re-

Helping Others Beat Shyness

You may not be shy, but one out of two people are. Be sensitive to the fact that others may not be as outgoing and confident. It's your job to make others comfortable around you. Be a host to humanity.

• Make sure no one person at a social gathering—including yourself—is the focus of attention. That makes it possible for everyone to have some of the attention some of the time.

• Like the host of any party, make it your job to bring out the best in others, in any situation. At school, teachers should make it a point to call on kids who are reluctant to speak up. At work, bosses should seek out employees who don't comment in meetings; encouragement to express ideas and creativity will improve any company. At parties, break the ice by approaching someone who is standing alone.

• Help others put their best foot forward. Socially competent people feel comfortable because they tend to steer conversation to their own interests. Find out what the shy person next to you is interested in; introduce the topic.

• Help others keep the conversation going. Shy people often don't speak up in ongoing conversations. Ask a shy person his or her opinion next time you are in a lively discussion.

sult from tail-spinning life upheavals. Divorce at mid-life might be one. "A whole new set of problems kick in with a failure of a relationship, especially if you are interested in establishing new relationships," says Pilkonis. For highly successful, career-defined people, being fired from a long-held job can be similarly debilitating, especially in the interviewing process.

Count in the Culture

Biology and relationship history are not the sole creators of shyness. Culture counts, too. Shyness exists universally, although it is not experienced or defined the same way from culture to culture. Even Zimbardo's earliest surveys hinted at cultural differences in shyness: Japanese and Taiwanese students consistently expressed the highest level of shyness, Jewish students the lowest. With these clues, Zimbardo took himself to Japan, Israel, and Taiwan to study college students. The cross-cultural studies turned up even greater cultural differences than the American survey. In Israel, only 30 percent of college-age students report being shy—versus 60 percent in Japan and Taiwan.

From conversations with foreign colleagues and parents, Zimbardo acquired unprecedented insights into how culture shapes behavior in general, and more specifically the cultural roots of shyness. The key is in the way parents attribute blame or praise in the performance of their children. When a child tries and fails at a task, who gets the blame? And when a child tries and succeeds, who gets the credit?

In Japan, if a child tries and succeeds, the parents get the credit. So do the grandparents, teachers, coaches, even Buddha. If there's any left over, only then is it given to the child. But if the child tries and fails, the child is fully culpable and cannot blame anyone else. An "I can't win" belief takes hold, so that children of the culture never take a chance or do anything that will make them stand out. As the Japanese proverb states, "the nail that stands out is pounded down." The upshot is a low-key interpersonal style. Kids are likely to be modest and quiet; they do little to call attention to themselves. In fact, in studies of American college students' individuation tendencies—the endorsement of behaviors that will make a person stand out, unique, or noticed—Asian students tend to score the lowest. They are much less likely to speak or act up in a social gathering for fear of calling attention to themselves.

In Israel, the attributional style is just the opposite. A child who tries gets rewarded, regardless of the outcome. Consider the

We Shall Overcome

1. Overcoming the Anxiety: To tame your racing heart and churning stomach, learn how to relax. Use simple breathing exercises that involve inhaling and exhaling deeply and slowly.

You can ride out the acute discomfort by staying around for a while. If you give into your distress and flee a party after only five minutes, you guarantee yourself a bad time. Stick around.

2. Getting Your Feet Wet: Nothing breeds success like success. Set up a nonthreatening social interaction that has a high probability of success and build from there. Call a radio show with a prepared comment or question. Call some sort of information line.

3. Face to Face: Then tackle the art of very, very small talk face-to-face. Start a casual, quick exchange with the person next to you, or the cashier, in the supermarket checkout line. Most people in such situations would be very responsive to passing the time in light conversation. Since half the battle is having something to say, prepare. Scan the newspaper for conversation topics, and practice what you are going to say a few times.

5. Smile and Make Eye Contact: When you smile you project a benign social force around you; people will be more likely to notice you and smile back. If you frown or look at your feet, you don't exist for people, or worse, you project a negative presence. Once you have smiled and made eye contact, you have opened up a window for the casual "This elevator is so slow"–type comment. Always maintain eye contact in conversation; it signals that you are listening and interested.

6. Compliment: The shortest route to social success is via a compliment. It's a way to make other people feel good about themselves and about talking to you. Compliment someone every day.

7. Know How to Receive Compliments: Thank the person right away. Then return the compliment: "That's great coming from you, I've always admired the way you dress." Use this as a jumping-off point for a real conversation. Elaborate, ask him where he

gets his ties or shops for suits.

8. Stop Assuming the Worst: In expecting the worst of every situation, shy people undermine themselves—they get nervous, start to stutter, and forget what they wanted to say. Chances are that once you actually throw yourself into that dreaded interaction it will be much easier than you thought. Only then will you realize how ridiculous your doomsday predictions are. Ask your workmate if he likes his job. Just do it.

9. Stop Whipping Yourself: Thoughts about how stupid you sound or how nobody really likes you run through your head in every conversation. No one would judge your performance as harshly as you do, Search for evidence to refute your beliefs about yourself. Don't get upset that you didn't ask someone to dance; focus on the fact that you talked to a woman you wanted to meet.

Don't overgeneralize your social mishaps. Say you start to stutter in conversation with someone at a party. Don't punish yourself by assuming that every other interaction that night or in your life will go the same way.

10. Lose the Perfectionism: Your jokes have to be hilarious, your remarks insightful and ironic. Truth is, you set standards so impossible they spawn performance anxiety and doom you to failure. Set more realistic standards.

11. Learn to Take Rejection: Rejection is one of the risks *everyone* takes in social interaction. Try not to take it personally; it may have nothing to do with you.

12. Find Your Comfort Zone: Not all social situations are for everybody. Go where your interests are. You might be happier at an art gallery, book club, or on a volleyball team than at a bar.

13. Comfort Is Not Enough: The goal in overcoming shyness is to break through your self-centeredness. In an interaction, focus on the other person. Make other people's comfort and happiness your main priority. If people think to themselves, "I really enjoyed being with her," when they leave you, then you have transformed your shyness into social competence. Congratulations.

Yiddish expression *kvell*, which means to engage in an outsize display of pride. If a child tries to make a kite, people *kvell* by pointing out what a great kite it is. And if it doesn't fly, parents blame it on the wind. If a child tries and fails in a competitive setting, parents and others might reproach the coach for not giving the child enough training. In such a supportive environment, a child senses that failure does not have a high price—and so is willing to take a risk. With such a belief system, a person is highly likely to develop *chutzpah*, a type of audacity whereby one always take a chance or risk—with or without the talent. Children of such a value system are more apt to speak up or ask someone to dance at a party without overwhelming self-consciousness.

Shyness, then, is a relative, culture-bound label. It's a safe bet that a shy Israeli would not be considered shy in Japan. Nancy Snidman brings the point home. In studying four-month-olds in Ireland and the U.S., she found no differences in degree of nervous system reactivity. But at age five, the Irish kids did not talk as much nor were they as loud as the American kids. The difference lies in the cultural expectations expressed in child-rearing. Using American norms of social behavior as the standard of comparison, the normal Irish child would be labeled shy. But, in their own culture, with their own norms of behavior, they are not. By the same token, American kids may be perceived as boorish by the Irish.

The Scarlet *S*

Shyness is un-American. We are, after all, the land of the free and the home of the brave. From the first settlers and explorers who came to the New World 500 years ago to our leadership in space exploration, America has always been associated with courageous and adventurous people ready to boldly go where others fear to tread. Our culture still values rugged individualism and the conquering of new environments, whether in outer space or in overseas markets. Personal attributes held high in our social esteem are leadership, assertiveness, dominance, independence, and risk-taking. Hence a stigma surrounding shyness.

The people given the most attention in our society are expressive, active, and sociable. We single out as heroes actors, athletes, politicians, television personalities, and rock stars—people expert at calling attention to themselves: Madonna, Rosanne, Howard Stern. People who are most likely to be successful are those who are able to obtain attention and feel comfortable with it.

What shy people don't want, above all

The Shy Brain

We all take time to get used to (or habituate to) a new stimulus (a job interview, a party) before we begin to explore the unfamiliar. After all, a novel stimulus may serve as a signal for something dangerous or important. But shy individuals sense danger where it does not exist. Their nervous system does not accommodate easily to the new. Animal studies by Michael Davis, Ph.D., of Yale University, indicate that the nerve pathways of shyness involve parts of the brain involved in the learning and expression of fear and anxiety.

Both fear and anxiety trigger similar physiologic reactions: muscle tension, increased heart rate, and blood pressure, all very handy in the event an animals has to fight or flee sudden danger. But there are important differences. Fear is an emotional reaction to a specific stimulus; it's quick to appear, and just as quick to dissipate when the stimulus passes. Anxiety is a more generalized response that takes much longer to dissipate.

Studies of cue conditioning implicate the **amygdala** as a central switchboard in both the association of a specific stimulus with the emotion of fear and the expression of that fear. Sitting atop the brain stem, the amygdala is crucial for relaying nerve signals related to emotions and stress. When faced with certain stimuli—notably strangers, authority figures, members of the opposite sex—the shy associate them with fearful reactions.

In contrast to such "explicit" conditioning is a process of "contextual" conditioning. It appears more slowly, lasts much longer. It is often set off by the context in which fear takes place. Exposure to that environment then produces anxiety-like feelings of general apprehension. Through contextual conditioning, shy people come to associate general environments—parties, group discussions where they will be expected to interact socially—with unpleasant feelings, even before the specific feared stimulus is present.

Contextual conditioning is a joint venture between the amygdala and the **hippocampus**, the sea horse–shaped cell cluster near the amygdala, which is essential to memory and spatial learning. Contextual conditioning can be seen as a kind of learning about unpleasant places.

But a crucial third party participates in contextual conditioning. It's the **bed nucleus of the stria terminalis (BNST)**. The long arms of its cells reach to many other areas of the brain, notably the **hypothalamus** and the brain stem, both of which spread the word of fear and anxiety to other parts of the body. The BNST is principally involved in the generalized emotional-behavioral arousal characteristic of anxiety. The BNST may be set off by the neurotransmitter corticotropin releasing factor (CRF).

Once alerted, the hypothalamus triggers the sympathetic nervous system, culminating in the symptoms of inner turmoil experienced by the shy—from rapid heartbeat to sweaty paleness. Another pathway of information, from the amygdala to the brain stem, freezes movement of the mouth.

The shy brain is not different in structure from yours and mine; it's just that certain parts are more sensitive. Everyone has a "shyness thermostat," set by genes and other factors. The pinpointing of brain structures and neurochemicals involved in shyness holds out the promise that specific treatment may eventually be developed to curb its most debilitating forms.

BNST
hypothalamus
amygdala
hippocampus

else, is to be the focus of attention. Thus, in elementary school, the shy child may not even ask the teacher for help. In college, the shy student is reluctant to ask a question in class. In adulthood, the shy employee is too embarrassed to make a formal presentation to those who grant promotions. In every cases, shyness undermines the ability to access the attention of others who would increase the likelihood of success. In a culture where everybody loves a winner, shyness is like entering a foot race with lead insoles.

Consider the findings of Stanford Business School professor Thomas Harrell. To figure out the best predictors of success in business, he gathered the records of Stanford B-School graduates, including their transcripts and letters of recommendation. Ten years out of school, the graduates were ranked from most to least successful based on the quality of their jobs. The only consistent and significant variable that could predict success (among students who were admittedly bright to start with) was verbal fluency—exactly what the typically tongue-tied shy person can't muster. The verbally fluent are able to sell themselves, their services, and their companies—all critical skills for running a corporation; think of Lee Iacocca. Shy people are probably those behind the scenes designing the cars, programs, and computers—impressive feats, but they don't pay as much as CEO.

The costs of shyness cut deeper than material success, and they take on different forms over a lifetime.

• A shy childhood may be a series of lost opportunities. Think of the child who wants so much to wear a soccer uniform and play just like all the other kids but can't muster the wherewithal to become part of a group. And if the parents do not find a way to help a child overcome feelings of nervousness and apprehension around others, the child may slip into more solitary activities, even though he really wants to be social. The self-selection into solitary activities further reduces the likelihood of the child developing social skills and self-confidence.

• Shy kids also have to endure teasing and peer rejection. Because of their general disposition for high reactivity, shy children make prime targets for bullies. Who better to tease and taunt than someone who gets scared easily and cries?

• Whether inherited or acquired, shyness predisposes to loneliness. It is the natural consequence of decades spent shunning others due to the angst of socializing. Reams of research show that loneliness and isolation can lead to mental and physical decline, even a hastened death.

• Without a circle of close friends or relatives, people are more vulnerable to risk. Lacking the opportunity to share feelings and fears with others, isolated people allow them to fester or escalate. What's more, they are prone to paranoia; there's no one around to correct their faulty thinking, no checks and balances on their beliefs. We all need someone to tell us when our thinking is ridiculous, that there is no Mafia in suburban Ohio, that no one is out to get you, that you've just hit a spate of bad luck.

• Shyness brings with it a potential for abusing alcohol and drugs as social lubricants. In Zimbardo's studies, shy adolescents report feeling greater peer pressure to drink or use drugs than do less shy adolescents. They also confide that they use drugs and alcohol to feel less self-conscious and to achieve a greater sense of acceptance.

• Call it the Hugh Grant Effect. Shyness is linked to sexual, uh, difficulties. Shy people have a hard time expressing themselves to begin with; communicating sexual needs and desires is especially difficult. Shy men may turn to prostitutes just to avoid the awkwardness of intimate negotiations. When Zimbardo asked them to describe their typical client, 20 San Francisco prostitutes said that the men who frequented them were shy and couldn't communicate their sexual desires to wives or girlfriends. And the shy guys made distinctive customers. They circled a block over and over again in their car before getting the nerve to stop and talk to the prostitute. To shy men, the allure of a prostitute is simple—she asks what you want, slaps on a price, and performs. No humiliation, no awkwardness.

Performance anxiety may also make the prospect of sex overwhelming. And because shy people avoid seeking help, any problems created by embarrassment or self-doubt will likely go untreated.

• Another cost—time. Shy people waste time deliberating and hesitating in social situations that others can pull off in an instant. Part of their problem is that they don't live in the present, observes Zimbardo, who is currently focusing on the psychology of time perspective. "Shy people live too much in their heads," obsessed with the past, the future, or both. A shy person in conversation is not apt to think about what is being said at the moment, but about how past conversations have initially gone well and then deteriorated—just as the current one threatens to. Says Zimbardo: "These are people who cannot enjoy that moment because everything is packaged in worries from the past—a Smithsonian archive of all the bad—that restructure the present."

Or shy people may focus all their thoughts and feelings on future consequences: If I say this, will he laugh at me? If I ask him something simple like where he is from, he'll be bored and think I'm a lousy conversationalist, so why bother anyway? The internal decision trees are vast and twisted. "Concern for consequences always makes you feel somewhat anxious. And that anxiety will impair the shy person's performance," says Zimbardo.

Factoring in past and future is wise, but obsession with either is undermining. Shy people need to focus on the now—the person you are talking to or dancing with—to appreciate any experience. "Dancing is a good example of being completely of the moment," comments Zimbardo. "It is not something you plan, or that you remember, you are just doing it." And enjoying it.

If the costs of shyness are paid by shy people, the benefits of shyness are reaped by others—parents, teachers, friends, and society as a whole.

Yet shy people are often gifted listeners. If they can get over their self-induced pressures for witty repartee, shy people can be great at conversation because they may actually be paying attention. (The hard part comes when a response is expected.) According to Harvard's Doreen Arcus, shy kids are apt to be especially empathic. Parents of the children she studies tell her that "even in infancy, the shy child seemed to be sensitive, empathic, and a good listener. They seem to make really good friends and their friends are very loyal to them and value them quite a bit." Even among children, friendships need someone who will talk and someone who will listen.

For any society to function well, a variety of roles need to be played. There is a place for the quiet, more reflective shy individual who does not jump in where angels fear to tread or attempt to steal the limelight from others. Yet as a culture we have devalued these in favor of boldness and expressiveness as a means of measuring worth.

The Future of Shyness

To put it bluntly, the future of shyness is bleak. My studies have documented that since 1975 its prevalence has risen from 40 percent to 48 percent. There are many reasons to expect the numbers to climb in the decades ahead.

Most significantly, technology is continually redefining how we communicate. We are engaging in a diminishing number of face-to-face interactions on a daily basis. When was the last time you talked to a bank teller? Or a gas station attendant? How often do you

call friends or colleagues when you know they aren't in just so you can leave a message on their machine? Voice mail, faxes, and E-mail give us the illusion of being "in touch," but what's to touch but the keyboard? This is not a Luddite view of technology, but a sane look at its deepest costs.

The electronic age was supposed to give us more time, but ironically it has stolen it from us. Technology has made us time-efficient—and redefined our sense of time and its value. It is not to be wasted, but to be used quickly and with a purpose.

Office encounters have become barren of social interaction. They are information-driven, problem-oriented, solution-based. No pleasantries. No backs slapped. We cut to the chase: I need this from you. Says Zimbardo, "You have to have an agenda." Some people don't even bother to show at the office at all; they telecommute.

The dwindling opportunities for face-to-face interaction put shy people at an increasing disadvantage. They no longer get to practice social skills within the comfort of daily routine. Dropping by a colleague's office to chat becomes increasingly awkward as you do it less and less. Social life has shrunk so much it can now be entirely encapsulated in a single, near-pejorative phrase: "face time," denoting the time employees may engage in eyeball-to-eyeball conversation. It's commonly relegated to morning meetings and after 4:00 P.M.

Electronic hand-held video games played solo now crowd out the time-honored social games of childhood. Even electronically simulated social interactions can't substitute—they do not permit people to learn the necessary give and take that is at the heart of all interpersonal relationships.

Technology is not the only culprit. The rise of organized sports for kids and the fall of informal sidewalk games robs kids of the chance to learn to work out their own relationship problems. Instead, the coach and the referee do it.

If technology is ushering in a culture of shyness, it is also the perfect medium for the shy. The Internet and World Wide Web are conduits for the shy to interact with others; electronic communication removes many of the barriers that inhibit the shy. You prepare what you want to say. Nobody knows what you look like. The danger, however, is that technology will become a hiding place for those who dread social interaction.

The first generation to go from cradle to grave with in-home computers, faxes, and the Internet is a long way from adulthood.

Helping Shy Kids

Infants with a touchy temperament are not necessarily doomed to become shy adults. Much depends on the parenting they receive.

Do not overprotect or overindulge: Although it may sound counterintuitive, you can help you child cope more effectively with shyness by allowing him or her to experience moderate amounts of anxiety in response to challenges. Rather than rush to your child's aid to soothe away every sign of distress, provide indirect support. Gradually expose your child to new objects, people, and places so that the child will learn to cope with his own unique level of sensitivity to novelty. Nudge, don't push, your child to continue to explore new things.

Show respect and understanding: Your children have private emotional lives separate from yours. It is important to show your shy child that you can understand and sympathize with her shyness, by talking with the child about her feelings of nervousness and being afraid. Then talk with her about what might be gained by trying new experiences *in spite of* being afraid. Revealing related experiences from your own childhood is a natural way to start the ball rolling. Overcoming fears and anxieties is not an easy process; the feelings may remain even after specific shy behaviors have been overcome. Key ingredients are sympathy, patience, and persistence.

Ease the tease: Shy children are especially sensitive to embarrassment. Compared to other children, they need extra attention, comfort, and reassurance after being teased and more encouragement to develop positive self-regard.

Help build friendships: Invite one or two playmates over to let the child gain experience in playing with different kids in the security of familiar surroundings. But allow them as much freedom as possible in structuring play routines. Shy kids sometimes do better when playing with slightly younger children.

Talk to teachers: Teachers often overlook a shy child or mistake quietness and passivity for disinterest or a lack of intelligence. Discuss what measure might be taken in the classroom or playground.

Prepare the child for new experiences: You can help to reduce fears and anxieties by helping your child get familiar with upcoming novel experiences. Take the child to a new school before classes actually start. Help rehearse activities likely to be performed in new situations, such as practicing for show-and-tell. Also role play with the child any anticipated anxiety-provoking situations, such as how to ask someone to dance at a party (if they'll let you) or speak up in a group at summer camp.

Find appropriate activities: Encourage your child to get involved in after-school activities as a means of developing a network of friends and social skills.

Provide indirect support: Ask the child the degree to which he wants you to be involved in his activities. For some kids, a parent cheering in the bleachers is humiliating. Better is indirect support—discussing the child's interests with him and letting him know of your pleasure and pride in him for participating.

Fit not fight: It's not as important to overcome shyness as to find a comfort zone consistent with your child's shyness. Rather than try to make your daughter outgoing, help her find a level of interaction that is comfortable and consistent with her temperament.

Own your temperament: Think how your own personality or interaction style operates in conjunction with your child's. If you aren't shy, understand that your child may need more time to feel comfortable before entering a novel situation or joining a social group. If you are shy, you may need to address your own shyness as a bridge to helping your child with hers.

Bottom Line: Talk, listen, support, and love shy children for who they are, not how outgoing you would like them to be.

We will have to wait at least another 20 years to accurately assess shyness in the wake of the new electronic age. But to do so, we must find a group of infants—shy and non-shy—and follow them through their life, rather than observe different people, from different generations, in different periods of their lives. Only then will we see the course of shyness over a lifetime. Stay tuned for PT's next shyness article, in 2015.

Social Perception

- Perception and Accuracy (Articles 8–10)
- Perception Processes (Articles 11 and 12)

A personnel director has the job of interviewing hundreds of prospective employees for her company every year. The total amount of time and money that will be invested in these new employees will be enormous; thus, the consequences of hiring the wrong people will be serious. In each interview, then, the personnel director tries to answer a number of important questions: How honest is this candidate? How dependable? How will he or she fit in with the other employees?

Sally has been dating Harry for several months, and things are starting to become more serious between them. As she begins to seriously consider the possibility that he may be "the one," Sally starts to think with extra care about what kind of person Harry really is: Is he just being especially nice during courtship; or is he a genuinely kind and considerate person? Was that time when he got really angry at another driver just an isolated incident, or does it indicate that Harry is someone who has the potential for violence?

Both of these examples are instances of social perception, or the process by which one individual makes inferences about another individual. As you might imagine, this is a very important ability for humans to have, because there are many times when it is important to reach an accurate understanding about what kind of person someone else is. When the behavior of others, such as

employees and spouses, has important implications for us, then the ability to successfully predict how such people will act in the future can be critical. It should not be surprising, then, to discover that social psychology has been interested in this topic for decades.

One approach to this topic has been to study "impression formation"—the process by which we form an initial impression of someone with whom we are not familiar. Research indicates that we form such impressions quite quickly, often on the basis of very little information. One kind of information that is often available in such situations—and which is therefore frequently used—is group membership, that is, the person's sex, race, age, social class, etc. Beyond such obvious kinds of information, we also use the person's words and actions to reach an initial impression.

There are problems facing us, however, when using another's actions in this way. It is not always easy to know the real cause of someone's behavior: Is it a reflection of his or her underlying personality, or was the behavior caused by factors outside the individual's control? Attempts to answer questions such as these are what social psychology calls making "attributions," and a number of theories have been proposed to help us understand how people make such determinations. Most of these approaches have emphasized the view that humans often act like scientists as they try to logically figure out the causes of events.

The subsections that make up this unit approach the question of social perception from two different angles. The first subsection is concerned with the question of accuracy in social perception. In "Spotting Lies: Can Humans Learn to Do Better?" Bella DePaulo considers the question of whether humans are able to distinguish truthful statements from lies and finds that the evidence for such an ability is not very strong. Despite humans' generally poor performance as lie detectors, however, DePaulo also argues that such performance might be improved through practice. The second selection, "The EQ Factor," describes a relatively new concept known as "emotional intelligence," or EQ. In contrast to IQ, which supposedly measures raw intelligence, EQ is said to tap a set of personality traits that reflect an intelligence in the realm of social interaction: empathy, emotional control, and accuracy in judgments of others. Above and beyond simple IQ, EQ may have a substantial impact on one's ability to function effectively in the world. The third subselection in this section, "EQ: What's Your Emotional Intelligence Quotient?" provides an interesting but very informal way to measure your own EQ.

The second unit subsection focuses on the actual processes by which social perception occurs. In the first, "Inferential Hopscotch: How People Draw Social Inferences from Behavior," the authors review recent research that indicates that drawing inferences actually consists of multiple steps. The initial step is typically rather quick and automatic; in it, the behavior is immediately interpreted as evidence of an underlying trait. In the more conscious and effortful second step, however, we deliberately try to take into account other factors that might have influenced the behavior. The final article, "Motivational Approaches to Expectancy Confirmation," deals with an interesting phenomenon known as the self-fulfilling prophecy—when our expectancies about people lead us to act differently toward them, and this behavior then prompts them to act in ways that confirm the expectancy. In this selection, John Copeland reviews recent research on motivational factors that can either make this phenomenon more likely, or less likely, to occur.

Looking Ahead: Challenge Questions

How do people go about detecting deception in others? What cues do we use to distinguish between someone telling the truth and someone telling a lie? Why aren't we more accurate in making such distinctions? How would you specifically go about improving the ability to detect deceit in others?

What are the traits that characterize people who are more socially successful than others? Does it make sense to lump all those traits together into something called "emotional intelligence"? Which of those traits would you think are more important? Which are less important?

What does it mean to say that some parts of the social inference process are "automatic" and some are "controlled"? Why is that distinction important for our understanding of the perception process?

How would you summarize the phenomenon known as "behavioral confirmation"? What is actually being "confirmed"? What circumstances make behavioral confirmation more likely to occur? Less likely? Why?

Spotting Lies:
Can Humans Learn to Do Better?

Bella M. DePaulo

Bella M. DePaulo is Professor of Psychology at the University of Virginia and recipient of a Research Scientist Development Award from the National Institute of Mental Health. Address correspondence to Bella DePaulo, Department of Psychology, Gilmer Hall, University of Virginia, Charlottesville, VA 22903; e-mail: bmd@virginia.edu.

Though cynicism may seem rampant, the empirical fact is that most people seem to believe most of what they hear most of the time. I have seen this repeatedly in the studies my colleagues and I have conducted on the detection of deception.[1] To determine whether people can separate truths from lies, we show them videotapes we have made of people we know to be lying or telling the truth. The topics of these lies and truths vary widely. For example, sometimes the people on the tape are talking about their feelings about other people they know; other times, the speakers are describing their opinions about controversial issues; in still other studies, they are talking to an artist about their preferences for various paintings, some of which are the artist's own work. When we show people ("judges") these tapes, we ask them to tell us, for each segment that they watch, whether they think the person on the tape (the "speaker") was lying or telling the truth. We also ask them to indicate, on rating scales, just how deceptive or truthful the speaker seemed to be. We might also ask them how they think the speaker really did feel and what impression the speaker was trying to convey about how he or she felt. For example, it might seem that the speaker was politely trying to give the impression that she liked the person she was describing, when in fact she detested that person.

Typically, the tapes that we play for our judges include equal numbers of truths and lies. Yet when judges watch or hear the tapes, they almost always think that many more of the messages are truths than lies. (One of the rare exceptions was a study in which the speakers on the tape were experienced salespersons pitching the kinds of products that they sell; in that study, the judges more often thought that the salespersons were lying.[2]) Similarly, judges typically believe that the speakers really do feel the way they are claiming to feel. When a speaker claims to like a painting, the judges are more inclined to believe that he or she really does like it than to infer that the kind words are a facade to cover genuine loathing.

Despite this compelling inclination to take what other people say at face value, judges are not totally blind to the differences between truths and lies. When we ask them to indicate just how deceptive or truthful the speakers seemed to be, judges reliably rate the lies as somewhat more deceptive than the truths. The ratings of both the lies and the truths are almost always on the truthful end of the scale; still, the lies seem to the judges to be a little less truthful than the truths.[3] When we study humans' ability to detect lies, it is this ability to distinguish truths from lies that we examine.

WOULD PEOPLE BE BETTER LIE DETECTORS IF THEY WERE LESS TRUSTING?

Generally, then, people seem to take each other at their word more often than they should. Carol Toris and I did a simple study to see whether people would be better lie detectors if they were forewarned of the possibility that another person might be lying to them.[4] Subjects played the role of interviewers and either were or were not forewarned that the applicants might lie to them. The forewarned interviewers did indeed become less trusting: They thought the applicants were generally more deceptive than did the interviewers whose suspicions had not been aroused. But the suspicious interviewers did not become any more accurate at distinguishing liars from truth tellers. That is, they did not rate the applicants who really were lying as any more deceptive than the ones who were telling the truth.

Robert Rosenthal and I have seen the same pattern in our studies of sex differences in detecting deceit.[5] In the way that they perceive the liars and the truth tellers on our videotapes, men are generally less trusting than women. For example, when judges watch subjects who are talking to an art student about paintings, the male judges are more likely than the female judges to think that the subjects are exaggerating their liking for the paintings; the women, in contrast, are more inclined to believe that the liking expressed by the subjects is genuine. Again, though, men and women do not differ in their abil-

From *Current Directions in Psychological Science*, June 1994, pp. 83-86. © 1994 by the American Psychological Association. Reprinted by permission of Cambridge University Press.

ities to distinguish liars from truth tellers, that is, to see the liars as relatively less trustworthy than the truth tellers.

WOULD PEOPLE BE BETTER LIE DETECTORS IF THEY HAD MORE EXPERIENCE AT IT?

To distinguish truths from lies may require some knowledge or sensitivity about the ways that lies differ from truths. Perhaps this sort of understanding comes with endless practice at trying to detect deceit. Roger Pfeifer and I studied the lie detection skills of federal law enforcement officers who had worked for years at jobs that routinely involved attempts to detect deceit.[6] These officers and undergraduate students who had no special experience or training at detecting deceit both listened to the same audiotapes of students who were lying or telling the truth about their opinions about controversial issues. Across this test of 32 lies and 32 truths, the officers were no more accurate than the students at discriminating truths from lies—they only thought they were. That is, the officers were more confident than the students, and their confidence increased over the course of the test, although their accuracy did not. A study of experienced customs inspectors told the same tale: They were no better than laypersons at discerning which potential "smugglers" to search in a mock customs inspection conducted at an airport.[7] Similarly, in studies of special groups of people who should be especially skilled lie detectors—members of the U.S. Secret Service, federal polygraphers, judges, police, psychiatrists, and special interest groups (e.g., business people and lawyers)—as well as students, Paul Ekman and Maureen O'Sullivan have found generally unimpressive levels of accuracy at detecting deceit.[8] Of those groups, only the Secret Service did particularly well.

Another kind of experience that intuitively might seem to predict skill at knowing when someone is lying is the kind that comes from getting to know someone over the course of a deepening relationship. Should not dating partners, spouses, and close friends be much more perceptive than strangers at spotting each other's lies? Once again, research has shown that experience is no guarantee of sensitivity to deceit. Compared with strangers, relational partners are more trusting of each other's truthfulness and more certain that their impressions of each other's truthfulness or deceptiveness are correct. But unless that trust is severed somehow, they are ordinarily not more accurate at detecting each other's deceit.[9]

Perhaps there is still another way in which experience might predict skill at detecting deception. Maybe any special skills that people have at detecting deceit are specific to the kinds of lies they are most experienced at hearing—the "I've heard that one before" phenomenon. My colleagues and I already knew from prior work in our lab that people lie differently to attractive people than to unattractive people. Interestingly, they lie more transparently to the former. We wanted to know whether the lies told to attractive people are especially transparent to judges who are themselves attractive. To test this idea, we asked judges who were themselves either attractive or unattractive to watch tapes of speakers who were lying and telling the truth to attractive and unattractive listeners.[10] The judges, however, could see only the speakers; they did not even know that the listeners varied systematically in attractiveness. Further, the speakers all lied and told the truth about the same topics—their opinions on controversial issues. These were not the stereotypical "gee, what beautiful eyes you have" kinds of lies. We found, once again, that the lies told to attractive listeners were easier to detect than were the lies told to unattractive listeners. More important, the lies told to attractive listeners were especially obvious to the judges who were themselves attractive. The unattrac-

tive judges, in contrast, did relatively better at detecting the lies told to the unattractive listeners.

There is other evidence, too, that skill at detecting lies may be specific to particular kinds of lies. For example, we have found that the ability to detect lies when liars are trying to hide their fond feelings is not related to the ability to detect lies when liars are trying to conceal ill will. We have also found that skill at detecting women's lies is unrelated to skill at detecting men's lies.[11] There is another interesting bit of evidence of specificity, which comes from a study in which Miron Zuckerman and his colleagues tried to train judges to be more accurate detectors of deceit.[12] The training procedure was very straightforward. Judges watched a segment in which a speaker was lying or telling the truth, and then they recorded their judgment as to whether the speaker was lying. Next, they were told whether the segment was in fact a lie or a truth. This procedure was repeated for several lies and truths told by the same speaker. Judges who were "trained" in this way did indeed become better at detecting deception, but only when watching the speaker they were trained on. Their new and improved deception detection skills did not generalize to different liars.

There is even evidence for specificity at a cultural level. Charles Bond and his colleagues have shown that both Americans and Jordanians can distinguish lies from truths when judging members of their own culture; however, they cannot differentiate each other's truths and lies.[13]

HOW DO LIES DIFFER FROM TRUTHS?

Intuitively, it may seem that the best way to train people to detect deceit is to instruct them about the kinds of behaviors that really do distinguish truths from lies and to give them practice at recognizing such

behaviors. This approach assumes that there are known differences between truths and lies, and in fact there are.[1]

Meta-analyses of the many studies of cues to deception reported in the literature indicate that when people are lying, they blink more, have more dilated pupils, and show more *adaptors* (self-manipulating gestures, such as rubbing or scratching) than they do when they are telling the truth. They also give shorter responses that are more negative, more irrelevant, and more generalized. They speak in a more distancing way (as if they do not really want to commit themselves to what they are saying), and they speak in a higher pitch. Though people who are about to tell a lie take more time to plan what they are about to say than do people who are about to tell the truth, the resulting statements tend to be more internally discrepant and more marred by hesitations, repetitions, grammatical errors, slips of the tongue, and other disfluencies. The lies seem rehearsed and lacking in spontaneity.[14]

There are, then, some important behavioral cues to deception. But for a variety of reasons, I am not optimistic about the prospects of teaching these cues directly, despite the fact that some limited successes have been reported. First, although these findings were obtained across a variety of studies, they are qualified in important ways. For example, it is possible to divide the studies into categories based on whether the liars were more or less motivated to get away with their lies. When this is done, it becomes apparent that the cues to deception differ. When people are more highly motivated to get away with their lies (compared with when they do not care as much), they shift their postures less, move their heads less, show fewer adaptors, gaze less, and even blink less when they are lying than when they are telling the truth. Their answers are also shorter and spoken more slowly. The overall impression they seem to convey is one of inhibition

and rigidity, as if they are trying too hard to control their behavior and thereby overcontrolling it. (It may be this dampening of expressiveness that accounts for another counterintuitive finding documented repeatedly in my lab—that is, that people who are most motivated to get away with their lies are, ironically, least likely to be successful at doing so when other people can see or hear any of their nonverbal cues.) Degree of liars' motivation is just one of the factors that will qualify conclusions about cues to deceit. There will be many others. For example, cues to deceit should vary with emotional state. The liar who feels guilty about a grave offense, for example, will probably lie in different ways than will a friend bubbling over with glee in an attempt to conceal a surprise birthday celebration.

Second, all these cues are associated with deceit only probabilistically. There is no one cue that always indicates that a person is lying. And each of the cues that is associated with deceit is also associated with other psychological states and conditions. For example, people speak in a higher pitch not only when they are lying but also when they are talking to children.

Third, as suggested by the training study in which improvement did not generalize to different liars, there are important individual differences in the ways that people lie. When Machiavellian people are rightly accused of lying, for example, they look their accusers in the eye while denying they have lied. It is the "low-Mach" types who conform to the cultural stereotype about lying and instead look away. Further, to determine when a person is lying, it is important to understand that person's usual ways of behaving. For instance, although halting and disfluent speech can be a sign of deceit, there are people who characteristically speak haltingly and disfluently; for them, verbal clutter is unlikely to indicate deceit unless it is even more marked than usual. Moreover, some people may be so skilled at lying that

it is virtually impossible for anyone to distinguish their lies from their truths. In the study of experienced salespersons, for example, the same kinds of judges (introductory psychology students) who could detect differences between the truths and lies of inexperienced liars could see no differences at all between the truths and lies told by experienced salespersons.[2] Even when the judges were given a hint that improved their lie detection success when they were observing inexperienced liars (namely, to pay special attention to tone of voice), they still could not differentiate the salespersons' lies and truths.

Does this mean that it is hopeless to try to refine people's sensitivity to the differences between truths and lies? Perhaps not. I think people know more about deception than it appears when experimenters ask them directly whether they think someone is lying. Sometimes people who cannot distinguish truths from lies by their ratings of deceptiveness can make a distinction by their ratings of some other attribute, such as ambivalence. Also, when people talk out loud as they try to decide whether someone is lying or not, they sound less confident when the message they are considering is a lie than when it is a truth; further, they are more likely to mention the possibility that the message is a lie when it really is.[15] Interviewers sometimes behave differently toward liars than toward truth tellers; for example, they might ask liars more questions that sound suspicious.[16] I think, then, that people have implicit knowledge about deception that they do not quite know how to access. Just how they can learn to access it is the question my students and I are currently pursuing.

Notes

1. B.M. DePaulo, J.I. Stone, and G.D. Lassiter, Deceiving and detecting deceit, in *The Self and Social Life*, B.R. Schlenker, Ed. (McGraw-Hill, New York, 1985).

2. P.J. DePaulo and B.M. DePaulo, Can at-

tempted deception by salespersons and customers be detected through nonverbal behavioral cues? *Journal of Applied Social Psychology, 19,* 1552–1577 (1989).

3. In studies in which judges simply indicate whether they think the speaker was lying or telling the truth, and lies and truths occur equally often, accuracy rarely exceeds 60%. A chance level of accuracy would be 50% in those studies.

4. C. Toris and B.M. DePaulo, Effects of actual deception and suspiciousness of deception on interpersonal perceptions, *Journal of Personality and Social Psychology, 47,* 1063–1073 (1984).

5. R. Rosenthal and B.M. DePaulo, Sex differences in eavesdropping on nonverbal cues, *Journal of Personality and Social Psychology, 37,* 273–285 (1979).

6. B.M. DePaulo and R.L. Pfeifer, On-the-job experience and skill at detecting deception, *Journal of Applied Social Psychology, 16,* 249–267 (1986).

7. R.E. Kraut and D. Poe, Behavioral roots of person perception: The deception judgments of customs inspectors and laypersons, *Journal of Personality and Social Psychology, 39,* 784–798 (1980).

8. P. Ekman and M. O'Sullivan, Who can catch a liar? *American Psychologist, 46,* 913–920 (1991).

9. S.A. McCornack and T.R. Levine, When lovers become leery: The relationship between suspiciousness and accuracy in detecting deception, *Communication Monographs, 57,* 219–230 (1990).

10. B.M. DePaulo, J. Tang, and J.I. Stone, Physical attractiveness and skill at detecting deception, *Personality and Social Psychology Bulletin, 13,* 177–187 (1987).

11. B.M. DePaulo and R. Rosenthal, Telling lies, *Journal of Personality and Social Psychology, 37,* 1713–1722 (1979).

12. M. Zuckerman, R. Koestner, and A.O. Alton, Learning to detect deception, *Journal of Personality and Social Psychology, 46,* 519–528 (1984).

13. C.F. Bond, Jr., A. Omar, A. Mahmoud, and R.N. Bonser, Lie detection across cultures, *Journal of Nonverbal Behavior, 14,* 189–204 (1990).

14. Other behavioral cues to deception have also been documented, but are based on fewer studies. For example, Ekman and his colleagues showed that nurses who were pretending to watch a pleasant film when the film was actually very gory smiled in different ways than the nurses who really were watching a pleasant film and telling the truth about it. The lying nurses were less likely to show smiles of genuine enjoyment ("Duchenne" smiles) and more likely to show "masking" smiles in which traces of their negative feelings were discernible. These data were reported in P. Ekman, W.V. Friesen, and M. O'Sullivan, Smiles while lying, *Journal of Personality and Social Psychology, 54,* 414–420 (1988).

15. K. Hurd and P. Noller, Decoding deception: A look at the process, *Journal of Nonverbal Behavior, 12,* 217–233 (1988).

16. D.B. Buller, K.D. Strzyzewski, and J. Comstock, Interpersonal deception: I. Deceivers' reactions to receivers' suspicions and probing, *Communication Monographs, 58,* 1–24 (1991).

Recommended Reading

DePaulo, B.M., Stone, J.I., and Lassiter, G.D. (1985). Deceiving and detecting deceit. In *The Self and Social Life,* B.R. Schlenker, Ed. (McGraw-Hill, New York).

Lewis, M., and Saarni, C., Eds. (1993). *Lying and Deception in Everyday Life* (Guilford Press, New York).

The EQ Factor

New brain research suggests that emotions, not IQ, may be the true measure of human intelligence

NANCY GIBBS

IT TURNS OUT THAT A SCIENTIST can see the future by watching four-year-olds interact with a marshmallow. The researcher invites the children, one by one, into a plain room and begins the gentle torment. You can have this marshmallow right now, he says. But if you wait while I run an errand, you can have two marshmallows when I get back. And then he leaves.

Some children grab for the treat the minute he's out the door. Some last a few minutes before they give in. But others are determined to wait. They cover their eyes; they put their heads down; they sing to themselves; they try to play games or even fall asleep. When the researcher returns, he gives these children their hard-earned marshmallows. And then, science waits for them to grow up.

By the time the children reach high school, something remarkable has happened. A survey of the children's parents and teachers found that those who as four-year-olds had the fortitude to hold out for the second marshmallow generally grew up to be better adjusted, more popular, adventurous, confident and dependable teenagers. The children who gave in to temptation early on were more likely to be lonely, easily frustrated and stubborn. They buckled under stress and shied away from challenges. And when some of the students in the two groups took the Scholastic Aptitude Test, the kids who had

---

Children who aren't accepted by classmates are up to eight times more likely to drop out

---

held out longer scored an average of 210 points higher.

When we think of brilliance we see Einstein, deep-eyed, woolly haired, a thinking machine with skin and mismatched socks. High achievers, we imagine, were wired for greatness from birth. But then you have to wonder why, over time, natural talent seems to ignite in some people and dim in others. This is where the marshmallows come in. It seems that the ability to delay gratification is a master skill, a triumph of the reasoning brain over the impulsive one. It is a sign, in short, of emotional intelligence. And it doesn't show up on an IQ test.

For most of this century, scientists have worshipped the hardware of the brain and the software of the mind; the messy powers of the heart were left to the poets. But cognitive theory could simply not explain the questions we wonder about most: why some people just seem to have a gift for living well; why the smartest kid in the

class will probably not end up the richest; why we like some people virtually on sight and distrust others; why some people remain buoyant in the face of troubles that would sink a less resilient soul. What qualities of the mind or spirit, in short, determine who succeeds?

The phrase "emotional intelligence" was coined by Yale psychologist Peter Salovey and the University of New Hampshire's John Mayer five years ago to describe qualities like understanding one's own feelings, empathy for the feelings of others and "the regulation of emotion in a way that enhances living." Their notion is about to bound into the national conversation, handily shortened to EQ, thanks to a new book, *Emotional Intelligence* (Bantam; $23.95) by Daniel Goleman. Goleman, a Harvard psychology Ph.D. and a New York *Times* science writer with a gift for making even the chewiest scientific theories digestible to lay readers, has brought together a decade's worth of behavioral research into how the mind processes feelings. His goal, he announces on the cover, is to redefine what it means to be smart. His thesis: when it comes to predicting people's success, brainpower as measured by IQ and standardized achievement tests may actually matter less than the qualities of mind once thought of as "character" before the word began to sound quaint.

At first glance, there would seem to be little that's new here to any close reader of

From *Time*, October 2, 1995, pp. 60-66, 68. © 1995 by Time Inc. Magazine Company. Reprinted by permission.

fortune cookies. There may be no less original idea than the notion that our hearts hold dominion over our heads. "I was so angry," we say, "I couldn't think straight." Neither is it surprising that "people skills" are useful, which amounts to saying, it's good to be nice. "It's so true it's trivial," says Dr. Paul McHugh, director of psychiatry at Johns Hopkins University School of Medicine. But if it were that simple, the book would not be quite so interesting or its implications so controversial.

Why do some people remain buoyant in the face of troubles that would sink others?

This is no abstract investigation. Goleman is looking for antidotes to restore "civility to our streets and caring to our communal life." He sees practical applications everywhere for how companies should decide whom to hire, how couples can increase the odds that their marriages will last, how parents should raise their children and how schools should teach them. When street gangs substitute for families and schoolyard insults end in stabbings, when more than half of marriages end in divorce, when the majority of the children murdered in this country are killed by parents and stepparents, many of whom say they were trying to discipline the child for behavior like blocking the TV or crying too much, it suggests a demand for remedial emotional education. While children are still young, Goleman argues, there is a "neurological window of opportunity" since the brain's prefrontal circuitry, which regulates how we act on what we feel, probably does not mature until mid-adolescence.

And it is here the arguments will break out. Goleman's highly popularized conclusions, says McHugh, "will chill any veteran scholar of psychotherapy and any neuroscientist who worries about how his research may come to be applied." While many researchers in this relatively new field are glad to see emotional issues finally taken seriously, they fear that a notion as handy as EQ invites misuse. Goleman admits the danger of suggesting that you can assign a numerical yardstick to a person's character as well as his intellect; Goleman never even uses the phrase EQ in his book. But he (begrudgingly) approved an "unscientific" EQ test in USA Today with choices like "I am aware of even subtle feelings as I have them," and "I can sense

the pulse of a group or relationship and state unspoken feelings."

"You don't want to take an average of your emotional skill," argues Harvard psychology professor Jerome Kagan, a pioneer in child-development research. "That's what's wrong with the concept of intelligence for mental skills too. Some people handle anger well but can't handle fear. Some people can't take joy. So each emotion has to be viewed differently."

EQ is not the opposite of IQ. Some people are blessed with a lot of both, some with little of either. What researchers have been trying to understand is how they complement each other; how one's ability to handle stress, for instance, affects the ability to concentrate and put intelligence to use. Among the ingredients for success, researchers now generally agree that IQ counts for about 20%; the rest depends on everything from class to luck to the neural pathways that have developed in the brain over millions of years of human evolution.

It is actually the neuroscientists and evolutionists who do the best job of explaining the reasons behind the most unreasonable behavior. In the past decade or so, scientists have learned enough about the brain to make judgments about where emotion comes from and why we need it. Primitive emotional responses held the keys to survival: fear drives the blood into the large muscles, making it easier to run; surprise triggers the eyebrows to rise, allowing the eyes to widen their view and gather more information about an unexpected event. Disgust wrinkles up the face and closes the nostrils to keep out foul smells.

Emotional life grows out of an area of the brain called the limbic system, specifically the amygdala, whence come delight and disgust and fear and anger. Millions of years ago, the neocortex was added on, enabling humans to plan, learn and remember. Lust grows from the limbic system; love, from the neocortex. Animals like reptiles that have no neocortex cannot experience anything like maternal love; this is why baby snakes have to hide to avoid being eaten by their parents. Humans, with their capacity for love, will protect their offspring, allowing the brains of the young time to develop. The more connections between limbic system and the neocortex, the more emotional responses are possible.

It was scientists like Joseph LeDoux of New York University who uncovered these cerebral pathways. LeDoux's parents owned a meat market. As a boy in Louisiana, he first learned about his future specialty by cutting up cows' brains for sweetbreads. "I found them the most interesting part of the cow's anatomy," he recalls. "They were visually pleasing—lots of folds, convolutions and patterns. The cerebellum was more interesting to look at

than steak." The butchers' son became a neuroscientist, and it was he who discovered the short circuit in the brain that lets emotions drive action before the intellect gets a chance to intervene.

A hiker on a mountain path, for example, sees a long, curved shape in the grass out of the corner of his eye. He leaps out of the way before he realizes it is only a stick that looks like a snake. Then he calms down; his cortex gets the message a few milliseconds after his amygdala and "regulates" its primitive response.

Without these emotional reflexes, rarely conscious but often terribly powerful, we would scarcely be able to function. "Most decisions we make have a vast number of possible outcomes, and any attempt to analyze all of them would never end," says University of Iowa neurologist Antonio Damasio, author of Descartes' Error: Emotion, Reason and the Human Brain. "I'd ask you to lunch tomorrow, and when the appointed time arrived, you'd still be thinking about whether you should come." What tips the balance, Damasio contends, is our unconscious assigning of emotional values to some of those choices. Whether we experience a somatic response—a gut feeling of dread or a giddy sense of elation— emotions are helping to limit the field in any choice we have to make. If the prospect of lunch with a neurologist is unnerving or distasteful, Damasio suggests, the invitee

Anxiety is a rehearsal for danger: A little anxiety helps focus the mind; too much can paralyze it

will conveniently remember a previous engagement.

When Damasio worked with patients in whom the connection between emotional brain and neocortex had been severed because of damage to the brain, he discovered how central that hidden pathway is to how we live our lives. People who had lost that linkage were just as smart and quick to reason, but their lives often fell apart nonetheless. They could not make decisions because they didn't know how they felt about their choices. They couldn't react to warnings or anger in other people. If they made a mistake, like a bad investment, they felt no regret or shame and so were bound to repeat it.

If there is a cornerstone to emotional

intelligence on which most other emotional skills depend, it is a sense of self-awareness, of being smart about what we feel. A person whose day starts badly at home may be grouchy all day at work without quite knowing why. Once an emotional response comes into awareness—or, physiologically, is processed through the neocortex—the chances of handling it appropriately improve. Scientists refer to "metamood," the ability to pull back and recognize that "what I'm feeling is anger," or sorrow, or shame.

Metamood is a difficult skill because emotions so often appear in disguise. A person in mourning may know he is sad, but he may not recognize that he is also angry at the person for dying—because this seems somehow inappropriate. A parent who yells at the child who ran into the street is expressing anger at disobedience, but the degree of anger may owe more to the fear the parent feels at what could have happened.

In Goleman's analysis, self-awareness is perhaps the most crucial ability because it allows us to exercise some self-control. The idea is not to repress feeling (the reaction that has made psychoanalysts rich) but rather to do what Aristotle considered the hard work of the will. "Anyone can become angry—that is easy," he wrote in the *Nicomachean Ethics*. "But to be angry with the right person, to the right degree, at the right time, for the right purpose, and in the right way—that is not easy."

Some impulses seem to be easier to control than others. Anger, not surprisingly, is one of the hardest, perhaps because of its evolutionary value in priming people to action. Researchers believe anger usually arises out of a sense of being trespassed against—the belief that one is being robbed

---

Deficient emotional skills may be the reason more than half of all marriages end in divorce

---

of what is rightfully his. The body's first response is a surge of energy, the release of a cascade of neurotransmitters called catecholamines. If a person is already aroused or under stress, the threshold for release is lower, which helps explain why people's tempers shorten during a hard day.

Scientists are not only discovering where anger comes from; they are also exposing myths about how best to handle it. Popular wisdom argues for "letting it all hang out" and having a good cathartic rant. But Goleman cites studies showing that dwelling on anger actually increases its power; the body needs a chance to process the adrenaline through exercise, relaxation techniques, a well-timed intervention or even the old admonition to count to 10.

Anxiety serves a similar useful purpose, so long as it doesn't spin out of control. Worrying is a rehearsal for danger; the act of fretting focuses the mind on a problem so it can search efficiently for solutions. The danger comes when worrying blocks thinking, becoming an end in itself or a path to resignation instead of perseverance. Over-worrying about failing increases the likelihood of failure; a salesman so concerned about his falling sales that he can't bring himself to pick up the phone guarantees that his sales will fall even further.

But why are some people better able to "snap out of it" and get on with the task at hand? Again, given sufficient self-awareness, people develop coping mechanisms. Sadness and discouragement, for instance, are "low arousal" states, and the dispirited salesman who goes out for a run is triggering a high arousal state that is incompatible with staying blue. Relaxation works better for high-energy moods like anger or anxiety. Either way, the idea is to shift to a state of arousal that breaks the destructive cycle of the dominant mood.

The idea of being able to predict which salesmen are most likely to prosper was not an abstraction for Metropolitan Life, which in the mid-'80s was hiring 5,000 salespeople a year and training them at a cost of more than $30,000 each. Half quit the first year, and four out of five within four years. The reason: selling life insurance involves having the door slammed in your face over and over again. Was it possible to identify which people would be better at handling frustration and take each refusal as a challenge rather than a setback?

The head of the company approached psychologist Martin Seligman at the University of Pennsylvania and invited him to test some of his theories about the importance of optimism in people's success. When optimists fail, he has found, they attribute the failure to something they can change, not some innate weakness that they are helpless to overcome. And that confidence in their power to effect change is self-reinforcing. Seligman tracked 15,000 new workers who had taken two tests. One was the company's regular screening exam, the other Seligman's test measuring their levels of optimism. Among the new hires was a group who flunked the screening test but scored as

"superoptimists" on Seligman's exam. And sure enough, they did the best of all; they outsold the pessimists in the regular group by 21% in the first year and 57% in the second. For years after that, passing Seligman's test was one way to get hired as a MetLife salesperson.

Perhaps the most visible emotional skills, the ones we recognize most readily, are the "people skills" like empathy, graciousness, the ability to read a social situation. Researchers believe that about 90% of emotional communication is nonverbal. Harvard psychologist Robert Rosenthal developed the PONS test (Profile of Nonverbal Sensitivity) to measure people's ability to read emotional cues. He shows subjects a film of a young woman expressing feelings—anger, love, jealousy, gratitude, seduction—edited so that one or another nonverbal cue is blanked out. In some instances the face is visible but not the body, or the woman's eyes are hidden, so that viewers have to judge the feeling by subtle cues. Once again, people with higher PONS scores tend to be more successful in their work and relationships; children who score well are more popular and successful in school, even when their IQs are quite average.

Like other emotional skills, empathy is an innate quality that can be shaped by experience. Infants as young as three months old exhibit empathy when they get upset at the sound of another baby crying. Even very young children learn by imitation; by watching how others act when they see someone in distress, these children acquire a repertoire of sensitive responses. If, on the other hand, the feelings they begin to express are not recognized and reinforced by the adults around them, they not only cease to express those feelings but they also become less able to recognize them in themselves or others.

Empathy too can be seen as a survival skill. Bert Cohler, a University of Chicago psychologist, and Fran Stott, dean of the Erikson Institute for Advanced Study in Child Development in Chicago, have found that children from psychically damaged families frequently become hypervigilant, developing an intense attunement to their parents' moods. One child they studied, Nicholas, had a horrible habit of approaching other kids in his nursery-school class as if he were going to kiss them, then would bite them instead. The scientists went back to study videos of Nicholas at 20 months interacting with his psychotic mother and found that she had responded to his every expression of anger or independence with compulsive kisses. The researchers dubbed them "kisses of death," and their true significance was obvious to Nicholas, who arched his back in horror at her approaching lips—and passed his own rage on to his classmates years later.

Empathy also acts as a buffer to cruelty, and it is a quality conspicuously lacking in child molesters and psychopaths. Goleman cites some chilling research into brutality by Robert Hare, a psychologist at the University of British Columbia. Hare found that psychopaths, when hooked up to electrodes and told they are going to receive a shock, show none of the visceral responses that fear of pain typically triggers: rapid heartbeat, sweating and so on. How could the threat of punishment deter such people from committing crimes?

It is easy to draw the obvious lesson from these test results. How much happier would we be, how much more successful as individuals and civil as a society, if we were more alert to the importance of emotional intelligence and more adept at teaching it? From kindergartens to business schools to corporations across the country, people are taking seriously the idea that a little more time spent on the "touchy-feely" skills so often derided may in fact pay rich dividends.

In the corporate world, according to

> In the corporate world, say personnel executives, IQ gets you hired, but EQ gets you promoted

personnel executives, IQ gets you hired, but EQ gets you promoted. Goleman likes to tell of a manager at AT&T's Bell Labs, a think tank for brilliant engineers in New Jersey, who was asked to rank his top performers. They weren't the ones with the highest IQs; they were the ones whose E-mail got answered. Those workers who were good collaborators and networkers and popular with colleagues were more likely to get the cooperation they needed to reach their goals than the socially awkward, lone-wolf geniuses.

When David Campbell and others at the Center for Creative Leadership studied "derailed executives," the rising stars who flamed out, the researchers found that these executives failed most often because of "an interpersonal flaw" rather than a technical inability. Interviews with top executives in the U.S. and Europe turned up nine so-called fatal flaws, many of them classic emotional failings, such as "poor working relations," being "authoritarian" or "too ambitious" and having "conflict with upper management."

At the center's executive-leadership seminars across the country, managers come to get emotionally retooled. "This isn't sensitivity training or Sunday-supplement stuff," says Campbell. "One thing they know when they get through is what other people think of them." And the executives have an incentive to listen. Says Karen Boylston, director of the center's team-leadership group: "Customers are telling businesses, 'I don't care if every member of your staff graduated with honors from Harvard,

One Way to Test Your EQ

UNLIKE IQ, WHICH IS GAUGED BY THE FAMOUS STANFORD-Binet tests, EQ does not lend itself to any single numerical measure. Nor should it, say experts. Emotional intelligence is by definition a complex, multifaceted quality representing such intangibles as self-awareness, empathy, persistence and social deftness.

Some aspects of emotional intelligence, however, can be quantified. Optimism, for example, is a handy measure of a person's self-worth. According to Martin Seligman, a University of Pennsylvania psychologist, how people respond to setbacks—optimistically or pessimistically—is a fairly accurate indicator of how well they will succeed in school, in sports and in certain kinds of work. To test his theory, Seligman devised a questionnaire to screen insurance salesmen at MetLife.

In Seligman's test, job applicants were asked to imagine a hypothetical event and then choose the response (A or B) that most closely resembled their own. Some samples from his questionnaire:

You forget your spouse's (boyfriend's/girlfriend's) birthday.
A. I'm not good at remembering birthdays.
B. I was preoccupied with other things.

You owe the library $10 for an overdue book.
A. When I am really involved in what I am reading, I often forget when it's due.
B. I was so involved in writing the report, I forgot to return the book.

You lose your temper with a friend.
A. He or she is always nagging me.
B. He or she was in a hostile mood.

You are penalized for returning your income-tax forms late.
A. I always put off doing my taxes.
B. I was lazy about getting my taxes done this year.

You've been feeling run-down.
A. I never get a chance to relax.
B. I was exceptionally busy this week.

A friend says something that hurts your feelings.
A. She always blurts things out without thinking of others.
B. My friend was in a bad mood and took it out on me.

You fall down a great deal while skiing.
A. Skiing is difficult.
B. The trails were icy.

You gain weight over the holidays, and you can't lose it.
A. Diets don't work in the long run.
B. The diet I tried didn't work.

Seligman found that those insurance salesmen who answered with more B's than A's were better able to overcome bad sales days, recovered more easily from rejection and were less likely to quit. People with an optimistic view of life tend to treat obstacles and setbacks as temporary (and therefore surmountable). Pessimists take them personally; what others see as fleeting, localized impediments, they view as pervasive and permanent.

The most dramatic proof of his theory, says Seligman, came at the 1988 Olympic Games in Seoul, South Korea, after U.S. swimmer Matt Biondi turned in two disappointing performances in his first two races. Before the Games, Biondi had been favored to win seven golds—as Mark Spitz had done 16 years earlier. After those first two races, most commentators thought Biondi would be unable to recover from his setback. Not Seligman. He had given some members of the U.S swim team a version of his optimism test before the races; it showed that Biondi possessed an extraordinarily upbeat attitude. Rather than losing heart after turning in a bad time, as others might, Biondi tended to respond by swimming even faster. Sure enough, Biondi bounced right back, winning five gold medals in the next five races.

—By Alice Park

Stanford and Wharton. I will take my business and go where I am understood and treated with respect.' "

Nowhere is the discussion of emotional intelligence more pressing than in schools, where both the stakes and the opportunities seem greatest. Instead of con-

---

Some EQ is innate. Infants as young as three months show empathy

---

stant crisis intervention, or declarations of war on drug abuse or teen pregnancy or violence, it is time, Goleman argues, for preventive medicine. "Five years ago, teachers didn't want to think about this," says principal Roberta Kirshbaum of P.S. 75 in New York City. "But when kids are getting killed in high school, we have to deal with it." Five years ago, Kirshbaum's school adopted an emotional literacy program, designed to help children learn to manage anger, frustration, loneliness. Since then, fights at lunchtime have decreased from two or three a day to almost none.

Educators can point to all sorts of data to support this new direction. Students who are depressed or angry literally cannot learn. Children who have trouble being accepted by their classmates are 2 to 8 times as likely to drop out. An inability to distinguish distressing feelings or handle frustration has been linked to eating disorders in girls.

Many school administrators are completely rethinking the weight they have been giving to traditional lessons and standardized tests. Peter Relic, president of the National Association of Independent Schools, would like to junk the SAT completely. "Yes, it may cost a heck of a lot more money to assess someone's EQ rather than using a machine-scored test to measure IQ," he says. "But if we don't, then we're saying that a test score is more important to us than who a child is as a human being. That means an immense loss in terms of human potential because we've defined success too narrowly."

This warm embrace by educators has left some scientists in a bind. On one hand, says Yale psychologist Salovey, "I love the idea that we want to teach people a richer understanding of their emotional life, to help them achieve their goals." But, he adds, "what I would oppose is training conformity to social expectations." The danger is that any campaign to hone emotional

Square Pegs in the Oval Office?

IF A HIGH DEGREE OF EMOTIONAL INTELLIGENCE IS A PREREQUISITE FOR OUTstanding achievement, there ought to be no better place to find it than in the White House. It turns out, however, that not every man who reached the pinnacle of American leadership was a gleaming example of self-awareness, empathy, impulse control and all the other qualities that mark an elevated EQ.

Oliver Wendell Holmes, who knew intelligence when he saw it, judged Franklin Roosevelt "a second-class intellect, but a first-class temperament." Born and educated as an aristocrat, F.D.R. had polio and needed a wheelchair for most of his adult life. Yet, far from becoming a self-pitying wretch, he developed an unbridled optimism that served him and the country well during the Depression and World War II—this despite, or because of, what Princeton professor Fred Greenstein calls Roosevelt's "tendency toward deviousness and duplicity."

Even a first-class temperament, however, is not a sure predictor of a successful presidency. According to Duke University political scientist James David Barber, the most perfect blend of intellect and warmth of personality in a Chief Executive was the brilliant Thomas Jefferson, who "knew the importance of communication and empathy. He never lost the common touch." Richard Ellis, a professor of politics at Oregon's Willamette University who is skeptical of the whole EQ theory, cites two 19th century Presidents who did not fit the mold. "Martin Van Buren was well adjusted, balanced, empathetic and persuasive, but he was not very successful," says Ellis. "Andrew Jackson was less well adjusted, less balanced, less empathetic and was terrible at controlling his own impulses, but he transformed the presidency."

Lyndon Johnson as Senate majority leader was a brilliant practitioner of the art of political persuasion, yet failed utterly to transfer that gift to the White House. In fact, says Princeton's Greenstein, L. B. J. and Richard Nixon would be labeled "worst cases" on any EQ scale of Presidents. Each was touched with political genius, yet each met with disaster. "To some extent," says Greenstein, "this is a function of the extreme aspects of their psyches; they are the political versions of Van Gogh, who does unbelievable paintings and then cuts off his ear."

History professor William Leuchtenburg of the University of North Carolina at Chapel Hill suggests that the 20th century Presidents with perhaps the highest IQs—Wilson, Hoover and Carter—also had the most trouble connecting with their constituents. Woodrow Wilson, he says, "was very high strung [and] arrogant; he was not willing to strike any middle ground. Herbert Hoover was so locked into certain ideas that you could never convince him otherwise. Jimmy Carter is probably the most puzzling of the three. He didn't have a deficiency of temperament; in fact, he was too temperate. There was an excessive rationalization about Carter's approach."

That was never a problem for John Kennedy and Ronald Reagan. Nobody ever accused them of intellectual genius, yet both radiated qualities of leadership with an infectious confidence and openheartedness that endeared them to the nation. Whether President Clinton will be so endeared remains a puzzle. That he is a Rhodes scholar makes him certifiably brainy, but his emotional intelligence is shaky. He obviously has the knack for establishing rapport with people, but he often appears so eager to please that he looks weak. "As for controlling his impulses," says Willamette's Ellis, "Clinton is terrible." —By Jesse Birnbaum.
Reported by James Carney/Washington and Lisa H. Towle/Raleigh

---

skills in children will end up teaching that there is a "right" emotional response for any given situation—laugh at parades, cry at funerals, sit still at church. "You can teach self-control," says Dr. Alvin Poussaint, professor of psychiatry at Harvard Medical School. "You can teach that it's better to talk out your anger and not use violence. But is it good emotional intelligence not to challenge authority?"

SOME PSYCHOLOGISTS GO further and challenge the very idea that emotional skills can or should be taught in any kind of formal, classroom way. Goleman's premise that children can be trained to analyze their feelings strikes Johns Hopkins' McHugh as an effort to reinvent the

encounter group: "I consider that an abominable idea, an idea we have seen with adults. That failed, and now he wants to try it with children? Good grief!" He cites the description in Goleman's book of an experimental program at the Nueva Learning Center in San Francisco. In one scene, two fifth-grade boys start to argue over the rules of an exercise, and the teacher breaks in to ask them to talk about what they're feeling. "I appreciate the way you're being assertive in talking with Tucker," she says to one student. "You're not attacking." This strikes McHugh as pure folly. "The author is presuming that someone has the key to the right emotions to be taught to children. We don't even know the

right emotions to be taught to adults. Do you really think a child of eight or nine really understands the difference between aggressiveness and assertiveness?"

The problem may be that there is an ingredient missing. Emotional skills, like intellectual ones, are morally neutral. Just as a genius could use his intellect either to cure cancer or engineer a deadly virus, someone with great empathic insight could use it to inspire colleagues or exploit them. Without a moral compass to guide people in how to employ their gifts, emotional intelligence can be used for good or evil. Columbia University psychologist Walter Mischel, who invented the marshmallow test and others like it,

observes that the knack for delaying gratification that makes a child one marshmallow richer can help him become a better citizen or—just as easily—an even more brilliant criminal.

Given the passionate arguments that are raging over the state of moral instruction in this country, it is no wonder Goleman chose to focus more on neutral emotional skills than on the values that should govern their use. That's another book—and another debate.

—Reported by Sharon E. Epperson and Lawrence Mondi/New York, James L. Graff/Chicago and Lisa H. Towle/Raleigh

EQ
What's your emotional intelligence quotient?

SPECIAL TO *UTNE READER*
Daniel Goleman
Daniel Goleman is a reporter for the New York Times and author of Emotional Intelligence *(Bantam, 1995).*

You've got the intellectual credentials: You did pretty well in school, maybe have a college diploma or even an advanced degree. You got high scores on your SATs and GREs, or even on that holy grail of the intellect, the IQ test. You may even be in Mensa, the select high-IQ club.

That's fine when it comes to intelligence of the academic variety. But how bright are you outside the classroom, when it comes to life's stickier moments? There you need other kinds of resourcefulness—most especially emotional intelligence, a different way of being smart.

TRY THE EQ TEST

So far, there's no single, well-validated paper-and-pencil test for emotional intelligence like an IQ test, but there are many situations in which the emotionally intelligent response is quantifiable. The following questions will give you a rough sense of what your EQ might be.

And listen, smarty-pants—answer honestly, on the basis of what you *really* would be most likely to do. Don't try to second-guess what seems right by using those old rules for psyching out multiple choice tests that helped you through school!

 1. You're on an airplane that suddenly hits extremely bad turbulence and begins rocking from side to side. What do you do?

a. Continue to read your book or magazine, or watch the movie, paying little attention to the turbulence.
b. Become vigilant for an emergency, carefully monitoring the stewardesses and reading the emergency instructions card.
c. A little of both a and b.
d. Not sure—never noticed.

 2. You've taken a group of 4-year-olds to the park, and one of them starts crying because the others won't play with her. What do you do?

a. Stay out of it—let the kids deal with it on their own.
b. Talk to her and help her figure out ways to get the other kids to play with her.
c. Tell her in a kind voice not to cry.
d. Try to distract the crying girl by showing her some other things she could play with.

 3. Assume you're a college student who had hoped to get an A in a course, but you have just found out you got a C- on the midterm. What do you do?

a. Sketch out a specific plan for ways to improve your grade and resolve to follow through on your plans.
b. Resolve to do better in the future.
c. Tell yourself it really doesn't matter much how you do in the course, and concentrate instead on other classes where your grades are higher.
d. Go to see the professor and try to talk her into giving you a better grade.

 4. Imagine you're an insurance salesman calling prospective clients. Fifteen people in a row have hung up on you, and you're getting discouraged. What do you do?

a. Call it a day and hope you have better luck tomorrow.
b. Assess qualities in yourself that may be undermining your ability to make a sale.
c. Try something new in the next call, and keep plugging away.
d. Consider another line of work.

From *Utne Reader,* November/December 1995, pp. 74-76. © 1995 by Daniel Goleman. Reprinted by permission.

5. You're a manager in an organization that is trying to encourage respect for racial and ethnic diversity. You overhear someone telling a racist joke. What do you do?

a. Ignore it—it's only a joke.
b. Call the person into your office for a reprimand.
c. Speak up on the spot, saying that such jokes are inappropriate and will not be tolerated in your organization.
d. Suggest to the person telling the joke he go through a diversity training program.

6. You're trying to calm down a friend who has worked himself up into a fury at a driver in another car who has cut dangerously close in front of him. What do you do?

a. Tell him to forget it—he's okay now and it's no big deal.
b. Put on one of his favorite tapes and try to distract him.
c. Join him in putting down the other driver, as a show of rapport.
d. Tell him about a time something like this happened to you and how you felt as mad as he does now, but then you saw the other driver was on the way to a hospital emergency room.

7. You and your life partner have gotten into an argument that has escalated into a shouting match; you're both upset and, in the heat of anger, making personal attacks you don't really mean. What's the best thing to do?

a. Take a 20-minute break and then continue the discussion.
b. Just stop the argument—go silent, no matter what your partner says.
c. Say you're sorry and ask your partner to apologize, too.
d. Stop for a moment, collect your thoughts, then state your side of the case as precisely as you can.

8. You've been assigned to head a working team that is trying to come up with a creative solution to a nagging problem at work. What's the first thing you do?

a. Draw up an agenda and allot time for discussion of each item so you make best use of your time together.
b. Have people take the time to get to know each other better.
c. Begin by asking each person for ideas about how to solve the problem, while the ideas are fresh.
d. Start with a brainstorming session, encouraging everyone to say whatever comes to mind, no matter how wild.

9. Your 3-year-old son is extremely timid, and has been hypersensitive about—and a bit fearful of—new places and people virtually since he was born. What do you do?

a. Accept that he has a shy temperament and think of ways to shelter him from situations that would upset him.
b. Take him to a child psychiatrist for help.
c. Purposely expose him to lots of new people and places so he can get over his fear.
d. Engineer an ongoing series of challenging but manageable experiences that will teach him he can handle new people and places.

10. For years you've been wanting to get back to learning to play a musical instrument you tried in childhood, and now, just for fun, you've finally gotten around to starting. You want to make the most effective use of your time. What do you do?

a. Hold yourself to a strict practice time each day.
b. Choose pieces that stretch your abilities a bit.
c. Practice only when you're really in the mood.
d. Pick pieces that are far beyond your ability, but that you can master with diligent effort.

READ THE FOLLOWING TIPS, THEN CHECK YOUR ANSWERS.

The basics of emotional intelligence include:
** Knowing your feelings and using them to make life decisions you can live with.
** Being able to manage your emotional life without being hijacked by it—not being paralyzed by depression or worry, or swept away by anger.
** Persisting in the face of setbacks and channeling your impulses in order to pursue your goals.
** Empathy—reading other people's emotions without their having to tell you what they are feeling.
** Handling feelings in relationships with skill and harmony—being able to articulate the unspoken pulse of a group, for example.

ANSWERS

 1. Anything but D—that answer reflects a lack of awareness of your habitual responses under stress. A=20, B=20, C=20, D=0.

 2. B is best. Emotionally intelligent parents use their children's moments of upsets as opportunities to act as emotional coaches, helping their children understand what made them upset, what they are feeling, and alternatives the child can try. A=0, B=20, C=0, D=0.

 3. A. One mark of self-motivation is being able to formulate a plan for overcoming obstacles and frustrations and follow through on it. A=20, B=0, C=0, D=0.

 4. C. Optimism, a mark of emotional intelligence, leads people to see setbacks as challenges they can learn from, and to persist, trying out new approaches rather than giving up, blaming themselves, or getting demoralized. A=0, B=0, C=20, D=0.

 5. C. The most effective way to create an atmosphere that welcomes diversity is to make clear in public that the social norms of your organization do not tolerate such expressions. Instead of trying to change prejudices (a much harder task), keep people from acting on them. A=0, B=0, C=20, D=0.

 6. D. Data on rage and how to calm it show the effectiveness of distracting the angry person from the focus of his rage, empathizing with his feelings and perspective, and suggesting a less anger-provoking way of seeing the situation. A=0, B=5, C=5, D=20.

 7. A. Take a break of 20 minutes or more. It takes at least that long to clear the body of the physiological arousal of anger—which distorts your perception and makes you more likely to launch damaging personal attacks. After cooling down you'll be more likely to have a fruitful discussion. A=20, B=0, C=0, D=0.

 8. B. Creative groups work at their peak when rapport, harmony, and comfort levels are highest—then people are freer to make their best contribution. A=0, B=20, C=0, D=0.

 9. D. Children born with a timid temperament can often become more outgoing if their parents arrange an ongoing series of manageable challenges to their shyness. A=0, B=5, C=0, D=20.

 10. B. By giving yourself moderate challenges, you are most likely to get into the state of flow, which is both pleasurable and where people learn and perform at their best. A=0, B=20, C=0, D=0.

WHAT YOUR SCORE MEANS (HYPOTHETICALLY):
200—Emotional genius
175—Empath
150—Gandhi
125—Freud
100—Average
 75—Have you tried psychotherapy?
 50—Emotionally challenged
 25—Neanderthal
  0—Newt

Emotional intelligence gives you a competitive edge. Even at Bell Labs, where everyone is smart, studies find that the most valued and productive engineers are those with the traits of emotional intelligence—not necessarily the highest IQ. Having great intellectual abilities may make you a superb fiscal analyst or legal scholar, but a highly developed emotional intelligence will make you a candidate for CEO or a brilliant trial lawyer.

Empathy and other qualities of the heart make it more likely that your marriage will thrive. Lack of those abilities explains why people of high IQ can be such disastrous pilots of their personal lives.

An analysis of the personality traits that accompany high IQ in men and women who also lack these emotional competencies portrays, well, the stereotypical nerd: critical and condescending, inhibited and uncomfortable with sensuality, emotionally bland. By contrast, men and women with the traits that mark emotional intelligence are poised and outgoing, committed to people and causes, sympathetic and caring, with a rich but appropriate emotional life—they're comfortable with themselves, others, and the social universe they live in.

A high IQ may get you into Mensa, but it won't make you a mensch.

Inferential Hopscotch: How People Draw Social Inferences From Behavior

Douglas S. Krull and Darin J. Erickson

Douglas S. Krull is an Assistant Professor of Psychology at the University of Missouri, Columbia. **Darin J. Erickson** is a graduate student at the University of Missouri, Columbia. Address correspondence to Douglas S. Krull, Department of Psychology, University of Missouri, Columbia, MO 65211; e-mail: psy261@mizzou1.

Tim and Sue observe an anxious-looking man in a dentist's waiting room. Tim decides that the man must have an anxious personality (a trait inference). In contrast, Sue decides that the man is anxious because he is waiting to see the dentist (a situational inference). Why might Tim and Sue have drawn such different inferences? Social inference researchers have long been interested in the different inferences that people draw when they view the same behavior. Early work on social inference focused on the tendency for peoples' inferences to be biased in favor of trait inferences. For example, when members of a debate team are assigned to argue for a particular political position, observers often infer that the debaters' true attitudes match their assigned position.[1] More recently, research has focused not only on *what* people infer (i.e., the final inference), but also on *how* they infer (i.e., the process by which inferences are drawn).

THE TRAIT INFERENCE PROCESS

The vast majority of recent work on social inference has investigated the process by which people draw inferences about an actor's personality. Research suggests that the trait inference process can be thought of as composed of three stages: behavior interpretation, trait inference, and situational revision.[2] First, people interpret, or derive meaning from, the actor's behavior ("John seems to be behaving in a very anxious manner"); next, they draw a trait inference that corresponds to the behavior ("John must have a very anxious personality"); finally, they may revise this inference to a greater or lesser degree by taking into account the situational forces that may have contributed to the actor's behavior ("John is waiting to see the dentist; perhaps he isn't such an anxious person after all"). These three stages seem to differ in the amount of effort required. Behavior interpretation and trait inference seem to be relatively spontaneous and effortless, whereas situational revision seems to be relatively effortful.[3] This process is depicted in Figure 1.

Stage 1: Behavior Interpretation

People tend to see what they expect to see.[4] Thus, many people in American society tend to interpret an ambiguous shove as more hostile when given by a black person than by a white person. However, people's expectations have less impact on their interpretations of behavior if the behavior is unambiguous. Trope[5] conducted an experiment in which participants interpreted facial expressions after being informed about the context in which the expressions took place. If the facial expressions were ambiguous, participants' context-based expectations influenced their interpretations of the emotions (e.g., participants interpreted a facial expression as happier if the context was "winning in a TV game show" and more fearful if the context was "a swarm of bees flying into the room"). If the facial expressions were unambiguous, participants' expectations had significantly less impact.

Stage 2: Trait Inference

People often think that you can judge a book by its cover, that people's actions reflect their personalities. Uleman, Winter, and their colleagues[6] conducted a series of investigations which suggest that when people view behavior, they may spontaneously draw inferences about the actor's personality. In these studies, participants read sentences (e.g., "The secretary solved the mystery halfway through the book") that suggest a particular trait (e.g., clever). Uleman and Winter proposed that if people spontaneously draw trait inferences upon reading the sentences (at encoding), then these traits should facilitate recall for the sentences (at retrieval). Studies of this hypothesis have found repeatedly that participants' recall is superior with trait cues than with no cues, and occasionally better with trait cues than with other types of

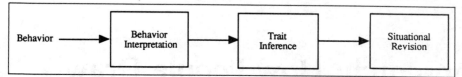

Fig. 1. The trait inference process.

cues (semantic), even when participants were not aware when reading the sentences that their memory for the sentences would be tested.

In a similar paradigm, Lupfer, Clark, and Hutcherson[7] conducted an experiment which suggests that trait inferences may be substantially effortless as well as spontaneous. If trait inference is substantially effortless, then people should be able to perform it even when their conscious resources are limited (i.e., when they are cognitively busy). Participants read sentences while they simultaneously rehearsed an easy set of numbers (which should not make people cognitively busy) or a difficult set of numbers (which should make people cognitively busy). Not only did trait-cued participants recall more sentences than noncued participants, but the trait-cued recall of participants in the difficult condition was not significantly different from the trait-cued recall of participants in the easy condition. This and other research suggests that when people view behavior, they may spontaneously and effortlessly interpret the behavior and infer that the actor's personality corresponds to the behavior ("John behaved in an anxious manner; John must have an anxious personality") even when they are distracted or preoccupied.

A relearning paradigm developed by Carlston and Skowronski[8] looks particularly promising for the further investigation of spontaneous trait inferences. These researchers first presented participants with person photos paired with personal statements that implied traits. For example, the following statement implies that the person in the photo is cruel: "I hate animals. Today I was walking to the pool hall and I saw this puppy. So I kicked it out of my way." Some participants were instructed to draw a trait inference (specific-impression condition), others were instructed to form an impression (general-impression condition), and others were told to simply look at the photos and statements (ostensibly to familiarize themselves with these materials for a later phase of the experiment; no-instruction condition). If these latter participants inferred traits, this would be evidence for spontaneity.

After a filler task, all participants were given photo–trait pairs and were instructed explicitly to memorize the trait associated with each photo. In some cases (relearning trials), these pairs corresponded to the photo–statement pairs presented earlier (e.g., the photo previously presented with the statement about kicking the puppy was paired with the word *cruel*). Thus, if the participants had previously inferred traits from the statements, they would be relearning the associations between the photos and the traits instead of learning these associations for the first time. In other cases, the photo–trait pairs did not correspond to the previous photo–statement pairs (control trials). Finally, participants were shown the photos and asked to recall the traits. Recall was higher for relearning trials than for control trials, suggesting that participants had inferred traits from the initial photo–statement pairs. In addition, this finding was similar across all three conditions (specific impression, general impression, no instruction), which suggests that trait inferences had occurred in the impression conditions, and spontaneous trait inferences had occurred in the no-instruction condition. Carlston and Skowronski also ruled out several alternative explanations. Thus, these results provide strong evidence that trait inferences can be drawn spontaneously.

Stage 3: Situational Revision

People may consider the situation in which the behavior took place when they draw trait inferences, but it is not easy for them to do so. Unlike behavior interpretation and trait inference, situational revision seems to be a relatively effortful process, and so people may not complete it when they lack either the ability or the motivation to do so. A program of research conducted by Gilbert and his colleagues[3] suggests that people may be unable to complete the situational revision stage sufficiently when they are cognitively busy (when they have limited conscious resources). In one study, participants viewed several videotape clips of an anxious-appearing woman who was ostensibly discussing anxiety-provoking topics (sexual fantasies) or calm topics (world travel) with an interviewer. The film was silent, but the discussion topics appeared in subtitles. Half the participants were required to memorize these topics (cognitively busy participants), and half were not. One might expect that participants would recognize that most people would be more anxious when discussing anxiety-provoking topics than calm topics, but, remarkably, participants who attempted to memorize the discussion topics were less able than the other participants to consider the effects of the topics when drawing inferences about the target. Thus, this study suggests that when people are preoccupied or distracted, they may draw biased trait inferences because they fail to sufficiently consider the situation in which the behavior took place.

An experiment by Webster[9] suggests that people may also revise their trait inferences insufficiently when they are unmotivated. Participants expected to answer questions about their impression of a speaker who expressed a negative view to-

ward student exchange programs. Before viewing the speaker, participants were informed that she was required to express a negative view, but Webster predicted that unmotivated participants would be less likely than motivated participants to consider this fact, and would be more likely to infer that the speaker's view reflected her true attitude. Half of the participants expected to perform a task involving multivariate statistics after the impression formation task, whereas the other half expected to perform a task involving comedy clips after the impression formation task. Webster predicted that participants who expected to view the statistics lecture would be motivated to "stretch the fun" on the (comparatively attractive) impression formation task, whereas participants who expected to view the comedy clips would be motivated to "get the (comparatively boring) impression formation task over with." As Webster predicted, participants in the statistics condition were better able to revise their inferences than were participants in the comedy clips condition, and were less likely to infer that the speaker's expressed view reflected her true attitude.

When people want to know about people, they seem to infer traits. What if people want to know about situations? Social inference researchers have learned much about the process by which people infer traits. Considerably less work has investigated how social inference proceeds when people are interested in learning about a situation, but some work suggests that situational inference may be a mirror image of the trait inference process.[10] In an experiment very similar to Gilbert's aforementioned anxious-woman experiment, participants viewed a silent videotape of an anxious-appearing interviewee. Half the participants attempted to estimate the interviewee's trait anxiety (trait goal); half attempted to estimate the degree of anxiety provoked by the interview topics (situational goal). Half of the participants in each of these conditions were made cognitively busy. For people with a trait goal, the results mirrored Gilbert's; that is, in an analysis that combined the dispositional and situational anxiety measures, busy participants inferred more dispositional anxiety than did nonbusy participants. However, the results were reversed for participants with a situational goal; that is, busy participants in this condition inferred more situational anxiety than did nonbusy participants. These results suggest that when people are interested in situations (rather than traits), they may spontaneously and effortlessly draw situational inferences (rather than trait inferences) from behavior. If people have the ability and motivation, they may revise these inferences by considering the actor's personality.

Considerable research suggests that when people have a trait goal, they interpret the actor's behavior, spontaneously and effortlessly draw a trait inference, and, if they have sufficient conscious resources and motivation, revise this inference by considering the situation in which the behavior took place. When people have a situational goal, they interpret the actor's behavior, may spontaneously and effortlessly draw a situational inference, and, if they have sufficient conscious resources and motivation, revise this inference by considering the actor's personality (see Fig. 2). It seems that people are able to draw either trait inferences or situational inferences from behavior when they are given either trait goals or situational goals, but what might create these goals in people's day-to-day lives? Social inference researchers have long maintained that people draw inferences to increase their ability to predict other people's behavior. Thus, a trait goal may be invoked when someone expects to interact with a person in the future ("I just met our new neighbors. They seem like friendly people."). When someone expects to enter a situation, a situational goal may be invoked ("Did you hear those people laughing? I can hardly wait to see that movie.").

Even when goals are not invoked by the immediate circumstances or people's current needs and motives, people may be predisposed to either trait inference or situational inference by their culture or personality.[11] A number of cross-cultural investigations have found that non-Westerners tend to form judgments that are more situational than those of Westerners. Shweder and Bourne[12] have suggested that non-Western people may be "culturally primed to see context and social relationships as a necessary condition for behavior," whereas Westerners may be "culturally primed to search for abstract summaries of the autonomous individual." Thus, Westerners' default process may be the trait inference process, whereas non-Westerners' default process may be the situational inference process. Even within a culture, some types of individuals may think more in terms of traits, and others may think more in terms of situational forces. For instance, Newman[13] has found that

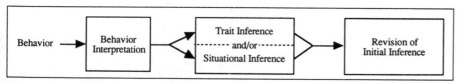

Fig. 2. The social inference process.

people who are high in idiocentrism (an individualistic view) are more likely than people who are low in idiocentrism to infer traits spontaneously from behavior.

CONCLUSION

In the past decade or so, social inference researchers have increased their attention on the process by which people draw inferences from behavior, particularly the trait inference process. This research suggests that when people are interested in learning about another person, they may spontaneously and effortlessly interpret behavior and draw an inference about the actor's personality. They may then revise their initial inference by considering the situation in which the behavior took place if they have the ability and motivation to do so. Less research has investigated how people draw inferences when they are interested in learning about situations. However, people with a situational goal may spontaneously and effortlessly interpret behavior and draw an inference about the situation, and may revise this inference by considering the actor's personality if they have the ability and motivation to do so. Thus, it seems that the social inference process may be flexible in that people may not be compelled to always travel the same inferential road. Social inference researchers have begun to investigate factors that might influence people's tendency to initially draw either trait or situational inferences (or perhaps both); some research suggests that people's current goals and motives may influence the process, and that individual differences and cultural factors may predispose people to either trait or situational inferences.

Further advances in the understanding of social inference processes and the influence of cultural factors and individual differences will have important implications at many levels of social science. Important benefits will accrue for psychologists, but also for political scientists and sociologists. For example, in politics, it may be that the tendency for conservatives to blame the poor for their plight and for liberals to blame the system reflects differences in social inference. Similarly, the default social inference process for an entire culture may influence its members' inferences and proposed solutions with regard to such ubiquitous social problems as homelessness, injustice, and violence.

Acknowledgments—We wish to thank Craig A. Anderson, Lori A. Krull, Jody C. Dill, and David Dubois for their valuable comments on earlier drafts of this manuscript.

Notes

1. This tendency to draw unwarranted trait inferences has been called correspondence bias, the fundamental attribution error, and overattribution bias. For a review, see E.E. Jones, *Interpersonal Perception* (Macmillan, New York, 1990).

2. See, e.g., D.T. Gilbert, B.W. Pelham, and D.S. Krull, On cognitive busyness: When person perceivers meet persons perceived, *Journal of Personality and Social Psychology, 54*, 733–740 (1988); Y. Trope, Identification and inferential processes in dispositional attribution, *Psychological Review, 93*, 239–257 (1986).

3. See, e.g., D.T. Gilbert, Thinking lightly about others: Automatic components of the social inference process, in *Unintended Thought: Limits of Awareness, Intention, and Control*, J.S. Uleman and J.A. Bargh, Eds. (Guilford Press, New York, 1989).

4. See, e.g., H.A. Sagar and J.W. Schofield, Racial and behavioral cues in black and white children's perceptions of ambiguously aggressive acts, *Journal of Personality and Social Psychology, 39*, 590–598 (1980). Note that contrast effects may also occur; e.g., L.L. Martin, J.J. Seta, and R.A. Crelia, Assimilation and contrast as a function of people's willingness and ability to expend effort in forming an impression, *Journal of Personality and Social Psychology, 59*, 27–37 (1990).

5. Trope, note 2.

6. For a review, see J.S. Uleman, Consciousness and control: The case of spontaneous trait inferences, *Personality and Social Psychology Bulletin, 13*, 337–354 (1987). Note that more recent work suggests that these spontaneous inferences may often be better thought of as summaries of behavior; e.g., J.N. Bassili, Traits as action categories versus traits as person attributes in social cognition, in *On-Line Cognition in Person Perception*, J.N. Bassili, Ed. (Erlbaum, Hillsdale, NJ, 1989).

7. M.B. Lupfer, L.F. Clark, and H.W. Hutcherson, Impact of context on spontaneous trait and situational attributions, *Journal of Personality and Social Psychology, 58*, 239–249 (1990). Note that trait inferences do require some conscious resources; see J.S. Uleman, L.S. Newman, and L. Winter, Can personality traits be inferred automatically? Spontaneous inferences require cognitive capacity at encoding, *Consciousness and Cognition, 1*, 72–90 (1992). See Bassili, note 6.

8. D.E. Carlston and J.J. Skowronski, Savings in the relearning of trait information as evidence for spontaneous inference generation, *Journal of Personality and Social Psychology, 66*, 840–856 (1994).

9. D.M. Webster, Motivated augmentation and reduction of the overattribution bias, *Journal of Personality and Social Psychology, 65*, 261–271 (1993).

10. D.S. Krull, Does the grist change the mill?: The effect of perceiver's goal on the process of social inference, *Personality and Social Psychology Bulletin, 19*, 340–348 (1993). See also G.A. Quattrone, Overattribution and unit formation: When behavior engulfs the person, *Journal of Personality and Social Psychology, 42*, 593–607 (1982); J.D. Vorauer and M. Ross, Making mountains out of molehills: An informational goals analysis of self- and social perception, *Personality and Social Psychology Bulletin, 19*, 620–632 (1993).

11. See, e.g., G.J.O. Fletcher and C. Ward, Attribution theory and processes: A cross-cultural perspective, in *The Cross-Cultural Challenge to Social Psychology*, M.H. Bond, Ed. (Sage, Beverly Hills, CA, 1988); J.G. Miller, Culture and the development of everyday social explanation, *Journal of Personality and Social Psychology, 46*, 961–978 (1984). Although the terms Western and non-Western have been used for simplicity, the cultural difference is perhaps better thought of as a distinction between cultures with an independent and with an interdependent view of the self.

12. R.A. Shweder and E. Bourne, Does the concept of the person vary cross-culturally? in *Cultural Conceptions of Mental Health and Therapy*, A.J. Marsella and G. White, Eds. (Reidel, Boston, 1982), pp. 129–130.

13. L.S. Newman, How individualists interpret behavior: Idiocentrism and spontaneous trait inference, *Social Cognition, 11*, 243–269 (1993). See Bassili, note 6.

Recommended Reading

Trope, Y., and Higgins, E.T., Eds. (1993). Special Issue: On Inferring Personal Dispositions From Behavior. *Personality and Social Psychology Bulletin, 19*.

Motivational Approaches to Expectancy Confirmation

John T. Copeland

John T. Copeland is an Assistant Professor of Psychology at Wabash College. Address correspondence to John T. Copeland, Wabash College, Crawfordsville, IN 47933; e-mail: copelanj@wabash.bitnet.

For some time now, social, personality, and cognitive psychologists have been interested in how our interpersonal expectations affect our thoughts, feelings, and behavior. A provocative finding in this research suggests that people often act in ways that preferentially confirm their expectations of others. Specifically, an individual who holds some expectation (who is generally referred to as a perceiver) about some other person (who is generally referred to as a target), through the course of their interaction, will often form expectancy-confirming impressions of the target (a phenomenon referred to as *perceptual confirmation*) and elicit expectancy-confirming behavior from the target (a phenomenon referred to as *behavioral confirmation*). Thus, expecting Jody to be a warm and friendly person, I may elicit warm and friendly behavior from her and form similar impressions of her. This expectancy confirmation is the essence of Merton's self-fulfilling prophecy and has been the subject of considerable laboratory and field studies by social psychologists.[1]

In a widely cited investigation of expectancy confirmation, Snyder, Tanke, and Berscheid had male perceivers engage in a dyadic, getting-acquainted conversation with female targets.[2] Before the conversation, each man was given a randomly assigned photograph, ostensibly of his woman partner. For half of the men, the picture portrayed the target woman as physically attractive; for the other half of the men, the picture portrayed the target as physically unattractive. In reality, the pictures were not of the targets, but of women who had participated in an earlier study. Snyder, Tanke, and Berscheid wanted to see if the beliefs, expectations, and stereotypes associated with physical attractiveness—namely, "what is beautiful is good"—would have an influence on the conversations between perceivers and targets.

Perceivers' reports indicated that the photo-induced expectations did indeed affect perceivers' postconversation impressions of targets. Men given attractive photos found their women partners to be more warm, open, and friendly than did men given unattractive photos—evidence of the perceptual confirmation of the men's physical attractiveness-based expectations. Additionally, independent judges, blind to experimental conditions, listened to only the targets' portion of the conversations. Judges' reports of targets' behavior indicated that the women in the attractive-photo condition actually behaved in a more warm and friendly manner than the women in the unattractive-photo condition—providing evidence of behavioral confirmation of perceivers' expectations. Analyses of perceivers' portions of the conversation, also by independent judges, indicated that the observed confirmation effects were due to differential behavior of the perceivers during the conversations. Specifically, men who expected to interact with attractive, warm, and friendly women behaved in a warm and friendly manner themselves, thus helping to elicit such behavior from those women. Thus, Snyder, Tanke, and Berscheid demonstrated that a "what is beautiful is good" stereotype can be self-fulfilling—behaviorally confirmed by targets because of perceivers' biased behavior.

Although this expectancy confirmation effect has important moderators and boundary conditions, it has been demonstrated in a variety of social settings, including the classroom, the workplace, and the psychological clinic. In addition to physical appearance, researchers have examined the confirmatory effects of other interpersonal expectations, such as those based on gender, race, and academic ability.[1] Although recent reviews and theoretical models have questioned the pervasiveness and extent of behavioral expectancy effects, most accounts of expectancy-influenced social encounters affirm the potential of such expectancies for producing biased outcomes.[3] Furthermore, expectancy confirmation phenomena have been linked to important deleterious social phenomena such as prejudice, discrimination, and the perpetuation of stereotypes. Thus, previous work on expectancy confirmation has focused on questions of

the process, outcomes, and boundary conditions of the phenomenon—the "how" and "how much" of expectancy confirmation.

The purpose of this review is to highlight a newly emerging theme in theory and research on expectancy confirmation. Recently, researchers interested in expectancy confirmation processes have turned their attention toward understanding the motivational antecedents of these processes—the "why" of expectancy confirmation. These efforts reflect an attempt to understand and explain, at a more parsimonious level, the diverse psychological and behavioral mechanisms that affect expectancy-influenced social interactions. Additionally, this motivational focus coincides with a renewed interest in motivational theories of social thinking and social behavior—theories being developed and explored in many psychological domains. Such theories postulate that much of thinking and behavior is purposeful and directed at achieving some more or less specific end. Thus, understanding psychological and behavioral processes requires understanding the needs, motives, goals, and plans that underlie such processes.

This review presents a sample of the emerging theory and research on the motivational moderators of expectancy confirmation. First, the role of impression formation goals—the extent to which people are concerned with gathering and integrating information about other people—is considered. Work on motives dealing with the regulation and facilitation of social interaction is then presented, including work on the moderating effects of self-presentation (e.g., ingratiation, self-promotion). Finally, the motivational and confirmatory implications of the social relationship between interactants is considered. Although covering the steps in the expectancy confirmation process and the pervasiveness of that process is beyond the scope of the current review, it

does represent a taste of the current motivational work in this area.

PERSON PERCEPTION AND IMPRESSION FORMATION

Impression formation is generally defined as the process of perceiving pieces of information about an individual (e.g., prior expectations, verbal and nonverbal behaviors) and integrating them into some coherent summary impression. Already a process of considerable study by cognitive and social psychologists for some time, impression formation as a motivational goal has recently become a focus of researchers interested in expectancy confirmation processes. These researchers postulate that social interactants' person perception and impression formation concerns moderate the extent of expectancy influences.

Snyder and his colleagues have taken a functional approach to studying the motivational foundations of expectancy confirmation.[4] At a general level, a functional approach is concerned with understanding the psychological functions served by an individual's beliefs and behaviors. A functional analysis of expectancy confirmation focuses on the psychological functions served by the beliefs and behaviors of a perceiver and a target. According to Snyder, perceivers motivated to form stable, predictable impressions of their target partners—perceivers whose behaviors serve the psychological function of acquiring and using social knowledge—are likely to confirm their expectations of targets.

In one study, Snyder and Haugen had male perceivers engage in a getting-acquainted conversation with female targets.[5] This was a conceptual replication of the earlier study by Snyder, Tanke, and Berscheid, but with a focus on obesity stereotypes. Each man was given a photograph, ostensibly of his partner, but, again, in reality, obtained in an earlier study. The picture portrayed the partner as being either obese or of

normal weight. Independent of the picture manipulation, each man was given one of three sets of motivational instructions. One third of the men were told to try to "get to know" their partners during their conversations—to form stable, predictable impressions of their partners. Another third of the men were told to "get along" well with their partners—to have smooth and pleasant conversations with them and try to avoid awkward points during their talk. Finally, one third of the men were given no specific motivational instructions for the conversations (a motivational control condition consisting of the traditional paradigmatic components but without any specific interaction objectives delivered to perceivers).

Analyses of perceivers' postconversation impression ratings revealed that relative to the men in the other motivational conditions, the men who were instructed to form stable, predictable impressions of their partners were more likely to form expectancy-confirming impressions of those targets. Specifically, for the men in this motivational condition, those given a picture of an obese target found their partners to be more unfriendly, reserved, and unenthusiastic than those given a picture of a normal-weight target found their partners. Additionally, the behavior of the women in this motivational condition was found by independent judges to be expectancy-consistent. In contrast, there was no evidence of either perceptual or behavioral confirmation in the other two motivational conditions. Perceivers who were instructed to "get along" with their targets as well as perceivers lacking any specific motivational instructions for their interaction neither formed confirming impressions nor elicited confirming behavior. Thus, perceivers whose behaviors served the psychological function of acquiring and using social knowledge were more likely to confirm their preinteraction expectations of targets.

Neuberg has focused on how ac-

curacy motives in person perception moderate expectancy confirmation.[6] Neuberg contrasts the goal of forming an accurate impression of a person with the goal of forming a rapid impression of a person. He believes that a perceiver motivated to form an accurate impression of a target will be less biased in information gathering about the target than will a perceiver motivated to form a rapid impression. As a result, the tendency for expectancy-confirming outcomes will be reduced for the former perceiver.

In a test of this hypothesis, Neuberg had perceivers serve as interviewers for a hypothetical job, with targets serving as applicants. Each interviewer talked with two targets, one at a time, and assessed their suitability for the job. Prior to the conversations, perceivers were led to believe that one of the targets was not well suited for the job, but no such information was given about the other target. Independent of the expectations, perceivers were given instructions either to form accurate impressions of the targets (accuracy goal) or to form impressions sufficient to decide on their suitability for the job (sufficiency goal).

Results indicated that accuracy motives had the predicted effects. Perceivers' postinterview impressions showed that expectancy confirmation occurred only in the sufficiency-goal condition, in which negative-expectancy targets were assessed less favorably than control targets. In contrast, perceivers motivated to form accurate impressions did not differ significantly in their impressions of the two targets. A substantially similar pattern of results was found from analyses of targets' actual behavior. Behavioral confirmation of perceivers' expectations occurred only in the sufficiency-goal condition. Indeed, in the accuracy-goal condition, there was evidence of behavioral disconfirmation: In the eyes of the independent judges, negative-expectancy targets performed better than the control targets.

These researchers have demonstrated that the extent to which perceivers are concerned with arriving at some understanding of their target partners will moderate expectancy effects. One distinction within this research seems to be between forming a stable, predictable impression of a target, as in the work of Snyder and Haugen, and forming an accurate impression of a target, as in Neuberg's work. When perceivers are motivated to form stable, predictable impressions of targets, we see the traditional expectancy confirmation effects. However, when perceivers are motivated to form accurate impressions, the effects are attenuated. The distinction between stability and accuracy appears to be important and has drawn the attention of these researchers.[5] Indeed, some recent theoretical accounts of expectancy confirmation highlight the potential accuracy of expectations and call into question the degree of confirmatory biases in social interaction.[7]

SELF-PRESENTATION AND INTERACTION FACILITATION

Researchers interested in the motivational antecedents of expectancy confirmation are also examining how interactants' self-presentational concerns and concerns with facilitating their social interactions affect the expectancy confirmation process. Briefly, self-presentational motives are concerns associated with managing one's image, one's appearance in the eyes of other people, or one's self-perception. Concerns about interaction facilitation center on having pleasant interactions with others, interactions unencumbered by awkward or uncomfortable exchanges. Both types of motives appear to play important roles in the moderation of expectancy effects.

In the previously discussed study by Snyder and Haugen, one third of the perceivers were instructed to get along well with their target partners.[5] As a result of this manipulation, there was no evidence of expectancy confirmation either in perceivers' postinteraction impressions of targets or in judges' ratings of targets' behavior. Perceivers whose behaviors served the psychological function of regulating and facilitating their social interaction avoided the cognitive and behavioral processes that generally lead to expectancy-confirming interaction outcomes.

In an investigation of the moderating role of ingratiation—a self-presentational goal—Neuberg, Judice, Virdin, and Carrillo had perceivers interview targets for a hypothetical job.[8] Half of the targets were portrayed in a negative light, and the other half were given no such portrayal. Independent of the expectancy manipulation, half of the interviewers were encouraged to get the applicants to like them (self-presentation), while the other half of the interviewers were given no explicit goal.

In the no-goal condition, the traditional expectancy confirmation effects were obtained. Interviewers were relatively cold and more challenging toward the negative-expectancy targets, causing these targets to perform less favorably during the interviews. However, in the liking-goal condition, interviewers behaved in a more warm and friendly manner toward the negative-expectancy targets than toward the no-expectancy targets, which led these interviewers to form expectancy-disconfirming impressions of the negatively labeled targets.

These studies suggest that perceivers motivated either to manage the impressions they give to targets or to have enjoyable social encounters will be less likely to effect a self-fulfilling prophecy than perceivers motivated to form impressions of targets. The interactions seem to be qualitatively different. Self-presentational and facilitative motives appear to inhibit both the tendency for perceivers to engage in expectancy-biased information seeking and tar-

gets' behavioral confirmation of perceivers' expectations.

THE PERCEIVER–TARGET RELATIONSHIP

Other researchers interested in the motivational underpinnings of expectancy confirmation focus on the relationship between a perceiver and a target in a particular interaction setting. These researchers claim that the interactants' roles, their relative power in the interaction setting, and the formality and structure of the interaction setting may affect both the motives of the interactants and the likelihood of expectancy-confirming outcomes.

Elsewhere, I have suggested that the relative power of perceiver and target moderates both motivation and expectancy confirmation.[9] In an investigation of this hypothesis, each perceiver was given one of two expectations about the target. Independent of the expectancy manipulation, one of the participants (either the perceiver or the target, as determined by random assignment to experimental conditions) had the power to choose whether the other would be a participant in a subsequent reward-laden phase of the study. When the perceivers had the power to affect the targets' outcomes, perceivers reported they were motivated primarily to acquire knowledge about targets, and targets reported they were motivated primarily to facilitate favorable interaction outcomes. These interactions resulted in both the perceptual and the behavioral confirmation of perceivers' experimentally delivered expectations about targets. However, when targets had control over perceivers' outcomes, the motive reports were reversed: Perceivers reported a primary concern with facilitating favorable interaction outcomes, and targets reported a primary concern with the acquisition of knowledge about perceivers. In these interactions, there were no signs of perceptual or behavioral

confirmation. Thus, power affected both subjects' motivations (at least, self-reported motivations) and the likelihood of subsequent expectancy confirmation.

In her situational taxonomy of expectancy situations, Harris has suggested that the formality and degree of structure in an interaction affect the extent to which expectancies will be influential.[10] Formality refers to the social formality of an interaction setting, the extent of adherence to explicit and fixed customs or social rules. Structure refers to how highly scripted an interaction is, the extent to which the roles are highly specified and articulated. Although these two dimensions are related, they are probably not redundant, as not all socially structured situations are formal (e.g., the players of a board game have structured roles, but they need not be formal roles).

Indirect support for Harris's hypothesis about the degree of structure was found in a study in which grade-school boys were paired for two different tasks.[11] For the structured task, the boys worked together to complete a color-by-number picture; for the less structured task, the boys worked together to plan and build their own Lego block design. Perceiver boys in this study also either were told that their partner would be difficult to work with or were given no such expectancy. Expectancy effects were weaker in the more structured task. During the color-by-number task, perceivers were less likely to form expectancy-confirming impressions and elicit expectancy-confirming behavior from targets than during the Lego task. From a motivational perspective, this result may have been due to perceivers' greater concern with completing the formal requirements of the more structured task. This concern may have kept perceivers too cognitively and behaviorally busy to engage in the expectancy confirmation processes that the less structured Lego task afforded.

Thus, aspects of the social relationship between a perceiver and a

target can have motivational ramifications and subsequent moderating effects on expectancy influences. The effects of these relationship factors are important to a thorough understanding of expectancy confirmation phenomena. Perceivers' and targets' motives may often be induced specifically because of the nature of the social relationship in a given interaction setting. When perceivers and targets will be concerned with impression formation or self-presentation may depend in large part on the nature of their social setting and the roles they are required to play.

DISCUSSION

Although most of the work covered in this review focuses on a perceiver's motives, other work not covered here focuses on the moderating role of a target's motives. To the extent that the same motives operate in other social contexts, these motivational approaches may add not only to our understanding of expectancy confirmation processes in particular, but also to what we know about social thinking and social behavior in general.

Acknowledgments—Support for the author's research described in this article was provided by a Dissertation Research Award from the American Psychological Association. The author would like to thank the anonymous reviewer who provided valuable comments on an earlier version of the manuscript. Preparation of the manuscript was aided through a Byron K. Trippet stipend.

Notes

1. J.M. Darley and R.H. Fazio, Expectancy-confirmation processes arising in the social interaction sequence, *American Psychologist, 35,* 867–881 (1980); R. Rosenthal, *On the Social Psychology of the Self-Fulfilling Prophecy: Further Evidence for Pygmalion Effects and Their Mediating Mechanisms* (M.S.S. Information Corporation Modular Publications, New York, 1974); M. Snyder, When belief creates reality, in *Advances in Experimental Social Psychology,* Vol. 18, L. Berkowitz, Ed. (Academic Press, Orlando, FL, 1984).

2. M. Snyder, E.D. Tanke, and E. Berscheid, Social perception and interpersonal behavior: On the self-fulfilling nature of social stereotypes, *Journal*

of *Personality and Social Psychology, 35,* 656–666 (1977).

3. L. Jussim, Social perception and social reality: A reflection-construction model, *Psychological Review, 98,* 54–73 (1991); E.E. Jones, *Interpersonal Perception* (W.H. Freeman, New York, 1990).

4. M. Snyder, Motivational foundations of behavioral confirmation, in *Advances in Experimental Social Psychology,* Vol. 25, M. Zanna, Ed. (Academic Press, San Diego, 1992).

5. M. Snyder and J.A. Haugen, *Why does behavioral confirmation occur? A functional perspective,* paper presented at the annual meeting of the American Psychological Association, Boston (August 1990).

6. S.L. Neuberg, The goal of forming accurate impressions during social interactions: Attenuating the impact of negative expectancies, *Journal of Personality and Social Psychology, 56,* 374–386 (1989).

7. Jussim, note 3.

8. S.L. Neuberg, T.N. Judice, L.M. Virdin, and M.A. Carrillo, Perceiver self-presentational goals as moderators of expectancy influences: Ingratiation and the disconfirmation of negative expectancies, *Journal of Personality and Social Psychology, 64,* 409–420 (1993).

9. J.T. Copeland, *Motivational implications of social power for behavioral confirmation,* paper presented at the annual meeting of the Midwestern Psychological Association, Chicago (May 1992).

10. M.J. Harris, Issues in studying the mediation of interpersonal expectancy effects: A taxonomy of expectancy situations, in *Interpersonal Expectations: Theory, Research, and Applications,* P.D. Blank, Ed. (Cambridge University Press, London, in press).

11. M.J. Harris, R. Milich, E.M. Corbitt, D.W. Hoover, and M. Brady, Self-fulfilling effects of stigmatizing information on children's social interactions, *Journal of Personality and Social Psychology, 63,* 41–50 (1992).

Recommended Reading

Hilton, J.L., and Darley, J.M. (1991). The effects of interaction goals on person perception. In *Advances in Experimental Social Psychology,* Vol. 24, M.P. Zanna, Ed. (Academic Press, San Diego).

Jussim, L. (1991). Social perception and social reality: A reflection-construction model. *Psychological Review, 98,* 54–73.

Snyder, M. (1992). Motivational foundations of behavioral confirmation. In *Advances in Experimental Social Psychology,* Vol. 25, M. Zanna, Ed. (Academic Press, San Diego).

Attitudes

Every year during professional football's Super Bowl, advertisers pay untold millions of dollars in order to show their commercials for beer, chips, beer, tires, beer, computers, and beer. The network showing the game also takes the opportunity to air countless advertisements promoting other programs on that network.

Every four years, during the presidential election, the airwaves are crowded with political advertisements in which candidates tout their own accomplishments, pose with cute children and cheering crowds, and display ominous, unflattering, black and white photographs of their opponents as grim-voiced announcers catalog the opponents' shortcomings.

The underlying reason for both of these phenomena is that the advertisers, networks, and candidates all share a common assumption: that attitudes are important. If attitudes toward a particular brand of beer can be made more favorable through cute commercials involving talking frogs, then people will buy more of that beer. If attitudes toward a television program can be made more favorable by showing funny clips from it every 12 minutes, then more people will watch the program. If attitudes toward a candidate can be made more positive—or attitudes toward the opponent more negative—then people will be more likely to vote for the candidate. To change someone's behavior, this argument goes, you must first change that person's attitude.

To one degree or another, social psychology has shared this view for decades. The study of attitudes and attitude change has been a central concern of the field for half a century—in fact, for a while that seemed to be *all* that social psychology studied. One major approach during this time has been to focus on where attitudes come from. The evidence from this research suggests that we acquire attitudes not only from careful consideration of the facts, but also through processes that are much less conscious and deliberate. Merely being exposed to some object frequently enough, for example, generally leads to a more favorable attitude toward it. It also appears that we some-

times arrive at our attitudes by looking at our behaviors, and then simply inferring what our attitudes must be based on our actions.

Another approach to the topic of attitudes has been to directly examine the basic assumption mentioned above, namely that attitudes are strongly associated with actual behavior. As it turns out, the link between attitudes and behavior is not as powerful or reliable as you might think, although under the right circumstances it is still possible to predict behavior from attitudes with considerable success. In fact, it is because of this link between attitudes and behavior that the last major approach to the topic—studying the factors that influence attitude *change*—has been popular for so long. Three of the four articles in this unit, in fact, focus on the issue of persuasion; in short, how does one person convince others to change their attitudes?

In "How Do You Persuade If Everyone Knows You Are Untrustworthy, Unbelievable, and Disliked?" Anthony Pratkanis and Elliot Aronson discuss the possibility that even disliked and noncredible individuals can be effective persuaders under the right circumstances. In particular, arguing for a position that seems at odds with your own self-interest often leads audiences to give greater credence to your message, and to change their own attitudes more toward the point of view you are expressing. The same authors address a different issue in "Mindless Propaganda, Thoughtful Persuasion"; in this selection, they discuss an influential theory in contemporary social psychology, the elaboration likelihood model. According to this approach, audiences react to persuasion attempts in two basic ways—either by thinking carefully about the message and attending to its arguments, or through a much more superficial processing of the message and its content. In "What's in a Brand?" Diane Crispell and Kathleen Brandenberg deal with a very practical kind of persuasion: advertising. It is very important for advertisers to understand the attitudes that consumers have toward brand names and what motivations underlie these atti-

gests that the way in which we make decisions and approach problems is influenced in part by our "regulatory focus"—whether we define success as the presence of positives (promotion-focused), or whether we see it more as the absence of negatives (prevention-focused). This general attitude toward the world helps determine the strategies we use in dealing with uncertainty: being promotion-focused leads us to seek rewards, even if it means taking chances, while being prevention-focused generally leads us to simply avoid punishments.

Looking Ahead: Challenge Questions

What is the difference between being "promotion-focused" and "prevention-focused"? How do these two general attitudes influence one's decision making? How would you describe yourself in terms of this model? Do you fit into one or the other of these categories?

Which characteristics of a communicator make him or her especially persuasive? Which characteristics make a communicator especially *in*effective? Are there any exceptions to these general rules, and if there are, what is responsible? If you could dream up the "ideal" communicator for some persuasive message, what would he or she be like?

When someone is paying careful attention to a persuasive message, what implications does this have for the message's success? That is, what factors will be especially important, or unimportant, in such cases? What are the implications when the audience is *not* carefully attending to the message? Could persuasion still occur? What would determine whether it did or not?

What determines your feelings toward certain products? Do you feel any "loyalty" to particular brands? Are there any brands that you would never buy? Why? Do you think your feelings toward particular brands will change as you grow older?

tudes; this selection considers some of the most important factors underlying brand loyalty.

The article "Attitude Affects Memory, Decisions, and Performance" is quite different from the others. It describes research by psychologist Tory Higgins, which sug-

Attitude Affects Memory, Decisions and Performance

Pollyannas and pessimists not only perceive the same event differently, their memories and emotions of the event differ.

Beth Azar

Monitor staff

Do you accentuate the positive or just try to avoid the negative? You probably do both depending on the situation, but most people lean toward one or the other. And those personal leanings help shape how people make decisions and approach problems, according to psychologist E. Tory Higgins, PhD, of Columbia University.

Traditional models of motivation revolve around pain and pleasure: People stop doing what's painful and continue doing what's pleasurable. Higgins proposes adding a second dimension to this model called "regulatory focus."

Two Focuses

He's found two types of regulatory focus: People who are "promotion-focused" view pain and pleasure in terms of the absence or presence of positives and try to promote positives.

People who are "prevention-focused" view pain and pleasure in terms of the presence or absence of negatives and try to prevent negatives (see figure). Higgins presented his theory at a Science Weekend address on outlook and cognition during the APA Annual Convention in Aug. 11–15.

The two types of focus are based on our evolutionary need for nurture and security, suggested Higgins. Nurture fosters a promotion focus, emphasizing the potential positives of life. Security fosters a prevention focus, emphasizing the potential negatives and a need to avoid them.

People can use both focus systems, but some people, known as "chronics," use one focus system predominantly. According to research by Higgins and his colleagues, either focus can affect what people remember about events, how they perform certain tasks and how they regulate their emotions.

Higgins found that people remember aspects of events that match their regulatory focus. For example, a promotion-focused person better remembers the details of a story about a man finding a $20 bill (presence of positive) than a story about getting stuck on a subway (presence of negative). For a prevention-focused person, memory is better for getting stuck on a subway.

When he has induced people to have a particular focus in a given situation, he has found the same effect on memory. In one study, he falsely told subjects he was testing the influence of exercise on physiology by collecting hormones from their saliva while they exercised.

Subjects rode an exercise bike with a cotton ball in their mouth that tasted either bitter or sweet. This promoted the pain or pleasure dimension.

Next subjects performed a mental exercise with a new cotton ball in their mouth and read four stories like the ones in his first study that represented the absence or presence of positive or the absence or presence of negative. The new cotton ball tasted neutral or maintained the taste they had before. This promoted a person's regulatory focus: Subjects experienced either sweet-sweet (presence of positive), sweet-neutral (absence of positive), bitter-bitter (presence of negative) or bitter-neutral (absence of negative).

Subjects then took a memory test about the stories. Higgins again found that subjects with an induced promotion focus—sweet-sweet and sweet-neutral—remembered the presence and absence of positive events better than the presence and absence of negative events. The opposite was true for the prevention-focused subjects—bitter-bitter, bitter-neutral. How people approach a goal or problem affects the strategies they use, according to other studies by Higgins. He asserts there are two basic strategies to problem-solving: approaching matches by seeing everything as an opportunity and avoiding mismatches by seeing everything as a potential hazard.

To test whether focus affects strategy, Higgins induced focus in a group of subjects who thought they were participating in a simple skills-test experiment. From a questionnaire given two months before the experiment, he selected two activities for each subject, one they liked and one they disliked. He told each subject they'd be doing two tasks, a memory recognition task and one of two other activi-

 From *APA Monitor*, November 1995, p. 27. © 1995 by the American Psychological Association. Reprinted by permission.

A four-pronged model of motivation

	Pain (negatives)	Pleasure (positives)	
Promotion focused	**Absence of positives**	**Presence of positives**	Promote Positives
Prevention focused	**Presence of negatives**	**Absence of negatives**	Prevent Negatives

ties—the one they liked, such as playing a game similar to the game show "Jeopardy," or the one they disliked, such as proofreading.

Higgins formed five groups by putting five different contingencies on the memory recognition task:

- **controls**—randomly chose which of the two alternate activities they did.
- **presence of positive**—if they did well on the recognition task, they would play "Jeopardy" instead of proofread.
- **absence of positive**—if they didn't do well on the memory task, they would not get to play "Jeopardy," and would have to proofread.
- **absence of negative**—if they didn't do poorly, they wouldn't

have to proofread, they would get to play "Jeopardy."
- **presence of negative**—if they did poorly, they would have to proofread instead of play "Jeopardy."

Everyone's goal, Higgins assumed, was do the task they liked. The strategies, however, would vary depending on the focus; they would either try to do well on the memory recognition task or try to avoid doing poorly. In the memory recognition task, subjects saw a sequence of nonsense words. They then saw another list and had to say whether a nonsense word was from the first list or not. He found that the promotion-focused subjects— the presence and absence of positive groups—tended to say "yes" to every word. The prevention-focused people,

tended to say "no" to every word. This makes sense, said Higgins, because promotion-focused people want correct answers, and the best way to get them is to look for word matches: They seek out more opportunities to find them. But for prevention-focused people, every opportunity is a chance to be wrong, which they want to avoid. So they avoid word mismatches by saying no to everything.

Using Both Strategies

Focus not only affects memory and strategies, it affects outlook and emotions, said Higgins.

He's found that promotion-focused people feel happy and satisfied when they see their lives are going well, and sad and disappointed during times of trouble. Prevention-focused people feel secure and calm when they perceive their lives as not going badly, and nervous and tense during adverse times.

For people who regularly use both systems, emotions crop up depending on the system they're using at the time.

For example, when people are sad, the promotion system isn't working. But it might be good for it to shut down, as it forces people to rethink their goals, Higgins said.

When prevention isn't working and fear sets in, it may mean the person has something legitimate to fear. But "when people get stuck at the extremes, people can get very depressed or anxious," said Higgins.

Learning more about these regulatory systems could help psychologists better understand how people regulate their lives he said.

How Do You Persuade If Everyone Knows You Are Untrustworthy, Unbelievable, and Disliked?

Anthony Pratkanis and Elliot Aronson

When you think about it, the professional propagandist has a difficult task. We commonly respond to persuasive messages by questioning the speaker's bias and noting how his or her self-interest is being served. This general skepticism can serve a useful purpose for the target of the appeal. By identifying a message as biased, the audience can prepare to defend its position and either to scrutinize carefully the contents of the message or to reject it out of hand depending on the circumstances. But from the propagandist's perspective, this constitutes a formidable obstacle to securing compliance. Accordingly, the propagandist finds it important not to *appear* to be a propagandist. In order to be successful, the communicator must appear unbiased and trustworthy. [W]e will look at two general strategies for making the untrustworthy, the unbelievable, and the disliked look trustworthy, believable, and liked.

The Chinese rhetorician Han Fei-Tzu, who advised rulers in the third century B.C., told the following story to illustrate how a ruler can improve the perception of his credibility.[1] The Duke of Wu wished to invade the country of Hu. The Duke pulled aside one of his most trusted counselors and asked him to argue in public that the Duke should attack Hu, which the counselor then did. The Duke immediately put the counselor to death as a dra-

matic way of reassuring the ruler of Hu that he had no intention of attacking. Assured that the Duke was a trustworthy leader—after all he just put one of his most trusted advisors to death—Hu disarmed. The Duke of Wu immediately launched a surprise attack and the country of Hu was captured.

One of the morals of Han Fei-Tzu's story is that communicators can make themselves seem trustworthy by apparently acting against their own self-interest. If we are led to believe that communicators have nothing to gain and perhaps something to lose by convincing us, we will trust them and they will be more effective. When the Duke of Wu put his counselor to death, he appeared to be arguing against his own self-interest—"No! Invading Hu—even though it may result in benefits to my country—is wrong. I believe this so strongly that I will put my favorite advisor to death for merely suggesting it." The problem—for the citizens of Hu—was that the Duke's position was an illusion; he had arranged it so that it would appear he was acting and arguing against his own self-interest. This leads us to the second moral of Han Fei-Tzu's story: When it comes to persuasion, appearances can be deceiving.

The strategy of acting or arguing against your own self-interest can be used to increase the perception of your trustworthiness without actually

From *Age of Propaganda: The Everyday Use and Abuse of Persuasion* by Anthony Pratkanis and Elliot Aronson, pp. 94–100. © 1992 by W. H. Freeman and Company. Reprinted by permission.

putting your best friend to death. An illustration may be helpful. Suppose a habitual criminal, recently convicted as a smuggler and peddler of cocaine, was delivering a talk on the harshness of the American judicial system and the overzealousness of its prosecutors. Would he influence you? Probably not. Most people would probably regard him as biased and untrustworthy. The cocaine peddler occupies a position clearly outside of the Aristotelian definition of a "good person." But suppose he was arguing that criminal justice was too *soft*— that criminals almost always beat the rap if they have a smart lawyer, and that even if criminals *are* convicted, the sentences normally meted out are too lenient. Would he influence you?

The evidence from one of our own experiments suggests that he probably would. In a study conducted in collaboration with Elaine Walster and Darcy Abrahams, we presented our subjects with a newspaper clipping of an interview with Joe "the Shoulder" Napolitano, who was identified in the manner described above.[2] In one experimental condition, Joe "the Shoulder" argued for stricter courts and more severe sentences. In another condition, he argued that courts should be more lenient and sentences less severe. We also ran a parallel set of conditions in which the same statements were attributed to a respected public official.

When Joe "the Shoulder" argued for more lenient courts, he was totally ineffective; indeed, he actually caused the subjects' opinions to change slightly in the opposite direction. But when he was arguing for stricter, more powerful courts, he was extremely effective—as effective as the respected public official delivering the same argument. This study demonstrates that Aristotle was not completely correct—a communicator can be an immoral person and still be effective, as long as it seems clear that the communicator has nothing to gain (and perhaps something to lose) by persuading us.

Why was Joe "the Shoulder" so effective in the experiment? Let's take a closer look. Most people would not be surprised to hear a known convict arguing in favor of a more lenient criminal justice system. Their knowledge of the criminal's background and self-interest would lead them to expect such a message. When they receive the opposite communication, however, these expectations are disconfirmed. To make sense of this contradiction, the members of the audience might conclude that the convict had reformed, or they could entertain the notion that the criminal is under some kind of pressure to make the anti-crime statements. In the absence of any evidence to substantiate these suppositions, however, another explanation becomes more reasonable: Maybe the truth of the issue is so compelling that, even though it apparently contradicts his background and self-interest, the spokesman sincerely believes in the position he espouses.

Evidence for this phenomenon comes from an experiment by Alice Eagly and her colleagues, who presented students with a description of a dispute between business interests and environmental groups over a company's polluting of a river.[3] The students then read a statement about the issue. In some conditions the spokesman was described as having a business background and was said to be speaking to a group of businessmen. In others, his background and audience were varied, thereby altering the subjects' expectations of his message. The results supported the reasoning above: When the message conflicted with their expectations, listeners perceived the communicator as being more sincere, and they were persuaded by his statement.

It is hard to imagine a more convincing spokesperson for an anti-smoking campaign than someone whose fortune was made off the habits of millions of American smokers. In fact, Patrick Reynolds, who inherited $2.5 million from the R. J. Reynolds Tobacco Company founded by his grandfather, has taken a strong public stand against smoking and has recently gone so far as to urge victims of smoking-related illnesses to file lawsuits against tobacco companies![4]

Similarly, among the most effective opponents of the nuclear arms race in recent years have been several professionals who have taken stands that seemingly contradict their backgrounds. These communicators—for example, J. Robert Oppenheimer, a respected nuclear physicist who, for many years, cautioned against the further development of nuclear technology; Carl Sagan, a trusted astronomer who has warned the world about nuclear winter; and Admiral Elmo Zumwalt, a former naval commander who campaigned for a halt to certain military developments—have been perceived as highly credible precisely because of the discontinuity between their messages and the apparent interests of their professions. First of all, they are experts. Second, since they have nothing to gain (and perhaps collegial esteem to lose) it seems that only the compelling need for disarmament lead them to speak out. Not only do we tend to take more notice of unexpected events, but we also attribute more credibility to speakers who appear to resist the pressures of their colleagues and who take stands in opposition to their backgrounds.

Today, one of the nation's most respected authorities on health issues is the former U.S. Surgeon General, Dr. C. Everett Koop. That was not the case when Koop was first appointed to the position in the early 1980s by President Reagan. Koop is an evangelical Christian whose position on abortion

and contraceptives caused many Americans, especially those with a more liberal bent, to worry that Koop would use his position to advance his own view of morality. As the full meaning of the AIDS epidemic began to be discovered, Dr. Koop made a dramatic recommendation: obviously the best way to avoid the AIDS virus is sexual abstinence or monogamy; however, if you plan to be sexually active you should use a condom. Koop's recommendation resulted in a firestorm from those on the Right and, especially, evangelical Christians. They believed that Koop's recommendation to use condoms promoted promiscuity. The firestorm did not end there. In the last days of his appointment, Koop released a report stating that there was no evidence that an abortion causes emotional harm to the woman—although Koop himself still believed that abortion was morally wrong. The report dismayed many in the Reagan administration, who had hoped to use evidence of emotional harm as an argument against abortion. However, C. Everett Koop turned out to be a man of impeccable integrity who had earned his reputation as a trustworthy source.

The Chinese philosopher Mencius, who lived in the fourth century B.C., provides us with another technique for increasing the perception of trustworthiness.5 Mencius had gained fame as a wise counselor. The king sent a polite note asking Mencius to come to court so that he might advise the king. Mencius replied that he was not well and was unable to come to court. The next day he walked conspicuously around town. The king was outraged and sent several men to find out why Mencius showed so little respect and to beseech him once more to come to court. Mencius would not receive the men and left to visit a friend. The king could stomach Mencius's impertinence no more and accused him of disloyalty. Mencius replied that far from being disloyal and disrespectful, he had shown the most loyalty and respect for the king in all the land. He could be useful to the king only if the king absolutely trusted his integrity and independence of mind. If the king suspected that he might do or say things merely to please, his counsel would be ignored.

Mencius's actions illustrate another way of increasing the perception of credibility: The apparent trustworthiness of a person can be *increased* and the apparent bias of the message *decreased* if the audience is absolutely certain the person is not trying to influence them. To illustrate, let us bring this discussion into the twentieth century. Suppose a stockbroker calls you up and gives you a hot tip on a particular stock. Will you buy? It's hard to be sure. On the one hand, the broker is probably an expert, and this might influence you to buy. On the other hand, the stockbroker has something to gain by giving you a tip (a commission), and this could lower her effectiveness. But suppose you accidently happened to *overhear* her telling a friend that a particular stock was about to rise. Because she was obviously not *trying* to influence you, you might be more readily influenced.

This is exactly what we discovered in an experiment by Elaine Walster and Leon Festinger.6 In this study, a conversation was staged between two graduate students in which one of them expressed his opinion on an issue. The situation was arranged so that an undergraduate student was allowed to overhear this conversation. In one experimental condition, it was clear to the undergraduate that the graduate students were aware of his presence in the next room; therefore, the undergraduate knew anything being said could conceivably be directed at him with the intention of influencing his opinion. In the other condition, the situation was arranged so that the undergraduate believed the graduate students were unaware of his presence in the next room. In this latter condition, undergraduates' opinions changed significantly more in the direction of the opinion expressed by the graduate students.

There are many tactics for making it appear that you are not really trying to influence someone. A few years back, the brokerage firm of E. F. Hutton ran a series of commercials in which, when one person began to pass on some stock advice from E. F. Hutton, a sudden hush fell over the room and everyone strained toward the speaker to better "overhear" the tip. The implication is clear: Everyone is getting in on advice that was not intended for them, and the information is all the more valuable as a result. Another example of this phenomenon is the "hidden camera" advertisements on television; if we are convinced a person has been caught unaware, we do not attribute a persuasive intent to the message. Believing the person is acting spontaneously, we are more persuaded by his or her testimony. Finally, politicians are notorious for claiming that, unlike their opponents, they are above "politics" and are merely taking the position that they do because they have the best interest of the public at heart. When communicators do not appear to be *trying* to influence us, their potential to do so is increased.

. . . [C]lever propaganda tactics can be used to manipulate our beliefs and behavior. . . . The second moral of Han Fei-Tzu's story—that appearances can be deceiving—is often all too true; but the acceptance of this moral can breed an unhealthy cynicism.

For this reason, it is good to pause and reflect on the behavior of people such as Dr. C. Everett Koop. In an era in which political self-interest appears to dominate—where, for example, congres-

sional leaders opposed to excessive military spending are in favor of shutting down military bases except, of course, for the ones in their district—it is refreshing to run into a public servant of high integrity. When Koop, as Surgeon General, was confronted with the AIDS crisis, he conducted a thorough investigation so that he could render an expert judgment. At great risk to his career and at the cost of alienating his friends and supporters, Dr. Koop spoke what he knew to be true. The cost to Dr. Koop's career for his honesty should not be downplayed. Although he made it clear that he would like to continue in public service and would enjoy a promotion to Secretary of Health and Human Services, Koop was not reappointed by the Bush Administration. His accomplishments should not be taken lightly either. There are untold Americans—perhaps the people who live next door to you, perhaps your own son or daughter, perhaps

even yourself—who will not die of AIDS but will go on to live long and productive lives as a result of Dr. Koop's actions. In this age of propaganda, Dr. Koop's behavior reminds us that there is still a place for Aristotle's communicator of good character.

Notes

1. Oliver, R. T. (1971). *Communication and culture in ancient India and China.* Syracuse, NY: Syracuse University Press.
2. Walster (Hatfield), E., Aronson, E., & Abrahams, D. (1966). On increasing the persuasiveness of a low prestige communicator. *Journal of Experimental Social Psychology, 2,* 325–342.
3. Eagly, A., Wood, W., & Chaiken, S. (1978). Causal inferences about communicators and their effect on opinion change. *Journal of Personality and Social Psychology, 36,* 424–435.
4. *Santa Cruz Sentinel,* January 13, 1987, p. A8.
5. Oliver, R. T. (1971), See note 1.
6. Walster (Hatfield), E., & Festinger, L. (1962). The effectiveness of "overheard" persuasive communications. Journal of Abnormal and Social Psychology, 65, 395–402.

What's in a Brand?

SUMMARY   Consumers and brands have relationships. Nurturing those relationships ensures a company's success. While juggling their many duties, brand managers must keep answering three questions: who buy the brand, what do they want from it, and why do they keep coming back. The answers are partly rational but are also based on emotional "cues" and cultural values.

Diane Crispell and Kathleen Brandenburg

Diane Crispell is executive editor of American Demographics, *and Kathleen Brandenburg is associate editor of* The Numbers News.

"He that steals my purse steals trash," says the villain Iago in Shakespeare's *Othello*. "But he that filches from me my good name . . . makes me poor indeed."

Iago didn't have much of a good name to filch, but businesses should heed his words nonetheless. A business's good name is often a brand name. Inside the customer's mind, a trusted brand is a promise of high quality and good things to come. But a tainted brand name can trigger memories of poor quality and bad service, driving customers away. That's why brand management can make or break a company's reputation.

To businesses, brands mean market share. Packaged-goods marketers know that a name can affect shelf placement in the supermarket. When customers spend an average of only four seconds examining a shelf, this can be important. And because people are willing to spend a little more to get something they trust, branded products can command premium prices.

In the 1990s, established brands face challenges that range from private-label products to deep-discount stores. Their managers must keep up with rapid changes in the way products are distributed, priced, and sold at the retail level. But brand managers' most important goal is protecting the brand's good name. To succeed, they must answer three questions: who buys the brand, what do they want from it, and why do they keep coming back.

WHO BUYS THE BRAND

Most Americans are brand-loyal to something. The annual Monitor poll conducted by Yankelovich Partners of Westport, Connecticut, reports that 74 percent of respondents "find a brand they like, then resist efforts to get them to change." Once consumers are convinced of the quality and value of a particular brand, it takes a lot of money and effort to change their minds.

Many people buy familiar brands even if they believe the product has no actual advantage. Just half of Americans think that specific brands of mayonnaise are different or better than others and worth paying more for, according to The Roper Organization. But 62 percent know what brand of mayonnaise they want when they walk in the store. Another 22 percent look around for the best price on a well-known brand. The same pattern applies to many products, including beer, coffee, and soup.

Brand behavior is complex. Not everyone is brand-conscious, and not all brand-conscious people are truly brand-driven. Depending on the product, 20 to 44 percent of Americans see no difference among brands or any reason to buy

> **Only half of Americans think brands of mayonnaise are different, but 62 percent have a favorite brand.**

higher-priced ones, according to Roper. And in a study conducted by Deloitte & Touche, only about 35 percent of consumers are willing to identify themselves as "label-seekers."

Managers, salespeople, and students are more likely than the average shopper to say that familiar labels are important to them when they shop. Clerical workers, factory workers, and homemakers are less likely to be interested in names. Asian Americans have a high interest in labels,

Reprinted with permission from *American Demographics*, May 1993, pp. 26-29, 31-32. © 1993 by American Demographics, Inc. For subscription information, please call (800) 828-1133.

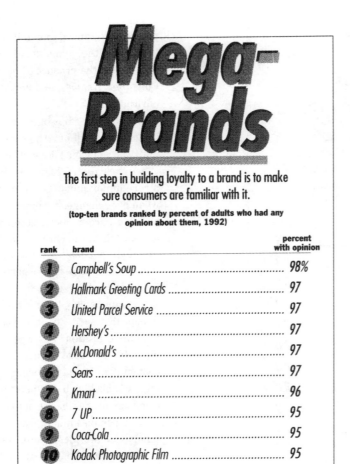

Mega-Brands

The first step in building loyalty to a brand is to make sure consumers are familiar with it.

(top-ten brands ranked by percent of adults who had any opinion about them, 1992)

rank	brand	percent with opinion
1	Campbell's Soup	98%
2	Hallmark Greeting Cards	97
3	United Parcel Service	97
4	Hershey's	97
5	McDonald's	97
6	Sears	97
7	Kmart	96
8	7 UP	95
9	Coca-Cola	95
10	Kodak Photographic Film	95

Source: Total Research Corporation, Princeton, New Jersey

"Pragmatists" (16 percent) are simply interested in getting value for their money.

The seven groups have different opinions about the quality of particular brands. Among luxury cars, for example, Intellects like the Lexus but give Cadillacs a mediocre rating. Sentimentals prefer Cadillacs and score the Lexus very low. The groups also shift over time in response to economic and social trends. Pragmatists, Conformists, and Actives are currently on the rise, while Popularity Seekers and Sentimentals are declining. Relief Seekers and Intellects are holding steady.

WHAT THEY WANT

Virtually everyone can identify a short list of "megabrands." The most familiar of all brands is Campbell Soup, according to To-

> When you see a can of Campbell's Tomato Soup, you react in ways that are rational, emotional, and cultural.

and blacks and Hispanics are slightly more interested than non-Hispanic whites. Label-seekers have an average amount of education, says Deloitte & Touche, but their household incomes are slightly higher than average.

In many ways, label-seekers are an elite group. They are more likely than average to own compact-disc players, microwave ovens, and home computers. They are also more likely to exercise regularly, participate in sports, and enjoy shopping. In fact, label-seekers list shopping as their fourth-favorite pastime, after TV, music, and reading.

Label-seekers say that a clothing store's selection is the most important reason to shop there, followed by quality and price. For others, selection is the most important criterion for dress clothing, but price is most important for casual clothes and shoes. Label-seekers and others agree that price is the most important thing when shopping for health-and-beauty aids.

But label-seekers rank selection second, while nonlabel-seekers mention location. In general, label-seekers see shopping as more of an exciting, emotionally fulfilling experience.

These hard-core brand shoppers are a minority of the population. But all shoppers fit into seven groups based on their definitions of brand quality, according to the Total Research Corporation of Princeton, New Jersey. "Conformists," at 12 percent of the population, choose the most popular brand because they want to belong to the crowd. "Popularity Seekers" (12 percent) go for trendy brands, while "Sentimentals" (12 percent) seek brands that emphasize comfort and good old-fashioned flavor. "Intellects" (17 percent) like upscale, cerebral, and technologically sophisticated brands, while "Relief Seekers" (17 percent) want something that offers escape from the pressures of life. "Actives" (15 percent) look for brands associated with a healthy, social lifestyle, and

tal Research: 98 percent of Americans have a positive, negative, or indifferent opinion about it. Other highly visible brands include Hallmark, United Parcel Service, Hershey's, McDonald's, Sears, Kmart, 7 UP, Coca-Cola, and Kodak. These names are cultural icons, and their managers enjoy powerful advantages over the competition.

When you see a can of Campbell's Tomato Soup, you react in ways that are rational, emotional, and cultural, according to Saatchi & Saatchi Advertising. Your rational mind thinks of tangible product qualities and features, such as the price of soup. Then your emotional side summons up a memory of the warm, comfortable feeling soup gives you. Finally, cultural influences make you consider the way you will be perceived by those who see Campbell on your pantry shelf.

A brand has many features, and people tend to evaluate the benefits of these features independently, says Saatchi & Saatchi executive vice president Penelope

Best Brands

Many well-known brands also rank high in quality.

(top-ten brands ranked by perceived quality using a 10-point scale, with 10 meaning "outstanding, extraordinary," 1992)

rank	high-quality brands	score
1	Disney World/Disneyland	8.5
2	Kodak Photographic Film	8.3
3	Hallmark Greeting Cards	8.2
4	United Parcel Service	8.2
5	Fisher-Price Toys	8.1
6	Levi's Jeans	8.0
7	Mercedes-Benz Automobiles	8.0
8	Arm & Hammer Baking Soda	8.0
9	AT&T Long-Distance Telephone	7.9
10	IBM Personal Computers	7.9

Source: Total Research Corporation, Princeton, New Jersey

Queen. To understand the rational side, the firm uses a conjoint, or trade-off, analysis technique that measures the relative value of each product attribute in the purchase decision. To understand the murkier emotional and cultural attractions of a brand, Queen conducts psychological interviews that explore societal influences and unconscious emotional needs.

Another ad agency, BBDO of New York, explores brand psychology in its own way. Its "Personal Drive Analysis" found that both Classico and Newman's Own spaghetti sauces are associated with upscale sophisticated adults. But people think of Classico in terms of "Italian" traits such as indulgence and romance, while they identify Newman's Own with the actor's individualistic and ambitious personality. BBDO uses this information to ensure that its advertising contains the appropriate emotional "cues" for each brand. Its methods can also reveal new niches by uncovering drives that current brands don't address.

Deep psychological motivations are an important part of why consumers buy, says Queen. But a brand's most powerful advantage is rooted in the human tendency to form habits and stick to routines. People's past experience with a brand is consistently the most important factor in their future brand choices, according to The Roper Organization. In the 17 years that Roper has been tracking the topic of brand choice, price and quality have almost always ranked second and third to past experience.

The reasons for choosing brands do change, albeit slowly. In 1985, quality temporarily moved into second place. In the Roper poll, price regained second place in 1986, and its lead over quality has widened considerably since then. In other words, quality is about as important to consumers as it was 17 years ago, but price is more important.

There are reasons for buying a product that go beyond experience, price, and quality. Recommendations from other

people have ranked fourth in all the Roper surveys. Other considerations are how well-known the product is, how it ranks in *Consumer Reports*, and how it affects the environment.

Whether it's a box of detergent or a car, most people will buy the same thing over and over as long as it satisfies their needs. When their needs change, rival brands get a rare opportunity. Often, needs change when lives change. A woman who becomes a single parent may watch every penny and switch to the cheapest detergent she can find. A couple who has a child will replace their two-seater sports car with a four-door sedan.

Sometimes people in transition switch brands that seem to have nothing to do with the transition. Forty percent of people who move to a new address also change their brand of toothpaste, according to Yankelovich Partners in Westport, Connecticut. "A change of that magnitude opens a person's mind," says Yankelovich senior vice president Watts Wacker. "Everything comes into question."

Most emotional relationships don't last unless both partners are adaptable and accommodating, and the relationship between brands and customers isn't any different. People won't be satisfied with the same skin-care product all their lives, for example. But the brand manager of a skin-care product can keep the relationship alive. One way is by extending the line of products sold under the brand name.

Like people, brands have a life span. They are born, they grow, they mature, they reach old age, and they die. One way to delay the process is to give them a makeover. For example, since its beginning, Tide detergent has become at least four products: original powder Tide, Liquid Tide, Tide with Bleach, and Ultra Tide. Each suits a particular market with a particular need.

The danger in line extensions is going too far. Levi's succeeded when it introduced looser-fitting jeans for middle-aged baby boomers, but it failed when it introduced a line of dress suits for men in the early 1980s. Loyal blue-jean buyers thought suits made by Levi's had to be

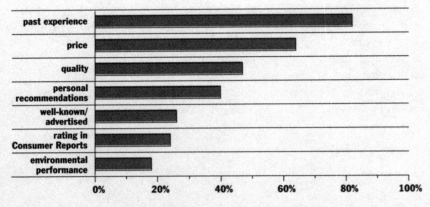

Tried It, Liked It

Knowing what to expect is the most common reason for buying a particular brand. Value and quality rank second and third.

(percent of adults who said that specified reasons were most important in deciding to buy a brand, 1992)

Source: The Roper Organization

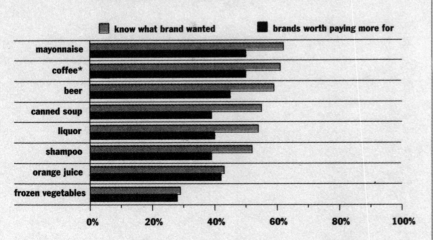

Air Share

In many product categories, some people who know what brand they will buy also think that particular brands are worth paying for.

(percent of adults who usually know which brand they will buy and who say that particular brands are worth paying more for, for selected product categories, 1992)

Coffee was referred to as "ground coffee" in the category brands worth paying more for.

Source: The Roper Organization

substandard in quality and design. As that perception took hold, Levi's began to lose jeans sales as well. It recalled the upscale line and scrambled to regain its traditional market.

Sometimes an old product can be rejuvenated simply by directing its advertising at a different market. Baby boomers who were raised on sweetened cereals are now health-conscious grown-ups. Kellogg's responded to this shift by repositioning Frosted Flakes as something that is still fun to eat but also good for you. Its advertisements show adults secretly admitting that they love the cereal.

KEEP THEM COMING BACK

Remember the old slogan for Alka-Seltzer: "Try it, you'll like it"? This is the essence of brand advertising. Success depends on finding people who are receptive to change and reaching them with advertising that reflects their attitudes toward the product.

Brand advertising should reflect two broad themes, according to a two-stage model developed by Larry Percy of Lintas: USA and John R. Rossiter of the Australian Graduate School of Management. The first theme is the reasons

> **Forty percent of people who move to a new address also change their brand of toothpaste.**

people buy (brand awareness), which in this model can be positive or negative. The second is the customer's level of involvement in the purchase decision (brand attitude), which can be high or low. Purchasing aspirin is a low-involvement decision, for example. Buying a house is a high-involvement decision.

Negative motivations include solving or avoiding problems and replenishing supplies of a product. Positive motivations include sensory gratification, intellectual stimulation, and social approval. Buying aspirin springs from a negative motivation, because one buys it to stop pain.

But cosmetics and vacations are positive buys.

There are four advertising strategies that match each of the four involvement-motivation combinations, say Percy and Rossiter. For a low-involvement, negative-motivational product like aspirin, advertising should stress the product's problem-solving benefits in a simple, emphatic manner. People don't necessarily have to like aspirin ads, but they must understand the product's benefits. For low-involvement, positive-motivational products like cosmetics, "emotional authenticity" is the key element and single benefit, say the authors. For this reason, the target audience must like the ad.

An automobile is usually a high-involvement purchase, say Percy and Rossiter. As such, its advertising should provide substantial information about the brand. But people buy cars for both positive and negative reasons, and the advertising should reflect this ambiguity. If the target audience needs no-nonsense transportation, the advertising should stress but not exaggerate product benefits while creating an initial positive attitude toward the brand. If the customer is looking for style or power, "emotional authenticity is paramount and should be tailored to lifestyle groups within the target audience." Moreover, "people must personally identify with the product."

In the final analysis, many brands are nothing more or less than an image that may imprint itself in consumers' minds forever. People were still ranking General Electric second in the food-blender market 20 years after it had stopped making them. Now that's brand loyalty.

TAKING IT FURTHER

The Total Research Corporation conducts the Equitrends survey. For more information, contact John Morton; telephone (609) 520-9100. For an insightful analysis of companies that have been successful (or not) with their brands, see *Managing Brand Equity: Capitalizing on the Value of a Brand Name*, by David A. Aaker of the University of California at Berkeley (The Free Press, 1991, $24.95). The Roper Organization conducts periodic surveys about a variety of brand-related attitudes; telephone (212) 599-0700. For Larry Percy and John R. Rossiter's "Model of Brand Awareness and Brand Attitude Advertising Strategies," see the July/August 1992 issue of *Psychology & Marketing* (John Wiley & Sons, Inc.).

Mindless Propaganda, Thoughtful Persuasion

Anthony Pratkanis and Elliot Aronson

Here are a five facts that professional persuaders have learned about modern propaganda:[1]

Ads that contain the words *new, quick, easy, improved, now, suddenly, amazing,* and *introducing* sell more products.

In supermarkets, merchandise placed on shelves at eye level sells best. Indeed, one study found that sales for products at waist level were only 74% as great and sales for products at floor level were only 57% as great as for those products placed at eye level.

Ads that use animals, babies, or sex appeal are more likely to sell the product than those that use cartoon characters and historical figures.

Merchandise placed at the end of a supermarket aisle or near the checkout aisle is more likely to be purchased.

Bundle pricing—for example, selling items at 2 for $1 instead of 50¢ each—often increases the customer's perception of product "value."

Why do these five techniques work? When you think about it, it makes little sense to purchase an item because it happens to be placed at the end of a supermarket aisle or on a shelf at eye level. You may not really need this conveniently located product, or the item you really want may be located on a top shelf. It makes little sense to be convinced by an ad because it uses a baby or contains certain words; such "information" is of little value in determining the quality of the product. A subtle rewording of the price does not add any value to the product. But that is the point—we consumers often don't think about the reasons we make the decisions we do. Studies show that about half of purchases in a supermarket are impulse buys and that upwards of 62% of all shoppers in discount stores buy at least one item on an unplanned basis.[2]

We often respond to propaganda with little thought and in a mindless fashion. Consider the experiments on mindlessness conducted by Ellen Langer and her colleagues.[3] Langer's collaborators walked up to persons busily using a university copy machine and said: "Excuse me: may I use the Xerox machine?" What would you do in such a situation? If you are like most people, it would depend on your mood. On some occasions you might think: *"Sure, why not? I'm a helpful person."* At other times, you might say to yourself: *"Is this person nuts or what? I got here first and have lots of work to do."* Indeed Langer's results indicate that both types of thinking were going on—a little over half of the people complied with this request.

Now, here's the interesting part. Langer found that she could get almost everyone to agree to let another person cut in front of them at the copy machine by adding one detail to the request—a *reason* for why the machine was needed. This makes sense. It takes a cold heart to deny someone, perhaps panic-stricken with an urgent need, the simple use of a copy machine. The odd thing about Langer's study is that although some of the reasons given made no sense at all, nearly everyone let the person cut in. For example, on some occasions Langer's collaborators would say, "Excuse me: May I use the Xerox machine, because I have to make copies." When you think about it, this is a pretty silly thing to say: Why would you need a copy machine if you were not planning to make copies? It is the same as no reason at all. But that is the point. Most of the people in the study did not think about it and mindlessly complied with the request.

We can also be influenced when we are being thoughtful. For example, most of us, at one time or another, have been panhandled, that is, stopped on the street by a passerby who asks for a quarter or any spare change. A common response is to ignore the request and continue to walk *mindlessly* down the street. Recently, we were panhandled in a novel manner. The panhandler asked, "Excuse me, do you have 17 cents that I could have?" What thoughts would run through your head in this situation? When it happened to us, our immediate thought was: *"Why does this person need exactly 17 cents? Is it for bus fare? Is it for a specific food purchase? Maybe the person came up short at the*

From *Age of Propaganda: The Everyday Use and Abuse of Persuasion* by Anthony Pratkanis and Elliot Aronson, pp. 25-32.
© 1992 by W. H. Freeman and Company. Reprinted by permission.

market." Suddenly the panhandler was a real individual with real needs, not someone we could mindlessly pass by. We were persuaded to part with a handful of change. Intrigued, we later sent our students out on the streets to panhandle for a local charity. They found that almost twice as many people contributed when asked for 17 or 37 cents compared to those who were asked for a quarter or any spare change.[4]

People can be persuaded both when they are in a mindless state *and* when they are thoughtful, but exactly how they are influenced in either of these two states differs considerably. Richard Petty and John Cacioppo argue that there are two routes to persuasion—*peripheral* and *central*.[5] In the peripheral route, a message recipient devotes little attention and effort to processing a communication. Some examples might include watching television while doing something else or listening to a debate on an issue that you don't care much about. In the peripheral route, persuasion is determined by simple cues, such as the attractiveness of the communicator, whether or not the people around you agree with the position presented, or the pleasure and pain associated with agreeing with the position. In contrast, in the central route, a message recipient engages in a careful and thoughtful consideration of the true merits of the information presented. For example, in the central route the person may actively argue against the message, may want to know the answer to additional questions, or may seek out new information. The persuasiveness of the message is determined by how well it can stand up to this scrutiny.

Let's see how the two routes to persuasion could be used to process one of the most influential and controversial television ads of the 1988 presidential election. This ad, prepared by the Bush campaign, told the story of Willie Horton, a black man who had been sent to prison for murder. During the time when Michael Dukakis, Bush's Democratic opponent, was governor of Massachusetts, Horton was released on a prison furlough program. While on furlough, Horton fled to Maryland, where he raped a white woman after stabbing her male companion.

The ad was influential because it required little thought for a person in the peripheral route to get the point. A typical response elicited by the ad went something like this: *"Dukakis let Horton out of prison to rape and kill. Dukakis is weak on crime, especially those committed by bad, black guys."* Although the response is simple, it was nonetheless effective for George Bush. Michael Dukakis was painted as a weak leader who was soft on crime; by comparison, George Bush looked strong and tough, capable of protecting us from the likes of Willie Horton.

However, no one was forced to think about this ad in the peripheral route. For example, in the central route to persuasion, the viewer might have asked *"Just how unusual is the Massachusetts prison furlough program? Do other states have similar programs? What is the success rate of such programs? Have instances like the Horton case happened in other states and with other governors? Can Dukakis really be held personally responsible for the decision to release Horton? How many prisoners were furloughed in Massachusetts without incident? Given that the cost of imprisoning someone for four years is approximately $88,000, or equal to the cost of four years of tuition for a student at Harvard with enough left over to buy the student a BMW upon graduation, is the furlough release program worth trying?"* In the central route, the Horton ad is potentially less effective (and might even have had the potential to damage the Bush campaign). The ad addressed few questions that a thoughtful viewer might raise.

This raises a crucial question: What determines which route to persuasion will be adopted? One factor identified by Petty and Cacioppo is the recipient's motivation to think about the message. In one experiment, Petty and Cacioppo, along with their student Rachel Goldman,[6] investigated the role of personal involvement in determining how we think about a message. Students at the University of Missouri heard a message advocating that their university adopt an exam that all students would need to pass in their senior year in order to graduate. Half of the students were told that their university's chancellor was considering adopting the comprehensive exam the following year, thereby making the issue of adopting the exam personally relevant for these students. The other half were told that the changes would not take effect for ten years and thus would not affect them personally.

To see how the personal relevance of an issue influenced thinking about a communication, Petty, Cacioppo, and Goldman prepared four different versions of the comprehensive exam message. Half of the messages were attributed to a source low in expertise—a local high school class. The other half of the messages were attributed to a source high in expertise—the Carnegie Commission on Higher Education. The researchers also varied the quality of arguments in the message, with half of the messages containing weak arguments (personal opinions and anecdotes) and the other half consisting of strong arguments (statistics and other data about the value of the exam).

This simple study can tell us a lot about the way people think about a persuasive message. Suppose

someone was operating in the central route to persuasion and was carefully scrutinizing the communication. When would that person be most persuaded? Given that the person was thinking carefully, he or she would not be persuaded by weak arguments and the source of the communication would not matter much; however, a strong message that stood up to close examination would be very effective. In contrast, the content of the message would not matter much to someone who was not thinking too much about the issue; instead, someone using the peripheral route would be most persuaded by a simple device such as a source that appears to be expert.

What did Petty, Cacioppo, and Goldman find? The personal relevance of the issue determined the route to persuasion. For those students for whom the issue of comprehensive exams was personally relevant, the strength of the message's argument was the most important factor determining whether or not they were persuaded. In contrast, for those students for whom the issue of the comprehensive exam was not personally relevant, the source of the communication mattered—the source high in expertise convinced; the one from the high school class failed to do so.

Petty and Cacioppo's two routes to persuasion should alert us to two important points—one about ourselves as human beings and one about propaganda in our modern world. In many ways, we are *cognitive misers*—we are forever trying to conserve our cognitive energy.[7] Given our finite ability to process information, we often adopt the strategies of the peripheral route for simplifying complex problems; we mindlessly accept a conclusion or proposition—not for any good reason but because it is accompanied by a simplistic persuasion device.

Modern propaganda promotes the use of the peripheral route to persuasion and is designed to take advantage of the limited processing capabilities of the cognitive miser. The characteristics of modern persuasion—the message-dense environment, the thirty-second ad, the immediacy of persuasion—make it increasingly more difficult to think deeply about important issues and decisions. Given that we often operate in the peripheral route, professional propagandists have free rein to use the type of tactics described at the beginning of this chapter and throughout this book to achieve, with impunity, whatever goal they may have in mind.

We have a state of affairs that may be called the *essential dilemma of modern democracy*. On the one hand, we, as a society, value persuasion; our government is based on the belief that free speech and discussion and exchange of ideas can lead to fairer and better decision making. On the other hand, as cognitive misers we often do not participate fully in this discussion, relying instead not on careful thought and scrutiny of a message, but on simplistic persuasion devices and limited reasoning. Mindless propaganda, not thoughtful persuasion, flourishes.

The antidote to the dilemma of modern democracy is not a simple one. It requires each of us to take steps to minimize the likelihood of our processing important information in the peripheral route. This might include increasing our ability to think about an issue through education or improving our ability to detect and understand propaganda by learning more about persuasion. It may mean alerting others to the personal importance of an issue so that many more citizens are encouraged to think deeply about a proposition. It could involve restructuring the way information is presented in our society so that we have the time and the ability to think before we decide. . . . Given the stakes, it behooves each of us to think carefully about how this dilemma can best be resolved.

Notes

1. Burton, P. W. (1981). *Which ad pulled best?* Chicago: Crain; Caples, J. (9174). *Tested advertising methods.* Englewood Cliffs, NJ: Prentice-Hall; Loudon, D. L., & Della Bitta, A. J. (1984). *Consumer behavior.* New York: McGraw-Hill; Ogilvy, D. (1983). *Ogilvy on advertising.* New York: Crown.
2. Ibid.
3. Langer, E., Blank, A., & Chanowitz, B. (1978). The mindlessness of ostensibly thoughtful action: The role of "placebic" information in interpersonal interaction. *Journal of Personality and Social Psychology, 36,* 635–642.
4. Santos, M., Leve, C., & Pratkanis, A. R. (August 1991). *Hey buddy, can you spare 17 cents? Mindfulness and persuasion.* Paper presented at the annual meeting of the American Psychological Association, San Francisco.
5. Petty, R. E., & Cacioppo, J. T. (1986). The elaboration likelihood model of persuasion. In L. Berkowitz (Ed.), *Advances in experimental social psychology* (Vol. 19; pp. 123–205). New York: Academic Press; Petty, R. E., & Cacioppo, J. T. (1986). *Communication and persuasion: Central and peripheral routes to attitude change.* New York: Springer-Verlag. See also Chaiken, S. (1980). Heuristic versus systematic information processing and the use of source versus message cues in persuasion. *Journal of Personality and Social Psychology, 39,* 752–766; Chaiken, S., Liberman, A., & Eagly, A. (1989). Heuristic versus systematic information processing within and beyond the persuasion context. In J. S. Uleman & J. A. Bargh (Eds.), *Unintended thought* (pp. 212–252). New York: Guilford.
6. Petty, R. E., Cacioppo, J. T., & Goldman, R. (1981). Personal involvement as a determinant of argument-based persuasion. *Journal of Personality and Social Psychology, 41,* 847–855.
7. Fiske, S. T., & Taylor, S. E. (1991). *Social cognition.* New York: McGraw-Hill.

Social Cognition

Pretend that I have just asked you your position on gun control, the name of your favorite television program, and how many children you plan on having. Now assume that I also ask you to estimate what proportion of the U.S. population holds the same attitude about guns, likes the same program, or plans on having that same number of children. If you are like most people, there is a good chance that your estimates of what the general population thinks on an issue will be influenced by your own opinion. In short, most of us believe that our own attitudes and preferences are relatively common in the population,

and that alternate attitudes and preferences are less common. This tendency to see our own preferences as being widely shared by others is referred to as the "false consensus effect."

This phenomenon is just one example of the kinds of topics that fall under the heading of social cognition, a broad topic that may loosely be defined as how people think about the social world. That is, the emphasis in this area is on the thought processes people engage in when they think about others. The emphasis in social cognition research, then, is usually on *how* people think, rather than

on the *content* of those thoughts. For example, one issue of importance to those who study social cognition is what happens to the information we acquire about other people. How is such information about people stored and organized in memory? How is it accessed and retrieved later on? After retrieval, how is it used to help us understand and interpret the world?

In response to questions such as these, considerable evidence now suggests that information about the self, other individuals, groups, places, and activities is stored in memory in the form of schemas—mental structures that contain information relevant to some concept or stimulus. These schemas are extremely important to us in a number of ways. For example, they influence the way in which we interpret and encode new information; in many instances, we are especially likely to notice and remember new information if it is consistent with information in existing schemas. Schemas also appear to exert an influence on the kinds of judgments we make about other people. Attitudes toward a new acquaintance who is a member of some identifiable group (for example, used car salesmen) can be significantly influenced if our preexisting schema for used car salesmen contains negative information (for example, "sneaky" or "slimy"). Much of the research in social cognition has been devoted, then, to understanding how cognitive structures such as schemas are formed, how they change, and how they affect our thoughts, feelings, and actions.

The five articles included in this unit illustrate the wide variety of issues that have been addressed within this area. The first selection, "Forbidden Thinking," describes one of the most interesting research areas in the field: a phenomenon known as "thought suppression." In a nutshell, this work is concerned with the process by which people try *not* to think about something—that is, how people suppress thoughts that they do not want to consciously entertain. As it turns out, thought suppression is a decidedly difficult thing to pull off and can lead to some surprising consequences. The following selection, "Road to Reward Is Rutted with Psychological Peril," describes some very practical problems that occur when people have to make decisions about an important personal matter: managing their investments. Because of some common cognitive biases, people often have difficulty making the most rational decisions where their money is concerned.

The next two selections address an important issue in contemporary social psychology, the distinction between automatic and controlled mental processes. In "Mindfulness and Mindlessness," Ellen Langer argues that it is surprisingly easy for us to act in "mindless" ways; when we do so, we ignore important information in a situation and simply respond in a habitual, automatic fashion. With the right prompting, however, we are also capable of acting in a "mindful" fashion and responding appropriately to situational information. The next selection, "Influences from the Mind's Inner Layers," treats the automatic vs. controlled distinction in a different way. Author Beth Azar summarizes recent research that indicates that existing schemas can be activated and influence our later judgments without any conscious awareness at all; in fact, stimuli presented too briefly to be consciously perceive (subliminally) can nevertheless activate cognitive structures and influence our behavior. The final selection in this unit, "In Japan, Blood Type Can Be Key to Success—or Failure," is a little different. It describes the stereotypes that many Japanese have about people with various blood types, illustrating that the power of cognitive schemas to affect our judgments of individuals is powerful indeed.

Looking Ahead: Challenge Questions

Why would people want to suppress certain thoughts? Why would it be difficult to accomplish this? Are there any methods that are more effective than others for suppressing unwanted thoughts? What are the consequences of trying unsuccessfully to suppress an unwanted thought?

Why is it difficult to make the most logical, unbiased decisions about your own monetary investments? Which cognitive biases contribute to this difficulty? Can you think of any situations, other than managing investments, in which such biases can interfere with rational decision making?

What is the difference between mindfulness and mindlessness? What causes us to enter one or the other of these two states? How would you compare this mindful/mindless distinction with the automatic/controlled distinction from the article by Beth Azar? Are the authors talking about the same thing? If not, how are they different?

Although stereotyping on the basis of blood types is not common in the United States (and may seem quite odd to most of us), we may have stereotyping systems that would seem equally odd or irrational to others. What examples of such systems can you think of?

Forbidden
THINKING

We all have dark impulses. None of us wants them. Yet attempts to suppress them can turn them into agents of harm. Be forewarned: Forces at work in our culture's value system may be making us more vulnerable to forbidden thoughts—and less able to cope with them.

Paul Roberts

Paul Roberts is a free-lance writer whose work has appeared in the New Republic, Newsweek, Adobe, *and other national magazines. He covers a broad range of topics, including environmental politics, science, and communication technologies, but has been interested in psychology since his days at the University of Washington. He lives with his wife and one-year-old daughter in Seattle; enjoys bicycling, climbing, and movie-watching; and insists that his thoughts are generally surprisingly pure.*

Have you ever thought of cheating on your spouse? What about slapping an obnoxious colleague? Or ramming some jerk on the freeway? Have you ever had thoughts about taboo or wild sex? Or divorce? Or leaving home? What about harming someone close? Or even harming yourself? Then there are the tamer varieties: Do you not fantasize about food, for example, when you are on a diet? Who has not gloated over someone else's misfortune or coveted a neighbor's house, car, or flashy lifestyle when we want to picture ourselves as perfectly content?

Few of us would dispute the notion that humans spend a great deal of time thinking thoughts we'd rather not have.

Most of us will never act out our forbidden impulses. Yet just the fact that we can think such thoughts may be so disturbing that we make Herculean efforts to repress them, to keep them secret. "I couldn't even tell my husband," recalls Beth, a gentle West Coast mother of three, after experiencing vivid thoughts about hurting her own children. "I spent a lot of time asking myself, 'What does this mean? Am I sick?'"

For as long as humankind has celebrated the creative powers of the mind, we've been forced to confront the darker side of the imagination: thoughts so mortifying, so frightening, so contrary to social custom and our own principles that we recoil in disgust or fear. In 1852, nearly three decades before the founding of modern psychology, author Herman Melville offered one of the more poignant observations on the life of the mind. "One trembles to think," he wrote, "of that mysterious thing in the soul, which...in spite of the individual's own innocent self, will still dream horrid dreams, and mutter unmentionable thoughts."

Reprinted with permission from *Psychology Today*, May/June 1995, pp. 34-40, 62, 64, 66. © 1995 by Sussex Publishers, Inc.

In times past, we blamed these dark impulses on the Devil, or on our own weak moral character. We regarded thoughts as but a step away from deeds, and admonished ourselves—or were admonished by others—to squelch the inappropriate notions at every turn. (No coincidence, surely, that five of the seven deadly sins—anger, avarice, envy, greed, and lust—refer specifically to states of mind.)

Even today, after more than a century of scientific exploration of the mind, Melville's "unmentionable thoughts" still raise vexing questions. What causes them? Do they reflect the "real" us? Should they be read as warning signs? Are some thoughts truly off-limits? If so, when does a thought cross the line, and how should it be dealt with?

We know the dangers of denial, and we understand the importance of accepting even the less-than-perfect parts of ourselves. Yet in a culture obsessed with, and increasingly defined by, stories of psychological dysfunction, and in a century punctuated with premeditated atrocity, some of what our own brains conjure up still has the power to terrify us. "For a lot of people, it's like discovering they have an animal inside them," says University of Washington sociologist Pepper Schwartz, Ph.D., who studies sexuality and sexual fantasies. "Oftentimes the feeling is 'My God! Am I one of those weirdos you read about in the paper?'"

Debated for centuries as a moral or philosophical question, the dilemma of forbidden thoughts has since become a compelling psychological subject, and research is yielding some intriguing, if not altogether reassuring, data. Forbidden thoughts—thoughts we feel we shouldn't have because they violate unwritten, yet ingrained, cultural codes—are universal, although the specific content varies across cultures, populations, and historical periods. Unwanted sexual fantasies, for example, typically involve behaviors our culture tells us are inappropriate, such as adultery, homosexuality, incest, and rape. Forbidden thoughts we might have about other people often involve stereotypes, which society frowns upon. Forbidden thoughts have an intuitive quality to them: It's the things we're not supposed to think about that often seem most alluring.

They're clearly linked to our decision-making mechanisms, our ability to distinguish "right" from "wrong," and our capacity to avoid dangerous, unfavorable outcomes. They may also be associated with our creative processes.

However, they can spin wildly out of control. In extreme cases, forbidden thoughts may become so powerful that they break out as actual behavior. More often, though, they get "stuck," become virtually impossible to dispel, and wreak havoc on our mental and physical health.

Much research has focused on the process of thought suppression—that is, on the ways we try to banish unwanted thoughts—and on the consequences of suppression. But researchers have also investigated how and why certain thoughts become forbidden in the first place. What emerges is an intriguing and complex picture of the mind, encompassing everything from genes and neurotransmitters to self-esteem and "family values." Ultimately, the dilemma of forbidden thinking rests on the courage to believe in ourselves.

Wired for Worry

Studies suggest that our individual vulnerability to forbidden thoughts is partly inherited, and that some of us are simply "wired" to dwell on worrisome thoughts. Yet studies also show that nearly all of us can be made vulnerable through a variety of external influences—influences that, in many cases, are intensifying. In fact, some psychologists speculate that our culture's increasingly fluid and permissive value systems may paradoxically be rendering us more vulnerable to forbidden thoughts—and less able to cope with them.

"At one time, we had much narrower standards of what thoughts were right and wrong—and nearly everything was wrong," says the University of Washington's Schwartz. "Today, it's far less clear where those lines are." And without those societal boundaries, many psychologists say, people may be overcompensating with unrealistic, self-imposed boundaries—and unwittingly making whole categories of thought "forbidden."

This is especially prevalent in the sexual arena. Ours is a culture that promotes sexual fulfillment and liberation while simultaneously insisting on restraint and "responsibility." Absent any clear standards for "healthy" thinking, some individuals attempt to ban their own sexual thoughts with such vigor that they close off an entire sector of experience.

The notion that we somehow create forbidden thoughts may sound strange. Yet many investigators argue that what we commonly refer to as "thought" doesn't begin as either "good" or "bad," but simply as a stream of randomly generated "value-free" images and symbols. "If we were somehow able to build a thought recorder, what we would record would be just about every kind of thought imaginable," argues psychologist David H. Barlow, Ph.D., director of the Center for Stress and Anxiety Disorders at the State University of New York–Albany. "Sexual thoughts, violent thoughts, some of them are very strange and bizarre—but for the most part, fleeting. They go in one ear and out the other, and a millisecond later you've forgotten about them."

Fleet Is Sweet

Where things get complicated, and where the trouble can start, is when thoughts aren't fleeting. For a variety of reasons, the brain seizes on a particular thought, holding it up for scrutiny and determining whether action is required. In some cases, however, this scrutinizing mechanism appears to go haywire. The partly processed thought somehow becomes permanent, or "intrusive," and can generate unpleasant emotional or physiological responses. In other words, researchers say, it's not the thought itself that is forbidden, but our reaction to it—a reaction that can involve intense feelings of shame, guilt, and even fear.

Precisely how this fixation occurs is not fully understood, but investigators have identified several main factors that can bring it on. Some fixation, for example, is clearly chemically induced. Research on individuals with obsessive-compulsive disorder (OCD), who appear genetically predisposed to focus, or "ruminate," on painful or strange thoughts, suggests that vulnerability has a neurological basis. Similar conclusions arise from studies on stress, a condition that can temporarily alter neurotransmitter flows and make subjects more likely to fixate on particularly unpleasant thoughts.

These findings could help explain why drugs like Prozac, Paxil, and Zoloft can inhibit or moderate the fixation process. The findings can also help explain fantasies like Beth's, which, according to Barlow and other researchers, are quite common among young, stressed-out parents.

Researchers have also identified certain higher-level cognitive factors that can influence the kinds of thoughts the brain latches on to, and how it interprets them. One factor may be what psychologists call "controllability." Closely related to self-esteem, controllability is the measure of an individual's sense of power, or control, over events in his or her life. The more in-control we feel, Barlow says, the less likely we are to interpret any event, whether external or coming from inside our heads, as worthy of concern or rumination. "On the other hand," warns Barlow, "if you feel that events are essentially out of your control, you're probably going to be much more vulnerable" to forbidden or unwanted thoughts. In other words, the vulnerable individual is likely to "read" more into a forbidden thought, just as a chronically anxious employee, for example, tends to read more into the boss's tone of voice or facial expression.

No Pain, No Gain

Worse, psychologists say that for low-controllability types, forbidden thoughts can unleash a damaging snowball effect. The more often people experience thoughts they deem uncomfortable or inappropriate, the more battered their sense of control and self-esteem become. And, notes Frank Fincham, Ph.D., a cognitive psychologist at the University of Wales, "how people react to unwanted thoughts depends a lot on his or her level of self-esteem."

Yet clearly, forbidden thoughts aren't simply the product of chemical imbalances or low self-esteem. A more central and complex factor, and one that researchers are just beginning to unravel, is the link between our forbidden thoughts and our larger system of values—our internalized template for judging right from wrong. A forbidden thought is, by definition, one that violates that template, and the resulting pain, researchers say, is part of what helps us to function as social beings. Displeasure over a fantasy of violence or adultery, for example, "may simply suggest that people approach life in a principled way," argues Norman Epstein, Ph.D., a psychologist in the family studies department at the University of Maryland. "If a thought like that pops into your head but you're not bothered by it at all, *that* could be a problem." The absence of this painful response may help explain some violent and other antisocial behavior.

Moreover, some psychologists see forbidden thoughts as part of the mind's process for testing and reaffirming its internal rules. Rape fantasies—both of raping and being raped—are quite common and are often interpreted by individuals as evidence of serious problems. But Schwartz argues that in many cases the brain may simply be teaching itself about consequences of rape. In the fantasy, Schwartz says, "maybe you're having someone who in real life you could never hope to have, or maybe you're dominating someone in a way that would hurt them." But sooner or later reality intrudes. "You realize the person is scared or is hurt," Schwartz says, "and in your mind, you back away."

Interestingly, just as individuals can "use" forbidden thoughts to explore the limits of their inner selves, many artists and authors use these thoughts to explore the outer limits of their culture. What are works like Henry Miller's *Tropic of Cancer* or David Lynch's film *Blue Velvet* (or just about anything by photographer Robert Mapplethorpe) but articulations of their creators's forbidden thoughts? One could argue, in fact, that many artistic, cultural, and political breakthroughs come about in part because an individual is willing to challenge the status quo to, in effect, "think the unthinkable."

Of course, few of us are paid for our unthinkable thoughts. More to the point, our culture offers few constructive rules or procedures for interpreting and coping with forbidden thoughts in a positive way. Instead, we're likely to construe them as unwholesome, as evidence of some deep psychosocial flaw, or as a prelude to antisocial or dangerous behavior. As such, psychologists say, our response is fairly predictable: We try to suppress them, usually with more energy than is realistically necessary, to prevent the worrisome thought from materializing into action.

The Trouble with Sin

Again, how strongly and negatively we react can depend on physiological or personality factors. But studies also suggest that past experiences, especially during upbringing, play an enormous role and that individuals from authoritarian backgrounds are far more likely to overreact to, and overcompensate for, forbidden thoughts. Research shows, for example, that persons raised in heavily religious households, where "evil" thoughts are regarded as evil deeds-in-waiting, are more likely than their non-religious counterparts to fixate on thoughts they feel are sinful or otherwise inappropriate. Their "God's will" world view may have produced a low sense of controllability and self-esteem, and thus a higher-than-average sense of vulnerability.

At the same time, such individuals grow up knowing precisely which thoughts are improper and therefore "worthy" of worry. "As a Catholic, there were whole domains of stuff that I wasn't supposed to think about,"

admits Thomas Borkovec, Ph.D., a distinguished professor of psychology at Penn State University who studies the phenomenon of worry. "When I did, I felt very guilty, and would try very hard to distract myself."

Unfortunately, it is precisely this response—attempting to avoid or suppress a forbidden thought—that can transform such thoughts from useful mental tools into agents of harm. Ever since Freud, psychologists and the lay public alike have understood that suppression of thoughts and feelings can have unintended consequences. But in the mid-1980s, research by University of Virginia psychologist Daniel Wegner, Ph.D., gave a whole new meaning to the word "backfire": the harder one tries *not* to think of a particular thought or image, Wegner found, the more likely it is to become intrusive and repetitive.

Beware the White Bear

Wegner's experiments were ingeniously simple. He set people in a room with a tape recorder and asked them to say whatever came to mind, with one caveat: They were not to think about a white bear. "People mentioned the bear about once a minute, despite the fact that they weren't supposed to be thinking about it," Wegner says. "They would try all sorts of tricks, but it would keep coming back to them."

Wegner and his colleagues aren't certain why this occurs. He suspects that in suppressing a thought, the mind is still "monitoring" the "contents of consciousness" for any vestige of the painful thought, and is thus more sensitive to that thought. Another theory is that in attempting to distract ourselves from one thought by thinking of another, the brain creates associations between the two thoughts. As a result, the distracting thought actually helps bring back the thought it was intended to mask. Still other researchers theorize that by suppressing a forbidden thought, the brain never gets a chance to fully process the thought. The individual then is never able to see that the forbidden thought is unrealistic and extremely unlikely to be translated into action. In short, without full processing, the thought may remain unresolved and will keep re-emerging in the consciousness for more processing—and more suppression.

Whatever the actual mechanics of suppression, Wegner says, it's an almost automatic response to unwanted or forbidden thoughts. People on a diet, he says, will suppress thoughts of food. Victims of traumatic experiences—accidents, loss of a loved one, broken relationships—will try to suppress painful memories. People with secrets, dark or otherwise, use suppression to keep the knowledge hidden.

Here again, researchers see a snowball effect. We tend to suppress most energetically thoughts that bring us the most pain, Wegner says, and yet, the harder we suppress, the more intrusive and unpleasant the thought becomes. In one provocative study, four researchers—C. Neil Macrae and Alan Milne at the University of Wales; Galen Bodenhausen, Ph.D., at Michigan State University; and Jolanda Jetten at the University of Nijmegen in the Netherlands—found that subjects attempting to suppress stereotypical, or prejudicial, thoughts made the thoughts *stronger* than be-

fore suppression. Psychologists call this unintended result an "ironic" process.

"The act of trying not to stereotype others ultimately increases the use of stereotypes," explains Bodenhausen. Other studies confirm his point: researchers have shown that governmental attempts at banishing Western thoughts from public discourse, as is the case in Iran, actually increase the number of times such ideas are discussed and, presumably, thought about.

In another study, Constantina Giannopoulos, M.A., and Michael Conway, Ph.D., at Montreal's Concordia University, asked subjects to suppress thoughts of food. They found the task far more difficult than did subjects under no such prohibition. In general, says Wegner, "The mental conditions we fear the most are the ones we tend to create through this process. It's a paradox, like trying desperately to get to sleep the night before something important."

CONFESS, DON'T SUPPRESS

What is startling even to researchers, however, is just how serious the consequences of suppression can be. In a well-known case, convicted serial killer Jeffrey Dahmer confided to psychologist Judith Becker that he had been tormented as a child by thoughts of torturing animals. (Clearly Dahmer was plagued by more than just thought suppression. "He found these thoughts repulsive and attempted to suppress them," notes Barlow. "And he basically ended up being haunted by them for the rest of his life."

Not unexpectedly, many researchers and therapists suggest that the way to loosen the grip of forbidden or unwanted thoughts begins with the de-suppression of them. Wegner and psychologist James Pennebaker, Ph.D., at Southern Methodist University, advocate confiding one's forbidden thoughts. They have found that subjects who do discuss their thoughts can feel better both emotionally and physically.

Part of it may simply be getting a troublesome thought off our "chests." But research by Roxane Cohen Silver, Ph.D., a psychologist at the University of California–Irvine who has worked with Vietnam vets and other trauma survivors, believes that sharing helps us realize we aren't alone in our anguish, that others have unwanted or forbidden thoughts as well. This, she says, can help reduce the stigma that often creates the forbidden thought in the first place. "The more that individuals who have experienced trauma think that their [mental] situation is unique," Silver says, "the less they're likely to talk about it, and the less likely they are to receive validation of their thoughts."

Unfortunately, de-suppression is only half the battle. In the first place, it's often hard to find someone to listen. Those we're willing to talk to—spouses, relatives, close friends—often lack the expertise or patience to realistically assess our thoughts. Indeed, friends and spouses may simply not be able to cope with especially disturbing thoughts. Generally, says Silver, research has shown that the more horrific and socially stigmatized the thought, the smaller the willing audience, and the more often the individual experiences the unwanted thoughts. The only place left to turn is the counselor, minister, or other trained listener—an option with its own social stigma attached.

WHAT LURKS IN MURK

The more daunting hurdle, however, may be finding new, more realistic mental "rules" to replace those that helped generate the forbidden thoughts. To be sure, rules against thoughts of, say, murder or child abuse still apply. But what about thoughts like divorce? You may have been raised in, and internalized the rules of, a culture where the "D-word" was never even spoken aloud. To even think of divorce was to admit your marriage was imperfect, that you were already planning to leave. Today the "rules" for thinking about divorce are vastly different. While the consequences of failed marriages remain clear, so do the dangers of staying married at all costs. Divorce is simultaneously stigmatized and regarded as a thinkable, potentially healthy option.

> **"While a too-rigid value system can create vulnerabilities to forbidden thoughts, so too can a system that is in a state of flux."**

The point, psychologists say, is that while a too-rigid value system can create vulnerabilities to forbidden thoughts, so, too, can a value system that is ill-defined or in a state of flux. This is especially evident in individuals who have begun to question their religious beliefs, to rebel against the authority of a parent or spouse, to resist the cultural attitudes they grew up with, or even to shuck off an old, unwanted self-image. Whatever the objective, many such individuals are, in essence, seeking to let themselves have thoughts that were once forbidden. (Not surprisingly, many of the popular new spiritual and self-help movement specifically encourage their adherents to avoid the terms "should" and "should not" in the context of thoughts and actions.)

CONSCIENCE IN CONFLICT

Such efforts may ultimately be wholesome and liberating. But they may also profoundly contradict many traditional teachings and attitudes, and could magnify confusion—and vulnerability—in persons whose past attitudes maintain a powerful, if unwanted, pull. They may find that the thoughts they want to have—about racial equality, for example—are at some level still "forbidden" by past experience and attitudes. At the same time, thoughts that were appropriate and encouraged under that previous world view—judging others via stereotype, for example—are now inappropriate, and thus also "forbidden."

In a sense, even before an individual has vanquished one set of forbidden thoughts, he or she may be busily creating a new one. "It can be a tough time," says the University of Maryland's Epstein. "You don't have a [belief system] to hold on to. Basically you know what you're trying to leave behind, but you haven't yet figured out what you're going into."

And, in reality, few people are torn between just two belief systems. Western culture, especially American culture, is a rich stew of competing value systems, distinct subcultures, and often radically different notions of "inappropriate" thoughts. What is correct thinking in one subculture may be intolerable in another, causing confusion for people moving between the two. A woman raised in a conservative rural community, for example, may have learned to "forbid" herself from desiring a professional career or equality with men. Yet if this same woman moves to an urban, liberal environment where such thoughts are encouraged, she may nonetheless find it difficult to have such "liberal" thoughts without guilt or self-doubt.

Indeed, cultural politics are rife with forbidden thoughts. Many liberal doctrines criticize traditional religion as "thought control," yet themselves set aside whole new categories of thought as "politically incorrect." Consider, for example, the internal conflicts of the "sensitive" male who views himself as respectful of women's rights and feelings and yet finds himself fantasizing about rape. Or consider the conflicts of an avowed feminist woman who finds herself fantasizing pleasurably about staying home with the kids. Or about being sexually dominated!

No category of thought may be as filled with contradictions, and so difficult to judge, as sexuality. We're bombarded daily with provocative images, stern warnings, new and often contradictory theories based as much on politics as science. We're told that sexual feelings are good, but that sexual feelings can get out of control. We're told the reason pornography is titillating is because our culture "forbids" sexuality, but that watching pornography corrupts our minds. We're told that lust is normal (Jimmy Carter admitted to it), but also that lust is a bad habit. That homosexuality is genetic, but also a chosen lifestyle and a sin. That adultery is fatal, but also a common, survivable social phenomenon. "It used to be that having sexual thoughts about anyone but your wife was wrong," observers Schwartz. "Now, it's as if we've been given more permission."

DO-IT-YOURSELF STANDARDS

Fluid societal boundaries not only make us vulnerable to forbidden thoughts, they simultaneously deny us the tools we need to cope with the unwanted intrusions. The only way to make sense of the chaos, some psychologists say, is not to blindly rely on culture to supply our mental standards. We must be willing to take matters into our own hands. That may mean seeking professional help, especially if we feel a thought is in danger of breaking out. A good rule of thumb: If a thought is causing pain, or interfering with your life, it's probably time to talk to someone.

In severe cases, where an individual is paralyzed by his or her reaction to forbidden thoughts, drugs or intensive therapy may be needed. In less serious instances, however, treatment centers on helping people to recreate or recover a healthier, more realistic perspective on their thoughts. And while these treatments are often conducted in the controlled environment of a therapist's office, psychologists say, they may also be effectively applied in everyday situations.

PERMISSIVE PERSPECTIVE

Some therapists, for example, give their clients "permission" to think the forbidden thought for a specified period of time each day, which, in less severe cases, allows our normal mental processes to wash away the anxiety associated with it. Others recommend what might be called the Big Picture approach. "What we try to do is have clients step back and look at their life as whole, to be objective," says Epstein. "To what degree are the thoughts having an impact on the way one leads one's life? Do they tend to live by basic principles? Do they tend to treat people in a fair way?" Often, he says, people troubled by forbidden thoughts "have highly unrealistic standards for themselves."

"Many liberal doctrines criticize religion as thought control, yet set aside whole new categories of thought as 'correct.' "

Generally, psychologists say, patients are helped to understand that life's stresses can produce impulsive, unwanted, but not necessarily deadly, thoughts. Work is a common source of forbidden thoughts. But family situations are probably the most fertile. This is particularly true in marriage or live-in relationships, where the work and stress of keeping a relationship together, raising children, managing money, keeping house, and coping with in-laws can occasionally give rise to less-than-savory thoughts about one's spouse.

The key is to consistently strive for a sense of perspective and realism. As Neil Jacobson, professor of psychology at the University of Washington puts it: "The fact is that to be married to someone is to sometimes think he is an asshole."

Whether we go it alone or seek counseling, psychologists say, confronting our forbidden thoughts ultimately requires courage. Courage to create, and live by, our own rules. Courage to face our own worst fears, and to question our own self-prohibitions with the same intensity and passion with which we question society's rules. But it is also the courage simply to believe in ourselves.

Forbidden thoughts may prevent us from committing heinous crimes and other regrettable acts. They may help us to survive as participants in an intricate social dance. But they can also serve as a means of undermining ourselves, of seeing ourselves in a primarily negative light. In the end, the most damaging "forbidden" thought, the one we have been trained to block at every turn, may simply be that we are really okay. "Most of us have had some pretty off-the-wall thoughts, and when we question ourselves, to some extent that's part of the mental health process," says Seattle therapist Michael Donnen. "But we have to learn to be gentle on ourselves."

Road to Reward Is Rutted with Psychological Peril

Though investors like profits, their own behavior traits work against them.

Johnathan Clements

Wall Street Journal

If you want to retire rich, your best bet is to save like crazy, invest in a broad collection of stocks, then close your eyes, clench your teeth and don't hold your breath while you wait.

Sound easy? For lots of investors, it isn't. In fact, when it comes to handling money, many of us aren't entirely rational. Here's what the experts in so-called behavioral finance have discovered:

We hate to lose: Stocks generate superior returns over the long haul, so it makes sense for folks with a long time horizon to own stocks. Yet many investors who are decades from retirement wouldn't dream of putting their money in the market.

"People get more pain out of losses than pleasure from gains, so they tend to be more risk averse than economists would expect," says Russell Fuller, president of RJF Asset Management in San Mateo, Calif.

Because investors find losses so painful, they tend to hang onto securities until they at least break even. "When you realize a loss, you kiss that money goodbye forever and you kick yourself," says Meir Statman, a finance professor at Santa Clara university. "That's the regret part, and it causes people to procrastinate."

Meanwhile, folks are often quick to sell their winners. If you own a stock that went from $10 to $50, "it's just a paper gain," Statman says. "Realized gains are more tangible."

Dollar-cost averaging, which involves investing a fixed amount in the stock market every month or every quarter, is often seen as a way of reducing risk. But like the reluctance to sell losers, dollar-cost averaging is really about regret, Statman argues.

"If I put all my money into stocks today and the market crashes tomorrow, I will feel just awful," he notes. Indeed, says Statman, if dollar-cost averaging is about risk control, why do investors also use the strategy when they are getting out of stocks? If investors really wanted to reduce risk, they would sell all their stocks immediately. But they don't do that, because they fear the market might surge the next day.

We often misread the past: "People like myself, who have been in the business since before the 1973–74 crash—we were terrified by that crash," says Fuller. "That's a very low-probability event. But many of the people in this business have spent the last 20 years worrying about that happening again."

More often, however, investors get swept up in the wave of the moment, getting more optimistic as stock prices rise or more nervous as prices fall. Similarly, investors flock to mutual funds with stellar one-year performance, even though it's impossible to assess whether a manager is lucky or smart based on such a short record.

"Investors are overconfident," argues Richard Thaler, an economics professor at the University of Chicago. "We know that most mutual funds underperform the index, yet people persist in putting most of their money in active portfolios" rather than index funds that simply try to match the performance of the market averages. "They think they can pick the winners."

We don't see the big picture: Money is money, right? Maybe not. After all, why is it that folks will happily run up credit card bills, but they're loath to borrow against the equity in their home, despite the lower cost involved?

Similarly, if you buy stocks, your gain may come from dividends, share-price appreciation or some combination of the two. Yet many investors are happy to spend their dividends but are deeply reluctant to dip into capital.

Investors, it seems, don't look at their entire portfolio. Instead, they divide money into different mental accounts.

For instance, "there's a tendency to look at investments in isolation," says Daniel Kahneman, a psychology professor at Princeton University. "Investors focus on the risk of individual securities." As a result, they tend to fret over the short-term performance of each investment, often leading to bad decisions.

From *St. Petersburg Times,* December 4, 1995, p. E4. Originally "Behavioral Specialists Put Investors on Couch" from *Wall Street Journal,* November 28, 1995. © 1995 by Dow Jones & Company, Inc. All rights reserved worldwide. Reprinted by permission.

Mindfulness and Mindlessness

Ellen Langer

Introduction

I don't like the idea of a unitary subject; I prefer the play of a kaleidoscope: you give it a tap and the little bits of colored glass form a new pattern.

(Roland Barthes, *The Grain of the Voice*)

One day, at a nursing home in Connecticut, elderly residents were each given a choice of houseplants to care for and were asked to make a number of small decisions about their daily routines. A year and a half later, not only were these people more cheerful, active, and alert than a similar group in the same institution who were not given these choices and responsibilities, but many more of them were still alive. In fact, less than half as many of the decision-making, plant-minding residents had died as had those in the other group. This experiment, with its startling results, began over ten years of research into the powerful effects of what my colleagues and I came to call *mindfulness*, and of its counterpart, the equally powerful but destructive state of *mindlessness*.[1] . . .

Social psychologists usually look for the ways in which behavior depends on context. When mindless, however, people treat information as though it were *context-free*—true regardless of circumstances. For example, take the statement: Heroin is dangerous. How true is this for a dying individual in intolerable pain?

Once alerted to the dangers of mindlessness and to the possibility of bringing about a more mindful attitude by such deceptively simple measures as those used in the nursing home experiment, I began to see this double-edged phenomenon at work in many different settings. For instance, consider the events that led to the 1985 crash of an Air Florida plane that killed seventy-four passengers. It was a routine flight from Washington, D.C., to Florida with an experienced flight crew. Pilot and copilot were in excellent physical health. Neither was tired, stressed, or under the influence. What went wrong? An extensive examination pointed to the crew's pre-takeoff control checks. As the copilot calls out each control on his list, the pilot makes sure the switches are where he wants them to be. One of these controls is an anti-icer. On this day, the pilot and copilot went over each of the controls as they had always done. They went through their routine and checked "off" when the anti-icer was mentioned. This time, however, the flight was different from their experience. This time they were not flying in the usual warm southern weather. It was icy outside.

As he went through the control checks, one by one as he always did, the pilot appeared to be thinking when he was not. The pre-takeoff routines of pilot and copilot have a lot in common with the tiresome safety demonstrations of flight attendants to experienced, glassy-eyed passengers. When we blindly follow routines or unwittingly carry out senseless orders, we are acting like automatons, with potentially grave consequences for ourselves and others.

From *The Production of Reality: Essays and Readings in Social Psychology* by Peter Kollock and Jodi O'Brien, 1994, chapter 2, pp. 94-98. Originally from *Mindfulness* by Ellen J. Langer, pp. 1, 3-4, 9-18. © 1989 by Ellen J. Langer. Reprinted by permission of Addison-Wesley Publishing Company, Inc.

When the Light's On and Nobody's Home

Out of time we cut "days" and "nights," "summers" and "winters." We say what each part of the sensible continuum is, and all these abstract whats are concepts.

The intellectual life of man consists almost wholly in his substitution of a conceptual order for the perceptual order in which his experience originally comes.

(William James, "The World We Live In")

Imagine that it's two o'clock in the morning. Your doorbell rings; you get up, startled, and make your way downstairs. You open the door and see a man standing before you. He wears two diamond rings and a fur coat, and there's a Rolls Royce behind him. He's sorry to wake you at this ridiculous hour, he tells you, but he's in the middle of a scavenger hunt. His ex-wife is in the same contest, which makes it very important to him that he win. He needs a piece of wood about three feet by seven feet. Can you help him? In order to make it worthwhile he'll give you $10,000. You believe him. He's obviously rich. And so you say to yourself, how in the world can I get this piece of wood for him? You think of the lumber yard; you don't know who owns the lumber yard; in fact you're not even sure where the lumber yard is. It would be closed at two o'clock in the morning anyway. You struggle but you can't come up with anything. Reluctantly, you tell him, "Gee, I'm sorry."

The next day, when passing a construction site near a friend's house, you see a piece of wood that's just about the right size, three feet by seven feet—a door. You could have just taken a door off its hinges and given it to him, for $10,000.

Why on earth, you say to yourself, didn't it occur to you to do that? It didn't occur to you because yesterday your door was not a piece of wood. The seven-by-three-foot piece of wood was hidden from you, stuck in the category called "door."

This kind of mindlessness, which usually takes more humdrum forms—"Why didn't I think of Susan? She can unclog sinks"—could be called "entrapment by category." It is one of three definitions that can help us understand the nature of mindlessness. The other two, which we will also explain, are automatic behavior and acting from a single perspective.

Trapped by Categories

We experience the world by creating categories and making distinctions among them. "This is a Chinese, not a Japanese, vase." "No, he's only a freshman." "The white orchids are endangered." "She's his boss now." In this way, we make a picture of the world, and of ourselves. Without categories the world might seem to escape us. Tibetan Buddhists call this habit of mind "The Lord of Speech":

We adopt sets of categories which serve as ways of managing phenomena. The most fully developed products of this tendency are ideologies, the systems of ideas that rationalize, justify and sanctify our lives. Nationalism, communism, existentialism, Christianity, Buddhism—all provide us with identities, rules of action, and interpretations of how and why things happen as they do.[3]

The creation of new categories, as we will see throughout this book, is a mindful activity. Mindlessness sets in when we rely too rigidly on categories and distinctions created in the past (masculine/feminine, old/young, success/failure). Once distinctions are created, they take on a life of their own. Consider: (1) First there was earth. (2) Then there was land, sea, and sky. (3) Then there were countries. (4) Then there was Germany. (5) Now there is East Germany versus West Germany. The categories we make gather momentum and are very hard to overthrow. We build our own and our shared realities and then we become victims of them—blind to the fact that they are constructs, ideas.

If we look back at the categories of an earlier age, once firmly established, it is easier to see why new ones might become necessary. The Argentinean writer Jorge Luis Borges quotes from an ancient Chinese encyclopedia in which the animals are classified as "(a) belonging to the Emperor, (b) embalmed, (c) tame, (d) suckling pigs, (e) sirens, (f) stray dogs, (g) included in the present classification, (h) frenzied, (i) innumerable, (j) drawn with a very fine camel brush, (k) et cetera, (l) having just broken the water pitcher, (m) that from a long way off look like flies."[4] To be mindless is to be trapped in a rigid world in which certain creatures always belong to the Emperor, Christianity is always good, certain people

are forever untouchable, and doors are only doors.

Automatic Behavior

Have you ever said "excuse me" to a store mannequin or written a check in January with the previous year's date? When in this mode, we take in and use limited signals from the world around us (the female form, the familiar face of the check) without letting other signals (the motionless pose, a calendar) penetrate as well.

Once, in a small department store, I gave a cashier a new credit card. Noticing that I hadn't signed it, she handed it back to me to sign. Then she took my card, passed it through her machine, handed me the resulting form, and asked me to sign it. I did as I was told. The cashier then held the form next to the newly signed card to see if the signatures matched.

Modern psychology has not paid much attention to how much complicated action may be performed automatically, yet as early as 1896 Leon Solomons and Gertrude Stein looked into this question. (This was *the* Gertrude Stein who, from 1893 to 1898, was a graduate student in experimental psychology at Harvard University, working under William James.) They studied what was then called "double personalities" and which later came to be known as "split personalities," and proposed that the mindless performance of the second personality was essentially similar to that of ordinary people. Ordinary people also engage in a great deal of complex behavior without consciously paying attention to it. Solomons and Stein conducted several experiments in which they were their own subjects, demonstrating that both writing and reading could be done automatically. They succeeded in writing English words while they were otherwise caught up in reading an absorbing story. With much practice, they were even able to take dictation automatically while reading. Afterward, they were completely unable to recall the words they had written but were nevertheless quite certain they had written something. To show that reading could take place automatically, the subject read aloud from a book while a captivating story was read to him or her. Again they found that, after a lot of practice, they could read aloud unhampered while giving full attention to the story being read to them.

Solomons and Stein concluded that a vast number of actions that we think of as intelligent, such as reading and writing, can be done quite automatically: "We have shown a general tendency on the part of normal people, to *act*, without any express desire or conscious volition, in a manner in general accord with the *previous habits* of the person."[5]

An experiment I conducted in 1978 with fellow psychologists Benzion Chanowitz and Arthur Blank explored this kind of mindlessness.[6] Our setting was the Graduate Center at the City University of New York. We approached people using a copying machine and asked whether they would let us copy something then and there. We gave reasons that were either sound or senseless. An identical response to both sound and senseless requests would show that our subjects were not thinking about what was being said. We made one of three requests: "Excuse me, may I use the Xerox machine?"; "Excuse me, may I use the Xerox machine because I want to make copies?"; "Excuse me, may I use the Xerox machine because I'm in a rush?"

The first and second requests are the same in *content*—What else would one do with a copying machine except make copies? Therefore if people were considering what was actually being said, the first two requests should be equally effective. Structurally, however, they are different. The redundant request ("Excuse me, may I use the Xerox machine because I want to make copies?") is more similar to the last one ("Excuse me, may I use the Xerox machine because I'm in a rush?") in that both state the request and give a reason. If people comply with the last two requests in equal numbers, this implies attention to structure rather than conscious attention to content. That, in fact, was just what we found. There was more compliance when a reason was given—whether the reason sounded legitimate or silly. People responded mindlessly to the familiar framework rather than mindfully attending to the content.

Of course, there are limits to this. If someone asked for a very large favor or if the excuse were unusually absurd ("because an elephant is after me"), the individual would be likely to think about what was said. It is not that people don't hear the request the rest of the time; they simply don't think about it actively.

In a similar experiment, we sent an interdepartmental memo around some university offices. The message either requested or demanded the return of the memo to a designated room—and that was all it said.[7] ("Please return this immediately to Room 247," or "This memo is to be returned to Room 247.") Anyone who read such a memo mindfully would ask, "If whoever sent the memo wanted it, why did he or she send it?" and therefore would not return the memo. Half of the memos were designed to look exactly like those usually sent between departments. The other half were made to look in some way different. When the memo looked like those they were used to, 90 percent of the recipients actually returned it. When the memo looked different, 60 percent returned it.

When I was discussing these studies at a university colloquium, a member of the audience told me about a little con game that operated along the same lines. Someone placed an ad in a Los Angeles newspaper that read, "It's not too late to send $1 to ————," and gave the person's own name and address. The reader was promised nothing in return. Many people replied, enclosing a dollar. The person who wrote the ad apparently earned a good sum.

The automatic behavior in evidence in these examples has much in common with habit.[8] Habit, or the tendency to keep on with behavior that has been repeated over time, naturally implies mindlessness. However, as we will see . . . mindless behavior can arise without a long history of repetition, almost instantaneously, in fact.

Acting From a Single Perspective

So often in our lives, we act as though there were only one set of rules. For instance, in cooking we tend to follow recipes with dutiful precision. We add ingredients as though by official decree. If the recipe calls for a pinch of salt and four pinches fall in, panic strikes, as though the bowl might now explode. Thinking of a recipe only as a rule, we often do not consider how people's tastes vary, or what fun it might be to make up a new dish.

The first experiment I conducted in graduate school explored this problem of the single perspective. It was a pilot study to examine the effectiveness of different requests for help. A fellow investigator stood on a busy sidewalk and told people passing by that she had sprained her knee and needed help. If someone stopped she asked him or her to get an Ace bandage from the nearby drugstore. I stood inside the store and listened while the helpful person gave the request to the pharmacist, who had agreed earlier to say that he was out of Ace bandages. After being told this, not one subject, out of the twenty-five we studied, thought to ask if the pharmacist could recommend something else. People left the drugstore and returned empty-handed to the "victim" and told her the news. We speculated that had she asked for less specific help, she might have received it. But, acting on the single thought that a sprained knee needs an Ace bandage, no one tried to find other kinds of help.

As a little test of how a narrow perspective can dominate our thinking, read the following sentence:

FINAL FOLIOS SEEM TO RESULT FROM YEARS OF DUTIFUL STUDY OF TEXTS ALONG WITH YEARS OF SCIENTIFIC EXPERIENCE.

Now count how many Fs there are, reading only once more through the sentence.

If you find fewer than there actually are (the answer is given in the notes),[9] your counting was probably influenced by the fact that the first two words in the sentence begin with F. In counting, your mind would tend to cling to this clue, or single perspective, and miss some of the Fs hidden within and at the end of words.

Highly specific instructions such as these or the request for an Ace bandage encourage mindlessness. Once we let them in, our minds snap shut like a clam on ice and do not let in new signals.

Notes

1. E. Langer & J. Rodin (1976), "The effects of enhanced personal responsibility for the aged: A field experiment in an institutional setting," *Journal of Personality and Social Psychology, 34,* 191-198; J. Rodin & E. Langer (1977), "Long-term effects of a control-relevant intervention among the institutionalized aged," *Journal of Personality and Social Psychology, 35,* 897-902.

2. C. Gersick & J. R. Hackman (1990), "Habitual routines in task-performing groups," *Organizational Behavior and Human Decision Processes, 47,* 65-97.

3. C. Trungpa (1973), *Cutting through spiritual materialism,* Boulder & London: Shambhala.

4. T'ai P'ing (978), *Kuang chi* [Extensive re-

cords made in the period of peace and prosperity]; cited in J. L. Borges (1967), *Libro de los seres imaginarios*, Buenos Aires: Editorial Kiersa S. A., Fauna China, p. 88.

5. L. Solomons & G. Stein (1896), "Normal motor automation," *Psychological Review, 36*, 492-572.

6. E. Langer, A. Blank, & B. Chanowitz (1978), "The mindlessness of ostensibly thoughtful action: The role of placebic information in interpersonal interaction, *Journal of Personality and Social Psychology, 36*, 635-642.

7. Langer et al. (1978).

8. To understand the more complex relationship between automatic information processing and mindlessness, compare E. Langer (1989), "Minding matters," in L. Berkowitz (Ed.), *Advances in experimental social psychology* (pp. 137-173), New York: Academic Press; and W. Schneider & R. M. Schiffrin (1977), "Controlled and automatic human information processing: I. Detection, search, and attention," *Psychological Review, 84*, 1-66.

9. The correct answer is 8. A similar quiz was printed on the business card of the Copy Service of Miami, Inc.

Influences from the Mind's Inner Layers

Research unveils the power that the unconscious mind has on judgment and behavior.

Beth Azar

Monitor staff

Without our knowledge, a force is at work tainting our perceptions and altering our behavior: That provocateur is our unconscious, and it plays a role in our attitudes, our demeanor and even our movements.

A decade's-worth of psychological research has documented that the mind reacts automatically to environmental cues before we consciously perceive them. These automatic reactions can influence our judgments and alter our behavior. Such findings counter the social-psychology assumption that thinking and behavior are consciously controlled.

"That unconsciously motivated thoughts can impact the manner in which we judge ourselves and others is still surprising," said psychologist Mahzarin Banaji, PhD, of Yale University. "These discoveries will change our view of human nature," giving the unconscious much more credit for our behavior.

Automatic Evaluations

Nothing is safe from the scrutinizing eye of the unconscious. The unconscious mind subtly evaluates whatever it perceives and colors our perception without us knowing it, argue psychologists John Bargh, PhD, and Shelly Chaiken, PhD, of New York University.

To study this automatic evaluation, researchers use a technique called priming. By exposing subjects to a prime—a stimulus such as a word or face—they trigger thoughts, feelings or ideas associated with the prime. They then examine how the prime unconsciously influences responses to another stimulus.

For example, researchers may present subjects with pairs of words or pictures. They flash the first item at the subjects for a quarter of a second, long enough for people to perceive it but not long enough for them to consciously form an opinion.

The second item is taken from a list of items that researchers know people find either pleasing or displeasing. For example, people universally rate the word "beautiful" as positive and the word "terrible" as negative.

After viewing or hearing the second item, subjects press a button indicating whether they regard it as positive or negative or, in some experiments, they pronounce the words "good" or "bad."

If people like or dislike both objects, they respond quickly. But if they like one and dislike the other, subjects respond detectably slower.

In her dissertation, graduate student Magda Garcia worked with Bargh and Chaiken to test how people evaluate novel words or pictures, such as "glojkrot," "gumok" or "taleer." When they paired "taleer"—a made up word--with "beautiful," reaction time was quicker than when they paired "taleer" with "terrible." This implies that when subjects see taleer, they unconsciously evaluate it positively and so are more ready to respond positively when they see the second word. If the word is obviously negative, they hesitate, causing the delay, Bargh said. It also turns out that English speakers like "wehsee" and "taleer" but dislike "glojkrot" and "gumok."

Bargh and Chaiken have yet to identify a word or object that people don't automatically evaluate as good or bad. Bargh believes these automatic evaluations may play a role in do-or-die situations where we must make a decision quicker than our conscious brains can act. It's unknown, however, whether they influence subsequent conscious judgments but there's no evidence to prove that, he added.

Gender Judgments

People make gender-biased judgments too, according to research by Banaji and Anthony Greenwald, PhD, of the University of Washington. In a series of studies, they found that words trigger unconscious gender stereotypes in men and women.

Subjects read a list of 72 names, presumably to judge how easy each name was to pronounce. Half of the list contained famous names, the other half nonfamous names, and

From *APA Monitor*, February 1996, pp. 1, 25. © 1996 by the American Psychological Association. Reprinted by permission.

each group contained equal numbers of male and female names. Two days later, subjects read a second list of 144 names, which contained the 72 names from the previous list and 72 new famous and nonfamous names, again half male and half female. Subjects had to judge each name on the second list as famous or nonfamous.

Although there were equal numbers of famous males and females, subjects consistently identified more men than women as famous. They most often mistakenly tagged nonfamous male names as famous if they saw the names on the first day.

Banaji and Greenwald's analysis revealed that subjects held men to a lower standard then women, said Banaji. "We have discovered that this bias is rooted in stricter criterion being set for judging female fame," she said.

Unconscious stereotypes can also influence behavior, such as body movement and manners, according to work by Bargh and his colleagues. He and graduate student Mark Chen began with the finding from previous experiments that the stereotypical image of an elderly person conveys notions of slowness and physical weakness. They secretly primed subjects with nonphysical elements of the elderly stereotype—forgetful, Florida, bingo—through what students thought was a language-ability test.

Unbeknownst to the subjects, the researchers timed them as they walked down a hallway after what they thought was the end of the experiment. Subjects primed with words related to the elderly stereotype walked slower than control subjects who saw unrelated words.

Bargh and Chen conducted a second experiment using polite or rude primes. After performing a language test that secretly primed subjects for one or the other behavior, subjects had to locate the experimenter outside the room. When they found the researcher, he was engaged in conversation with another student—who was clandestinely working for the researcher.

The two kept talking for up to 10 minutes or until the subject interrupted.

Sixty-seven percent of subjects primed with rude words interrupted within the allotted time, while 84 percent of the patience-primed subjects waited the entire 10 minutes. Subjects claimed they were unaware that the priming task influenced their behavior.

The priming words activate the same concepts that real-life events—such as seeing another person act rude or polite—would spark, said Bargh. These findings show that our surroundings can have striking unconscious influences on our behavior.

Approach or Avoid?

Our automatic reactions to environmental cues might be linked to an evolutionary need to quickly assess whether to approach or avoid a situation, suggests Bargh. Research by him and others find that our positive or negative evaluations of situations enhance arm-muscle movements toward or away from the body respectively.

For example, in priming tasks, people hesitate to pull a lever toward them in response to a negative word, but are quick to pull it toward them in response to a positive word.

Immediate avoidance reactions—that appear unconsciously—can be viewed by others as condescending facial expressions and can seriously affect an interaction, said Bargh. Picture this: you meet someone and because of his or her gender, race or even shirt color, you have an automatic, unconscious avoidance reaction that shows up on your face. That person may notice and react in kind and you're left wondering why they're so cold. Your unconscious reaction just colored the entire interaction.

Bargh and his colleagues say that these types of experiments point to a parallel-processing model of action and reaction. The environment triggers three forms of preconscious analysis: perceptual, evaluative and motivational.

Words, people and events trigger stereotypes that color our perceptions and our behavior. We automatically and unconsciously evaluate even novel or nonsense stimuli as bad or good, and our evaluation affects whether we approach or avoid.

"A large portion of our everyday thinking and feeling and actions must be guided by factors that operate outside conscious awareness," said Banaji. Understanding how such unconscious reactions operate will help us better understand how to control them or apply them to our benefit.

In Japan, Blood Type Can Be Key to Success—Or Failure

Newspaper profiles of politicians include their blood type. Job applicants are likely to be asked theirs.

Washington Post

TOKYO—Mika Matsui finds out on the first date. First two hours, max. There's no sense getting your hopes up if Mr. Wonderful is the wrong blood type.

Her last boyfriend was type O. Never again. O's are way too needy. Type A's are too boring. B's are sweet, but they don't like her. So it's the AB man she's looking for because "he's interesting to talk to, very kind and very nice."

"I don't believe in horoscopes, but I think blood type describes character most accurately," said Matsui, 29, a clerical worker for a large Tokyo company. "Check it out yourself."

Japan has an obsession with blood types. The blood in your veins is supposed to determine how well you live and love, how well you manage money, whether you will succeed at marriage or sumo wrestling. Great marriages or lousy careers are attributed to blood type.

Newspaper and magazine profiles of major political candidates always include their blood type. Job applications often ask for blood type. During World War II, Japan's imperial army and navy are said to have formed battle groups by blood type. The manager of a Japanese major league baseball team studies his players' blood types. Japanese television this year carried a sitcom about the life of a businessman called *I Am Type O*.

The Japanese buy almost 2-million blood type condoms every year.

"This is a little farfetched, but according to the survey we conducted, it was reported that the type A tends to have a very simple attitude toward sex, so we took a clue from that," said Katsuyoshi Yatsunagi, spokesman for Jex, the company that manufactures the condoms. Thus, type A condoms are standard shape, come in pink only and are 0.03 millimeters thick. Condoms for type B are slightly narrower, thicker and ribbed. For type O, the condoms are covered with a diamond-shaped pattern. Yatsunagi said he wasn't sure how colors figured into the blood type theory.

Estelle Viskovich, a stylist at the Sin Den, a popular Tokyo beauty salon, said all new customers are asked to fill out a questionnaire that includes blood type. "We thought it was cute to ask," said Viskovich, an Australian. "We think it's weird if you don't know your star sign; the Japanese think it's weird if you don't know your blood type."

Telling a Japanese person you don't know your blood type invites suspicion, Viskovich said: "It's like you're withholding information."

A Japanese company, Pokka Corp., marketed soft drinks by blood type a couple of years ago. Company spokesman Toshihiko Tarutani said the soda was intended to be little more than a "fun" marketing gimmick, but it sold more than 1.4-million cases a year in 1993 and 1994.

There are key chains and chewing gum, calendars, magazines and books, all geared toward the blood type phenomenon. While schoolgirls are the chief consumers of most products categorized by blood type, some of Japan's biggest corporations have looked into increasing their productivity by creating single-type work groups. One of the most influential companies in the country,

From *St. Petersburg Times*, January 3, 1996, pp. 1A, 14A. Originally from *The Washington Post*. © 1996 by The Washington Post. Reprinted by permission.

What Type Are You?

Selected supposed traits of the blood type:

TYPE A

Positive traits: Orderly, law-abiding, fastidious, soft-spoken, fashionable, calm.
Negative traits: Picky, selfish, secretive, pessimistic, inflexible, reckless when drunk.
Suitable careers: Accountant, librarian, economist, novelist, computer programer, gossip columnist.

TYPE B

Positive: Independent, flexible, candid, sensitive, passionate, persuasive.
Negative: Unpredictable, indiscreet, lazy, impatient, overbearing, can't wake up.
Suitable careers: Cook, hairdresser, military leader, talk show host, journalist, golfer.

TYPE AB

Positive: Rational, calculating, honest, diplomatic, organized, strong ESP.
Negative: Unforgiving, playboy, easily offended, too conservative, nitpicker, hard to know.
Suitable careers: Bartender, attorney, teacher, sales representative, social worker, witch.

TYPE O

Positive: Healthy, idealistic, goal-oriented, clear-sighted, good at sports, sexy.
Negative: Status-seeking, jealous, greedy, unreliable, obsessive lover, can't shut up.
Suitable careers: Banker, politician, gambler, minister, investment broker, baseball player.

—Source: "You Are Your Blood Type," by Toshitaka Nomi and Alexander Besher.

Mitsubishi Electric Corp., created a project development team of five ABs who were supposed to be creative and enterprising. The team was called the "Fantastic Project" and was eventually disbanded without producing much more than publicity.

Toshitaka Nomi, whose 30 books on blood types have sold more than 6-million copies in Japan, has been asked to give more than 1,000 speeches at some of Japan's biggest corporations, including Hitachi, Toyota, Nissan and several major banks. Nomi gave many of the speeches at training seminars where his theories were being studied as a potential management tool.

A person's blood type is determined by what kind of antigen, a type of protein, he has on the surface of his red blood cells. If a person has an A antigen, his blood is type A; if he has a B antigen, he's type B. People with both are type AB, and those with neither are type O. The most common type is O, followed by A, B and AB.

There is not one molecule of solid scientific evidence that blood type is related to character. Scientists say blood type is about as relevant to personality as hair color is to snorkeling ability. Of course, that's what they say about horoscopes, too—but it didn't stop Nancy Reagan from planning the president's schedule around his stars. And it hasn't stopped the Japanese from believing in blood types.

"All culture is not based upon Western science," said Marc Micozzi, a physician and director of the National Museum of Health and Medicine at Walter Reed Army Medical Center in Washington.

John Stone, a cardiologist at the Emory University School of Medicine who also writes poetry, said he "would not go to the mat" for the Japanese blood type theories. But the artist in him likes it: "It's a straw; we're all clutching at straws to try to explain ourselves."

According to Nomi's book *You Are Your Blood Type*, type O's are powerful leaders, goal-oriented, enthusiastic, optimistic and good at business. Famous O's include Ronald Reagan, Queen Elizabeth, Prince Charles and Al Capone.

Type A's, according to Nomi, are perfectionist, orderly, detail-oriented, industrious, idealistic, soft-spoken and careful. Former presidents Jimmy Carter, Lyndon Johnson and Richard Nixon shared A blood, if not much else. Despite much that separates them, Adolf Hitler was and Pope John Paul II is type A. And some of the most famous blood in recent history was type A: that of O. J. Simpson and his late ex-wife, Nicole Brown Simpson.

Nomi says type B's are flexible, passionate, creative, unconventional and have excellent concentration, like golfer Jack Nicklaus. Type ABs are supposed to be natural leaders, great organizers, diplomatic, rational and imaginative. John Kennedy and Marilyn Monroe shared AB blood.

"For the moment, we don't know why this is happening," Nomi said. "But we have so much evidence that links blood type to character, the next step is for the scientists to find out what causes this."

Japanese psychologists and social scientists have been proposing and exploring blood type theories since the 1920s. The Japanese public has always been receptive, but it wasn't until Nomi's father came along that blood types became a national obsession.

In 1971, Masahiko Nomi published a book on the subject based on 25 years of personal observations about blood type and character. When the book sold 1.2-million copies, the Nomi family got into the blood type business for good.

They started sending out questionnaires, asking blood type and a series of questions designed to reveal personality traits. Since 1971 they have sent seven major questionnaires and elicited responses from nearly 250,000 people; those responses are the bricks and mortar of Toshitaka Nomi's writings. About 15 years ago, he said, he sent a questionnaire to every member of Japan's Parliament and received responses from 98 percent of them. (The members were disproportionately type O, the classic leadership type.)

"I would say more than half the Japanese people are very interested in blood types," Nomi said, "see some truth in it and are prepared to use it in their daily life."

Social Influence

After World War II, members of the Nazi high command were put on trial for war crimes, in particular their genocidal slaughter of millions of "undesirables": Jews, Gypsies, and homosexuals, among others. One argument that they offered in their defense was that they were "only following orders"—that is, as soldiers during wartime they had no choice but to obey the orders of their superior officers. As a result, so the argument went, they did not bear the ultimate responsibility for their actions. This argument was not especially effective, however, and many of the defendants were convicted and, in some cases, executed for their crimes. In essence, then, the war crimes judges rejected the notion that people can give up their individual moral responsibility when they are given immoral orders.

A decade later, in one of the most famous social psychological investigations ever, Stanley Milgram reexamined this issue, and his results were highly disturbing. Milgram found that normal everyday Americans—not Nazi monsters—would follow the orders of an experimenter to administer what they thought were extremely intense electric shocks to an innocent victim as part of a research project. In some cases, a substantial percentage of the participants would administer what they thought were 450-volt shocks to a man with a heart condition who was screaming hysterically to be released from the experiment.

Although many of the participants were in a state of extreme anxiety and discomfort over their terrible behavior, they nevertheless continued to obey the experimenter. As had the Nazis during World War II, these American citizens seemed to give up their moral responsibility when they decided to follow the orders of the experimenter.

This research is just one example, although a highly dramatic one, of the phenomenon that social psychologists call social influence—the ability of a person or group to change the behavior of others. Traditionally, a distinction has been drawn among three different types of social influence: conformity, compliance, and obedience. *Conformity* refers to those times when individuals will change their attitudes or behaviors because of perceived group pressure—that is, they feel pressure to conform to the attitude or behavior of some group that is at least somewhat important to them. If, for instance, everyone in your group of friends adopts a particular style of clothing, or adopts a particular attitude toward another group, you may feel some pressure to conform your behavior to theirs, even if no one in the group ever asks you to. *Compliance*, on the other hand, refers to those times when individuals change their behavior in response to a direct request from others. We are often faced with direct requests intended to change our behavior, whether they come from family, friends, teachers, bosses, or door-to-door salesmen. Considerable research has been conducted to determine what kinds of strategies by "requesters" are the most effective in prompting actual compliance. Finally, *obedience* refers to those times when individuals change their behavior in response to a direct order from another person; thus, unlike compliance, in which you are asked to make a behavioral change, in obedience you are commanded to do so. The research by Milgram is a good example of an obedience situation.

The four selections in this unit illustrate, sometimes dramatically, the powerful ways in which social influence can operate. In "Making Sense of the Nonsensical: An Analysis of Jonestown," Neal Osherow analyzes one of the most horrific and bewildering events of the past quarter-century: the 1978 mass suicide of over 900 followers of the cult leader Jim Jones. What could lead so many people to end their lives in order to follow the wishes of this man? Osherow argues that a variety of social psychological processes, including some that were also considered in other units, probably operated to produce this bizarre event.

In "The Committed Heart," Anthony Pratkanis and Elliot Aronson discuss one of the most effective compliance strategies, the "foot in the door" technique. In this method, people are induced to commit themselves to some small action that most people would agree to do (the foot in the door); they then are asked to perform some more costly act, which was the real goal all along. As the authors demonstrate, salespeople have been aware of the usefulness of this approach for a long time. In the next selection, "What Is the Influence of One Flower Given?" the same authors describe another compliance-inducing strategy: the use of the reciprocity norm. By doing something for you initially (such as giving you a flower), other people can invoke the powerful reciprocity norm, which holds that we should return favors that are done for us. As a result, we become more likely to comply with a subsequent request from the one who has done us the favor.

In the final selection, "Suspect Confessions," Richard Jerome profiles a social psychologist who specializes in investigating a particular kind of compliance situation—the police interrogation. The work of social psychologist Richard Ofshe suggests that some of the techniques used by police during questioning can be so powerful that suspects will sometimes comply (confess) even when they are innocent of the crimes! This article provides a fascinating glimpse into just how powerful some compliance-inducing tactics can be.

Looking Ahead: Challenge Questions

Which social psychological principles of social influence can you identify in the typical operation of cults? For example, what evidence is there for *conformity* pressures? How are such pressures created? Which strategies for inducing *compliance* are commonly used in cult groups? Are there any other societal groups (ones we would not label as cults) that use the same kind of techniques?

How would a salesperson use the "foot in the door" technique to increase compliance? Which other compliance techniques used by salespeople can you identify? Why don't customers see through these techniques more frequently and refuse to fall for them? What steps could customers take to protect themselves from such techniques?

Are the techniques described in "Suspect Confessions" fair tactics for the police to use? Why? More generally, what sort of restrictions, if any, should be placed on the use of social influence techniques in our society?

Making Sense of the Nonsensical: An Analysis of Jonestown

Neal Osherow

University of California, Santa Cruz

> Those who do not remember the past are condemned to repeat it.
> —quotation on placard over Jim Jones's rostrum at Jonestown

Close to one thousand people died at Jonestown. The members of the Peoples Temple settlement in Guyana, under the direction of the Reverend Jim Jones, fed a poison-laced drink to their children, administered the potion to their infants, and drank it themselves. Their bodies were found lying together, arm in arm; over 900 perished.

How could such a tragedy occur? The image of an entire community destroying itself, of parents killing their own children, appears incredible. The media stories about the event and full-color pictures of the scene documented some of its horror but did little to illuminate the causes or to explain the processes that led to the deaths. Even a year afterwards, a CBS Evening News broadcast asserted that "it was widely assumed that time would offer some

explanation for the ritualistic suicide/murder of over 900 people. . . . One year later, it does not appear that any lessons have been uncovered" (CBS News, 1979).

The story of the Peoples Temple is not enshrouded in mystery, however. Jim Jones had founded his church over twenty years before, in Indiana. His preaching stressed the need for racial brotherhood and integration, and his group helped feed the poor and find them jobs. As his congregation grew, Jim Jones gradually increased the discipline and dedication that he required from the members. In 1965, he moved to northern California; about 100 of his faithful relocated with him. The membership began to multiply, new congregations were formed, and the headquarters was established in San Francisco.

Behind his public image as a beloved leader espousing interracial harmony, "Father," as Jones was called, assumed a messiah-like presence in the Peoples Temple. Increasingly, he became the personal object of the members' devotion, and he used their numbers and obedience to gain political influence and power. Within the Temple, Jones demanded absolute loyalty, enforced a taxing regimen, and delivered sermons forecasting nuclear holocaust and an apocalyptic destruction of the world, promising his followers that they alone would

emerge as survivors. Many of his harangues attacked racism and capitalism, but his most vehement anger focused on the "enemies" of the Peoples Temple—its detractors and especially its defectors. In mid-1977, publication of unfavorable magazine articles, coupled with the impending custody battle over a six-year-old Jones claimed as a "son," prompted emigration of the bulk of Temple membership to a jungle outpost in Guyana.

In November, 1978, Congressman Leo Ryan responded to charges that the Peoples Temple was holding people against their will at Jonestown. He organized a trip to the South American settlement; a small party of journalists and "Concerned Relatives" of Peoples Temple members accompanied him on his investigation. They were in Jonestown for one evening and part of the following day. They heard most residents praise the settlement, expressing their joy at being there and indicating their desire to stay. Two families, however, slipped messages to Ryan that they wanted to leave with him. After the visit, as Ryan's party and these defectors tried to board planes to depart, the group was ambushed and fired upon by Temple gunmen— five people, including Ryan, were murdered.

As the shootings were taking place at the jungle airstrip, Jim Jones

I am very grateful to Elliot Aronson for his assistance with this essay. His insights, suggestions, and criticism were most valuable to its development. Also, my thanks to Elise Bean for her helpful editing.

From *Readings About the Social Animal*, 4/e, edited by Elliot Aronson, chapter 2, pp. 68-86. © 1993 by Scientific American Books. Reprinted by permission of W. H. Freeman and Company.

gathered the community at Jonestown. He informed them that the Congressman's party would be killed and then initiated the final ritual: the "revolutionary suicide" that the membership had rehearsed on prior occasions. The poison was brought out. It was taken.

Jonestown's remoteness caused reports of the event to reach the public in stages. First came bulletins announcing the assassination of Congressman Ryan along with several members of his party. Then came rumors of mass-deaths at Jonestown, then confirmations. The initial estimates put the number of dead near 400, bringing the hope that substantial numbers of people had escaped into the jungle. But as the bodies were counted, many smaller victims were discovered under the corpses of larger ones—virtually none of the inhabitants of Jonestown survived. The public was shocked, then horrified, then incredulous.

Amid the early stories about the tragedy, along with the lurid descriptions and sensational photographs, came some attempts at analysis. Most discussed the charisma of Jim Jones and the power of "cults." Jones was described as "a character Joseph Conrad might have dreamt up (Krause, 1978), a "self-appointed messiah" whose "lust for dominion" led hundreds of "fanatic" followers to their demise (Special Report: The Cult of Death, *Newsweek*, 1978a).

While a description in terms of the personality of the perpetrator and the vulnerability of the victims provides some explanation, it relegates the event to the category of being an aberration, a product of unique forces and dispositions. Assuming such a perspective distances us from the phenomenon. This might be comforting, but I believe that it limits our understanding and is potentially dangerous. My aim in this analysis is not to blunt the emotional impact of a tragedy of this magnitude by subjecting it to academic examination. At the same time, applying social psychological theory and research makes it more conceivable and comprehensible, thus bringing it closer (in kind rather than in degree) to processes each of us en-

counters. Social psychological concepts can facilitate our understanding: The killings themselves, and many of the occurrences leading up to them, can be viewed in terms of obedience and compliance. The processes that induced people to join and to believe in the Peoples Temple made use of strategies involved in propaganda and persuasion. In grappling with the most perplexing questions—Why didn't more people leave the Temple? How could they actually kill their children and themselves?—the psychology of self-justification provides some insight.

Conformity

The character of a church . . . can be seen in its attitude toward its detractors.
—Hugh Prather, Notes to Myself

At one level, the deaths at Jonestown can be viewed as the product of obedience, of people complying with the orders of a leader and reacting to the threat of force. In the Peoples Temple, whatever Jim Jones commanded, the members did. When he gathered the community at the pavilion and the poison was brought out, the populace was surrounded by armed guards who were trusted lieutenants of Jones. There are reports that some people did not drink voluntarily but had the poison forced down their throats or injected (Winfrey, 1979). While there were isolated acts of resistance and suggestions of opposition to the suicides, excerpts from a tape, recorded as the final ritual was being enacted, reveal that such dissent was quickly dismissed or shouted down:

JONES: I've tried my best to give you a good life. In spite of all I've tried, a handful of people, with their lies, have made our life impossible. If we can't live in peace then let's die in peace. (Applause) . . . We have been so terribly betrayed.
What's going to happen here in the matter of a few minutes is that one of the people on that plane is going to shoot the pilot—I know

that. I didn't plan it, but I know it's going to happen. . . . So my opinion is that you be kind to children, and be kind to seniors, and take the potion like they used to in ancient Greece, and step over quietly, because we are not committing suicide—it's a revolutionary act. . . . We can't go back. They're now going back to tell more lies. . . .
FIRST WOMAN: I feel like that as long as there's life, there's hope.
JONES: Well, someday everybody dies.
CROWD: That's right, that's right!
JONES: What those people gone and done, and what they get through will make our lives worse than hell. . . . But to me, death is not a fearful thing. It's living that's cursed. . . . Not worth living like this.
FIRST WOMAN: But I'm afraid to die.
JONES: I don't think you are. I don't think you are.
FIRST WOMAN: I think there were too few who left for 1,200 people to give them their lives for those people who left. . . . I look at all the babies and I think they deserve to live.
JONES: But don't they deserve much more—they deserve peace. The best testimony we can give is to leave this goddam world. (Applause)
FIRST MAN: It's over, sister. . . . We've made a beautiful day. (Applause)
SECOND MAN: If you tell us we have to give our lives now, we're ready. (Applause) [*Baltimore Sun*, 1979.]

Above the cries of babies wailing, the tape continues, with Jones insisting upon the need for suicide and urging the people to complete the act:

JONES: Please get some medication. Simple. It's simple. There's no convulsions with it. . . . Don't be afraid to die. You'll see people land out here. They'll torture our people.
SECOND WOMAN: There's nothing to worry about. Everybody keep calm and try to keep your children calm. . . . They're not crying from pain; it's just a little bitter tasting . . .
THIRD WOMAN: This is nothing to cry about. This is something we could all rejoice about. (Applause)

JONES: Please, for God's sake, let's get on with it. . . . This is a revolutionary suicide. This is not a self-destructive suicide. (Voices praise "Dad." Applause)
THIRD MAN: Dad has brought us this far. My vote is to go with Dad. . . .
JONES: We must die with dignity. Hurry, hurry, hurry. We must hurry. . . . Stop this hysterics. Death is a million times more preferable to spending more days in this life. . . . If you knew what was ahead, you'd be glad to be stepping over tonight . . .
FOURTH WOMAN: It's been a pleasure walking with all of you in this revolutionary struggle. . . . No other way I would rather go than to give my life for socialism. Communism, and I thank Dad very much.
JONES: Take our life from us. . . . We didn't commit suicide. We committed an act of revolutionary suicide protesting against the conditions of an inhuman world [*Newsweek*, 1978b, 1979].

If you hold a gun at someone's head, you can get that person to do just about anything. As many accounts have attested,[1] by the early 1970s the members of the Peoples Temple lived in constant fear of severe punishment—brutal beatings coupled with public humiliation—for committing trivial or even inadvertent offenses. But the power of an authority need not be so explicitly threatening in order to induce compliance with its demands, as demonstrated by social psychological research. In Milgram's experiments (1963), a surprisingly high proportion of subjects obeyed the instructions of an experimenter to administer what they thought were very strong electric shocks to an-

---

[1]The reports of ex-Peoples Temple members who defected create a very consistent picture of the tactics Jim Jones employed in his church. Jeanne Mills (1979) provides the most comprehensive personal account, and there are affidavits about the Peoples Temple sworn to by Deborah Blakey (May 12, 1978 and June 15, 1978) and Yolanda Crawford (April 10, 1978). Media stories about the Peoples Temple, which usually rely on interviews with defectors, and about Jonestown, which are based on interviews with survivors, also corroborate one another. (See especially Kilduff and Tracy (1977), *Newsweek* (1978a), Lifton (1979), and Cahill (1979).

other person. Nor does the consensus of a group need be so blatantly coercive to induce agreement with its opinion, as Asch's experiments (1955) on conformity to the incorrect judgments of a majority indicate.

Jim Jones utilized the threat of severe punishment to impose the strict discipline and absolute devotion that he demanded, and he also took measures to eliminate those factors that might encourage resistance or rebellion among his followers. Research showed that the presence of a "disobedient" partner greatly reduced the extent to which most subjects in the Milgram situation (1965) obeyed the instructions to shock the person designated the "learner." Similarly, by including just one confederate who expressed an opinion different from the majority's, Asch (1955) showed that the subject would also agree far less, even when the "other dissenter's" judgment was also incorrect and differed from the subject's. In the Peoples Temple, Jones tolerated no dissent, made sure that members had no allegiance more powerful than to himself, and tried to make the alternative of leaving the Temple an unthinkable option.

Jeanne Mills, who spent six years as a high-ranking member before becoming one of the few who left the Peoples Temple, writes: "There was an unwritten but perfectly understood law in the church that was very important: 'No one is to criticize Father, his wife, or his children' " (Mills, 1979). Deborah Blakey, another long-time member who managed to defect, testified:

Any disagreement with [Jim Jones's] dictates came to be regarded as "treason." . . . Although I felt terrible about what was happening, I was afraid to say anything because I knew that anyone with a differing opinion gained the wrath of Jones and other members. [Blakey, June 15, 1978.]

Conditions in the Peoples Temple became so oppressive, the discrepancy between Jim Jones's stated aims and his practices so pronounced,

that it is almost inconceivable that members failed to entertain questions about the church. But these doubts went unreinforced. There were no allies to support one's disobedience of the leader's commands and no fellow dissenters to encourage the expression of disagreement with the majority. Public disobedience or dissent was quickly punished. Questioning Jones's word, even in the company of family or friends, was dangerous—informers and "counselors" were quick to report indiscretions, even by relatives.

The use of informers went further than to stifle dissent; it also diminished the solidarity and loyalty that individuals felt toward their families and friends. While Jones preached that a spirit of brotherhood should pervade his church, he made it clear that each member's personal dedication should be directed to "Father." Families were split: First, children were seated away from parents during services; then, many were assigned to another member's care as they grew up; and ultimately, parents were forced to sign documents surrendering custody rights. "Families are part of the enemy system," Jones stated, because they hurt one's total dedication to the "Cause" (Mills, 1979). Thus, a person called before the membership to be punished could expect his or her family to be among the first and most forceful critics (Cahill, 1979).

Besides splitting parent and child, Jones sought to loosen the bonds between wife and husband. He forced spouses into extramarital sexual relations, which were often of a homosexual or humiliating nature, or with Jones himself. Sexual partnerships and activities not under his direction and control were discouraged and publicly ridiculed.

Thus, expressing any doubts or criticism of Jones—even to a friend, child, or partner—became risky for the individual. As a consequence, such thoughts were kept to oneself, and with the resulting impression that nobody else shared them. In addition to limiting one's access to in-

formation, this "fallacy of uniqueness" precluded the sharing of support. It is interesting that among the few who successfully defected from the Peoples Temple were couples such as Jeanne and Al Mills, who kept together, shared their doubts, and gave each other support.

Why didn't more people leave? Once inside the Peoples Temple, getting out was discouraged; defectors were hated. Nothing upset Jim Jones so much; people who left became the targets of his most vitriolic attacks and were blamed for any problems that occurred. One member recalled that after several teen-age members left the Temple, "We hated those eight with such a passion because we knew any day they were going to try bombing us. I mean Jim Jones had us totally convinced of this" (Winfrey, 1979).

Defectors were threatened: Immediately after she left, Grace Stoen headed for the beach at Lake Tahoe, where she found herself looking over her shoulder, checking to make sure that she hadn't been tracked down (Kilduff and Tracy, 1977). Jeanne Mills reports that she and her family were followed by men in cars, their home was burglarized, and they were threatened with the use of confessions they had signed while still members. When a friend from the Temple paid a visit, she quickly examined Mills' ears—Jim Jones had vowed to have one of them cut off (Mills, 1979). He had made ominous predictions concerning other defectors as well: Indeed, several ex-members suffered puzzling deaths or committed very questionable "suicides" shortly after leaving the Peoples Temple (Reiterman, 1977; Tracy, 1978).

Defecting became quite a risky enterprise, and, for most members, the potential benefits were very uncertain. They had little to hope for outside of the Peoples Temple; what they had, they had committed to the church. Jim Jones had vilified previous defectors as "the enemy" and had instilled the fear that, once outside of the Peoples Temple, members'

stories would not be believed by the "racist, fascist" society, and they would be subjected to torture, concentration camps, and execution. Finally, in Guyana, Jonestown was surrounded by dense jungle, the few trails patrolled by armed security guards (Cahill, 1979). Escape was not a viable option. Resistance was too costly. With no other alternatives apparent, compliance became the most reasonable course of action.

The power that Jim Jones wielded kept the membership of the Peoples Temple in line, and the difficulty of defecting helped to keep them in. But what attracted them to join Jones's church in the first place?

Persuasion

Nothing is so unbelievable that oratory cannot make it acceptable.
—Cicero

Jim Jones was a charismatic figure, adept at oratory. He sought people for his church who would be receptive to his messages and vulnerable to his promises, and he carefully honed his presentation to appeal to each specific audience.

The bulk of the Peoples Temple membership was comprised of society's needy and neglected: the urban poor, the black, the elderly, and a sprinkling of ex-addicts and ex-convicts (Winfrey, 1979). To attract new members, Jones held public services in various cities. Leaflets would be distributed:

PASTOR JIM JONES . . . Incredible! . . . Miraculous! . . . Amazing! . . . The Most Unique Prophetic Healing Service You've Ever Witnessed! Behold the Word Made Incarnate In Your Midst!
God works as tumorous masses are passed in every service. . . . Before your eyes, the crippled walk, the blind see! [Kilduff and Javers, 1978.]

Potential members first confronted an almost idyllic scene of blacks and whites living, working, and worshipping together. Guests were

greeted and treated most warmly and were invited to share in the group's meal. As advertised, Jim Jones also gave them miracles. A number of members would recount how Jones had cured them of cancer or other dread diseases; during the service Jones or one of his nurses would reach into the member's throat and emerge with a vile mass of tissue—the "cancer" that had been passed as the person gagged. Sometimes Jim Jones would make predictions that would occur with uncanny frequency. He also received revelations about members or visitors that nobody but those individuals could know—what they had eaten for dinner the night before, for instance, or news about a far-off relative. Occasionally, he performed miracles similar to more well-established religious figures:

There were more people than usual at the Sunday service, and for some reason the church members hadn't brought enough food to feed everyone. It became apparent that the last fifty people in line weren't going to get any meat. Jim announced, "Even though there isn't enough food to feed this multitude, I am blessing the food that we have and multiplying it—just as Jesus did in biblical times."
Sure enough, a few minutes after he made this startling announcement, Eva Pugh came out of the kitchen beaming, carrying two platters filled with fried chicken. A big cheer came from the people assembled in the room, especially from the people who were at the end of the line.
The "blessed chicken" was extraordinarily delicious, and several of the people mentioned that Jim had produced the best-tasting chicken they had ever eaten. [Mills, 1979.]

These demonstrations were dramatic and impressive; most members were convinced of their authenticity and believed in Jones's "powers." They didn't know that the "cancers" were actually rancid chicken gizzards, that the occurrences Jones "forecast" were staged, or that sending people to sift through a person's

garbage could reveal packages of certain foods or letters of out-of-town relatives to serve as grist for Jones' "revelations" (Kilduff and Tracy, 1977; Mills, 1979). Members were motivated to believe in Jones; they appreciated the racial harmony, sense of purpose, and relief from feelings of worthlessness that the Peoples Temple provided them (Winfrey, 1979; Lifton, 1979). Even when suspecting that something was wrong, they learned that it was unwise to voice their doubts:

> One of the men, Chuck Beikman . . . jokingly mentioned to a few people standing near him that he had seen Eva drive up a few moments earlier with buckets from the Kentucky Fried Chicken stand. He smiled as he said, "The person that blessed this chicken was Colonel Sanders."
>
> During the evening meeting Jim mentioned the fact that Chuck had made fun of his gift. "He lied to some of the members here, telling them that the chicken had come from a local shop," Jim stormed. "But the Spirit of Justice has prevailed. Because of his lie Chuck is in the men's room right now, wishing that he was dead. He is vomiting and has diarrhea so bad he can't talk!"
>
> An hour later a pale and shaken Chuck Beikman walked out of the men's room and up to the front, being supported by one of the guards. Jim asked him, "Do you have anything you'd like to say?"
>
> Chuck looked up weakly and answered, "Jim, I apologize for what I said. Please forgive me."
>
> As we looked at Chuck, we vowed in our hearts that we would never question any of Jim's "miracles"—at least not out loud. Years later, we learned that Jim had put a mild poison in a piece of cake and given it to Chuck. [Mills, 1979.]

While most members responded to presentations that were emotional, one-sided, and almost sensational in tone, those who eventually assumed positions of responsibility in the upper echelons of the Peoples Temples were attracted by different considerations. Most of these people were white and came from upper-middle-class backgrounds—they in-

cluded lawyers, a medical student, nurses, and people representing other occupations that demanded education and reflected a strong social consciousness. Jones lured these members by stressing the social and political aspects of the church, its potential as an idealistic experiment with integration and socialism. Tim Stoen, who was the Temple's lawyer, stated later, "I wanted utopia so damn bad I could die" (Winfrey, 1979). These members had the information and intelligence to see through many of Jones's ploys, but, as Jeanne Mills explains repeatedly in her book, they dismissed their qualms and dismissed Jones's deception as being necessary to achieve a more important aim—furthering the Cause: "For the thousandth time, I rationalized my doubts. 'If Jim feels it's necessary for the Cause, who am I to question his wisdom?' " (Mills, 1979).

It turned out to be remarkably easy to overcome their hesitancy and calm their doubts. Mills recalls that she and her husband initially were skeptical about Jones and the Peoples Temple. After attending their first meeting, they remained unimpressed by the many members who proclaimed that Jones had healed their cancers or cured their drug habits. They were annoyed by Jones' arrogance, and they were bored by most of the long service. But in the weeks following their visit, they received numerous letters containing testimonials and gifts from the Peoples Temple, they had dreams about Jones, and they were attracted by the friendship and love they had felt from both the black and the white members. When they went back for their second visit, they took their children with them. After the long drive, the Mills's were greeted warmly by many members and by Jones himself. "This time . . . my mind was open to hear his message because my own beliefs had become very shaky" (Mills, 1979). As they were driving home afterwards, the children begged their parents to join the church:

> We had to admit that we enjoyed the service more this time and we told the children that we'd think it over. Somehow, though, we knew that it was only a matter of time before we were going to become members of the Peoples Temple. [Mills, 1979.]

Jim Jones skillfully manipulated the impression that his church would convey to newcomers. He carefully managed its public image. He used the letter-writing and political clout of hundreds of members to praise and impress the politicians and press that supported the Peoples Temple, as well as to criticize and intimidate its opponents (Kasindorf, 1978). Most importantly, Jones severely restricted the information that was available to the members. In addition to indoctrinating members into his own belief system through extensive sermons and lectures, he inculcated a distrust of any contradictory messages, labelling them the product of enemies. By destroying the credibility of their sources, he inoculated the membership against being persuaded by outside criticism. Similarly, any contradictory thoughts that might arise within each member were to be discredited. Instead of seeing them as having any basis in reality, members interpreted them as indications of their own shortcomings or lack of faith. Members learned to attribute the apparent discrepancies between Jones's lofty pronouncements and the rigors of life in the Peoples Temple to their personal inadequacies rather than blaming them on any fault of Jones. As ex-member Neva Sly was quoted: "We always blamed ourselves for things that didn't seem right" (Winfrey, 1979). A unique and distorting language developed within the church, in which "the Cause" became anything that Jim Jones said (Mills, 1979). It was spoken at Jonestown, where a guard tower was called the "playground" (Cahill, 1979). Ultimately, through the clever use of oratory, deception, and language, Jones could speak of death as "stepping over," thereby camouflaging a hopeless act of self-

destruction as a noble and brave act of "revolutionary suicide," and the members accepted his words.

Self-Justification

Both salvation and punishment for man lie in the fact that if he lives wrongly he can befog himself so as not to see the misery of his position.
—Tolstoy, "The Kreutzer Sonata"

Analyzing Jonestown in terms of obedience and the power of the situation can help to explain why the people *acted* as they did. Once the Peoples Temple had moved to Jonestown, there was little the members could do other than follow Jim Jones's dictates. They were comforted by an authority of absolute power. They were left with few options, being surrounded by armed guards and by the jungle, having given their passports and various documents and confessions to Jones, and believing that conditions in the outside world were even more threatening. The members' poor diet, heavy workload, lack of sleep, and constant exposure to Jones's diatribes exacerbated the coerciveness of their predicament; tremendous pressures encouraged them to obey.

By the time of the final ritual, opposition or escape had become almost impossible for most of the members. Yet even then, it is doubtful that many *wanted* to resist or to leave. Most had come to believe in Jones—one woman's body was found with a message scribbled on her arm during the final hours: "Jim Jones is the only one" (Cahill, 1979). They seemed to have accepted the necessity, and even the beauty, of dying—just before the ritual began, a guard approached Charles Garry, one of the Temple's hired attorneys, and exclaimed, "It's a great moment . . . we all die" (Lifton, 1979). A survivor of Jonestown, who happened to be away at the dentist, was interviewed a year following the deaths:

If I had been there, I would have been the first one to stand in that line and take that poison and I would have been proud to take it. The thing I'm sad about is this; that I missed the ending. [Gallagher, 1979.]

It is this aspect of Jonestown that is perhaps the most troubling. To the end, and even beyond, the vast majority of the Peoples Temple members *believed* in Jim Jones. External forces, in the form of power or persuasion, can exact compliance. But one must examine a different set of processes to account for the members' internalizing those beliefs.

Although Jones's statements were often inconsistent and his methods cruel, most members maintained their faith in his leadership. Once they were isolated at Jonestown, there was little opportunity or motivation to think otherwise—resistance or escape was out of the question. In such a situation, the individual is motivated to rationalize his or her predicament; a person confronted with the inevitable tends to regard it more positively. For example, social psychological research has shown that when children believe that they will be served more of a vegetable they dislike, they will convince themselves that it is not so noxious (Brehm, 1959), and when a person thinks that she will be interacting with someone, she tends to judge a description of that individual more favorably (Darley and Berscheid, 1967).

A member's involvement in the Temple did not begin at Jonestown—it started much earlier, closer to home, and less dramatically. At first, the potential member would attend meetings voluntarily and might put in a few hours each week working for the church. Though the established members would urge the recruit to join, he or she felt free to choose whether to stay or to leave. Upon deciding to join, a member expended more effort and became more committed to the Peoples Temple. In small increments, Jones increased the demands made on the member, and only after a long se-

quence did he escalate the oppressiveness of his rule and the desperation of his message. Little by little, the individual's alternatives became more limited. Step by step, the person was motivated to rationalize his or her commitment and to justify his or her behavior.

Jeanne Mills, who managed to defect two years before the Temple relocated in Guyana, begins her account, *Six Years With God* (1979), by writing: "Every time I tell someone about the six years we spent as members of the Peoples Temple, I am faced with an unanswerable question: 'If the church was so bad, why did you and your family stay in for so long?" Several classic studies from social psychological research investigating processes of self-justification and the theory of cognitive dissonance (see Aronson, 1980, chapter 4; Aronson, 1969) can point to explanations for such seemingly irrational behavior.

According to dissonance theory, when a person commits an act or holds a cognition that is psychologically inconsistent with his or her self-concept, the inconsistency arouses an unpleasant state of tension. The individual tries to reduce this "dissonance," usually by altering his or her attitudes to bring them more into line with the previously discrepant action or belief. A number of occurrences in the Peoples Temple can be illuminated by viewing them in light of this process. The horrifying events of Jonestown were not due merely to the threat of force, nor did they erupt instantaneously. That is, it was *not* the case that something "snapped" in people's minds, suddenly causing them to behave in bizarre ways. Rather, as the theory of cognitive dissonance spells out, people seek to *justify* their choices and commitments.

Just as a towering waterfall can begin as a trickle, so too can the impetus for doing extreme or calamitous actions be provided by the consequences of agreeing to do seemingly trivial ones. In the Peoples Temple, the process started with the effects of undergoing a severe initiation to join the church, was reinforced by the ten-

dency to justify one's commitments, and was strengthened by the need to rationalize one's behavior.

Consider the prospective member's initial visit to the People's Temple, for example. When a person undergoes a severe initiation in order to gain entrance into a group, he or she is apt to judge that group as being more attractive, in order to justify expending the effort or enduring the pain. Aronson and Mills (1959) demonstrated that students who suffered greater embarrassment as a prerequisite for being allowed to participate in a discussion group rated its conversation (which actually was quite boring) to be significantly more interesting than did those students who experienced little or no embarrassment in order to be admitted. Not only is there a tendency to justify undergoing the experience by raising one's estimation of the goal—in some circumstances, choosing to experience a hardship can go so far as to affect a person's perception of the discomfort or pain he or she felt. Zimbardo (1969) and his colleagues showed that when subjects volunteered for a procedure that involves their being given electric shocks, those thinking that they had more choice in the matter reported feeling less pain from the shocks. More specifically, those who experienced greater dissonance, having little external justification to account for their choosing to endure the pain, described it as being less intense. This extended beyond their impressions and verbal reports; their performance on a task was hindered less, and they even recorded somewhat lower readings on a physiological instrument measuring galvanic skin responses. Thus the dissonance-reducing process can be double-edged: Under proper guidance, a person who voluntarily experiences a severe initiation not only comes to regard its ends more positively, but may also begin to see the means as less aversive: "We begin to appreciate the long meetings, because we were told that spiritual growth comes from self-sacrifice" (Mills, 1979).

Once involved, a member found ever-increasing portions of his or her time and energy devoted to the Peoples Temple. The services and meetings occupied weekends and several evenings each week. Working on Temple projects and writing the required letters to politicians and the press took much of one's "spare" time. Expected monetary contributions changed from "voluntary" donations (though they were recorded) to the required contribution of a quarter of one's income. Eventually, a member was supposed to sign over all personal property, savings, social security checks, and the like to the Peoples Temple. Before entering the meeting room for each service, a member stopped at a table and wrote self-incriminating letters or signed blank documents that were turned over to the church. If anyone objected, the refusal was interpreted as denoting a "lack of faith" in Jones. Finally, members were asked to live at Temple facilities to save money and to be able to work more efficiently, and many of their children were raised under the care of other families. Acceding to each new demand had two repercussions: In practical terms, it enmeshed the person further into the Peoples Temple web and made leaving more difficult; on an attitudinal level, it set the aforementioned processes of self-justification into motion. As Mills (1979) describes:

> We had to face painful reality. Our life savings were gone. Jim had demanded that we sell the life insurance policy and turn the equity over to the church, so that was gone. Our property had all been taken from us. Our dream of going to an overseas mission was gone. We thought that we had alienated our parents when we told them we were leaving the country. Even the children whom we had left in the care of Carol and Bill were openly hostile toward us. Jim had accomplished all this in such a short time! All we had left now was Jim and the Cause, so we decided to buckle under and give our energies to these two.

Ultimately, Jim Jones and the Cause would require the members to give their lives.

What could cause people to kill their children and themselves? From a detached perspective, the image seems unbelievable. In fact, at first glance, so does the idea of so many individuals committing so much of their time, giving all of their money, and even sacrificing the control of their children to the Peoples Temple. Jones took advantage of rationalization processes that allow people to justify their commitments by raising their estimations of the goal and minimizing its costs. Much as he gradually increased his demands, Jones carefully orchestrated the members' exposure to the concept of a "final ritual." He utilized the leverage provided by their previous commitments to push them closer and closer to its enactment. Gaining a "foot in the door" by getting a person to agree to a moderate request makes it more probable that he or she will agree to do a much larger deed later, as social psychologists—and salespeople—have found (Freedman and Fraser, 1966). Doing the initial task causes something that might have seemed unreasonable at first appear less extreme in comparison, and it also motivates a person to make his or her behavior appear more consistent by consenting to the larger request as well.

After indoctrinating the members with the workings of the Peoples Temple itself, Jones began to focus on broader and more basic attitudes. He started by undermining the members' belief that death was to be fought and feared and set the stage by introducing the possibility of a cataclysmic ending for the church. As several accounts corroborate (see Mills, 1979; Lifton, 1979; Cahill, 1979), Jones directed several "fake" suicide drills, first with the elite Planning Commission of the Peoples Temple and later with the general membership. He would give them wine and then announce that it had been poisoned and that they would soon die. These became tests of faith, of the members' willingness to follow Jones even to death. Jones would ask people if they were ready to die and on occasion would have the mem-

bership "decide" its own fate by voting whether to carry out his wishes. An ex-member recounted that one time, after a while

> Jones smiled and said, "Well, it was a good lesson. I see you're not dead." He made it sound like we needed the 30 minutes to do very strong, introspective type of thinking. We all felt strongly dedicated, proud of ourselves.... [Jones] taught that it was a privilege to die for what you believed in, which is exactly what I would have been doing. [Winfrey, 1979.]

After the Temple moved to Jonestown, the "White Nights," as the suicide drills were called, occurred repeatedly. An exercise that appears crazy to the observer was a regular, justifiable occurrence for the Peoples Temple participant. The reader might ask whether this caused the members to think that the actual suicides were merely another practice, but there were many indications that they knew that the poison was truly deadly on that final occasion. The Ryan visit had been climatic, there were several new defectors, the cooks—who had been excused from the prior drills in order to prepare the upcoming meal—were included, Jones had been growing increasingly angry, desperate, and unpredictable, and, finally, everyone could see the first babies die. The membership was manipulated, but they were not unaware that this time the ritual was for real.

A dramatic example of the impact of self-justification concerns the physical punishment that was meted out in the Peoples Temple. As discussed earlier, the threat of being beaten or humiliated forced the member to comply with Jones's orders: A person will obey as long as he or she is being threatened and supervised. To affect a person's *attitudes*, however, a mild threat has been demonstrated to be more effective than a severe threat (Aronson and Carlsmith, 1963) and its influence has been shown to be far longer lasting (Freedman, 1965). Under a mild threat, the individual has more difficulty attributing his or her behavior to such a minor external restraint, forcing the person to alter his or her attitudes in order to justify the action. Severe threats elicit compliance, but, imposed from the outside, they usually fail to cause the behavior to be internalized. Quite a different dynamic ensues when it is not so clear that the action is being imposed upon the person. When an individual feels that he or she played an active role in carrying out an action that hurts someone, there comes a motivation to justify one's part in the cruelty by rationalizing it as necessary or by derogating the victim by thinking that the punishment was deserved (Davis and Jones, 1960).

Let's step back for a moment. The processes doing on at Jonestown obviously were not as simple as those in a well-controlled laboratory experiment; several themes were going on simultaneously. For example, Jim Jones had the power to impose any punishments that he wished in the Peoples Temple, and, especially towards the end, brutality and terror at Jonestown were rampant. But Jones carefully controlled how the punishments were carried out. He often called upon the members themselves to agree to the imposition of beatings. They were instructed to testify against fellow members, bigger members told to beat up smaller ones, wives or lovers forced to sexually humiliate their partners, and parents asked to consent to and assist in the beatings of their children (Mills, 1979; Kilduff and Javers, 1978). The punishments grew more and more sadistic, the beatings so severe as to knock the victim unconscious and cause bruises that lasted for weeks. As Donald Lunde, a psychiatrist who has investigated acts of extreme violence, explains:

> Once you've done something that major, it's very hard to admit even to yourself that you've made a mistake, and subconsciously you will go to great lengths to rationalize what you did. It's very tricky defense mechanism exploited to the hilt by the charismatic leader. [*Newsweek*, 1978a.]

A more personal account of the impact of this process is provided by Jeanne Mills. At one meeting, she and her husband were forced to consent to the beating of their daughter as punishment for a very minor transgression. She relates the effect this had on her daughter, the victim, as well as on herself, one of the perpetrators:

> As we drove home, everyone in the car was silent. We were all afraid that our words would be considered treasonous. The only sounds came from Linda, sobbing quietly in the back seat. When we got into our house, Al and I sat down to talk with Linda. She was in too much pain to sit. She stood quietly while we talked with her. "How do you feel about what happened tonight?" Al asked her.
>
> "Father was right to have me whipped," Linda answered. "I've been so rebellious lately, and I've done a lot of things that were wrong.... I'm sure Father knew about those things, and that's why he had me hit so many times."
>
> As we kissed our daughter goodnight, our heads were spinning. It was hard to think clearly when things were so confusing. Linda had been the victim, and yet we were the only people angry about it. She should have been hostile and angry. Instead, she said that Jim had actually helped her. We knew Jim had done a cruel thing, and yet everyone acted as if he were doing a loving thing in whipping our disobedient child. Unlike a cruel person hurting a child, Jim had seemed calm, almost loving, as he observed the beating and counted off the whacks. Our minds were not able to comprehend the atrocity of the situation because none of the feedback we were receiving was accurate. [Mills, 1979.]

The feedback one received from the outside was limited, and the feedback from inside the Temple member was distorted. By justifying the previous actions and commitments, the groundwork for accepting the ultimate commitment was established.

Conclusion

> Only months after we defected from Temple did we realize the full extent of the cocoon in which we'd lived. And only then did we understand the fraud, sadism, and emotional blackmail of the master manipulator.
>
> —Jeanne Mills, Six Years with God

Immediately following the Jonestown tragedy, there came a proliferation of articles about "cults" and calls for their investigation and control. From Synanon to Transcendental Meditation, groups and practices were examined by the press, which had a difficult time determining what constituted a "cult" or differentiating between those that might be safe and beneficial and those that could be dangerous. The Peoples Temple and the events at Jonestown make such a definition all the more problematic. A few hours before his murder, Congressman Ryan addressed the membership: "I can tell you right now that by the few conversations I've had with some of the folks . . . there are some people who believe this is the best thing that ever happened in their whole lives" (Krause, 1978). The acquiescence of so many and the letters they left behind indicate that this feeling was widely shared—or at least expressed—by the members.

Many "untraditional"—to mainstream American culture—groups or practices, such as Eastern religions or meditation techniques, have proven valuable for the people who experience them but may be seen as very strange and frightening to others. How can people determine whether they are being exposed to a potentially useful alternative way of living their lives or if they are being drawn to a dangerous one?

The distinction is a difficult one. Three questions suggested by the previous analysis, however, can provide important clues: Are alternatives being provided or taken away? Is one's access to new and different information being broadened or denied? Finally, does the individual assume personal responsibility and control or is it usurped by the group or by its leader?

The Peoples Temple attracted many of its members because it provided them an alternative way of viewing their lives; it gave many people who were downtrodden a sense of purpose, and even transcendence. But it did so at a cost, forcing them to disown their former friendships and beliefs and teaching them to fear anything outside of the Temple as "the enemy." Following Jones became the *only* alternative.

Indeed, most of the members grew increasingly unaware of the possibility of any other course. Within the Peoples Temple, and especially at Jonestown, Jim Jones controlled the information to which members would be exposed. He effectively stifled any dissent that might arise within the church and instilled a distrust in each member for contradictory messages from outside. After all, what credibility could be carried by information supplied by "the enemy" that was out to destroy the Peoples Temple with "lies"?

Seeing no alternatives and having no information, a member's capacity for dissent or resistance was minimized. Moreover, for most members, part of the Temple's attraction resulted from their willingness to relinquish much of the responsibility and control over their lives. These were primarily the poor, the minorities, the elderly, and the unsuccessful—they were happy to exchange personal autonomy (with its implicit assumption of personal responsibility for their plights) for security, brotherhood, the illusion of miracles, and the promise of salvation. Stanley Cath, a psychiatrist who has studied the conversion techniques used by cults, generalizes: "Converts have to believe only what they are told. They don't have to think, and this relieves tremendous tensions" (*Newsweek*, 1978a). Even Jeanne Mills, one of the better-educated Temple members, commented:

> I was amazed at how little disagreement there was between the members of this church. Before we joined the church, Al and I couldn't even agree on whom to vote for in the presidential election. Now that we all belonged to a group, family arguments were becoming a thing of the past. There was never a question of who was right, because Jim was always right. When our large household met to discuss family problems, we didn't ask for opinions. Instead, we put the question to the children, "What would Jim do?" It took the difficulty out of life. There was a type of "manifest destiny" which said the Cause was right and would succeed. Jim was right and those who agreed with him were right. If you disagreed with Jim, you were wrong. It was as simple as that. [Mills, 1979.]

Though it is unlikely that he had any formal exposure to the social psychological literature, Jim Jones utilized several very powerful and effective techniques for controlling people's behavior and altering their attitudes. Some analyses have compared his tactics to those involved in "brainwashing," for both include the control of communication, the manipulation of guilt, and dispensing power over people's existence (Lifton, 1979), as well as isolation, an exacting regimen, physical pressure, and the use of confessions (Cahill, 1979). But using the term brainwashing makes the process sound too esoteric and unusual. There *were* some unique and scary elements in Jones' personality—paranoia, delusions of grandeur, sadism, and a preoccupation with suicide. Whatever his personal motivation, however, having formulated his plans and fantasies, he took advantage of well-established social psychological tactics to carry them out. The decision to have a community destroy itself was crazy, but those who performed the deed were "normal" people who were subjected to a tremendously impactful situation, the victims of powerful internal forces as well as external pressures.

Postscript

Within a few weeks of the deaths at Jonestown, the bodies had been trans-

ported back to the United States, the remnants of the Peoples Temple membership were said to have disbanded, and the spate of stories and books about the suicide/murders had begun to lose the public's attention. Three months afterwards, Michael Prokes, who had escaped from Jonestown because he was assigned to carry away a box of Peoples Temple funds, called a press conference in a California motel room. After claiming that Jones had been misunderstood and demanding the release of a tape recording of the final minutes [quoted earlier], he stepped into the bathroom and shot himself in the head. He left behind a note, saying that if his death inspired another book about Jonestown, it was worthwhile (*Newsweek*, 1979).

Postscript

Jeanne and Al Mills were among the most vocal of the Peoples Temples critics following their defection, and they topped an alleged "death list" of its enemies. Even after Jonestown, the Mills's had repeatedly expressed fear for their lives. Well over a year after the Peoples Temple deaths, they and their daughter were murdered in their Berkeley home. Their teen-aged son, himself an ex-Peoples Temple member, has testified that he was in another part of the large house at the time. At this writing, no suspect has been charged. There are indications that the Mills's knew their killer—there were no signs of forced entry, and they were shot at close range. Jeanne Mills had been quoted as saying, "It's going to happen. If not today, then tomorrow." On the final tape of Jonestown, Jim Jones had blamed Jeanne Mills by name, and had promised that his followers in San Francisco "will not take our death in vain" (*Newsweek*, 1980).

References

ARONSON, E. *The social animal* (3rd ed.) San Francisco: W. H. Freeman and Company, 1980.

ARONSON, E. The theory of cognitive dissonance: A current perspective. In L. Berkowitz (ed.), *Advances in experimental social psychology*. Vol. 4. New York: Academic Press, 1969.

ARONSON E., AND CARLSMITH, J. M. Effect of the severity of threat on the devaluation of forbidden behavior. Journal of Abnormal and Social Psychology. 1963, 66, 584–588.

ARONSON, E., AND MILLS, J. The effects of severity of initiation on liking for a group. *Journal of Abnormal and Social Psychology.* 1959, 59, 177–181.

ASCH, S. Opinions and social pressure. *Scientific American*, 1955, 193. (Also reprinted in this volume.)

Tape hints early decision by Jones on mass suicide. *Baltimore Sun.* March 15, 1979.

BLAKEY, D. Affidavit: Georgetown, Guyana. May 12, 1978.

BLAKEY, D. Affidavit: San Francisco. June 15, 1978.

BREHM, J. Increasing cognitive dissonance by a *fait-accompli. Journal of Abnormal and Social Psychology*, 1959, 58, 379–382.

CAHILL, T. In the valley of the shadow of death. *Rolling Stone.* January 25, 1979.

Committee on Foreign Affairs, U.S. House of Representatives, Report of a staff investigative group. *The assassination of Representative Leo J. Ryan and the Jonestown, Guyana tragedy.* Washington, D.C.: Government Printing Office, May 15, 1979. (Many of the other press reports are reprinted in this volume.)

CRAWFORD, Y. Affidavit: San Francisco. April 10, 1978.

DARLEY, J., AND BERSCHEID, E. Increased liking as a result of the anticipation of personal contact. *Human Relations*, 1967, **20**, 29–40.

DAVIS, K., AND JONES, E. Changes in interpersonal perception as a means of reducing cognitive dissonance. Journal of Abnormal and Social Psychology, 1960, 61, 402–410.

"Don't be afraid to die" and another victim of Jonestown. *Newsweek*, March 10, 1980.

A fatal prophecy is fulfilled. *Newsweek*, March 10, 1980.

FREEDMAN, J. Long-term behavioral effects of cognitive dissonance. *Journal of Experimental Social Psychology*, 1965, **1**, 145–155.

FREEDMAN, J., AND FRASER, S. Compliance without pressure: The foot-in-the-door technique. *Journal of Personality and Social Psychology*, 1966, **4**, 195–202.

GALLAGHER, N. Jonestown: The survivors' story. *New York Times Magazine*, November 18, 1979.

KASINDORF, J. Jim Jones: The seduction of San Francisco. *New West*, December 18, 1978.

KILDUFF, M., AND JAVERS, R. *The suicide cult.* New York: Bantam, 1978, and *San Francisco Chronicle.*

KILDUFF, M., AND TRACY, P. Inside Peoples Temple. *New West*, August 1, 1977.

KRAUSE, C. *Guyana massacre.* New York: Berkley, 1978, and *Washington Post.*

LIFTON, R. J. Appeal of the death trip. *New York Times Magazine*, January 7, 1979.

MILGRAM, S. Behavioral study of obedience. *Journal of Abnormal and Social Psychology*, 1963, 67, 371–378. (Also reprinted in E. Aronson (ed.), *Readings about the social animal.*)

MILGRAM, S. Liberating effects of group pressure. *Journal of Personality and Social Psychology*, 1965, **1**, 127–134.

MILLS, J. *Six years with God.* New York: A & W Publishers, 1979.

REITERMAN, T. Scared too long. *San Francisco Examiner*, November 13, 1977.

The sounds of death. *Newsweek*, December 18, 1978b.

Special report: The cult of death. *Newsweek*, December 4, 1978a.

TRACY, P. Jim Jones: The making of a madman. *New West*, December 18, 1978.

WINFREY, C. Why 900 died in Guyana. *New York Times Magazine*, February 25, 1979.

YOUNG, S. Report on Jonestown. *The CBS Evening News with Walter Cronkite.* November 16, 1979.

ZIMBARDO, P. *The cognitive control of motivation.* Glenview, Ill.: Scott Foresman, 1969.

ZIMBARDO, P., EBBESON, E., AND MASLACH, C. *Influencing attitudes and changing behavior* (2nd ed.). Reading, Mass.: Addison-Wesley, 1977.

The Committed Heart

Anthony Pratkanis and Elliot Aronson

A visit from the encyclopedia salesman can illustrate many persuasion tactics. The "free" road atlas given for listening to the sales representative invokes the norm of reciprocity. The features of the volumes are described in glowing, influential words. The salesman encourages you to generate dozens of good reasons (at least you think so) for owning a set of encyclopedias. The fact that your children and other loved ones don't already have access to a world of knowledge makes you feel a little guilty.

But perhaps one of the most powerful inducers to buy occurs "after" the sales presentation. The salesman continues:

"Well, if there are no more questions about the books, that will conclude the presentation. Oh yes, one more thing. My boss would really like it if I could get your opinion about our encyclopedias. Would you mind completing a form with me?"

You respond, "OK."

"It's a series of questions about what *you* would like in an encyclopedia. It would really help if you would respond as *if you were buying a set today.*"

The salesman goes on to ask a series of questions. "Which color binding do you like—white, maroon, or black? With or without gold leaf? With or without double-strength binding?" and so on. You answer each question mindlessly as the salesman checks off your responses on a preprinted official form.

At the end of the inquiry he asks, "Would you mind initialing this sheet as a way of authorizing your answers?" Again, you do so in a half-mindless state.

From that point on, that formal-looking paper is treated as *your* order for a set of encyclopedias. The salesman suggests, "Let's see how much it would cost to buy *your* set of encyclopedias today; hmmmmm, with a 5% discount that would be___," as he hands you a slip of paper with a handwritten number on it. As you read it, the salesman asks, "Shall I order *your* set today?" You stammer, half-confused, "Well, 'em, I'd . . . well."

We don't know if you will buy that set of encyclopedias today or not. Many of us will undoubtedly see through his ploys. But we bet this procedure of "taking your order" will increase encyclopedia sales and will do so because of the feelings it engenders. In general, it is important to all of us to be "persons of our word," that is, to be self-consistent and to honor our commitments. Granted, we did not say we would buy an encyclopedia, but the salesman seems to think so—perhaps we *did* indicate we would like one. When we go back on our word, we often feel uneasy, even when it is a seemingly flimsy commitment like the one given to the encyclopedia salesman. To maintain a positive view of ourselves, we act on our commitments. The rationalization trap has captured another unsuspecting victim.

Preying on our sense of commitment as a way to induce persuasion is often accomplished in small doses. Suppose you would like to enlist someone's aid in a massive undertaking, but you know the job you have in mind for the person is so difficult, and will require so much time and effort, the person surely will decline. What should you do? One possibility is to get the person involved in a much smaller aspect of the job, one so easy that he or she wouldn't dream of refusing to do it. This action serves to commit the individual to "the cause." Once people are thus committed, the likelihood of their complying with the larger request increases.

This phenomenon was demonstrated by Jonathan Freedman and Scott Fraser.[1] They attempted to induce several home owners to put up a huge, unattractive sign in their front yards reading "Drive Carefully." Because of the ugliness and obtrusiveness of the sign, most residents refused to put it up; only 17% complied. A different group of residents, however, were first "softened up" by an experimenter who "put his foot in the door" by getting them to sign a petition favoring safe driving. Because signing a petition is an easy thing to do, virtually all who were asked agreed to sign. A few weeks later, a different experimenter went to each resident with the ugly "Drive Carefully" sign. More than 55% of these residents allowed the sign to be put up on their property.

Thus, when individuals commit themselves in a small way, the likelihood they will commit themselves further in that direction is increased. This process of using small favors to encourage people to accede to larger requests has been dubbed the *foot-in-the-door* technique (a technique opposite in form to the door-in-the-face tactic). It is effective because having done the smaller favor sets up pressures toward agreeing to do the larger favor; in effect, we comply

From *Age of Propaganda: The Everyday Use and Abuse of Persuasion* by Anthony Pratkanis and Elliot Aronson, pp. 183-188.
© 1992 by W. H. Freeman and Company. Reprinted by permission.

with the large request to be consistent with our earlier commitment.

Similar results using this technique have been found in studies of charitable donations and voting. For example, people induced to wear a lapel pin publicizing an American Cancer Society fund-raising drive were approximately twice as likely to give a donation the next day as were those who were simply approached for a contribution.[2] Other investigators have found that the chances of getting people to vote on election day could be increased just by asking them if they planned to go to the polls.[3] In this study, the researchers contacted potential voters and asked them to predict if they would vote in an election to be held on the upcoming Tuesday. All of those contacted, perhaps out of a desire to appear civic-minded, said "yes," they would be voting. The respondents then acted on this commitment, with 86.7% of them voting in the election compared to 61.5% of those not asked to make self-predictions.

Car dealers also know how to use commitment to sell automobiles. Indeed, when Robert Cialdini temporarily joined the sales force of an automobile dealer, he discovered a common and successful ploy called *lowballing* or "throwing the customer a lowball."[4]

The technique works this way. Suppose you enter an automobile showroom intent on buying a new car. You've already priced the car you want at several dealers—you know you can purchase it for about $9,300. Lo and behold, the salesman tells you he can sell you one for $8,942. Excited by the bargain, you agree to the deal and write out a check for the downpayment. While the salesman takes your check to the sales manager to consummate the deal, you rub your hands in glee as you imagine yourself driving home in your shiny new car. But alas, ten minutes later, the salesman returns with a forlorn look on his face—it seems he made a calculation error and the sales manager caught it. The price of the car is actually $9,384. You can get it cheaper elsewhere; moreover, the decision to buy is not irrevocable. And yet, far more people in this situation will go ahead with the deal than if the original asking price had been $9,384—even though the reason for purchasing the car from this dealer (the bargain price) no longer exists.

What is going on in this situation? There are at least three important things to notice. First, while the customer's decision to buy is certainly reversible, a commitment was emphasized by the act of signing a check for the downpayment and handing it over to the salesman. Second, this commitment triggered the anticipation of a pleasant or interesting experience: driving out with a new car. To have the anticipated event thwarted (by not going ahead

with the deal) would have produced disappointment. Third, although the final price is substantially higher than the customer thought it would be, it is only slightly higher than the price somewhere else. Under these circumstances, the customer in effect says, "Oh, what the hell. I'm already here, I've already filled out the forms—why wait?

Commitment can be self-perpetuating, resulting in an escalating commitment to an often failing course of action. Once a small commitment is made, it sets the stage for ever increasing commitments. The original behavior needs to be justified, so attitudes are changed; this change in attitudes influences future decisions and behavior. The result is a seemingly irrational commitment to a poor business plan, a purchase that makes no sense, a war that has no realistic objectives, or an arms race gone out of control.

The processes of escalating commitment may have been an important factor in the deepening U.S. involvement in the war in Vietnam. As a analysis the *Pentagon Papers* by the news magazine *Time* stated:

> Yet the bureaucracy, the Pentagon Papers indicate, always demanded new options; each option was to apply more force. Each tightening of the screw created a position that must be defended; once committed, the military pressure must be maintained.[5]

In a thought-provoking analysis of the *Pentagon Papers*, Ralph White suggested that previous commitments blinded our leaders to information incompatible with the decisions they had already made.[6] As White put it, "There was a tendency, when actions were out of line with ideas, for decision-makers to align their ideas with their actions." To take just one of many examples, the decision by the Joint Chiefs of Staff to continue to escalate the bombing of North Vietnam was made at the price of ignoring crucial evidence from the CIA and other sources that made it clear that bombing would not break the will of the North Vietnamese people but, quite the contrary, would only strengthen their resolve. White surmises the reason the Joint Chiefs prevailed in their efforts to escalate the bombing was that their advice was consonant with decisions already made and with certain key assumptions that later proved to be erroneous. In other words, the Joint Chiefs' escalation of the war was in part an attempt to reduce their own dissonance about their previous war efforts, a process reminiscent of what happened after Mrs. Keech's end-of-the-world prophecy failed and after the city of Santa Cruz was informed about an impending, destructive earthquake.

As with other self-motives and emotions, commitment and consistency have their purpose and value.

5. SOCIAL INFLUENCE

No one wants to live in a society of inconsistent, two-faced liars! However, commitments can form a persuasion trap—we commit ourselves, sometimes inadvertently, sometimes inappropriately, and then live out our commitments in all honesty. The clever propagandist will know how to secure our commitment and set a rationalization trap.

In such cases, it may be useful to ask, "How did I get myself into this situation?" Fortunately, many states require that consumers be given a period of time to "change their minds" about a particular purchase—a time to rethink mistaken commitments. It may also help us if we remember that the most honorable action is always that of not honoring dishonorable commitments.

Notes

1. Freedman, J., & Fraser, S. (1966). Compliance without pressure: The foot-in-the-door technique. Journal of Personality and Social Psychology, 4, 195–202.
2. Pliner, P., Hart, H., Kohl, J., & Saari, D. (1974). Compliance without pressure: Some further data on the foot-in-the-door technique. Journal of Experimental Social Psychology, 10, 17–22.
3. Greenwald, A. G., Carnot, C. G., Beach, R., & Young, B. (1987). Increasing voting behavior by asking people if they expect to vote. Journal of Applied Psychology, 72, 315–318.
4. Cialdini, R. B., Cacioppo, J. T., Bassett, R., & Miller, J. (1978). Low-ball procedure for compliance: Commitment then cost. Journal of Personality and Social Psychology, 36, 463–476.
5. Pentagon papers: The secret war. (1971, June 28). Time, p. 12.
6. White, R. (November 1971). Selective inattention. Psychology Today, pp. 47–50, 78–84.

What Is the Influence of One Flower Given?

Anthony Pratkanis and Elliot Aronson

A. C. Bhaktivedanta spent much of his life in India as a manager of a successful pharmaceutical company. In the early 1960s, after leaving his wife and family and accepting the name of Swami Prabhupada, he came to America and founded the International Society for Krishna Consciousness, a movement devoted to improving the world's spiritual health by chants and love for Lord Krishna. Starting from a storefront mission on Manhattan's Lower East Side, the swami, in less than a decade, was able to gather the resources to establish a worldwide network of more than a hundred Hare Krishna temples and communes, including forty located in the United States.

Swami Prabhupada's primary source of income during this period of rapid expansion came from public donations and sales of religious merchandise, including his two most popular items, *Back to Godhead* magazine and a designer edition of the *Bhagavad Gita*. What makes the Hare Krishna's success so remarkable was the sales force the swami recruited to sell the society's merchandise. The swami selected young people—often teenagers, many of them with psychological problems—dressed them in saffron robes, holy beads, and B. F. Goodrich sandals, shaved the heads of the males, fed them a diet consisting primarily of vegetables (most notably dahl and chickpeas), and then sent them into the marketplace singing, dancing, and chanting the Hare Krishna. Would you buy a copy of the *Bhagavad Gita* (or anything else, for that matter) from a chanting, orange-clad, stubble-headed sales agent? Not likely. The Hare Krishna sales force breaks just about every persuasion rule (save one) . . . they were low in source credibility, low in interpersonal attraction and liking, and high in vested self-interest.

How did the swami get thousands of people to part with their hard-earned cash to finance his spiritual kingdom? Robert Cialdini, one of the world's leading authorities on influence tactics, wondered how he did it, too.[1] At first, Cialdini notes, the Hare Krishnas were quite unsuccessful in their solicitations. Indeed, many towns enacted laws and ordinances prohibiting Krishna begging and even banned them from certain parts of town, especially airports. Occasionally violence would erupt between Krishnas and townspeople. All of this turned around, according to Cialdini, when the Krishnas discovered one of society's most effective persuasion devices, one capable both of overcoming the Krishnas' negative image and of placing of an overpriced copy of the *Bhagavad Gita* into the hands of many a weary traveler. Their technique made use of what is called the *norm of reciprocity*.

A norm is a specific guide to conduct—for example, tip 15% of the dinner bill; don't cut in front of people standing in line at the movies; don't urinate in public; don't read other people's mail. If we break a norm, we most likely receive some form of social sanction and disapproval—a glaring look, gossip and ridicule, shunning and ostracism, and sometime even physical punishment, jail, banishment, or death. (Note the reaction of some people to the Krishnas because they broke society's dress and social interaction norms.) As a consequence of these sanctions, even a young child begins to learn not to break the norms. Indeed, when put in a position of transgressing a norm, we often feel highly anxious—a feeling that we would like to avoid. We may end up obeying the norm almost automatically without much thought as to why.

Often norms can be associated with a specific role (cooking is women's work; businessmen are competitive) or a specific culture (eat with a fork [as opposed to chopsticks]; don't goldbrick [overproduce] in this workshop). Other norms are widely shared and appear in many cultures and societies (incest is taboo; honor your commitments). The norm of reciprocity is one such norm. It states: "If I do something for you, then you are obligated to return the favor and do something for me." Perhaps one reason why this norm is found in so many cultures is its value to a society. The norm of reciprocity regulates exchange in a culture; it insures that the person who makes the first exchange will not be cheated.

From *Age of Propaganda: The Everyday Use and Abuse of Persuasion* by Anthony Pratkanis and Elliot Aronson, pp. 178-183. © 1992 by W. H. Freeman and Company. Reprinted by permission.

5. SOCIAL INFLUENCE

A study by Dennis Regan illustrates the persuasive power of the norm of reciprocity—a tactic so powerful that it can overcome the effects of being disliked.[2] In his experiment, two male students reported for a study that supposedly was investigating "aesthetic judgments." One of the men was really an accomplice who, at the beginning of the study, attempted to make himself unlikable (by being rude and inconsiderate to another person) or likable (by being kind and considerate to another). After both "subjects" rated art slides for about five minutes, the accomplice slipped out of the room for a couple of minutes and returned either empty-handed or carrying two Cokes and said, "I asked him [the experimenter] if I could get myself a Coke, and he said it was OK, so I bought one for you, too." At the end of the study, the accomplice asked the real subject if he would like to buy some raffle tickets. The results showed that when the accomplice gave the other student a Coke and thus invoked the norm of reciprocity, he sold nearly twice as many raffle tickets, compared to when no Coke was given and regardless of how socially attractive he was perceived to be!

How did the Krishnas use the norm of reciprocity to solicit money? Quite simply, they gave the influence target a gift of a flower. As Cialdini, who spent hours at the airport observing the Krishnas in action, tells it, the sect member would spy a "victim," who would suddenly find a flower pressed into his or her hand or pinned to a jacket. If the target attempted to give it back, the Krishna would refuse by saying, "It is our gift to you." Only then was the request made for a donation. The gift of a flower established a feeling of obligation and indebtedness. How could this favor be repaid? Quite obviously by providing Society with a donation or with the purchase of an attractive edition of *Bhagavad Gita*.

Hare Krishnas are not the only ones to employ the norm of reciprocity for persuasion purposes. This may have started on a mass scale with the well-known "Fuller-brushman," a fixture of the 1930s who went from door to door selling brushes. He always began by giving the home owner a small inexpensive brush as a way to establish the reciprocity norm. A phenomenon of the 1950s, Tupperware parties, began with a gift from the company (typically a small Tupperware item) and a gift from the party host (refreshments), thereby obligating the party goer to both company and host (who receives a gift from the company if you and your friends buy enough). A recent television ad for an antacid began with an authoritative looking man stating, "We believe in our product so much, that, after watching this ad, if you would like to try our product just call us toll-free and we will send you a

pack." Marketers know that a free sample—a taste of sausage or orange juice at the supermarket or a trial packet of cold medicine or shampoo in the mail—can greatly increase product sales. Sales presentations for such things as vacuum cleaners, automobiles, encyclopedias, and beachfront property in Florida often begin with a free prize, such as a road atlas, a transistor radio, or a trial magazine subscription. Charities and political parties frequently mail free gifts of buttons and bumper stickers with catchy slogans when they ask for a contribution. Many university professors will receive . . . [free book copies] in the hopes that they will assign it to their classes.

One ingenious variation in the use of the norm of reciprocity occurs in negotiations and has been dubbed the door-in-the-face technique. Here's how it works. Imagine that you worked for a local blood bank and you wanted to increase blood donations. Using the *door-in-the-face* technique, you would begin by asking for a very extreme favor—say, donate blood once every two months for at least three years. Such a request would surely be rejected (hence the name "door-in-the-face") but might lead to more acceptances of a compromise—say, donating one unit of blood—than would otherwise be the case. This is exactly what Robert Cialdini and Karen Ascani found.[3] In one study, they asked passersby on a University of Arizona walkway to either (1) donate a unit of blood sometime tomorrow or (2) donate a unit of blood once every two months for a period of three years and, when this request was rejected by the passerby, to merely donate a unit of blood sometime tomorrow. The results showed that more people agreed to give blood and actually gave more blood when they received the extreme request first.

The door-in-the-face technique makes use of two basic psychological processes. First, the large request sets up a contrast effect, similar to the one that occurs with decoys—giving a pint of blood doesn't seem nearly so bad when compared to donating at regular intervals for the next three years. Second, the immediate concession by the requester invokes the norm of reciprocity. The requester is implicitly saying, "I just reduced my request from three years of blood donations to just once; now it is your turn to reciprocate my concession." And many an influence target does just that!

Car dealers have learned the value of the door-in-the-face technique. Dealers often pad the asking price for an automobile by adding an extra price sticker that raises the price of a car by as much as a few thousand dollars. Early in the negotiations, the dealer will graciously concede this extra charge. Now it is *your turn* to reciprocate and to pay *more* for that car.

In general, the norm of reciprocity is successful as a persuasion device because it directs our thoughts and carries its own motivation to act on those thoughts. We are directed to think "How can I repay my obligation?" as opposed to "Is this a good deal?" Our primary motivation is to avoid the uneasy feeling that comes from transgressing the norm. Other norms can similarly motivate our thinking. . . .

Notes

1. Cialdini, R. B. (1984). *Influence.* New York: Morrow.
2. Regan, D. T. (1971). Effects of a favor and liking on compliance. *Journal of Experimental Social Psychology, 7,* 627–639.
3. Cialdini, R. B., & Ascani, K. (1976). Test of a concession procedure for inducing verbal, behavioral, and further compliance with a request to give blood. *Journal of Applied Psychology, 61,* 295–300.

SUSPECT CONFESSIONS

He's made mincemeat of false memories.
But the social psychologist Richard Ofshe has a more pressing
question: Why do innocent people admit to crimes
they didn't commit?

Richard Jerome

Richard Jerome is a senior writer at People *magazine.*

THROUGH A THICKENING FOG, RICHARD J. OFSHE WINDS his white BMW homeward into the Oakland hills, leaving behind the University of California at Berkeley, where he is a professor of social psychology. In florid tones refined by 30 years at the lectern, Ofshe is expounding on his latest area of interest, the ways in which police interrogations can elicit false confessions. Specifically, he is bemoaning the case of Jessie Lloyd Misskelley Jr., a teen-ager from a squalid Arkansas trailer park who confessed – falsely, Ofshe maintains – to taking part in the ghastly murder of three 8-year-old boys. In spite of Ofshe's voluminous expert testimony on his behalf, Misskelley, who has an I.Q. in the 70's, was sentenced to life plus 40 years in prison.

"It was like walking straight into 'Deliverance,' " Ofshe says, casually veering around another hairpin turn. "The trial was a travesty. The conduct of the judge was outrageous."

At 54, Ofshe has acquired a muted celebrity for his work on extreme influence tactics and thought control. He shared in the 1979 Pulitzer Prize in public service after assisting The Point Reyes (Calif.) Light in its exposé of Synanon, a Bay Area drug rehabilitation group that evolved into an armed cult. More recently, Ofshe has been an aggressive and influential debunker of "recovered memory," the theory whereby long-repressed traumas are retrieved by patients undergoing what Ofshe calls exceedingly manipulative psycho-

therapy. As such, Ofshe is a vivid figure in "Remembering Satan," Lawrence Wright's book about the case of Paul Ingram, a former Olympia, Wash., sheriff's deputy now serving 20 years in prison primarily because he became convinced that the accusations of one of his daughters, who claimed that he had indulged in a 17-year binge of satanism, incest and infanticide, were true. Ofshe, a champion of Ingram, dissects the affair in his recent book, "Making Monsters: False Memories, Psychotherapy and Sexual Hysteria," written with Ethan Watters.

But for the most part, Ofshe has set aside violent cults and overzealous shrinks and is fixated on the third of his bêtes noires: false confessions. According to Ofshe and a considerable body of literature, modern interrogation tactics are so subtly powerful that police can – entirely unwittingly – coerce innocent suspects into admitting to the most heinous crimes. Sometimes, Ofshe says, a suspect admits guilt simply to escape the stress of the interrogation. More rarely, a suspect comes to believe that he actually committed the crime in question, though he has no memory of it.

For Ofshe, exorcising both kinds of false confession from the American justice system has become an almost obsessive quest. All told, he has consulted or testified in more than 80 criminal cases involving suspects from whom, he concluded, confessions were coerced; in most of these cases, the physical evidence strongly suggested innocence. Although he makes money at it overall – $40,000 in 1993 – he sometimes works pro bono. With dark, disdaining eyes set against a shock of gray curls and a swirling beard, Ofshe looks vaguely sinister – a wily Renaissance pol, perhaps, or Claudius in a

From *The New York Times Magazine,* August 13, 1995, pp. 28-31. © 1995 by The New York Times Company. Reprinted by permission.

road company of Hamlet. Confession, he points out, is the anchor of a trial in which there is no hard evidence. "And false confession," he says, "ranks third after perjury and eyewitness error as a cause of wrongful convictions in American homicide cases."

His numbers are based on several studies, most recently work by the sociologist Michael L. Radelet of the University of Florida, Hugo Adam Bedau, professor of philosophy at Tufts University, and Constance E. Putnam, a Boston-based writer. In their 1992 book, "In Spite of Innocence," the authors review more than 400 cases in which innocent people were convicted of capital crimes in the United States. Fourteen percent were caused by false confession. "If it happened just one-half of 1 percent of the time," Ofshe says, "it still means that hundreds, or perhaps thousands, of people each year are being unjustly imprisoned. Even if one innocent man or woman is convicted, it's too many. And it's unnecessary because this is a fixable problem"—fixable, he adds, if only police interrogations were electronically recorded, a requirement now only in Alaska and Minnesota.

"Now I don't think for one second," Ofshe stresses, "that the detectives and prosecutors in cases of false confessions want to bring about that result. But because they don't understand the mistake as it is being made, the case moves forward and takes everyone along with it."

THE BMW IS NOW TUCKED SAFELY UNder Ofshe's red Ferrari, which sits on a raised hoist in the garage of his hillside home, a quasi-Mediterranean mix of stone and stucco. Inside, rock music from a new stereo system tumbles down the coiled stairs of a three-and-a-half-story central rotunda, into a cherry-paneled library where Ofshe, propped like a pasha on a brown leather couch, surveys his domain with a reverent sigh: "I never thought I'd ever get to have a house like this."

It mirrors its inhabitant: spare, opulent, imposing yet accessible. One can well appreciate that Ofshe's fondest boyhood memory is of the austere charms of the Frick Collection mansion. His father, a dress designer, moved the family from the Bronx to Queens when Ofshe was a child. Ofshe attended Queens College, then went to graduate school at Stanford. "I honestly can't tell you now what led me to psychology," he says. "I suppose I'm a watcher. I'm comfortable observing people and lecturing at them — but I am absolutely incapable of making small talk, a gift I consider one of the great mysteries of life."

During graduate school, Ofshe was married briefly and then, as he puts it, "got un-married." (He married his present wife, Bonnie Blair, a successful designer of sweaters, in 1981.) Ofshe gravitated toward social psychology; his work on cults grew out of a study of utopian societies

he undertook in the early 1970's. One such community was Synanon, begun as a drug treatment center by Charles Dederich. But by 1978, Dederich had accumulated a substantial arsenal, as well as a large cadre of loyal followers. By this time, The Point Reyes Light, a weekly based near Ofshe's summer home, had begun an investigative series on Synanon, on which Ofshe collaborated. As a result of the media exposure, Synanon lost its tax-exempt status and disintegrated. Dederich sued Ofshe three times unsuccessfully for libel, prompting him to retaliate with a malicious prosecution suit. " 'When this is over, I'll be the one driving the red Ferrari,' " Ofshe says he told people at the time. The Ferrari, he now confides, "accounts for a small percentage of my settlement. A very small percentage."

Material success aside, Ofshe seems to revel most in the validation of his work by respected media outlets. It takes little prodding for him to express his glee at Lawrence Wright's description of him as "Zeus-like" in "Remembering Satan" — which first appeared as an article in The New Yorker, a magazine Ofshe clearly reveres. And he is quick to point out that the television movie of Wright's book, currently being filmed, features him as the central character — as played by William Devane.

What saves this self-absorption from being insufferable is Ofshe's interest in helping people he considers innocent. He first focused on police interrogation in 1987, after a phone call from Joseph G. Donahey Jr., a veteran Florida attorney. Donahey was representing Thomas F. Sawyer, a Clearwater golf course groundskeeper who in 1986, after an uncommonly grueling 16-hour interrogation, confessed to the brutal murder of a neighbor; the police convinced Sawyer that he'd lost all memory of the incident during an alcoholic blackout. (Sawyer, against whom there was no physical evidence, had quickly recanted.) "Donahey realized something was terribly wrong with Tom's confession," Ofshe says. "At first I was skeptical. But once I read the transcript of the interrogation, it became obvious what had happened to Tom."

Ofshe spent 300 hours analyzing the Sawyer interrogation — which, by a lucky quirk, was taped in its entirety — and concluded it was "a tour de force of psychological coercion." Sawyer's police interrogators, Peter Fire and John Dean, invited Sawyer to the station house on the premise that he was being asked to "assist" with their investigation. Then, Ofshe says, they flattered him into providing his own hypothetical murder scenario. The detectives then used leading questions to shape the groundskeeper's responses, eventually tossing his answers back as evidence of his guilt. Consider the following dialogue, slightly condensed, on the position of the victim's body:

FIRE: And he would put her in the bed how? Like she's doing what?

SAWYER: Sleeping.
FIRE: O.K. What would you put her on? Her. . . .
SAWYER: On her back.
FIRE: Put her on her back? . . .
SAWYER: I'd put her on her back sleeping.
FIRE: Put her on her back, sleeping?
SAWYER: Don't you sleep on your back?
FIRE: No. . . .
SAWYER: I don't sleep on my side.
FIRE: Well, what other way could you put her?
SAWYER: Face down.
FIRE: O.K. Face down. . . .
SAWYER: I'd put her on her stomach. . . .
FIRE: You hit the nail on the head. You put her on her stomach.

Deception, typically by lying about the presence of witnesses or physical evidence or about polygraph results, is a common interrogation tactic, Ofshe says, and it was used baldly against Sawyer. ("We found a lot of hairs and fibers on her body," Fire insisted at one point. "We have your hair. . . . There's a lot of evidence. There's a lot of evidence. A lot of evidence.")

"If you're dealing with middle-class types," Ofshe says, "or at least middle-class types socialized by my mother, they're hearing: 'It's inevitable that you'll be caught and punished to the max.' I have no interest in stripping police of tactics that make perfect sense — when those tactics are supported by compelling physical evidence. But the same things that can convince a guilty person that he's been caught can convince someone who's innocent that he's caught."

Under this intense barrage, Sawyer, who for hours steadfastly maintained his innocence, exhibited his first trace of self-doubt: "I honestly believe that I didn't do it. . . . I don't remember doing it. If I did, and I don't think I did. . . . You almost got me convinced I did, but. . . . "

"He went from straight denial to 'I couldn't have done something like this,' " Ofshe says. "And finally, when he confessed, it was so beautiful, so perfect in the way he verbalized it: 'I guess all the evidence is in, I guess I must have done it.' "

Strong evidence of a false confession, Ofshe says, is when the narrative is at odds with the known facts of the case or has been clearly fed to the suspect, however inadvertently, by the police themselves. "Sawyer was wrong about almost everything," Ofshe says, "except for several details" — like the position of the victim's body — "that were clearly introduced by Fire and Dean."

Ultimately, Ofshe's testimony helped exonerate Sawyer, whose confession was suppressed in 1989 after the groundskeeper had spent 14 months in jail awaiting trial. Shortly thereafter, Ofshe — by now increasingly sought by desperate defense attorneys — helped free Mark Nunez, Leo Bruce and Dante Parker, who, fingered by a psychiatric patient and subjected to a highly coercive interrogation, had falsely confessed to killing nine people

at a Buddhist temple outside Phoenix. In Flagstaff, Ofshe was instrumental in winning the 1988 acquittal of George Abney, a graduate student with a history of depression, who had admitted to the ritualistic murder of a Navajo woman. In the Phoenix case, the real murderer was eventually caught and prosecuted.

"WHAT SOME OF THE PSYCHOLOGISTS SAY IS I put you in a room, you're all emotional and at the end of five or six hours, I've fed you everything," Lieut. Ralph M. Lacer is saying in his Oakland police office, several miles from Ofshe's home. "Well, if I was on the jury, I'd be rolling my eyes saying: 'Who is the dumb [expletive] who thinks this is gonna go over?' "

Fiftyish, ruddy and blond, the bespectacled Lacer was one of the interrogating officers in the high-profile case of Bradley Page, a handsome Berkeley student who had admitted — falsely, so Page and his attorneys maintained — to murdering his girlfriend, Roberta (BiBi) Lee, in a fit of anger in 1984. After two trials, the second of which Ofshe consulted on, Page was convicted of manslaughter. (He was released, after serving part of a six-year sentence, in February.)

Only part of the Page interrogation was recorded. From 11:50 A.M. to 1:10 P.M. on Dec. 10, 1984, Lacer and his partner, Sgt. Jerry Harris, taped Page as he gave them a firm, lucid account of his movements during the time since Lee had disappeared a month before — none of which included bludgeoning her to death. Then the detectives shut off the machine until 7:07 P.M., by which time Page was highly emotional, confessing to murder, albeit in vague, halting language peppered with "might haves," "would haves" and other subjunctive phrases that left Ofshe highly suspicious. Lacer freely acknowledges that Page's admission of guilt, made in the absence of hard evidence, was the heart and soul of the case against him. "If we hadn't gotten the confession," Lacer says, "Brad would've walked."

I raise Ofshe's argument, that taping interrogations in full might resolve any ambiguities.

"First of all, a tape is inhibiting," Lacer counters. "It's hard to get at the truth. And say we go for 10 hours — we have 10 hours of tape that maybe boil down to 15 or 20 minutes of you saying, 'Yes, I killed Johnny Jones.' You bet the public defender's going to have the jury listen to all 10 hours of that tape and by that time the jury won't remember what it's all about."

According to Lacer, the craft of interrogation is learned through experience. "Every day when you stop someone on the street, you're interrogating them," he says. " 'Where do you live? Where you headed to?' We definitely try to establish rapport — basically, I want to get you to talk to me. But when we bring a suspect in, we keep the room bare, a table and two or three chairs, a locked door."

I glance around, aware for the first time that the

interview is unfolding in the ideal interrogation setting. I ask Lacer what would happen if a person being questioned invokes his constitutional right of silence or, if he is not under arrest, his right to simply walk out the door.

"Well, that would be the end of the situation," he says. "But many times it won't happen, and here's why: I see you've got a wedding ring on, Rich. Well, say Mrs. Rich ends up dead in the house. We call you down and you say, 'I don't think I want to talk to you guys, I'm out of here.' Well, the thing is, your in-laws find out that you took that route and they know right away who killed your wife.

"Now most of the time, the suspect will set up barriers. Like you got your legs crossed — that's kind of a psychological barrier. And I lean forward, violate your personal space, get closer and closer and pretty soon we're nose to nose." As Lacer edges toward me, his eyes, though still genial, bear into mine.

"Now remember, I'm just talking, not yelling or bullying," he says. "It's not going to help matters if I suddenly say '[Expletive], that's a [expletive] black sweater you have on — I threw away the last black sweater I had like that!' " You can maybe bully a little bit verbally by saying: 'Rich, that last story was [expletive]. Let's not even go into that again.' " Lacer's eyes turn caustic through his aviator glasses.

"Now as far as yelling," he says, chummy again, "about the only time we do it here in Oakland is if someone's talking over you or if they're going off on a tangent, and I'd say, 'Hey Rich, let's get back to the *subject!* " His voice slices through the claustrophobia of the room — a ferocity all the more unnerving because it booms from Lacer's amiable shell.

"We've been in a room together for a while, Rich," he says, chuckling. "Do you feel like confessing to anything?"

"LACER RATIONALIZES THAT SOMEONE LIKE Bradley Page — or you and I — cannot be made to confess," Ofshe says on the day after my encounter with the Oakland lieutenant. "Because it is in many ways one of the worst professional errors you can make — like a physician amputating the wrong arm."

Prevention, he adds, is surprisingly simple: "Above all, no confession ought be accepted unless it has been corroborated with clear-cut and powerful evidence. And you must never instigate a high-pressure, accusatory interrogation unless you have a good and sound reason to do it." Another safeguard, Ofshe reiterates, is to record interrogations. Early last year, the professor helped win a significant victory in the same Clearwater courthouse where the Sawyer case was heard. Relying substantially on Ofshe's testimony, Judge Claire K. Luten formed a forceful opinion that the confession of Francis Dupont, an alcoholic drifter who had admitted to murdering a friend, was psychologically coerced. Moreover, Luten ruled that the failure to tape the interrogation of Dupont was in direct violation of due process.

"I'd be content to devote myself to that issue until I am too old to work on it," Ofshe says.

In a sense, this is Ofshe's moment, for never has the nation been more attuned to what happens in a courtroom. Yet for the plain citizen — the juror — he is also a problematic figure, a bearded academic speaking in tones of unassailable authority about social psychology, a discipline that resounds with squishy inexactitude. Ofshe's theories about false confession, however well researched, risk being perceived as just another set of legal loopholes. And his "one innocent man or woman" might well be shrugged off — probably not worth the trouble and surely not worth the risk.

For which reason Ofshe emphasizes the most basic preventive to false confession: if you find yourself being questioned about a crime you know you did not commit, resist at all costs the impulse to be helpful, no matter how charming or forbidding the interrogator might be.

"I tell my classes," Ofshe says, "that if they ever find themselves in that situation, remember the four magic words of the criminal justice system: 'I want a lawyer.' "

Social Relationships

A young man stands on a narrow suspension bridge that stretches over a river 230 feet below. The bridge is only five feet wide, over 400 feet long, and it constantly swings and sways in the wind. Even for someone without a fear of heights, crossing this bridge while looking at the river far below, is definitely an arousing experience. In fact, a considerable number of the people who visit this popular tourist spot every year find themselves unable to cross the bridge at all. While standing on the bridge, the young man is approached by an attractive young woman who asks him to participate in a psychology research project she is working on—all he has to do is write a brief imaginative story in response to a picture she gives him. He does so, and when he is finished, the experimenter gives him her phone number in case he wants to learn more about the experiment.

A few miles away, another young man stands on another bridge—but this one is not scary at all. It is solidly built, does not sway and wobble, and stands only 10 feet above a peaceful stream. The same attractive woman approaches this man with the same request, and, again she gives him her phone number when the experiment ends. Who do you think is more likely to call the young woman later? When this experiment was actually carried out, the results were clear—men on the arousing bridge were much more likely than men on the safe bridge to call the female experimenter later on. Not only that, but the stories the men on the arousing bridge wrote were noticeably different; they contained significantly more references to sex. In short, the men on the arousing bridge apparently reacted in a very different way to the young woman—they experienced a greater sense of physical attraction to her, and acted on that attraction later on by calling her up. Even though men on the sturdy bridge met the same young woman, they did not experience the same physical attraction.

This experiment is just one example of some of the work done by psychologists who study social relationships. This area of social psychology turns out to be a very broad one indeed, and a wide variety of topics fall under its umbrella. One research question, for example, that has attracted a lot of attention is this: What are the factors that influence the initial attraction (both romantic and nonromantic) that we feel for another person? Considerable research indicates that being similar to the other person is important, as is the sheer physical attractiveness of that other. Living or working in close proximity to other people also increases the likelihood of attraction to them.

Other researchers have tackled issues such as identifying the processes that are important for maintaining friendships over time. The level of self-disclosure in the relationship seems to be important, as does the general feeling by both participants that what they are receiving from the relationship is roughly equivalent to what their partner is receiving; that is, issues of fairness seem to play a crucial role. Still, other investigators have concerned themselves with the question of long-term romantic relationships: Which factors lead to initial romantic attraction; Which factors contribute to long-term satisfaction; and How do couples deal with conflict and disagreements in long-term relationships?

The selections in this unit are divided into two sections. The first subsection addresses the general issue of affiliation—the tendency that humans have to enjoy and seek out social contact. In the first selection, "A Nation of Hermits: The Loss of Community," Tori DeAngelis discusses evidence that modern American society is displaying a decline in the amount of affiliation between its members. Some possible social psychological reasons for, and consequences of, this decline are presented. The next article, "Laughs: Rhythmic Bursts of Social Glue," takes a very different approach. In this essay, Natalie Angier presents interesting research that suggests that social laughter serves a valuable function in maintaining community. By regularly indicating to our interaction partners that we are experiencing positive emotions, social laughter helps smooth our social interactions.

The second subsection focuses on articles that deal in one way or another with the topic of love. In "Up from Gorilla Land: The Hidden Logic of Love and Lust," Robert Wright analyzes love and sex from the standpoint of evolutionary psychology. This approach argues that human behavior today is shaped by evolutionary forces that have existed for hundreds of thousands of years. The differing selection pressures on men and women during that time have led to distinctly different mating strategies for the two sexes, and thus two very different approaches to love. In "The Lessons of Love," Beth Livermore reviews a number of social psychological approaches to this topic; in addition to evolutionary forces, she also examines evidence for the role of culture in influencing love and research exploring attachment and emotion. Finally, in "What Makes Love Last?" the work of John Gottman is described. Gottman argues that the way in which couples deal with conflict in their relationship, and the emotions

that result from that conflict, are of critical importance in determining whether they will stay together.

Looking Ahead: Challenge Questions

Do you agree that modern American society is characterized by a deterioration of community? What evidence do you see of that? What evidence is not consistent with this view? If it is true, however, which factors do you think have contributed to this decline? What remedies for such a decline seem possible?

What function does social laughter serve? What kind of evidence is there for the argument that it plays a fun-

damental role in governing social interaction? What would a social interaction completely lacking in laughter be like?

What do you think of the evolutionary psychologists' explanation for some of the differences between men and women in the area of sexual behavior? What is their strongest evidence? Their weakest evidence? Can their findings be explained in any other way?

What is meant by the term "love styles"? What are the six different styles of love, and how do they differ from one another? Can you think of people in your life who illustrate each style?

Is conflict in a marriage always a negative thing? What does the research evidence suggest about the best way to handle conflicts when they arise?

A Nation of Hermits: The Loss of Community

Today's mobile, urban and impersonal lifestyle is creating a culture of loneliness.

Tori DeAngelis

Monitor staff

It wasn't long ago that people made friends with the mailman, the barber or the grocer who cut their meat for them on Saturdays.

But today, such community intimacy seems part of the past. In a culture where we can pull money from a machine and never interact with a human bank teller, enter a crowded subway without meeting another's eyes, and call telephone assistance only to get information from a computerized voice, it's truly possible to be alone in a crowd.

A blend of social trends has led to this hermit's lifestyle: mass flight from rural areas to the cities and suburbs; the advent of depersonalizing technology at home and at work; and the breakdown of the family, through divorce and career moves. Census figures show that more than 75 percent of Americans now live in cities and suburbs, while national surveys find that a quarter of Americans say they've felt lonely in the last month.

Psychologists are examining this uniquely modern problem, looking at the effects of isolation and technology's role in it (see sidebar), and developing theories on the psychosocial damage that such alienation can inflict.

While social isolation is in part the product of nonhuman forces such as technology and industrialization, social psychologists emphasize the human dimensions of the problem. In particular, they cite the country's so-cial mobility as a prime reason for increased separation in our culture.

"Compared to most other societies, our bonds are much more tentative and fragile," says Roy Baumeister, PhD, professor of psychology and an E. B. Smith professor in liberal arts at Case Western Reserve University.

"We can get out of almost any relationship, and the possibility of moving away, changing jobs and losing touch with everyone we once lived with is much more common than it used to be."

Frequent change of dwelling "puts a lot of pressure on the individual to be the 'right kind of person,'" adds Mark Leary, PhD, a psychology professor at Wake Forest University. "Every time you move to a new place and start a new job, you have to reestablish your identity again."

The pressure of that dynamic can easily lead to social isolation. It is anxiety-provoking to adapt continuously to new situations, so people don't try as hard to reach out, says Mihaly Csikszentmihalyi, PhD, a University of Chicago psychology professor. Csikszentmihalyi has conducted numerous studies on enhancing use of one's free time and the effects of culture on daily life. He has written a number of popular books on his research, including *Flow: The Psychology of Optimal Experience,* on tapping the positive aspects of human potential.

In life-enhancement workshops he conducts with middle-aged businessmen, Csikszentmihalyi hears complaints that they have no friends: that because everyone moves in different directions, they have no chance to establish connections.

In addition, beginning with Stanley Milgram, PhD, in the 1970s, social psychologists have noted the phenomenon that living in crowded areas can "produce a kind of sensory and cognitive overload that causes [people] to withdraw," Leary said.

Certain people tend to be lonelier and hence more prone to isolation than others, psychologists have also found. About 2 percent of people are "social phobics," who "are so nervous about social interactions that they live relatively isolated lives and are unhappy in that isolation," Leary said. People who tend to be rejected by others, beginning in childhood, are also more likely to experience isolation.

Studies by University of Tennessee psychologist Warren Jones, PhD, find that college students—who "live in an environment full of attractive, intelligent, pleasant people with whom to associate"—are among the loneliest members of society. The reasons are twofold, Jones believes: They tend to be overly idealistic, expecting too much from potential mates and friends. And they reject possible friends and partners because they're "overcome with their own social anxiety and fear of rejection, and rationalize that fear by saying their friends aren't good enough, attractive enough and so on."

Whatever its etiology, Baumeister and Leary stress that emotional and social isolation cuts into a basic human drive: the need to belong. In an

From *APA Monitor*, September 1995, pp. 1, 46. © 1995 by the American Psychological Association. Reprinted by permission.

Though Technology Can Isolate, It Can Also Provide Social Glue

It seems intuitively obvious that technology contributes to a sense of isolation by teaching people to focus more attention on the cold glare of a computer or TV screen than on the warmth of a friendly face.

Yet research by psychologists paints a mixed picture of technology's effect on people—and one that's not entirely negative.

In studies on the effects of the much-maligned television on people's mood states, University of Chicago researcher Mihaly Czikszentmihalyi, PhD, has found that indeed, TV can have negative effects—at least for some. Watching the tube makes people feel "passive, weak, rather irritable, and sad, "especially if they have little else going on in their lives, he said.

"If you don't have a job you like, or a good family and friends, the more TV you watch, the less good you feel."

But if a person likes her job and has a happy personal life, "watching TV is a positive experience—people can watch what they want, then do something else." Unfortunately, people who are less educated, have worse jobs and worse relationships watch more TV and are more negatively affected by it—a vicious circle, Czikszentmihalyi says. Just as TV doesn't always serve to foster isolation, computers can be a positive connective experience, too, a team of Carnegie-Mellon University researchers is finding.

In a study launched in September 1994, psychologists Robert Kraut, PhD, and Sara Kiesler, PhD, computer scientist William Scherlis, PhD, and economist Tridas Mukhopadhyay, PhD, are examining the effects of introducing personal computers with e-mail links into the homes of 50 Pittsburgh families.

The team is looking in part at whether using the Internet creates "a different or similar kind of community to the real world," according to Kraut.

The team's initial speculation—that those who use the Net more often might be lonelier and more socially isolated—is proving invalid. The only personality variable that predicts use is a person's openness to new experiences. In addition, younger people, whites and those with positive attitudes toward the computer before the study used the Net more often than others.

All the families in the study report engaging in "a substantial amount of interpersonal communication" using the computer, both with people they're already close to and others they've "met" through the Net, Kraut said.

"They see it as a pleasurable activity in is own right," he says. "It's yet one more channel that allows people to communicate."

—Tori DeAngelis

article published in the May *American Psychologist,* the two review a wide range of psychological literature to argue that "belonging" is a fundamental human motivation.

They conclude that the need to belong is an evolutionary strategy that fits people's survival and reproductive needs. For instance, children who stay with adults stand a better chance of surviving to adolescence because they'll be better protected. Likewise, adults who form bonds both with members of their peer group and a romantic partner are more likely to have children and add to community life than those who don't, they note.

The need to belong has two major components, both supported by a wealth of research, Leary and Baumeister note. People need frequent personal contacts with others. They also need an interpersonal bond marked by stability, emotional concern and continuity.

The importance of both aspects is pronounced in situations where only one is present. In "commuter marriages," for instance, the second dimension of caring and stability is present, but not the frequent personal contact. Both partners feel stressed,

even though they report they don't doubt each other's love.

"Just having the other person there seems tremendously powerful," Baumeister says. Likewise, having frequent personal contact but a dearth of emotional bonding—as in the case of a prostitute and his or her client—is unsatisfying, he believes.

So when a culture pushes some of its citizens toward isolation, Baumeister believes "it goes against human nature" in the most profound sense. "The data on happiness are pretty clear: People who live in social isolation are very rarely happy."

As Harmful as Smoking

A range of studies show that being isolated and feeling lonely contribute powerfully to problems in psychological and physical well-being.

In reviewing a decade of literature on social support, University of Michigan sociologist James House, PhD, found that the effects of social isolation on health are as great as the health effects of such factors as cigarette smoking, obesity and high-blood pressure. More strikingly, even, those

with a low quantity and quality of social relationships die earlier than others, House found.

Psychologist-researcher Janice Kiecolt-Glaser, PhD, has found that lonely people are more likely to have problems in immune functioning than others. In a 1992 study of 48 adults, she found that those who reported lower social support had a weaker immune response to a hepatitis-B vaccine than others. Her findings ran along a continuum: The less social support subjects reported, the weaker their immune response.

In another recent study, Kiecolt-Glaser tested natural-killer cell activity—which shows how well the body is fighting infection—in 75 medical students a month before they took a final exam, the day of the exam and again when the students returned from vacation. All the students experienced a drop in killer-cell activity during the examinations. But students who reported that they were lonely had significantly lower levels than others.

Recent qualitative research by Kipling Williams, PhD, suggests that social ostracism can have serious psychosocial consequences. Subjects he

interviewed who were long-term sufferers of ostracism blamed a range of devastating outcomes on the experience of being shunned, including anorexia, suicidal feelings and prostitution.

Even criminal activity may be affected by a lack of belonging, according to research by psychologists sociologist Robert Sampson, PhD, and criminal justice expert John Laub, PhD. In a 1993 study, they found that having a good marriage and stable job was a strong deterrent effect on adult crime—suggesting that the obverse may foster criminal behavior.

Fortunately, people have many ways of coping with alienation, from attending church to joining the local baseball team, said Leary.

"Research on patterns of churchgoing suggest it's the social opportunities—the pancake suppers, the youth groups—that really keep people coming back," he said. And in an age when fewer people are attending church and joining other traditional institutions, support groups, book clubs and even aerobics classes have become sources of camaraderie, he said.

The adage "no man is an island" rings especially true in the 1990s when social conditions are leading to a greater possibility of isolation for more people, Baumeister said.

Without meaningful relationships, "even if a person has enough food, enough money, freedom, all the things they needed to read and be stimulated by, they still wouldn't be happy," he said.

Laughs: Rhythmic Bursts of Social Glue

Natalie Angier

BALTIMORE

Here is a sampling of knee slappers to jump-start your day:

"Got to go now!"

"I see your point."

"It must be nice."

"Look! It's Andre."

Hey, wait a minute. Where are the guffaws, the chuckles, at the very least a polite titter or two? Get me laughtrack! Doesn't this deadbeat crowd know that such lines are genuine howlers, field-tested fomenters of laughter among ordinary groups of people in ordinary social settings?

We're not talking Aristophanes here, or even Phyllis Diller. We're talking the sort of laughter that we give and receive every day while strolling with friends in the park, or having lunch in the company cafeteria, or chatting over the telephone. The sort of social laughter that punctuates casual conversations so regularly and unremarkably that we never think about or notice it—but that we would surely, sorely miss if it were gone.

One person who has thought about and noticed laughter in great detail is Dr. Robert R. Provine, a professor of neurobiology and psychology at the University of Maryland Baltimore County. Dr. Provine has become a professional laugh-tracker, if you will, an anthropologist of our amusement, asking the deliciously obvious questions that science has not deigned to consider before. He has analyzed what, physically, a laugh is, what its vocal signature looks like and how it differs from the auditory shape of a spoken word or a cry or any other human utterance.

He has asked when people laugh and why, what sort of comments elicit laughter, whether women laugh more than men, whether a person laughs more while speaking or while listening. He has studied the rules of laughter: when in a conversation a laugh will occur, and when, for one reason or another, the brain decides it is taboo. He has compared human laughter to the breathy, panting vocalizations that chimpanzees make while they are being chased or tickled, and that any primatologist or caretaker will firmly describe as chimpanzee laughter.

Dr. Provine has eavesdropped on 1,200 bouts of laughter among people in malls and other public places, noting down the comments that preceded each laugh and compiling a list of what he calls his "greatest hits" of laugh generators, which include witless-isms like those quoted above. In so doing he has made a discovery at once startling and perfectly sensible: most of what we laugh at in life is not particularly funny or clever but merely the stuff of social banter, the glue that binds a group together. Even the comparatively humorous laugh-getters are not exactly up to Seinfeld, lines like, "She's got a sex disorder: she doesn't like sex"; or "You don't have to drink. Just buy us drinks." It is probably a good thing that our laugh-meters are set so low, because very few of us are natural wits, and those that are often get into bad moods and refuse to say a single clever thing for entire evenings at a time.

Dr. Provine, a tall man with a well-groomed academic-issue beard who in profile looks faintly like the actor Fernando Rey, is neither clownish nor severe, somehow remaining animated about his subject without becoming silly. He can laugh loudly on command to demonstrate his points, which is something many people refuse to do. In videos, when Dr. Provine is shown approaching strangers on the Baltimore waterfront, telling them he is studying laughter and asking them to laugh for him. Usually, people give sidelong glances to their companions, grin, fuss with their hair, and as he persists, they grow annoyed. "I can't laugh on command," they complain. "Tell me a joke first."

To Dr. Provine, that difficulty reveals something important about the nature of laughter. We can smile on command, albeit stiffly, and we can certainly talk on command, but laughter has an essential spontaneous element to it. It is a vocalization of a mood state, rather than a cognitive act, and as such it is difficult

to fake, just as it is hard to force out tears. Those who are good at laughing on cue, said Dr. Provine, often have stage experience.

Dr. Provine summarizes much of his recent research in the current issue of American Scientist, and he recently presented results at the annual meeting of the Society for Neuroscience in San Diego. His work departs sharply from the well-mined territory of humor analysis, in which scholars gather at conferences to discuss the ontology of Woody Allen or Monty Python and leave one with a distinct taste of sawdust in the mouth. Dr. Provine is not interested in formal comic material, or why some like Lenny Bruce and others Red Skelton, but in laughter as a universal social act.

"His work is extremely interesting, insightful," said Dr. William F. Fry, a psychiatrist at the Stanford University School of Medicine. "He's doing the sort of things that should have been done 300 years ago." Dr. Fry is no joke himself, having studied the aerobic, physical and emotional benefits that accrue when a person laughs. One hundred laughs, he discovered, is equivalent to 10 minutes spent rowing.

Lest it appear that Dr. Provine is in the business of amusing himself and making strangers uncomfortable, he elaborates on the many quite serious questions that the study of laughter addresses. Laughter gives you a foothold on the neurobiology of behavior, he said. "It is species-typical, everybody does it, and it is simple in structure, which gives you powerful leverage on the neurology behind it," he said.

"Looking at a common human behavior that is socially interesting gives us the opportunity to go back and forth between the neural circuitry and a higher social act," he said. Dr. Provine compares studying a simple system like laughter for clues to more complex types of human behavior to biologists' use of a simple organism like yeast or nematodes for delving into the thicket of genetics or brain development.

He points out that linguists and scientists who study speech are always searching for the deep underlying structure to language, those phonemes that might be recognized as language units by everybody, regardless of whether they are French, Chinese or New Guinean. But finding the common currency of language has proved quite difficult. "If you're interested in the mechanisms of speech, wouldn't it be useful to look at a vocalization that all individuals produce in the same way, such as laughter?" he asks rhetorically.

Laughter also has the useful property of being contagious, he said. When you hear laughter, you tend to start laughing yourself—hence the logic behind the sitcom's ubiquitous laugh-track. And it is easy to assess whether the brain's circuitry for recognizing laughter has been activated, Dr. Provine said. "You don't need to use electrodes, or wait for clinical cases of brain lesions," to study laughter recognition, he said. All you have to do is see if the person laughs on hearing laughter.

A hundred laughs: as beneficial as 10 minutes of rowing.

The infectiousness of laughter also makes it a particularly interesting social activity to explore. Few behaviors, short of shouting "Fire" in a movie theater, can have such a dramatic, swelling impact on group behavior as can the burst of a merry chime of laughter. Indeed Dr. Provine came to laughter research after studying another highly contagious human behavior: yawning.

Before he could hope to get at any neural circuitry, Dr. Provine first had to do the basics, starting with what a laugh looks like. He brought re-

corded samples of human laughter to the sound analysis laboratory at the National Zoo in Washington, where the usual subjects of research are bird songs and monkey screams. There he and colleagues generated laugh waveforms and laugh frequency spectrums. They determined that the average laugh consisted of short bursts of vowel-based notes—haha or hehe—each note lasting about 75 milliseconds and separated by rests of 210 milliseconds. Whether a person laughs with a shy giggle, a joyous musical peal, or a braying hee-haw, "the key is the burst of vowel-like sounds produced in a regular rhythmic pattern," he said.

Eavesdropping on giggles is serious research.

A typical laugh also has a decrescendo structure, starting strong and ending soft. A laugh played backward, going from low to high bursts, sounds slightly strange, almost frightening, and yet it is still clearly recognizable as a laugh, just as a birdsong played backward would be; the same cannot be said for a human conversation played backwards. "Laughter has more in common with animal calls than with what we think of as modern speech," Dr. Provine said.

Dr. Provine and his students also began gathering hundreds of episodes of everyday laughter. They were startled by the ordinariness of the comments that would elicit laughter. Equally surprising was how often people laughed at their own statements. The standard image of the comedian is the deadpan performer who hardly grins while the audience members convulse in laughter. But the average speaker chattering away laughs 46 percent more frequently than do those listening to the spiel.

There proved to be wide variations based on sex in the ratio of speaker-to-listener laughter. A man talking to a male listener laughs only slightly more than his companion will in response. If a woman is talking to a woman, she laughs considerably more than does her audience. By contrast, a male speaker with a female hanging on his words laughs 7 percent less often than does his appreciative hearer. And the biggest discrepancy of all is found when a woman speaks to a man, in which case she laughs 127 percent more than her male associate, who perhaps is otherwise occupied with planning a witty rejoinder.

Speakers and listeners alike abide by rules while laughing. Laughter almost never intrudes upon the phrase structure of speech. It never interrupts a thought. Instead, it occurs as a kind of punctuation, to reflect natural pauses in speech.

This is true for listeners as well as the talkers: they do not laugh in the middle of a speaker's phrase, Dr. Provine said. And in fact to do so may be evidence of psychological abnormality; a crazy person may not wait for you to finish speaking before interrupting with a booming HA!

The lawfulness of the relationship between laughter and speech, said Dr. Provine, indicates a segregation of brain processes devoted to one or the other. "It suggests that you have mutually exclusive but interacting vocal processes," he said. "And it seems speech is dominant over laughter, because laughter does not intrude on speech."

What, then, is the purpose of all this lawfully punctuating chuckling? Laughter is, above all, a social act, Dr. Provine said. You are far more likely to talk to yourself while alone than laugh to yourself (unless you are watching television or reading, in which case you are engaged vicariously in a social event). Dr. Provine sees laughter as a within-group modulator, something designed to influence the tenor of an assemblage, to synchronize mood and possibly subsequent actions.

Joyous laughter can help solidify friendships and pull people into the fold.

The flip side of mirthful laughter may not be tears, but jeering, malicious laughter, used not to include people in one's group, but to exclude the laughable misfit. To make his point about the downside of laughter, and how it can turn deadly, Dr. Provine shows a clip from the movie "Goodfellas," a scene in which the volatile Joe Pesci character laughs together with his fellow thugs before smashing a bottle of alcohol into a poor intruder's face.

Despots historically have feared the power of laughter; comedians during the Nazi era in Germany, for example, were kept on the Gestapo's shortest leash. "Fashions on laughter change, but one thing that stays the same is, you can't laugh at people in power," Dr. Provine said. The sanction holds for the personal as well as the political. Laugh at your boss, and you may be the recipient of that practical joke known as the little pink slip.

Up from Gorilla Land

The Hidden Logic of Love and Lust

If you want to understand the emotional spigots that turn on the attractions, passions, and infatuations that course through you, it helps to think of yourself as a gene machine with a single-minded evolutionary past. But this common goal implies different tendencies for men and women. Men, at heart, are quantity creatures; women go for quality.

Robert Wright

IN RECENT YEARS A SMALL BUT GROWING GROUP OF SCHOLARS HAS TAKEN THE WORK OF DARWIN AND HIS SUCCESSORS AND CARRIED IT INTO THE SOCIAL SCIENCES WITH THE AIM OF OVERHAULING THEM. THESE EVOLUTIONARY PSYCHOLOGISTS ARE TRYING, IN A SENSE, TO DISCERN HUMAN NATURE, A DEEP UNITY WITHIN MEMBERS OF OUR SPECIES. IN CULTURE AFTER CULTURE, WE SEE A THIRST FOR SOCIAL APPROVAL, A CAPACITY FOR GUILT. YOU MIGHT CALL THESE, AND MANY OTHER HUMAN UNIVERSALS, "THE KNOBS OF HUMAN NATURE." THE EXACT TUNINGS OF THESE KNOBS DIFFER FROM PERSON TO PERSON; ONE PERSON'S GUILT KNOB IS SET LOW AND ANOTHER PERSON'S IS PAINFULLY HIGH.

How do these knobs get set? Genetic differences among individuals sure play a role, but perhaps a larger role is played by a species-wide developmental program that absorbs information from the social environment and adjusts the maturing mind accordingly. Oddly, future progress in grasping the importance of the environment will probably come from thinking about genes.

The questions addressed by evolutionary psychologists range from the mundane to the spiritual and touch on just about everything that matters: racism, friendship, neurosis, sibling rivalry, war, altruism, guilt, the unconscious mind, even social climbing. No human behavior, however, affects the transmission of genes more obviously than sex. So no parts of human psychology are clearer candidates for

evolutionary explanation than the states of mind that lead to sex: raw lust, dreamy infatuation, sturdy love, and so on—the basic forces amid which people all over the world have come of age.

The recently popular premise that men and women are basically identical in nature seems to have fewer and fewer defenders. A whole school of feminists—the "difference feminists"—now accept that men and women are deeply different.

The first step toward understanding the basic imbalance of the sexes is to assume hypothetically the role natural selection plays in designing a species. Suppose you're in charge of instilling, in the minds of human beings, rules of behavior that will guide them through life, the object of the game being to make each person behave in such a way that he or she is likely to have

lots of offspring—offspring, moreover, who themselves have lots of offspring.

When playing the Administrator of Evolution, and trying to maximize genetic legacy, you may quickly discover that this goal implies different tendencies for men and women. Men can reproduce hundreds of times a year, assuming they can persuade enough women to cooperate, and assuming there aren't any laws against polygamy—which there assuredly weren't in the ancestral environment where much of our evolution took place.

Women, on the other hand, can't reproduce more than once a year. The asymmetry lies partly in the high price of eggs; in all species they're bigger and rarer than minuscule, mass-produced sperm. But the asymmetry is exaggerated by the

From *Psychology Today*, March/April 1995, pp. 26-29. Excerpted from *The Moral Animal: Why We Are the Way We Are* by Robert Wright. © 1994 by Robert Wright. Reprinted by permission of Pantheon Books, a division of Random House, Inc.

details of mammalian reproduction: the egg's lengthy conversion into an organism happens inside the female, and she can't handle many projects at once.

So while there are various reasons why it could make Darwinian sense for a woman to mate with more than one man, there comes a time when having more sex just isn't worth the trouble. Better to get some rest and grab a bite to eat. For a man, unless he's really on the brink of collapse or starvation, that time never comes. Each new partner offers a very real chance to get more genes into the next generation—a much more valuable prospect, in the Darwinian calculus, than a nap or a meal. As the evolutionary psychologists Martin Daly and Margo Wilson have put it, for males "there is always the possibility of doing better."

There's a sense in which a female can do better, too, but it has to do with quality, not quantity. Giving birth involves a huge commitment of time and energy, and nature has put a low ceiling on how many such enterprises she can undertake. So each child, from her (genetic) point of view, is an extremely precious gene machine. Its ability to survive is of mammoth importance. It makes Darwinian sense, then, for a woman to be selective about the man who is going to help her build each gene machine. She should size up an aspiring partner before letting him in on the investment, asking herself what he'll bring to the project.

The reason: At some point, extensive male parental investment entered our evolutionary lineage. Fathers everywhere help feed, teach, support, and defend their children. Throw this into the equation, and suddenly the female is concerned not only with the male's genetic investment, but with what resources he'll bring to the offspring after it materializes.

In 1989, psychologist David Buss published a pioneering study of mate preferences in 37 cultures around the world. He found that in every culture, females placed more emphasis than males on a potential mate's financial prospects. Actually, women may not be attuned so much to a man's wealth as to his social status; among hunter-gatherers, status often translates into influence over the divvying up of resources, such as meat after a big kill. In

modern societies, in any event, wealth and status often go hand in hand, and seem to make an attractive package in the eyes of the average woman. It's no surprise that flowers and other tokens of affection are more prized by women than by men.

One might imagine that this analysis is steadily losing its relevance. After all, as more women enter the work force, they can better afford to premise their marital decisions on something other than the man's income. But though a modern women can reflect on her wealth and her independently earned status, and try to gauge marital decisions accordingly, that doesn't mean she can easily override the deep aesthetic impulses that had such value in the ancestral environment. In fact, modern women do not override them. Psychologists have shown that the tendency of women to place greater emphasis than men on a mate's financial prospects persists regardless of the income of the woman in question.

In judging potential partners, women needn't literally ask about these issues, or even be aware of them. Much of our species' history took place before our ancestors were smart enough to ask much of anything.

In the case of sexual attraction, everyday experience suggests that natural selection has wielded its influence largely via emotional spigots that turn on and off such feelings as tentative attraction, fierce passion, and swoon-inducing infatuation. A woman doesn't size up a man and say, "He seems like a worthy contributor to my genetic legacy." She just sizes him up and feels attracted to him—or doesn't. All the "thinking" has been done—unconsciously, metaphorically—by natural selection. Genes leading to attractions that wound up being good for her ancestors' genetic legacies have flourished. Understanding the often unconscious nature of genetic control is the first step toward understanding that—in many realms, not just sex—we're all puppets, and our best hope for even partial liberation is to try to decipher the logic of the puppeteer.

It would be misleading to say that men are selective about mates, but in theory they are at least *selectively* selective. They will, on the one hand, have sex with just about anything that moves, given an easy chance. In one experiment, three-fourths of the men approached by an unknown woman on a college campus agreed to have sex with her, whereas none of the women approached by an unknown man were willing to do so.

On the other hand, when it comes to finding a female for a long-term joint venture, discretion makes sense. Males can undertake only so many ventures over the course of a lifetime, so the genes that the partner brings to the project—genes for robustness, brains, whatever—are worth scrutinizing.

The distinction was nicely drawn by a study in which both men and women were asked about the minimal level of intelligence they would accept in a person they were "dating." The average response, for both males and females, was: average intelligence. They were also asked how smart a person would have to be before they would consent to sex. The women said: Oh, in that case, markedly *above* average. The men said: Oh, in that case, markedly *below* average.

Men will, on the one hand, have sex with just about anything that moves, given an easy chance.

In the psychology laboratory, David Buss has found further evidence that men do dichotomize between short-term and long-term partners. Cues suggesting promiscuity (a low-cut dress, perhaps, or aggressive body language) make a woman more attractive as a short-term mate and less attractive as a long-term mate. Cues suggesting a lack of sexual experiences work the other way around.

Psychologist Donald Symons believes that the lifestyle of the modern philandering bachelor—seducing and abandoning available women year after year, without making any of them targets for ongoing investment—is not a distinct, evolved sexual strategy. It is just what happens when you take the male mind, with its preference for varied sex partners, and set it down in a big city replete with contraceptive technology.

Still, even if the ancestral environment wasn't full of single women sitting alone after one-night stands muttering, "Men are scum," there were reasons to guard against males who exaggerate commitment, only to leave after fathering a child. Divorce happens even

among modern-day hunter-gatherers (whose lifestyle mirrors that of our ancestors), and polygyny is often an option. Given such prospects, a woman's genes would be well served by her early and careful scrutiny of a man's likely devotion. Gauging of a man's commitment does seem to be a part of human female psychology; and male psychology does seem inclined to sometimes encourage a false reading. One study found that males, markedly more than females, report depicting themselves as more kind, sincere, and trustworthy than they actually are.

Though both men and women seek general genetic quality, tastes may in other ways diverge. Just as women have special reason to focus on a man's ability to provide resources, men have special reason to focus on the ability to produce babies. That means, among other things, caring greatly about the age of a potential mate, since fertility declines until menopause, when it falls off abruptly. The last thing evolutionary psychologists would expect to find is that a plainly postmenopausal woman is sexually attractive to the average man. They don't find it: In everyone of Buss's 37 cultures, males preferred younger mates (and females preferred older mates). The importance of youth in a female mate may help explain the extreme male concern with physical attractiveness. Women can afford to be more open-minded about looks: an oldish man, unlike an oldish woman, is probably fertile.

When it comes to assessing character—to figuring out if you can trust a mate—a male's discernment may again differ from a female's, because the kind of treachery that threatens his genes is different from the kind that threatens hers. Whereas the woman's natural fear is the withdrawal of his investment, his natural fear is that the investment is misplaced. Not long for this world are the genes of a man who spends his time rearing children who aren't his.

All of this sounds highly theoretical—and of course it is. But this theory is readily tested. David Buss placed electrodes on men and women and had them envision their mates doing various disturbing things. When men imagined their partner committing sexual infidelity, their heart rates took leaps of a magnitude typically induced by three successive cups of coffee. They sweated. Their brows wrinkled. When they imagined a budding emotional attachment, they calmed down, though not quite to their normal level. For women things were reversed: envisioning *emotional* infidelity—redirected love, not supplementary sex—brought the deeper physiological distress.

The logic behind male jealousy isn't what it used to be. These days some adulterous women use contraception and thus don't dupe their husbands into spending two decades shepherding another man's genes. But the weakening of the logic hasn't weakened the jealousy. For the average husband, the fact that his wife inserted a diaphragm before copulating with her tennis instructor will not be a major source of consolation.

The classic example of an adaptation that has outlived its logic is the sweet tooth. Our fondness for sweetness was designed for an ancestral environment in

---

Gauging a man's commitment does seem to be a part of human female psychology.

---

which fruit existed but candy didn't. Now that a sweet tooth can bring obesity, people try to control their cravings, and sometimes they succeed. But few people find it easy. Similarly, the basic impulse toward jealousy is very hard to erase. Still, people can muster some control over the impulse, and, moreover, can muster some

control over some forms of its expression, such as violence, given a sufficiently powerful reason. Prison, for example.

This raises two final points. First, to say something is a product of natural selection is not to say that it is unchangeable. Just about any manifestation of human nature can be changed, given an apt alteration of the environment—though the required alteration will in some cases be prohibitively drastic.

Contrary to expectations, evolutionary psychologists subscribe to a cardinal doctrine of twentieth-century psychology: the potency of early social environment in shaping the adult mind. But if we want to know, say, how levels of ambition or insecurity get adjusted by early experience, we must first ask why natural selection made them adjustable. A guiding assumption of many evolutionary psychologists is that the most radical differences among people are the ones most likely to be traceable to environment.

Second, to say that something is "natural" is not to say that it is good. Nature isn't a moral authority, and we needn't adopt any "values" that seem implicit in its workings—natural selection's indifference to the suffering of the weak, for example, is not something we need emulate. But if we want to pursue values that are at odds with natural selection's, we need to know what we're up against. If we want to change some disconcertingly stubborn parts of our moral code, it would help to know where they come from. And where they ultimately come from is human nature, however complexly that nature is refracted by the many layers of circumstance and cultural inheritance through which it passes.

THE LESSONS OF LOVE

Yes, we've learned a few things. We now know that it is the insecure rather than the confident who fall in love most readily. And men fall faster than women. And who ever said sex had anything to do with it?

Beth Livermore

As winter thaws, so too do icicles on cold hearts. For with spring, the sap rises—and resistance to love wanes. And though the flame will burn more of us than it warms, we will return to the fire—over and over again.

Indeed, love holds central in everybody's everyday. We spend years, sometimes lifetimes pursuing it, preparing for it, longing for it. Some of us even die for love. Still, only poets and songwriters, philosophers and playwrights have traditionally been granted license to sift this hallowed preserve. Until recently. Over the last decade and a half, scientists have finally taken on this most elusive entity. They have begun to parse out the intangibles, the *je ne sais quoi* of love. The word so far is—little we were sure of is proving to be true.

OUT OF THE LAB, INTO THE FIRE

True early greats, like Sigmund Freud and Carl Rogers, acknowledged love as important to the human experience. But not till the 1970s did anyone attempt to define it—and only now is it considered a respectable topic of study.

One reason for this hesitation has been public resistance. "Some people are afraid that if they look too close they will lose the mask," says Arthur Aron, Ph.D., professor of psychology at the University of California, Santa Cruz. "Others believe we know all that we need to know." But mostly, to systematically study love has been thought impossible, and therefore a waste of time and money.

No one did more to propagate this false notion than former United States Senator William Proxmire of Wisconsin, who in 1974 launched a very public campaign against the study of love. As a member of the Senate Finance Committee, he took it upon himself to ferret out waste in government spending. One of the first places he looked was the National Science Foundation, a federal body that both funds research and promotes scientific progress.

Upon inspection, Proxmire found that Ellen Berscheid, Ph.D., a psychologist at the University of Minnesota who had already broken new ground scrutinizing the social power of physical attractiveness, had secured an $84,000 federal grant to study relationships. The proposal mentioned romantic love. Proxmire loudly denounced such work as frivolous—tax dollars ill spent.

The publicity that was given Proxmire's pronouncements not only cast a pall over all behavioral science research, it set off an international firestorm around Berscheid that lasted the next two years. Colleagues were fired. Her office was swamped with hate mail. She even received death threats. But in the long run, the strategy backfired, much to Proxmire's chagrin. It generated increased scientific interest in the study of love, propelling it forward, and identified Berscheid as the keeper of the flame. Scholars and individuals from Alaska to then-darkest Cold War Albania sent her requests for information, along with letters of support.

Berscheid jettisoned her plans for very early retirement, buttoned up the country house, and, as she says, "became a clearinghouse" for North American love research. "It became eminently clear that there were people who really did want to learn more about love. And I had tenure."

PUTTING THE SOCIAL INTO PSYCHOLOGY

This incident was perfectly timed. For during the early 1970s, the field of social psychology was undergoing a revolution of sorts—a revolution that made the study of love newly possible.

For decades behaviorism, the school of psychology founded by John B. Watson, dominated the field. Watson argued that only overt actions capable of direct observation and measurement were worthy of study. However, by the early seventies, dissenters were openly calling this approach far too narrow. It excluded unobservable mental events such as ideas and emotions. Thus rose cognitive science, the study of the mind, or perception, thought, and memory.

Now psychologists were encouraged to ask human subjects what they thought and how they felt about things. Self-report questionnaires emerged as a legitimate research tool. Psychologists were encouraged to escape laboratory confines—to study real people in the real world. Once out there, they discovered that there was plenty to mine.

Throughout the seventies, soaring divorce rates, loneliness, and isolation began to dominate the emotional landscape of America. By the end of that decade, love had become a pathology. No longer was the question "What is love?" thought to be trivial. "People in our culture dissolve unions when love disappears, which has a lasting effect on society," says Berscheid. Besides, "we already understood the mating habits of the stickleback fish." It was time to turn to a new species.

Today there are hundreds of research papers on love. Topics range from romantic ideals to attachment styles of the

Reprinted with permission from *Psychology Today*, March/April 1993, pp. 30-34, 36-39, 80. © 1993 by Sussex Publishers, Inc.

young and unmarried. "There were maybe a half dozen when I wrote my dissertation on romantic attraction in 1969," reports Aron. These days, a national association and an international society bring "close relationship" researchers close together annually. Together or apart they are busy producing and sharing new theories, new questionnaires to use as research instruments, and new findings. Their unabashed aim: to improve the human condition by helping us to understand, to repair, and to perfect our love relationships.

SO WHAT *IS* LOVE?

"If there is anything that we have learned about love it is its variegated nature," says Clyde Hendrick, Ph.D., of Texas Tech University in Lubbock. "No one volume or theory or research program can capture love and transform it into a controlled bit of knowledge."

Instead, scholars are tackling specific questions about love in the hopes of nailing down a few facets at a time. The expectation is that every finding will be a building block in the base of knowledge, elevating understanding.

Elaine Hatfield, Ph.D., now of the University of Hawaii, has carved out the territory of passionate love. Along with Berscheid, Hatfield was at the University of Minnesota in 1964 when Stanley Schacter, formerly a professor there and still a great presence, proposed a new theory of emotion. It said that any emotional state requires two conditions: both physiological arousal and relevant situational cues. Already studying close relationships, Hatfield and Berscheid were intrigued. Could the theory help to explain the turbulent, all-consuming experience of passionate love?

Hatfield has spent a good chunk of her professional life examining passionate love, "a state of intense longing for union with another." In 1986, along with sociologist Susan Sprecher, she devised the Passionate Love Scale (PLS), a questionnaire that measures thoughts and feelings she previously identified as distinctive of this "emotional" state.

Lovers rate the applicability of a variety of descriptive statements. To be passionately in love is to be preoccupied with thoughts of your partner much of the time. Also, you likely idealize your partner. So those of you who are passionately in love would, for example,

give "I yearn to know all about—" a score somewhere between "moderately true" and "definitely true" on the PLS.

True erotic love is intense and involves taking risks. It seems to demand a strong sense of self.

The quiz also asks subjects if they find themselves trying to determine the other's feelings, trying to please their lover, or making up excuses to be close to him or her—all hallmarks of passionate, erotic love. It canvasses for both positive and negative feelings. "Passionate lovers," explains Hatfield, "experience a roller coaster of feelings: euphoria, happiness, calm, tranquility, vulnerability, anxiety, panic, despair."

For a full 10 percent of lovers, previous romantic relationships proved so painful that they hope they will never love again.

Passionate love, she maintains, is kindled by "a sprinkle of hope and a large dollop of loneliness, mourning, jealousy, and terror." It is, in other words, fueled by a juxtaposition of pain and pleasure. According to psychologist Dorothy Tennov, who interviewed some 500 lovers, most of them expect their romantic experiences to be bittersweet. For a full 10 percent of them, previous romantic relationships proved so painful that they hope never to love again.

Contrary to myths that hold women responsible for romance, Hatfield finds that both males and females love with equal passion. But men fall in love faster. They are, thus, more romantic. Women are more apt to mix pragmatic concerns with their passion.

And people of all ages, even four-year-old children, are capable of "falling passionately in love." So are people of any ethnic group and socioeconomic stratum capable of passionate love.

Hatfield's most recent study, of love in three very different cultures, shows that

romantic love is not simply a product of the Western mind. It exists among diverse cultures worldwide.

Taken together, Hatfield's findings support the idea that passionate love is an evolutionary adaptation. In this scheme, passionate love works as a bonding mechanism, a necessary kind of interpersonal glue that has existed since the start of the human race. It assures that procreation will take place, that the human species will be perpetuated.

UP FROM THE SWAMP

Recent anthropological work also supports this notion. In 1991, William Jankowiak, Ph.D., of the University of Nevada in Las Vegas, and Edward Fischer, Ph.D., of Tulane University published the first study systematically comparing romantic love across 166 cultures.

They looked at folklore, indigenous advice about love, tales about lovers, love potion recipes—anything related. They found "clear evidence" that romantic love is known in 147, or 89 percent, of cultures. Further, Jankowiak suspects that the lack of proof in the remaining 19 cultures is due more to field workers' oversights than to the absence of romance.

Unless prompted, few anthropologists recognize romantic love in the populations that they study, explains Jankowiak. Mostly because romance takes different shapes in different cultures, they do not know what to look for. They tend to recognize romance only in the form it takes in American culture—a progressive phenomenon leading from flirtation to marriage. Elsewhere, it may be a more fleeting fancy. Still, reports Jankowiak, "when I ask them specific questions about behavior, like 'Did couples run away from camp together?', almost all of them have a positive response."

For all that, there is a sizable claque of scholars who insist that romantic love is a cultural invention of the last 200 years or so. They point out that few cultures outside the West embrace romantic love with the vigor that we do. Fewer still build marriage, traditionally a social and economic institution, on the individualistic pillar of romance.

Romantic love, this thinking holds, consists of a learned set of behaviors; the phenomenon is culturally transmitted from one generation to the next by example, stories, imitation, and direct instruc-

LOVE ME TENDER

How To Make Love to a Man
(what men like, in order of importance)

taking walks together
kissing
candle-lit dinners
cuddling
hugging
flowers
holding hands
making love
love letters
sitting by the fireplace

How To Make Love to a Woman
(what women like, in order of importance)

taking walks together
flowers
kissing
candle-lit dinners
cuddling
declaring "I love you"
love letters
slow dancing
hugging
giving surprise gifts

tion. Therefore, it did not rise from the swamps with us, but rather evolved with culture.

THE ANXIOUS ARE ITS PREY

Regardless whether passionate, romantic love is universal or unique to us, there is considerable evidence that what renders people particularly vulnerable to it is anxiety. It whips up the wherewithal to love. And anxiety is not alone; in fact, there are a number of predictable precursors to love.

To test the idea that emotions such as fear, which produces anxiety, can amplify attraction, Santa Cruz's Arthur Aron recorded the responses of two sets of men to an attractive woman. But one group first had to cross a narrow 450-foot-long bridge that swayed in the wind over a 230-foot drop—a pure prescription for anxiety. The other group tromped confidently across a seemingly safe bridge. Both groups encountered Miss Lovely, a decoy, as they stepped back onto terra firm.

Aron's attractive confederate stopped each young man to explain that she was doing a class project and asked if he would complete a questionnaire. Once he finished, she handed him her telephone number, saying that she would be happy to explain her project in greater detail.

Who called? Nine of the 33 men on the suspension bridge telephoned, while only two of the men on the safe bridge called. It is not impossible that the callers simply wanted details on the project, but Aron suspects instead that a combustible mix of excitement and anxiety prompted the men to become interested in their attractive interviewee.

Along similar if less treacherous lines, Aron has most recently looked at eleven possible precursors to love. He compiled the list by conducting a comprehensive literature search for candidate items. If you have a lot in common with or live and work close to someone you find attractive, your chances of falling in love are good, the literature suggests.

Other general factors proposed at one time or another as good predictors include being liked by the other, a partner's positive social status, a partner's ability to fill your needs, your readiness for entering a relationship, your isolation from others, mystery, and exciting surroundings or circumstances. Then there are specific cues, like hair color, eye expression, and face shape.

Love depends as much on the perception of being liked as on the presence of a desirable partner. Love isn't possible without it.

To test the viability and relative importance of these eleven putative factors, Aron asked three different groups of people to give real-life accounts of falling in love. Predictably, desirable characteristics, such as good looks and personality, made the top of the list. But proximity, readiness to develop a relationship, and exciting surroundings and circumstances ranked close behind.

The big surprise: reciprocity. Love is at heart a two-way event. The perception of being liked ranked just as high as the presence of desirable characteristics in

the partner. "The combination of the two appears to be very important," says Aron. In fact, love just may not be possible without it.

Sprecher and his colleagues got much the same results in a very recent cross-cultural survey. They and their colleagues interviewed 1,667 men and women in the U.S., Russia, and Japan. They asked the people to think about the last time they had fallen in love or been infatuated. Then they asked about the circumstance that surrounded the love experience.

Surprisingly, the rank ordering of the factors was quite similar in all three cultures. In all three, men and women consider reciprocal liking, personality, and physical appearance to be especially important. A partner's social status and the approval of family and friends are way down the list. The cross-cultural validation of predisposing influences suggests that reciprocal liking, desirable personality and physical features may be universal elements of love, among the *sine qua non* of love, part of its heart and soul.

FRIENDSHIP OVER PASSION

Another tack to the intangible of love is the "prototype" approach. This is the study of our conceptions of love, what we "think" love is.

In 1988, Beverly Fehr, Ph.D., of the University of Winnipeg in Canada conducted a series of six studies designed to determine what "love" and "commitment" have in common. Assorted theories suggested they could be anything from mutually inclusive to completely separate. Fehr asked subjects to list characteristics of love and to list features of commitment. Then she asked them to determine which qualities were central and which more peripheral to each.

People's concepts of the two were to some degree overlapping. Such elements as trust, caring, respect, honesty, devotion, sacrifice, and contentment were deemed attributes of both love and commitment. But such other factors as intimacy, happiness, and a desire to be with the other proved unique to love (while commitment alone demanded perseverance, mutual agreement, obligation, and even a feeling of being trapped).

The findings of Fehr's set of studies, as well as others', defy many expectations. Most subjects said they consider

caring, trust, respect, and honesty central to love—while passion-related events like touching, sexual passion, and physical attraction are only peripheral. "They are not very central to our concept of love," Fehr shrugs.

Recently, Fehr explored gender differences in views of love—and found remarkably few. Both men and women put forth friendship as primary to love. Only in a second study, which asked subjects to match their personal ideal of love to various descriptions, did any differences show up. More so than women, men tended to rate erotic, romantic love closer to their personal conception of love.

Both men and women deem romance and passion far less important than support and warm fuzzies . . .

Still, Fehr is fair. On the whole, she says, "the essence, the core meaning of love differs little." Both genders deem romance and passion far less important than support and warm fuzzies. As even Nadine Crenshaw, creator of steamy romance novels, has remarked, "love gets you to the bathroom when you're sick."

LOVE ME TENDER

Since the intangible essence of love cannot be measured directly, many researchers settle for its reflection in what people do. They examine the behavior of lovers.

Clifford Swensen, Ph.D., professor of psychology at Purdue University, pioneered this approach by developing a scale with which to measure lovers' behavior. He produced it from statements people made when asked what they did for, said to, or felt about people they loved . . . and how these people behaved towards them.

Being supportive and providing encouragement are important behaviors to all love relationships—whether with a friend or mate, Swensen and colleagues found. Subjects also gave high ratings to self-disclosure, or talking about personal matters, and a sense of agreement on important topics.

But two categories of behaviors stood out as unique to romantic relationships.

Lovers said that they expressed feelings of love verbally; they talked about how they enjoyed being together, how they missed one another when apart, and other such murmurings. They also showed their affection through physical acts like hugging and kissing.

Elaborating on the verbal and physical demonstrations of love, psychologist Raymond Tucker, Ph.D., of Bowling Green State University in Ohio probed 149 women and 48 men to determine "What constitutes a romantic act?" He asked subjects, average age of 21, to name common examples. There was little disagreement between the genders.

Both men and women most often cited "taking walks" together. For women, "sending or receiving flowers" and "kissing" followed close on its heels, then "candle-lit dinners" and "cuddling." Outright declarations of "I love you came in a distant sixth. (Advisory to men: The florists were right all along. Say it with flowers instead.)

. . . as one romance novelist confides, "love gets you to the bathroom when you're sick."

For men, kissing and "candle-lit dinners" came in second and third. If women preferred demonstrations of love to outright declarations of it, men did even more so; "hearing and saying 'I love you didn't even show up among their top ten preferences. Nor did "slow dancing or giving or receiving surprise gifts," although all three were on the women's top-ten list. Men likewise listed three kinds of activity women didn't even mention: "holding hands," "making love"—and "sitting by the fireplace." For both sexes, love is more tender than most of us imagined.

All in all, says Tucker, lovers consistently engage in a specific array of actions. "I see these items show up over and over and over again." They may very well be the bedrock behaviors of romantic love.

SIX COLORS OF LOVE

That is not to say that once in love we all behave alike. We do not. Each of us

has a set of attitudes toward love that colors what we do. While yours need not match your mate's, you best understand your partner's approach. It underlies how your partner is likely to treat you.

There are six basic orientations toward love, Canadian sociologist John Allen Lee first suggested in 1973. They emerged from a series of studies in which subjects matched story cards, which contain statements projecting attitudes, to their own personal relationships. In 1990 Texas Tech's Clyde Hendrick, along with wife/colleague Susan Hendrick, Ph.D., produced a Love Attitude Scale to measure all six styles. You may embody more than one of these styles. You are also likely to change style with time and circumstance.

Both men and women prefer demonstrations of love to outright declarations of it.

You may, for example, have spent your freewheeling college years as an Eros lover, passionate and quick to get involved, setting store on physical attraction and sexual satisfaction. Yet today you may find yourself happy as a Storge lover, valuing friendship-based love, preferring a secure, trusting relationship with a partner of like values.

There are Ludus lovers, game-players who like to have several partners at one time. Their partners may be very different from one another, as Ludus does not act on romantic ideals. Mania-type lovers, by contrast, experience great emotional highs and lows. They are very possessive—and often jealous. They spend a lot of their time doubting their partner's sincerity.

Pragma lovers are, well, pragmatic. They get involved only with the "right" guy or gal—someone who fills their needs or meets other specifications. This group is happy to trade drama and excitement for a partner they can build a life with. In contrast, Agape, or altruistic, lovers form relationships because of what they may be able to give to their partner. Even sex is not an urgent concern of theirs. "Agape functions on a more spiritual level," Hendrick says.

The Hendricks have found some gender difference among love styles. In general, men are more ludic, or game-playing. Women tend to be more storgic,

THE COLORS OF LOVE

How do I love thee? At least six are the ways.

There is no one type of love; there are many equally valid ways of loving. Researchers have consistently identified six attitudes or styles of love that, to one degree or another, encompass our conceptions of love and color our romantic relationships. They reflect both fixed personality traits and more malleable attitudes. Your relative standing on these dimensions may vary over time—being in love NOW will intensify your responses in some dimensions. Nevertheless, studies show that for most people, one dimension of love predominates.

Answering the questions below will help you identify your own love style, one of several important factors contributing to the satisfaction you feel in relationships. You may wish to rate yourself on a separate sheet of paper. There are no right or wrong answers, nor is there any scoring system. The test is designed to help you examine your own feelings and to help you understand your own romantic experiences.

After you take the test, if you are currently in a relationship, you may want to ask your partner to take the test and then compare your responses. Better yet, try to predict your partner's love attitudes before giving the test to him or her.

Studies show that most partners are well-correlated in the areas of love passion and intensity (Eros), companionate or friendship love (Storge), dependency (Mania), and all-giving or selfless love (Agape). If you and your partner aren't a perfect match, don't worry. Knowing your styles can help you manage your relationship.

Directions: Listed below are several statements that reflect different attitudes about love. For each statement, fill in the response on an answer sheet that indicates how much you agree or disagree with that statement. The items refer to a specific love relationship. Whenever possible, answer the questions with your current partner in mind. If you are not currently dating anyone, answer the questions with your most recent partner in mind. If you have never been in love, answer in terms of what you think your responses would most likely be.

FOR EACH STATEMENT:

A = Strongly agree with the statement
B = Moderately agree with the statement
C = Neutral, neither agree nor disagree
D = Moderately disagree with the statement
E = Strongly disagree with the statement

Eros

Measures passionate love as well as intimacy and commitment. It is directly and strongly correlated with satisfaction in a relationship, a major ingredient in relationship success. Eros gives fully, intensely, and takes risks in love; it requires substantial ego strength. Probably reflects secure attachment style.

1. My partner and I were attracted to each other immediately after we first met.

2. My partner and I have the right physical "chemistry" between us.

3. Our lovemaking is very intense and satisfying.

4. I feel that my partner and I were meant for each other.

5. My partner and I became emotionally involved rather quickly.

6. My partner and I really understand each other.

7. My partner fits my ideal standards of physical beauty/handsomeness.

Ludus

Measures love as an interaction game to be played out with diverse partners. Relationships do not have great depth of feeling. Ludus is wary of emotional intensity from others, and has a manipulative or cynical quality to it. Ludus is negatively related to satisfaction in relationships. May reflect avoidant attachment style.

8. I try to keep my partner a little uncertain about my commitment to him/her.

9. I believe that what my partner doesn't know about me won't hurt him/her.

10. I have sometimes had to keep my partner from finding out about other partners.

11. I could get over my affair with my partner pretty easily and quickly.

12. My partner would get upset if he/she knew of some of the things I've done with other people.

13. When my partner gets too dependent on me, I want to back off a little.

14. I enjoy playing the "game of love" with my partner and a number of other partners.

Storge

Reflects an inclination to merge love and friendship. Storgic love is solid, down to earth, presumably enduring. It is evolutionary, not revolutionary, and may take time to develop. It is related to satisfaction in long-term relationships.

15. It is hard for me to say exactly when our friendship turned to love.

16. To be genuine, our love first required caring for a while.

17. I expect to always be friends with my partner.

18. Our love is the best kind because it grew out of a long friendship.

19. Our friendship merged gradually into love over time.

20. Our love is really a deep friendship, not a mysterious, mystical emotion.

21. Our love relationship is the most satisfying because it developed from a good friendship.

Pragma

Reflects logical, "shopping list" love, rational calculation with a focus on desired attributes of a lover. Suited to computer-matched dating. Related to satisfaction in long-term relationships.

22. I considered what my partner was going to become in life before I committed myself to him/her.

23. I tried to plan my life carefully before choosing my partner.

24. In choosing my partner, I believed it was best to love someone with a similar background.

25. A main consideration in choosing my partner was how he/she would reflect on my family.

26. An important factor in choosing my partner was whether or not he/she would be a good parent.

27. One consideration in choosing my partner was how he/she would reflect on my career.

28. Before getting very involved with my partner, I tried to figure out how compatible his/her hereditary background would be with mine in case we ever had children.

Mania

Measures possessive, dependent love. Associated with high emotional expressiveness and disclosure, but low self-esteem; reflects uncertainty of self in the relationship. Negatively associated with relationship satisfaction. May reflect anxious/ambivalent attachment style.

29. When things aren't right with my partner and me, my stomach gets upset.

30. If my partner and I break up, I would get so depressed that I would even think of suicide.

31. Sometimes I get so excited about being in love with my partner that I can't sleep.

32. When my partner doesn't pay attention to me, I feel sick all over.

33. Since I've been in love with my partner, I've had trouble concentrating on anything else.

34. I cannot relax if I suspect that my partner is with someone else.

35. If my partner ignores me for a while, I sometimes do stupid things to try to get his/her attention back.

Agape

Reflects all-giving, selfless, nondemanding love. Associated with altruistic, committed, sexually idealistic love. Like Eros, tends to flare up with "being in love now."

36. I try to always help my partner through difficult times.

37. I would rather suffer myself than let my partner suffer.

38. I cannot be happy unless I place my partner's happiness before my own.

39. I am usually willing to sacrifice my own wishes to let my partner achieve his/hers.

40. Whatever I won is my partner's to use as he/she chooses.

41. When my partner gets angry with me, I still love him/her fully and unconditionally.

42. I would endure all things for the sake of my partner.

Adapted from Hendrick, Love Attitudes Scale

more pragmatic—and more manic. However, men and women seem to be equally passionate and altruistic in their relationships. On the whole, say the Hendricks, the sexes are more similar than different in style.

Personality traits, at least one personality trait, is strongly correlated to love style, the Hendricks have discovered. People with high self-esteem are more apt to endorse eros, but less likely to endorse mania than other groups. "This finding fits with the image of a secure, confident eros lover who moves intensely but with mutuality into a new relationship," they maintain.

When they turned their attention to ongoing relationships, the Hendricks' found that couples who stayed together over the course of their months-long study were more passionate and less game-playing than couples who broke up. "A substantial amount of passionate love" and "a low dose of game-playing" love are key to the development of satisfying relationships—at least among the college kids studied.

YOUR MOTHER MADE YOU DO IT

The love style you embrace, how you treat your partner, may reflect the very first human relationship you ever had—probably with Mom. There is growing evidence supporting "attachment theory," which holds that the rhythms of response by a child's primary care giver affect the development of personality and influence later attachment processes, including adult love relationships.

First put forth by British psychiatrist John Bowlby in the 1960s and elaborated by American psychologist Mary Ainsworth, attachment theory is the culmination of years of painstaking observation of infants and their adult caregivers—and those separated from them—in both natural and experimental situations. Essentially it suggests that there are three major patterns of attachment; they develop within the first year of life and

stick with us, all the while reflecting the responsiveness of the caregiver to our needs as helpless infants.

Those whose mothers, or caregivers, were unavailable or unresponsive may grow up to be detached and nonresponsive to others. Their behavior is Avoidant in relationships. A second group takes a more Anxious-Ambivalent approach to relationships, a response set in motion by having mothers they may not have been able to count on—sometimes responsive, other times not. The lucky among us are Secure in attachment, trusting and stable in relationships, probably the result of having had consistently responsive care.

While attachment theory is now driving a great deal of research on children's social, emotional, and cognitive development, University of Denver psychologists Cindy Hazan and Philip Shaver set out not long ago to investigate the possible effect of childhood relationships on adult attachments. First, they developed descriptive statements that reflect each of the three attachment styles. Then they asked people in their community, along with college kids, which statements best describe how they relate to others. They asked, for example, about trust and jealousy, about closeness and desire for reciprocation, about emotional extremes.

The distribution of the three attachment styles has proved to be about the same in grown-ups as in infants, the same among collegians as the fully fledged. More than half of adult respondents call themselves Secure; the rest are split between Avoidant and Ambivalent. Further, their adult attachment patterns predictably reflect the relationship they report with their parents. Secure people generally describe their parents as having been warm and supportive. What's more, these adults predictably differ in success at romantic love. Secure people reported happy, long-lasting relationships. Avoidants rarely found love.

Secure adults are more trusting of their romantic partners and more confident of a partner's love, report Australian psychologists Judith Feeney and Patricia Noller of the University of

Queensland. The two surveyed nearly 400 college undergraduates with a questionnaire on family background and love relationships, along with items designed to reveal their personality and related traits.

In contrast to the Secure, Avoidants indicated an aversion to intimacy. The Anxious-Ambivalent participants were characterized by dependency and what Feeney and Noller describe as "a hunger" for commitment. Their approach resembles the Mania style of love. Each of the three groups reported differences in early childhood experience that could account for their adult approach to relationships. Avoidants, for example, were most likely to tell of separations from their mother.

It may be, Hazan and Shaver suggest, that the world's greatest love affairs are conducted by the Ambitious-Ambivalents—people desperately searching for a kind of security they never had.

THE MAGIC NEVER DIES

Not quite two decades into the look at love, it appears as though love will not always mystify us. For already we are beginning to define what we think about it, how it makes us feel, and what we do when we are in love. We now know that it is the insecure, rather than the confident, who fall in love more readily. We know that outside stimuli that alter our emotional state can affect our susceptibility to romance; it is not just the person. We now know that to a certain extent your love style is set by the parenting you received. And, oh yes, men are more quickly romantic than women.

The best news may well be that when it comes to love, men and women are more similar than different. In the face of continuing gender wars, it is comforting to think that men and women share an important, and peaceful, spot of turf. It is also clear that no matter how hard we look at love, we will always be amazed and mesmerized by it.

PSYCHOLOGISTS
AT THE "LOVE LAB"
ARE USING SCIENCE
TO UNCOVER THE
REAL REASON
WHY MARRIAGES
SUCCEED OR FAIL.

What Makes Love Last?

Alan AtKisson

Alan AtKisson is a writer, songwriter, and consultant living in Seattle, Washington. He and partner, Denise Benitez, recently celebrated their ninth wedding anniversary by hiking in the North Cascades.

My old friends Karen and Bill, married since 1955, recently celebrated another anniversary. "I wore the same nightgown I wore on our wedding night," confessed Karen to me over the phone. "Just as I have every anniversary for thirty-nine years."

"I wore pajamas on our wedding night," offered Bill. "But last night I didn't wear nothin'." They laughed, and even over three thousand miles of telephone wire I felt the strength of their love for one another.

Long-lasting marriages like Bill's and Karen's are becoming increasingly rare. Not only do more than 50 percent of all first marriages in the United States end in divorce (make that 60 percent for repeat attempts), but fewer people are even bothering to tie the slippery knot in the first place. One fourth of Americans eighteen or older—about 41 million people—have never married at all. In 1970, that figure was only one sixth.

But even while millions of couples march down the aisle only to pass through the therapist's office and into divorce court, a quiet revolution is taking place when it comes to understanding how long-term love really works. Inside the laboratories of the Family Formation Project at the University of Washington in Seattle—affectionately dubbed the Love Lab—research psychologists are putting our most cherished relationship theories under the scientific microscope. What they're discovering is that much of what we regard as conventional wisdom is simply wrong.

"Almost none of our theory and practice [in marital therapy] is founded on empirical scientific research," contends the Love Lab's head, John Gottman, an award-winning research psychologist trained both as a therapist and a mathematician. Indeed, it is this lack of solid research, Gottman believes, that contributes to a discouraging statistic: for 50 percent of married couples who enter therapy, divorce is still the end result.

Gottman believes that, although relationship counseling has helped many people, much of it just doesn't work. Not satisfied with warm and fuzzy ideas about how to "get the love you want," Gottman is scouting for numbers, data, *proof*—and he's finding it.

From *New Age Journal,* September/October 1994, pp. 74-79, 146-148. © 1994 by New Age Publishing, Inc. Reprinted by permission.

For the past twenty years, in a laboratory equipped with video cameras, EKGs, and an array of custom-designed instruments, Gottman and his colleagues have been intensely observing what happens when couples interact. He watches them talk. He watches them fight. He watches them hash out problems and reaffirm their love. He records facial expressions and self-reported emotions, heart rhythms and blood chemistry. He tests urine, memories, and couples' ability to interpret each other's emotional cues. Then he pours his data, like so many puzzle pieces, into a computer. The resulting picture, he says, is so clear and detailed it's like "a CAT scan of a living relationship." [See "Putting Love to the Test," at right.]

What Gottman and his colleagues have discovered—and summarized for popular audiences in a new book, *Why Marriages Succeed or Fail* (Simon & Schuster) —is mind-boggling in its very simplicity. His conclusion: Couples who stay together are . . . well . . . *nice* to each other more often than not. "[S]atisfied couples," claims Gottman, "maintained a five-to-one ratio of positive to negative moments" in their relationship. Couples heading for divorce, on the other hand, allow that ratio to slip below one-to-one.

If it ended there, Gottman's research

Fighting, whether rare or frequent, is sometimes the healthiest thing a couple can do for their relationship.

might remain just an interesting footnote. But for him and his colleagues, this discovery is just the beginning. In fact, Gottman's novel and methodical approach to marriage research is threatening to turn much of current relationship therapy on its head. He contends that many aspects of wedded life often considered critical to long-term success— how intensely people fight; whether they face conflict or avoid it; how well they solve problems; how compatible they are socially, financially, even sexually

—are less important than people (including therapists) tend to think. In fact, Gottman believes, none of these things matter to a marriage's longevity as much as maintaining that crucial ratio of five to one.

If it's hard to believe that the longevity of your relationship depends primarily on your being five times as nice as you are nasty to each other, some of Gottman's other conclusions may be even more surprising. For example:

❤ Wildly explosive relationships that vacillate between heated arguments and passionate reconciliations can be as happy—and long-lasting—as those that seem

more emotionally stable. They may even be more exciting and intimate.

❤ Emotionally inexpressive marriages, which may seem like repressed volcanoes destined to explode, are actually very successful—so long as the couple maintains that five-to-one ratio in what they do express to each other. In fact, too much emotional catharsis among such couples can "scare the hell out of them," says Gottman.

❤ Couples who start out complaining about each other have some of the most stable marriages over time, while those who don't fight early on are more likely to hit the rocky shoals of divorce.

Putting Love to the Test

How the "Love Lab" researchers decode blood, sweat, and tears.

THE STUDIO APARTMENT IS TINY, BUT IT affords a great view of Seattle's Portage Bay. The ambiance is that of a dorm room tastefully furnished in late-'80s Sears, Roebuck. A cute kitchen table invites you to the window. A Monet print graces one wall. Oh, and three video cameras—suspended from the ceiling like single-eyed bats—follow your every move.

Welcome to the "Love Lab," wherein Professor John Gottman and a revolving crew of students and researchers monitor the emotions, behaviors, and hormones of married couples. Today, lab coordinator Jim Coan—a calm, clear-eyed, pony-tailed young man in Birkenstocks who started out as a student volunteer three years ago—is giving me the tour.

The Love Lab is actually two labs. I have entered through the "Apartment Lab," whose weekly routine Coan describes: A volunteer couple arrives on a Sunday morning, prepared to spend the day being intensely observed (for which they are modestly compensated). Special microphones record every sound they make; videotape captures every subtle gesture. The only true privacy is found in the bathroom, but even there science has a presence: A cooler by the toilet has two

little urine collection bottles, today marked "Bill" and "Jeannie."

At the end of a relaxed day doing whatever they like (and being watched doing it), the couple welcomes a house guest—a psychologist who listens to the story of how they met, fell in love, and began building a life together. This "oral history," which most people greatly enjoy telling, will later be closely scrutinized: Gottman and company have learned that how fondly a couple remembers this story can predict whether they will stay together or divorce.

Then, after a sleep-over on the Lab's hide-a-bed (cameras and microphones off) and a blood sample, a technician takes the pair out for breakfast, gives them their check, and sends them on their way. The videotapes will later be analyzed in voluminous detail. Every affectionate gesture, sarcastic jab, or angry dispute will be recorded and categorized using Gottman's "specific affect" emotional coding system (the lab folks call it SPAFF for short). At the same time, the couple's blood and urine will be sent to another lab and tested for stress hormone levels. Finally, in four years or so (depending on the study), the lab will follow up with the

❤ Fighting, whether rare or frequent, is sometimes the healthiest thing a couple can do for their relationship. In fact, blunt anger, appropriately expressed, "seems to immunize marriages against deterioration."

❤ In happy marriages, there are no discernible gender differences in terms of the quantity and quality of emotional expression. In fact, men in happy marriages are more likely to reveal intimate personal information about themselves than women. (When conflict erupts, however, profound gender differences emerge.)

❤ Men who do housework are likely to have happier marriages, greater physical health, even better sex lives than men who don't. (This piece of news alone could cause a run on aprons.)

❤ Women are made physically sick by a relentlessly unresponsive or emotionally contemptuous husband. Gottman's researchers can even tell just how sick: They can predict the number of infectious diseases women in such marriages will suffer over a four-year period.

❤ How warmly you remember the story of your relationship foretells your chances for staying together. In one study that involved taking oral histories

from couples about the unfolding of their relationship, psychologists were able to predict—with an astonishing 94 percent accuracy—which couples would be divorced within three years.

THE THREE VARIETIES OF MARRIAGE

In person, Gottman is a fast-talking, restless intellect, clearly in love with his work. Now in his late forties and seven years into a second marriage (to clinical psychologist Julie Schwartz), he seems very satisfied. Yet, in his book, he sheds

---

couple to see if they're still together—and take another look at the data they gathered to see if a predictable pattern can be discerned.

OTHER COUPLES WHO VISIT THE FAMILY Formation Project, as the "Love Lab" is more formally known, merely pass the pleasant apartment on their way to a less cozy destination: the "Fixed Lab." Here they are seated ("fixed") in plain wooden chairs and hooked up with a dizzying array of instruments—EKG electrodes, finger-pulse detectors, and skin galvanometers ("a fancy word for sweat detectors," says Coan). A thick black spring stretched across their chests registers breathing. Their chair itself is a "jiggleometer," recording every fidget and tremor.

A "facilitator" first interviews the pair about what issues cause conflict in their marriage, then gets them talking about the most contentious ones. Video cameras focus on the couple's faces and chests. Computers track the complex streams of data coming in through the sensors and displays them on a color monitor in a rainbow of blips and graphs.

After fifteen minutes of surprisingly "normal" and often emotional conversa-

tion, the couple are stopped by the facilitator, who plays back the videotape for them. While watching, each partner rates his or her own emotional state at every moment during the conversation, using a big black dial with a scale running from "extremely negative" through "neutral" to "extremely positive." Then the pair watch the tape again, this time in an attempt to similarly judge their partner's emotional state (with widely varying levels of success).

Later, students trained by Coan will review the tape using a specially designed dial and the SPAFF coding system, to chart the feelings being displayed. It's eerie to see the range of human emotional expression represented on a high-tech instrument panel: disgust, contempt, belligerence, domination, criticism, anger, tension, tense humor ("very popular, that one," Coan tells me), defensiveness, whining, sadness, stonewalling, interest, validation, affection, humor, joy, and positive or negative surprise (students made Gottman aware of the two different kinds). In the middle is a neutral setting for when couples are merely exchanging information without noticeable emotion.

BACK IN THE APARTMENT LAB, COAN SHOWS me videos of couples who have agreed to be involved with the media. Two young parents from Houston discuss the stress around caring for their new baby, and Coan gives me the play-by-play: "He's being very defensive here" or "See that deep sigh? She's feeling sad now" or "Now that was a nice validation."

Coan says that most people seem to enjoy the lab experience—and even get some benefit from it (though it's not meant to be therapeutic). Amazingly, even with sensors attached to their ears and fingers and chests, the couples seem to forget that they're being watched. They giggle and cry and manage to create a genuine closeness while fixed under a physiological microscope.

"It's a real privilege to work here," Coan says thoughtfully. Even in a short visit, I feel it too. The observation of intimacy, both its joy and its pain, is more than just scientific video voyeurism. It's as though the love these couples are trying so devotedly to share with each other seeps out of the box, a gift to the watchers.

— A. A.

the mantle of guru in the first sentence: "My personal life has not been a trail of great wisdom in understanding relationships," he says. "My expertise is in the scientific observation of couples."

Gottman began developing this expertise some twenty years ago, when a troubled couple who came to him for help didn't respond well to conventional therapy. In frustration, Gottman suggested that they try videotaping the sessions. "Both the couple and I were astonished by the vividness and clarity on the tape of the pattern of criticism, contempt, and defensiveness they repeatedly fell into," he recalls. "It shocked them into working harder . . . [and] it gave me my life's work."

Struck by the power of impartial observation, Gottman became fascinated with research. His goal: to systematically describe the differences between happy and unhappy couples, and from those observations develop a scientific theory capable of predicting marital success. This seemed a daunting task, both because "marriage is so subjective" and because "personality theory, in psychology, has been a failure at predicting anything."

The result of Gottman's passion is a veritable mountain of data: tens of thousands of observations involving thousands of couples, gathered by the Love Lab's researchers and stored in its computer data-bases. The geography of that mountain reveals a surprising pattern: Successful marriages come in not one but three different varieties, largely determined by how a couple handles their inevitable disagreements. Gottman calls these three types of stable marriages *validating, volatile,* and *conflict-avoiding.*

Validating couples are what most people (including most therapists) have in mind when they think of a "good marriage." Even when these couples don't agree, they "still let their partner know that they consider his or her opinions and emotions valid." They "compromise often and calmly work out their problems to mutual satisfaction as they arise." And when they fight, they know how to listen, acknowledge their differences, and negotiate agreement without screaming at each other. "These couples," Gottman notes, "look and sound a lot like two psychotherapists engaging in a dialogue."

But where modern therapy often goes wrong, says Gottman, is in assuming that this is the only way a marriage can work—and trying to force all couples

Couples who start out complaining about each other have some of the most stable marriages over time.

into the validating mold. While "viewing this style of marriage as the ideal has simplified the careers of marital therapists," it hasn't necessarily helped their clients, he says, who may fall into the other two types of stable pattern.

Volatile couples, in contrast to validating ones, thrive on unfiltered emotional intensity. Their relationships are full of angry growls and passionate sighs, sudden ruptures and romantic reconcilia-

Men who do housework are likely to have happier marriages, greater physical health, even better sex lives than men who don't.

tions. They may fight bitterly (and even unfairly), and they may seem destined for divorce to anyone watching them squabble. But Gottman's data indicate that this pessimism is often misplaced: These couples will stay together if "for every nasty swipe, there are five caresses." In fact, "the passion and relish with which they fight seems to fuel their positive interactions even more." Such couples are more romantic and affectionate than most—but they are also more vulnerable to a decay in that all-important five-to-one ratio (and at their worst, to violence). Trying to change the style of their relationship not only isn't necessary, Gottman says, it probably won't work.

Nor will conflict-avoiding couples, the third type of stable marriage, necessarily benefit from an increase in their emotional expression, he says. Gottman likens such unions to "the placid waters of a summer lake," where neither partner wants to make waves. They keep the peace and minimize argument by constantly agreeing to disagree. "In these relationships, solving a problem usually means ignoring the difference, one partner agreeing to act more like the other . . . or most often just letting time take its course." The universal five-to-one ratio must still be present for the couple to stay together, but it gets translated into a

Four Keys to a Happy Relationship

DESPITE ALL HIS SOPHISTICATED ANALYSIS of how relationships work (and don't work), researcher John Gottman's advice to the lovelorn and fight-torn is really quite simple.

LEARN TO CALM DOWN.
This will cut down on the flooding response that makes further communication so difficult. "The most brilliant and philosophically subtle therapy in the world will have no impact on a couple not grounded in their own bodies to hear it," he says. Once couples are calm enough, suggests Gottman, they can work on three other basic "keys" to improving their relationship.

LEARN TO SPEAK AND LISTEN NONDEFENSIVELY.
This is tough, Gottman admits, but defensiveness is a very dangerous response, and it needs to be interrupted. One of the most powerful things you can do—in addition to working toward the ideal of listening with empathy and speaking without blame—is to "reintro-

much smaller number of swipes and caresses (which are also less intensely expressed). This restrained style may seem stifling to some, but the couple themselves can experience it as a peaceful contentment.

Things get more complicated when the marriage is "mixed"—when, say, a volatile person marries someone who prefers to minimize conflict. But Gottman suggests that, even in these cases, "it may be possible to borrow from each marital style and create a viable mixed style." The most difficult hurdle faced by couples with incompatible fighting styles lies in confronting that core difference

---

duce praise and admiration into your relationship." A little appreciation goes a long way toward changing the chemistry between people.

VALIDATE YOUR PARTNER.
Validation involves "putting yourself in your partner's shoes and imagining his or her emotional state." Let your partner know that you understand how he or she feels, and why, even if you don't agree. You can also show validation by acknowledging your partner's point of view, accepting appropriate responsibility, and apologizing when you're clearly wrong. If this still seems too much of a stretch, at least let your partner know that you're *trying* to understand, even if you're finding it hard.

PRACTICE, PRACTICE, PRACTICE.
Gottman calls this "overlearning," doing something so many times that it becomes second nature. The goal is to be able to calm yourself down, communicate nondefensively, and validate your partner automatically—even in the heat of an argument.

---

and negotiating which style (or combination of styles) they will use. If they can't resolve that primary conflict, it may be impossible to tip the overall balance of their relational life in the direction of five-to-one.

The important thing here is to find a compatible fighting style—not to stop fighting altogether. Gottman is convinced that the "one" in that ratio is just as important as the "five": "What may lead to temporary misery in a marriage —disagreement and anger—may be healthy for it in the long run." Negativity acts as the predator in the ecosystem of marriage, says Gottman. It's the lion that feeds on the weakest antelopes and makes the herd stronger. Couples who never disagree at all may start out happier than others, but without some conflict to resolve their differences, their marriages may soon veer toward divorce because their "ecosystem" is out of balance.

THE FOUR HORSEMEN OF THE APOCALYPSE

Even the most stable marriages of any style can fall apart, and Gottman and company have observed an all-too-predictable pattern in their decline and fall. He likens the process to a cascade—a tumble down the rapids—that starts with the arrival of a dangerous quartet of behaviors. So destructive is their effect on marital happiness, in fact, that he calls these behaviors "The Four Horsemen of the Apocalypse."

The first horseman is criticism: "attacking someone's personality or character" rather than making some specific complaint about his or her behavior. The difference between saying, say, "I wish you had taken care of that bill" (a healthy and specific complaint) and "You never get the bills paid on time!" (a generalizing and blaming attack) is very significant to the listener. Criticism often engenders criticism in return and sets the stage for the second horseman: contempt.

"What separates contempt from criticism," explains Gottman, "is the intention to insult and psychologically abuse your partner." Negative thoughts about the other come out in subtle put-downs, hostile jokes, mocking facial expressions, and name-calling ("You are such an idiot

---

around money"). By now the positive qualities that attracted you to this person seem long ago and far away, and instead of trying to build intimacy, you're ushering in the third horseman.

Defensiveness comes on the heels of contempt as a seemingly reasonable response to attack—but it only makes things worse. By denying responsibility, making excuses, whining, tossing back counter-attacks, and other strategies ("How come I'm the one who always pays the bills?!"), you just accelerate your speed down river. Gottman also warns that it's possible to skip straight to the third horseman by being oversensitive about legitimate complaints.

Once stonewalling (the fourth horseman) shows up, things are looking bleak. Stonewallers simply stop communicating, refusing to respond even in self-defense. Of course, all these "horsemen" drop in on couples once in a while. But when a partner habitually shuts down and withdraws, the final rapids of negativity (what Gottman calls the "Distance and Isolation Cascade") can quickly propel the marriage through whirlpools of hopelessness, isolation, and loneliness over the waterfall of divorce. With the arrival of the fourth horseman, one or both partners is thinking negative thoughts about his or her counterpart most of the time, and the couple's minds—as well as their bodies—are in a perpetual state of defensive red alert.

The stress of conflict eventually sends blood pressure, heart rate, and adrenaline into the red zone—a phenomenon Gottman calls *flooding*. "The body of someone who feels flooded," he writes, "is a confused jumble of signals. It may be hard to breathe.... Muscles tense up and stay tensed. The heart beats fast, and it may seem to beat harder." Emotionally, the flooded person may feel a range of emotions, from fear to anger to confusion.

The bottom line is that flooding is physically uncomfortable, and stonewalling becomes an attempt to escape that discomfort. When flooding becomes chronic, stonewalling can become chronic, too. Eighty-five percent of the time the stonewaller (among heterosexual couples) is the man. The reason for this gender discrepancy is one of many physiological phenomena that Gottman sees as critical to understanding why mar-

Women are made physically sick by a relentlessly unresponsive or emotionally contemptuous husband. Gottman's researchers can even tell just how sick.

riages go sour, and what people can do to fix them.

Though flooding happens to both men and women, it affects men more quickly, more intensely, and for a longer period of time. "Men tend to have shorter fuses and longer-lasting explosions than women," says Gottman. Numerous observations in the laboratory have shown that it often takes mere criticism to set men off, whereas women require something at least on the level of contempt. The reasons for this are left to speculation. "Probably this difference in wiring had evolutionary survival benefits," Gottman conjectures. An added sensitivity to threats may have kept males alert and ready to repel attacks on their families, he suggests, while women calmed down more quickly so they could soothe the children.

Whatever its origin, this ancient biological difference creates havoc in contemporary male-female relationships, because men are also "more tuned in to the internal physiological environment than women," Gottman reports. (For example, men are better at tapping along with their heartbeat.) Men's bodily sensitivity translates into greater physical discomfort during conflict. In short, arguing hurts. The result: "Men are more likely to withdraw emotionally when their bodies are telling them they're upset." Meanwhile, "when men withdraw, women get upset, and they pursue [the issue]"—which gets men more upset.

Here is where physiology meets sociology. Men, says Gottman, need to rely on physiological cues to know how they're feeling. Women, in contrast, rely on social cues, such as what's happening in the conversation.

In addition, men are trained since early

childhood not to build intimacy with others, while women "are given intense schooling on the subject" from an equally early age. Socially, the genders are almost totally segregated (in terms of their own choices of friendships and playmates) from age seven until early adulthood. Indeed, it would seem that cross-gender relationships are set up to fail. "In fact," Gottman writes, "our upbringing couldn't be a worse training ground for a successful marriage."

Yet the challenge is far from insurmountable, as millions of marriages prove. In fact, Gottman's research reveals that "by and large, in happy marriages there are *no* gender differences in emotional expression!" In these marriages, men are just as likely to share intimate emotions as their partners (indeed they may be more likely to reveal personal information about themselves). However, in unhappy marriages, "all the gender differences we've been talking about

Men's bodily sensitivity translates into greater physical discomfort during conflict. The result: Men are more likely to withdraw emotionally.

emerge"—feeding a vicious cycle that, once established, is hard to break.

Married couples who routinely let the Four Horsemen ransack their living rooms face enormous physical and psychological consequences. Gottman's studies show that chronic flooding and negativity not only make such couples more likely to get sick, they also make it very difficult for couples to change how they relate. When your heart is beating rapidly and your veins are constricting in your arms and legs (another evolutionary stress response), it's hard to think fresh, clear thoughts about how you're communicating. Nor can the brain process new information very well. Instead, a flooded person

relies on "overlearned responses"—old relationship habits that probably just fan the flames.

All this physiological data has enormous implications for relationship therapists as well as their clients. Gottman believes that "most of what you see currently in marital therapy—not all of it, but most of it—is completely misguided."

For example, he thinks it's an exercise in futility when "the therapist says 'Calm down, Bertha. Calm down, Max. Let's take a look at this and analyze it. Let's remember the way we were with our mothers.' Bertha and Max can do it in the office because he's doing it for them. But once they get home, and their heart rates get above 100 beats per minute, whew, forget about it."

Teaching psychological skills such as interpreting nonverbal behavior also misses the mark. "We have evidence that husbands in unhappy marriages are terrible at reading their wives' nonverbal behavior. But they're great at reading other people's nonverbal behavior. In other words, they have the social skills, but they aren't using them." The problem isn't a lack of skill; it's the overwhelming feelings experienced in the cycle of negativity. Chronic flooding short-circuits a couple's basic listening and empathy skills, and it undermines the one thing that can turn back the Four Horsemen: the repair attempt.

HEADING OFF DISASTER

Repair attempts are a kind of "metacommunication"—a way of talking about how you're communicating with each other. "Can we please stay on the subject?" "That was a rude thing to say." "We're not talking about your father!" "I don't think you're listening to me." Such statements, even when delivered in a grouchy or complaining tone, are efforts to interrupt the cycle of criticism, contempt, defensiveness, and stonewalling and to bring the conversation back on track.

"In stable relationships," explains Gottman, "the other person will respond favorably: 'Alright, alright. Finish.' The agreement isn't made very nicely. But it does stop the person. They listen, they accept the repair attempt, and they actually change" the way they're relating.

Repair attempts are "really critical," says Gottman, because "everybody screws up. Everybody gets irritated, defensive, contemptuous. People insult one another," especially their spouses. Repair attempts are a way of saying "we've got to fix this before it slides any deeper into the morass." Even people in bad marriages make repair attempts; the problem is, they get ignored.

Training people to receive repair attempts favorably—even in the middle of a heated argument—is one of the new frontiers in relationship therapy. According to Gottman, "Even when things are going badly, you've got to focus not on the negativity but on the repair attempt. That's what couples do in happy mar-

> *Even people in bad marriages make repair attempts; the problem is, they get ignored.*

riages." He's convinced that such skills can be taught: One colleague has even devised a set of flash cards with a variety of repair attempts on them, ranging from "I know I've been a terrible jerk, but can we take this from the top?" to "I'm really too upset to listen right now." [See Upfront, July/August 1993.] Even in mid-tempest, couples can use the cards to practice giving, and receiving, messages about how they're communicating.

Breaking the Four Horsemen cycle is critical, says Gottman, because "the more time [couples] spend in that negative perceptual state, the more likely they are to start making long-lasting attributions about this marriage as being negative." Such couples begin rewriting the story of how they met, fell in love, made commitments. Warm memories about how "we were so crazy about each other" get replaced with "I was *crazy* to marry him/her." And once the story of the marriage has been infected with negativity, the motivation to work on its repair declines. Divorce becomes much more likely (and predictable—consider that 94 percent accuracy rate in the oral history study).

Of course, not all relationships can, or should, be saved. Some couples are trapped in violent relationships, which "are in a class by themselves." Others may suffer a fundamental difference in their preferred style—validating, volatile, or conflict-avoidant—that leaves them stuck in chronic flooding. With hard work, some of these marriages can be saved; trying to save others, however, may do more harm than good.

In the end, the hope for repairing even a broken marriage is to be found, as usual, in the courage and effort people are willing to invest in their own growth and change. "The hardest thing to do," says Gottman, "is to get back to the fundamentals that really make you happy." Couples who fail to do this allow the Four Horsemen to carry them far from the fundamentals of affection, humor, appreciation, and respect. Couples who succeed cultivate these qualities like gardeners. They also cultivate an affirming story of their lives together, understanding that that is the soil from which everything else grows.

The work may be a continuous challenge, but the harvest, as my long-married friends Bill and Karen would say, is an enormous blessing: the joy in being truly known and loved, and in knowing how to love.

The Lovers' Library

A slew of new books appearing in 1994 address some of the most entrenched problems facing long-term lovers:

■ *Hot Monogamy: Essential Steps to More Passionate, Intimate Lovemaking*, by Patricia Love and Jo Robinson (Dutton, 1994). This is a wonderful guide to enriching your sex life in a host of imaginative ways, and to reducing the shame and anxiety caused by differences in sexual appetite. (Also available as an excellent workshop on cassette from The Sounds True Catalog, 800-333-9185.)

■ *When Opposites Attract: Right Brain/Left Brain Relationships and How to Make Them Work*, by Rebecca Cutter (Dutton, 1994). A very helpful and thorough guide to dealing with the wide range of problems that can stem from fundamental differences in brain wiring.

■ *The Couple's Comfort Book: A Creative Guide for Renewing Passion, Pleasure, and Commitment*, by Jennifer Louden (HarperSanFrancisco, 1994). A highly usable compendium of nurturing and imaginative things to do together, cross-referenced so you can hop around the book and design your own program of relationship rebirth.

Prejudice, Discrimination, and Stereotyping

- Prejudice (Articles 31 and 32)
- Discrimination (Articles 33 and 34)
- Stereotyping (Articles 35 and 36)

In colonial America, relatively few people were allowed to vote. Women couldn't. Blacks couldn't. Even white men, if they lacked property, couldn't. It took many years, the Civil War, and the passage of constitutional amendments for this particular form of discrimination to eventually pass from the scene. Even so, many would argue today that discrimination against women, minorities, and those at the lower end of the economic spectrum continues, although usually in less obvious forms. The tendency for humans to make negative judgments about others on the basis of their membership in some social group, and then to act on those judgments, is a powerful one.

As the title implies, this unit covers three distinct but related topics: prejudice, discrimination, and stereotyping. *Prejudice* refers to the negative attitude that is directed toward some people simply because they are members of some particular social group. Thus, the feelings of distaste that one might experience when encountering a member of some minority group would be an example of prejudice. In such a case, the prejudiced feelings would also probably influence the way in which our hypothetical person evaluated and judged everything that the minority group member did. In contrast, *discrimination* refers to a negative action directed toward the members of some particular social group. That is, while prejudice refers only to negative feelings, discrimination crosses the line into actual behavior. Thus, yelling a racial slur, or failing to hire someone because of her religion, would be examples of discrimination. As you might imagine, however, those who hold prejudiced attitudes are generally more likely

to engage in discriminatory behavior as well. The third concept—*stereotyping*—is more cognitive in tone than the other two. Stereotyping refers to the tendency that people have to see all members of a specific social group as being alike—that is, to not recognize the differences that exist and to exaggerate the similarities. Thus, stereotypes per se are distinct from the negative feelings and negative behavior that characterize prejudice and discrimination.

The first unit subsection considers the topic of prejudice, and both articles are concerned with a recent and highly influential approach to studying prejudice. In "Prejudice Is a Habit That Can Be Broken," Beth Azar reports on research suggesting that everyone—prejudiced and nonprejudiced alike—is aware of racial stereotypes and has that knowledge automatically activated by encountering a member of that race. What distinguishes prejudiced and nonprejudiced people is what comes next; prejudiced people largely accept those stereotypes and act on them, while nonprejudiced people consciously inhibit these initial responses and substitute other, more tolerant values. In the second selection, "Breaking the Prejudice Habit," psychologist Patricia Devine takes this argument a bit further and describes some of her own research that supports the idea that nonprejudiced people often find themselves wrestling with conflicting impulses: their immediate prejudiced reaction and their conscious rejection of that response.

The second subsection tackles the issue of discrimination. In "Psychologists Examine Attacks on Homosexuals," author Peter Freiberg discusses an extreme form of discrimination: actual physical violence directed against members of an out-group, in this case, gay males and lesbians. This article not only documents the extent of this frequently overlooked form of discrimination, but it also discusses the role played by the victims' social support network in affecting their responses to the attack. Discrimination does not always take such a blatant form, of course, and in "Crimes against Humanity," Ward Churchill makes the case that the actual language used to describe members of social groups can help perpetuate racial and ethnic prejudice. To illustrate, he offers numerous examples of the ways in which Native Americans are routinely demeaned in U.S. society, especially in the area of sports symbolism.

The third subsection consists of two articles that address stereotyping. In the first, "Whites' Myths about Blacks," specific misconceptions that are part of the stereotypical view of African Americans are detailed. This stereotype contains beliefs about work ethic, willingness to take personal responsibility, and the degree to which African Americans still face discrimination. The final article in this section, "Gendered Media: The Influence of Media on Views of Gender," analyzes the ways in which men and women are typically depicted in television, movies, and magazines. Author Julia Wood contends that images of women in mass media help to create and maintain society's gender stereotypes; she notes that women in the media tend to be young, thin, beautiful, and passive.

Looking Ahead: Challenge Questions

What kind of evidence supports the view that both prejudiced and nonprejudiced people are familiar with negative racial stereotypes? Do you agree that nonprejudiced people must deliberately and consciously attempt to substitute tolerant values for their own unconscious stereotyped beliefs? Does this research suggest any possible solutions to the problem of prejudice in society?

How much power does the use of racially demeaning language have in perpetuating prejudice and discrimination? What did you find the most convincing evidence in the article "Crimes against Humanity?" The least convincing?

What factors contribute to violence against gay males and lesbians? What factors determine the degree to which such violence influences the psychological health of the victims?

Besides men and women, what other social groups are depicted in the media in ways that might perpetuate stereotypes? Racial groups? Occupations? Different age groups? How powerful do you think such depictions are?

Aside from media depictions, where do you think that the information in social stereotypes comes from? For example, although you may not accept it as true, you probably are aware of certain traits that supposedly characterize various racial and ethnic groups. Where did you learn this information?

Prejudice Is a Habit That Can Be Broken

*Peoples' responses are based on cultural stereotypes,
even if they don't believe in those stereotypes.*

Beth Azar

Monitor staff

A black youth sits next to you on an empty subway car. An openly gay man interviews with you for a job in your office. A Hispanic woman asks you for directions. How should you react? How *do* you react?

Few people openly admit they should or would react with prejudice to situations like these. And yet, blatant and more subtle forms of prejudice occur every day. People may withhold promotions from minority persons or may be less willing to give directions or the time of day to someone of a different race.

Even people who score low on the Modern Racism Scale—a widely used test of prejudice—tend to show subtle bias when interacting with certain ethnic groups. They may avoid eye contact and physical closeness or act less friendly.

Automatic Prejudice

Some people claim that prejudice hasn't actually declined over the past 20 years, but is just better disguised. Several researchers addressed these problems and potential solutions in symposia on prejudice and stereotyping.

A powerful technique lets researchers "get inside the heads of subjects" and record subtle unconscious or unadmitted biases, said Russell Fazio, PhD, of Indiana University. The technique, called "priming," records people's subconscious reactions to stimuli.

Subjects are primed by a word or picture, then asked to respond to another stimulus—often a word. For example, a prime could be the face of a white person. After researchers show subjects the face, they ask them to perform certain tasks. The subjects may have to judge adjectives as positive or negative or fill in missing letters to form words.

Priming is based on the idea that thinking of a word activates a spot in the brain where the word is stored as well as connections to other words and ideas related to that word.

So after seeing a prime word people access terms or ideas related to the prime faster than terms or ideas unrelated to the prime. For example, if people are primed with "dog" they will be faster at recognizing "cat" than "car." Researchers get this priming effect even if the prime is shown so quickly that the subject doesn't remember seeing it.

Researchers find prejudicial reactions in many people after numerous priming tasks—even people who claim not to be prejudiced. For example, people primed with a photo of an Asian person holding a sign that says "N_P" most often fill in the blank letter with an "i" to spell NIP—a derogatory term for Asians.

In a recent experiment, Fazio and his colleagues briefly presented high-resolution color images of black and white faces, then had subjects identify obviously positive or negative adjectives as positive or negative by pressing one of two buttons. For example, a subject would see "attractive" and would press the "positive" button. The faster the response, the more related the adjective would be to the prime in the subjects' mind.

They found a highly significant interaction between the race of the person in the photo and the speed of subjects' reaction to positive and negative adjectives. When white subjects saw a black face and then a negative adjective, they responded faster than when they saw a white face. The opposite occurred for positive adjectives.

On average, whites displayed negativity toward blacks, and vice versa, said Fazio. However, there were many individual differences, with some white subjects reacting highly negatively toward blacks and others reacting as positively toward blacks as blacks themselves.

They found that the automatic responses in white subjects predicted subtle nonverbal behaviors in a 10-minute, one-on-one interaction with a black experimenter. The experimenter rated subjects on friendliness, paying attention to such nonverbal behaviors as eye contact, personal distance and smiling. People's scores correlated with their scores on the priming task.

These subtle prejudicial responses don't necessarily mean people will act in an openly biased fashion. Fazio and other prejudice researchers have found that some people are motivated

 From *APA Monitor*, October 1995, p. 28. © 1995 by the American Psychological Association. Reprinted by permission.

'Powerful' People are More Apt to Stereotype

People stereotype other races and cultures to preserve a sense of self and a feeling of personal power, according to research by Steven Spencer, PhD, and Susan Fiske, PhD.

Spencer, of the State University of New York, Buffalo, conducted a series of studies that put subjects in situations that threatened their self-esteem. In one study, subjects took an intelligence test and received either a positive or negative score manipulated by the experimenter. The experimenters rated the subjects' self-esteem using a standard questionnaire. Then subjects rated the qualifications of a hypothetical Jewish-American woman for a job.

Subjects who thought they'd scored low on the intelligence test more often rated the job candidate negatively. A self-esteem test taken afterward showed significant increases in self-esteem after subjects engaged in stereotyping.

He also found that people were more likely to stereotype in such self-esteem-threatening situations if they scored high on the Modern Racism Scale—a standard questionnaire.

"Stereotyping seems to be automatic for some people when they sense a threat to their self-esteem," said Spencer.

Fiske theorizes that people in positions of power tend to engage in more stereotyping. The powerful—bosses, supervisors, managers—are rarely stereotyped themselves because power demands attention and stereotyping demands that one not pay attention.

Two processes make the powerful prone to stereotyping others, said Fiske, of the University of Massachusetts, Amherst. First, because they're powerful, they stereotype by default—they simply don't pay attention to information that makes people unique. Second, when the powerful must justify decisions they make about other people, they stereotype by design. They don't have time to see people as unique so they hear and see only things that confirm their stereotypes.

To test these theories, Fiske and graduate student Stephanie Goodwin had subjects judge hypothetical job applicants. Half of the subjects were given a lot of power in the decision and half were given little power. They reviewed applications from a Hispanic and a white woman.

They found that subjects with the most decision-making power paid less attention to individualizing information and more attention to stereotype-confirming information. For example, the powerful would ignore personal references about the Hispanic woman's efficiency and pay particular attention to references that implied she was ignorant or unreliable. As power increased, use of stereotyping information increased, said Fiske.

The researchers conducted a second study examining whether a dominant personality had any effect on stereotyping. All the subjects had equal power but the researchers found that people with dominant personalities ignored individualizing information and paid particular attention to stereotyping information, just as the powerful subjects had in the previous study.

Fiske imagines the powerful driving around in a fog and tuned into one radio station—the one that confirms their stereotypes.

—Beth Azar

to control overt prejudice depending on the situation. For example, people will temper their answers to the Modern Racism Scale to look less prejudice if the interviewer is black.

There seem to be three types of people: those who are openly prejudiced and show it in their overt and covert actions; those who believe they are not prejudiced and try to act that way, but show some covert signs of bias; and those who believe they are not prejudiced and whose covert actions show no signs of bias.

Not Just Attitude

Patricia Devine, PhD, believes that breaking down prejudice is a process. Like every bad habit, it goes away in stages. Devine is professor of psychology at the University of Wisconsin, Madison. She believes people's responses are based on cultural stereotypes, even if they don't believe in those stereotypes. Low-prejudice people are especially vulnerable to conflict between their beliefs and unintentional responses, said Devine. She asked high- and low-prejudice people how they thought they should respond in interactions with people of different races or sexual orientation.

She then gave them a set of hypothetical interactions and asked them how they would respond in certain situations. She asked, for example, if they would feel uncomfortable being interviewed by a gay man, a black man or a woman. As expected, low-prejudice people thought they should, and would, respond with less prejudice than high-prejudice people did.

However, many low-prejudice people admitted they would respond with more prejudice than they thought they should. When asked how subjects felt immediately after they answered the questions, low-prejudice people who saw a discrepancy between their beliefs and their actions felt guilty, annoyed, and frustrated and were critical of themselves.

The bigger the discrepancy between beliefs and actions, the more people engaged in guilt and other self-directed negative responses. She takes this as evidence that many people who claim to be unprejudiced truly don't want to be.

To test whether self-directed negative responses can help people overcome automatic prejudiced responses, she tested people's responses to racial jokes. She had subjects listen to racial jokes and had those who laughed compare their response to their beliefs about prejudice. The low-prejudice people felt guilty and, as a result, found a second set of jokes less amusing.

"The comparison activates a self-regulatory process," said Devine. "If people don't recognize the discrepancy, however, they won't feel guilt and this process won't activate." Her work shows that even people with a nonprejudice attitude often fail to bring their behaviors in line. "Prejudice appears to be a habit that can be broken," said Devine. "We need to teach people to become skilled rather than try to change their attitudes."

Breaking the Prejudice Habit

Patricia G. Devine, PhD,
University of Wisconsin, Madison

Patricia G. Devine, PhD, is Professor of Psychology at the University of Wisconsin, Madison. Before becoming Professor, she was a Visiting Fellow at Yale University and an Associate Professor at Wisconsin.

Dr. Devine received the Gordon Allport Intergroup Relations Prize from the Society for the Psychological Study of Social Issues in 1990 and the APA Distinguished Scientific Award for Early Career Contribution to Psychology in 1994. She is the author or coauthor of several journal articles and is the coeditor of *Social Cognition: Impact on Social Psychology* (Academic Press, 1994). Her research interests include prejudice and intergroup relations, stereotyping, dissonance, and resistance to persuasion. Dr. Devine received her PhD in Social Psychology from Ohio State University in 1986.

Legal scholars, politicians, legislators, social scientists, and lay people alike have puzzled over the paradox of racism in a nation founded on the fundamental principle of human equality. Legislators responded with landmark legal decisions (e.g., Supreme Court ruling on school desegregation and the Civil Rights laws) that made overt discrimination based on race illegal. In the wake of the legislative changes, social scientists examined the extent to which shifts in whites' attitudes kept pace with the legal changes. The literature, however, reveals conflicting findings. Whereas overt expressions of prejudice on surveys declined (i.e., verbal reports), more subtle indicators (i.e., nonverbal measures) continue to reveal prejudice even among those who say they renounced prejudice. A central challenge presented to contemporary prejudice researchers is to explain the disparity between verbal reports and the more subtle measures.

Some reject the optimistic conclusion suggested by survey research and argue that prejudice in America is not declining; it is only changing form—becoming more subtle and disguised. By this argument, most (if not all) Americans are assumed to be racist, with only the *type* of racism differing between people. Such conclusions are based on the belief that *any* response that results in differential treatment between groups is taken as evidence of prejudice. However, this definition fails to consider *intent* or motive and is based on the assumption that nonthoughtful (e.g., nonverbal) responses are, by definition, more trustworthy than thoughtful responses. Indeed, nonverbal measures are assumed to be good indicators of prejudice precisely because they do not typically involve careful thought and people do not control them in the same way that they can control their verbally reported attitudes.

Rather than dismiss either response as necessarily untrustworthy, my colleagues and I have tried to understand the origin of both thoughtful and nonthoughtful responses. By directly addressing the disparity between thoughtful and nonthoughtful responses, our approach offers a more optimistic analysis regarding prospects for prejudice reduction than the extant formulations. To foreshadow, our program of research has been devoted to understanding (a) how and why those who truly renounce prejudice may continue to experience prejudice-like thoughts and feelings and (b) the nature of the rather formidable challenges and obstacles that must be overcome before one can succeed in reducing the disparity between thoughtful and nonthoughtful responses.

Automatic and Controlled Processes in Prejudice

The distinction between automatic and controlled cognitive processes has been central to our analysis in prejudice reduction. Automatic processes occur unintentionally, spontaneously, and unconsciously. We have evidence that both low- and high-prejudiced people are vulnerable to automatic stereotype activation. Once the stereotype is well-learned, its influence is hard to avoid because it so easily comes to mind. Controlled processes, in contrast, are under the intentional control of the individual. An important aspect of such processes is that their initiation and use requires time and sufficient cognitive *capacity*. Nonprejudiced responses require inhibiting the spontaneously activated stereotypes and deliberately activating personal beliefs to serve as the basis for responses. Without sufficient time or cognitive capacity, responses may well be stereotype-based and, therefore, appear prejudiced.

The important implication of the automatic/controlled process distinction is that if one looks only at nonthoughtful, automatic responses, one may well conclude that all white Americans are prejudiced. We have found important differences between low- and high-prejudiced people based on the personal beliefs that each hold, despite similar knowledge of and vulnerability to the activation of cultural stereotypes. Furthermore, low-prejudiced people have established and internalized nonprejudiced personal standards for how to treat members of stereotyped groups. When given sufficient time, low-prejudiced people censor responses based on the stereotype and, instead, respond based on their beliefs. High-prejudiced people, in contrast, do not reject the stereotype and are not personally motivated to overcome its effect on their behavior.

A strength of this approach is that it delineates the role of both thoughtful and nonthoughtful processes in response to stereotyped group members. Eliminating prejudice requires over-

From *Psychological Science Agenda*, January/February 1996, pp. 10-11. © 1996 by the American Psychological Association. Reprinted by permission.

coming a lifetime of socialization experiences, which, unfortunately, promote prejudice. We have likened reducing prejudice to the breaking of a habit in that people must first make a decision to eliminate the habit and then *learn* to inhibit the habitual (prejudiced) responses. Thus, the change from being prejudiced to nonprejudiced is not viewed as an all or none event, but as a process during which the low-prejudiced person is especially vulnerable to conflict between his or her enduring negative responses and endorsed nonprejudiced beliefs. For those who renounce prejudice, overcoming the "prejudice habit" presents a formidable task that is likely to entail a great deal of internal conflict over a protracted period of time.

Prejudice With and Without Compunction

In subsequent work, we examined the nature and consequences of the internal conflict associated with prejudice reduction. Specifically, we have focused on the challenges faced by those individuals who have internalized nonprejudiced personal standards and are trying to control their prejudiced responses, but sometimes fail. We have shown that people high and low in prejudice (as assessed by a self-report technique) have qualitatively different affective reactions to the conflict between their verbal reports concerning how they *should* respond in situations involving contact with members of stereotyped groups and how they say they actually *would* respond. Low-prejudiced people, for example, believe that they should not feel uncomfortable sitting next to an African American on a bus. High-prejudiced people disagree, indicating that it's acceptable to feel uncomfortable in this situation. When actual responses violate personal standards, low-prejudiced people experience guilt or "prejudice with compunction," but high-prejudiced individuals do not. For low-prejudiced people, the coexistence of such conflicting reactions threatens their nonprejudiced self-concepts. Moreover, these guilt feelings play a functional role in helping people to "break the prejudice habit." That is, violations combined

with guilt have been shown to help low-prejudiced people to use controlled processes to inhibit the prejudiced responses and to replace them with responses that are based on their personal beliefs.

Interpersonal Dynamics of Intergroup Contact

Until recently, our research has focused rather exclusively on the nature of internal conflict associated with prejudice reduction efforts. However, many of the challenges associated with prejudice reduction are played out in the interpersonal arena, and we believe it's important to explore the relevance of our work to issues of intergroup tension. Thus, one of our current lines of research is devoted to exploring the nature of the challenges created by the intergroup contact when people's standards are "put on the line."

In interpersonal intergroup contact situations, we have found that although low-prejudiced people are highly motivated to respond without prejudice, there are few guidelines for "how to do the intergroup thing well." As a result, many experience doubt and uncertainty about how to express their nonprejudiced attitudes in intergroup situations. Thus, for low-prejudiced people, their high motivation to respond without prejudice may actually interfere with their efforts to convey accurately their nonprejudiced intentions. Under these circumstances, they become socially anxious; this anxiety disrupts the typically smooth and coordinated aspects of social interaction. Their interaction styles become awkward and strained resulting in nonverbal behaviors such as decreased eye contact and awkward speech patterns. These are exactly the types of subtle responses that have typically been interpreted as signs of prejudice or antipathy. Indeed, it is not possible to distinguish between the type of tension that arises out of antipathy toward the group or social anxiety based on these signs alone.

We argue that it may be important to acknowledge that there are qualitatively distinct forms of intergroup tension experienced by majority group members, which are systematically related to their self-reported level of prejudice. For some, the tension can arise out of

antipathy, as was always thought in the prejudice literature, but for others, the tension arises out of anxiety over trying to do the intergroup thing well. Functionally then, we have different starting points for trying to reduce intergroup tension. Strategies for attempting to reduce intergroup tension differ when the problem is conceived as one of improving skills rather than one of changing negative attitudes.

Conclusion

To sum up, although it is not easy and clearly requires effort, time, and practice, prejudice appears to be a habit that can be broken. In contrast to the prevailing, pessimistic opinion that little progress is being made toward the alleviation of prejudice, our program of research suggests that many people appear to be embroiled in the difficult or arduous process of overcoming their prejudices. During this process, low-prejudiced people are confronted with rather formidable challenges from within, as people battle their spontaneous reactions, and from the interpersonal settings in which people's standards are put on the line. We are sanguine that by developing a realistic analysis of the practical challenges faced by those who renounce prejudice, we may be able to identify strategies that may facilitate their prejudice reduction efforts.

It is important to recognize that we are not claiming to have solved the problem of intergroup prejudice, nor are we suggesting that prejudice has disappeared. The past several years have witnessed a disturbing increase in the incidence of hate crimes against minorities. And a sizable proportion of white Americans continue to embrace old-fashioned forms of bigotry. Nevertheless, we hope that by developing an understanding of the challenges associated with breaking the prejudice habit, we may gain insight into the reasons low-prejudiced people establish and internalize nonprejudiced standards. Armed with this knowledge, we may be able to encourage high-prejudiced people to renounce prejudice. And when they do, we will be in a better position to understand their challenges and, perhaps, to assist them in their efforts,

Psychologists Examine Attacks on Homosexuals

Gays and lesbians bore the brunt of hate violence in 1994 compared to their relative numbers in society.

Peter Freiberg

Peter Freiberg is a freelance writer in Hudson, N.Y.

In San Francisco, two gay men holding hands during a walk home were confronted by men in a car. After a passenger asked why they were holding hands and a few words were exchanged, the driver maneuvered the vehicle onto the sidewalk, pinning one of the men against the wall while the passenger shot him in the chest.

In Minneapolis, an identified caller assailed two lesbians as "homos" and warned they would be beaten up. Shortly thereafter, their cars were vandalized and their home burglarized.

In New York, a gay photographer was stabbed to death with a kitchen knife in his apartment by a man he met in Greenwich Village. Police arrested a man who had a long record of pick-up related crimes against gay men.

These three incidents, culled from the files of police and groups dedicated to fighting homophobic violence, are among hundreds of incidents reported last year in what some activists and social scientists call an "epidemic" of hate crimes against gay people.

Such bias-motivated crimes against gays—little noticed even a decade ago—are now drawing increasing attention from law enforcement agencies, elected officials and civil-rights groups. In response, psychologists are focusing on antigay hate crimes in their public policy advocacy, research and clinical work.

FBI's latest report show that 11 percent of the 7,587 bias-motivated crimes reported by law enforcement agencies in 1993 were against gay people or people perceived to be gay.

But actual statistics are thought to be even higher (see sidebar). Klanwatch, a Southern Poverty Law Center project that monitors hate crimes, said its figures indicate that gays and lesbians bore the brunt of hate violence in 1994 compared to their relative numbers in society. A study by the New York City Gay and Lesbian Anti-Violence Project said gay organizations in nine cities reported 2,031 antigay incidents in 1993—substantially more than the FBI's figure—and 2,064 such incidents in 1994.

"Among the assault victims, [more than] 25 percent were gay or lesbian," Klanwatch said in a recent report. Of 18 bias-related murders Klanwatch verified last year, 11 were motivated by antigay bias.

Educating the Public

Clinton Anderson, officer for lesbian and gay concerns at the American Psychological Association, says that psychologists' research on antigay violence in particular and bias crime in general has played a major role in educating the public.

Psychologist Anthony D'Augelli, PhD, a professor at Pennsylvania State University, is one psychologist studying the extent of harassment of young gay people and its impact on their mental health.

In a national study, D'Augelli surveyed 194 lesbian, gay male and bisexual youths between ages 15 and 21. The research, he said, provides evidence that victimization—verbal abuse, threats of attack and assaults—has deleterious effects on mental health.

"The more people get put upon, the worse they do in terms of mental health," he said. But victimization, he said, did not seem to be directly linked to suicide attempts.

Family support and self-esteem are two major variables determining how much antigay hate crimes impact mental health, D'Augelli said. Family support, defined as positive reactions to a youth's sexual orientation, "buffered the adolescent against the harmful effects of victimization on mental health," D'Augelli said.

But family support, he found, only seemed to help people ward off the effects of "low-level" victimization, such as name-calling. If the victimization is moderate—such as property destruction—or high—physical attacks—family support does not appear to buffer the individual against the mental health problems engendered by victimization, according to a paper D'Augelli wrote with psychologist Scott Hershberger, PhD, of Penn-

From *APA Monitor*, June 1995, pp. 30-31. © 1995 by Peter Freiberg. Reprinted by permission.

Victims of Hate Crimes Come from All Beliefs, Races, Religions

The April bombing of an Oklahoma City federal building turned the spot light on white supremacist and other groups whose members spout racist, anti-Semitic and often antigay rhetoric and sometimes commit hate crimes.

While hate-crime statistics are incomplete, enough data have accumulated to confirm that bias-motivated violence has become a serious issue and that victims come from all races, religions, ethnic groups and sexual orientations.

In its latest report, which covers 1993, the FBI said that of 7,587 bias-motivated criminal incidents reported by law enforcement agencies, 62 percent were motivated by racial bias; 17 percent by religious bias; 11 percent by sexual-orientation bias; and the remainder by ethnicity/national origin bias.

Of the 9,372 reported victims in 1993, 67 percent were targets of crimes against persons. Six of every 10 victims were attacked because of their race, with blacks making up 38 percent of the victims. Of the incidents motivated by religious bias, 88 percent were anti-Semitic. Intimidation

was the single most frequently reported hate crime, accounting for 34 percent of the total.

But Bryan Levin, legal director of Klanwatch, a division of the Southern Poverty Law Center that monitors hate crimes, estimates that the actual number of hate crimes is five times as high as the FBI's numbers.

The FBI, Levin says, has been "making an assiduous effort" to obtain statistics, but it must depend on voluntary submission by local law enforcement agencies, many of which do not supply information.

Local agencies that do collect hate crime data vary greatly in how they list such crimes. According to Klanwatch, more than half of all bias-motivated crimes are not reported to law enforcement; of those that are, many are not classified by police and prosecutors as hate crimes.

Joe Roy, chief investigator for Klanwatch, says available figures "understate the true level of violent hate crimes."

At the same time, Levin notes that passage of the federal Hate Crimes Sta-

tistics Act of 1990, together with the U.S. Supreme Court's 1993 ruling that hate-crime laws are constitutional, have encouraged "greater recognition and acceptance by law enforcement of this type of crime."

Hate-crime laws—which raise penalties for crimes motivated by bias—are on the books in more than 40 states, although only about half include sexual orientation. Levin cautions, however, that laws can do only so much. "This isn't a problem that is limited to the criminal justice system." Asserting that education is crucial, Levin says, "We're just on the verge now of sending a clear message that status-motivated violence is intolerable in our society, but we have a long way to go."

According to a Klanwatch report issued last March, one hate group—the neo-Nazi Aryan Nation—has shown "phenomenal growth," which means, experts say, that more violent attacks are ahead.

—Peter Freiberg

sylvania State University. These problems include tension, anxiety, depression, stress, fear for safety and distrust of society, D'Augelli said. Similarly, self-esteem—which included how comfortable a youth is with being a gay male or lesbian—also appears to "provide something of a buffer" in the face of a verbal assault, D'Augelli says.

In two surveys at Penn State in 1987 and 1990, D'Augelli found extensive verbal, property and physical victimization among 121 lesbian, gay male and bisexual undergraduates he studied. Eighty percent had experienced verbal insults, one third had objects thrown at them, 31 percent reported being chased or followed, 13 percent reported being spat upon and nearly one-fifth said they had been physically assaulted—punched, hit or kicked—because of their sexual orientation; 22 percent of the sample also reported a sexual assault as a result of their sexual orientation. Most harassers were fellow students.

Such violence, says D'Augelli, leads victims as well as more closeted gays to conceal their sexual orientation from heterosexual counterparts on campus.

"The costs associated with hiding and fear," he says, "are likely high, leading to emotional stresses, social difficulties and academic problems."

Gregory Herek, PhD, a research psychologist at the University of California at Davis and nationally recognized authority on antigay bias crimes, found similar evidence of the impact of hate crimes. In his pilot study of 147 Sacramento-area gay people, he found that about 29 percent had experienced a bias-related crime against their person. Compared to other respondents who had experienced no hate crimes against their person, these victims showed significantly higher levels of depression, anxiety, anger and symptoms associated with post-traumatic stress disorder. These preliminary results, Herek says, will be tested in a much

larger study of 2,200 lesbians and gay men.

Counseling the Victims

Psychologists and counselors are already dealing with the consequences of such crimes. Bea Hanson, director of social services for the New York City Gay and Lesbian Anti-Violence Project, says most survivors need short-term "crisis work" rather than long-term therapy. The project is one of 23 such groups in the country.

This "crisis work," Hanson says, is primarily advocacy—helping victims report crimes to police, obtaining medical attention and following the case through the courts. When therapy is requested, it is usually short-term. But some victims do need long-term therapy. Psychologist Linda Garnets, PhD, a Santa Monica clinician, says the principal risk is that the survivor may feel "there's something wrong with me that caused me to be

targeted as a gay person," she said. The psychologist's main task is to help the survivor reaffirm the positive value of a gay or lesbian identity, and help them feel the anger rather than blame themselves.

Psychologist Glenda Russell, PhD, a Boulder, Colo., clinician, says an antigay hate crime starts the victim not only questioning "the safety of the world but the goodness of being gay." It feeds into what society tells us about lesbians and gays all the time, which is that lesbians and gays are bad," says Russell.

That's why, Russell says, the psychologist needs to separate out the external event from the person's internal feelings.

"You can't just tend to how it feels to the person to have been bashed, and you can't just tend to the homophobia out there that caused the bashing," Russell said. "The therapist really has to work with both the internal and external aspects."

That also applies to the causes of antigay violence, says Herek. While research needs to be done on assailants' attitudes, he says, "it's not always the case that you can cite individual homophobia as the motivation in these attacks."

Many factors, including the need for acceptance by friends and society's attitudes towards gays, influence the mostly young male perpetrators. "It's very complicated," says Herek, "but I do think . . . that it's society's homophobia, or heterosexism, that fosters these attacks because they set up gay people as targets."

So when a group of young men is hanging around looking for a target, says Herek, gay people are more likely victims because gays are "not valued greatly and [are] somewhat acceptable to attack; because of society's antipathy towards them.

Crimes Against Humanity

If nifty little "pep" gestures like the "Indian Chant" and the "Tomahawk Chop"
are just good clean fun, then let's spread the fun around, shall we?

Ward Churchill

During the past couple of seasons, there has been an increasing wave of controversy regarding the names of professional sports teams like the Atlanta "Braves," Cleveland "Indians," Washington "Redskins," and Kansas City "Chiefs." The issue extends to the names of college teams like Florida State University "Seminoles," University of Illinois "Fighting Illini," and so on, right on down to high school outfits like the Lamar (Colorado) "Savages." Also involved have been team adoption of "mascots," replete with feathers, buckskins, beads, spears and "warpaint" (some fans have opted to adorn themselves in the same fashion), and nifty little "pep" gestures like the "Indian Chant" and "Tomahawk Chop."

A substantial number of American Indians have protested that use of native names, images and symbols as sports team mascots and the like is, by definition, a virulently racist practice. Given the historical relationship between Indians and non-Indians during what has been called the "Conquest of America," American Indian Movement leader (and American Indian Anti-Defamation Council founder) Russell Means has compared the practice to contemporary Germans naming their soccer teams the "Jews," "Hebrews," and "Yids," while adorning their uniforms with grotesque caricatures of Jewish faces taken from the Nazis' anti-Semitic propaganda of the 1930s. Numerous demonstrations have occurred in conjunction with games—most notably during the November 15, 1992 match-up between the Chiefs and Redskins in Kansas City—by angry Indians and their supporters.

In response, a number of players—especially African Americans and other minority athletes—have been trotted out by professional team owners like Ted Turner, as well as university and public school officials, to announce that they mean not to insult but to honor native people. They have been joined by the television networks and most major newspapers, all of which have editorialized that Indian discomfort with the situation is "no big deal," insisting that the whole thing is just "good, clean fun." The country needs more such fun, they've argued, and "a few disgruntled Native Americans" have no right to undermine the nation's enjoyment of its leisure time by complaining. This is especially the case, some have argued, "in hard times like these." It has even been contended that Indian outrage at being systematically degraded—rather than the degradation itself—creates "a serious barrier to the sort of intergroup communication so necessary in a multicultural society such as ours."

Okay, let's communicate. We are frankly dubious that those advancing such positions really believe their own rhetoric, but, just for the sake of argument, let's accept the premise that they are sincere. If what they say is true, then isn't it time we spread such "inoffen-

From *Z Magazine*, March 1993, pp. 43-47. © 1993 by Ward Churchill. Reprinted by permission.

siveness" and "good cheer" around among *all* groups so that *everybody* can participate *equally* in fostering the round of national laughs they call for? Sure it is—the country can't have too much fun or "intergroup involvement—so the more, the merrier. Simple consistency demands that anyone who thinks the Tomahawk Chop is a swell pastime must be just as hearty in their endorsement of the following ideas—by the logic used to defend the defamation of American Indians—should help us all really start yukking it up.

First, as a counterpart to the Redskins, we need an NFL team called "Niggers" to honor Afro-Americans. Half-time festivities for fans might include a simulated stewing of the opposing coach in a large pot while players and cheerleaders dance around it, garbed in leopard skins and wearing fake bones in their noses. This concept obviously goes along with the kind of gaiety attending the Chop, but also with the actions of the Kansas City Chiefs, whose team members—prominently including black team members—lately appeared on a poster looking "fierce" and "savage" by way of wearing Indian regalia. Just a bit of harmless "morale boosting," says the Chiefs' front office. You bet.

So that the newly-formed Niggers sports club won't end up too out of sync while expressing the "spirit" and "identity" of Afro-Americans in the above fashion, a baseball franchise—let's call this one the "Sambos"—should be formed. How about a basketball team called the "Spearchuckers?" A hockey team called the "Jungle Bunnies?" Maybe the "essence" of these teams could be depicted by images of tiny black faces adorned with huge pairs of lips. The players could appear on TV every week or so gnawing on chicken legs and spitting watermelon seeds at one another. Catchy, eh? Well, there's "nothing to be upset about," according to those who love wearing "war bonnets" to the Super Bowl or having "Chief Illiniwik" dance around the sports arenas of Urbana, Illinois.

And why stop there? There are plenty of other groups to include. "Hispanics?" They can be "represented" by the Galveston "Greasers" and San Diego "Spics," at least until the Wisconsin "Wetbacks" and Baltimore "Beaners" get off the ground. Asian Americans? How about the "Slopes," "Dinks," "Gooks," and "Zipperheads?" Owners of the latter teams might get their logo ideas from editorial page cartoons printed in

Cleveland "Indians"

the nation's newspapers during World War II: slant-eyes, buck teeth, big glasses, but nothing racially insulting or derogatory, according to the editors and artists involved at the time. Indeed, this Second World War-vintage stuff can be seen as just another barrel of laughs, at least by what current editors say are their "local standards" concerning American Indians.

Let's see. Who's been left out? Teams like the Kansas City "Kikes," Hanover "Honkies," San Leandro "Shylocks," Daytona "Dagos," and Pittsburgh "Polacks" will fill a certain social void among white folk.

Have a religious belief? Let's all go for the gusto and gear up the Milwaukee "Mackerel Snappers" and Hollywood "Holy Rollers." The Fighting Irish of Notre Dame can be rechristened the "Drunken Irish" or "Papist Pigs." Issues of gender and sexual preference can be addressed through creation of teams like the St. Louis "Sluts," Boston "Bimbos," Detroit "Dykes," and the Fresno "Fags." How about the Gainesville "Gimps" and Richmond "Retards," so the physically and mentally impaired won't be excluded from our fun and games?

Now, don't go getting "overly sensitive" out there. None of this is demeaning or insulting, at least not when it's being done to Indians. Just ask the folks who are doing it, or their apologists like Andy Rooney in the national media. They'll tell you—as in fact they *have* been telling you—that there's been no harm done, regardless of what their victims think, feel, or say. The situation is exactly the same as when those with precisely the same mentality used to insist that Step 'n' Fetchit was okay, or Rochester on the Jack Benny Show, or Amos and Andy, Charlie Chan, the Frito Bandito, or any of the other cutsey symbols making up the lexicon of American racism. Have we communicated yet?

Let's get just a little bit real here. The notion of "fun" embodied in rituals like the Tomahawk Chop must be understood for what it is. There's not a single non-Indian example used above which can be considered socially acceptable in even the most marginal sense. The reasons are obvious enough. So why is it different where American Indians are concerned? One can only conclude that, in contrast to the other groups at issue, Indians are (falsely) perceived as being too few, and therefore too weak, to defend themselves effectively against racist and otherwise offensive behavior.

Fortunately, there are some glimmers of hope. A few teams and their fans have gotten the message and have responded appropriately. Stanford University, which opted to drop the name "Indians" from Stanford, has experienced no resulting drop-off in attendance. Meanwhile, the local newspaper in Portland, Oregon recently decided its long-standing editorial policy prohibiting use of racial epithets should include derogatory team names. The Redskins, for instance, are now referred to as "the Washington team," and will continue to be described in this way until the franchise adopts an inoffensive moniker (newspaper sales in Portland have suffered no decline as a result).

Such examples are to be applauded and encouraged. They stand as figurative beacons in the night, proving beyond all doubt that it is quite possible to indulge in the pleasure of athletics without accepting blatant racism into the bargain.

Yuma "Indians"

Nuremberg Precedents

On October 16, 1946, a man named Julius Streicher mounted the steps of a gallows. Moments later he was dead, the sentence of an international tribunal composed of representatives of the United States, France, Great Britain, and the Soviet Union having been imposed. Streicher's body was then cremated, and—so horrendous were his crimes thought to have been—his ashes dumped into an unspecified German river so that "no one should ever know a particular place to go for reasons of mourning his memory."

Julius Streicher had been convicted at Nuremberg, Germany of what were termed "Crimes Against Humanity." The lead prosecutor in his case—Justice Robert Jackson of the United States Supreme Court—had not argued that the defendant had killed anyone, nor that he had personally committed any especially violent act. Nor was it contended that Streicher had held any particularly important position in the German government during the period in which the so-called Third Reich had exterminated some 6,000,000 Jews, as well as several million Gypsies, Poles, Slavs, homosexuals, and other untermenschen (subhumans).

The sole offense for which the accused was ordered put to death was in having served as publisher/editor of a Bavarian tabloid entitled *Der Sturmer* during the early-to-mid 1930s, years before the Nazi genocide actually began. In this capacity, he had penned a long series of virulently anti-Semitic editorials and "news" stories, usually accompanied by cartoons and other images graphically depicting Jews in extraordinarily derogatory fashion. This, the prosecution asserted, had done much to "dehumanize" the targets of his distortion in the mind of the German public. In turn, such dehumanization had made it possible—or at least easier—for average Germans to later indulge in the outright liquidation of Jewish "vermin." The tribunal agreed, holding that Streicher was therefore complicit in genocide and deserving of death by hanging.

During his remarks to the Nuremberg tribunal, Justice Jackson observed that, in implementing its sentences, the participating powers were morally and legally binding themselves to adhere forever after to the same standards of conduct that were being applied to Streicher and the other Nazi leaders. In the alternative, he said, the victorious allies would have committed "pure murder" at Nuremberg—no different in substance from that carried out by those they presumed to judge—rather than establishing the "permanent benchmark for justice" which was intended.

Yet in the United States of Robert Jackson, the indigenous American Indian population had already been reduced, in a process which is ongoing to this day, from perhaps 12.5 million in the year 1500 to fewer than 250,000 by the beginning of the 20th century. This was accomplished, according to official sources, "largely through the cruelty of [EuroAmerican] settlers," and an informal but clear governmental policy which had made it an articulated goal to "exterminate these red vermin," or at least whole segments of them.

Bounties had been placed on the scalps of Indians—any Indians—in places as diverse as Georgia, Kentucky, Texas, the Dakotas, Oregon, and California, and had been maintained until resident Indian populations were decimated or disappeared altogether. Entire peoples such as the Cherokee had been reduced to half their size through a policy of forced removal from their homelands east of the Mississippi River to what were then considered less preferable areas in the West.

Others, such as the Navajo, suffered the same fate while under military guard for years on end. The

United States Army had also perpetrated a long series of wholesale massacres of Indians at places like Horseshoe Bend, Bear River, Sand Creek, the Washita River, the Marias River, Camp Robinson, and Wounded Knee.

Through it all, hundreds of popular novels—each competing with the next to make Indians appear more grotesque, menacing, and inhuman—were sold in the tens of millions of copies in the U.S. Plainly, the Euro-American public was being conditioned to see Indians in such a way as to allow their eradication to continue. And continue it did until the Manifest Destiny of the U.S.—a direct precursor to what Hitler would subsequently call Lebens-raumpolitik (the politics of living space)—was consummated.

By 1900, the national project of "clearing" Native Americans from their land and replacing them with "superior" Anglo-American settlers was complete; the indigenous population had been reduced by as much as 98 percent while approximately 97.5 percent of their original territory had "passed" to the invaders. The survivors had been concentrated, out of sight and mind of the public, on scattered "reservations," all of them under the self-assigned "plenary" (full) power of the federal government. There was, of course, no Nuremberg-style tribunal passing judgment on those who had fostered such circumstances in North America. No U.S. official or private citizen was ever imprisoned—never mind hanged—for implementing or propagandizing what had been done. Nor had the process of genocide afflicting Indians been completed. Instead, it merely changed form.

Between the 1880s and the 1980s, nearly half of all Native American children were coercively transferred from their own families, communities, and cultures to those of the conquering society. This was done through compulsory attendance at remote boarding schools, often hundreds of miles from their homes, where native children were kept for years on end while being systematically "deculturated" (indoctrinated to think and act in the manner of Euro Americans rather than as Indians). It was also accomplished through a pervasive foster home and adoption program—including "blind" adoptions, where children would be permanently denied information as to who they were/are and where they'd come from—placing native youths in non-Indian homes.

Westminster "Warriors"

The express purpose of all this was to facilitate a U.S. governmental policy to bring about the "assimilation" (dissolution) of indigenous societies. In other words, Indian cultures as such were to be caused to disappear. Such policy objectives are directly contrary to the United Nations 1948 Convention on Punishment and Prevention of the Crime of Genocide, an element of international law arising from the Nuremberg proceedings. The forced "transfer of the children" of a targeted "racial, ethnical, or religious group" is explicitly prohibited as a genocidal activity under the Convention's second article.

Article II of the Genocide Convention also expressly prohibits involuntary sterilization as a means of "preventing births among" a targeted population. Yet, in 1975, it was conceded by the U.S. government that its Indian Health Service (IHS) then a subpart of the Bureau of Indian Affairs (BIA), was even then conducting a secret program of involuntary sterilization that had affected approximately 40 percent of all Indian women. The program was allegedly discontinued, and the IHS was transferred to the Public Health Service, but no one was punished. In 1990, it came out that the IHS was inoculating Inuit children in Alaska with Hepatitis-B vaccine. The vaccine had already been banned by the World Health Organization as having a demonstrated correlation with the HIV-Syndrome which is itself correlated to AIDS. As this is written, a "field test" of Hepatitis-A vaccine, also HIV-correlated, is being conducted on Indian reservations in the northern plains region.

The Genocide Convention makes it a "crime against humanity" to create conditions leading to the destruction of an identifiable human group, as such. Yet the BIA has utilized the government's plenary prerogatives to negotiate mineral leases "on behalf of" Indian peoples paying a fraction of standard royalty rates. The result has been "super profits" for a number of preferred U.S. corporations. Meanwhile, Indians, whose reservations ironically turned out to be in some of the most mineral-rich areas of North America, which makes us, the nominally wealthiest segment of the continent's population, live in dire poverty.

By the government's own data in the mid-1980s, Indians received the lowest annual and lifetime per capita incomes of any aggregate population group in the United States. Concomitantly, we suffer the highest

rate of infant mortality, death by exposure and malnutrition, disease, and the like. Under such circumstances, alcoholism and other escapist forms of substance abuse are endemic in the Indian community, a situation which leads both to a general physical debilitation of the population and a catastrophic accident rate. Teen suicide among Indians is several times the national average.

The average life expectancy of a reservation-based Native American man is barely 45 years; women can expect to live less than three years longer.

Such itemizations could be continued at great length, including matters like the radioactive contamination of large portions of contemporary Indian Country, the forced relocation of traditional Navajos, and so on. But the point should be made: Genocide, as defined in international law, is a continuing fact of day-to-day life (and death) for North America's native peoples. Yet there has been —and is—only the barest flicker of public concern about, or even consciousness of, this reality. Absent any serious expression of public outrage, no one is punished and the process continues.

A salient reason for public acquiescence before the ongoing holocaust in Native North America has been a continuation of the popular legacy, often through more effective media. Since 1925, Hollywood has released more than 2,000 films, many of them rerun frequently on television, portraying Indians as strange, perverted, ridiculous, and often dangerous things of the past. Moreover, we are habitually presented to mass audiences one-dimensionally, devoid of recognizable human motivations and emotions; Indians thus serve as props, little more. We have thus been thoroughly and systematically dehumanized.

Nor is this the extent of it. Everywhere, we are used as logos, as mascots, as jokes: "Big Chief writing tablets, "Red Man" chewing tobacco, "Winnebago" campers, "Navajo and "Cherokee" and "Pontiac" and "Cadillac" pickups and automobiles. There are the Cleveland "Indians," the Kansas City "Chiefs," the Atlanta "Braves" and the Washington "Redskins" professional sports teams—not to mention those in thousands of colleges, high schools, and elementary schools across the country—each with their own degrading caricatures and parodies of Indians and/or things In-

Lamar High School
"Home of the Savages"

dian. Pop fiction continues in the same vein, including an unending stream of New Age manuals purporting to expose the inner works of indigenous spirituality in everything from pseudo-philosophical to do-it-yourself styles. Blond yuppies from Beverly Hills amble about the country claiming to be reincarnated 17th century Cheyenne Ushamans ready to perform previously secret ceremonies.

In effect, a concerted, sustained, and in some ways accelerating effort has gone into making Indians unreal. It is thus of obvious importance that the American public begin to think about the implications of such things the next time they witness a gaggle of face-painted and war-bonneted buffoons doing the "Tomahawk Chop" at a baseball or football game. It is necessary that they think about the implications of the grade-school teacher adorning their child in turkey feathers to commemorate Thanksgiving. Think about the significance of John Wayne or Charleton Heston killing a dozen "savages" with a single bullet the next time a western comes on TV. Think about why Land-o-Lakes finds it appropriate to market its butter with the stereotyped image of an "Indian princess" on the wrapper. Think about what it means when non-Indian academics profess—as they often do—to "know more about Indians than Indians do themselves." Think about the significance of charlatans like Carlos Castaneda and Jamake Highwater and Mary Summer Rain and Lynn Andrews churning out "Indian" bestsellers, one after the other, while Indians typically can't get into print.

Think about the real situation of American Indians. Think about Julius Streicher. Remember Justice Jackson's admonition. Understand that the treatment of Indians in American popular culture is not "cute" or "amusing" or just "good, clean fun."

Know that it causes real pain and real suffering to real people. Know that it threatens our very survival. And know that this is just as much a crime against humanity as anything the Nazis ever did. It is likely that the indigenous people of the United States will never demand that those guilty of such criminal activity be punished for their deeds. But the least we have the right to expect—indeed, to demand—is that such practices finally be brought to a halt.

Whites' myths about blacks

Though some white views have softened, mistaken beliefs persist

After the riots last spring, the *Los Angeles Times* asked city residents a simple, open-ended question. What did Angelenos think was "the most important action that must be taken" to begin a citywide healing process? Poll results from nearly 900 residents showed that the two most *unpopular* antidotes were the standard solutions favored by liberals or conservatives: "more government financial aid" and a "crackdown on gangs, drugs and lawlessness." Slightly more in favor were the human-capital remedies of the economists to "improve education" and "improve the economy." But the No. 1 solution was the psychologists' remedy. What the city most needed, residents concluded, was to "renew efforts among groups to communicate [with] and understand each other."

That prescription sounds squishy, yet in all the post-riot analysis there may have been too much talk about the ostensibly "tangible" roots of the riots (such as cutbacks in urban aid or weak job markets) and too little discussion of racial misunderstanding and ethnic stereotyping. In 1964, Martin Luther King Jr. warned that "we must learn to live together as brothers or perish together as fools," and the famed 1968 Kerner Commission report emphasized that narrowing racial inequalities would require "new attitudes, new understanding and, above all, new will." In the intervening years, however, those new attitudes and understanding have been all too lacking. And continuing strife in cities may only further stoke racial prejudice and hostilities.

Changing times. At first glance, recent trends in white attitudes toward blacks are deceptively upbeat. Fifty years ago, a *majority* of white Americans supported segregation and discrimination against blacks; just 25 years ago, 71 percent of whites felt blacks were moving too fast in their drive for equality. Today, by contrast, overwhelming majorities of whites support the principle of equal treatment for the races in schools, jobs, housing and other public spheres. Moreover, several national surveys taken after the riots contain encouraging signs of interracial accord. Most whites and blacks agree the Rodney King verdict and the violence that followed it were both unjust. The same polls show little evidence the riots initially made whites less sympathetic to the plight of poor blacks. For instance, both whites and blacks agree by large margins that jobs and training are more effective ways to prevent future unrest than strengthening police forces.

Yet much of the black-white convergence may be misleading for two reasons. For starters, blacks are still far more likely than whites to identify race discrimination as a pervasive problem in American society, especially when it comes to police and the criminal-justice system. At the same time, it seems probable that the riots at best only temporarily shifted whites' views of blacks. Annual polls taken by the National Opinion Research Center have found consistently since 1973 that most whites believe the government spends enough or too much to improve the condition of blacks (65 percent of whites thought so in 1991). Yet a *New York Times*/CBS survey taken *after* the riots found that a hefty majority of the American public (61 percent) now believes that the government spends too little to improve the condition of blacks.

In all likelihood, white prejudices are now evolving a bit like a virus. While the most virulent forms have been largely stamped out, new and more resistant strains continue to emerge. In the old racist formula, the innate "inferiority" of blacks accounted for their plight; in the modern-day cultural version, a lack of ambition and laziness do. Some modern-day stereotypes are simply false; others contain a kernel of truth but are vastly overblown. Regrettably, a large group of whites continues to harbor core myths about blacks based almost solely on their impressions of the most disadvantaged. Some examples:

■ **The work ethic.** The white myth: Blacks lack motivation. A 1990 NORC poll found that 62 percent of whites rated blacks as lazier than whites, and 78 percent thought them more likely to prefer welfare to being self-supporting.

Fact: For most of this century, blacks were actually *more* likely to work than whites. A greater percentage of black men than white men were in the work force from 1890 until after World War II, and black women outpaced white women until mid-1990. As late as 1970, black males ages 20 to 24 had higher labor-force participation rates than their white counterparts.

Today, the labor-force participation of the races is closer. After a 25-year influx of white women into the job market, white and black women participate in the labor force at nearly identical rates. Black men are slightly less likely than white men to be in the work force—69.5 percent vs. 76.4 percent. The only large gap between the two races occurs among teenagers: Last year, 55.8 percent of white teens were in the labor force, compared with 35.4 percent of black teens.

Blacks, who make up 12 percent of the population, are disproportionately represented on the welfare rolls; 40 percent of recipients of Aid to Families with Dependent Children are black, while 55 percent are white or Hispanic. However, numerous surveys have failed to find any evidence that most blacks prefer welfare to work.

In 1987, under the supervision of University of Chicago sociologist William Julius Wilson, the NORC surveyed 2,490 residents of Chicago's inner-city

From *U.S. News & World Report*, November 9, 1992, pp. 41, 43-44. © 1992 by U.S. News & World Report. Reprinted by permission.

poverty tracts, including 1,200 blacks, 500 Puerto Ricans and 400 Mexicans. Roughly 80 percent of black parents surveyed said they preferred working to welfare, even when public aid provided the same money and medical coverage.

The most that can be said for white suspicions about black motivation is that a small segment of blacks has a more casual attitude toward welfare than do their low-income ethnic peers. In Wilson's survey, black parents were about twice as likely as Mexican parents to believe people have a right to welfare without working. And inner-city black fathers who did not finish high school and lacked a car were, in practice, twice as likely to be unemployed as were similarly situated Mexicans.

■ **Crime and the police.** The white myth: Blacks are given to violence and resent tough law enforcement. The 1990 NORC survey found that half of whites rated blacks as more violence-prone than whites. An 11-city survey of police in ghetto precincts taken after the 1960s riots showed 30 percent of white officers believed "most" blacks "regard the police as enemies."

Fact: The vast majority of blacks have long held favorable attitudes toward the police. As Samuel Walker reports in the 1992 edition of "The Police in America," 85 percent of blacks rate the crime-fighting performance of police as either good or fair, just below the 90 percent approval rating given by whites. Some blacks, especially young males, tend to hold hostile views toward the police, and ugly encounters with young blacks often stand out in the minds of cops. Yet studies consistently show that white officers have "seriously overestimated the degree of public hostility among blacks," says Walker. Even *after* the recent riots, a *Los Angeles Times* poll found that 60 percent of local blacks felt the police did a good job of holding down crime, not much below the white figure of 72 percent.

Blacks, or at least young black males, do commit a disproportionate share of crime; blacks account for roughly 45 percent of all arrests for violent crime. Still, the disparity between black and white arrest rates results partly from the fact that blacks *ask* police to arrest juveniles and other suspects more often than whites do. The vast majority of victims of black crime are themselves black, and it is blacks, more than whites, who are likely to be afraid to walk alone at night or to feel unsafe at home. In fact, one of the gripes blacks have with cops is underpolicing. Walker writes: "Black Americans are nearly as likely as whites to ask for more, not less, police protection."

■ **Job and housing bias.** The white myth: Blacks no longer face widespread job and housing discrimination. Three of four respondents in a 1990 Gallup Poll said that "blacks have as good a chance as white people in my community" to get any job for which they are qualified, and a survey last year found that 53 percent of Americans believed that blacks actually got "too much consideration" in job hiring. In June, a national survey by the Federal National Mortgage Association reported that most whites also believe blacks have as good a chance as whites in their community to get housing they can afford.

Fact: Researchers have documented the persistence of discrimination by testing what happens when pairs of whites and blacks with identical housing needs and credentials—apart from their race—apply for housing. The most recent national study, funded by the Department of Housing and Urban Development, found that in 1989, real-estate agents discriminated against black applicants slightly over half the time, showing them fewer rental apartments than they showed whites, steering them to minority neighborhoods, providing them with less assistance in finding a mortgage and so on. According to University of Chicago sociologist Douglas Massey, 60 to 90 percent of the housing units presented to whites were not made available to blacks. Even more disappointing, the evaluators found no evidence that discrimination had declined since HUD's last national study in 1977. And last week, the Federal Reserve Board reported that black applicants are currently twice as likely to be rejected for mortgages as economically comparable whites.

In the workplace, discrimination seems slightly less pervasive. Still, a 1991 Urban Institute analysis of matched white and black male college students who applied for 476 entry-level jobs in Chicago and Washington found "entrenched and widespread" discrimination in the hiring process; 1 white applicant in 5 advanced further than his equally qualified black counterpart.

■ **Taking responsibility.** The white myth: Blacks blame everyone but themselves for their problems. Since 1977, a majority of whites have agreed that the main reason blacks tend to "have worse jobs, income and housing than whites" is that they "just don't have the motivation or willpower to pull themselves up out of poverty." Fifty-seven percent of whites ascribed to that belief when NORC last asked the question, in 1991.

Fact: When it comes to apportioning blame, blacks neither presume that big government is the answer to their problems nor shy away from self-criticism. A 1992 Gallup Poll of 511 blacks found that just 1 in 4 blacks believed the most important way they could improve conditions in their communities was to "put more pressure on government to address their problems"; 2 of 3 opted for trying harder

either to "solve their communities' problems themselves" or to "better themselves personally and their families."

In fact, blacks are almost as likely as whites to "blame the victim" and invoke the virtues of individual responsibility. In a 1988 Gallup Poll asking, "Why do you think poor blacks have not been able to rise out of poverty—is it mainly the fault of blacks themselves or is it the fault of society?" 30 percent of blacks responded that black poverty was the fault of blacks themselves; 29 percent of whites said the same. A 1992 poll for the *Washington Post* found that 52 percent of blacks—and 38 percent of whites—agreed that "if blacks would try harder, they could be just as well off as whites." Often, the status of race relations is a secondary concern for black voters. A poll released just last week by the Joint Center for Political and Economic Studies found that black and white voters both ranked the economy, public education and health care as their "most important" issues. Only 14 percent of blacks and 5 percent of whites cited the state of race relations.

A development with uncertain consequences is that both whites and blacks exaggerate the extent of white stereotyping. Both groups display a classic polling phenomenon—the "I'm OK, but you're not" syndrome. Whites are likely to overestimate other whites' support for racial segregation; blacks are likely to exaggerate whites' beliefs that blacks have no self-discipline or are prone to violent crime. Moreover, blacks and whites are far more sanguine about race relations and police fairness in their own communities than they are about other areas or the nation at large. A *New York Times*/CBS News poll after the L.A. riots found that just 1 in 4 Americans thought race relations were good nationwide, but 3 out of 4 believed race relations were generally good in their communities.

The downside to this syndrome is that it could make it easier for whites and blacks in suburban and upscale neighborhoods to write off blacks in poorer areas. A *Los Angeles Times* poll taken days after the riots found that nearly 80 percent of city residents felt they would suffer few if any hardships because of the riots' aftereffects, and 2 out of 3 respondents said their lives were already back to normal.

On the other hand, the fact that whites and blacks mix more at work, at home and socially than in previous decades suggests that increases in interracial contact could eventually help diminish stereotyping by both races. More tolerance will not solve the nation's race problem by itself. But it sure wouldn't hurt if, one day, "them" became "us."

BY JEANNYE THORNTON AND DAVID WHITMAN WITH DORIAN FRIEDMAN

Gendered Media: The Influence of Media on Views of Gender

Julia T. Wood

Department of Communication, University of North Carolina at Chapel Hill.

THEMES IN MEDIA

Of the many influences on how we view men and women, media are the most pervasive and one of the most powerful. Woven throughout our daily lives, media insinuate their messages into our consciousness at every turn. All forms of media communicate images of the sexes, many of which perpetuate unrealistic, stereotypical, and limiting perceptions. Three themes describe how media represent gender. First, women are underrepresented, which falsely implies that men are the cultural standard and women are unimportant or invisible. Second, men and women are portrayed in stereotypical ways that reflect and sustain socially endorsed views of gender. Third, depictions of relationships between men and women emphasize traditional roles and normalize violence against women. We will consider each of these themes in this section.

Underrepresentation of Women

A primary way in which media distort reality is in underrepresenting women. Whether it is prime-time television, in which there are three times as many white men as women (Basow, 1992 p. 159), or children's programming, in which males outnumber females by two to one, or newscasts, in which women make up 16% of newscasters and in which stories about men are included 10 times more often than ones about women ("Study Reports Sex Bias," 1989), media misrepresent actual proportions of men and women in the population. This constant distortion tempts us to believe that there really are more men than women and, further, that men are the cultural standard.

Other myths about what is standard are similarly fortified by communication in media. Minorities are even less visible than women, with African-Americans appearing only rarely (Gray, 1986; Stroman, 1989) and other ethnic minorities being virtually nonexistent. In children's programming when African-Americans do appear, almost invariably they appear in supporting roles rather than as main characters (O'Connor, 1989). While more African-Americans are appearing in

---

MEDIA'S MISREPRESENTATION OF AMERICAN LIFE

The media present a distorted version of cultural life in our country. According to media portrayals:

White males make up two-thirds of the population. The women are less in number, perhaps because fewer than 10% live beyond 35. Those who do, like their younger and male counterparts, are nearly all white and heterosexual. In addition to being young, the majority of women are beautiful, very thin, passive, and primarily concerned with relationships and getting rings out of collars and commodes. There are a few bad, bitchy women, and they are not so pretty, not so subordinate, and not so caring as the good women. Most of the bad ones work outside of the home, which is probably why they are hardened and undesirable. The more powerful, ambitious men occupy themselves with important business deals, exciting adventures, and rescuing dependent females, whom they often then assault sexually.

From *Gendered Lives: Communication, Gender, and Culture* by Julia T. Wood, chapter 9, pp. 231-244, 250-259. © 1994 by Wadsworth Publishing Company, Inc. Reprinted by permission.

prime-time television, they are too often cast in stereotypical roles. In the 1992 season, for instance, 12 of the 74 series on commercial networks included large African-American casts, yet most featured them in stereotypical roles. Black men are presented as lazy and unable to handle authority, as lecherous, and/or as unlawful, while females are portrayed as domineering or as sex objects ("Sights, Sounds, and Stereotypes," 1992). Writing in 1993, David Evans (1993, p. 10) criticized television for stereotyping black males as athletes and entertainers. These roles, wrote Evans, mislead young black male viewers into thinking success "is only a dribble or dance step away," and blind them to other, more realistic ambitions. Hispanics and Asians are nearly absent, and when they are presented it is usually as villains or criminals (Lichter, Lichter, Rothman, & Amundson, 1987).

Also underrepresented is the single fastest growing group of Americans—older people. As a country, we are aging so that people over 60 make up a major part of our population; within this group, women significantly outnumber men (Wood, 1993c). Older people not only are underrepresented in media but also are represented inaccurately. In contrast to demographic realities, media consistently show fewer older women than men, presumably because our culture worships youth and beauty in women. Further, elderly individuals are frequently portrayed as sick, dependent, fumbling, and passive, images not borne out in real life. Distorted depictions of older people and especially older women in media, however, can delude us into thinking they are a small, sickly, and unimportant part of our population.

The lack of women in the media is paralleled by the scarcity of women in charge of media. Only about 5% of television writers, executives, and producers are women (Lichter, Lichter, & Rothman, 1986). Ironically, while two-thirds of journalism graduates are women, they make up less than 2% of those in corporate management of newspapers and only about 5% of newspaper publishers ("Women in Media," 1988). Female film directors are even more scarce, as are executives in charge of MTV. It is probably not coincidental that so few women are behind the scenes of an industry that so consistently portrays women negatively. Some media analysts (Mills, 1988) believe that if more women had positions of authority at executive levels, media would offer more positive portrayals of women.

Stereotypical Portrayals of Women and Men

In general, media continue to present both women and men in stereotyped ways that limit our perceptions of human possibilities. Typically men are portrayed as active, adventurous, powerful, sexually aggressive, and largely uninvolved in human relationships. Just as consistent with cultural views of gender are depictions of women as sex objects who are usually young, thin, beautiful, passive, dependent, and often incompetent and dumb. Female characters devote their primary energies to improving their appearances and taking care of homes and people. Because media pervade our lives, the ways they misrepresent genders may distort how we see ourselves and what we perceive as normal and desirable for men and women.

Stereotypical portrayals of men. According to J. A. Doyle (1989, p. 111), whose research focuses on masculinity, children's television typically shows males as "aggressive, dominant, and engaged in exciting activities from which they receive rewards from others for their 'masculine' accomplishments." Relatedly, recent studies reveal that the majority of men on prime-time television are independent, aggressive, and in charge (McCauley, Thangavelu, & Rozin, 1988). Television programming for all ages disproportionately depicts men as serious, confident, competent, powerful, and in high-status positions. Gentleness in men, which was briefly evident in the 1970s, has receded as established male characters are redrawn to be more tough and distanced from others (Boyer, 1986). Highly popular films such as *Lethal Weapon, Predator, Days of Thunder, Total Recall, Robocop, Die Hard,* and *Die Harder* star men who embody the stereotype of extreme masculinity. Media, then, reinforce long-standing cultural ideals of masculinity: Men are presented as hard, tough, independent, sexually aggressive, unafraid, violent, totally in control of all emotions, and—above all—in no way feminine.

Equally interesting is how males are *not* presented. J. D. Brown and K. Campbell (1986) report that men are seldom shown doing housework. Doyle (1989) notes that boys and men are rarely presented caring for others. B. Horovitz (1989) points out they are typically represented as uninterested in and incompetent at homemaking, cooking, and child care. Each season's new ads for cooking and cleaning supplies include several that caricature men as incompetent buffoons, who are klutzes in the kitchen and no better at taking care of children. While children's books have made a limited attempt to depict women engaged in activities outside of the home, there has been little parallel effort to show men involved in family and home life. When someone is shown taking care of a child, it is usually the mother, not the father. This perpetuates a negative stereotype of men as uncaring and uninvolved in family life.

Stereotypical portrayals of women. Media's images of women also reflect cultural stereotypes that depart markedly from reality. As we have already seen, girls and women are dramatically underrepresented. In prime-time television in 1987, fully two-thirds of the speaking parts were for men. Women are portrayed as significantly younger and thinner than women in the population as a whole, and most are

JILL

I remember when I was little I used to read books from the boys' section of the library because they were more interesting. Boys did the fun stuff and the exciting things. My mother kept trying to get me to read girls' books, but I just couldn't get into them. Why can't stories about girls be full of adventure and bravery? I know when I'm a mother, I want any daughters of mine to understand that excitement isn't just for boys.

depicted as passive, dependent on men, and enmeshed in relationships or housework (Davis, 1990). The requirements of youth and beauty in women even influence news shows, where female newscasters are expected to be younger, more physically attractive, and less outspoken than males (Craft, 1988; Sanders & Rock, 1988). Despite educators' criticism of self-fulfilling prophesies that discourage girls from success in math and science, that stereotype was dramatically reiterated in 1992 when Mattel offered a new talking Barbie doll. What did she say? "Math class is tough," a message that reinforces the stereotype that women cannot do math ("Mattel Offers Trade-In," 1992). From children's programming, in which the few existing female characters typically spend their time watching males do things (Feldman & Brown, 1984; Woodman, 1991), to MTV, which routinely pictures women satisfying men's sexual fantasies (Pareles, 1990; Texier, 1990), media reiterate the cultural image of women as dependent, ornamental objects whose primary functions are to look good, please men, and stay quietly on the periphery of life.

Media have created two images of women: good women and bad ones. These polar opposites are often juxtaposed against each other to dramatize differences in the consequences that befall good and bad women. Good women are pretty, deferential, and focused on home, family, and caring for others. Subordinate to men, they are usually cast as victims, angels, martyrs, and loyal wives and helpmates. Occasionally, women who depart from traditional roles are portrayed positively, but this is done either by making their career lives invisible, as with Claire Huxtable, or by softening and feminizing working women to make them more consistent with traditional views of femininity. For instance, in the original script, Cagney and Lacey were conceived as strong, mature, independent women who took their work seriously and did it well. It took 6 years for writers Barbara Corday and Barbara Avedon to sell the script to CBS, and even then they had to agree to subdue Cagney's and Lacey's abilities to placate producer Barney Rosenzweig, who complained, "These women aren't soft enough. These women aren't feminine enough" (Faludi, 1991, p. 150). While female

viewers wrote thousands of letters praising the show, male executives at CBS continued to force writers to make the characters softer, more tender, and less sure of themselves (Faludi, 1991, p. 152). The remaking of Cagney and Lacey illustrates the media's bias in favor of women who are traditionally feminine and who are not too able, too powerful, or too confident. The rule seems to be that a woman may be strong and successful if and only if she also exemplifies traditional stereotypes of femininity—subservience, passivity, beauty, and an identity linked to one or more men.

The other image of women the media offer us is the evil sister of the good homebody. Versions of this image are the witch, bitch, whore, or nonwoman, who is represented as hard, cold, aggressive—all of the things a good woman is not supposed to be. Exemplifying the evil woman is Alex in *Fatal Attraction*, which grossed more than $100 million in its first four months (Faludi, 1991, p. 113). Yet Alex was only an extreme version of how bad women are generally portrayed. In children's literature, we encounter witches and mean stepmothers as villains, with beautiful and passive females like Snow White and Sleeping Beauty as their good counterparts.

Prime-time television favorably portrays pretty, nurturing, other-focused women, such as Claire Huxtable on "The Cosby Show," whose career as an attorney never entered storylines as much as her engagement in family matters. Hope in "Thirtysomething" is an angel, committed to husband Michael and daughter Janey. In the biographies written for each of the characters when the show was in development, all male characters were defined in terms of their career goals, beliefs, and activities. Hope's biography consisted of one line: "Hope is married to Michael" (Faludi, 1991, p. 162). Hope epitomizes the traditional woman, so much so in fact that in one episode she refers to herself as June Cleaver and calls Michael "Ward," thus reprising the traditional family of the 1950s as personified in "Leave It to Beaver" (Faludi, 1991, p. 161). Meanwhile, prime-time typically represents ambitious, independent women as lonely, embittered spinsters who are counterpoints to "good" women.

Stereotypical Images of Relationships Between Men and Women

Given media's stereotypical portrayals of women and men, we shouldn't be surprised to find that relationships between women and men are similarly depicted in ways that reinforce stereotypes. Four themes demonstrate how media reflect and promote traditional arrangements between the sexes.

Women's dependence/men's independence. Walt Disney's award-winning animated film *The Little Mermaid* vividly embodies females' dependence on males for identity. In this feature film, the mermaid quite literally gives up her identity as a mermaid in order to

become acceptable to her human lover. In this children's story, we see a particularly obvious illustration of the asymmetrical relationship between women and men that is more subtly conveyed in other media productions. Even the Smurfs, formless little beings who have no obvious sex, reflect the male-female, dominant-submissive roles. The female smurf, unlike her male companions, who have names, is called only Smurfette, making her sole identity a diminutive relation to male smurfs. The male dominance/female subservience pattern that permeates mediated representations of relationships is no accident. Beginning in 1991, television executives deliberately and consciously adopted a policy of having dominant male characters in all Saturday morning children's programming (Carter, 1991).

Women, as well as minorities, are cast in support roles rather than leading ones in both children's shows and the commercials interspersed within them (O'Connor, 1989). Analyses of MTV revealed that it portrays females as passive and waiting for men's attention, while males are shown ignoring, exploiting, or directing women (Brown, Campbell, & Fisher, 1986). In rap music videos, where African-American men and women star, men dominate women, whose primary role is as objects of male desires (Pareles, 1990; Texier, 1990). News programs that have male and female hosts routinely cast the female as deferential to her male colleague (Craft, 1988; Sanders & Rock, 1988). Commercials, too, manifest power cues that echo the male dominance/female subservience pattern. For instance, men are usually shown positioned above women, and women are more frequently pictured in varying degrees of undress (Masse & Rosenblum, 1988; Nigro, Hill, Gelbein, & Clark, 1988). Such nonverbal cues represent women as vulnerable and more submissive while men stay in control.

In a brief departure from this pattern, films and television beginning in the 1970s responded to the second wave of feminism by showing women who were independent without being hard, embittered, or without close relationships. Films such as *Alice Doesn't Live Here Anymore, Up the Sandbox, The Turning Point, Diary of a Mad Housewife,* and *An Unmarried Woman* offered realistic portraits of women who sought and found their own voices independent of men. Judy Davis's film, *My Brilliant Career,* particularly embodied this focus by telling the story of a woman who chooses work over marriage. During this period, television followed suit, offering viewers prime-time fare such as "Maude" and "The Mary Tyler Moore Show," which starred women who were able and achieving in their own rights. "One Day at a Time," which premiered in 1974, was the first prime-time program about a divorced woman.

By the 1980s, however, traditionally gendered arrangements resurged as the backlash movement against feminism was embraced by media (Haskell, 1988; Maslin, 1990). Thus, film fare in the 1980s included *Pretty Woman,* the story of a prostitute who becomes a good woman when she is saved from her evil ways by a rigidly stereotypical man, complete with millions to prove his success. Meanwhile, *Tie Me Up, Tie Me Down* trivialized abuse of women and underlined women's dependence on men with a story of a woman who is bound by a man and colludes in sustaining her bondage. *Crossing Delancey* showed successful careerist Amy Irving talked into believing she needs a man to be complete, a theme reprised by Cher in *Moonstruck.*

Television, too, cooperated in returning women to their traditional roles with characters like Hope in "Thirtysomething," who minded house and baby as an ultratraditional wife, and even Murphy Brown found her career wasn't enough and had a baby. Against her protests, Cybill Shepherd, who played Maddie in "Moonlighting," was forced to marry briefly on screen, which Susan Faludi (1991, p. 157) refers to as part of a "campaign to cow this independent female figure." Popular music added its voice with hit songs like "Having My Baby," which glorified a woman who defined herself by motherhood and her relationship to a man. The point is not that having babies or committing to relationships is wrong; rather, it is that media virtually require this of women in order to present them positively. Media define a very narrow range for womanhood.

Joining the campaign to restore traditional dominant-subordinate patterns of male-female relationships were magazines, which reinvigorated their focus on women's role as the helpmate and supporter of husbands and families (Peirce, 1990). In 1988, that staple of Americana, *Good Housekeeping,* did its part to revive women's traditional roles with a full-page ad ("The Best in the House," 1988) for its new demographic edition marketed to "the new traditionalist woman." A month later, the magazine followed this up with a second full-page ad in national newspapers that saluted the "new traditionalist woman," with this copy ("The New Traditionalist," 1988): "She has made her commitment. Her mission: create a more meaningful life for herself and her family. She is the New Traditionalist— a contemporary woman who finds her fulfillment in traditional values." The long-standing dominant-submissive model for male-female relationships was largely restored in the 1980s. With only rare exceptions, women are still portrayed as dependent on men and subservient to them. As B. Lott (1989, p. 64) points out, it is women who "do the laundry and are secretaries to men who own companies."

Men's authority/women's incompetence. A second recurrent theme in media representations of relationships is that men are the competent authorities who save women from their incompetence. Children's litera-

PAUL

I wouldn't say this around anyone, but personally I'd be glad if the media let up a little on us guys. I watch those guys in films and on TV, and I just feel inadequate. I mean, I'm healthy and I look okay, and I'll probably make a decent salary when I graduate. But I am no stud; I can't beat up three guys at once, women don't fall dead at my feet; I doubt I'll make a million bucks; and I don't have muscles that ripple. Every time I go to a film, I leave feeling like a wimp. How can any of us guys measure up to what's on the screen?

ture vividly implements this motif by casting females as helpless and males as coming to their rescue. Sleeping Beauty's resurrection depends on Prince Charming's kiss, a theme that appears in the increasingly popular gothic romance novels for adults (Modleski, 1982).

One of the most pervasive ways in which media define males as authorities is in commercials. Women are routinely shown anguishing over dirty floors and bathroom fixtures only to be relieved of their distress when Mr. Clean shows up to tell them how to keep their homes spotless. Even when commercials are aimed at women, selling products intended for them, up to 90% of the time a man's voice is used to explain the value of what is being sold (Basow, 1992, p. 161; Bretl & Cantor, 1988). Using male voice-overs reinforces the cultural view that men are authorities and women depend on men to tell them what to do.

Television further communicates the message that men are authorities and women are not. One means of doing this is sheer numbers. As we have seen, men vastly outnumber women in television programming. In addition, the dominance of men as news anchors who inform us of happenings in the world underlines their authority ("Study Reports Sex Bias," 1989). Prime-time television contributes to this image by showing women who need to be rescued by men and by presenting women as incompetent more than twice as often as men (Boyer, 1986; Lichter et al., 1986).

Consider the characters in "The Jetsons," an animated television series set in the future. Daughter Judy Jetson is constantly complaining and waiting for others to help her, using ploys of helplessness and flattery to win men's attention. *The Rescuers,* a popular animated video of the 1990s, features Miss Bianca (whose voice is that of Zsa Zsa Gabor, fittingly enough), who splits her time evenly between being in trouble and being grateful to male characters for rescuing her. These stereotypical representations of males and females reinforce a number of harmful beliefs. They suggest, first, that men are more competent than women. Compounding this is the message that a woman's power lies in her looks and conventional

femininity, since that is how females from Sleeping Beauty to Judy Jetson get males to assist them with their dilemmas (McCauley, Thangavelu, & Rozin, 1988). Third, these stereotypes underline the requirement that men must perform, succeed, and conquer in order to be worthy.

Women as primary caregivers/men as breadwinners. A third perennial theme in media is that women are caregivers and men are providers. Since the backlash of the 1980s, in fact, this gendered arrangement has been promulgated with renewed vigor. Once again, as in the 1950s, we see women devoting themselves to getting rings off of collars, gray out of their hair, and meals on the table. Corresponding to this is the restatement of men's inability in domestic and nurturing roles. Horovitz (1989), for instance, reports that in commercials men are regularly the butt of jokes for their ignorance about nutrition, child care, and housework.

When media portray women who work outside of the home, their career lives typically receive little or no attention. Although these characters have titles such as lawyer or doctor, they are shown predominantly in their roles as homemakers, mothers, and wives. We see them involved in caring conversations with family and friends and doing things for others, all of which never seem to conflict with their professional responsibilities. This has the potential to cultivate unrealistic expectations of being "superwoman," who does it all without her getting a hair out of place or being late to a conference.

Magazines play a key role in promoting pleasing others as a primary focus of women's lives. K. Peirce's (1990) study found that magazines aimed at women stress looking good and doing things to please others. Thus, advertising tells women how to be "me, only better" by dyeing their hair to look younger; how to lose weight so "you'll still be attractive to him"; and how to prepare gourmet meals so "he's always glad to come home." Constantly, these advertisements empha-

JOANNE

I'd like to know who dreams up those commercials that show men as unable to boil water or run a vacuum. I'd like to tell them they're creating monsters. My boyfriend and I agreed to split all chores equally when we moved in together. Ha! Fat chance of that. He does zilch. When I get on his case, he reminds me of what happened when the father on some show had to take over housework and practically demolished the kitchen. Then he grins and says, "Now, you wouldn't want that, would you?" Or worse yet, he throws up Hope or one of the other women on TV, and asks me why I can't be as sweet and supportive as she is. It's like the junk on television gives him blanket license for doing nothing.

size pleasing others, especially men, as central to being a woman, and the message is fortified with the thinly veiled warning that if a woman fails to look good and please, her man might leave (Rakow, 1992).

There is a second, less known way in which advertisements contribute to stereotypes of women as focused on others and men as focused on work. Writing in 1990, Gloria Steinem, editor of *Ms.*, revealed that advertisers control some to most of the *content* in magazines. In exchange for placing an ad, a company receives "complimentary copy," which is one or more articles that increase the market appeal of its product. So a soup company that takes out an ad might be given a three-page story on how to prepare meals using that brand of soup; likewise, an ad for hair coloring products might be accompanied by interviews with famous women who choose to dye their hair. Thus, the message of advertisers is multiplied by magazine content, which readers often mistakenly assume is independent of advertising.

Advertisers support media, and they exert a powerful influence on what is presented. To understand the prevalence of traditional gender roles in programming, magazine copy, and other media, we need only ask what is in the best interests of advertisers. They want to sponsor shows that create or expand markets for their products. Media images of women as sex objects, devoted homemakers, and mothers buttress the very roles in which the majority of consuming takes place. To live up to these images, women have to buy cosmetics and other personal care products, diet aids, food, household cleaners, utensils and appliances, clothes and toys for children, and so on. In short, it is in advertisers' interests to support programming and copy that feature women in traditional roles. In a recent analysis, Lana Rakow (1992) demonstrated that much advertising is oppressive to women and is very difficult to resist, even when one is a committed feminist.

Women's role in the home and men's role outside of it are reinforced by newspapers and news programming. Both emphasize men's independent activities and, in fact, define news almost entirely as stories about and by men ("Study Reports Sex Bias," 1989). Stories about men focus on work and/or their achievements (Luebke, 1989), reiterating the cultural message that men are supposed to do, perform. Meanwhile the few stories about women almost invariably focus on their roles as wives, mothers, and homemakers ("Study Reports Sex Bias," 1989). Even stories about women who are in the news because of achievements and professional activities typically dwell on marriage, family life, and other aspects of women's traditional role (Foreit et al., 1980).

Women as victims and sex objects/men as aggressors. A final theme in mediated representations of relationships between women and men is representation of women as subject to men's sexual desires. The

irony of this representation is that the very qualities women are encouraged to develop (beauty, sexiness, passivity, and powerlessness) in order to meet cultural ideals of femininity contribute to their victimization. Also, the qualities that men are urged to exemplify (aggressiveness, dominance, sexuality, and strength) are identical to those linked to abuse of women. It is no coincidence that all but one of the women nominated for Best Actress in the 1988 Academy Awards played a victim (Faludi, 1991, p. 138). Women are portrayed alternatively either as decorative objects, who must attract a man to be valuable, or as victims of men's sexual impulses. Either way, women are defined by their bodies and how men treat them. Their independent identities and endeavors are irrelevant to how they are represented in media, and their abilities to resist exploitation by others are obscured.

This theme, which was somewhat toned down during the 1970s, returned with vigor in the 1980s as the backlash permeated media. According to S. A. Basow (1992, p. 160), since 1987 there has been a "resurgence of male prominence, pretty female sidekicks, female homemakers." Advertising in magazines also communicates the message that women are sexual objects. While men are seldom pictured nude or even partially unclothed, women habitually are. Advertisements for makeup, colognes, hair products, and clothes often show women attracting men because they got the right products and made themselves irresistible. Stars on prime-time and films, who are beautiful and dangerously thin, perpetuate the idea that women must literally starve themselves to death to win men's interest (Silverstein et al., 1986).

Perhaps the most glaring examples of portrayals of women as sex objects and men as sexual aggressors occur in music videos as shown on MTV and many other stations. Typically, females are shown dancing provocatively in scant and/or revealing clothing as they try to gain men's attention (Texier, 1990). Frequently, men are seen coercing women into sexual activities and/or physically abusing them. Violence against women is also condoned in many recent films. R. Warshaw (1991) reported that cinematic presentations of rapes, especially acquaintance rapes, are not presented as power-motivated violations of women but rather as strictly sexual encounters. Similarly, others (Cowan, Lee, Levy, & Snyder, 1988; Cowan & O'Brien, 1990) have found that male dominance and sexual exploitation of women are themes in virtually all R- and X-rated films, which almost anyone may now rent for home viewing. These media images carry to extremes long-standing cultural views of masculinity as aggressive and femininity as passive. They also make violence seem sexy (D. Russell, 1993). In so doing, they recreate these limited and limiting perceptions in the thinking of another generation of women and men.

In sum, we have identified basic stereotypes and

themes in media's representations of women, men, and relationships between the two. Individually and in combination these images sustain and reinforce socially constructed views of the genders, views that have restricted both men and women and that appear to legitimize destructive behaviors ranging from anorexia to battering. Later in this chapter, we will probe more closely how media versions of gender are linked to problems such as these. . . .

Pathologizing the Human Body

One of the most damaging consequences of media's images of women and men is that these images encourage us to perceive normal bodies and normal physical functions as problems. It's understandable to wish we weighed a little more or less, had better developed muscles, and never had pimples or cramps. What is neither reasonable nor healthy, however, is to regard healthy, functional bodies as abnormal and unacceptable. Yet this is precisely the negative self-image cultivated by media portrayals of women and men. Because sex sells products (Muro, 1989), sexual and erotic images are the single most prominent characteristic of advertising (Courtney & Whipple, 1983). Further, advertising is increasingly objectifying men, which probably accounts for the rise in men's weight training and cosmetic surgery. Media, and especially advertising, are equal opportunity dehumanizers of both sexes.

Not only do media induce us to think we should measure up to artificial standards, but they encourage us to see normal bodies and bodily functions as pathologies. A good example is the media's construction of premenstrual syndrome (PMS). Historically, PMS has not been a problem, but recently it has been declared a disease (Richmond-Abbott, 1992). In fact, a good deal of research (Parlee, 1973, 1987) indicates that PMS affected very few women in earlier eras. After the war, when women were no longer needed in the work force, opinion changed and the term *premenstrual tension* was coined (Greene & Dalton, 1953) and used to define women as inferior employees. In 1964, only one article on PMS appeared; in 1988–1989, a total of 425 were published (Tavris, 1992, p. 140). Drug companies funded research and publicity, since selling PMS meant selling their remedies for the newly created problem. Behind the hoopla, however, there was and is little evidence to support the currently widespread belief that PMS is a serious problem for a significant portion of the female population. Facts aside, the myth has caught on, carrying in its wake many women and men who now perceive normal monthly changes as abnormal and as making women unfit for positions of leadership and authority. Another consequence of defining PMS as a serious problem most women suffer is that it leads to labeling women in general as deviant and unreliable (Unger & Crawford, 1992), an image that fortifies long-held biases against women.

Menopause is similarly pathologized. Carol Tavris (1992, p. 159) notes that books describe menopause "in terms of deprivation, deficiency, loss, shedding, and sloughing," language that defines a normal process as negative. Like menstruation, menopause is represented as abnormalcy and disease, an image that probably contributes to the negative attitudes toward it in America. The cover of the May 25, 1992, *Newsweek* featured an abstract drawing of a tree in the shape of a woman's head. The tree was stripped of all leaves, making it drab and barren. Across the picture was the cover-story headline "Menopause." From first glance, menopause was represented negatively—as desolate and unfruitful. The article focused primarily on the problems and losses of menopause. Only toward the end did readers find reports from anthropologists, whose cross-cultural research revealed that in many cultures menopause is not an issue or is viewed positively. Women in Mayan villages and the Greek island of Evia do not understand questions about hot flashes and depression, which are symptoms often associated with menopause in Western societies ("Menopause," 1992, p. 77). These are not part of their experience in cultures that do not define a normal change in women as a pathology. Because Western countries, especially America, stigmatize menopause and define it as "the end of womanhood," Western women are likely to feel distressed and unproductive about the cessation of menstruation (Greer, 1992).

Advertising is very effective in convincing us that we need products to solve problems we are unaware of until some clever public relations campaign persuades us that something natural about us is really unnatural and unacceptable. Media have convinced millions of American women that what every medical source considers "normal body weight" is really abnormal and cause for severe dieting (Wolf, 1991). Similarly, gray hair, which naturally develops with age, is now something all of us, especially women, are supposed to cover up. Facial lines, which indicate a person has lived a life and accumulated experiences, can be removed so that we look younger—a prime goal in a culture that glorifies youth (Greer, 1992).

Body hair is another interesting case of media's convincing us that something normal is really abnormal. Beginning in 1915, a sustained marketing campaign informed women that underarm hair was unsightly and socially incorrect. (The campaign against leg hair came later.) *Harper's Bazaar*, an upscale magazine, launched the crusade against underarm hair with a photograph of a woman whose raised arms revealed clean-shaven armpits. Underneath the photograph was this caption: "Summer dress and modern dancing combine to make necessary the removal of objectionable hair" (Adams, 1991). Within a few years, ads promoting removal of underarm hair appeared in most women's magazines, and by 1922, razors and depilatories were

firmly ensconced in middle America as evidenced by their inclusion in the women's section of the Sears Roebuck catalog.

Media efforts to pathologize natural physiology can be very serious. As we have seen in prior chapters, the emphasis on excessive thinness contributes to severe and potentially lethal dieting, especially in Caucasian women (Spitzack, 1993). Nonetheless, the top female models in 1993 are skeletal, more so than in recent years (Leland & Leonard, 1993). Many women's natural breast size exceeded the cultural ideal in the 1960s when thin, angular bodies were represented as ideal. Thus, breast reduction surgeries rose. By the 1980s, cultural standards changed to define large breasts as the feminine ideal. Consequently, breast augmentation surgeries accelerated, and fully 80% of implants were for cosmetic reasons ("The Implant Circus," 1992). In an effort to meet the cultural standards of beautiful bodies, many women suffered unnecessary surgery, which led to disfigurement, loss of feeling, and sometimes death for women when silicone implants were later linked to fatal conditions. Implicitly, media argue that our natural state is abnormal and objectionable, a premise that is essential to sell products and advice for improving ourselves. Accepting media messages about our bodies and ourselves, however, is not inevitable: We can reflect on the messages and resist those that are inappropriate and/or harmful. We would probably all be considerably happier and healthier if we became more critical in analyzing media's communication about how we should look, be, and act.

Normalizing Violence Against Women

Since we have seen that media positively portray aggression in males and passivity in females, it's important to ask whether media messages contribute to abuse of and violence against women. There is by now fairly convincing evidence (Hansen & Hansen, 1988) that exposure to sexual violence through media is linked to greater tolerance, or even approval, of violence. For instance, P. Dieter (1989) found a strong relationship between females' viewing of sexually violent MTV and their acceptance of sexual violence as part of "normal" relationships. He reasoned that the more they observe positive portrayals of sexual violence, the more likely women are to perceive this as natural in relationships with men and the less likely they are to object to violence or to defend themselves from it. In short, Dieter suggests that heavy exposure to media violence within relationships tends to normalize it, so that abuse and violence are considered natural parts of love and sex.

Dieter's study demonstrates a direct link between sexual aggression and one popular form of media, MTV. Research on pornography further corroborates connections between exposure to portrayals of violence against women and willingness to engage in or accept it in one's own relationships (Russell, 1993). Before we discuss this research, however, we need to clarify what we will mean by the term pornography, since defining it is a matter of some controversy. Pornography is not simply sexually explicit material. To distinguish pornography from erotica, we might focus on mutual agreement and mutual benefit. If we use these criteria, pornography may be defined as materials that favorably show subordination and degradation of a person such as presenting sadistic behaviors as pleasurable, brutalizing and pain as enjoyable, and forced sex or abuse as positive. Erotica, on the other hand, depicts consensual sexual activities that are sought by and pleasurable to all parties involved (MacKinnon, 1987). These distinctions are important, since it has been well established that graphic sexual material itself is not harmful, while sexually violent materials appear to be (Donnerstein, Linz, & Penrod, 1987).

Pornographic films are a big business, outnumbering other films by 3 to 1 and grossing over $365 million a year in the United States alone (Wolf, 1991). The primary themes characteristic of pornography as a genre are extremes of those in media generally: sex, violence, and domination of one person by another, usually women by men (Basow, 1992, p. 317). More than 80% of X-rated films in one study included scenes in which one or more men dominate and exploit one or more women; within these films, three-fourths portray physical aggression against women, and fully half explicitly depict rape (Cowan et al., 1988). That these are linked to viewers' own tendencies to engage in sexual violence is no longer disputable. According to recent research (Demare, Briere, & Lips, 1988; Donnerstein et al., 1987; Malamuth & Briere, 1986), viewing sexually violent material tends to increase men's beliefs in rape myths, raises the likelihood that men will admit they might themselves commit rape, and desensitizes men to rape, thereby making forced sex more acceptable to them. This research suggests that repeated exposure to pornography influences how men think about rape by transforming it from an unacceptable behavior with which they do not identify into one they find acceptable and enticing. Not surprisingly, the single best predictor of rape is the circulation of pornographic materials that glorify sexual force and exploitation (Baron & Straus, 1989). This is alarming when we realize that 18 million men buy a total of 165 different pornographic magazines every month in the United States (Wolf, 1991, p. 79).

It is well documented that the incidence of reported rape is rising and that an increasing number of men regard forced sex as acceptable (Brownmiller, 1993; Soeken & Damrosch, 1986). Studies of men (Allgeier, 1987; Koss & Dinero, 1988; Koss, Dinero, Seibel, & Cox, 1988; Koss, Gidycz, & Wisniewski, 1987; Lisak & Roth, 1988) have produced shocking findings: While the majority of college men report not having raped anyone, a stunning 50% admit they have coerced,

manipulated, or pressured a woman to have sex or have had sex with her after getting her drunk; 1 in 12 men at some colleges has engaged in behaviors meeting the legal definition of rape or attempted rape; over 80% of men who admitted to acts that meet the definition of rape did not believe they had committed rape; and fully one-third of college men said they would commit rape if they believed nobody would find out.

Contrary to popular belief, we also know that men who do commit rape are not psychologically abnormal. They are indistinguishable from other men in terms of psychological adjustment and health, emotional well-being, heterosexual relationships, and frequency of sexual experiences (Segel-Evans, 1987). The only established difference between men who are sexually violent and men who are not is that the former have "hypermasculine" attitudes and self-concepts—their approval of male dominance and sexual rights is even stronger than that of nonrapists (Allgeier, 1987; Koss & Dinero, 1988; Lisak & Roth, 1988; Wood, 1993a). The difference between sexually violent men and others appears to be only a matter of degree.

We also know something about women who are victims of rape and other forms of sexual violence. Between 33% and 66% of all women have been sexually abused before reaching age 18 (Clutter, 1990; Koss, 1990). The majority of college women—up to 75%—say they have been coerced into some type of unwanted sex at least once (Koss, Gidycz, & Wisniewski, 1987; Poppen & Segal, 1988; Warshaw, 1988). A third of women who survive rape contemplate suicide (Koss et al., 1988). It is also clear that the trauma of rape is not confined to the time of its actual occurrence. The feelings that accompany rape and sexual assault—fear, a sense of degradation and shame, anger, powerlessness, and depression—endure far beyond the act itself (Brownmiller, 1975; Wood, 1992b, 1993f). Most victims of rape continue to deal with the emotional aftermath of rape for the rest of their lives (Marhoefer-Dvorak, Resick, Hutter, & Girelli, 1988).

What causes rape, now the fastest growing violent crime in the United States (Doyle, 1989; Soeken & Damrosch, 1986)? According to experts (Costin & Schwartz, 1987; Koss & Dinero, 1988; Koss, Gidycz, & Wisniewski, 1987; Scott & Tetreault, 1987; Scully, 1990), rape is not the result of psychological deviance or uncontrollable lust. Although rape involves sex, it is not motivated by sexual desire. Authorities agree that rape is an aggressive act used to dominate and show power over another person, be it a man over a woman or one man over another, as in prison settings where rape is one way inmates brutalize one another and establish a power hierarchy (Rideau & Sinclair, 1982). Instead, mounting evidence suggests that rape is a predictable outcome of views of men, women, and relationships between the sexes that our society inculcates in mem-

bers (Brownmiller, 1975; Costin & Schwartz, 1987; Scott & Tetreault, 1987; South & Felson, 1990).

Particularly compelling support for the cultural basis of rape comes from cross-cultural studies (Griffin, 1981; Sanday, 1986), which reveal that rape is extremely rare in cultures that value women and feminine qualities and that have ideologies that promote harmonious interdependence among humans and between them and the natural world. Rape is most common in countries, like the United States, that have ideologies of male supremacy and dominance and a disrespect of women and nature. Cultural values communicated to us by family, schools, media, and other sources constantly encourage us to believe men are superior, men should dominate women, male aggression is acceptable as a means of attaining what is wanted, women are passive and should defer to men, and women are sex objects. In concert, these beliefs legitimize violence and aggression against women.

While the majority of media communication may not be pornographic, it does echo in somewhat muted forms the predominant themes of pornography: sex, violence, and male domination of women. As we have seen, these same motifs permeate media that are part of our daily

MYTHS AND FACTS ABOUT RAPE

Myth	Fact
Rape is a sexual act that results from sexual urges.	Rape is an aggressive act used to dominate another.
Rapists are abnormal.	Rapists have not been shown to differ from nonrapists in personality, psychology, adjustment, or involvement in interpersonal relationships.
Most rapes occur between strangers.	Eighty percent to 90% of rapes are committed by a person known to the victim (Allgeier, 1987).
Most rapists are African-American men, and most victims are Caucasian women.	More than three-fourths of all rapes occur within races, not between races. This myth reflects racism.
The way a woman dresses affects the likelihood she will be raped.	The majority—up to 90%—of rapes are planned in advance and without knowledge of how the victim will dress (Scully, 1990).
False reports of rapes are frequent.	The majority of rapes are never reported (Koss, Gidycz, & Wisniewski, 1987). Less than 10% of rape reports are judged false, the same as for other violent crimes.
Rape is a universal problem.	The incidence of rape varies across cultures. It is highest in societies with ideologies of male dominance and a disregard for nature; it is lowest in cultures that respect women and feminine values (Griffin, 1981).

lives, which generally portray males as dominating in number, status, authority, and will. Substantial violence toward women punctuates movies, television—including children's programming—rock music, and music videos, desensitizing men and women alike to the *un*naturalness and unacceptability of force and brutality between human beings. Thus, the research that demonstrates connections between sex-stereotypical media and acceptance of sexual violence is consistent with that showing relationships between more extreme, pornographic media and acceptance of and use of violence. . . .

REFERENCES

Adams, C. (1991, April). The straight dope. *Triangle Comic Review*, p. 26.

Allgeier, E. R. (1987). Coercive versus consensual sexual interactions. In V. P. Makosky (Ed.), *The G. Stanley Hall Lecture Series* (Vol. 7, pp. 7–63). Washington, DC: American Psychological Association.

Baron, L., & Straus, M. A. (1989). *Four theories of rape in American society.* New Haven, CT: Yale University Press.

Basow, S. A. (1992). *Gender: Stereotypes and roles* (3rd ed.). Pacific Grove, CA: Brooks/Cole.

The best in the house. (1988, October 19). *New York Times*, p. 52Y.

Boyer, P. J. (1986, February 16). TV turns to the hard-boiled male. *New York Times*, pp. H1, H29.

Bretl, D., & Cantor, J. (1988). The portrayal of men and women in U.S. commercials: A recent content analysis and trend over 15 years. *Sex Roles, 18*, 595–609.

Brown, J. D., & Campbell, K. (1986). Race and gender in music videos: The same beat but a different drummer. *Journal of Communication, 36*, 94–106.

Brown, J. D., Campbell, K., & Fisher, L. (1986). American adolescents and music videos: Why do they watch? *Gazette, 37*, 9–32.

Brownmiller, S. (1975). *Against our wills: Men, women, and rape.* New York: Simon and Schuster.

Brownmiller, S. (1993, January 4). Making female bodies the battlefield. *Newsweek*, p. 37.

Carter, B. (1991, May 1). Children's TV, where boys are king. *New York Times*, pp. A1, C18.

Clutter, S. (1990, May 3). Gender may affect response and outrage to sex abuse. *Morning Call*, p. D14.

Costin, F., & Schwartz, N. (1987). Beliefs about rape and women's social roles: A four-nation study. *Journal of Interpersonal Violence, 2*, 46–56.

Courtney, A. E., & Whipple T. W. (1983). *Sex stereotyping in advertising.* Lexington, MA: D. C. Heath.

Cowan, G., Lee, C., Levy, D., & Snyder, D. (1988). Dominance and inequality in X-rated videocassettes. *Psychology of Women Quarterly, 12*, 299–311.

Cowan, G., & O'Brien, M. (1990). Gender and survival vs. death in slasher films: A content analysis. *Sex Roles, 23*, 187–196.

Craft, C. (1988). *Too old, too ugly, and not deferential to men: An anchorwoman's courageous battle against sex discrimination.* Rockland, CA: Prima.

Davis, D. M. (1990). Portrayals of women in prime-time network television: Some demographic characteristics. *Sex Roles, 23*, 325–332.

Demare, D., Briere, J., & Lips, H. M. (1988). Violent pornography and self-reported likelihood of sexual aggression. *Journal of Research in Personality, 22*, 140–153.

Dieter, P. (1989, March). *Shooting her with video, drugs, bullets, and promises.* Paper presented at the meeting of the Association of Women in Psychology, Newport, RI.

Donnerstein, E., Linz, D., & Penrod, S. (1987). *The question of pornography: Research findings and policy implications.* New York: Free Press.

Doyle, J. A. (1989). *The male experience* (2nd ed.). Dubuque, IA: William C. Brown.

Evans, D. (1993, March 1). The wrong examples. *Newsweek*, p. 10.

Faludi, S. (1991). *Backlash: The undeclared war against American women.* New York: Crown.

Feldman, N. S., & Brown, E. (1984, April). *Male vs. female differences in control strategies: What children learn from Saturday morning television.* Paper presented at the meeting of the Eastern Psychological Association, Baltimore, MD. (Cited in Basow, 1992.)

Foreit, K. G., Agor, T., Byers, J., Larue, J., Lokey, H., Palazzini, M., Patterson, M., & Smith, L. (1980). Sex bias in the newspaper treatment of male-centered and female-centered news stories. *Sex Roles, 6*, 475–480.

Gray, H. (1986). Television and the new black man: Black male images in prime-time situation comedies. *Media, Culture, and Society, 8*, 223–242.

Greene, R., & Dalton, K. (1953). The premenstrual syndrome. *British Medical Journal, 1*, 1007–1014.

Greer, G. (1992). *The change: Women, aging, and menopause.* New York: Alfred Knopf.

Griffin, S. (1981). *Pornography and silence: Culture's revenge against nature.* New York: Harper and Row.

Hansen, C. H., & Hansen, R. D. (1988). How rock music videos can change what is seen when boy meets girl: Priming stereotypic appraisal of social interactions. *Sex Roles, 19*, 287–316.

Haskell, M. (1988, May). Hollywood Madonnas. *Ms.*, pp. 84, 86, 88.

Horovitz, B. (1989, August 10). In TV commercials, men are often the butt of the jokes. *Philadelphia Inquirer*, pp. 5b, 6b.

The implant circus. (1992, February 18). *Wall Street Journal*, p. A20.

Koss, M. P. (1990). The women's mental health research agenda: Violence against women. *American Psychologist, 45*, 374–380.

Koss, M. P., & Dinero, T. E. (1988). Predictors of sexual aggression among a national sample of male college students. In V. I. Quinsey & R. Orentky (Eds.), *Human sexual aggression* (pp. 133–147). New York: Academy of Sciences.

Koss, M. P., Dinero, T. E., Seibel, C. A., & Cox, S. L. (1988). Stranger and acquaintance rape: Are there differences in the victim's experience? *Psychology of Women Quarterly, 12*, 1–24.

Koss, M. P., Gidycz, C. J., Wisniewski, N. (1987). The scope of rape: Incidence and prevalence of sexual aggression and victimization in a national sample of higher education students. *Journal of Consulting and Clinical Psychology, 55*, 162–170.

Leland, J., & Leonard, E. (1993, February 1). Back to Twiggy. *Newsweek*, pp. 64–65.

Lichter, S. R., Lichter, L. S., & Rothman, S. (1986, September/October). From Lucy to Lacey: TV's dream girls. *Public Opinion*, pp. 16–19.

Lichter, S. R., Lichter, L. S., Rothman, S., & Amundson, D. (1987, July/August). Prime-time prejudice: TV's images of blacks and Hispanics. *Public Opinion*, pp. 13–16.

Lisak, D., & Roth, S. (1988). Motivational factors in nonincarcerated sexually aggressive men. *Journal of Personality and Social Psychology, 55*, 795–802.

Lott, B. (1989). Sexist discrimination as distancing behavior: II. Prime-time television. *Psychology of Women Quarterly, 13*, 341–355.

MacKinnon, C. A. (1987). *Feminism unmodified: Discourses on life and law.* Cambridge, MA: Harvard University Press.

Malamuth, N. M., & Briere, J. (1986). Sexual violence in the media: Indirect effects on aggression against women. *Journal of Social Issues, 42*, 75–92.

Marhoefer-Dvorak, S., Resick, P., Hutter, C., & Girelli, S. (1988). Single-versus multiple-incident rape victims: A comparison of psychological reactions to rape. *Journal of Interpersonal Violence, 3*, 145–160.

Maslin, J. (1990, June 17). Bimbos embody retro rage. *New York Times*, pp. H13, H14.

Masse, M. A., & Rosenblum, K. (1988). Male and female created they them: The depiction of gender in the advertising of traditional women's and men's magazine's. *Women's Studies International Forum, 11*, 127–144.

Mattell offers trade-in for "Teen Talk" Barbie. (1992, October 13). *Raleigh News and Observer*, p. A3.

McCauley, C., Thangavelu, K., & Rozin, P. (1988). Sex stereotyping of occupations in relation to television representations and census facts. *Basic and Applied Social Psychology, 9*, 197–212.

Menopause. (1992, May 25). *Newsweek*, pp. 71–80.

Mills, K. (1988). *A place in the news: From the women's pages to the front page.* New York: Dodd, Mead.

Modleski, T. (1982). *Loving with a vengeance: Mass-produced fantasies for women.* New York: Methuen.

Muro, M. (1989, April 23). Comment: New era of eros in advertising. *Morning Call*, pp. D1, D16.

The new traditionalist. (1988, November 17). *New York Times*, p. Y46.

Nigro, G. N., Hill, D. E., Gelbein, M. E., & Clark, C. L. (1988). Changes in the facial prominence of women and men over the last decade. *Psychology of Women Quarterly, 12*, 225–235.

O'Connor, J. J. (1989, June 6). What are commercials selling to children? *New York Times*, p. 28.

Pareles, J. (1990, October 21). The women who talk back in rap. *New York Times*, pp. H33, H36.

Parlee, M. B. (1973). The premenstrual syndrome. *Psychological Bulletin, 80*, 454–465.

Parlee, M. B. (1979, May). Conversational politics. *Psychology Today*, pp. 48–56.

Peirce, K. (1990). A feminist theoretical perspective on the socialization of teenage girls through *Seventeen* magazine. *Sex Roles, 23*, 491–500.

Rakow, L. F. (1986). Rethinking gender research in communication. *Journal of Communication, 36*, 11–26.

Richmond-Abbott, M. (1992). *Masculine and feminine: Gender roles over the life cycle.* New York: McGraw-Hill.

Rideau, W., & Sinclair, B. (1982). Prison: The sexual jungle. In A. Scacco, Jr. (Ed.), *Male Rape* (pp. 3–29). New York: AMS Press.

Russell, D. E. H. (Ed.). (1993). *Feminist views on pornography.* Colchester, VT: Teachers College Press.

Sanday, P. R. (1986). Rape and the silencing of the feminine. In S. Tomaselli & R. Porter (Eds.), *Rape* (pp. 84–101). Oxford, UK: Basil Blackwell.

Sanders, M., & Rock, M. (1988). *Waiting for prime time: The women of television news.* Urbana, IL: University of Illinois Press.

Scott, R., & Tetreault, L. (1987). Attitudes of rapists and other violent offenders toward women. *Journal of Social Psychology, 124*, 375–380.

Scully, D. (1990). *Understanding sexual violence: A study of convicted rapists.* Boston, MA: Unwin Hyman.

Segel-Evans, K. (1987). Rape prevention and masculinity. In F. Abbott (Ed.), *New men, new minds: Breaking male tradition* (pp. 117–121). Freedom, CA: Crossing Press.

Sights, sounds and stereotypes. (1992, October 11). *Raleigh News and Observer*, pp. G1, G10.

Silverstein, B., Perdue, L., Peterson, B., & Kelly, E. (1986). The role of the mass media in promoting a thin standard of bodily attractiveness for women. *Sex Roles, 14*, 519–532.

Soeken, K., & Damrosch, S. (1986). Randomized response technique: Application to research on rape. *Psychology of Women Quarterly, 10*, 119–126.

South, S. J., & Felson, R. B. (1990). The racial patterning of rape. *Social Forces, 69*, 71–93.

Spitzack, C. (1993). The spectacle of anorexia nervosa. *Text and Performance Quarterly, 13*, 1–21.

Stroman, C. A. (1989). To be young, male and black on prime-time television. *Urban Research Review, 12*, 9–10.

Study reports sex bias in news organizations. (1989, April 11). *New York Times*, p. C22.

Tavris, C. (1992). *The mismeasure of woman.* New York: Simon and Schuster.

Texier, C. (1990, April 22), Have women surrendered in MTV's battle of the sexes? *New York Times*, pp. H29, H31.

Unger, R., & Crawford, M. (1992). *Women and gender: A feminist psychology.* New York: McGraw-Hill.

Warshaw, R. (1988). *I never called it rape.* New York: Harper and Row.

Wolf, N. (1991). *The beauty myth.* New York: William Morrow.

Women in media say careers hit "glass ceiling." (1988, March 2). *Easton Express*, p. A9.

Wood, J. T. (1992b). Telling our stories: Narratives as a basis for theorizing sexual harassment. *Journal of Applied Communication Research, 4*, 349–363.

Wood, J. T. (1993a). Engendered relationships: Interaction, caring, power, and responsibility in close relationships. In S. Duck (Ed.), *Processes in close relationships: Contexts of close relationships* (Vol. 3). Beverly Hills, CA: Sage.

Wood, J. T. (1993c). *Who cares: Women, care, and culture.* Carbondale, IL: Southern Illinois University Press.

Wood, J. T. (1993f). Defining and studying sexual harassment as situated experience. In G. Kreps (Ed.), *Communication and sexual harassment in the workplace.* Cresskill, NJ: Hampton Press.

Woodman, S. (1991, May). How super are heros? *Health*, pp. 40, 49, 82.

Aggression

- Biological Factors (Articles 37 and 38)
- Aggression in Childhood and Adolescence (Articles 39 and 40)
- Mass Media Effects (Articles 41 an 42)

The evidence that human beings are capable of great violence is all around us—all you have to do is read a newspaper or watch the evening news. Every day, people are shot, stabbed, beaten, or otherwise treated in a violent manner by friends, family, or strangers. People are attacked for the color of their skin, their political ideas, their membership in a rival gang, or just because they were in the wrong place at the wrong time. Nations war against other nations, and in civil conflicts nations war against themselves. Faced with millions and millions of victims, it is hard to disagree with the conclusion that the capacity for aggression is fundamental to human nature.

Of course, it may depend on what you mean by aggression. As it turns out, coming up with one clear definition of aggression has been very difficult. For example, does aggression require a clear intention to harm? That is, must I *intend* to hurt you in order for my behavior to be called aggressive? Must aggression be physical in nature, or can my verbal attacks on you also be labeled aggressive? Does aggression have to be directed toward a human being? What about violence toward animals, or even inanimate objects, such as when I become angry during a round of golf and bend my putter around a tree? Even after decades of research on this topic, social

psychologists still disagree on what exactly defines an aggressive act.

Although social psychology does not completely ignore the role of biological factors in aggression (and two of the selections in this unit in fact address this topic), its usual focus is on identifying the environmental factors that influence aggressive behavior. One approach to understanding a form of aggression known as *hostile aggression* (aggression carried out for its own sake) has been to identify situational factors that cause unpleasant emotional states, which might then cause aggressive actions. For example, the failure to reach an important goal might lead to the unpleasant feeling of frustration, and these feelings can then trigger aggression. Hot and uncomfortable environments might also contribute to unpleasant emotional states, and thus contribute to heightened aggression.

In contrast to hostile aggression, which is carried out for its own sake, *instrumental aggression* is carried out in order to attain some other goal or objective. This form of aggression is often explained in terms of social learning theory, which holds that people can learn to carry out aggressive actions when they observe others doing so, and when those others are rewarded for their actions. Thus, this theory contends that people frequently learn to use aggression as a tool for getting something they want. One place where such behaviors can be learned, of course, is the mass media, and many studies (and congressional hearings) have been carried out to determine the role of television and other media in teaching violence to children.

The selections in this unit are divided into three subsections. The first subsection focuses on biological factors in aggression, an approach that has only recently become more common in the social psychological literature. In "The Biology of Violence," Robert Wright offers a thoughtful analysis of some controversies in this area. Drawing upon both evolutionary psychology and biological research on serotonin levels, Wright offers the interesting idea that environment and biology work together to help produce aggression; the environmental conditions of those low in social status may influence their serotonin levels, which may then influence violence. In the second article, "A Violence in the Blood," Sarah Richardson describes the analysis of several generations of a Dutch family in order to explore the role of genetic factors in fostering aggression.

The second subsection deals with aggression during childhood and adolescence. In the first essay, "Big. Bad. Bully." author Hara Estroff Marano provides a detailed summary of the research on children who bully their smaller and weaker peers. Although bullies do not appear to have a substantially different self-concept or lower self-esteem, they do seem to be different in some ways. They seem to have greater suspicion of others, and they have more difficulty with emotional self-control. In the second selection, "In an Angry World, Lessons for Emotional Self-Control," Daniel Goleman describes one recent program designed precisely to help children develop better control over their emotions, especially when they are provoked.

The final subsection deals with the issue of violence in mass media. "Televised Violence and Kids: A Public Health Problem?" provides an overview of some of the most famous and influential research in this area: a longitudinal study that found evidence that childhood viewing of television violence produced heightened aggression as an adult. The second selection, "Frankenstein Must be Destroyed: Chasing the Monster of TV Violence," takes a more skeptical look at this same research and concludes that its findings are not as powerful or convincing as many believe.

Looking Ahead: Challenge Questions

What is the evidence that genetic factors can influence the aggressive behaviors of individuals? What is the evidence that biological factors can play such a role? What is the *difference* between genetic and biological influences on aggression? Are biological and environmental explanations of aggression mutually exclusive?

What seems to be the most important factor in creating bullies? How strong is that evidence? Do you think that the program to teach self-control ("In an Angry World, Lessons for Emotional Self-Control") would be effective with bullies? Why or why not?

Do you think that seeing violence on television causes children to become more violent? Have *you* been made more violent by your television viewing? How might society use the results of social psychological research to reduce aggression in our culture? Is there any danger in using psychological research for such a purpose?

BRAVE NEW WORLD DEPT.

THE BIOLOGY OF VIOLENCE

Is inner-city violence a response to the social ravages of poverty, or a biochemical syndrome that may be remedied with drugs? Fallout from that debate derailed the Bush Administration's Violence Initiative, but a school of new Darwinians is proposing an answer that will unsettle both sides.

ROBERT WRIGHT

FREDERICK GOODWIN has learned a lot during a lifetime of studying human behavior, but no lesson is more memorable than the one driven home to him over the past three years: becoming known as someone who compares inner-city teen-agers to monkeys is not a ticket to smooth sailing in American public life. As of early 1992, Goodwin's career had followed a steady upward course. He had been the first scientist to demonstrate clinically the antidepressant effects of lithium, and had become known as a leading, if not the leading, expert on manic-depressive illness. He had risen to become head of the Alcohol, Drug Abuse and Mental Health Administration, the top position for a psychiatrist in the federal government, and was poised to be the point man in a policy that the Bush Administration was proudly unveiling: the Federal Violence Initiative. The idea was to treat violence as a public-health problem—to identify violently inclined youth and provide therapy early, before they had killed. The initiative had the strong support of the Secretary of Health and Human Services, Louis Sullivan, and Goodwin planned to make it his organization's main focus.

Then, in early 1992, while discussing the initiative before the National Mental Health Advisory Council, Goodwin made his fateful remarks. Speaking impromptu—and after a wholly sleepless night, he later said—he got off onto an extended riff about monkeys. In some monkey populations, he said, males kill other males and then, with the competition thus muted, proceed to copulate prolifically with females. These "hyperaggressive" males, he said, seem to be also "hypersexual." By a train of logic that was not entirely clear, he then arrived at the suggestion that "maybe it isn't just a careless use of the word when people call certain areas of certain cities jungles." Goodwin elaborated a bit on his obscure transition from monkeys to underclass males, but no matter; these few fragments are what came to form the standard paraphrase of his remarks. As the Los Angeles *Times* put it, Goodwin "made comparisons between inner-city youths and violent, oversexed monkeys who live in the wild."

As if a few seemingly racist quotes weren't enough of a public-relations bonanza for opponents of the Violence Initiative, Goodwin also injected what some took to be Hitlerian overtones. He talked about "genetic factors" inclining human beings toward violence, and suggested that one way to spot especially troublesome kids might be to look for "biological markers" of violent disposition. Within months, the Violence Initiative was abandoned, amid charges of racism. And Goodwin, facing the same charges, was reassigned to head the National Institute of Mental Health—not a huge demotion, but a conspicuous slap on the wrist. Finally, last year, he left that job for a position in academe after intermittent coolness from the Clinton Administration. Though no Clinton official ever told him he was a political liability, Goodwin found himself no longer invited to meetings he had once attended—meetings on violence, for example.

Goodwin is a victim of a vestigial feature of the American liberal mind: its undiscerning fear of the words "genetic" and "biological," and its wholesale hostility to Darwinian explanations of behavior. It turns out, believe it or not, that comparing violent inner-city males to monkeys isn't necessarily racist, or even necessarily right wing. On the contrary, a truly state-of-the-art comprehension of the comparison yields what is in many ways an archetypally liberal view of the "root causes" of urban violence. This comprehension comes via a young, hybrid academic discipline known as evolutionary psychology. Goodwin himself actually has little familiarity with the field, and doesn't realize how far to the left one can be dragged by a modern Darwinian view of the human mind. But he's closer to realizing it than the people whose outrage has altered his career.

As it happens, the nominally dead Federal Violence Initiative isn't really dead. Indeed, one of the few things Goodwin and his critics agree on is that its "life" and "death" have always been largely a question of labelling. Goodwin, who recently broke a thirty-month silence on the controversy, makes the point while dismissing the sinister aims attributed to the program. "They've made it sound like a cohesive new program that had some uniform direction to it and was directed by one person—namely, me," he told me. "The word 'initiative,' in bureaucratese, is simply a way of pulling stuff together to argue for budgets. In effect, that's what this was—a budget-formulation document, at Sullivan's request." Goodwin's critics

Originally from *The New Yorker*, March 13, 1995, pp. 68-77. © 1995 by Robert Wright. Reprinted by permission.

look at the other side of the coin: just as the bulk of the Violence Initiative predated the name itself, the bulk of it survived the name's deletion. Thus the war against the violence initiative—lower case—must go on.

THE person who was most responsible for turning Goodwin's monkey remarks into a life-changing and policy-influencing event is a psychiatrist named Peter Breggin, the founder and executive director of the Center for the Study of Psychiatry, in Bethesda, Maryland, just outside Washington. The center doubles as Breggin's home, and the center's research director, Ginger Ross Breggin, doubles as Breggin's wife. (Goodwin says of Peter Breggin, in reference to the center's lack of distinct physical existence, "People who don't know any better think he's a legitimate person.") Both Breggins take some credit for Goodwin's recent departure from government. "We've been all over the man for three years," Ginger Breggin observes.

Goodwin and Peter Breggin interned together at SUNY Upstate Medical Center in the nineteen-sixties. Both took a course taught by Thomas Szasz, the author of "The Myth of Mental Illness," which held that much of psychiatry is merely an oppressive tool by which the powers that be label inconvenient behavior "deviant." Szasz had formed his world view back when the most common form of oppression was locking people up, and Breggin, since founding his center, in 1971, has carried this view into the age of psychopharmacology. He fought lithium, Goodwin's initial claim to fame. He fought the monoamine-oxidase inhibitors, a somewhat crude generation of antidepressants, and now he fights a younger, less crude generation of them. "Talking Back to Prozac," written in collaboration with his wife and published last June, is among the anti-psychopharmacology books he has recently churned out. So is "The War Against Children," published last fall, in which the Breggins attack Goodwin, the Violence Initiative, and also the drug Ritalin. In Breggin's view, giving Ritalin to "hyperactive" children is a way of regimenting spirited kids rather than according them the attention they need—just as giving "anti-aggression" drugs to inner-city kids would be an excuse for continued neglect. And Breg-

gin is convinced that such drugs will be used in precisely this fashion if the Goodwins of the world get their way. This is the hidden agenda of the Violence Initiative, he says. And Goodwin concedes that pharmacological therapy was a likely outcome of the initiative.

Breggin's all-embracing opposition to psychopharmacology has earned him a reputation among psychiatrists as a "flat-earther." Some, indeed, go further in their disparagement, and Breggin is aware of this. "I am not a kook," he will tell a reporter whether or not the reporter has asked. People try to discredit him, Breggin says, because he is a threat to their interests—to the money made by drug companies, which insidiously bias research toward chemical therapy, and to the power of Goodwin and other "biological psychiatrists," who earn their status by "medicalizing" everything they see. "How is it that some spiritually passionate people become labeled schizophrenic and find themselves being treated as mental patients?" he asks in a 1991 book, "Toxic Psychiatry."

Breggin says he is struck by the parallels between the Violence Initiative and Nazi Germany: "the medicalization of social issues, the declaration that the victim of oppression, in this case the Jew, is in fact a genetically and biologically defective person, the mobilization of the state for eugenic purposes and biological purposes, the heavy use of psychiatry in the development of social-control programs." This is the sort of view that encouraged some members of the Congressional Black Caucus to demand that Goodwin be disciplined; it also helped get Breggin on Black Entertainment Television, and led to such headlines in black newspapers as "PLOT TO SEDATE BLACK YOUTH."

Breggin's scenario, the question of its truth aside, did have the rhetorical virtue of simple narrative form. ("He made a nice story of it," Goodwin says, in a tone not wholly devoid of admiration.) There has lately been much interest in, and much federally funded research into, the role that the neurotransmitter serotonin plays in violence. On average, people with low serotonin levels are more inclined toward impulsive violence than people with normal levels. Since Goodwin was a co-author of the first paper noting the correlation between serotonin and violence, he would seem to

have a natural interest in this issue. And, since the "serotonin-reuptake inhibitors," such as Eli Lilly's Prozac, raise serotonin levels, there would seem to exist a large financial incentive to identify low serotonin as the source of urban ills. Hence, from Breggin's vantage point it all fell into place—a confluence of corporate and personal interests that helped make serotonin the most talked-about biochemical in federal violence research. But, Breggin says, we musn't lose sight of its larger significance: serotonin is "just a code word for biological approaches."

IT was in the late seventies that Goodwin and several colleagues stumbled on the connection between serotonin and violence, while studying servicemen who were being observed for possible psychiatric discharge. Since then, low serotonin has been found in other violent populations, such as children who torture animals, children who are unusually hostile toward their mothers, and people who score high for aggression on standardized tests. Lowering people's serotonin levels in a laboratory setting made them more inclined to give a person electrical shocks (or, at least, what experimenters deceived them into thinking were electrical shocks).

It isn't clear whether serotonin influences aggression per se or simply impulse control, since low serotonin correlates also with impulsive arson and with attempted suicide. But serotonin level does seem to be a rough predictor of misbehavior—a biological marker. In a study of twenty-nine children with "disruptive behavior disorders," serotonin level helped predict future aggression. And in a National Institutes of Health study of fifty-eight violent offenders and impulsive arsonists serotonin level, together with another biochemical index, predicted with eighty-four-per-cent accuracy whether they would commit crimes after leaving prison.

It doesn't take an overactive imagination to envision parole boards screening prisoners for biological markers before deciding their fate—just as Goodwin had suggested that using biological markers might help determine which children need antiviolence therapy. These are the kinds of scenarios that make Breggin worry about a world in which the government labels some people ge-

netically deficient and treats them accordingly. In reply, Goodwin stresses that a "biological" marker needn't be a "genetic" one. Though N.I.H. studies suggest that some people's genes are conducive to low serotonin, environmental influences can also lower serotonin, and federal researchers are studying these. Thus a "biological" marker may be an "environmental" marker, not a "genetic" one. To this Breggin replies, "It's not what they believe, it's not in a million years what they really believe." This attempt to cast biological research as research into environment "shows their desperation, because this was never their argument until they got attacked," he says. "It's a political move."

In truth, federal researchers, including Goodwin, were looking into "environmental influences" on biochemistry well before being attacked by Breggin. Still, they do often employ a narrower notion of the term's meaning that Breggin would like. When Goodwin talks about such influences, he doesn't dwell on the sort of social forces that interest Breggin, such as poverty and bad schools. He says, for example, that he has looked into "data on head injuries, victims of abuse, poor prenatal nutrition, higher levels of lead," and so on.

In other words, he is inclined to view violence as an illness, whether it is the product of aberrant genes or of pathological—deeply unnatural—circumstances, or both. This is not surprising, given his line of work: he is a psychiatrist, a doctor; his job is to cure people, and people without pathologies don't need curing. "Once I learned that seventy-nine per cent of repeated violent offenses were by seven per cent of youth, it began to look to me like a clinical population, a population that had something wrong with it that resulted in this behavior," he says. Other federal researchers on violence tend to take the same approach. After all, most of them work at one of the National Institutes of Health, whether the National Institute of Mental Health, the National Institute on Alcohol Abuse and Alcoholism, or some other affiliate. For the Violence Initiative to be successful in the pragmatic aims that Goodwin acknowledges—as a way "to argue for budgets" for the Department of Health and Human Services—it pretty much had to

define violence as a pathology, characteristic of inner-city kids who have something "wrong" with them.

Breggin would rather depict violence as the not very surprising reaction of normal people to oppressive circumstances. A big problem with biological views of behavior generally, he says, is that they so often bolster the medical notions of "deviance" and "pathology"—and thus divert attention from the need to change social conditions.

But "biological" views don't have to be "medical" views. This is where the field of evolutionary psychology enters the picture, and modern Darwinian thought begins to diverge from Goodwin's sketchier and more dated ideas about human evolution. Evolutionary psychologists share Goodwin's conviction that genes, neurotransmitters such as serotonin, and biology more generally are a valid route to explaining human behavior; and they share his belief in the relevance of studying nonhuman primates. Yet they are much more open than he is to the Bregginesque view that inner-city violence is a "natural" reaction to a particular social environment.

To most N.I.H. researchers, evolutionary psychology is terra incognita. Goodwin, for one, professes only vague awareness of the field. But the field offers something that should intrigue him: a theory about what serotonin is, in the deepest sense—why natural selection designed it to do the things it does. This theory would explain, for example, the effect that Prozac has on people. More to the point, this theory would explain the link that Goodwin himself discovered between low serotonin and violence.

THE two acknowledged experts on human violence within evolutionary psychology are Martin Daly and Margo Wilson, of McMaster University, in Ontario. Their 1988 book, "Homicide," barely known outside Darwinian-social-science circles, is considered a classic within them. Listening to Margo Wilson talk about urban crime is like entering a time warp and finding yourself chatting with Huey Newton or Jane Fonda in 1969. "First of all, what's a crime?" she asks. It all depends on "who are the rule-makers, who's in power. We call it theft when somebody comes into

your house and steals something, but we don't call it theft when we get ripped off by political agendas or big-business practices." And as for gang violence: "It's a coalition of males who are mutually supporting each other to serve their interests against some other coalition. How is that different from some international war?"

To hear this sort of flaming liberal rhetoric from a confirmed Darwinian should surprise not just Peter Breggin but anyone familiar with intellectual history. For much of this century, many people who took a Darwinian view of human behavior embraced the notorious ideology of social Darwinism. They emphatically did not view social deviance as some arbitrary and self-serving designation made by the ruling class; more likely, crime was a sign of "unfitness," of an innate inability to thrive legitimately. The "unfit" were best left to languish in jail, where they could not reproduce. And "unfit" would-be immigrants—those from, say, Eastern Europe, who were congenitally ill equipped to enrich American society—were best kept out of the country.

What permits Margo Wilson to sound a quite different theme is two distinguishing features of evolutionary psychology. First, evolutionary psychologists are not much interested in genetic differences, whether among individuals or among groups. The object of study is, rather, "species-typical mental adaptations"—also known as "human nature." A basic tenet of evolutionary psychologists is that there is such a thing as human nature—that people everywhere have fundamentally the same minds.

A second tenet of evolutionary psychologists is respect for the power of environment. The human mind, they say, has been designed to adjust to social circumstances. The vital difference between this and earlier forms of environmental determinism is the word "designed." Evolutionary psychologists believe that the developmental programs that convert social experience into personality were created by natural selection, which is to say that those programs lie in our genes. Thus, to think clearly about the influence of environment we must think about what sorts of influences would have been favored by natural selection.

If, for example, early social rejection makes people enduringly insecure, then we should ask whether this pattern of development might have had a genetic payoff during evolution. Maybe people who faced such rejection saw their chances of survival and reproduction plummet unless they became more socially vigilant—neurotically attentive to nourishing their social ties. Thus genes that responded to rejection by instilling this neurotic vigilance, this insecurity, would have flourished. And eventually those genes could have spread through the species, becoming part of human nature.

These two themes—universal human nature and the power of environment—are related. It is belief in the power of environment—of family milieu, cultural milieu, social happenstance—that allows evolutionary psychologists to see great variation in human behavior, from person to person or from group to group, without reflexively concluding that the explanation lies in genetic variation. The explanation lies in the genes, to be sure. Where else could a program for psychological development ultimately reside? But it doesn't necessarily lie in differences among different people's genes.

This is the perspective that Martin Daly and Margo Wilson bring to the subject of violence. They think about genes in order to understand the role of environment. And one result of this outlook is agreement with Peter Breggin that inner-city violence shouldn't be labelled a "pathology." In a paper published last year Daly and Wilson wrote, "Violence is abhorrent. . . . Violence is so aversive that merely witnessing an instance can be literally sickening. . . ." There is thus "but a short leap to the metaphorical characterization of violence itself as a sort of 'sickness' or 'dysfunction.'" But, they insisted, this leap is ill advised. Violence is eminently functional—something that people are designed to do.

Especially men. From an evolutionary point of view, the leading cause of violence is maleness. "Men have evolved the morphological, physiological and psychological means to be effective users of violence," Daly and Wilson wrote. The reason, according to modern evolutionary thought, is simple. Because a female can reproduce only once a year, whereas a male can reproduce many times a year, females are the scarcer

sexual resource. During evolution, males have competed over this resource, with the winners impregnating more than their share of women and the losers impregnating few or none. As always with natural selection, we're left with the genes of the winners—in this case, genes inclining males toward fierce combat. One reflection of this history is that men are larger and stronger than women. Such "sexual dimorphism" is seen in many species, and biologists consider it a rough index of the intensity of male sexual competition.

To say that during evolution men have fought over women isn't to say that they've always fought directly over women, with the winner of a bout walking over and claiming his nubile trophy. Rather, human beings are somewhat like our nearest relatives, the chimpanzees: males compete for status, and status brings access to females. Hence skills conducive to successful status competition would have a "selective advantage"—would be favored by natural selection. As Daly and Wilson have put it, "if status has persistently contributed to reproductive success, and a capacity for controlled violence has regularly contributed to status, then the selective advantage of violent skills cannot be gainsaid."

It's easy to find anecdotal evidence that status has indeed tended to boost the reproductive success of males. (It was Henry Kissinger who said that power is an aphrodisiac, and Representative Pat Schroeder who observed that a middle-aged congresswoman doesn't exert the same animal magnetism on the opposite sex that a middle-aged congressman does.) But more telling is evidence drawn from hunter-gatherer societies, the closest thing to real-life examples of the pre-agrarian social context for which the human mind was designed. Among the Ache of Paraguay, high-status men have more extramarital affairs and more illegitimate children than low-status men. Among the Aka Pygmies of central Africa, an informal leader known as a *kombeti* gets more wives and offspring than the average Aka. And so on. The Aka, the Ache, and Henry Kissinger all demonstrate that violence against other men is hardly the only means by which male status is sought. Being a good hunter is a primary route to status among the Ache, and be-

ing a wily social manipulator helps in all societies (even, it turns out, in chimp societies, where males climb the status ladder by forging "political" coalitions). Still, in all human societies questions of relative male status are sometimes settled through fighting. This form of settlement is, of course, more prevalent in some arenas than others—more in a bikers' bar than in the Russian Tea Room, more in the inner city than on the Upper East Side. But, as Daly and Wilson note, one theme holds true everywhere: men compete for status through the means locally available. If men in the Russian Tea Room don't assault one another, that's because assault isn't the route to status in the Russian Tea Room.

According to Daly and Wilson, a failure to see the importance of such circumstances is what leads well-heeled people to express patronizing shock that "trivial" arguments in barrooms and ghettos escalate to murder. In "Homicide" they wrote, "An implicit contrast is drawn between the foolishness of violent men and the more rational motives that move sensible people like ourselves. The combatants are in effect denigrated as creatures of some lower order of mental functioning, evidently governed by immediate stimuli rather than by foresightful contemplation." In truth, Daly and Wilson say, such combatants are typical of our species, as it has been observed around the world: "In most social milieus, a man's reputation depends in part upon the maintenance of a credible threat of violence." This fact is "obscured in modern mass society because the state has assumed a monopoly on the legitimate use of force. But wherever that monopoly is relaxed—whether in an entire society or in a neglected underclass—then the utility of that credible threat becomes apparent." In such an environment, "a seemingly minor affront is not merely a 'stimulus' to action, isolated in time and space. It must be understood within a larger social context of reputations, face, relative social status, and enduring relationships. Men are known by their fellows as . . . people whose word means action and people who are full of hot air."

That a basic purpose of violence is display—to convince peers that you will defend your status—helps explain an otherwise puzzling fact. As Daly and Wilson note, when men kill men whom

they know, there is usually an audience. This doesn't seem to make sense—why murder someone in the presence of witnesses?—except in terms of evolutionary psychology. Violence is in large part a performance.

Thus the dismay often inspired by reports that a black teen-ager killed because he had been "dissed" is naïve. Nothing was more vital to the reproductive success of our male ancestors than respect, so there is nothing that the male mind will more feverishly seek to neutralize than disrespect. All men spend much of their lives doing exactly this; most are just lucky enough to live in a place where guns won't help them do it. These days, well-educated men do their status maintenance the way Goodwin and Breggin do it, by verbally defending their honor and verbally assailing the honor of their enemies. But back when duelling was in vogue even the most polished of men might occasionally try to kill one another.

THIS view from evolutionary psychology in some ways jibes with a rarely quoted point that Goodwin made during his rambling remarks on monkeys: that inner-city violence may be caused by a "loss of structure in society"; in an environment where violence is deemed legitimate, the male inclination for violence may reassert itself. Of monkeys, Goodwin had said, "that is the natural way of it for males, to knock each other off," and the implicit comparison was supposed to be with all human males, not just black ones; his point was that many black males now live in neighborhoods where social restraints have dissolved. This is the sense in which Goodwin says he meant to compare the inner cities to jungles, and the transcript of his remarks bears him out. His poor choice of imagery still haunts him. "If I had said that in the Wild West, where there was no structure, there was a hell of a lot of violence, no one would have noticed."

There is a crucial difference between this emphasis on social milieu as rendered by Goodwin and as rendered by evolutionary psychologists; namely, they don't abandon it when they start thinking about the interface between biology and environment. Whereas pondering this interface steers Goodwin's thoughts

toward "pathology"—the biological effects of malnutrition, or brain damage due to child abuse—evolutionary psychologists try to figure out how normal, everyday experience affects the biochemistry of violence.

Consider serotonin. In particular, consider an extensive study of serotonin in monkeys done by Michael McGuire, an evolutionary psychologist, and his colleagues at U.C.L.A. Vervet monkeys have a clear male social hierarchy: low-status males defer to high-status males over access to limited resources, including females. McGuire found that the highest-ranking monkeys in the male social hierarchy have the highest serotonin levels. What's more, the lower-ranking males tend to be more impulsively violent. Other studies have linked low serotonin to violence in monkeys even more directly.

At first glance, such findings might appear to be what Peter Breggin, and many liberals, would consider their worst nightmare. If this biochemical analogy between monkeys and human beings is indeed valid, the lesson would seem to be this: some individuals are born to be society's leaders, some are born to be its hoodlums; the chairman of I.B.M. was born with high serotonin, the urban gang member was born with low serotonin. And what if it turns out that blacks on average have less serotonin than whites do?

There certainly is evidence that some sort of analogy between the social lives of monkeys and human beings is in order. McGuire has found that officers of college fraternities have higher serotonin levels than the average frat-house resident, and that college athletes perceived as team leaders have higher levels than their average teammate. But grasping the import of the analogy requires delving into the details of McGuire's monkey research.

When McGuire examines a dominant male monkey before he becomes a dominant—before he climbs the social hierarchy by winning some key fights with other males—serotonin level is often unexceptional. It rises during his ascent, apparently in response to sometimes inconspicuous social cues. Indeed, his serotonin may begin to creep upward before he physically challenges any

higher-ranking males; the initial rise may be caused by favorable attention from females (who play a larger role in shaping the male social hierarchy than was once appreciated). When, on the other hand, a dominant male suffers a loss of status, his serotonin level drops.

What's going on here? There is no way to look inside a monkey's mind and see how serotonin makes him feel. But there is evidence that in human beings high serotonin levels bring high self-esteem. Raising self-esteem is one effect of Prozac and other serotonin boosters, such as Zoloft. And, indeed, high-ranking monkeys—or, to take a species more closely related to us, high-ranking chimpanzees—tend to behave the way people with high self-esteem behave: with calm self-assurance; assertively, yes, but seldom violently. (This subtle distinction, as Peter Kramer notes in "Listening to Prozac," is also seen in human beings. Prozac may make them more socially assertive, but less irritable, less prone to spontaneous outbursts.) To be sure, an alpha-male chimp may periodically exhibit aggression—or, really, a kind of ritual mock-aggression—to remind everyone that he's the boss, but most alphas tend not to be as fidgety and perturbable as some lower-ranking apes, except when leadership is being contested.

All this suggests a hypothesis. Maybe one function of serotonin—in human and nonhuman primates—is to regulate self-esteem in accordance with social feedback; and maybe one function of self-esteem is, in turn to help primates negotiate social hierarchies, climbing as high on the ladder as circumstance permits. Self-esteem (read serotonin) keeps rising as long as one encounters social success, and each step in this elevation inclines one to raise one's social sights a little higher. Variable self-esteem, then, is evolution's way of preparing us to reach and maintain whatever level of social status is realistic, given our various attributes (social skills, talent, etc.) and our milieu. High serotonin, in this view, isn't nature's way of destining people from birth for high status; it is nature's way of equipping any of us for high status should we find ourselves possessing it. The flip side of this hypothesis is that low self-esteem (and low serotonin) is evolution's way of equipping us for low status should our situation not be conducive to elevation.

This *doesn't* mean what an earlier generation of evolutionists would have thought: that Mother Nature wants people with low status to endure their fate patiently for "the greater good." Just the opposite. A founding insight of evolutionary psychology is that natural selection rarely designs things for the "good of the group." Any psychological inclinations that offer a way to cope with low status provide just that—a way to cope, a way to make the best of a bad situation. The purpose of low self-esteem isn't to bring submission for the sake of social order; more likely, its purpose is to discourage people from conspicuously challenging higher-status people who are, by virtue of their status, in a position to punish such insolence.

AND what about the antisocial tendencies, the impulsive behavior linked with low serotonin in both human beings and monkeys? How does evolutionary psychology explain them? This is where the demise of "good of the group" logic opens the way for especially intriguing theories. In particular: primates may be designed to respond to low status by "breaking the rules" when they can get away with it. The established social order isn't working in their favor, so they circumvent its strictures at every opportunity. Similarly, inner-city thugs may be functioning as "designed": their minds absorb environmental input reflecting their low socioeconomic standing and the absence of "legitimate" routes to social elevation, and incline their behavior in the appropriately criminal direction.

The trouble with breaking rules, of course, is the risk of getting caught and punished. But, as Daly and Wilson note by quoting Bob Dylan, "When you ain't got nothin', you got nothin' to lose." In the environment of our evolution, low status often signified that a male had had little or no reproductive success to date; for such a male, taking risks to raise status could make sense in Darwinian terms. In hunter-gatherer societies, Daly and Wilson write, "competition can sometimes be fiercest near the bottom of the scale, where the man on track for total [reproductive] failure has nothing to lose by the most dangerous competitive tactics, and may therefore throw caution to the winds." Even as low self-esteem

keeps him from challenging dominant males, he may behave recklessly toward those closer to him on the social ladder. Thus may the biochemistry of low status, along with the attendant states of mind, encourage impulsive risk-taking.

This theory, at any rate, would help make sense of some long-unexplained data. Psychologists found several decades ago that artificially lowering people's self-esteem—by giving them false reports about scores on a personality test—makes them more likely to cheat in a subsequent game of cards. Such risky rule-breaking is just the sort of behavior that makes more sense for a low-status animal than for a high-status animal.

To say that serotonin level is heavily influenced by social experience isn't to say that a person's genetic idiosyncrasies aren't significant. But it is to say that they are at best half the story. There are not yet any definitive studies on the "heritability" of serotonin level—the amount of the variation among people that is explained by genetic difference. But the one study that has been done suggests that less than half the variation in the population studied came from genetic differences, and the rest from differences in environment. And even this estimate of heritability is probably misleadingly high. Presumably, self-esteem correlates with many other personal attributes, such as physique or facial attractiveness. Impressive people, after all, inspire the sort of feedback that raises self-esteem and serotonin. Since these attributes are themselves quite heritable—traceable largely to a person's distinctive genes—some of the "heritability" estimate for serotonin may reflect genes not for high serotonin per se but for good looks, great body, and so on. (The technical term for this oblique genetic effect is "reactive heritability.")

At least some of the variation in serotonin level is grounded more directly in genetic difference. N.I.H. researchers have identified a human gene that helps convert tryptophan, an amino acid found in some grains and fruits, into serotonin, and they have found a version of the gene that yields low serotonin levels. Still, there is no reason to believe that different ethnic groups have different genetic endowments for serotonin. Indeed, even if it turned out that American blacks on average had lower serotonin than

whites, there would be no cause to implicate genes. One would expect groups that find themselves shunted toward the bottom of the socioeconomic hierarchy to have low serotonin. That may be nature's way of preparing them to take risks and to evade the rules of the powers that be.

This Darwinian theory integrating serotonin, status, and impulsive violence remains meagerly tested and is no doubt oversimplified. One complicating factor is modern life. People in contemporary America are part of various social hierarchies. An inner-city gang leader may get great, serotonin-boosting respect ("juice," as the suggestive street slang calls it) from fellow gang members while also getting serotonin-sapping signs of disrespect when he walks into a tony jewelry store, or even when he turns on the TV and sees that wealthy, high-status males tend to bear no physical or cultural resemblance to him. The human mind was designed for a less ambiguous setting— a hunter-gatherer society, in which a young man's social reference points stay fairly constant from day to day. We don't yet know how the mind responds to a world of wildly clashing status cues.

Another hidden complexity in this Darwinian theory lies in the fact that serotonin does lots of things besides mediate self-esteem and impulsive aggression. Precisely what it does depends on the part of the brain it is affecting and the levels of other neurotransmitters. Over-all serotonin level is hardly the subtlest imaginable chemical index of a human being's mental state. Still, though we don't yet fathom the entire biochemistry of things like self-esteem, impulsiveness, and violence, there is little doubt among evolutionary psychologists that the subject is fathomable—and that it will get fathomed much faster if biomedical researchers, at N.I.H. and elsewhere, start thinking in Darwinian terms.

IF evolutionary psychologists are right in even the broad contours of their outlook, then there is good news and bad news for both Frederick Goodwin and Peter Breggin. For Goodwin, the good news is that his infamous remarks were essentially on target: he was right to compare violent inner-city males—or any other violent human males—to nonhuman primates (though he exag-

gerated the incidence of actual murder among such primates). The bad news is that his Violence Initiative, in failing to pursue that insight, in clinging to the view of violence as pathology, was doomed to miss a large part of the picture; the bulk of inner-city violence will probably never be explained by reference to head injuries, poor nutrition, prenatal exposure to drugs, and bad genes. If violence is a public-health problem, it is so mainly in the sense that getting killed is bad for your health.

Evolutionary psychology depicts all kinds of things often thought to be "pathological" as "natural": unyielding hatred, mild depression, a tendency of men to treat women as their personal property. Some Darwinians even think that rape may in some sense be a "natural" response to certain circumstances. Of course, to call these things "natural" isn't to call them beyond self-control, or beyond the influence of punishment. And it certainly isn't to call them good. If anything, evolutionary psychology might be invoked on behalf of the doctrine of Original Sin: we are in some respects born bad, and redemption entails struggle against our nature.

Many people, including many social scientists and biomedical researchers, seem to have trouble with the idea of a conflict between nature and morality. "I think this is a source of resistance to evolutionary ways of thinking," says John Tooby, a professor at the University of California at Santa Barbara, who along with his wife, Leda Cosmides, laid down some of the founding doctrines of evolutionary psychology. "There's a strong tendency to want to return to the romantic notion that the natural is the good." Indeed, "one modern basis for establishing morals is to try to ground them in the notion of sickness. Anything people don't like, they accuse the person doing it of being sick."

Thomas Szasz couldn't have said it better. Herein lies evolutionary psychology's good news for Peter Breggin: yes, it is indeed misleading to call most violence a pathology, a disorder. The bad news for Breggin is that, even though

the causes of violence are broadly environmental, as he insists, they are nonetheless biological, because environmental forces are mediated biologically—in this case by, among other things, serotonin. Thus, a scientist can be a "biological determinist" or a "biological reductionist" without being a genetic determinist. He or she can say—as Daly and Wilson and Tooby and Cosmides do—that human behavior is driven by biological forces impinging on the brain, yet can view those forces largely as a reflection of a person's distinctive environment.

This confronts Breggin with a major rhetorical complication. Much of his success in arousing opposition to the Violence Initiative lay in conveniently conflating the terms "biological" and "genetic." He does this habitually. In suggesting that the initiative grew out of Goodwin's long-standing designs, Breggin says he has Baltimore *Evening Sun* articles from 1984 in which "Goodwin is talking about crime and violence being genetic and biological." In truth, these articles show Goodwin saying nothing about genes—only that violence has some biological correlates and might respond to pharmacological treatment. In Breggin's mind, "genetic" and "biological" are joined at the waist.

That these terms are not, in fact, inseparable—that something utterly biological, like serotonin level, may differ between two people because of environmental, not genetic, differences—poses a second problem for Breggin. The best way to illuminate the environmental forces he stresses may be to study the biological underpinnings of behavior, and that is a prospect he loathes. If serotonin is one chemical that converts poverty and disrespect into impulsiveness or aggression or low self-esteem, then it, along with other chemicals, may be a handy index of all these things—something whose level can be monitored more precisely than the things themselves. (Studies finding that blacks on average don't suffer from low self-esteem

are based on asking black people and white people how they feel about themselves—a dubious approach, since expressions of humility seem to be more highly valued in white suburban culture than in black urban culture.)

That Breggin may be wrong in the way he thinks about biology and behavior doesn't mean that the unsettling scenarios he envisions are far-fetched. The government may well try to use biochemical "markers" to select violently inclined kids for therapy, or to screen prisoners for parole. (Then again, if these chemicals aren't simple "genetic markers," but rather are summaries of the way genes and environment have together molded a person's state of mind, how are they different from a standard psychological evaluation, which summarizes the same thing?) There may also be attempts to treat violently inclined teenagers with serotonin-boosting drugs, as Breggin fears. And, though some teenagers might thus be helped into the mainstream economy, these drugs could also become a palliative, a way to keep the inner city tranquil without improving it. The brave new world of biochemical diagnosis and therapy is coming; and, for all the insight evolutionary psychology brings, it won't magically answer the difficult questions that will arise.

The point to bear in mind is simply that less eerie, more traditionally liberal prescriptions for urban violence continue to make sense after we've looked at black teen-agers as animals—which, after all, is what human beings are. The view from evolutionary psychology suggests that one way to reduce black violence would be to make the inner cities places where young men have nonviolent routes to social status and the means and motivation to follow them. Better-paying jobs, and better public schools, for example, wouldn't hurt. Oddly enough, thinking about genes from a Darwinian standpoint suggests that inner-city teen-agers are victims of their environment.

A Violence in the Blood

Five generations of aggressive men in a Dutch family have led researchers to a gene that seems to lie at the root of the violence.

Sarah Richardson

One day in 1978 a woman walked into University Hospital in Nijmegen, the Netherlands, with a problem: the men in her family. Many of them—including several of her brothers and a son—seemed to have some sort of mental debility. Gradually, as the clinical geneticists who counseled the woman got to know her and her family, the details of the strange behavior of the woman's male kin emerged. One had tried to rape his sister; another had tried to run his boss down with a car; a third had forced his sisters to undress at knife point. Furthermore, the violent streak had a long history. In 1962 the woman's granduncle had prepared a family tree that identified nine other males with the same disorder, tracing it as far back as 1870. The granduncle, who was not violent himself—he worked in an institution for the learning disabled—had apparently come to suspect that something was terribly wrong with his family.

Three decades later, and 15 years after the woman's first office visit, geneticist Han Brunner and his colleagues at the Nijmegen hospital think they've figured out what that something is. Some of the men in the woman's family, they say, suffer from a genetic defect on the X chromosome—a defect that cripples an enzyme that may help regulate aggressive behavior. If Brunner and his colleagues are right, it would be the first time a specific gene has been linked to aggression. That means their finding cannot fail to be controversial.

The geneticists' first clue to the origin of the aggressive behavior in the Dutch family was simply that all the violent family members were men; moreover, the trait seemed to be handed down from mother to son. That pattern immediately suggested that the root of the disorder was a defect on the X chromosome. Men are vulnerable to such a defect because they only have one X chromosome. Women have two X chromosomes, so as long as the second one is normal they don't feel the effects of a defect on the first. But they can carry the defect and pass it on to their sons.

> *"We can't say a genetic defect causes the aggressive behavior. It is only one element."*

The second clue to the nature of the disorder came from the IQs of the affected men, which were typically about 85, on the border of what is considered mental retardation. (Only one of the five men examined by the geneticists had even completed primary school.) X-linked mental retardation is a well-known phenomenon; it comes in many forms and is caused by many different genetic defects, but aggressive behavior is one of its more common symptoms. The Nijmegen geneticists had often seen X-linked retardation. At first, all they could do for the worried woman who had walked into their office was tell her that her male relatives appeared to have a mild form of it, traceable to a defect on the X chromosome—precise location unknown.

By 1988, though, two things had happened to change the situation. The men in the family were continuing to be violent in a way that didn't seem mild and that frightened the women enough to seek help again. "The youngest generation of women were reaching their twenties," says Brunner, who joined the Nijmegen group in 1984, "and they wanted to know if they were carriers." By then, a key gene-mapping technique had improved enough to allow the geneticists to tell them.

The technique is called genetic linkage analysis. It consists essentially in analyzing a chromosome to find an identifiable stretch of DNA that is always inherited along with a still-unidentified genetic defect—to find, that is, a "genetic marker" that lies near the defect on the chromosome. Over the course of four years, Brunner and his colleagues analyzed the X chromosomes of 28 members of the Dutch family. Finally they found a marker. "It was on the short arm of the X chromosome," says Brunner, "and the match with the clinical condition was absolutely perfect." The violent men examined by the researchers all had the marker, and so did some of the women—they, presumably, were carriers of the genetic defect. None of the nonviolent men had it. The chance of such a coincidence occurring randomly, says Brunner, is about 1 in 5,000.

The researchers still did not know the nature of the genetic defect itself, but now they had a clue. Although hundreds of genes, most of them unidentified, lay in the vicinity of the marker, one was of particular interest. It was known to code for an enzyme called monoamine oxidase A, or MAOA. MAOA's job is to break down three important neurotransmitters—chemicals that trigger or inhibit the transmission of nerve impulses. One of the three is norepinephrine, which raises blood pressure and increases alertness as part of the body's "fight or flight" response. The other two neurotransmitters that MAOA breaks down are serotonin and dopamine, which are also involved in regulating mood and alertness, and imbalances of which are often found in

Reprinted with permission from *Discover* magazine, October 1993, pp. 30-31. © 1993 by The Walt Disney Company.

patients with psychiatric disorders. The MAOA gene thus seemed like a good place to look for a defect associated with mental retardation and aggressive behavior.

If the violent men were suffering from defective MAOA, Brunner and his colleagues reasoned, excess levels of the neurotransmitters would accumulate in their bodies and in their urine. So the researchers tested the men's urine. They found excess levels of all three neurotransmitters. They also found extraordinarily low levels of breakdown products—the substances normally left over after MAOA has done its work.

Brunner and his colleagues don't know how MAOA deficiency might result in a lower IQ, but they think the excess neurotransmitters may amount to a kind of biochemical hair trigger that predisposes the men to violence when they are under stress. (Two of the men, for example, committed arson following the death of a close relative.) "We can't say a genetic defect *causes* the behavior," says Brunner. "It is only one element. What we observe in these men is a lowered threshold for this type of behavior."

Even that seemingly measured conclusion is likely to excite controversy, however; the very notion that there might be biological roots to aggression carries such emotional freight these days that last year the National Institutes of Health was forced by a public outcry to cancel a conference on the subject. Skeptics point out that even though the Dutch study was confined to one family—which may limit its significance, they say—Brunner's group did not attempt to measure the influence of a shared environment on the violent men.

Yet the possibility that MAOA deficiency might be associated with behavioral abnormalities was predicted as far back as the late seventies, on the basis of experiments with rats and mice. And some researchers who have studied the enzyme are impressed with Brunner's results. Xandra Breakefield, a neurogeneticist at Massachusetts General Hospital who has cloned the MAOA gene, is now collaborating with Brunner to pinpoint the genetic defect in the Dutch family. Breakefield wants to find out whether the Dutch disorder is a "rare,

esoteric illness," as she puts it, "or a relatively common deficiency." Rare or not, she says, MAOA deficiency may one day be treatable, either through dietary restrictions designed to limit the body's synthesis of neurotransmitters, or through drugs that block their action.

Even if MAOA deficiency turns out to explain more than the strange history of one Dutch family, though, it is not likely to be anything remotely resembling a generalized biological root for aggressive behavior. Such behavior must have many causes. "There is no such thing as an aggression gene," says Brunner. "Rather there is a balanced system known as the brain. If it's disturbed, you may have this type of behavior."

But Brunner and his colleagues are convinced they have found one particular form of disturbance that leads to aggression. "When we started," Brunner points out, "we were unaware of the huge literature linking MAOA deficiency and aggression in rats and mice. We weren't looking for what we found, and I think that strengthens our credibility."

Big. Bad. Bully.

No, it's not just boys being boys. It takes a special breed of person to cause pain to others. But the one most hurt by bullying is the bully himself—though that's not at first obvious and the effects worsen over the life cycle. Yes, females can be bullies too. They just favor a different means of mean.

Hara Estroff Marano

On the first day of spring in 1993, honor student Curtis Taylor took his seat in the eighth-grade classroom he had grown to hate in the Oak Street Middle School in Burlington, Iowa. For three years other boys had been tripping him in the hallways, knocking things out of his hands. They'd even taken his head in their hands and banged it into a locker. Things were now intensifying. The name-calling was harsher. Some beloved books were taken. His bicycle was vandalized twice. Kids even kicked the cast that covered his broken ankle. And in front of his classmates, some guys poured chocolate milk down the front of his sweatshirt. Curtis was so upset he went to see a school counselor. He blamed himself for the other kids not liking him.

That night, Curtis went into a family bedroom, took out a gun, and shot himself to death. The community was stunned. The television cameras rolled, at least for a few days. Chicago journalist Bob Green lingered over the events in his column, and then he printed letters from folks for whom the episode served largely as a reminder of their own childhood humiliations at the hands of bullies.

Months later, in Cherokee County, Georgia, 15-year-old Brian Head grew tired of the same teasing and deeds. The denouement was only slightly more remarkable. He shot himself to death—in front of his classmates. He walked to the front of the classroom and pulled the trigger. The Georgia death came on the heels of five bullying-related suicides in a small town in New Hampshire. Within days, the story got lost in the cacophony of breaking events.

Just over a decade earlier, in late 1982, a near identical series of events unfolded in the northern reaches of Norway. Three boys between the ages of 10 and 14 killed themselves, one newspaper reported, to avoid continued severe bullying from schoolmates. But the story would not die. Nor would it shrivel into self-pity. An entire nation erupted. The following fall, scarcely nine months later, a campaign against bullying was in full swing in all of Norway's primary and junior high schools, launched by the minister of education. And its architect, Dan Olweus, Ph.D., a psychologist who, in 1970, had pioneered the systematic study of bullying, became something of a national hero in Sweden.

The difference between the American and the Scandinavian experience could arguably be summed up in four words: Mighty Morphin Power Rangers. A nation whose toys are given to slashing robots in half seems to have more tolerance for violence as a solution to problems. Most Americans do not take bullying very seriously—not even school personnel, a surprising finding given that most bullying takes place in schools. If Americans think at all about it, they tend to think that bullying is a given of childhood, at most a passing stage, one inhabited largely by boys who will, simply, inevitably, be boys.

"They even encourage it in boys," observes Gary W. Ladd, Ph.D., a professor of psychology at the University of Illinois and one of a growing cadre of Americans studying the phenomenon. "That's what parents always ask me," says psychologist David Schwartz, Ph.D., of Vanderbilt University, "isn't it just a case of boys being boys?" The same parents harbor the belief that kids should somehow always be able to defend themselves—to "stand up for themselves," "fight back," "not be pushed around by anyone"—and those who don't or can't almost deserve what they get. Bullying is just good old boyhood in a land of aggressive individualists.

Nothing could be further from the truth.

First in Scandinavia, then in England, Japan, the Netherlands, Canada, and finally, the United States, researchers have begun scrutinizing the phenomenon of bullying. What they are finding is as sad as it is alarming:

- Bullies are a special breed of children. The vast majority of children (60 to 70 percent) are never involved in bullying, either as perpetrators or victims. Early in development, most children acquire internal restraints against such behavior. But those who bully do it consistently.

- Their aggression starts at an early age.

- It takes a very specific set of conditions to produce a child who can start fights, threaten or intimidate a peer ("Give me the jump rope or I'll kill you"), and actively inflict pain upon others.

- Bullying causes a great deal of misery to others, and its effects on victims last for decades, perhaps even a lifetime.

- The person hurt most by bullying is the bully himself, though that's not at first obvious, and the negative effects increase over time.

- Most bullies have a downwardly

Reprinted with permission from *Psychology Today*, September/October 1995, pp. 50-57, 62, 64, 66, 68-70, 74, 76, 79, 82. © 1995 by Sussex Publishers, Inc.

spiraling course through life, their behavior interfering with learning, friendships, work, intimate relationships, income, and mental health.

• Bullies turn into antisocial adults, and are far more likely than nonaggressive kids to commit crimes, batter their wives, abuse their children—and produce another generation of bullies.

• Oh yes, girls can be bullies too. The aggression of girls has been vastly underestimated because it takes a different form. It is a far more subtle and complex means of meanness than the overt physical aggression boys engage in.

To understand the behavior of bullies is to see how aggression is learned and how well the lesson is taken to heart. The existence of bullies tells us that the social needs of human beings are vastly undervalued, at least in Western culture. For the social life of kids, often thought as an ac-

cessory to childhood, turns out to be crucial to healthy development. In the long run, bullying can be a way—a desperate and damaging way—for some people to maintain a circle of human contacts.

And bullying always has a very long run. Bullying may begin in childhood, but it continues into adulthood; it is among the most stable of human behavior styles.

What's a Bully and Who Is It?

There is no standard definition of a bully, but Dan Olweus has honed the definition to three core elements—bullying involves a pattern of *repeated aggressive behavior* with *negative intent* directed from one child to another where there is a *power difference*. There's either a larger child or several children picking on one, or a child who is clearly more dominant (as opposed to garden-variety aggression, where there may be similar acts but be-

tween two people of equal status). By definition, the bully's target has difficulty defending him- or herself, and the bully's aggressive behavior is intended to cause distress, observes Olweus, professor of psychology at the University of Bergen.

The chronicity of bullying is one of its more intriguing features. It is the most obvious clue that there comes to be some kind of a social relationship between a bully and his victims—and most bullies are boys, while victims are equally girls and boys. And it suggests that, contrary to parents's beliefs, bullying is not a problem that sorts itself out naturally.

The aggression can be physical—pushes and shoves and hitting, kicking, and punching. Or it can be verbal—name-calling, taunts, threats, ridicule, and insults. Bullies not only say mean things *to* you, they say mean things *about* you to others. Often enough, the intimidation that starts

How To Handle a Bully

What Children Can Do:

• A wise line of defense is avoidance. Know when to walk away. It is thoroughly adaptive behavior to avoid a bully. Being picked on is not character-building.
• Use humor to defuse a bully who may be about to attack. Make a joke: "Look, Johnny, lay off. I don't want you to be late for school."
• Or tell the bully assertively. "Get a life. Leave me alone." And walk away. This may be the best defense for girls.
• Recruit a friend. Observers find that having a friend on the playground is one of the most powerful protectives, especially for boys.
• In general, seek out the friendly children and build friendships with them.

What Parents Can Do:

• See that your child has a grounding in assertive behavior. The real first line of defense against a bully is self-confidence.
• Spread the word that bullying is bad for bullies.
• Ask your children how peers treat them. Children often are ashamed to bring up the subject. Parents must.
• Enroll your child in a social-skills group where children learn and practice skills in different situations.
• Model good relationships at home. Help siblings get along.

• Increase the social opportunities of all kids, but especially victimized ones. Invite other children, and groups of children, over to the house. Encourage sleepovers. This is your job; parents are social engineers.
• Enroll your child in classes or groups that develop competencies in activities that are valued by peers. Even kids who don't love sports may like karate, tae kwon do, and similar activities.
• Shut off the TV; much programming reinforces the idea that aggression is the only way to deal with conflicts.
• Empathy helps. Instill in all kids a sense of the distress that a victim experiences.
• Help your child come up with a set of clever verbal comebacks to be used in the event of victimization by verbally abusive peers.
• See that kids in groups have plenty of things to do. Provide play materials. Buy a soccer ball. Paint a hopscotch pattern on the sidewalk. Bullying flourishes when kids are together and having nothing else to do.
• Do not tell or teach a kid to fight back. Fighting back is the *worst defense*. In most instances, victimized children really are weaker and smaller than the bully—thus their fears of losing these fights may be quite real. Besides, not all bullying takes the form of physical aggression. Counter-aggression to any form of bullying actually increases the likelihood of continued victimization.
• Do not expect kids to work it out on their own. Bullying is not simply a problem of

individuals. Given the influence of the peer groups and reputational factors in maintaining the behavior of bullies and victims, it is extremely unrealistic to expect kids to alter the dynamics of bullying by themselves.
• Always intervene. Adults have a crucial role to play in the socialization of children. And consistency counts. Any time adults do not intervene they are essentially training others to solve problems through aggression.
• Intervene at the level of the group. Let all kids know bullying is not OK. Declare emphatically: "This is not acceptable behavior. You can't do this here."
• Talk to your child's teachers to find out what is normal behavior for children of that age group and to find out what the class atmosphere is like.
• Talk to other parents: where there's one victimized child there are likely to be others.
• Get the school involved. At the very least, ask that the school declare bullying off-limits. A change in the atmosphere of the school is not only possible, but helpful in reducing bullying.
• Go to the school administration and demand that bullies be transferred to other classes or schools. Every child has the right to a safe school environment.
• If all else fails, see that your child is transferred to another school. The same child may thrive in a different school with a group of children having different values.

with a fist is later accomplished with no more than a nasty glance. The older bullies get, the more their aggression takes the form of verbal threats and abuse.

Figures differ from study to study, from country to country, and especially from school to school, but from 15 to 20 percent of children are involved in bullying more than once or twice a term, either as bullies or victims. In one Canadian study, 15 percent of students reported that they bullied others more than once or twice during the term. According to large-scale studies Olweus conducted in Norway in 1983, 7 percent of students bullied others "with some regularity." But since then, bully problems have increased, he told PSYCHOLOGY TODAY. By 1991, they had gone up a whopping 30 percent.

Bullies, for the most part, are different from you and me. Studies reliably show that they have a distinctive cognitive makeup—a hostile attributional bias, a kind of paranoia. They perpetually attribute hostile intentions to others. The trouble is, they perceive provocation where it does not exist. That comes to justify their aggressive behavior. Say someone bumps them and they drop a book. Bullies don't see it as an accident; they see it as a call to arms. These children act aggressively because they process social information inaccurately. They endorse revenge.

That allows them a favorable attitude toward violence and the use of violence to solve problems. Whether they start out there or get there along the way, bullies come to believe that aggression is the best solution to conflicts. They also have a strong need to dominate, and derive satisfaction from injuring others. Bullies lack what psychologists call prosocial behavior—they do not know how to relate to others. No prosocial attitudes hold them in check; they do not understand the feelings of others and thus come to deny others's suffering.

Bullies are also untroubled by anxiety, an emotion disabling in its extreme form but in milder form the root of human restraint. What may be most surprising is that bullies see themselves quite positively—which may be because they are so little aware of what others truly think of them. Indeed, a blindness to the feelings of others permeates their behavioral style and outlook.

Every attempt to trace aggression to its roots indicates that it starts in the preschool years and thrives in elementary and middle school. Up to grade six, Olweus reports bullies are of average popularity. They tend

to have two or three friends—largely other aggressive kids. And it's their physical strength other kids admire. As they get older, though, their popularity with classmates wanes; by high school they are hanging out only with other toughs. They may get what they want through aggression, and be looked up to for being tough, but they are not *liked*.

If their self-confidence survives increasing rejection by peers, it may be because bullies are unable to perceive themselves correctly in social situations, a part of their social blindness. Reports child psychologist Melissa De Rosier, Ph.D., of the University of North Carolina: "Bullies are clueless as to how little they are liked. They are out of touch with what kids think." As something of a threat to others, they are not likely to learn just exactly how other kids feel about them. And with their deficits in social cognition, they certainly don't see the impact of their own behavior on others.

It's possible that bullying is not the same in all the world's cultures and that American children suffer more severely at the hands of bullies—a suggestion borne out by the fact that bullies register less popular with peers here, especially as they get older, than they do in Scandinavia. There may be an intensity to bullying here that does not exist elsewhere. Dominance may be more valued; competition more accepted. Victimization may be more extreme. This intensity has many observers worried because violence is worsening in the U.S. and other countries. While that doesn't necessarily mean bullying is getting worse, there are disturbing signals. "Clinically, I see an increment in the aggressive fantasies kids now bring to therapy," confides Schwartz. "They talk about their dolls tearing the skin off each other."

Bullying exists, to greater or lesser degrees, in virtually every Westernized culture. It is a serious problem in Japan. It happens in China. No one knows for sure, because the same methodology has not been applied in every country, but there may be more bullies per capita in the U.S., England, Canada, and Ireland than in other countries. And bullying's not partial to cities; if anything, it's more common in the one-room schoolhouse than in urban settings.

But no matter where they live, bullies find one place especially congenial to their nefarious activities: school. Most bullying occurs on the school playground, especially its unsupervised corners, and in the long and crowded corridors of most schools.

Above all else, says Dan Olweus, bullying is a school problem.

It's not that bullying worsens at adolescence; in fact, it tends to lessen. But that's when sensitivity to rejection by peers takes a painful leap forward. Curtis Taylor probably could have told you that.

They Don't Pick on Just Anyone

Up until about age seven, studies suggest, bullies pick on anyone. After that, they single out specific kids to prey on. And those bullied at one age tend to be bullied later on. Olweus calls them "whipping boys." Even the term is searing. Between ages eight and 16, about 8 or 9 percent of kids are the consistent targets of bullies.

And, says Illinois's Gary Ladd, bullies engage in a "shopping process" to find them. At the beginning of the school year, when children do not know each other well, about 22 percent of children report having a victimization experience on more than a moderate level, Ladd finds. But by the end of the school year, only 8 percent of kids wind up being regularly singled out by bullies. About half of all kids are victimized at least once a year.

Moreover, the younger a child, the more likely he or she is to experience aggression at the hands of peers. For if there's one thing bullies do, it's pick on children who are younger and smaller than they are. And weaker. Most bullies are physically strong and they specifically seek out kids who are ill-equipped to fight back.

Those who become targets also bear a particular set of psychological characteristics. They are more sensitive, cautious, and quiet than other kids, Olweus finds, and more anxious. They also have a negative view of violence. It's not just that they're nonaggressive, for lots of kids are nonaggressive. But these kids withdraw from confrontations of any kind and cry when attacked. They radiate what one researcher calls "an anxious vulnerability." Faced with conflict, they are gripped with fear. Their fearfulness and physical weakness probably set them up.

"The big question," says Ladd, "is where does victimization start. Do kids emit signals for others to test them? Or is it that bullies pick out those they see they can dominate?" He finds clues in the fact that some kids are victimized later in the school year but not early on. "Something increases their likelihood of being picked on—probably, vulnerabilities revealed in a class environment. Maybe they don't do well in gym, or fumble a reading task."

And they easily acquiesce to the demands of bullies: They cry and assume defensive postures. Not only do they not fight back, they hand over their possessions—handsomely rewarding their attackers psychologically and materially—powerfully reinforcing them. The reinforcement is doubled: Bullies are unlikely to be punished by retaliation.

It's one thing to be submissive when challenged, but researchers now know that the children who become bully victims are submissive even before they're picked on. At Vanderbilt University, where he is a research associate, child psychologist David Schwartz conducted a novel study of children, none of whom knew each other at the outset. He silently monitored and videotaped them in a series of play sessions. "Even in the first two sessions, before bully–victim situations develop, these kids behaved submissively," Schwartz reports.

In nonconfrontational situations they showed themselves to be "pervasively nonassertive." Schwartz catalogues the ways. They didn't make overtures to others, didn't initiate conversation. They made no attempts to verbally persuade their peers—no demands, requests, or even suggestions. They were thoroughly socially incompetent, spending time in passive play, playing parallel to their peers, rather than with them.

Being submissive in nonaggressive contexts kicks off a dizzying downward spiral of events. It sets them up as easy targets. "It seems to mark these kids for later victimization," says Schwartz. "And that only made them more submissive." Here's the catch—being victimized leads to feeling bad, feeling anxious, which then increases vulnerability to *further* victimization. This is the spiral Curtis Taylor couldn't—and shouldn't have been expected to—untangle by himself.

To say that victims are socially incompetent is not to say that they are to blame for the aggressive behavior of bullies. It is simply to recognize that certain patterns of social behavior make some children vulnerable, say investigators. After all, even the most passive child isn't victimized unless there's a bully in the room.

Just as certain as there will always be a bully around, victimization can lead to a host of social-psychological difficulties. No one likes a bully, but no one likes a victim either. The failure—or inability—of victims to stick up for themselves seems to make other kids highly uncomfortable. After all, says Ladd, "part of growing up is learning how to stick up for yourself." Gradually,

whipping boys become more and more isolated from their peers. While bullying is painful, it is the social isolation that probably is most damaging to victims. An emerging body of research shows that social isolation, to say nothing of active rejection, is a severe form of stress for humans to endure. And rejection deprives these kids of the very opportunities they need to acquire and practice social competence.

Victims are rejected not only by the bullies but typically by other peers as well. Few children like them; many dislike them. In answering questionnaires they confide they are very lonely. They typically develop a negative view of school and hate going. They suffer headaches, stomachaches, and other somatic complaints. "We ask them how they feel in school," Ladd reports. "It's clear they're pretty unhappy. They want to get away from that environment." Eventually, achievement suffers. Regardless of their grades, a disproportionate number of rejected kids drop out of school. These children internalize the very negative views of themselves others hold of them, Olweus finds.

"There are lots of kids in schools who are being victimized and, as a result, are not living up to their potential, not getting as much out of the school experience as they could," says Ladd. "They get very negative views of themselves and their abilities. That's a waste of human beings, and a threat to the health and wealth of the country."

Olweus, who has followed thousands of Norwegian children into adulthood, finds that by age 23, some "normalization" takes place. By then, those who once were victims are free to choose or create their own social and physical environments. However, they are still susceptible to depression and to negative feelings about themselves.

Victimization, everyone agrees is bad for kids. But it sometimes has effects that are not entirely negative. It can proud children into finding a way to salvage a sense of self-respect. There are those whom victimization by bullies drives deeper into the world of books and to excel in schoolwork—both activities with long-term payoffs—although it's scarcely a predictable outcome and a terribly aversive route to excellence.

In Olweus's studies, victims have close relationships with their parents and tend to come from overprotective families. As a result, they get no practice in handling conflict, one of the basic facts of social

life, and no confidence in their ability to negotiate the world on their own. Overprotection prevents them from learning the skills necessary to avoid exploitation by others.

Dance Macabre

Increasingly, researchers are coming to see bullying and victimization less as the products of individual characteristics and more as an outgrowth of unique interactive chemistry. Over time, bullies and their victims become a twosome—a dyad, in the lingo of social science. Like husbands and wives, mothers and infants, and other lovers, they come to have an ongoing relationship, they interact frequently, and there is a special dynamic operating.

What makes normal dyadic relationship so enthralling for both parties—and for infants is the medium in which growth takes place—is the intricate pattern of *mutual responsiveness,* of action and response, the synchrony of give and take that gets established. It sets up its own gravitational field; it draws the two together and validates each as a special person. If that's not quite how it goes with bullies and their victims, still these children develop a history with each other, and the behavior of each reinforces the other. Call it the bully–victim dance.

That's how Toronto psychologist Debra Pepler, Ph.D., sees it. "There is a relationship. There is a repeatedness over time. Then a glance or comment can work, setting up a whole terrifying sequence of emotions such as anxiety," where once there was the verbal threat of aggression, or even the real thing. Then the submissiveness signals to the bully that his aggression is working. Once selected for aggression, victims seem to reward their attackers with submission.

Other researchers describe victims who actually pester the bully. There is, for example, the kid who runs after the bully: "Aren't you going to tease me today? I won't get mad." Both bullies and victims are disliked by their peers. They may be seeking each other for social contact—just because no one else will.

An Underground Activity

Bullying inhabits a covert kids-only world—right under the noses of adults. "Teachers tell us it doesn't happen in their school or classroom," reports Ladd, "when in fact it does"—a point he teases out by giving separate questionnaires to students and teachers. "To some degree the teachers simply don't want to admit it. But there is

also evidence that kids know just how anti-social their behavior is and often choose corners out of the ken of their teachers."

Nor do most parents know about it when their kids are victimized. Like Curtis Taylor, kids often think it is their own fault. So there is deep shame and humiliation. Moreover, the fear of reprisals keeps kids from saying a word. And tragically, says Ladd, the pace of parenting today doesn't leave a whole lot of room for parents to sit down every evening with their children and find out how their day went, to talk about how they are being treated by their peers.

He wishes they would, because when he asks, he hears. "We ask kids to tell us something fun that happened at school. Then we ask, 'tell us about something that happened that was nasty.' Out pour stories about harassment, exclusion, rejection, victimization. A lot of the parents look like they're hearing about it for the first time."

When Toronto's Debra Pepler wanted to get a detailed glimpse into the world of bullies, she planted a video camera in schools and trained it on the playground, where the kids were monitored by remote microphones. In 52 hours of tape, Pepler, of York University, documented over 400 episodes of bullying, from brushes of mild teasing to 37 solid minutes of kicking and punching. The average episode, however, lasted 37 seconds. Teachers noticed and intervened in only one out of 25 episodes. The child in the 37-minute incident, says Pepler, is repeatedly kicked and thrown around by two kids (although in the vast majority of instances, bullying is one-on-one). "What's so strange to me is that *he stays in it*. There are lots of opportunities for him to get away. At one point a teacher even tries to break it up, and *all three* of them say, 'Oh no, we're just having fun.'

"In showing other kids the tapes, I confirmed what I felt—it's so important for children to be members of a social group that to receive negative attention is better than to receive no attention at all. It's actually self-confirming. There's a sense of who I am; I am at least somebody with a role in the group. I have no way of identifying myself if nobody pays attention to me."

Or as one seventh-grade boy said to her about the victim, "It's just like he's getting paid for it to stay a part of that group. It's like being a prostitute. You do something you don't want to do and you get paid a lot of money for it." Some victims "really do silly things that feed into their victimization," she agrees. Olweus sharply disagrees. He contends that the way kids were selected for the study renders the findings

"atypical." "In my experience," he insists, "the overwhelming majority of victims derive no satisfaction from victimization."

Nevertheless, Pepler's studies suggest bullying is far more common among kids than most adults either observe or admit. In a mid-sized school it happens once every seven minutes. And 4 percent of bullies are armed, at least in Toronto, an ethnically balanced city. Probably because bullying is such a covert activity, schools seem to have a hard time figuring out what to do about it. There are only scattered efforts in U.S. schools to institute any anti-bully programs, and, unlike in Scandinavia, rarely have they been tested for effectiveness.

Bullying may thrive underground, but it is a psychologically distinctive experience. It's painful. It's scary. Victims feel a great loss of control. Ask anyone who's ever been victimized even once—the memory tends to survive well into adulthood.

Not All Bullies Are Alike

Until recently, a bully was just a bully. But researchers are turning up differences among them that provide strong clues as to how the behavior takes shape. There seem to be two distinct types of bully, distinguished by how often they themselves are bullied.

To make matters slightly more complex, different researchers have different names for them and draw slightly different boundary lines. There are those bullies who are out-and-out aggressive and don't need situations of conflict to set them off, called "proactive aggressors" in some studies, "effectual aggressors" in others. Classic playground bullies fall into this camp. Their behavior is motivated by future reward—like "get me something." It's goal oriented, instrumental. Or perhaps these bullies have high thresholds of arousal and need some increase in arousal level. Hard as it is to believe, these bullies have friends—primarily other bullies. What they don't have at all is empathy; cooperation is a foreign word. They are missing prosocial feelings.

Then there are those bullies who are sometimes aggressors, sometimes victims: "reactive bullies," "ineffectual aggressors," or, in Olweus's lexicon, "provocative" victims. Regardless of who starts a fight, these kids prolong the battle, says David Perry, Ph.D., professor of psychology at Florida Atlantic University in Boca Raton. They get angry easily and escalate conflict into aggression, but end up losing. Their behavior is motivated by perceived provocation.

Perry claims that half of all bullies are hotheads. Any way the bully pie is sliced,

these highly reactive aggressors are the worst off. They engage in the highest levels of conflict—they give it and they get it. And they place great value on controlling their adversaries. But their emotional make-up is distinct: They are easily emotionally aroused and can't handle conflict. "Peers are good at describing their characteristics," Perry reports. "They get emotionally upset, they show distress easily, they are quick to become oppositional and defiant. They are quick to cry. And they are named most likely to lose fights amid exaggerated cries of frustration and distress."

And they are the least liked. Of all children, they are the most rejected in the peer group—which puts them at risk of developing the kinds of externalizing, antisocial problems bullies develop, as well as the internalizing problems, like anxiety and depression, that are common to victims. Whether these bullies have the most trouble in life isn't clear, but they do have the fewest friends.

Why do they keep at it, when they always lose? Most of all, says Perry, they have problems of emotional regulation; they have low thresholds of arousal in the first place, and they can't calm themselves down once conflict starts. They get invested in their fights. Their high level of arousal keeps them from recognizing it's time to get up and walk away when they are clearly losing. "Their emotions may be preempting their cognitions, or arousal may be distorting their cognition," Perry says.

Most of all, they are targets because they're fun for other bullies to pick on; they provide lots of theatrical value. They get provoked because they react in ways that are rewarding to bullies—*they get a response*. Getting a response is the bully's ultimate reward.

These hotheads, says Perry, seem to have a low threshold of irritability. "They seem to exist in a mood state of readiness." They frequently take an oppositional stance in situations.

The ineffectual bullies bear an uncanny resemblance to psychobiologist Gary W. Kraemer's monkeys. Kraemer, an associate professor at the University of Wisconsin, and a researcher at the famed Harlow Primate Laboratory, is working with two of the lab's populations of rhesus monkeys. One group is reared from birth by their monkey mothers. The other is nurtured by lab workers for the first month after birth, then reared with their monkey peers.

Human "mothers," Kraemer finds, do a swell job of raising physically robust monkeys. But only the monkey moms raise so-

cially competent ones. The human-reared monkeys are either impulsively aggressive or inordinately reclusive—their behavior varies unpredictably. They have a collage of changes in the way they see the world, deficits in cognitive problem-solving that endure no matter how much social interaction with their peers the monkeys later get.

"Peer-reared monkeys can't anticipate what is going to happen next in social interactions," says Kraemer. "They look like a wild cannon. Something will set them off. And they have no 'off' button. Once in agonistic encounters, they have a hard time stopping." These monkeys not only display unregulated aggression and antisocial behavior, they contribute to the instability of the whole group. They just don't "get" the rhythms of relationships.

In addition to behaving like reactive bullies, they have an array of enduring neurochemical changes in the brain. There is chaos in specific neurotransmitter systems—the serotonin, norepinephrine, and dopamine pathways. "The norepinephrine system is not developed at all," says Kraemer. "The serotonin system is strange." To Kraemer, these monkeys are proof that social relations—specifically the early caregiver–infant attachment process, the *dance* of mother and child—actually structures the developing nervous system. It gets incorporated within, becoming the prototype for all social behavior. In the connection between mother and infant lies the pattern and desire for connecting with others.

"To the degree that caregivers are unpredictable, random, and asynchronous, then social behavior is not likely to be internally regulated," Kraemer says. "Social activity is not an accessory in life; it's reproduced in your brain." That's one reason, he believes, that aggression begins early and winds up such a durable approach to life.

Of the human-reared monkeys, he says, "You can give them all the Prozac in the world but you can never get them back on the usual trajectory. It will reduce the duration and frequency of repetitive behaviors, but it doesn't increase the proportion of social behavior. The entire system is dysregulated. You can make a symptom go away, but that doesn't restore normalcy."

In the normal course of events, says Kraemer, human children develop dominance hierarchies, although they are not very rigid. But in bullies, the process becomes supervening. Even when failure is evident, they continue. "There is certainly a dysregulation of something. Bullies and victims are breaking the normal harmony. Theirs is a different dance."

If his studies suggest that aggression begins in the early caregiver–child interaction, there's an arsenal of human research making the very same case.

Aw, C'mon—Isn't It Just Boys Being Boys?

Sure lots of boys engage in all kinds of competition and rough-and-tumble play; those are non-threatening physical ways of establishing dominance hierarchies, a goal that actually promotes social stability.

But the line between fun and fisticuffs gets erased only when there's a bully in the pack; the bully may misconstrue some borderline gesture or movement as intentionally hostile. When push turns to shove, when meanness intrudes on play—when someone selects a target and inflicts pain and the payoff is someone else's humiliation—then it's outright bullying.

And that's not a healthy way of interacting, not for the victims, but especially not for the bullies. There are huge costs to them. It is the first and perhaps most identifiable stop on a trajectory that leads almost directly to criminal behavior. Bullying is just another word for antisocial behavior, and it's part of a more general rule-breaking stance. According to long-term studies conducted by Olweus, 60 percent of boys who were named as bullies in grades six to nine have at least one court conviction by age 24.

Kids who are aggressive in childhood tend to be aggressive in adolescence and later. In a decades-long look at boys in London, those who were bullies at age 14 were largely bullies at age 18—and at 32. In a classic long-term study that is still ongoing, University of Michigan psychologist Leonard Eron, Ph.D., and colleagues have been following 518 children in upstate New York from the age of eight. All are now in their 40s. The most astonishing finding is that the kids who were named by their peers—*at age eight*—as most aggressive commit more crimes, and more serious crimes, as adults. They have more driving offenses. More court convictions. More alcoholism. More antisocial personality disorder. More use of mental health services.

When young, says Eron, these kids have intelligence levels equal to those of their normal peers. But by age 19, aggressive behavior gets in the way of developing intellectual skills. At age 30, they and their spouses were interviewed. "There is significantly more abusive behavior," says Eron, who's girding for another round of assessment. "They don't achieve socially, economically, or professionally. They never

learned prosocial behavior, and that interferes with every activity." Their work histories are erratic, at best—the behaviors that make them troublesome among peers make them disruptive among co-workers. The longer the haul, the more the bully suffers.

"Parents should be concerned about bullying," Eton adds. "These kids are not just harming others; they're harming themselves."

"Over time, aggression is a marker of every negative outcome that there is," adds Vanderbilt's Schwartz. Bullies get locked into patterns of aggressive and hostile response that are very rewarding to them—but that sharply circumscribe who they get to hang out with. As they go through high school, increasingly their behavior is acceptable only to others like themselves; fortified with their hostile cognitive style and growing contempt for the values of others, they spin their way to outcast lifestyle.

There's sex, drugs, and booze to keep them busy—and they take up with all of them earlier than most other kids, studies show. They drop out of school, hang out with aggressive peers, and that drives further deviance; the link with others like them may be what turns a bully into a criminal. However criminals are made, the point can not be clearer—bullies's social style drives their downward drift through life.

If bullying is bad for those who give it as well as those who get it, then just exactly why do kids do it? "It's a great strategy for getting what you want," says Illinois's Gary Ladd. You push the little girl off the tricycle, you get the tricycle. "A lot of aggressive kids think aggression works. They think about one outcome, but not about the others."

People do have a need to control their environment, and perhaps some enter life with differences in that need, as occurs with other traits. The great psychological benefit to bullying, says Ladd, is that bullies feel powerful, in control. "They've picked a little microcosm in which to exert control." But it's a helluva way to get your own way.

"These kids are experts at using short-term payoffs," says psychologist Gerald R. Patterson, Ph.D., a founder of the Oregon Social Learning Center in Eugene, and a pioneer in family studies of aggression. "They're not very good at long-range things that are in their best interest."

For all those boys who engage in bullying as a way of gaining status, the last laugh is on them. Their trophy is a sham. What looks like power and status turns out not to be that at all. The proof is in their testosterone levels.

Richard E. Tremblay, Ph.D., is a psychologist at the University of Montreal who

has been conducting long-term studies of over a thousand bullies and other aggressive kids. Among one group of 178 kids that has passed the threshold of adolescence, Tremblay checked out hormone-behavior links by measuring the boys's levels of testosterone. What he found set him on his ear. The boys who were rated (by peers and teachers) most physically aggressive at ages six to 12 had lower testosterone levels at age 13 than ordinary peers. The "multiproblem fighters," or hothead bullies, proved to have the lowest testosterone levels of all.

How could these consistently aggressive boys register so low on testosterone? Tremblay admits to having been puzzled. The mistake, he realized, is all those direct extrapolations from animal studies of dominance in which testosterone equals aggression. He has come to believe that testosterone does not reflect brute force but is a barometer of social success. "Physical aggression that is not accompanied by social well-being and social success—being designated a leader by peers—is not associated with high testicular activity."

Among humans, he says, physical aggression leads increasingly to rejection by peers, parents, even the school system. By the end of elementary school, half of bullies are not in their age-appropriate grade.

"They are losers," he states emphatically. "Their testosterone status at puberty reflects the fact that they are not dominating their environment. The human behaviors of dominance are not the same as animal ones," he insists. In humans, even in beefy boys, social dominance has less and less to do with physical aggression—and more and more with language. "While aggression is important for attaining high social status," says Tremblay, "it is not the only strategy. And when sustained, it is not decisive at all." And that is precisely where bullies are weak. Their general intelligence starts out about on a par with that of other kids, but their verbal intelligence is low.

Tremblay pauses to register his bemusement. "I started out studying aggression in adult criminals. Then I found I had to look at adolescents. Now I'm looking at young children. If you had told me I was going to be studying two-year-olds, I would have said that you were crazy."

But he has come to believe that the lifestyle of aggression is pretty much a done deal by age two. And with that, the Terrible Twos just got a lot worse. "Physical aggression is normal at that age. It builds up from nine months and reaches its highest frequency at age two. And then you learn that it hurts when aggressed. Adults intervene

and indicate that it is the wrong behavior. Language skills increase, and physical aggression decreases. If you don't get it by age two, then you become aggressive. There's something about language." It may be that language skills are socially acquired in the caregiver–child interaction. And some kids get more of that than others.

Hey—What About the Girls?

Bullying has been studied largely in boys because they are so much more overtly aggressive. The problem, contends psychologist Nicki R. Crick, Ph.D., is that aggression has always been defined strictly in terms of what boys do that's mean. And that's just one more instance of male bias distorting the way things really are. She and her colleagues now know that "girls are just as capable of being mean as boys are.

"The research shows that boys engage in physical aggression such as kicking, hitting, pushing, shoving, and verbal aggression like name-calling and making fun of kids more than girls do," notes Crick. "The interpretation is that boys are just a lot more aggressive than girls are. But if you go back to the textbook definition of aggression, it's 'the intent to hurt or harm.'

"For the past three years we've been looking at the ways girls try to harm others. We've identified a form of aggression unique to females, what we call relational aggression, hurting others through damaging or manipulating their relationships in aversive ways." Like:

• Spreading vicious rumors in the peer group to get even with someone so that other people will reject that person.

• Telling others to stop liking someone in order to get even with him or her.

• Trying to control or dominate a person by using social exclusion as a form of retaliation: "You can't come to my birthday party if you don't do x, y, and z."

• Threatening to withdraw friendship in order to get one's way, control another's behavior, or hurt someone: "I won't be your friend if…"

• Giving someone the silent treatment and making sure that they know they're being excluded as a form of retaliation.

It makes intuitive sense to Crick. "If you want to hurt someone and you want it to be effective, shouldn't it be something they really value? Numerous studies have shown that women and girls really value relationships, establishing intimacy and dyadic relations with other girls. That led us to looking at the use of relationships as the vehicle for harm, because if you take that away from a girl, you're really getting

at her." Similarly, boys's aggression, plays into goals shown to be important to boys in the face of their peers—physical dominance and having things, or instrumentality.

In studies of children ranging from three years of age to 12, she has determined that parents, teachers, and kids themselves see these behaviors as problematic. They regard them as mean and manipulative. "This behavior cuts across all socioeconomic and all age groups. Adults do these things too." In fact, Crick's studies show that relational aggression becomes a more normative angry behavior for girls the older they get. Particularly as girls move into adolescence, themes of social exclusion increase in frequency in girls's conflicts with their peers.

While Crick's studies show that 27 percent of aggressive kids, mostly boys, engage in *both* overt and relational aggression, the majority of aggressive kids—73 percent—engage in one or the other, not both. Relational aggression is far more characteristic of girls, at least throughout the school years. Taking relational aggression into account leads to a startling conclusion: Girls (22 percent) and boys (27 percent) are aggressive in almost equal numbers.

Just as in the case with physical aggression, neither relational bullies nor their victims do well in the short or long haul. They're unhappy with their relationships. They feel emotionally upset and are at risk for social and emotional problems. Being the target of such aggression leaves victims subject to anxiety when meeting people and set on a path to avoiding others.

Being the social bully puts girls at risk of being increasingly rejected over time. Others grow tired of their behavior, weary of being manipulated. While most relationally aggressive kids are rejected by most others, a few are "controversial"—that is, they are well-liked by some kids and actively disliked by others. Either way, their own behavior brings them problems because it strictly limits the pool of potential friends.

Being the friend of a relationally aggressive girl—and 75 percent of them have at least one friend—is no picnic. Their friendships are hotbeds of conflict and betrayal. While there's more intimacy in their friendships—more self-disclosure, telling secrets, talking about their feelings—there's also more more negativity and aggression. Such girls don't buffer their friends from their aggressiveness; they do it to them, too.

They also construct coalitions and demand exclusivity, getting jealous when a friend pays attention to anyone else. "We think that intimacy is for them a medium of control," says Crick. "They want to be inti-

mate because that is how they get information to use to control others."

Only rarely do relational bullies form a friendship with one of their own kind; they typically choose a very nonaggressive peer. Normally, friendship is a highly positive experience and buffers people from a host of ills. But friendship with a relational bully can be a passage to psychopathology.

If other researchers have missed such behaviors, it's because they are subtle and sophisticated, and far less visible than the black-eyed bullying of boys. They also create fewer problems for society; these behaviors may be harmful, but relational bullies don't wind up in the criminal justice system.

Of Peers and Cheers

So you or your kid is not a bully or a victim. There's still no room for smugness. Even observing aggression from the sidelines is not a neutral activity.

The nature of bullying is such that even kids who aren't antisocial get drawn into it. "I no longer think of bullying as something that happens just between two people," says Toronto's Debra Pepler, even though over 90 percent of episodes involve a single bully and victim. "Peers are so often present when we observe it on the playground. It's really in some sense an interaction that unfolds in a context rather than in isolation. I hesitate to say this, but there's the entertainment and the theater value of it. The other kids may feel a part of that. They may feel anxious, excited, afraid—but that feeds into the interaction."

In 85 percent of the episodes of bullying, says Pepler, other children are involved in some capacity or as audience. "If you're going to establish dominance, the only way to do it is with other children around. In the longer episodes, there's a tremendous building of excitement and arousal."

Sometimes the roles peers play in promoting bullying is less marginal. Two bullies kick a kid to the ground and bystander peers, through a process of social contagion, join in, particularly if it's a kid they dislike. The group is empowered by the numbers, their individual responsibility diluted to the vanishing point.

Take the "slam book" that circulated in one Toronto classroom. Each page bore a heading: who's the stupidest, who's the ugliest, who's the most unpopular, and so on. "Almost all the girls in the class nominated someone," says Pepler. "It had a huge negative impact on the kids being named. Most of the girls in this class were really nice kids. Eight of the 10 involved would never have done it on their own. But because of the im-

portance of being part of a group, they engaged in antisocial behavior that just wasn't a part of their person."

Antonius Cillessen, Ph.D., calls group dynamics "the hidden purpose" of much bullying. A psychologist at the University of Connecticut, he finds that peer groups fan the flames of bullying by conferring reputations that keep bullies and victims frozen in their roles. They especially reinforce victimization. "When children have negative expectations of another child, they act more negatively to that child. This negative behavior then seems to trigger a reciprocally negative reaction from the target child," thus creating a self-fulfilling prophecy.

No matter what victims do, even if they change their behavior, their peers filter observations of them through their negative expectations—and still give a negative interpretation to those kids's actions. As peers see them, they can't do *anything* right.

Cillessen is concerned. The power of reputational factors among peers is so strong that what look like obvious remedies will not solve bullying problems. For example, teaching victims social skills—more assertive and socially competent ways of interacting—is necessary but not sufficient. Their peers's perceptions still remain the same, and they act accordingly. His studies furnish proof that bullying can be tackled only with a school-wide program.

How They Get That Way

Most kids try aggression in the course of growing up. And most give it up. But some, says David Perry, "are encouraged by parental behaviors or by neglect." In other words, bullies are made, not born.

There is no big bang, no one crisis of development. It's largely in the nuances of parent–child interaction. And so unexceptional, so mundane is the process that it's taken Gerald Patterson over 20 years of observing parents and children together to nail it down. But he distills it into four words: the coercion parenting model. It gets played out in relatively trivial—but frequent—bouts of disobedience.

Marginally skilled parents—many parents are, he says, and their numbers are increasing—come up against an active, willful, "difficult" child. The mother says something reasonable to the child: "Would you close the door, please." The child doesn't do it; he is noncompliant. "The core of aggressive behavior in children and adults is noncompliance," Patterson says.

The child goes over to the TV set and turns it on. Five minutes later, the mother asks again: Please close the door. The kid ig-

nores her again. Then the parent shouts and threatens, "If you don't close the door, I'm going to spank you." At some point, the kid may get up and close the door, says Patterson, but he has the mother reduced to four or five minutes of yelling. "The child is controlling the mother by his noncompliance. Then the mother gets so upset at the back talk and noncompliance that she strikes out and hits the child. These are not crazy parents. They get caught in a process that is controlling their behavior."

The basic problem with their parenting is that it's noncontingent. The noncompliance (say, a two-year-old hits his sister) goes unpunished—until the parent is so full of hostility she lashes out unpredictably. "Instead of being contingent, these parents natter and scold. They threaten but don't follow through and say, 'Okay, that misbehavior will cost you…' and name some chore. And if the child still doesn't do it, 'I'm going to lock up your bicycle'—and really do it. And start the process all over again the next day. They don't do that." The inconsistent use of ineffective punishment winds up intermittently rewarding defiance.

Given the lack of a consistent adult response, a child cannot develop trust in a caregiver, sowing the seeds for a hostile view of the world. Noncontingent parenting breeds in kids the expectation that others will treat them unfairly and unpredictably.

The use of physical punishment as a solution to aggression only teaches the child the same solution—and fosters resentment. Their experiences may leave them overwhelmed with intense retaliatory feelings.

But it isn't just the discipline. In between the inconsistent parenting there's a lack of parental monitoring of children's behavior. And that comes across as uncaring. Children of parents who use such a discipline style may become more worried about how to get their own way, meet their own needs. They don't—can't—think about other people very much.

Here's the kicker: Bullies are more aggressive as kids, so they often receive harsh punishment from parents, which teaches them how to be even more aggressive.

"Noncontingent parenting is unable to stop deviant or aggressive behavior," Patterson emphasizes. "What goes along with it that makes it a Greek tragedy is that the families that get swept up in it not only inadvertently reinforce antisocial behavior, they fail to reinforce prosocial behavior. They don't sit down with their kid, give him a nod, a hug—the kinds of things good parents normally do hundreds of times a day." They don't engage in the dance.

That dance is "extremely important to foster growth," Patterson says. "These kids get slowed in language development. The child doesn't learn to ask for things; he takes things," living on the edge of his impulses.

To cite parenting practices as "the primary proximal cause" for the earliest form of antagonistic behavior, as Patterson does, is not to rerun blame-mom views of what's wrong with people. It's a meticulous analysis of the ways that children learn to join the society of others, to curb their impulses. All that's needed, says Patterson, are nonhostile, nonthreatening, nonphysical sanctions for rule-breaking applied consistently.

Patterson admits that the reams of data he and others have collected show that the coercion-parenting model doesn't fit for girls unless they are overtly aggressive. Relational aggression begins differently.

Starting this fall, Nicki Crick is looking into the family relationships of relationally aggressive children. "We think that these behaviors may get modeled for kids. Say mom doesn't speak to dad when she's mad at him. She punishes him by giving him the silent treatment, or she may withdraw love. There are family variables that might increase a kid's need to control, or need to have affection, such as discipline."

She also thinks parents may be directly teaching kids to make hostile attributions. Kids learn a worldview from their parents: Is the world a nice or a mean place?

No matter how bullies get that way, there is ultimately only one way to stop bullying: to establish a climate in which aggressive behavior is not tolerated—and enforce it. As a nation, Sweden is leading the way. As of July 1994, it outlawed bullying, following a suggestion of Olweus, himself a Swede. Norway may soon do it, too.

Big Bullies

What do bullies do when they grow up? In one sense, they never grow up; they are locked in an infantile pattern of noncompliance, frozen into one way of handling problems. Lacking social skills, and especially the ability to handle conflict, their relationships are likely to be unstable and short-lived. But when they do take partners, they often become spouse abusers.

Bullying is virtually a *sine qua non* of domestic violence. Battered wives commonly describe what their husbands do as bullying, reports University of Washington psychologist Neil Jacobson, Ph.D. Bullying and battering share a dark mission. "Battering is using violence or the threat of violence to control another's behavior," says Jacobson. "That is the essence of bullying—it's just directed to one's significant other."

While no one has directly observed bullying transforming itself into battering, the evidence points to a direct convergence of bullying and battering behavior across the life cycle. The life histories of adult batterers parallel the course bullies's lives take as development unfolds. Batterers are likely to have been delinquent as adolescents.

There is an even more remarkable suggestion that bullying and spouse abuse are two stops along the same dead-end street. Batterers and bullies both sort themselves into distinct types that share certain peculiarities of behavior and biology. Jacobson observes two batterer types among adult men: calculating cobras and reactive hotheads. In a kind of disharmonic convergence, they resemble proactive and reactive bullies, and Kraemer's motherless monkeys.

Like batterers, bullies tend to minimize their own aggressive actions. They make identical cognitive distortions, and attribute hostility to others where it doesn't exist. This misinterpretation gives bullies and batterers alike a way to justify violence. It is the greasy gear with which they typically shift onto others the blame for their own misdeeds.

But as if bullies aren't bad enough, they tend to have children who are bullies. Not only do they model aggression as a solution to conflict, but they are likely to lash out at their children, use physical means— and so hand-feed to the next generation a belief that the world is an uncaring place, an excuse for another go at hostility.

Power, Yes. Persecution, No.

Bullying is a conflict in which aggression is used to demonstrate power. But aggression and power are not synonyms. "I don't think we want our children to learn lessons about aggression and violence when they have power," says Pepler. "Aggression is the wrong way to use power. There are wonderful ways to be leaders without being aggressive."

Tremblay points to what he defines as "tough leaders." These are boys who are aggressive but have prosocial skills. They don't get their way by physical aggression or verbal abuse. In new situations they quickly take over and establish dominance by verbal fluency. In his studies, they are the most socially successful, the best-liked—and have the highest testosterone levels of all.

Bullies wind up being very costly to society, says Gerald Patterson: "We're talking about the production of marginally skilled adults who will be at the margins of society even if they don't commit crimes. They cost the rest of us a lot." They have more accidents; more illness; shorter, less productive lives; pay less in taxes; and use more welfare services. In school they tended to get lots of services, things that were not very effective.

But the most profound case against bullying is made by Dan Olweus. He sees it as a blow to the very soul of freedom. "Bullying violates fundamental democratic principles," he argues. If two kids were merely to challenge each other, they'd fight fair, one would win and the other lose, they'd shake hands, and that would be the end of that. Like our Presidential elections. "But the problem is that bullies seek out the victims and persecute them. They follow them up, wait for them in order to harass them. It is a basic democratic right for a child to feel safe in school and to be spared the oppression and repeated, intentional humiliation implied in bullying."

In an Angry World, Lessons for Emotional Self-Control

Daniel Goleman

NEW HAVEN—East Rock School abuts the sidewalk with a forbidding, windowless wall, suggesting a defensive posture against the dangers of the neighborhood. But inside, the tone is warmer: the walls are hung with banners proclaiming, "Parents, teachers, students together," and, "East Rock Welcomes You," part of a citywide campaign to get parents and neighbors to drop by, help out and get involved in their schools.

Down the hall in Sue Fineman's classroom, Life Skills, an experiment, is in progress, giving children lessons in the emotions. The aim is to help them understand and control responses like aggressiveness and impulsiveness.

Ms. Fineman leads her seventh graders through responses to a hypothetical situation: "Someone bumps into you and knocks your books out of your hand. How can you prevent a problem?"

Cory, a shy girl, ventures, "You could say, 'Would you please pick them up . . .' " Then, sheepishly, retracts it: "Maybe that would make it worse."

Adrielle suggests instead: "Try: 'Excuse me, you knocked my books out of my hand. Could you help me pick them up?' "

Ebie, looking demure, proposes, "You could just ignore them and pick up the books yourself."

Their teacher praises their answers: "That's great; you didn't accuse them. These are all answers that would de-escalate things."

The scenario is a pointed one. Research by Dr. Kenneth Dodge at Vanderbilt University on the children who most often get into fights finds a consistent perceptual skew: they misinterpret neutral events, like a bump, as hostile, and so attack in the mistaken belief they have already been attacked themselves. One remedy for this pre-emptive strike mentality is to have such children realize there are alternatives to knee-jerk aggression.

The New Haven program was begun in 1990 by a group of Yale psychologists at the urgent request of the New Haven superintendent at the time, who was concerned about skyrocketing rates of problems like dropouts, fights and teen-age pregnancies. Today, disciplinary referrals are down, as are the number of children reporting they are sexually active. The program already has parallels in a scattering of schools from New Jersey to California, and the numbers are rising. The need to build children's emotional abilities is felt most everywhere, not just in impoverished neighborhoods like the one East Rock serves. national studies show a marked decline among America's children in emotional abilities like handling conflict and planning ahead.

Behavior Erodes For Rich and Poor

These classes in emotional literacy point to an array of competences that appear to be slowly eroding among American children, according to the results of a random sample of 2,000 children assessed by their teachers and parents in 1976 and again in 1989.

In the study, by Dr. Thomas Achenbach of the University of Vermont, American children, on average, showed increases in apathy, impulsiveness, disobedience, anxiety, having a hot temper and close to three dozen other indicators of troubled emotional lives.

While the rates of decline were similar among children from well-to-do families and those living in poverty, the problems were far worse to begin with among children of the inner cities. In recent years in New Haven, a city of dying industries and endemic poverty, the odds an eighth grader would graduate from high school were just 50-50. The city has the fourth highest teen-age pregnancy rate and the highest rate of pediatric AIDS in the coun-

From *New York Times*, December 6, 1995, p. B8. © 1995 by The New York Times Company. Reprinted by permission.

try; a quarter of sixth-grade girls have reportedly had intercourse.

The New Haven schools in 1995–96, the sixth year of this experiment in helping children survive these ominous tides, are perhaps the only school district in America—certainly the only one of its size—where all 19,000 students are methodically schooled in the emotional skills deemed essential for resisting the centripetal forces of destruction.

The rationale for such emotional literacy programs was articulated in a 1992 report, finished as the New Haven program was taking shape, by a consortium of child specialists organized by the W. T. Grant Foundation. After studying the proliferating school programs that were part of successive "wars" on violence, drugs and other school problems, the consortium concluded that a great many of the programs had little or no impact, and that some made things worse.

But the standouts shared certain common features. They were taught over many years, repeating basics in ways appropriate to students' changing comprehension. They emphasized tightening bonds to families and neighborhoods. And they inculcated a core set of emotional and social abilities.

With these principles in mind, a team of Yale psychologists patched together the curriculum, borrowing from a few of the better programs and creating lessons where none existed. A result is the methodical schooling in emotional competence that makes the Life Skills approach—part of a broader "social development" curriculum—unique among strategies to prevent ills like dropping out, violence and pregnancy.

A Simple Poster, A Lot of Science

One poster seems inescapable at New Haven's East Rock Middle School, enshrined on the wall of virtually every classroom. Alongside the red-yellow-green lights of a traffic signal, the text reads:

When you have a problem...
STOP, CALM DOWN, THINK before you act
Say the PROBLEM and how you FEEL
Find a POSITIVE GOAL
Think of lots of SOLUTIONS
Think ahead to the CONSEQUENCES
Go ahead and TRY THE BEST PLAN.

It's in the air at East Rock. The students call it "the stoplight" or "think before you act." Teachers invoke the stoplight when a student frets about a problem like being left out of a game or about some dispute. Sal Punzo, the principal, drills home the concept when he talks to children sent to his office for discipline, running them through other ways they might have handled whatever it was that got them in trouble.

The stoplight poster, one of the more pervasive Life Skills props, urges impulse control, the calming of anger or anxiety, and the broadening of children's repertory of emotional response.

A premise of emotional literacy is that such crucial skills can become second nature for children if these lessons are repeated over and over, especially at the moments of upset when children need them most. The rationale hinges on a new understanding of the emotional brain.

Regulated by circuitry running between the prefrontal lobes behind the forehead and the limbic centers deep in the brain, these emotional capacities are, neurologically speaking, largely independent of higher cortical intelligences measured by I.Q. tests, like verbal fluency.

Though the limbic centers, the source of emotional impulse, are developed by the time a child reaches puberty, the areas of the prefrontal lobes that are the source of emotional self-control and skillful social response continue to develop into adolescence.

In this continuing development, new neurons are not added, but the number of synapses—the connec-

tions between brain cells—continue to increase. Emotional learning, like all other learning, strengthens synaptic connections.

For example, repeated experience in childhood has been found to improve a crucial emotional skill, the knack of soothing oneself. This ability can be monitored by the activity of the vagus nerve, which at one end regulates the heart and at the other sends signals that prime the "fight or flight" response. A University of Washington team led by Dr. John Gottman observed parents and children interacting; they found that emotionally adept parenting led to an improvement in the children's vagal nerve functioning.

Bright Spots In Discipline

Just how much all this matters, though, is hard to judge. The first class of New Haven seniors who have had this curriculum from kindergarten onward will not graduate until 2003.

But Mr. Punzo, the energetic, wiry principal at East Rock, says there has been a gradual improvement in the tone of the school, which includes grades one through eight. He cites a decline in the numbers of middle school students sent to him for discipline: for the school year ending in 1994 the total was 176 referrals; a year later, the number was down to 121.

Some bright spots emerged in a recent study comparing the New Haven schools in the years ending in 1992 and 1994: a 5 percent drop in reported sexual intercourse among sixth graders, an 11 percent drop in fights for sixth graders and an 8 percent decline for eighth graders; a 5 percent rise in 10th graders who say they think they will finish high school. The dropout rate among high school students fell from about 15 percent a year to 12 percent.

But "even though these are the areas the program is designed to help, there are many other potential causes for these changes," cautions Dr. Mary Schwab-Stone, a psychia-

trist at the Yale Child Studies Center who directs the Collaborative for the Advancement of Social and Emotional Learning, which seeks to help spread emotional literacy programs.

While it is too early to say what the precise impact is on the New Haven children's lives, there is already promising news from the handful of careful comparisons done on more modest pilot programs in emotional literacy.

They show marked improvements in critical elements of emotional intelligence like impulse control and managing anger and anxiety, empathy and sensitivity to others' perspectives, resolving conflicts and cooperation.

Perhaps the most compelling testimony comes from the students themselves. Corey Wilson, a baby-faced seventh grader with his hair in neat rows of pink- and blue-rib-

boned pigtails, told of being at the corner store with a friend who was stealing candy, and who tried to get him to steal some, too. "I said I don't want to do that," Corey said. "If I get caught, my mom will get mad and I'll miss out on all kinds of stuff. So I just left the store."

"They call that," Corey added with a tone of pride, " 'Think before you act.' "

TELEVISED VIOLENCE AND KIDS: A PUBLIC HEALTH PROBLEM?

When Leonard Eron surveyed every 8-year-old child in Columbia County, New York, in 1960, he found something he wasn't looking for: an astonishing, and unmistakable, correlation between the amount of violence the youngsters saw on television and the aggressiveness of their behavior.

More than three decades and two follow-up studies later, after several related research projects and countless hearings and conferences, the work of Eron and his ISR colleague, L. Rowell Huesmann, has become an "overnight sensation." As leading researchers on the effects of media violence on the young, they have been making the rounds of TV talk and news programs and radio call-in shows, while fielding almost daily calls from reporters.

Their message is ultimately a simple one: Aggression is a learned behavior, it is learned at an early age, and media violence is one of its teachers. But because it is a learned behavior, there is hope that it can be unlearned, or never taught in the first place.

Both Eron and Huesmann are professors of psychology at the University of Michigan and research scientists at ISR's Research Center for Group Dynamics. Huesmann is also a professor of communication and acting chair of the Depart-ment of Communication. Their talents and interests have complemented each other since they met at Yale in the early 1970s. Eron's research interest is aggression, while Huesmann, who minored in mathematics as a U-M undergraduate in the early '60s, brings his prowess in data analysis and expertise in cognitive mechanisms and development to the team.

"I wanted to measure child-rearing practices as they related to aggression" in the 1960 survey, says Eron. "The parents knew what the study was about and, in the interviews, we were asking sensitive questions about how parents punished their children, what their disagreements were, and so forth. So we wanted to buffer those with what we called 'Ladies' Home Journal' questions — Had they read Dr. Spock? How often did their child watch TV? What were his or her favorite shows?

"But the computer was unaware of our humor and analyzed those TV programs," he adds. "And, lo and behold, the more aggressive that kids were in school, the higher the violence content of the shows they watched."

But that still left the chicken-and-egg ambiguity. Did watching violent TV make kids more aggressive, or did more aggressive kids watch violent TV?

That's where time, and Huesmann, came in. In 1970, the U.S. Surgeon General formed a committee on television and social behavior, and asked Eron to re-survey as many of the Columbia County kids as he could find. Eron, in turn, sought the services of Huesmann, then an assistant professor at Yale.

"How can they say their programs have no effect on behavior when they're in the business of selling ads?"

—Leonard Eron

"The analysis of long-term data on children's behavior required some sophisticated mathematical and statistical analysis," says Huesmann, "and that was the area in which I was trained."

The project also struck another responsive chord, he says: "The models that had been advanced to explain the long-terms effects of television violence were lacking an explanation of how the effects of watching television violence could last way into adulthood."

So it was back to the Hudson Valley of upstate New York in 1971. They found about 500 of

From *ISR Newsletter,* Vol. 18, No. 1, February 1994, pp. 5-7. © 1994 by the Regents of the University of Michigan Institute for Social Research. Reprinted by permission.

the now 19-year-olds from the original sample of 875 youngsters. The results were just as powerful, if not more so.

"The correlation between violence-viewing at age 8 and how aggressive the individual was at 19 was higher than the correlation between watching violence at age 8 and behaving aggressively at age 8," says Eron. "There was no correlation between violence-viewing at age 19 and aggressiveness at 19. It seems there was a cumulative effect going on here."

Its persistence was documented once more in 1981, when 400 of the subjects were surveyed again, along with 80 of their offspring. The 30-year-old men who had been the most aggressive when they were 8 had more arrests for drunk

---

"The evidence is overwhelming. The strength of the relationship is the same as cigarettes causing lung cancer. Is there any doubt about that?"

—Leonard Eron

---

driving, more arrests for violent crime, were more abusive to their spouses . . . and had more aggressive children. And of the 600 subjects whose criminal justice records were reviewed, those who watched more violence on TV when they were 8 had been arrested more often for violent crimes, and self-reported more fights when consuming alcohol.

In other words, their viewing choices and behavior as 8-year-olds were better predictors of their behavior at age 30 than either what they watched on TV or how aggressively they behaved later in life.

"Children learn programs for how to behave that I call scripts," says Huesmann. "In a new social situation, how do

you know how to behave? You search for scripts to follow. Where is a likely place for those scripts to come from? From what you've observed others doing in life, films, TV. So, as a child, you see a Dirty Harry movie, where the heroic policeman is shooting people right and left. Even years later, the right kind of scene can trigger that script and suggest a way to behave that follows it. Our studies have come up with a lot of evidence that suggests that's very possible. Moreover, we find that watching TV violence affects the viewer's beliefs and attitudes about how people are going to behave."

The longitudinal data were so compelling that the 1993 report of the American Psychological Association's Commission on Violence and Youth, which Eron chaired, stated unequivocally that there is "absolutely no doubt that higher levels of viewing violence on television are correlated with increased acceptance of aggressive attitudes and increased aggressive behavior."

"The evidence is overwhelming," says Eron. "The strength of the relationship is the same as cigarettes causing lung cancer. Is there any doubt about that?"

Only among those who profit from tobacco, just as TV and movie industry executives have generated most of the criticism of the ISR colleagues' work. While the media in general were fascinated by the damning data, especially after the APA report was released last August, the visual media in particular were equally eager to defend themselves and defuse the evidence.

This is not a message the industry wants to hear. Its position is that the off-on switch is the ultimate defense, and parents wield it. Eron says that's unrealistic.

"Parents can't do it all by themselves, especially in these days

of single-parent families and two parents working," he says. "They can't be with their children all the time."

If the industry can't or won't regulate itself, should the government intervene? It's an obvious question to ask and a difficult one to answer, especially for believers in the First Amendment.

"The scientific evidence clearly shows that long-term exposure to TV violence makes kids behave more aggressively," says Huesmann, "but it doesn't show the same effect on adults. What you watch now won't have nearly the effect of what you saw when you were 8. What we're talking about is regulating what kids see, not adults, and there are reasonable precedents for this — alcohol and tobacco regulations, for example."

"What we're talking about is regulating what kids see, not adults, and there are reasonable precedents for this—alcohol and tobacco regulations, for example."

—L. Rowell Huesmann

In their view, watching TV violence is every bit as dangerous to kids as smoking and drinking. They see it as a matter of public health, not free speech. And they are grimly amused by the industry's protestations of exculpability. "How can they say their programs have no effect on behavior when they're in the business of selling ads?" Eron asks.

Then there are those who wonder how it is that Detroit and Windsor, Ontario, which face each other across the Detroit River and receive the same TV signals, have such disparate crime rates. "If we said TV violence is the only cause, then they'd have an

argument," says Eron. "But we don't say that."

They are, in fact, well aware that any number of psychological, physiological and macro-social factors are simmering in the stew of violence. "TV is really a minor part of our research," says Eron, "although it's gotten the most play. We're interested in how children learn aggression. Violence on TV is only one cause, but it's a cause we can do something about."

Two projects they are currently involved in show signs of making progress toward that end. Huesmann is directing the second phase of a study begun in 1977 that looks, he says, at "whether the effects of media violence generalize across different countries and cultures."

Researchers are collecting longitudinal data on subjects in Poland, Australia, Finland and Israel, as well as the United States. Meanwhile, Eron, Huesmann and three researchers at the University of Illinois (where Huesmann spent 20 years before returning to U-M in 1992) are conducting an ambitious study of inner-city schools "in which we are trying to change the whole school atmosphere," says Eron.

In the former study, almost 2,000 children were interviewed and tested in either first or third grade and for two consecutive years thereafter. "In all countries, the children who watched more violence were the more aggressive," says Huesmann. "This was a study showing that this was a real effect across countries and not a special, one-time study of Columbia County."

The only exceptions were found in Australia and Israel. In Australia, there was a correlation between watching violence and behaving aggressively, but it was not as persistent as in other countries. In Israel, the correlation was stronger for city-raised children than for those growing up in kibbutzes. Huesmann suspects that the communal nature of the kibbutz, with its attendant reinforcement of pro-social behaviors, neutralized the effect of televised violence. And Australia? "We have no good explanation," he says.

"As a child, you see a Dirty Harry movie, where the heroic policeman is shooting people right and left. Even years later, the right kind of scene can trigger that script and suggest a way to behave that follows it."

—L. Rowell Huesmann

Perhaps the second phase, revisiting subjects who are now in their early 20s, will provide one. Interviewing is almost complete in the United States and Finland and began in Poland this winter as one of the collaborative projects between ISR and ISS [Institute for Social Studies], its Polish sibling. Work will begin in Israel near the end of 1994.

The project in Illinois attempts to measure the relative influence of multiple contexts, including schools, peers,

families, and neighborhoods, and the cost-effectiveness of targeting each. "This is a public health model," says Eron, "from primary prevention to tertiary prevention."

Both teachers and students will be taught techniques for handling aggression and solving problems. Youngsters who are believed to be at high risk for becoming aggressive will also be seen in groups of six by research staffers. And half of those youngsters will receive family therapy as well, what Eron calls "an increased dosage" of treatment.

"We don't think just working with kids in the schools will help much," Eron says. "Studies show kids change attitudes, but there's no data to show they change behavior. In this program, we're trying to change the whole school atmosphere. We're also trying to see what the cost-effectiveness is. Is it enough to have a school program? Or do you always have to do family therapy, which is the most costly? Does it really add to the effectiveness of the treatment?"

The problem clearly isn't simple, but some of the data are nonetheless clear. "Over the years, Rowell and I have testified at many congressional hearings," says Eron, "and now it's having an effect. The public sentiment is there's too much of this stuff, and we've got the data to show it. I think we are having an impact, finally."

Eron himself estimates that TV is only responsible for perhaps 10% of the violent behavior in this country. "But," he says, "if we could reduce violence by 10%, that would be a great achievement."

Frankenstein Must Be Destroyed
Chasing the Monster of TV Violence

Brian Siano

Brian Siano is a writer and researcher living in Philadelphia. His column, "The Skeptical Eye," appears regularly in The Humanist. He can be contacted via E-mail at revpk@cellar.org.

Here's the scene: Bugs Bunny, Daffy Duck, and a well-armed Elmer Fudd are having a stand-off in the forest. Daffy the rat-fink has just exposed Bugs' latest disguise, so Bugs takes off the costume and says, "That's right, Doc, I'm a wabbit. Would you like to shoot me now or wait until we get home?"

"Shoot him now! Shoot him now!" Daffy screams.

"You keep out of this," Bugs says. "He does not have to shoot you now."

"He does so have to shoot me now!" says Daffy. Full of wrath, he storms up to Elmer Fudd and shrieks, "And I *demand* that you shoot me now!"

Now, if you *aren't* smiling to yourself over the prospect of Daffy's beak whirling around his head like a roulette wheel, stop reading right now. This one's for a very select group: those evil degenerates (like me) who want to corrupt the unsullied youth of America by showing them violence on television.

Wolves' heads being conked with mallets in Tex Avery's *Swing Shift Cinderella*. Dozens of dead bodies falling from a closet in *Who Killed Who?* A sweet little kitten seemingly baked into cookies in Chuck Jones' *Feed the Kitty*. And best of all, Wile E. Coyote's unending odyssey of pain in *Fast and Furrious* and *Hook, Line, and Stinker*. God, I love it. The more explosions, crashes, gunshots, and defective ACME catapults there are, the better it is for the little tykes.

Shocked? Hey, I haven't even gotten to "The Three Stooges" yet.

The villagers are out hunting another monster—the Frankenstein of TV violence. Senator Paul Simon's hearings in early August 1993 provoked a fresh round of arguments in a debate that's been going on ever since the first round of violent kids' shows—"Sky King," "Captain Midnight," and "Hopalong Cassidy"—were on the air. More recently, Attorney General Janet Reno has taken a hard line on TV violence. "We're fed up with excuses," she told the Senate, arguing that "the regulation of violence is constitutionally permissible" and that, if the networks don't do it, "government should respond." Reno herself presents a fine example, given her rotisserielike tactics with the Branch Davidian sect in Waco, or her medieval record on prosecuting "satanic ritual abuse" cases in Florida. (At least she wasn't as befuddled as Senator Ernest Hollings, who kept referring to "Beavis and Butt-head" as "Buffcoat and Beaver.")

Simon claims to have become concerned with this issue because, three years ago, he turned on the TV in his hotel room and was treated to the sight of a man being hacked apart with a chainsaw. (From his description, it sounds like the notorious scene in Brian de Palma's *Scarface*—itself censored to avoid an X-rating—but Simon never said what network, cable, or pay-per-view channel he saw it on.) This experience prompted him to sponsor a three-year antitrust exemption for the networks, which was his way of encouraging them to voluntarily "clean house." But at the end of that period, the rates of TV violence hadn't changed enough to satisfy him, so Simon convened open hearings on the subject in 1993.

If Simon was truly concerned with the content of television programming, the first question that comes to mind is why he gave the networks an antitrust exemption in the first place. Thanks to Reagan-era deregulation, ownership of the mass media has become steadily more concentrated in the hands of fewer and fewer corporations. For example, the Federal Com-

From *The Humanist*, January/February 1994, pp. 20-25. © 1994 by Brian Siano. Reprinted by permission.

munications Commission used to have a "seven-and-seven" rule, whereby no company was allowed to own more than seven radio and seven television stations. In 1984, this was revised to a "12-and-12-and-12" rule: 12 FM radio stations, 12 AM radio stations, and 12 TV stations. It's a process outlined by Ben Bagdikian in his fine book *The Media Monopoly*. The net result is a loss of dissident, investigative, or regional voices; a mass media that questions less; and a forum for public debate that includes only the powerful.

This process could be impeded with judicious use of antitrust laws and stricter FCC controls—a return to the "seven-and-seven" rule, perhaps. But rather than hold hearings on this subject—a far greater threat to the nation's political well-being than watching *Aliens* on pay-per-view—Simon gave the networks a three-year *exemption* from antitrust legislation.

There's a reason we should be concerned about this issue of media ownership: television influences people. That's its *job*. Advertisers don't spend all that money on TV commercials because they have no impact. Corporations don't dump money into PBS shows like "The McLaughlin Group" or "Firing Line" unless they are getting their point across. *Somebody* is buying stuff from the Home Shopping Network and keeping Rush Limbaugh's ratings up. Then, too, we all applaud such public-service initiatives as "Don't Drink and Drive" ads, and I think most of us would be appalled if Donatello of the *Teenage Mutant Ninja Turtles* lit up a Marlboro or chugged a fifth of Cutty Sark. So it's not unreasonable to wonder whether violent television might be encouraging violent behavior.

The debate becomes even more impassioned when we ask how children might be affected. The innocent, trusting little tykes are spending hours bathed in TV's unreal colors, and their fantasy lives are inhabited by such weirdos as Wolverine and Eek the Cat. Parents usually want their kids to grow up sharing their ideals and values, or at least to be well-behaved and obedient. Tell parents that their kids are watching "Beavis and Butt-head" in their formative years and you set off some major alarms.

There are also elitist, even snobbish, attitudes toward pop culture that help to rationalize censorship. One is that the corporate, mass-market culture of TV isn't important enough or "art" enough to deserve the same free-speech protection as James Joyce's *Ulysses* or William Burrough's *Naked Lunch*. The second is that rational, civilized human beings are supposed to be into Shakespeare and Scarlatti, not Pearl Jam and "Beavis and Butt-head." Seen in this "enlightened" way, the efforts of Paul Simon are actually for *our own good*. And so we define anything even remotely energetic as "violent," wail about how innocent freckle-faced children are being defiled by such fare as "NYPD Blue," and call for a Council of Certified Nice People who will decide what the rest of us get to see. A recent *Mother Jones* article by Carl Cannon (July/August 1993) took just this hysterical tone, citing as proof "some three thousand research studies of this issue."

Actually, there aren't 3,000 studies. In 1984, the *Psychological Bulletin* published an overview by Jonathan Freedman of research on the subject. Referring to the "2,500 studies" figure

bandied about at the time (it's a safe bet that 10 years would inflate this figure to 3,000), Freedman writes:

> The reality is more modest. The large number refers to the complete bibliography on television. References to television and aggression are far fewer, perhaps around 500. . . . The actual literature on the relation between television violence and aggression consists of fewer than 100 independent studies, and the majority of these are laboratory experiments. Although this is still a substantial body of work, it is not vast, and there are only a small number of studies dealing specifically with the effects of television violence outside the laboratory.

The bulk of the evidence for a causal relationship between television violence and violent behavior comes from the research of Leonard Eron of the University of Illinois and Rowell Huesmann of the University of Michigan. Beginning in 1960, Eron and his associates began a large-scale appraisal of how aggression develops in children and whether or not it persists into adulthood. (The question of television violence was, originally, a side issue to the long-term study.) Unfortunately, when the popular press writes about Eron's work, it tends to present his methodology in the simplest of terms: *Mother Jones* erroneously stated that his study "followed the viewing habits of a group of children for twenty-two years." It's this sort of sloppiness, and overzealousness to prove a point, that keeps people from understanding the issues or raising substantial criticisms. Therefore, we must discuss Eron's work in some detail.

The first issue in Eron's study was how to measure aggressiveness in children. Eron's "peer-nominated index" followed a simple strategy: asking each child in a classroom questions about which kids were the main offenders in 10 different categories of classroom aggression (that is, "Who pushes or shoves children?"). The method is

> *There are elitist and snobbish attitudes toward pop culture that help to rationalize censorship.*

consistent with other scales of aggression, and its one-month test-retest reliability is 91 percent. The researchers also tested the roles of four behavioral dimensions in the development of aggression: *instigation* (parental rejection or lack of nurturance),

reinforcement (punishment versus reward), *identification* (acquiring the parents' behavior and values), and *sociocultural norms*.

Eron's team selected the entire third-grade population of Columbia County, New York, testing 870 children and interviewing about 75 to 80 percent of their parents. Several trends became clear almost immediately. Children with less nurturing parents were more aggressive. Children who more closely identified with either parent were less aggressive. And children with low parental identification who were punished tended to be *more* aggressive (an observation which required revision of the behavioral model).

Ten years later, Eron and company tracked down and re-interviewed about half of the original sample. (They followed up on the subjects in 1981 as well.) Many of the subjects—now high-school seniors—demonstrated a persistence in aggression over time. Not only were the "peer-nominated" ratings roughly consistent with the third-grade ratings, but the more aggressive kids were three times as likely to have a police record by adulthood.

Eron's team also checked for the influences on aggression which they had previously noted when the subjects were eight. The persistent influences were parental identification and socioeconomic variables. Some previously important influences (lack of nurturance, punishment for aggression) didn't seem to affect the subjects' behavior as much in young adulthood. Eron writes of these factors:

> Their effect is short-lived and other variables are more important in predicting later aggression. Likewise, contingencies and environmental conditions can change drastically over 10 years, and thus the earlier contingent response becomes irrelevant.

It's at this stage that Eron mentions television as a factor:

> One of the best predictors of how aggressive a young man would be at age 19 was the violence of the television programs he preferred when he was 8 years old. Now, because we had longitudinal data, we could say with more certainty, on the basis of regression analysis, partial correlation, path analysis, and so forth, that there indeed was a cause-and-effect relation. *Continued research, however, has indicated that the causal effect is probably bidirectional: Aggressive children prefer violent television, and the violence on television causes them to be more aggressive.*   [italics added]

Before we address the last comment, I should make one thing clear. Eron's research is sound. The methods he used to measure aggression are used by social scientists in many other contexts. His research does not ignore such obvious factors as the parents' socioeconomic status. And, as the above summary makes clear, Eron's own work makes a strong case for the positive or negative influence of parents in the development of their children's aggressiveness.

Now let's look at this "causal effect" business. Eron's data reveals that aggressive kids who turn into aggressive adults

like aggressive television. But this is a correlation; it is not proof of a causal influence. If aggressive kids liked eating strawberry ice cream more often than the class wusses did, that too would be a predictor, and one might speculate on some anger-inducing chemical in strawberries.

Of course, the relation between representational violence and its influence on real life isn't as farfetched as that. The problem lies in determining precisely the nature of that relation, as we see when we look at the laboratory studies conducted by other researchers. Usually, the protocol for these experiments involves providing groups of individuals with entertainment calibrated for violent content, and studying some aspect of behavior after exposure—response to a behavioral test, which toys the children choose to play with, and so forth. But the results of these tests have been somewhat mixed. Sometimes the results are at variance with other studies, and many have methodological problems. For example, which "violent" entertainment is chosen? Bugs Bunny and the "Teenage Mutant Ninja Turtles" present action in very different contexts, and in one study, the Adam West "Batman" series was deemed nonviolent, despite those *Pow! Bam! Sock!* fistfights that ended every episode.

Many of the studies report that children do demonstrate higher levels of interpersonal aggression shortly after watching violent, energetic entertainment. But a 1971 study by Feshbach and Singer had boys from seven schools watch preassigned violent and nonviolent shows for six weeks. The results were not constant from school to school—and the boys watching the *nonviolent* shows tended to be more aggressive. Another protocol, carried out in Belgium as well as the United States, separated children into cottages at an institutional school and exposed certain groups to violent films. Higher aggression was noted in *all* groups after the films were viewed, but it returned to a near-baseline level after a week or so. (The children also rated the less violent films as less exciting, more boring, and sillier than the violent films—indicating that maybe kids *like* a little rush now and then.) Given the criticisms of the short-term-effects studies, and the alternate interpretations of the longitudinal studies, is this matter really settled?

Eron certainly thinks so. Testifying before Simon's committee in August, he declared that "the scientific debate is over" and called upon the Senate to reduce TV violence. His statement did not include any reference to such significant factors as parental identification—which, as his own research indicates, can change the way children interpret physical punishment. And even though Rowell Huesmann concurred with Eron in similar testimony before a House subcommittee, Huesmann's 1984 study of 1,500 youths in the United States, Finland, Poland, and Australia argued that, assuming a causal influence, television might be responsible for 5 percent of the violence in society. At *most*.

This is where I feel one has to part company with Leonard Eron. He is one of the most respected researchers in his field, and his work points to an imperative for parents in shaping and sharing their children's lives. But he has lent his considerable authority to such diversionary efforts as Paul Simon's and

urged us to address, by questionable means, what only *might* be causing a tiny portion of real-life violence.

Some of Eron's suggestions for improving television are problematic as well. In his Senate testimony, Eron proposed restrictions on televised violence from 6:00 AM to 10:00 PM—which would exclude pro football, documentaries about World War II, and even concerned lawperson Janet Reno's proudest moments. Or take Eron's suggestion that, in televised drama, "perpetrators of violence should not be rewarded for violent acts." I don't know what shows Eron's been watching, but all of the cop shows I remember usually ended with the bad guys getting caught or killed. And when Eron suggests that "gratuitous violence that is not necessary to the plot should be reduced or abandoned," one has to ask just *who* decides that it's "not necessary"? Perhaps most troubling is Eron's closing statement:

For many years now Western European countries have had monitoring of TV and films for violence by government agencies and have *not* permitted the showing of excess violence, especially during child viewing hours. And I've never heard complaints by citizens of those democratic countries that their rights have been violated. If something doesn't give, we may have to institute some such monitoring by government agencies here in the U.S.A. If the industry does not police itself, then there is left only the prospect of official censorship, distasteful as this may be to many of us.

The most often-cited measure of just how violent TV programs are is that of George Gerbner, dean of the Annenberg School of Communications at the University of Pennsylvania. Few of the news stories about TV violence explain how this index is compiled, the context in which Gerbner has conducted his studies, or even some criticisms that could be raised.

Gerbner's view of the media's role in society is far more nuanced than the publicity given the violence profile may indicate. He sees television as a kind of myth-structure/religion for modern society. Television dramas, situation comedies, news shows, and all the rest create a shared culture for viewers, which "communicates much about social norms and relationships, about goals and means, about winners and losers." One portion of Gerbner's research involves compiling "risk ratios" in an effort to discern which minority groups—including children, the aged, and women—tend to be the victims or the aggressors in drama. This provides a picture of a pecking order within society (white males on top, no surprise there) that has remained somewhat consistent over the 20-year history of the index.

In a press release accompanying the 1993 violence index, Gerbner discusses his investigations of the long-term effects of television viewing. Heavy viewers were more likely to express feelings of living in a hostile world. Gerbner adds, "Violence is a demonstration of power. It shows who can get away with what against whom."

In a previous violence index compiled for cable-television programs, violence is defined as a "clear-cut and overt episode of physical violence—hurting or killing or the threat of hurting and/or killing—in any context." An earlier definition reads: "The overt expression of physical force against self or other compelling action against one's will on pain of being hurt or killed, or actually hurting or killing." These definitions have been criticized for being too broad; they encompass episodes of physical comedy, depiction of accidents in dramas, and even violent incidents in documentaries. They also include zany cartoon violence; in fact, the indexes for Saturday-morning programming tend to be substantially higher than the indexes for prime-time programming. Gerbner argues that, since he is analyzing cultural norms and since television entertainment is a deliberately conceived expression of these norms, his definition serves the purposes of his study.

> *Stories of media-inspired violence are atypical of the norm; the vast majority of people don't take a movie or TV show as a license to kill.*

The incidents of violence (total number = R) in a given viewing period are compiled by Gerbner's staff. Some of the statistics are easy to derive, such as the percentage of programs with violence, the number of violent scenes per hour, and the actual duration of violence, in minutes per hour. The actual violence index is calculated by adding together the following stats:

$\%P$ — the *percentage* of programs in which there is violence;

$2(R/P)$ — twice the number of violent episodes per program;

$2(R/H)$ — twice the number of violent episodes per *hour;*

$\%V$ — percentage of *leading characters* involved in violence, either as victim or perpetrator; and

$\%K$ — percentage of leading characters involved in an actual *killing,* either as victim or perpetrator.

But if these are the factors used to compile the violence profile, it's difficult to see how they can provide a clear-cut mandate for the specific content of television drama. For example, two of the numbers used are averages; why are they arbitrarily doubled and then added to percentages? Also, because

the numbers are determined by a definition which explicitly separates violence from dramatic context, the index says little about actual television content outside of a broad, overall gauge. One may imagine a television season of nothing but slapstick comedy with a very high violence profile.

This is why the violence profile is best understood within the context of Gerbner's wider analysis of media content. It does not lend itself to providing specific conclusions or guidelines of the sort urged by Senator Paul Simon. (It is important to note that, even though Simon observed little change in prime-time violence levels during his three-year antitrust exemption, the index for all three of those years was *below* the overall 20-year score.)

Finally, there's the anecdotal evidence—loudly trumpeted as such by Carl Cannon in *Mother Jones*—where isolated examples of entertainment-inspired violence are cited as proof of its pernicous influence. Several such examples have turned up recently. A sequence was edited out of the film *The Good Son* in which MacCaulay Culkin drops stuff onto a highway from an overhead bridge. (As we all know, nobody ever did this before the movie came out.) The film *The Program* was re-edited when some kids were killed imitating the film's characters, who "proved their courage" by lying down on a highway's dividing line. Perhaps most notoriously, in October 1993 a four-year-old Ohio boy set his family's trailer on fire, killing his younger sister; the child's mother promptly blamed MTV's "Beavis and Butt-head" for setting a bad example. But a neighbor interviewed on CNN reported that the family didn't even have cable television and that the kid had a local rep as a pyromaniac months before. This particular account was not followed up by the national media, which, if there were no enticing 'Beavis and Butt-head" angle, would never have mentioned this fire at a low-income trailer park to begin with.

Numerous articles about media-inspired violence have cited similar stories—killers claiming to be Freddy Kreuger, kids imitating crimes they'd seen on a cop show a few days before, and so forth. In many of these cases, it is undeniably true that the person involved took his or her inspiration to act from a dramatic presentation in the media—the obvious example being John Hinckley's fixation on the film *Taxi Driver*. (Needless to say, Bible-inspired crimes just don't attract the ire of Congress.) But stories of media-inspired violence are striking mainly because they're so *atypical* of the norm; the vast majority of people don't take a movie or a TV show as a license to kill. Ironically, it is the *abnormality* of these stories that ensures they'll get widespread dissemination and be remembered long after the more mundane crimes are forgotten.

Of course, there are a few crazies out there who will be un-favorably influenced by what they see on TV. But even assuming that somehow the TV show (or movie or record) shares some of the blame, how does one predict what future crazies will take for inspiration? What guidelines would ensure that people write, act, or produce something that *will not upset a psy-*

chotic? Not only is this a ridiculous demand, it's insulting to the public as well. We would all be treated as potential murderers in order to gain a hypothetical 5 percent reduction in violence.

In crusades like this—where the villagers pick up their torches and go hunting after Frankenstein—people often lose sight of what they're defending. I've read reams of statements from people who claim to know what television does to kids; but what do *kids* do with television? Almost none of what I've read gives kids any credit for thinking. None of these people seems to remember what being a kid is like.

When *Jurassic Park* was released, there was a huge debate over whether or not children should be allowed to see it. Kids like to see dinosaurs, people argued, but this movie might scare them into catatonia. There was even the suspicion that Steven Spielberg and company were being sneaky and underhanded by making a film about dinosaurs that was terrifying. These objections were actually taken seriously. But kids like dinosaurs because they're big, look really weird, and scare the hell out of everything around them. Dinosaurs *kick ass*. What parent would tell his or her child that dinosaurs were *cute*? (And how long have these "concerned parents" been *lying* to their kids about the most fearsome beasts ever to shake the earth?)

Along the same lines, what kid hasn't tried to gross out everyone at the dinner table by showing them his or her chewed-up food? Or tried using a magnifying glass on an ant-hill on a hot day? Or clinically inspected the first dead animal he or she ever came across? Sixty years ago, adults were ter-rified of *Frankenstein* and fainted at the premiere of *King Kong*. But today, *Kong* is regarded as a fantasy story, *Godzilla* can be shown without the objections of child psychologists, and there are breakfast cereals called Count Chocula and Franken-berry. Sadly, there are few adults who seem to remember how they identified more with the monsters. Who wanted to be one of those stupid villagers waving torches at Frankenstein? That's what our *parents* were like.

But it's not just an issue of kids liking violence, grossness, or comic-book adventure. About 90 percent of the cartoon shows I watched as a child were the mass-produced sludge of the Hanna-Barbera Studios—like "Wacky Races," "The Jet-sons," and "Scooby Doo, Where Are You?" I can't remember a single memorable moment from any of them. But that Bugs Bunny sequence at the beginning of this article (from *Rabbit Seasoning*, 1952, directed by Chuck Jones) was done from memory, and I have no doubt that it's almost verbatim.

I know that, even at the age of eight or nine, I had some rudimentary aesthetic sense about it all. There was something hip and complex about the Warner Bros. cartoons, and some trite, insulting *sameness* to the Hanna-Barbera trash, although I couldn't quite understand it then. Bugs Bunny clearly wasn't made for kids according to some study on social-interaction development. Bugs Bunny was meant to make adults laugh as much as children. Kids can also enjoy entertainment ostensibly created for adults—in fact, that's often the most rewarding kind. I had no trouble digesting *Jaws*, James Bond, and Clint East-

wood "spaghetti westerns" in my preteen years. And I'd have no problems with showing a 10-year-old *Jurassic Park*, because I know how much he or she would love it.

Another example: Ralph Bakshi's brilliant "Mighty Mouse" series was canceled after the Reverend Donald Wildmon claimed it showed the mouse snorting coke. Kids don't organize mass write-in campaigns, and I hate to see them lose something wonderful just because some officious crackpot decides it was corrupting their morals. Perhaps aspartame-drenched shows like "Barney and Friends" or "Widget" (a purple, spermy little alien who can do magic) encourage children to be good citizens, but they also encourage kids to be docile and unimaginative—just the sort of "good citizens" easily manipulated by the likes of Wildmon.

I don't enjoy bad television with lots of violence, but I'd rather not lose *decent* shows that use violence for good reason. Shows like "Star Trek," "X-Men," or the spectacular "Batman: The Animated Series" can give kids a sense of adventure while teaching them about such qualities as courage, bravery, and heroism. Even better, a healthy and robust spirit of irreverence can be found in Bugs Bunny, "Ren and Stimpy," and "Tiny Toons." Some of these entertainments—like adventure stories and comic books of the past—can teach kids how to be really *alive*.

Finally, if we must have a defense against the pernicious influence of the mass media, it cannot be from the Senate's legislation or the pronouncements of social scientists. It must begin with precisely the qualities I described above—especially irreverence. One good start is Comedy Central's "Mystery Science Theater 3000," where the main characters, forced to watch horrendous movies, fight back by heckling them. Not surprisingly, children love the show, even though most of the jokes go right over their curious little heads. They recognize a kindred spirit in "MST 3000." Kids want to stick up for themselves, maybe like Batman, maybe like Bugs Bunny, or even like Beavis and Butt-head—but always against a world made by adults.

You know, *adults*—those doofuses with the torches, trying to burn up Frankenstein in the old mill.

Helping

Early in the semester, you volunteer to participate in a psychology experiment being conducted at your school. When you arrive at the appointed time and place you are greeted by the experimenter, who explains that the research project requires you to complete a series of questionnaires measuring different aspects of your personality. The experimenter gives you the questionnaires and then returns to his office for the 30 minutes it will take you to complete them. After 5 minutes or so, you hear a loud crash in the hallway, and then you hear what sounds like a person groaning softly. What do you do?

Most of us have a very clear idea about what we would do—we would leave the room, look for the person who apparently fell, and try to help him or her. And sure enough, when research like this is conducted, that is what happens . . . some of the time. When students are alone in the room when the crash occurs, they are quite likely to help, just as we might expect. When several students are in the room together, however, they are less likely to help; in fact, the *more* people in the room, the *less* helping occurs. Thus, there is something about being in a group of people that makes us less likely to respond to the needs of another during an emergency. Weird.

Weird it may be, but research like this is one example of the kind of work that is done by social psychologists who study helping behavior. This particular kind of experiment is an attempt to understand a phenomenon known as "bystander intervention"—when bystanders actively get involved during an emergency to try to help the victim. Research has consistently demonstrated that having a large number of bystanders can actually reduce the amount of aid that is given, in part because each person takes less and less responsibility for helping the victim.

Other approaches to helping have tried to uncover the different kinds of motivations that lead people to help.

Some people seem to help, for example, because they have a strong sense of obligation to care for others who are in need; this sense of obligation is often created early in life. Sometimes people help in order to reduce the level of arousing distress they feel when they see a victim; thus, helping the other person actually serves to help oneself as well. Helping that also provides a benefit to the helper is usually termed "egoistic" helping. There is also evidence that sometimes people help simply for the goal of easing another's burden, and they are not doing so to achieve personal gain. Helping of this kind is usually referred to as "altruistic" helping, because its ultimate goal is to benefit another.

The first selection in this unit, "The Roots of Good and Evil," examines the behavior of some of our closest biological relatives—chimpanzees—to determine whether some of the helping we offer to each other might have its roots in our evolutionary heritage. As in human society, chimpanzee communities also develop norms of behavior that protect the general good and punish those who violate the rules.

In "Volunteerism and Society's Response to the HIV Epidemic," psychologists Mark Snyder and Allen Omoto focus on a particular form of helping: volunteerism. Each year millions of people donate their time and energy to their communities in some way, and in this selection the authors consider the various motives that can lead people to volunteer, and the motives that can lead them to continue volunteering over the long haul.

"Getting By with a Little Help from Some Friends" approaches the question of helping by looking at the ways in which cooperation and helping behavior can be encouraged in children. One powerful technique is modeling—that is, for adults who are in frequent contact with children (parents, teachers, etc.) to display helpful behav-

ior themselves. Providing this kind of example can reinforce children's preexisting ability to empathize with others.

Finally, in "Mobilization and Deterioration of Social Support Following Natural Disasters," authors Krzysztof Kaniasty and Fran Norris examine the kind of help social support networks provide in times of extreme need, such as in the aftermath of natural disasters. While support networks generally provide needed assistance to individuals in such situations, the severity of the disaster can also overwhelm the ability of the networks to help.

Looking Ahead: Challenge Questions

What kind of evidence is there for the notion that our concepts of helping and cooperation spring from our evolutionary history? How valid, do you think, is a comparison of human and chimpanzee behavior?

What kind of motivations lead people to volunteer their time and energy to help others? Would you call these motivations "egoistic" or "altruistic"? What factors seem to be especially important in determining whether people continue their volunteering or not?

How can parents encourage children to develop an empathic, caring outlook toward others? How can schools and teachers do this? Is there any chance of success in creating such an outlook in neglected and abused teenagers?

When considering the social support received after a natural disaster, what is the "rule of relative needs" and the "rule of relative advantage"? How do these rules determine who receives support? How capable are social support networks of providing needed aid for as long as necessary following a disaster?

The Roots of Good and Evil

What can chimps tell us about our moral nature?

GEOFFREY COWLEY

T'S A LAZY AFTERNOON IN LAW- renceville, Ga., and everything should be going Jimoh's way. As the top-ranking male in a group of 20 chimpanzees maintained by the Yer- kes Primate Research Center, this muscular, black-haired 29-year-old is every female's favorite escort. And today Peony, one of his own favorites, has a red swelling on her rump, signaling a period of sexual readiness. As the rest of the group lounges, Jimoh sidles up to her, sporting an erection, and the two are briefly united. But when a pair of youngsters sense they're missing out on some fun, they bound over to throw dirt and pound on the amorous couple. Jimoh could throttle the punks, but the alpha male withdraws with a look of calm resignation and waits for a more auspicious moment to mate. "He has to be very tolerant of the ju- veniles," explains primatologist Frans de Waal. "He can't afford to alienate their moms."

Shifting view: Can't afford to alienate their moms? Until recently, no serious scientist would have uttered such a thought. As ev- eryone knew, humans were cultural ani- mals, born and raised to restrain them- selves. Other primates were just plain animals. But the conventional view—both of them and of us—is shifting. A growing number of researchers are studying human and animal social conventions just as they would diets or mating patterns—not as fixed ideals but as biological adaptations. And their findings suggest that the roots of morality are far older than we are. As de Waal shows in his new book, "Good Na- tured" *(296 pages. Harvard University Press. $24.95)*, we're much like other primates when it comes to sharing resources, settling differences and enforcing order. Unfortu- nately, as other scholars are discovering,

the ethical impulses we share with our furry cousins can undermine our best efforts to create a stable community.

De Waal has spent two decades toppling misconceptions about chimpanzee society. He has shown, for example, that males achieve dominance not through sheer force but through shrewd politics. In his new book, he builds on that insight, arguing that the hier- archy is a "mutual contract" between leaders and subordinates. De Waal recounts how Ji- moh once caught Socko, an adolescent male, mating with a female he had been pursuing himself. "He chased him all around the en- closure—Socko screaming and defecating in fear." But when the females in the group joined in an angry howl of protest, Jimoh called off the attack and walked away with a nervous grin. "One never hears [such a pro- test] when a mother punishes her own off- spring, or when an adult male controls a tiff among juveniles," de Waal writes. "Thinking in terms of rules and violations may help us [understand it]."

It may also help us understand the chimps' food-sharing rituals. Visit the lush, 117-acre Yerkes field station on an August afternoon and you'll find de Waal's re- search assistant Mike Seres clipping fresh shoots of bush clover, honeysuckle, sweet gum and muscadine. When he tosses the bundles into the chimps' compound, the rules of rank are briefly suspended. Within minutes, the chimps who haven't secured their own branches gather around someone who has. Despite an occasional skirmish, everyone ends up with something to chew on. De Waal has found that physical attacks increase ninefold when branches are tossed into a pen—but not for the reason you'd expect. The chimps use violence not to se- cure food but, more often, to rebuff food seekers who have previously failed to

share. The implicit moral rule: "Those who seek favors must grant them."

As moral actions go, punishing ill deeds is pretty rudimentary. But chimps some- times rise above side-taking to exhibit what de Waal calls "community concern." A creature that can survive only in a group is right to perceive social disarray as a threat to its own well-being. And as de Waal re- counts from experience, chimps are exceed- ingly sensitive to disharmony among their group mates. High-ranking males often act as beat cops, quelling disputes before they escalate into riots. Females practice a sort of diplomacy, drawing angry rivals together and encouraging them to reconcile. And when rivals embrace, signaling an end to their hostilities, the entire colony may erupt in joyous pandemonium.

Seeds of civilization: Chimps may not think consciously about harmony; they pur- sue it as instinctively as they do sex. But de Waal sees in their communal spirit the seeds of civilization. "Human morality can be looked at as community concern made explicit," he writes. "Our ancestors began to understand how to preserve peace and order—hence how to keep their group unit- ed against external threats. . . . They came to judge behavior that systematically un- dermined the social fabric as wrong, and behavior that made a community worth- while to live in as right."

Alas, that's not to say that charity comes naturally to us and cruelty doesn't. Social impulses may flourish when they're useful to individuals, but you can count on them to wither when they're not. Mutualism is the rule among groups of Olympic marmots, furry rodents that eke out their living in the rocky meadows of the Olympic Mountains. The woodchuck, a related species found in lush lowland forests, is less dependent on

 From *Newsweek*, February 26, 1996, pp. 52-54. © 1996 by Newsweek, Inc. All rights reserved. Reprinted by permission.

its neighbors—and it treats them accordingly. It's the same for chimps and humans. "Different environments require different degrees of moral solidarity," says John Tooby, an anthropologist at the University of California, Santa Barbara. "We tend to be convivial when it pays."

When it doesn't pay, ruthlessness is often the rule. The famed Jane Goodall observed male chimps in Africa patrolling the borders of their territories, mounting gang attacks on members of neighboring groups. "Males race forward and jointly attack mother-infant pair," reads one of her team's field notes. "Mother loses half an ear. . . . Infant alive and calling for four minutes while being eaten." To anyone who follows the news, that death-squad dynamic should sound chillingly familiar.

If we're quick to deny outsiders any moral consideration, we're even quicker to cheat on our comrades when we think we can get away with it. The chimps at Yerkes may understand rank and reciprocity, but they'll gladly slip out of sight to cop some illicit sex, or feign illness to avoid sharing a choice piece of food. If you think humans are different, consider that a 1994 poll found one American in four would steal $10 million if he knew he wouldn't get caught. Freeloading is hard to get away with in a small group; as de Waal has found in his food-provisioning experiments, cheaters are easily identified, and no one forgets who they are. Throughout vast stretches of evolutionary history, our own ancestors lived in groups of less than 100, where face-to-face accountability would have been the norm. But with the advent of agriculture 10,000 years ago, populations exploded. For the first time, groups of primates had to codify social norms and create governments and religions to administer them.

Not suprisingly, these brave new institutions have turned out to be as troublesome as they are necessary. As our collective efforts make life more comfortable, each of us ends up with more to lose, and the case for self-sacrifice starts to ring hollow. As Dartmouth political scientist Roger Masters observes in his new book, "Machiavelli, Leonardo, and the Science of Power" *(384 pages. Notre Dame Press. $32.95),* "the very success of [civic] institutions re-creates the pressures that made [them] necessary in the first place." It's comforting to know that notions of right and wrong are part of our animal heritage. But it's not at all clear that our innate moral sense is up to the challenges we've created.

Volunteerism and Society's Response to the HIV Epidemic

Mark Snyder and Allen M. Omoto

Mark Snyder is Professor of Psychology at the University of Minnesota. **Allen M. Omoto** is Assistant Professor of Psychology at the University of Kansas. Address correspondence to Mark Snyder, Department of Psychology, University of Minnesota, 75 East River Road, Minneapolis, MN 55455-0344, or Allen M. Omoto, Department of Psychology, 426 Fraser Hall, University of Kansas, Lawrence, KS 66045-2160.

In 1981, the Centers for Disease Control reported the first case of what would come to be known as AIDS. Now, barely a decade later, there are over 200,000 confirmed cases of AIDS in the United States and an estimated 1.5 million Americans infected with HIV (the virus that causes AIDS). The World Health Organization projects that, by the year 2000, 30 to 40 million adults and children worldwide will have been infected with HIV, and most of them are expected to develop AIDS.[1] Clearly, with neither a vaccine nor a cure in sight, the full impact of AIDS, as devastating and profound as the epidemic has been, has yet to be felt, and will surely touch all of our lives.

Society has responded to the HIV epidemic on a number of fronts, including at least three for which the skills and expertise of psychologists, as scientists and practitioners, can be tapped: (a) providing psychological services for persons living with AIDS (PWAs), (b) developing behavior change campaigns to reduce the likelihood of HIV transmission, and (c) implementing public education programs to address matters of prejudice and discrimination associated with AIDS and PWAs.[2] In our research, we are examining a remarkable social phenomenon born of the HIV epidemic—AIDS volunteerism and its implications for each of these fronts.

A critical component of society's response has been the development of community-based grass-roots organizations of volunteers involved in caring for PWAs and in educating the public about HIV, AIDS, and PWAs. Volunteers fill many roles; some provide emotional and social support as "buddies" to PWAs, whereas others help PWAs with their household chores or transportation needs. Volunteers also staff information, counseling, and referral hotlines; make educational presentations; raise funds; and engage in social, legal, and political advocacy. In the United States, AIDS volunteer programs have emerged in every state, in cities large and small, and in rural areas as well. AIDS volunteerism is a compelling testimonial to human kindness and to the power of communities of "ordinary people" to unite and organize in response to extraordinary events.[3]

As remarkable as AIDS volunteerism is, it actually is part of a pervasive social phenomenon in American society. A recent Gallup Poll estimated that, in 1989, 98.4 million American adults engaged in some form of volunteerism, with 25.6 million giving 5 or more hours per week to volunteer work—volunteer services worth some $170 billion.[4] In addition to working on HIV-related issues, volunteers provide companionship to the elderly, health care to the sick, tutoring to the illiterate, counseling to the troubled, food to the hungry, and shelter to the homeless.

Although the study of helping has long been a mainstay of research in the psychological sciences, volunteerism is a form of prosocial action about which there is little systematic literature.[5] Volunteerism is, however, marked by several distinctive features. Volunteers typically seek out their opportunities to help, often deliberate long and hard about the form and the extent of their involvements, and may carefully consider how different volunteer opportunities fit with their own needs, goals, and motivations. Many forms of volunteerism also entail commitments to ongoing helping relationships that have considerable duration and require sizable personal costs in time, energy, and expense.

We view AIDS volunteerism not only as an intriguing social phenomenon, but also as paradigmatic of sustained and potentially costly helping behavior. In one survey,[6] we found that AIDS volunteers overwhelmingly had actively sought out

From *Current Directions in Psychological Science,* August 1992, pp. 113-116. © 1992 by the American Psychological Association.
Reprinted by permission of Cambridge University Press.

their volunteer opportunities (over 80% indicated that they had approached their AIDS organizations on their own initiative). Moreover, their involvement represented a substantial and recurring time commitment (on average, 4 hr per week) that extended over a considerable length of time (1½ years on average, and often spanning several years). Finally, these volunteers were giving of themselves in trying and stressful circumstances (spending time with PWAs and confronting the tragic realities of serious illness and death) and doing so at some personal cost (with many reporting feeling stigmatized as a result of their AIDS work).

THREE STAGES OF THE VOLUNTEER PROCESS

In our research, we are seeking to understand the social and psychological aspects of volunteerism. Our research is grounded in a three-stage conceptual model of the *volunteer process,* a model that specifies psychological and behavioral features associated with each stage and speaks to activity at three levels of analysis: the individual volunteer, the organizational context, and the broader social system.[7]

The first stage of the volunteer process involves *antecedents* of volunteerism and addresses the questions "who volunteers?" and "why do they volunteer?" In the case of AIDS, considerations at the antecedents stage focus on the attitudes, values, and motivations that dispose people to serve as AIDS volunteers, as well as the needs and goals that AIDS volunteer work may fulfill for individuals.

The second stage concerns *experiences* of volunteers and the dynamics of the helping relationships that develop between volunteers and the people with whom they work. In the specific case of AIDS, it is important to recognize that these relationships are carried out against the stressful backdrop of chronic illness and even death. Of additional concern are the effects of AIDS volunteers on the general treatment and coping processes of PWAs, as well as changes that occur in volunteers themselves.

The third stage focuses on *consequences* of volunteerism and is concerned with how volunteer work affects volunteers, members of their social networks, and society at large. For AIDS volunteers, it is possible that their work has not only beneficial effects on personal attitudes, knowledge, and behaviors, but also negative consequences of stigmatization and social censure. When it comes to societal issues, moreover, AIDS volunteerism may possess the potential for encouraging social change as volunteers transmit their new attitudes and behavior to their friends and associates and, by extension, to the broader social system.

BASIC RESEARCH AND PRACTICAL PROBLEMS

In our research, we are engaged in a coordinated program of cross-sectional and longitudinal field studies coupled with experiments conducted in the laboratory and sampling from diverse populations of volunteers and nonvolunteers. Thus, we have conducted a national survey of currently active AIDS volunteers, querying them about their motivations for volunteering, their experiences, and the consequences of their involvement in AIDS volunteerism, thereby generating cross-sectional data relevant to the three stages of the volunteer process. In an extended longitudinal study, we are also tracking new volunteers over the course of their service providing emotional support and living assistance to PWAs; in this long-term study, we are examining the same people at all stages of the volunteer process. Finally, we are conducting laboratory experiments and field intervention studies, each relevant to one or more stages of the volunteer process.

At each stage of our conceptual model, relevant psychological theories and the evidence of basic research are helping us to frame research questions, the answers to which, we hope, will have implications for addressing practical issues related to volunteerism, as well as for building bridges between basic research and practical application. To illustrate the ways in which our research builds these bridges, let us examine two important practical matters that are rooted in different stages of the volunteer process and the theoretically informed answers to them derived from our program of research. Specifically, we examine issues of volunteer recruitment and retention.

The Recruitment of Volunteers

Recruitment is one of the key concerns at the antecedents stage. There are many formidable barriers that can keep prospective volunteers from getting involved; in the case of AIDS, not only are there limits of time and energy but also, for many people, fear of AIDS and death and concerns about stigmatization. What, then, motivates people to volunteer to staff an AIDS hotline or to be buddies for PWAs?

Guided by a functionally oriented theory of motivation (which proposes that apparently similar acts of volunteerism may reflect markedly different underlying motivations), we have been examining the motivations of AIDS volunteers. We have utilized exploratory and confirmatory factor analytic techniques in developing and validating a self-report inventory to assess five primary motivations for AIDS volunteerism, each one reliably measured by five different items.[8] The first set of motivations involves personal *values* (e.g., "because of my humanitarian obligation to help others"). The second set invokes considerations related to *understanding* (e.g., "to learn about how people cope with AIDS"). The third set taps *community concern* and reflects people's sense of obligation to or concern about a community or social group-

ing (e.g., "because of my concern and worry about the gay community"). The fourth set concerns *personal development* and centers on issues of personal growth (e.g., "to challenge myself and test my skills"). The fifth category assesses *esteem enhancement* and includes considerations about current voids or deficits in one's life (e.g., "to feel better about myself").[9]

The development of this motivational inventory has made possible a more thorough analysis of the psychology of AIDS volunteerism. This work has revealed that, despite what appears to be a commonality of purpose in being a volunteer, there is striking individual-to-individual variability in the motivations that are most and least important. An appreciation of different motivations, moreover, has great practical import for volunteer recruitment. Because volunteering serves different psychological functions for different people, volunteer organizations would be well advised to tailor their recruitment messages to particular motivations of selected sets of potential volunteers. In recruiting volunteers who would be motivated by esteem enhancement, for instance, recruitment appeals could stress how AIDS volunteerism provides many opportunities for people to work through personal fears, anxieties, and doubts rather than, say, stressing humanitarian obligations and images of kindness (which could be used to appeal to prospective volunteers motivated by value-based concerns).

The Retention of Volunteers

Why do some volunteers continue to donate their time and services, and why do others stop? A persistent frustration in volunteer programs is the high rate of attrition (i.e., dropout) of volunteers. As difficult as it may be to recruit volunteers, it is sometimes even more difficult to ensure their continued service. Considerations of the expe-

riences and consequences stages of the volunteer process may shed light on matters of attrition and longevity of service because the experiences associated with volunteer work and the consequences that result from it likely influence volunteers' effectiveness, their satisfaction, and the length of time they ultimately remain active. To examine some of these possibilities, we recontacted one set of AIDS volunteers a year after they had told us about their work. At that time, approximately one half of the original sample was still active with their AIDS organizations, and we proceeded to ask both quitters and stayers about their experiences as volunteers and the consequences of their work.[8]

We found no differences between the quitters and stayers in reported satisfaction with their service and commitment to the purposes of their AIDS organizations. Where quitters and stayers differed, however, was in their perceptions of the costs of their volunteer work. Despite having engaged in satisfying and rewarding volunteer work, quitters more than stayers said they felt that volunteering had taken up too much time and—an important point—caused them to feel embarrassed, uncomfortable, or stigmatized. The negative consequences and not the rewards of the work, then, distinguished quitters from volunteers who continued to serve.

Bringing our analysis full circle, we also found that initial motivations for volunteering were related to attrition and length of service. To the extent that people espoused esteem enhancement or personal development reasons for their work (rather than community concern, values, or understanding), they were likely to still be active volunteers at our 1-year follow-up; moreover, esteem enhancement and understanding motivations proved valuable as predictors of the total length of service of these volunteers. Thus, volunteer attrition seemed not to be associated with the relatively "self-less" or other-focused motivations, as one

might expect, but with more "selfish" desires of feeling good about oneself and acquiring knowledge and skills. Good, and perhaps romanticized, intentions related to humanitarian concern simply may not be strong enough to sustain volunteers faced with the tough realities and personal costs of working with PWAs. Therefore, volunteer organizations, in combating attrition, may want to remind volunteers of the personal rewards of their work rather than underscoring how volunteer efforts benefit clients and society. Similarly, volunteers may be better prepared for their work by having the potential costs of volunteerism made explicit to them at the outset; in this way, volunteers could be "prepared for the worst" and thereby "inoculated" against the negative impact of the personal costs of their service.

CONCLUSIONS

To conclude, let us explicitly address a recurring theme in our research—the relation between basic research and practical problems. Our research is simultaneously basic and applied. As much as it informs applied concerns with the current and potential roles of volunteerism in society's response to AIDS, our work also speaks directly to theoretical concerns about the nature of helping relationships and, more generally, the dynamics of individual and collective action in response to societal needs. With a dual focus on applied and theoretical concerns, our program of research embodies the essential components of *action research,* in which basic and applied research mutually inform and enrich one another and, under optimal circumstances, basic research is advanced and effective social action is undertaken.[10]

It is said that a society is judged by how it responds in times of need. Clearly, the age of AIDS is a time of the greatest need. The HIV epidemic represents not only a medical crisis, but also a broader set of challenges

to individuals and to society. Among these challenges are those to researchers in the social and behavioral sciences. By all accounts, the number of AIDS cases will only increase in the years ahead, and, as medical advances extend the life expectancy of PWAs, more and more people will be living with AIDS and living *longer* with AIDS. As the HIV epidemic continues and intensifies, so too will the importance of contributions of theory-based research relevant to all facets of AIDS. Ultimately, when the history of the HIV epidemic is written, we hope that the psychological sciences will have proven themselves integral to society's collective response to AIDS.

Acknowledgments—This research and the preparation of this manuscript have been supported by grants from the American Foundation for AIDS Research (No. 000741-5 and 000961-7) and from the National Institute of Mental Health (No. 1 RO1 MH47673) to Mark Snyder and Allen M. Omoto. We thank the volunteers and staff of the Minnesota AIDS Project (Minneapolis, MN) and the Good Samaritan Project (Kansas City, MO) for their cooperation and participation in this research.

Notes

1. AIDS spreading faster than thought, *The Kansas City Star*, p. A-3 (February 12, 1992).

2. G.M. Herek and E.K. Glunt, An epidemic of stigma: Public reaction to AIDS, *American Psychologist*, 43, 886–891 (1988); S.F. Morin, AIDS: The challenge to psychology, *American Psychologist*, 43, 838–842 (1988).

3. P.S. Arno, The nonprofit sector's response to the AIDS epidemic: Community-based services in San Francisco, *American Journal of Public Health*, 76, 1325–1330 (1988); S.M. Chambré, The volunteer response to the AIDS epidemic in New York City: Implications for research on voluntarism, *Nonprofit and Voluntary Sector Quarterly*, 20, 267–287 (1991); J.A. Dumont, Volunteer visitors for patients with AIDS, *The Journal of Volunteer Administration*, 8, 3–8 (1989); P.M. Kayal, Gay AIDS voluntarism as political activity, *Nonprofit and Voluntary Sector Quarterly*, 20, 289–331 (1991); S.C. Ouellette Kobasa, AIDS and volunteer associations: Perspectives on social and individual change, *The Milbank Quarterly*, 68 (S2), 280–294 (1990); D. Lopez and G.S. Getzel, Strategies for volunteers caring for persons with AIDS, *Social Casework*, 68, 47–53 (1987).

4. Independent Sector, *Giving and Volunteering in the United States* (Gallup Organization for Independent Sector, Washington, DC, 1990).

5. For perspectives on the literature on volunteerism, see S.M. Chambré, Kindling points of light: Volunteering as public policy, *Nonprofit and Voluntary Sector Quarterly*, 18, 249–268 (1989); E.G. Clary and M. Snyder, A functional analysis of altruism and prosocial behavior: The case of volunteerism, *Review of Personality and Social Psychology*, 12, 119–148 (1991); J. Van Til, *Mapping the Third Sector: Voluntarism in a Changing Social Economy* (Foundation Center, New York, 1988).

6. A.M. Omoto, M. Snyder, and J.P. Berghuis, The psychology of volunteerism: A conceptual analysis and a program of action research, in *The Social Psychology of HIV Infection*, J.B. Pryor and G.D. Reeder, Eds. (Erlbaum, Hillsdale, NJ, 1992).

7. A.M. Omoto and M. Snyder, Basic research in action: Volunteerism and society's response to AIDS, *Personality and Social Psychology Bulletin*, 16, 152–165 (1990); Omoto, Snyder, and Berghuis, note 6.

8. M. Snyder and A.M. Omoto, Who helps and why? The psychology of AIDS volunteerism, in *Helping and Being Helped: Naturalistic Studies*, S. Spacapan and S. Oskamp, Eds. (Sage, Newbury Park, CA, 1991); M. Snyder and A.M. Omoto, AIDS volunteers: Who volunteers and why do they volunteer? in *Leadership and Management*, V.A. Hodgkinson and R.D. Sumariwalla, Eds. (Independent Sector, Washington, DC, 1991).

9. Similar sets of motivations have also emerged from other attempts to measure the motives of AIDS volunteers. See, e.g., M.J. Williams, Gay men as "buddies" to persons living with AIDS and ARC, *Smith College Studies in Social Work*, 59, 38–52 (1988); L.M. Wong, S.C. Ouellette Kobasa, J.B. Cassel, and L.P. Platt, *A new scale identifies 6 motives for AIDS volunteers*, poster presented at the annual meeting of the American Psychological Society, Washington, DC (June 1991). On the motivations served by volunteerism in general, see E.G. Clary, M. Snyder, and R.D. Ridge, Volunteers' motivations: A functional strategy for the recruitment, placement, and retention of volunteers, *Nonprofit Management and Leadership* (in press).

10. K. Lewin, *Field Theory in Social Science* (Harper, New York, 1951; original work published 1944); Omoto and Snyder, note 7.

Recommended Reading

Omoto, A.M., Snyder, M., and Berghuis, J.P. (1992). The psychology of volunteerism: A conceptual analysis and a program of action research. In *The Social Psychology of HIV Infection*, J.B. Pryor and G.D. Reeder, Eds. (Erlbaum, Hillsdale, NJ).

Snyder, M., and Omoto, A.M. (1991). Who helps and why? The psychology of AIDS volunteerism. In *Helping and Being Helped: Naturalistic Studies*, S. Spacapan and S. Oskamp, Eds. (Sage, Newbury Park, CA).

Getting By with a Little Help from Some Friends

Teaching empathy and kindness is catching on as part of a national movement to give children prosocial values.

Bridget Murray

Monitor staff

Instead of hounding at-risk adolescents to stay out of trouble, a new psychologist-driven program at 10 New York City homes for abused and neglected teen-agers is teaching them to care for one another and lift each others' spirits.

Clinical psychologist Michael Schulman, PhD, has launched the Caring Profile Values Modification Program at the Leake and Watts Services Group Homes to help troubled adolescents replace their angry feelings toward others with gentle, empathic ones.

Many of the teens feel betrayed by loved ones and equate love with painful vulnerability, says Schulman, an author of the 1994 book "Bringing up a Moral Child." He and the Leake and Watts staff he's training are helping the 100 teens who live in the homes to see that caring emotions can be uplifting.

"We encourage kids to find and re-experience the joy of loving someone, whether it's a family member or friend," says Schulman. "We remind them that loving is what makes life worthwhile and that it's worth the risk."

As part of a growing national movement to teach prosocial values to America's youth, Schulman and other psychologists are teaching youngsters how to care for others and are encouraging parents and teachers to do the same.

"Kids are being taught that being attractive or athletic doesn't necessarily make you a good person, but being caring does," said Schulman.

Boosting Natural Empathy

Ideally, teaching gentleness and morality should start in the home when children are young, says psychologist Carolyn Zahn-Waxler, PhD, of the National Institute of Mental Health. She has found that children show signs of empathy when they're as young as one year old.

In a 1992 study of 27 mothers and their one-year-old children, Zahn-Waxler found that, by age two, all but one of the children had displayed a caring behavior like hugging, kissing or patting someone in distress, during or after an argument, injury, crying spell or illness.

Many of them displayed empathic gestures like sad, concerned facial expressions or made reassuring statements like "I'm sorry." Girls tended to show more empathy, which Zahn-Waxler says may relate to gender-role socialization.

It's parents' responsibility to nurture this naturally occurring empathy and teach children prosocial values, Zahn-Waxler notes. Parents who teach caring are most likely to have empathic children, she says.

 From *APA Monitor*, January 1996, p. 41. © 1996 by the American Psychological Association. Reprinted by permission.

"It's children's innate ability to feel for others that makes it possible for parents to effectively teach and model altruistic behavior," said Zahn-Waxler.

Parents can teach gentleness along with the ABC's, she says. They can tune children into the hurt of others in daily life and, if their children harm others, can alert them of it and explain the harm done. However, parents should try not to be hyper-vigilant, Zahn-Waxler says. It's important not to find fault with the child.

Her research shows that children who have been abused or neglected or exposed to physical and verbal cruelty between family members often have trouble behaving kindly.

Parents' own modeling of altruistic acts strongly influences their children's lifelong altruism, other research finds. In a late 1980s study of 162 volunteers at a Minneapolis telephone crisis-counseling agency, psychologist E. Gil Clary, PhD, of the College of St. Catherine found that those who reported lower levels of parental altruism—defined as warm, giving behaviors toward their children and others—were more likely to leave the agency in a six-month period than those who reported high levels of parental altruism.

High levels were equated with strong parental commitment to charity and causes such as sheltering the homeless. Lower levels were equated with erratic charitable giving and lukewarm affiliations with causes. Parental actions proved much more influential than parental speeches. Children model what their parents do much more than what they say, Clary notes.

"Parents who model helpfulness will develop [in children] the psychological structures that make children caring adults," says Clary. "Instead of seeing others as strangers, they'll see them as neighbors—people who share the same earth and live within the same walls."

In the same study, Clary also found that volunteers who underwent group training were more likely to continue volunteering. They felt more connected to the agency socially because they were friendlier with their fellow volunteers.

"KIDS ARE BEING TAUGHT THAT BEING ATTRACTIVE OR ATHLETIC DOESN'T NECESSARILY MAKE YOU A GOOD PERSON, BUT BEING CARING DOES."
MICHAEL SCHULMAN, PhD
NEW YORK CITY

Caring at School

Similarly, schools are seeking to build stronger social bonds between students. School psychologist Eva Mekler, PhD, who co-authored "Bringing Up a Moral Child" with Schulman, explains to the children she works with in the New York City school system that a classroom is a community where everybody must treat each other decently.

Mekler fosters friendliness in students who would otherwise maltreat or ostracize one another. She encourages them to look for facial expressions and gestures that signify hurt in someone who feels angry or insulted. Instead of ignoring someone else's pain, she tells students to try to understand it and show kindness.

Schulman describes the steps to building a caring school community in his book, "Schools as Moral Communities." He believes schools should:

- make clear in their mission statements that they are devoted to caring about everyone's feelings and to moral excellence;
- provide staff training for teachers to help them deal with students' unpleasant behaviors, such as hurtful teasing;
- add a moral perspective to social studies courses to examine historic peacemaking efforts of leaders such as Mohandas Gandhi; and
- hold workshops for students to discuss moral issues and help them resolve their conflicts with others.

Tom Lickona, PhD, who specializes in character education at the State University of New York-Cortland and directs its Center for the Fourth and Fifth Rs (respect and responsibility), believes that schools are important shapers of students' common moral sense, and can enhance parents' moral training or even serve as sole moral providers. Through the center, he is running summer character-education workshops for New York State school teachers.

Schools must "tout core values of respect, responsibility and honesty from the cafeteria to the school bus," he says. They should encourage students to tutor others and provide community service to build their sense of knowing the good, desiring the good and doing the good.

Standards of Kindness

Knowing the good is difficult for the 13- to 20-year-olds who live in the Leake and Watts Homes. They're usually assigned to the homes by the city welfare agency because their parents can no longer support them or deal with them. Sometimes they're there because their parents are ill or dying, other times because their parents reject them. Many bear scars of beatings, rapes, neglect and constant criticism from parents and other family members.

To counteract their bitterness, the community at the homes is built around concern for other's feelings. Sarcasm, violence, bullying, exploitation and name-calling are forbidden, and caring gestures such as empathic listening, welcoming newcomers and talking about feelings are modeled by

the staff. Even when teens come home after curfew, staff members still greet them pleasantly before discussing their tardiness.

Schulman encourages teens to tap into one another's feelings in group therapy and offer comfort to peers who feel depressed. To encourage commitment to community values, those who do well in school and follow house rules such as cleaning up the kitchen and bathroom, using the phone during "calling hours" and smoking outside the house, receive material rewards like more television time and clothing money.

Children develop a conscience through internalizing adults' standards of kindness and fairness, feeling empathic and developing personal standards of right and wrong, he believes.

"The children that come to the homes are used to verbal and physical aggression—at first they're skeptical of the caring environment but after a while they appreciate the emotional safety," said Schulman. "For some kids this is the first time somebody's really talked to them and been concerned about their emotions."

Mobilization and Deterioration of Social Support Following Natural Disasters

Krzysztof Kaniasty and Fran H. Norris

Krzysztof Kaniasty is an Associate Professor of Psychology at Indiana University of Pennsylvania. **Fran H. Norris** is an Associate Professor of Psychology at Georgia State University. Address correspondence to Krys Kaniasty, Department of Psychology, Indiana University of Pennsylvania, Indiana, PA 15705; e-mail: kaniasty@iup.bitnet.

When natural disasters strike, the victims face a double jeopardy: To cope with their threats and losses, they need to marshal social support at the time when their social networks are most likely to be disrupted and potentially unable to carry out their supportive roles. The stress that challenges victims of natural disasters, such as floods, hurricanes, tornadoes, or earthquakes, is multifaceted.[1] It often involves immediate trauma arising from exposure to death and injury, extreme physical force, and life-threatening situations. Disaster stress often entails the destruction or loss of tangible goods and possessions that are of substantial monetary value or symbolic and emotional significance. It threatens and shatters various valued resources needed to sustain physical and psychological health. Not surprisingly, then, research has documented reliable increases in physical and psychological symptomatology experienced by victims.[2]

Disasters engulf whole communities. Victimization is shared. At the extreme, a disaster evolves into a devastating collective trauma, "a blow to the tissues of social life that damages the bonds linking people together and impairs the prevailing sense of communality."[3] Almost every definition of disaster speaks of the disruption of social structure or sense of community. With equal consistency, however, empirical and lay reports use labels such as "altruistic" or "therapeutic" community and postdisaster "utopia" or "heroism" when describing higher than usual levels of solidarity, fellowship, and altruism that emerge immediately after the impact. Therefore, natural disasters pose an interesting paradox for researchers of social support. On the one hand, disasters elicit outpourings of immense mutual helping; on the other hand, disasters impede the exchange of support because they disrupt social networks through death or injury, relocation, changes in routine activities, and physical destruction of environments conducive for social interactions.[4]

This review of a growing area of interdisciplinary research investigating mutual helping following catastrophic events is an attempt to describe postdisaster processes that originate with an instant mobilization of supportive behaviors but often lead to deterioration of helping resources, leaving some victims with a perceived sense of loss in their social relationships at a time when they need these relationships the most. To understand this phenomenon, we must look more closely at the dynamic transactions between characteristics of the stressor and social support. Although disasters occur suddenly, the stress they cause is not only acute. Disasters create continuous challenges for victims and their communities. The literature distinguishes explicitly among several postimpact stages: The salient heroic phase, with its therapeutic features of increased cohesiveness and altruism, is soon replaced by the disillusionment and reconstruction phases. It is then that the victims discover that the need for assistance far exceeds the availability of resources and realize that the increased sense of benevolence was short-lived. President Clinton, during his visit to the areas of the Great Flood of '93, appropriately remarked, "Folks are brave and good-humored and courageous. But then the reality of the losses sinks in and grief takes over."[5] Social support is not a static property of a person or the environment. Its quantity, quality, and functions depend on individuals and the stressor demands they face. As a "rise and fall of utopia," natural disaster is an excellent example of an event that moves across time from an initial rush of spontaneous helping to a long-term depletion of supportive resources.

POSTDISASTER MOBILIZATION OF SUPPORT

It is important to differentiate various manifestations of social support. We distinguish among three

From *Current Directions in Psychological Science*, June 1995, pp. 94-98. © 1995 by the American Psychological Association.
Reprinted by permission of Cambridge University Press.

general categories: received support (actual receipt of help), perceived support (the belief that help would be available if needed), and social embeddedness (quantity and type of relationships with other people). It could be said that the instant mobilization of help following disaster is the domain of received support, whereas a lingering sense of deterioration and disruption of the indigenous social fabric is the domain of perceived support and embeddedness.

The mutual help in emergent postdisaster helping communities is not distributed equally or randomly. Priority is given to those victims who are most exposed to the disaster's destructive powers. In fall 1990, 1 year after Hurricane Hugo devastated large areas of North and South Carolina (September 22, 1989), we interviewed 1,000 victims and nonvictims.[6] Disaster exposure, operationalized as loss (of property and belongings) and harm (injury or threat to life), was strongly associated with the amount of help received. The between-group differences were pervasive: Victims received much more help than nonvictims, and high-exposure victims received more support than low-exposure victims. The importance of loss and harm in predicting the receipt of assistance is consistent with the *rule of relative needs*. Relative needs, most often operationalized as the severity of experienced stressor, serve as an impetus in mobilizing support from other people.

Kin networks are the most utilized sources of support to disaster victims. Nonkin informal networks, such as friends, neighbors, or religious congregations, also appear to play a vital role in assisting victims, particularly when kin ties are weak or absent.[4] In a study of widespread flooding that occurred in southeastern Kentucky in 1981 and 1984, we found that victims received more help from kin than nonkin sources.[7] Interestingly, the extent of loss significantly predicted help only from nonkin sources. Thus, helping

among immediate family and relatives may not follow a rule of relative needs, and may be allocated somewhat irrespectively of the extent of losses experienced.

According to the contemporary models of stress, social support is an asset in that it promotes preservation or recovery of physical and psychological resources that are needed for successful coping. Studies that have examined the role of social support among victims of natural disasters generally show that inadequate levels of social support are associated with greater distress.[4,8,9] If social networks are to play their protective and restorative functions, they have to provide resources that are most challenged by stressful circumstances. Consequently, in the study of Hurricane Hugo, we found that the greatest difference in support received by victims and nonvictims was in the realm of tangible help.[6] Victims helped each other extensively by cleaning properties, doing household chores, sharing shelter, and lending needed tools, equipment, or money. They also received much more help than nonvictims in the form of guidance and information. Victims need to know how to assess their emotions, where to go for organized aid, and how to protect their properties. All these supportive acts are specific and well matched to the ecological demands of the event. This point is important because receipt of support should be most beneficial to psychological well-being if the specific demands of the stressor and supportive provisions are congruent with each other.

Of course, being surrounded by people who are loving and understanding is imperative for disaster victims, many of whom not only have lost valuables of material or symbolic significance but also have been exposed to death and injury. Not surprisingly, then, emotional help was, in absolute terms, the most frequently exchanged helping behavior among Hugo victims. However, victims were not as different from nonvictims in amount of

emotional support received as they were in amount of tangible and informational support received. Analyses of the concomitants of support receipt indicated that the levels of emotional help were determined less by disaster impact and more by person characteristics than tangible and information help. Possibly, people desire emotional support at all times, whereas their need for tangible aid and advice is determined more by demands of the stressor.

Besides the rule of relative needs, the *rule of relative advantage* surfaced in the post-Hugo helping community: Female, younger, married, white, and more educated persons typically received more help than their male, older, unmarried, black, and less educated counterparts. Relative advantage (person characteristics) interacted with relative needs (stressor) to produce two patterns of differential mobilization of support. The first, a *pattern of neglect*, emerged among less educated persons and blacks, who received proportionately less help than equally affected victims who were more educated and white. These findings are not isolated incidents peculiar to the context of Hurricane Hugo. Bolin and Bolton,[10] based on the examination of four disasters that struck culturally and ethnically diverse sites, concluded that the poor and minorities had the greatest difficulties securing adequate assistance and recovering from disaster. Often-publicized examples of altruism and solidarity that the public can marshal in times of crisis should not obscure the fact that the pattern of neglect is equally real.

Fortunately, a few victims of Hurricane Hugo experienced a *pattern of concern*: The oldest respondents (over 70 years old), when faced with threats to their lives and health, received relatively more help than similarly affected victims from younger age groups. However, older victims did not experience such a pattern of concern when faced with property loss. Findings of other studies also point to the limits of this spe-

cial regard for the elderly. Some researchers reported that older victims may, in fact, experience neglect and receive considerably less help from all sources than younger people.[11] The Kentucky floods elicited such a pattern: Elderly flood victims received very little help—much less than they had expected.[7] Evidently, when the need for support is not manifested as a threat to their health, older victims may be overlooked by altruistic communities.

POSTDISASTER DETERIORATION OF SUPPORT

Our study of the Kentucky floods had two unique features. First, pre- as well as postdisaster measures were available because the floods occurred in the midst of an ongoing panel study of older adults in the area. This afforded an excellent opportunity to examine changes in perceptions of social support as a direct result of disaster. Second, we operationalized disaster victimization at both individual and community levels because disasters are community events with potential psychological and social consequences even for people who incur no direct losses.

The results indicated that postflood perceptions of social support declined from preflood levels. Personal losses (extent of damages at the household level) were associated with substantial declines in expectations of how much support would be available from kin and nonkin sources. Similarly, in other disaster contexts, Solomon and her colleagues found that some victims experienced a profound loss of perceived availability of support.[9] In the case of the Kentucky floods, the need for support may simply have exceeded its availability. Therefore, decline in postflood perceptions of support availability may have constituted a veridical assessment of temporary inability (most of these effects

were limited to 3 to 6 months post-disaster) of social networks to provide adequate support. Interestingly, these declines were not limited to people personally affected by the disaster (i.e., primary victims). Natural disasters most often affect entire indigenous networks. Consequently, in the Kentucky floods study, we found that community destruction (extent of damages at the county level) was negatively associated with postdisaster perceptions of support, suggesting that declines in perceived availability of support were also experienced by secondary victims, that is, people who resided in the flooded areas but did not sustain personal losses.

There was also a strong communitywide tendency to experience declines in social embeddedness. Destruction of the physical environment may have disrupted activities, such as visiting, shopping, religious services, and recreation, that maintain a sense of social embeddedness and promote companionship. Our initial analyses of a sample of 400 Floridians interviewed about 6 months after Hurricane Andrew (August 1992) destroyed their neighborhoods in South Miami suggest that victims experienced disruption of routine social activities, loss of opportunities for fun and leisure, and less satisfaction with their social lives. Relocation or job loss removed relatives, friends, or neighbors from readily accessible social networks. Physical fatigue, emotional irritability, and scarcity of resources augmented the potential for interpersonal conflicts, isolation, and loneliness. In the most tragic cases, like after the Buffalo Creek dam collapse, the sense of community may be completely shattered—and with it "the power it gave people to care for one another in moments of need, to console one another in moments of distress, and to protect one another in moments of danger."[12] Small or great, annual or centennial, natural disasters impair the capacity of a community's naturally occurring support systems,

making support exchanges difficult, strenuous, or even impossible.

The deterioration of perceived social support and sense of embeddedness is one path through which natural disasters exert their adverse effects on psychological well-being. We tested a theoretical model stipulating that victims experience the impact of the disaster both directly, through immediate loss and exposure to trauma, and indirectly, through deterioration of their social supports (see Fig. 1). Using data from the Kentucky floods,[7] we found convincing evidence for this mediating model: The disaster-induced erosion of social support to a great extent accounted for increased depressive symptomatology among both primary and secondary victims. The loss of social support has also mediated psychological consequences of Hurricanes Hugo and Andrew.[13]

This *deterioration model of social support* recognizes the potential of the stressor to curtail support and in this way is conceptually different from the more prominent stress-

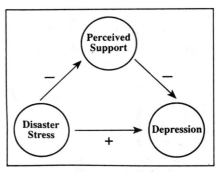

Fig. 1. Deterioration model of social support.

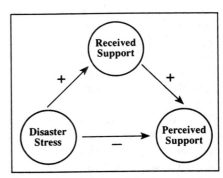

Fig. 2. Deterioration deterrence model.

buffering model of social support. The model assumes that the changes in support contribute to the detrimental effects of stress rather than counteract them. In fact, declines in perceived social support may be the reason why stress-buffering processes are not operating, or are very limited, in the context of natural disasters.[8,9] After all, if the belief that support is available is undermined, how could it protect against the impact of the stressor? Of course, those victims whose initial high levels of support do not deteriorate, or even increase, could enjoy the benefits of perceived support as a buffer of stress.

Is the deterioration of perceived social support inevitable, or can it be counteracted by higher levels of received support? We addressed this question with the data from Hurricane Hugo, whose victims received relatively high levels of help.[14] Figure 2 depicts the *deterioration deterrence model*, which closely resembles more general stress-suppressor or support-mobilization models.[15] If postdisaster support mobilization has occurred, the disaster stress should be positively related to received support. This received support, in turn, should be positively related to perceived support. Thus, the receipt of support deters the otherwise negative relation between stress and perceived support. Structural equation modeling analyses provided quite strong support for this conceptualization. For all types of support examined—emotional, informational, tangible—the sign of the path coefficient from disaster stress to perceived support was negative (indicating deterioration), whereas the path from disaster stress to received support was positive (indicating mobilization). And, most important, there was a large positive coefficient for the path from received support to perceived support. Thus, when received support is low relative to needs, disaster victims' perceptions of support will deteriorate. However, when received support is adequate for those needs, di-

saster victims will maintain their expectations of available support.

SUMMARY MODEL

Figure 3 illustrates the processes linking the stress of natural disasters, person characteristics, social supports, and psychological distress. First, there is a deterioration process wherein disaster victims whose needs are unmet experience a decline in perceived support and a consequent increase in distress (see Paths a and b). Fortunately, the mobilization of received support may deter this deterioration and preserve victims' ongoing perceptions that support is available (see Paths c and

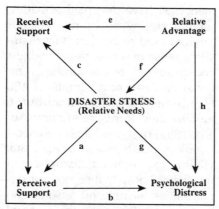

Fig. 3. Schematic framework depicting paths linking stress, person characteristics, social supports, and psychological distress.

d). These beliefs of being reliably connected to other people will shield victims from experiencing intense distress (Path b). Patterns of concern and neglect may also emerge; that is, the mobilization of support may be influenced by victims' relative advantage (Path e) as well as their relative needs (Path c). As illustrated via Paths f, g, and h, other mechanisms operate as well.

We recognize that the processes we have described may not generalize easily to other stressful life events, especially those confined to lone individuals. However, these

dynamics may apply to other community-level events in which the distinction between the victim and the supporter is just a matter of speech, not reality. Any time a resource is scarce, various rules that influence its distribution come into play. At best, the emergent altruistic community is insufficient to meet all the community needs; at worst, it may inadvertently exclude many citizens who are in need. Mobilizing indigenous support is a very difficult task. Therefore, we must explore ways to provide the resources that help people help each other.

Acknowledgments—Preparation of this review and some of the research reported in it were supported by Grant No. MH45069 (Hurricane Hugo) and Grant No. MH51278 (Hurricane Andrew) from the National Institute of Mental Health, Fran H. Norris, Principal Investigator.

Notes

1. The focus of this review is on helping behavior from indigenous social networks following natural disasters. In some cases, human-induced catastrophes (e.g., a collapse of a dam) share many features with natural disasters, and therefore could be included here. However, because of space limitations, we excluded from this review research on technological disasters that either do not have well-defined low points ("worst is over") and are not associated with immediate and clear damages (e.g., nuclear power plant accident, toxic waste spill) or are confined to relatively small groups of individuals (e.g., transportation disasters). For definitional issues, see, e.g., R. Gist and B. Lubin, Eds., *Psychosocial Aspects of Disaster* (Wiley, New York, 1989).

2. See, e.g., A. Rubonis and L. Bickman, Psychological impairment in the wake of disaster: The disaster-psychopathology relationship, *Psychological Bulletin, 109,* 384–399 (1991).

3. K. Erikson, Loss of communality at Buffalo Creek, *American Journal of Psychiatry, 133,* 302–305 (1976), p. 302.

4. See, e.g., T. Drabek and W. Key, *Conquering Disaster: Family Recovery and Long-Term Consequences* (Irvington Publishers, New York, 1984); S.D. Solomon, Mobilizing social support networks in times of disaster, in *Trauma and Its Wake: Vol. 2. Traumatic Stress Theory, Research, and Intervention,* C. Figley, Ed. (Brunner/Mazel, New York, 1986).

5. J. Adler, Troubled waters, *Newsweek* (July 26, 1993), p. 23.

6. K. Kaniasty and F. Norris, In search of altruistic community: Patterns of social support mobilization following Hurricane Hugo, *American Journal of Community Psychology* (in press).

7. K. Kaniasty, F. Norris, and S. Murrell, Received and perceived social support following natural disaster, *Journal of Applied Social Psychology, 20,* 85–114 (1990); K. Kaniasty and F. Norris, A test of the social support deterioration model in the context of natural disaster, *Journal of Personality and Social Psychology, 64,* 395–408 (1993).

8. See, e.g., J. Cook and L. Bickman, Social support and psychological symptomatology following a natural disaster, *Journal of Traumatic Stress, 3,* 541–556 (1990); M. Cowan and S. Murphy, Iden-

tification of postdisaster bereavement risk predictors, *Nursing Research, 34,* 71–75 (1985).

9. S.D. Solomon, M. Bravo, M. Rubio-Stipec, and G. Canino, Effect of family role on response to disaster, *Journal of Traumatic Stress, 6,* 255–269 (1993).

10. R. Bolin and P. Bolton, *Race, Religion, and Ethnicity in Disaster Recovery* (University of Colorado, Boulder, 1986).

11. T. Kilijanek and T.E. Drabek, Assessing long-term impacts of a natural disaster: A focus on the elderly, *The Gerontologist, 19,* 555–566 (1979).

12. Erikson, note 3, p. 305.

13. G. Ironson, D. Greenwood, C. Wynings, A. Baum, M. Rodriquez, C. Carver, C. Benight, J. Evans, M. Antoni, A. LaPerriere, M. Kumar, M. Fletcher, and N. Schneiderman, *Social support, neuroendocrine, and immune functioning during Hurricane Andrew,* paper presented at the annual meeting of the American Psychological Association, Toronto, Canada (August 1993); K. Kaniasty and F. Norris, *Social support from family and friends following catastrophic events: The role of cultural factors,* paper presented at the 7th International Conference on Personal Relationships, Groningen, The Netherlands (July 1994).

14. F. Norris and K. Kaniasty, *Receipt of help and perceived social support in times of stress: A test of the social support deterioration deterrence model,* manuscript submitted for publication (1994).

15. See M. Barrera, Models of social support and life stress: Beyond the buffering hypothesis, in *Life Events and Psychological Functioning,* L.H. Cohen, Ed. (Sage Publications, Newbury Park, CA, 1988).

Group Processes

In 1961 President John F. Kennedy and a group of his senior advisers held a series of secret meetings to plan a dramatic military action. The plan under consideration was an invasion of Cuba, and the goal was to overthrow the Communist regime of Fidel Castro. This was not to be a massive invasion, however, utilizing the United States' heavy superiority in numbers and technology; such a move would be too provocative. Instead, the plan called for the U.S. to secretly train and equip a relatively small force of anti-Castro Cubans—exiles driven from their homeland because of Castro's rise to power. This small force of about 1,400 men would begin the invasion by landing at the Bahia de Cochinos, or the Bay of Pigs. Seizing control of radio stations, they would broadcast news of Cuba's liberation and would then sweep across the country picking up support from the Cuban people until they would constitute a force so compelling that Castro could not endure.

They never had a chance. Supplies that were supposed to sustain the invaders failed to arrive; the tiny invading force was completely overwhelmed by the larger, better-trained Cuban military; and the anticipated uprising by the Cuban people never happened. Within three days the entire force had been captured or killed. Instead of a dramatic military success, the United States, and President Kennedy, suffered a humiliating political defeat in the eyes of the world; in fact, the phrase "Bay of Pigs" has come to signify any plan or action that comes to a disastrous end. In the aftermath of this debacle, moreover, it seemed painfully obvious that the plan was doomed

from the start. The nagging question, then, was how could some of the smartest people in the country come to agree on a plan that in retrospect seemed to have no chance at all of succeeding? How could the group go so wrong?

That question is one of the many that social psychology has asked about groups, and the processes that occur when people meet in groups. In fact, a very interesting line of research into how groups can reach such bad decisions—a phenomenon known as "groupthink"—was directly inspired by the Bay of Pigs fiasco. According to this approach, highly cohesive groups frequently develop a mind-set characterized by secretiveness, overconfidence, and illusions of invulnerability; this in turn can lead them into decisions that overlook what should be obvious flaws. Other approaches to group decision making have focused on another common phenomenon: the fact that when groups have to choose a course of action, they often make a choice that is more extreme than the decision that each individual would make alone. That is, one effect of group discussion is to polarize the attitudes of the group members.

In addition to the issue of how groups make decisions, another topic of interest has been the impact that groups can have on the *behavior* of the individuals who make up the group. For example, it frequently happens that individuals work faster and more productively when in the presence of others than they do when they are alone— at least if the task they are working on is relatively simple, or if it is a task with which they have had a lot of practice. In contrast, on a new task, or one which is very complex, the presence of other people can hurt performance. Researchers who study this phenomenon, called *social facilitation,* have identified a variety of possible explanations for its occurrence.

The selections in this unit represent several different approaches to the study of group processes. The first two selections address the issue of group decision making. In "Group Decision Fiascoes Continue: Space Shuttle *Challenger* and a Revised Groupthink Framework," the authors use the decision to launch the ill-fated space shuttle *Chal-*

lenger as an example of groupthink. They trace how some of the cognitive biases that characterize groupthink were present during the discussions leading up to the decision to launch. In "Blowup," author Malcolm Gladwell takes a different approach, and argues that modern systems, both mechanical and social, are so complex that certain kinds of accidents are virtually unavoidable.

Other selections focus on issues that have a special relevance to group processes in the business world. "'90s Style Brainstorming" discusses a solution to some of the problems that occur in face-to-face meetings devoted to exploring possible plans of action. To prevent some of the conformity pressures and social loafing that can take place in such meetings, some companies have used technology to "level the playing field" in such encounters. In "The New Post-Heroic Leadership," John Huey reports on an emerging leadership style in complex organizations. Rather than attempting to maintain all control and responsibility in the hands of a single "leader," this style encourages more democratic and cooperative sharing of such responsibility.

Looking Ahead: Challenge Questions

What are the most important characteristics of a group experiencing groupthink? How do those characteristics ultimately influence the decisions reached by the group? Other than the Bay of Pigs and *Challenger* disasters, can you think of any well-known group decisions that might be examples of groupthink? Can you think of any examples from groups in your own life? What do you think of the argument in "Blowup" that complex systems today cannot be understood well enough to avoid all disasters?

What are the problems with traditional brainstorming techniques? How can technology solve those problems? Are there any new problems for groups or leaders created by the use of such technological solutions?

What does it mean to be a real leader? Can a leader really *be* a leader if he or she gives up responsibility to others? How well do you think the "post-heroic" leadership style would work in groups with which you are familiar?

Group Decision Fiascoes Continue: Space Shuttle Challenger and a Revised Groupthink Framework

Gregory Moorhead, Richard Ference and Chris P. Neck

In this article, the authors review the events surrounding the tragic decision to launch the space shuttle Challenger. Moorhead and his colleagues assert that the decision-making process demonstrates *groupthink,* a phenomenon wherein cohesive groups become so concerned with their own process that they lose sight of the true requirements of their task. The authors review the events in light of this concept, suggesting that the groupthink concept needs to be expanded to consider time pressures, which were surely present in the Challenger situation, as well as the kind of leadership patterns that exist in a group.

In 1972, a new dimension was added to our understanding of group decision making with the proposal of the groupthink hypothesis by Janis (1972). Janis coined the term "groupthink" to refer to "a mode of thinking that people engage in when they are deeply involved in a cohesive in-group, when the members' striving for unanimity override their motivation to realistically appraise alternative courses of action" (Janis, 1972, p. 8). The hypothesis was supported by his hindsight analysis of several political-military fiascoes and successes that are differentiated by the occurrence or non-occurrence of antecedent conditions, groupthink symptoms, and decision making defects.

In a subsequent volume, Janis further explicates the theory and adds an analysis of the Watergate transcripts and various published memoirs and accounts of principals involved, concluding that the Watergate cover-up decision also was a result of groupthink (Janis, 1983). Both volumes propose prescriptions for preventing the occurrence of groupthink, many of

which have appeared in popular press, in books on executive decision making, and in management textbooks. Multiple advocacy decision-making procedures have been adopted at the executive levels in many organizations, including the executive branch of the government. One would think that by 1986, 13 years after the publication of a popular book, that its prescriptions might be well ingrained in our management and decision-making styles. Unfortunately, it has not happened.

On January 28, 1986, the space shuttle Challenger was launched from Kennedy Space Center. The temperature that morning was in the mid-20's, well below the previous low temperatures at which the shuttle engines had been tested. Seventy-three seconds after launch, the Challenger exploded, killing all seven astronauts aboard, and becoming the worst disaster in space flight history. The catastrophe shocked the nation, crippled the American space program, and is destined to be remembered as the most tragic national event since the assassination of John F. Kennedy in 1963.

The Presidential Commission that investigated the accident pointed to a flawed decision-making process as a primary contributory cause. The decision was made the night before the launch in the Level I Flight Readiness Review meeting. Due to the work of the Presidential Commission, information concerning that meeting is available for analysis as a group decision possibly susceptible to groupthink.

In this paper, we report the results of our analysis of the Level I Flight Readiness Review meeting as a decision-making situation that displays evidence of groupthink. We review the antecedent conditions, the groupthink symptoms, and the pos-

From *Psychology Is Social: Readings and Conversations in Social Psychology, 3/e,* by Edward Krupat, 1994, chapter 5, pp. 185-195. Originally from *Human Relations,* 1991, pp. 539-550. © 1991 by Plenum Publishing Company. Reprinted by permission.

sible decision-making defects, as suggested by Janis (1983). In addition, we take the next and more important step by going beyond the development of another example of groupthink to make recommendations for renewed inquiry into group decision-making processes.

THEORY AND EVIDENCE

The meeting(s) took place throughout the day and evening from 12:36 pm (EST), January 27, 1986 following the decision to not launch the Challenger due to high crosswinds at the launch site. Discussions continued through about 12:00 midnight (EST) via teleconferencing and Telefax systems connecting the Kennedy Space Center in Florida, Morton Thiokol (MTI) in Utah, Johnson Space Center in Houston, and the Marshall Space Flight Center. The Level I Flight Readiness Review is the highest level of review prior to launch. It comprises the highest level of management at the three space centers and at MTI, the private supplier of the solid rocket booster engines.

To briefly state the situation, the MTI engineers recommended not to launch if temperatures of the O-ring seals on the rocket were below 53 degrees Fahrenheit, which was the lowest temperature of any previous flight. Laurence B. Mulloy, manager of the Solid Rocket Booster Project at Marshall Space Flight Center, states:

> The bottom line of that, though, initially was that Thiokol engineering, Bob Lund, who is the Vice President and Director of Engineering, who is here today, recommended that 51-L [the Challenger] not be launched if the O-ring temperatures predicted at launch time would be lower than any previous launch, and that was 53 degrees. (*Report of the Presidential Commission on the Space Shuttle Accident,* 1986, p. 91–92).

This recommendation was made at 8:45 pm, January 27, 1986 (*Report of the Presidential Commission on the Space Shuttle Accident,* 1986). Through the ensuing discussions the decision to launch was made.

Antecedent Conditions

The three primary antecedent conditions for the development of groupthink are: a highly cohesive group, leader preference for a certain decision, and insulation of the group from qualified outside opinions. These conditions existed in this situation.

Cohesive Group. The people who made the decision to launch had worked together for many years. They were familiar with each other and had grown through the ranks of the space program. A high degree of *esprit de corps* existed between the members.

Leader Preference. Two top level managers actively promoted their pro-launch opinions in the face of opposition. The commission report states that several managers at space centers and MTI pushed for launch, regardless of the low temperatures.

Insulation from Experts. MTI engineers made their recommendations relatively early in the evening. The top level decision-making group knew of their objections but did not meet with them directly to review their data and concerns. As Roger Boisjoly, a Thiokol engineer, states in his remarks to the Presidential Commission:

> and the bottom line was that the engineering people would not recommend a launch below 53 degrees Fahrenheit.... From this point on, management formulated the points to base their decision on. There was never one comment in favor, as I have said, of launching by any engineer or other nonmanagement person.... I was not even asked to participate in giving any input to the final decision charts (*Report of the Presidential Commission on the Space Shuttle Accident,* 1986, p. 91–92).

This testimonial indicates that the top decision-making team was insulated from the engineers who possessed the expertise regarding the functioning of the equipment.

Janis identified eight symptoms of groupthink. They are presented here along with evidence from the *Report of the Presidential Commission on the Space Shuttle Accident* (1986).

Invulnerability. When groupthink occurs, most or all of the members of the decision-making group have an illusion of invulnerability that reassures them in the face of obvious dangers. This illusion leads the group to become overly optimistic and willing to take extraordinary risks. It may also cause them to ignore clear warnings of danger.

The solid rocket joint problem that destroyed Challenger was discussed often at flight readiness review meetings prior to flight. However, Commission member Richard Feynman concluded from the testimony that a mentality of overconfidence existed due to the extraordinary record of success of space flights. Every time we send one up it is successful. Involved members may seem to think that on the next one we can lower our standards or take more risks because it always works (*Time,* 1986).

The invulnerability illusion may have built up over time as a result of NASA's own spectacular history. NASA had not lost an astronaut since 1967 when a flash fire in the capsule of Apollo 1 killed three. Since that time NASA had a string of 55 successful missions. They had put a man on the moon, built and launched Skylab and the shuttle, and retrieved defective satellites from orbit. In the minds of most Americans and apparently their own, they could do no wrong.

Rationalization. Victims of groupthink collectively construct rationalizations that discount warnings and other forms of negative feedback. If these signals were taken seriously when presented, the group members would be forced to reconsider their assumptions each time they re-commit themselves to their past decisions.

In the Level I flight readiness meeting when the Challenger was given final launch approval, MTI engineers presented evidence that the joint would fail. Their argument was based on the fact that in the coldest previous launch (air temperature 30 degrees) the joint in question experienced serious erosion and that no data existed as to how the joint would perform at colder temperatures. Flight center officials put forth numerous tech-

nical rationalizations faulting MTI's analysis. One of these rationalizations was that the engineer's data were inconclusive. As Mr. Boisjoly emphasized to the Commission:

> I was asked, yes, at that point in time I was asked to quantify my concerns, and I said I couldn't. I couldn't quantify it. I had no data to quantify it, but I did say I knew that it was away from goodness in the current data base. Someone on the net commented that we had soot blow-by on SRM-22 [Flight 61-A, October, 1985] which was launched at 75 degrees. I don't remember who made the comment, but that is where the first comment came in about the disparity between my conclusion and the observed data because SRM-22 [Flight 61-A, October 1985] had blow-by at essentially a room temperature launch. I then said that SRM-15 [Flight 51-C, January, 1985] had much more blow-by indication and that it was indeed telling us that lower temperature was a factor. I was asked again for data to support my claim, and I said I have none other than what is being presented (*Report of the Presidential Commission on the Space Shuttle Accident,* 1986, p. 89).

Discussions became twisted (compared to previous meetings) and no one detected it. Under normal conditions, MTI would have to prove the shuttle boosters readiness for launch, instead they found themselves being forced to prove that the boosters were unsafe. Boisjoly's testimony supports this description of the discussion:

> This was a meeting where the determination was to launch, and it was up to us to prove beyond a shadow of a doubt that it was not safe to do so. This is in total reverse to what the position usually is in a preflight conversation or a flight readiness review. It is usually exactly the opposite of that. (*Report of the Presidential Commission on the Space Shuttle Accident,* 1986, p. 93).

Morality. Group members often believe, without question, in the inherent morality of their position. They tend to ignore the ethical or moral consequences of their decision.

In the Challenger case, this point was raised by a very high level MTI manager, Allan J. McDonald, who tried to stop the launch and said that he would not want to have to defend the decision to launch. He stated to the Commission:

> I made the statement that if we're wrong and something goes wrong on this flight, I wouldn't want to have to be the person to stand up in front of board in inquiry and say that I went ahead and told them to go ahead and fly this thing outside what the motor was qualified to. (*Report of the Presidential Commission on the Space Shuttle Accident,* 1986, p. 95).

Some members did not hear this statement because it occurred during a break. Three top officials who did hear it ignored it.

Stereotyped Views of Others. Victims of groupthink often have a stereotyped view of the opposition of anyone with a competing opinion. They feel that the opposition is too stupid or too weak to understand or deal effectively with the problem.

Two of the top three NASA officials responsible for the launch displayed this attitude. They felt that they completely understood the nature of the joint problem and never seriously considered the objections raised by the MTI engineers. In fact they denigrated and badgered the opposition and their information and opinions.

Pressure on Dissent. Group members often apply direct pressure to anyone who questions the validity of these arguments supporting a decision or position favored by the majority. These same two officials pressured MTI to change its position after MTI originally recommended that the launch not take place. These two officials pressured MTI personnel to prove that it was not safe to launch, rather than to prove the opposite. As mentioned earlier, this was a total reversal of normal preflight procedures. It was this pressure that top MTI management was responding to when they overruled their engineering staff and recommended launch. As the Commission report states:

> At approximately 11 p.m. Eastern Standard Time, the Thiokol/NASA teleconference resumed, the Thiokol management stating that they had reassessed the problem, that the temperature effects were a concern, but that the data was admittedly inconclusive (p. 96).

This seems to indicate the NASA's pressure on these Thiokol officials forced them to change their recommendation from delay to execution of the launch.

Self-Censorship. Group members tend to censor themselves when they have opinions or ideas that deviate from the apparent group consensus. Janis feels that this reflects each member's inclination to minimize to himself or herself the importance of his or her own doubts and counter-arguments.

The most obvious evidence of self-censorship occurred when a vice president of MTI, who had previously presented information against launch, bowed to pressure from NASA and accepted their rationalizations for launch. He then wrote these up and presented them to NASA as the reasons that MTI had changed its recommendation to launch.

Illusion of Unanimity. Group members falling victim to groupthink share an illusion of unanimity concerning judgments made by members speaking in favor of the majority view. This symptom is caused in part by the preceding one and is aided by the false assumption that any participant who remains silent is in agreement with the majority opinion. The group leader and other members support each other by playing up points of convergence in their thinking at the expense of fully exploring points of divergence that might reveal unsettling problems.

No participant from NASA ever openly agreed with or even took sides with MTI in the discussion. The silence from NASA was probably amplified by the fact that the meeting was a teleconference linking the participants at three different locations. Obviously, body language which might have been evidenced by dissenters was not visible to others who might also have held a dissenting opinion. Thus, silence meant agreement.

Mindguarding. Certain group members assume the role of guarding the minds of others in the group. They attempt to shield the group from adverse information that might destroy

the majority view of the facts regarding the appropriateness of the decision.

The top management at Marshall knew that the rocket casings had been ordered redesigned to correct a flaw 5 months previous to this launch. This information and other technical details concerning the history of the joint problem was withheld at the meeting.

Decision-Making Defects

The result of the antecedent conditions and the symptoms of groupthink is a defective decision-making process. Janis discusses several defects in decision making that can result.

Few Alternatives. The group considers only a few alternatives, often only two. No initial survey of all possible alternatives occurs. The Flight Readiness Review team had a launch/no-launch decision to make. These were the only two alternatives considered. Other possible alternatives might have been to delay the launch for further testing, or to delay until the temperatures reached an appropriate level.

No Re-Examination of Alternatives. The group fails to re-examine alternatives that may have been initially discarded based on early unfavorable information. Top NASA officials spent time and effort defending and strengthening their position, rather than examining the MTI position.

Rejecting Expert Opinions. Members make little or no attempt to seek outside experts opinions. NASA did not seek out other experts who might have some expertise in this area. They assumed that they had all the information.

Rejecting Negative Information. Members tend to focus on supportive information and ignore any data or information that might cast a negative light on their preferred alternative. MTI representatives repeatedly tried to point out errors in the rationale the NASA officials were using to justify the launch. Even after the decision was made, the argument continued until a NASA official told the MTI representative that it was no longer his concern.

No Contingency Plans. Members spend little time discussing the possible consequences of the decision and, therefore, fail to develop contingency plans. There is no documented evidence in the Rogers Commission Report of any discussion of the possible consequences of an incorrect decision.

The major categories and key elements of the groupthink hypothesis have been presented (albeit somewhat briefly) along with evidence from the discussions prior to the launching of the Challenger, as reported in the President's Commission to investigate the accident. The antecedent conditions were present in the decision-making group, even though the group was in several physical locations. The leaders had a preferred solution and engaged in behaviors designed to promote it rather than critically appraise alternatives. These behaviors were evidence of most of the symptoms leading to a defective decision-making process.

DISCUSSION

This situation provides another example of decision making in which the group fell victim to the groupthink syndrome, as have so many previous groups. It illustrates the situation characteristics, the symptoms of group think, and decision-making defects as described by Janis. This situation, however, also illustrates several other aspects of situations that are critical to the development of groupthink that need to be included in a revised formulation of the groupthink model. First, the element of time in influencing the development of groupthink has not received adequate attention. In the decision to launch the space shuttle Challenger, time was a crucial part of the decision-making process. The launch had been delayed once, and the window for another launch was fast closing. The leaders of the decision team were concerned about public and congressional perceptions of the entire space shuttle program and its continued funding and may have felt that further delays of the launch could seriously impact future funding. With the space

Figure 1   Revised groupthink framework

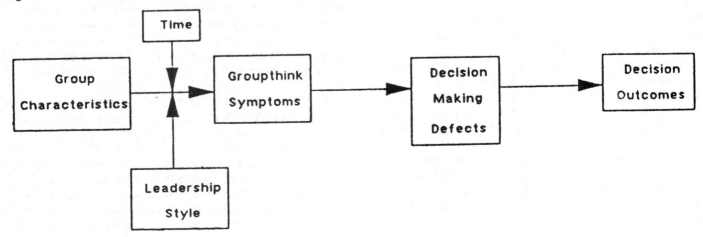

window fast closing, the decision team was faced with a launch now or seriously damage the program decision. One top level manager's response to Thiokol's initial recommendation to postpone the launch indicates the presence of time pressure:

> With this LCC (Launch Commit Criteria), i.e., do not launch with a temperature greater [sic] than 53 degrees, we may not be able to launch until next April. We need to consider this carefully before we jump to any conclusions. (*Report of the Presidential Commission on the Space Shuttle Accident*, 1986, p. 96).

Time pressure could have played a role in the group choosing to agree and to self-censor their comments. We propose that in certain situations when there is pressure to make a decision quickly, the elements may combine to foster the development of groupthink.

The second revision needs to be in the role of the leadership of the decision-making group. In the space shuttle Challenger incident, the leadership of the group varied from a shared type of leadership to a very clear leader in the situation. This may indicate that the leadership role needs to be clearly defined and a style that demands open disclosure of information, points of opposition, complaints, and dissension. We propose the leadership style is a crucial variable that moderates the relationship between the group characteristics and the development of the symptoms. Janis (1983) is a primary form of evidence to support the inclusion of leadership style in the enhanced model. His account of why the *same* group succumbed to groupthink in one decision (Bay of Pigs) and not in another (Cuban Missile Crisis) supports the depiction of leadership style as a moderator variable. In these decisions, the only condition that changed was the leadership style of the President. In other words, the element that seemed to distinguish why groupthink occurred in the Bay of Pigs decision and not in the Cuban Missile Crisis situation is the president's change in his behavior.

These two variables, time and leadership style, are proposed as moderators of the impact of the group characteristics on groupthink symptoms. This relationship is portrayed graphically in Fig. 1. In effect, we propose that the groupthink symptoms result from the group characteristics, as proposed by Janis, but only in the presence of the moderator variables of time and certain leadership styles.

Time, as an important element in the model, is relatively straightforward. When a decision must be made within a very short time frame, pressure on members to agree, to avoid time-consuming arguments and reports from outside experts, and to self-censor themselves may increase. These pressures inevitably cause group members to seek agreement. In Janis's original model, time was included indirectly as a function of the antecedent condition, group cohesion. Janis (1983) argued that time pressures can adversely affect decision quality in two ways. First, it affects the decision makers' mental efficiency and judgment, interfering with their ability to concentrate on complicated discussions, to absorb new information, and to use imagination to anticipate the future consequences of alternative courses of action. Second, time pressure is a source of stress that will have the effect of inducing a policy-making group to become more cohesive and more likely to engage in groupthink.

Leadership style is shown to be a moderator because of the importance it plays in either promoting or avoiding the development of the symptoms of the groupthink. The leader, even though she or he may not promote a preferred solution, may allow or even assist the group seeking agreement by not forcing the group to critically appraise all alternative courses of action. The focus of this leadership variable is on the degree to which the leader allows or promotes discussion and evaluation of alternatives. It is not a matter of simply not making known a preferred solution; the issue is one of stimulation of critical thinking among the group.

Impact on Prescriptions for Prevention

The revised model suggests that more specific prescriptions for prevention of groupthink can be made. First, group members need to be aware of the impact that a short decision time frame has on decision processes. When a decision must be made quickly, there will be more pressure to agree, i.e., discouragement of dissent, self-censorship, avoidance of expert opinion, and assumptions about unanimity. The type of leadership suggested here is not one that sits back and simply does not make known her or his preferred solution. This type of leader must be one that requires all members to speak up with concerns, questions, and new information. The leader must know what some of these concerns are and which members are likely to have serious doubts so that the people with concerns can be called upon to voice them. This type of group leadership does not simply assign the role of devil's advocate and step out of the way. This leader actually plays the role or makes sure that others do. A leader with the required style to avoid groupthink is not a laissez faire leader or non-involved participative leader. This leader is active in directing the activities of the group but does not make known a preferred solution. The group still must develop and evaluate alternative courses of action, but under the direct influence of a strong, demanding leader who forces critical appraisal of all alternatives.

Finally, a combination of the two variables suggests that the leader needs to help members to avoid the problems created by the time element. For example, the leader may be able to alter an externally imposed time frame for the decision by negotiating an extension or even paying late fees, if necessary. If an extension is not possible, the leader may need to help the group eliminate the effects of time on the decision processes. This can be done by forcing attention to issues rather than time, encouraging dissension and confrontation, and

scheduling special sessions to hear reports from outside experts that challenge prevailing views within the group.

Janis presents, in both editions of his book, several recommendations for preventing the occurrence of groupthink. These recommendations focus on the inclusion of outside experts in the decision-making process, all members taking the role of devil's advocate and critically appraising all alternative courses of action, and the leader not expressing a preferred solution. The revised groupthink framework suggests several new prescriptions that may be helpful in preventing further decision fiascoes similar to the decision to launch the space shuttle Challenger.

REFERENCES

Time. Fixing NASA. June 9, 1986.
Janis, I. L. (1983) *Victims of groupthink.* Boston: Houghton Mifflin.
Janis, I. L. (1983) *Groupthink* (2nd ed., revised). Boston: Houghton Mifflin.
Report of the Presidential Commission on the Space Shuttle Accident. Washington, D.C.: July 1986.

BLOWUP

Who can be blamed for disasters like the Challenger explosion, a decade ago?
No one, according to the new risk theorists, and we'd better get used to it.

MALCOLM GLADWELL

IN the technological age, there is a ritual to disaster. When planes crash or chemical plants explode, each piece of physical evidence—of twisted metal or fractured concrete—becomes a kind of fetish object, painstakingly located, mapped, tagged, and analyzed, with findings submitted to boards of inquiry that then probe and interview and soberly draw conclusions. It is a ritual of reassurance, based on the principle that what we learn from one accident can help us prevent another, and a measure of its effectiveness is that Americans did not shut down the nuclear industry after Three Mile Island and do not abandon the skies after each new plane crash. But the rituals of disaster have rarely been played out so dramatically as they were in the case of the Challenger space shuttle, which blew up over southern Florida on January 28th ten years ago.

Fifty-five minutes after the explosion, when the last of the debris had fallen into the ocean, recovery ships were on the scene. They remained there for the next three months, as part of what turned into the largest maritime salvage operation in history, combing a hundred and fifty thousand square nautical miles for floating debris, while the ocean floor surrounding the crash site was inspected by submarines. In mid-April of 1986, the salvage team found several chunks of charred metal that confirmed what had previously been only suspected: the explosion was caused by a faulty seal in one of the shuttle's rocket boosters, which had allowed a stream of flame to escape and ignite an external fuel tank.

Armed with this confirmation, a special Presidential investigative commission concluded the following June that the deficient seal reflected shoddy engineering and lax management at NASA and its prime contractor, Morton Thiokol. Properly chastised, NASA returned to the drawing board, to emerge thirty-two months later with a new shuttle—Discovery—redesigned according to the lessons learned from the disaster. During that first post-Challenger flight, as America watched breathlessly, the crew of the Discovery held a short commemorative service. "Dear friends," the mission commander, Captain Frederick H. Hauck, said, addressing the seven dead Challenger astronauts, "your loss has meant that we could confidently begin anew." The ritual was complete. NASA was back.

But what if the assumptions that underlie our disaster rituals aren't true? What if these public post mortems don't help us avoid future accidents? Over the past few years, a group of scholars has begun making the unsettling argument that the rituals that follow things like plane crashes or the Three Mile Island crisis are as much exercises in self-deception as they are genuine opportunities for reassurance. For these revisionists, high-technology accidents may not have clear causes at all. They may be inherent in the complexity of the technological systems we have created.

This month, on the tenth anniversary of the Challenger disaster, such revisionism has been extended to the space shuttle with the publication, by the Boston College sociologist Diane Vaughan, of "The Challenger Launch Decision" (Chicago), which is the first truly definitive analysis of the events leading up to January 28, 1986. The conventional view is that the Challenger accident was an anomaly, that it happened because people at NASA had not done their job. But the study's conclusion is the opposite: it says that the accident happened because people at NASA had done exactly what they were supposed to do. "No fundamental decision was made at NASA to do evil," Vaughan writes. "Rather, a series of seemingly harmless decisions were made that incrementally moved the space agency toward a catastrophic outcome."

No doubt Vaughan's analysis will be hotly disputed in the coming months, but even if she is only partly right the implications of this kind of argument are enormous. We have surrounded ourselves in the modern age with things like power plants and nuclear-weapons systems and airports that handle hundreds of planes an hour, on the understanding that the risks they represent are, at the very least, manageable. But if the potential for catastrophe is actually found in the normal functioning of

Originally from *The New Yorker*, January 22, 1996, pp. 32-36. © 1996 by Malcolm Gladwell. Reprinted by permission.

complex systems, this assumption is false. Risks are not easily manageable, accidents are not easily preventable, and the rituals of disaster have no meaning. The first time around, the story of the Challenger was tragic. In its retelling, a decade later, it is merely banal.

PERHAPS the best way to understand the argument over the Challenger explosion is to start with an accident that preceded it—the near-disaster at the Three Mile Island (T.M.I.) nuclear-power plant in March of 1979. The conclusion of the President's commission that investigated the T.M.I. accident was that it was the result of human error, particularly on the part of the plant's operators. But the truth of what happened there, the revisionists maintain, is a good deal more complicated than that, and their arguments are worth examining in detail.

The trouble at T.M.I. started with a blockage in what is called the plant's polisher—a kind of giant water filter. Polisher problems were not unusual at T.M.I., or particularly serious. But in this case the blockage caused moisture to leak into the plant's air system, inadvertently tripping two valves and shutting down the flow of cold water into the plant's steam generator.

As it happens, T.M.I. had a backup cooling system for precisely this situation. But on that particular day, for reasons that no one really knows, the valves for the backup system weren't open. They had been closed, and an indicator in the control room showing they were closed was blocked by a repair tag hanging from a switch above it. That left the reactor dependent on another backup system, a special sort of relief valve. But, as luck would have it, the relief valve wasn't working properly that day, either. It stuck open when it was supposed to close, and, to make matters even worse, a gauge in the control room which should have told the operators that the relief valve wasn't working was itself not working. By the time T.M.I.'s engineers realized what was happening, the reactor had come dangerously close to a meltdown.

Here, in other words, was a major accident caused by five discrete events. There is no way the engineers in the control room could have known about any of them. No glaring errors or spectacularly bad decisions were made that exacerbated those events. And all the malfunctions—the blocked polisher, the shut valves, the obscured indicator, the faulty relief valve, and the broken gauge—were in themselves so trivial that individually they would have created no more than a nuisance. What caused the accident was the way minor events unexpectedly interacted to create a major problem.

This kind of disaster is what the Yale University sociologist Charles Perrow has famously called a "normal accident." By "normal" Perrow does not mean that it is frequent; he means that it is the kind of accident one can expect in the normal functioning of a technologically complex operation. Modern systems, Perrow argues, are made up of thousands of parts, all of which interrelate in ways that are impossible to anticipate. Given that complexity, he says, it is almost inevitable that some combinations of minor failures will eventually amount to something catastrophic. In a classic 1984 treatise on accidents, Perrow takes examples of well-known plane crashes, oil spills, chemical-plant explosions, and nuclear-weapons mishaps and shows how many of them are best understood as "normal." If you saw last year's hit movie "Apollo 13," in fact, you have seen a perfect illustration of one of the most famous of all normal accidents: the Apollo flight went awry because of the interaction of failures of the spacecraft's oxygen and hydrogen tanks, and an indicator light that diverted the astronauts' attention from the real problem.

Had this been a "real" accident—if the mission had run into trouble because of one massive or venal error—the story would have made for a much inferior movie. In real accidents, people rant and rave and hunt down the culprit. They do, in short, what people in Hollywood thrillers always do. But what made Apollo 13 unusual was that the dominant emotion was not anger but bafflement—bafflement that so much could go wrong for so little apparent reason. There was no one to blame, no dark secret to unearth, no recourse but to re-create an entire system in place of one that had inexplicably failed. In the end, the normal accident was the more terrifying one.

WAS the Challenger explosion a "normal accident"? In a narrow sense, the answer is no. Unlike what happened at T.M.I., its explosion was caused by a single, catastrophic malfunction: the so-called O-rings that were supposed to prevent hot gases from leaking out of the rocket boosters didn't do their job. But Vaughan argues that the O-ring problem was really just a symptom. The cause of the accident was the culture of NASA, she says, and that culture led to a series of decisions about the Challenger which very much followed the contours of a normal accident.

The heart of the question is how NASA chose to evaluate the problems it had been having with the rocket boosters' O-rings. These are the thin rubber bands that run around the lips of each of the rocket's four segments, and each O-ring was meant to work like the rubber seal on the top of a bottle of preserves, making the fit between each part of the rocket snug and airtight. But from as far back as 1981, on one shuttle flight after another, the O-rings had shown increasing problems. In a number of instances, the rubber seal had been dangerously eroded—a condition suggesting that hot gases had almost escaped. What's more, O-rings were strongly suspected to be less effective in cold weather, when the rubber would harden and not give as tight a seal. On the morning of January 28, 1986, the shuttle launchpad was encased in ice, and the temperature at liftoff was just above freezing. Anticipating these low temperatures, engineers at Morton Thiokol, the manufacturer of the shuttle's rockets, had recommended that the launch be delayed. Morton Thiokol brass and NASA, however, overruled the recommendation, and that decision led both the President's commission and numerous critics since to accuse NASA of egregious—if not criminal—misjudgment.

Vaughan doesn't dispute that the decision was fatally flawed. But, after reviewing thousands of pages of transcripts and internal NASA documents, she can't find any evidence of people acting negligently, or nakedly sacrificing

safety in the name of politics or expediency. The mistakes that NASA made, she says, were made in the normal course of operation. For example, in retrospect it may seem obvious that cold weather impaired O-ring performance. But it wasn't obvious at the time. A previous shuttle flight that had suffered worse O-ring damage had been launched in seventy-five-degree heat. And on a series of previous occasions when NASA had proposed—but eventually scrubbed for other reasons—shuttle launches in weather as cold as forty-one degrees, Morton Thiokol had not said a word about the potential threat posed by the cold, so its pre-Challenger objection had seemed to NASA not reasonable but arbitrary. Vaughan confirms that there was a dispute between managers and engineers on the eve of the launch but points out that in the shuttle program disputes of this sort were commonplace. And, while the President's commission was astonished by NASA's repeated use of the phrases "acceptable risk" and "acceptable erosion" in internal discussion of the rocket-booster joints, Vaughan shows that flying with acceptable risks was a standard part of NASA culture. The lists of "acceptable risks" on the space shuttle, in fact, filled six volumes. "Although [O-ring] erosion itself had not been predicted, its occurrence conformed to engineering expectations about large-scale technical systems," she writes. "At NASA, problems were the norm. The word 'anomaly' was part of everyday talk. . . . The whole shuttle system operated on the assumption that deviation could be controlled but not eliminated."

What NASA had created was a closed culture that, in her words, "normalized deviance" so that to the outside world decisions that were obviously questionable were seen by NASA's management as prudent and reasonable. It is her depiction of this internal world that makes her book so disquieting: when she lays out the sequence of decisions which led to the launch—each decision as trivial as the string of failures that led to T.M.I.—it is difficult to find any precise point where things went wrong or where things might be improved next time. "It can truly be said that the Challenger launch decision was a rule-based decision," she concludes. "But the cul-

tural understandings, rules, procedures, and norms that always had worked in the past did not work this time. It was not amorally calculating managers violating rules that were responsible for the tragedy. It was conformity."

THERE is another way to look at this problem, and that is from the standpoint of how human beings handle risk. One of the assumptions behind the modern disaster ritual is that when a risk can be identified and eliminated a system can be made safer. The new booster joints on the shuttle, for example, are so much better than the old ones that the over-all chances of a Challenger-style accident's ever happening again must be lower—right? This is such a straightforward idea that questioning it seems almost impossible. But that is just what another group of scholars has done, under what is called the theory of "risk homeostasis."

It should be said that within the academic community there are huge debates over how widely the theory of risk homeostasis can and should be applied. But the basic idea, which has been laid out brilliantly by the Canadian psychologist Gerald Wilde in his book "Target Risk," is quite simple: under certain circumstances, changes that appear to make a system or an organization safer in fact don't. Why? Because human beings have a seemingly fundamental tendency to compensate for lower risks in one area by taking greater risks in another.

Consider, for example, the results of a famous experiment conducted several years ago in Germany. Part of a fleet of taxicabs in Munich was equipped with antilock brake systems (A.B.S.), the recent technological innovation that vastly improves braking, particularly on slippery surfaces. The rest of the fleet was left alone, and the two groups—which were otherwise perfectly matched—were placed under careful and secret observation for three years.

You would expect the better brakes to make for safer driving. But that is exactly the opposite of what happened. Giving some drivers A.B.S. made no difference at all in their accident rate; in fact, it turned them into markedly inferior drivers. They drove faster. They

made sharper turns. They showed poorer lane discipline. They braked harder. They were more likely to tailgate. They didn't merge as well, and they were involved in more near-misses. In other words, the A.B.S. systems were not used to reduce accidents; instead, the drivers used the additional element of safety to enable them to drive faster and more recklessly without increasing their risk of getting into an accident. As economists would say, they "consumed" the risk reduction, they didn't save it.

Risk homeostasis doesn't happen all the time. Often—as in the case of seat belts, say—compensatory behavior only partly offsets the risk-reduction of a safety measure. But it happens often enough that it must be given serious consideration. Why are more pedestrians killed crossing the street at marked crosswalks than at unmarked crosswalks? Because they compensate for the "safe" environment of a marked crossing by being less viligant about oncoming traffic. Why did the introduction of childproof lids on medicine bottles lead, according to one study, to a substantial increase in fatal child poisonings? Because adults became less careful in keeping pill bottles out of the reach of children.

Risk homeostasis also works in the opposite direction. In the late nineteen-sixties, Sweden changed over from driving on the left-hand side of the road to driving on the right, a switch that one would think would create an epidemic of accidents. But, in fact, the opposite was true. People compensated for their unfamiliarity with the new traffic patterns by driving more carefully. During the next twelve months, traffic fatalities dropped seventeen per cent—before returning slowly to their previous levels. As Wilde only half-facetiously argues, countries truly interested in making their streets and highways safer should think about switching over from one side of the road to the other on a regular basis.

It doesn't take much imagination to see how risk homeostasis applies to NASA and the space shuttle. In one frequently quoted phrase, Richard Feynman, the Nobel Prize-winning physicist who served on the Challenger commission, said that at NASA decision-making was "a kind of Russian roulette." When the O-rings began to have problems and nothing happened, the agency be-

gan to believe that "the risk is no longer so high for the next flights," Feynman said, and that "we can lower our standards a little bit because we got away with it last time." But fixing the O-rings doesn't mean that this kind of risk-taking stops. There are six whole volumes of shuttle components that are deemed by NASA to be as risky as O-rings. It is entirely possible that better O-rings just give NASA the confidence to play Russian roulette with something else.

This is a depressing conclusion, but it shouldn't come as a surprise. The truth is that our stated commitment to safety, our faithful enactment of the rituals of disaster, has always masked a certain hypocrisy. We don't really want the safest of all possible worlds. The national fifty-five-mile-per-hour speed limit probably saved more lives than any other single government intervention of the past twenty-five years. But the fact that Congress lifted it last month with a minimum of argument proves that we would rather consume the recent safety advances of things like seat belts and air bags than save them. The same is true of the dramatic improvements that have been made in recent years in the design of aircraft and flight-navigation systems. Presumably, these innovations could be used to bring down the airline-accident rate as low as possible. But that is not what consumers want. They want air travel to be cheaper, more reliable, or more convenient, and so those safety advances have been at least partly consumed by flying and landing planes in worse weather and heavier traffic conditions.

What accidents like the Challenger should teach us is that we have constructed a world in which the potential for high-tech catastrophe is embedded in the fabric of day-to-day life. At some point in the future—for the most mundane of reasons, and with the very best of intentions—a NASA spacecraft will again go down in flames. We should at least admit this to ourselves now. And if we cannot—if the possibility is too much to bear—then our only option is to start thinking about getting rid of things like space shuttles altogether.

'90s Style Brainstorming

Alice LaPlante

Throw those flip charts, overhead projectors and typed agendas out the conference room window. Networked PCs are bringing high tech to the meeting room. But is corporate America ready for the onslaught?

IF PEOPLE ARE to achieve some degree of happiness in their work, the 19th-century British critic John Ruskin wrote, "they must be fit for it. They must not do too much of it. And they must have a sense of success in it."

All of which points to the dreaded meeting as the toothache of corporate life. According to a study by the University of Southern California, in Los Angeles:

○ The average meeting takes place in the company conference room at 11 a.m. and lasts an hour and 30 minutes.
○ It is attended by nine people—two managers, four co-workers, two subordinates and one outsider—who have received two-hour prior notification.
○ It has no written agenda, and its purported purpose is completed only 50 percent of the time.
○ A quarter of meeting participants complain they waste between 11 and 25 percent of the time discussing irrelevant issues.
○ A full third of them feel pressured to publicly espouse opinions with which they privately disagree.
○ Another third feel they have minimal or no influence on the discussion.
○ Although 36 percent of meetings result in a "complete" resolution of the topic at hand, participants considered only one percent of those conclusions to be particularly "creative."
○ A whopping 63 percent of meeting attendees feel that underlying issues outside the scope of the official agenda are the real subjects under discussion.
○ Senior executives spend 53 percent of their time in meetings, at an average rate of $320 per person per hour.

Happily, help is on the way.

"Electronic Brainstorming"— Here's How It Works

A new type of software—labeled, awkwardly enough, GDSS, for group decision support system—promises to change all of this. Here's the scenario: A U-shaped conference table contains between 12 and 20 "meeting stations" made up of PCs or Macintosh computers and their associated point-and-click devices (such as mice) or drawing tools (such as light pens). A large—usually 60-inch—color monitor is located at one end of the table where it can be easily viewed by everyone in the room. A facilitator calls the meeting to order, and instead of talking (whispering, shouting), participants type their ideas, comments or reactions on their keyboards. Their input appears simultaneously on every screen in the room, as well as on the monitor at the head of the table. Input is anonymous. Every-one gets a chance to contribute. No one can dominate the airspace—because there is none. With everyone typing simultaneously, it's virtually impossible for someone to grab the floor and hold onto it to the dismay of the other participants.

Public relations giant Hill & Knowl-ton raves about the results. A key H&K client had suddenly initiated Chapter 11 bankruptcy proceedings; the client needed to spin the news in such a way that the stock price would not be disastrously affected or thousands of suppliers and distributors frightened off until

E*nthusiasts of GDSS like to express their amazement at its tremendous power to disarm meeting blowhards and bullies.*

the reorganization was complete. Timing was critical. "This was an urgent situation. We were under a very tight deadline to come up with a plan," says Mayer G. Becker, an H&K vice-president. Becker had seen a demo of VisionQuest, a GDSS package from Innovative Solutions Inc., at a computer trade show. Becker liked what he saw. Last November, he took nine of his account team colleagues to the Chicago offices of Lante Corp., a systems design firm that had built a dedi-

Reprinted with permission from *Forbes ASAP*, October 25, 1993, pp. 45-46, 53-54, 60-61. © 1993 by Forbes, Inc.

cated electronic brainstorming room for its own use.

The H&K account team members sat down around the conference table at networked PCs and began typing their thoughts into the system. "Within 10 minutes, we had 47 excellent ideas," says Becker. "By the end of the hour, we had discussed them, voted on them, ranked them in order of priority and walked out with printed documentation in hand."

As Hill & Knowlton discovered, GDSS offers myriad benefits. Personal and organizational influence go out the window. One person can't dominate this type of meeting. You can't raise your voice. You can't stare down an underling who says something you don't like. It's no wonder that more ideas—and more surprising conclusions—can be generated in a much shorter time. Studies show that computer-assisted meetings substantially cut down on meeting time, according to Virginia Johnson, director of human relations at 3M Co. and a member of the 3M Management Institute in Austin. She adds that "many major companies are in the experimental phase of using these technologies."

Just ask Carl DiPietro, a consultant specializing in computer-assisted meetings who first introduced the idea to the Marriott Corp. in 1992 while he was vice-president of human resources there. He claims to have held more than 5,000 electronically enhanced meetings with more than 100 different clients since starting his own meeting consulting firm last year in Bethesda, Md. DiPietro carries with him to customer sites 12 to 20 notebook computers equipped with Ethernet networking packs, a more powerful "lunch box" portable to act as a Novell LAN server, and VisionQuest software. Within minutes, he is able to transform a conventional conference room into a wired forum, ready to untangle deadlocked management teams.

How to Avoid the "Abilene Paradox" and the "Football Phenomenon"

One of the strengths of meetingware is that it helps organizations avoid what DiPietro calls the "Abilene paradox." "We've all heard this type of

saga," he says. A Texas family gathers one Sunday morning to decide what to do for the day. No one has any ideas— or if they do, they're afraid to speak up. "Finally, the patriarch of the family suggests going to Abilene—which is 100 miles away—on the hottest day of a Texas summer. Everyone agrees, with relief, and they take a long, hot, joyless trip there and back." At the end of the day it turns out that no one wanted to go to Abilene—not even the person who suggested it. "But everyone just fell in line with the suggestion. This happens all the time. We make decisions by observing other people's behaviors rather than based on our own ideas or beliefs."

Another conference room scenario is one DiPietro characterizes as the "football phenomenon." All hell breaks loose during the last five minutes of a meeting, and grand conclusions are reached that bear little resemblance to the discussions of the preceding three hours. Worse still is the case of the person who volunteers to write up the minutes of the meeting, walks off with the flip chart and two months later sends around a memo that reflects nothing of what the participants thought occurred.

Indeed, anyone who has used a GDSS generally gets around to expressing amazement at its tremendous power to disarm the "meeting bully."

"With the anonymity, the ideas become more important than who said them or how they were said," says Susanna Opper, president of Susanna

Products and Vendors

CM/1 (V.1.0) provides a graphical "map" to meetings that combines a Windows-based hypertext interface with an object-oriented database to allow groups to collaborate and organize ideas, arguments and solutions during brainstorming sessions. It runs on Novell NetWare LANs and is priced starting at $1,500.

Corporate Memory Systems (512) 795-9999
8920 Business Park Drive, Suite 145, Austin, TX 78759

GroupSytems V is electronic meeting software that captures anonymous text-based ideas from a group simultaneously and displays the results in a shared-screen environment. Pricing starts at $24,900 for a 20-user license, and the software is available for Novell, Banyan, Token Ring, Ethernet and TCP/IP networks.

Ventana (602) 325-8228
1430 E. Fort Lowell Road, Suite 301, Tucson, AZ 85719

OptionFinder is an interactive group decision support system that allows each meeting participant to vote using a numeric keypad attached to a PC. The program collects, calculates and graphically displays results instantaneously. It supports as many as 250 simultaneous users and is available in both wired and wireless versions. Pricing starts at $8,995.

Option Technologies (612) 450-1700
1275 Knollwood Lane, Mendota Heights, MN 55118

VisionQuest is electronic meeting support software that allows anonymous brainstorming, voting, allocation and documentation of meetings. Licenses are priced from $400 to $30,000 and up, and are available for DOS, Windows and Notes environments, and run over Novell, 3Com, Banyan, PC-LAN, LAN Manager, LANtastic and LAN Server networks.

Collaborative Technologies (512) 794-8858
8920 Business Park Drive, Suite 100, Austin, TX 78759

Opper and Associates, a New York-based consulting firm that focuses on groupware, such as Lotus Notes, and meetingware, such as VisionQuest. "Someone lower down in an organization, who might not be as respected because of his job or minority status, or because she is a woman, is someone who isn't normally listened to. This technology gives them a voice."

But Is It for You?

All of this sounds good, even terrific—so what's the catch?

For one thing, it's easy for this type of technology to disrupt or even dominate a meeting. Johnson, of 3M's Meeting Management Institute, warns that "for the most part, this technology is well ahead of the acceptance level of the average meeting-goer."

Walter Parrish, a facilitator for Tulsa, Okla.-based Texaco, uses Group-Systems V, a GDSS from Ventana Corp., Tucson, Ariz., in approximately 25 percent of the meetings he coordinates, but he doesn't recommend it for shorter conferences involving high-level executives. "When people aren't very computer literate—which includes some of upper management—there's a bias against these tools. You have to fight for it," he says.

For this reason, some consultants and meeting facilitators prefer to bypass full-blown GDSS products in favor of scaled-down technologies. Westinghouse Electric Corp., for example, prefers a simple electronic voting keypad for its ease of use (see Westinghouse case study).

Hudi Cantrell, an information technology manager at Hewlett Packard Co., has noticed that extroverts tend to "drop out" of electronic meetings because they are so dismayed with their inability to use their strong verbal skills. "You tend to get much more input from shyer people, but you also lose others." Cantrell says balanced use of these tools is the answer. In most HP meetings where GroupSystems V is used the electronic portion represents between only 25 and 50 percent of the meeting, she says.

Marke Tebbe, president of Lante Corp., which assisted Hill & Knowlton with its initial VisionQuest session, agrees: "The best meetings are a combination of the two. You use these tools to brainstorm and prioritize ideas, then you discuss them in the usual way."

Will an old-style manager be comfortable with this? "Probably not," says Opper. "We're talking about leveling the hierarchy, and that's a scary thing." But opening up a meeting in this way doesn't imply that a senior manager is going to opt for democratic rule. "People simply want their day in court. They can understand if the decision-making authority still resides elsewhere," says DiPietro.

In the brainstorming session Lante conducted for Hill & Knowlton, participants used VisionQuest's voting tools to get a sense of how the group ranked the ideas that had been generated, but in the end the results—and final decisionmaking authority—were left to the three managers who headed the account. Old-fashioned leadership still counts, in other words.

Calculations, Weightings and Grunt Work

One of GDSS's nicest features is its voting and calculation mechanism. DiPietro can ask participants to prioritize a list of projects using a scale of, say, one to 10. "Or I'll say, 'You have $1 million in your budget; allocate the money among these projects.' The computer does all the calculations, weightings and grunt work. It displays the results on the screen. You have a clear picture of what everyone thinks."

Be aware, however, that people will undoubtedly find ways to manipulate the technology to suit their own purposes. Lante's Tebbe, who uses VisionQuest or GroupSystems V every other week with his 10-member management team, realized that one meeting participant—a fast typist—was pretending to be more than one person when he vehemently agreed or disagreed with an idea being discussed. "He'd type 'Oh, I agree,' and then 'Ditto, ditto' or 'What a great idea' all in quick succession, using different variations of upper-case and lower-case letters and punctuation," recalls Tebbe. "He tried to make it seem like a lot of people

were concurring, but it was just him." How did Tebbe discover this ploy? "The person sitting next to him got suspicious and began watching his screen," he says.

Meeting experts also say to be wary of the productivity numbers bandied about by meetingware vendors. According to Lisa Neal, a senior research engineer with Electronic Data Systems' Center for Advanced Research, Cambridge, Mass., a lot of the hype surrounding computer-assisted meetings is meaningless. "People say, 'We generated so many more ideas in so much time, so we had 50 percent time savings.' That's meaningless because it says nothing about the quality of those ideas."

Indeed, it's often difficult to define a successful meeting, says Dave Hoffman, an information systems programmer who works in organizational development for Texaco, in Houston, on meeting technologies. Texaco uses GroupSystems V and in the last two years has spent approximately $300,000 to build a room for electronically facilitated meetings. It's equipped with a U-shaped table that contains embedded networked PCs, letting participants see each other and their personal screens easily. A large monitor mounted at the front of the room also displays group output.

"We'd had meetings where people walked out extremely satisfied, yet they hadn't accomplished anything," says Hoffman. "At other times, people would leave a meeting room very frustrated and unhappy, yet in my opinion they had accomplished a lot." How do you initially determine a solution's quality? Only time will tell.

Still, EDS's Neal has discovered that people place more value on the result of electronic brainstorming. She asks participants to fill out questionnaires immediately after a meeting, and then again two to three weeks later. When asked why they are more satisfied, respondents often say they feel they've moved forward—even if they haven't accomplished what they set out to. "But something happened, even if it's just identification of the next step," says Neal.

Last words of advice? When experimenting with this technology, say Opper and others, "forget about the demos that the vendors want to show

you. Take a real business problem to one of these electronic meeting rooms, bring a real work team eager to discuss something that matters, and prepare to be amazed."

Case Study: How GE Rates the Boss—Safely

A year ago, Bob Flynn's boss read an article about electronic brainstorming. Intrigued, he asked Flynn, information services manager at General Electric Co.'s Capacitor and Power Protection unit in Fort Edward, N.Y., to investigate. Flynn brought in VisionQuest for a three-month trial run.

One project in particular had loaded consequences. At the direction of Joe McSweeney, the plant general manager, Flynn divided the plant's 45 work group leaders into six groups and led them through a no-holds-barred evaluation of the plant's management. The outline revealed that the employees viewed McSweeney as creative, entrepreneurial and "a bureaucracy basher," eager to remove organizational barriers to innovative and good ideas, says Flynn.

On the downside, it emerged that "people felt he was so impatient to get things done that he interceded in a decision that should have been theirs to make." A week after the electronic ratings were completed McSweeney stood before his management team and responded, point by point, to the comments. "He was absolutely sincere about really wanting this feedback," says Flynn.

Extroverts tend to "drop out" of electronic meetings because they can't use their strong verbal skills—and often can't type fast enough.

McSweeney and other GE managers were so impressed by this new type of software that they made VisionQuest a standard tool for many important meetings at the site. "This takes the mechanics out of arriving at a con-

sensus," says Flynn. "We don't need flip charts, we don't need tape recorders, we don't need someone writing down their version of what's happening."

However, VisionQuest is not a panacea for every meeting, says Flynn. "We have one guy—a very strong personality—who tends to dominate traditional meetings. Because he can't do that using VisionQuest, he isn't terribly inclined to participate or use this tool." Instead of typing his comments on the keyboard, Flynn says, the backslider calls things out, starts a discussion, changes the topic and leads everyone down a different path. How should facilitators respond when confronted with this type of behavior? "Let it go; then eventually steer people back to the matter at hand," he says—especially when, as is the case with this example, the person happens to be a valuable and active contributor. With people like this, "you have to be flexible until they become more comfortable with the tool," says Flynn.

Case Study: How Hewitt Associates Balances Decisions between Opposing Interests

Today, discussions of benefit packages often require the input of the CEO, CFO and other senior executives. Surprised at the upper-level involvement? Don't be. "After capital expenditures and direct pay, benefits are the largest single expense many employers have," says Jack Bruner, flexibility compensation practice leader for Hewitt Associates, an international firm of consultants and actuaries specializing in employee benefit and compensation programs.

Getting top managers in a room necessitates that complex negotiations be conducted quickly. "We need to be as efficient as possible," says Bruner, who uses VisionQuest to facilitate meetings with clients. "This tool allows them to dump all of their best ideas with amazing quickness, take a preliminary vote, then discuss the top 10 of those 50 ideas before coming to a consensus."

Founded in 1940, the $357 million Lincolnshire, Ill.-based Hewitt employs more than 3,500 associates in 60 offices worldwide, and has provided benefits consulting services to 75 percent of

America's largest companies. About half of the clients work with electronic brainstorming tools like VisionQuest.

The first time Bruner used VisionQuest was with client Kraft General Foods to help brainstorm ideas for a new employee benefits program that would later be presented to Kraft's senior managers. Bruner sat the 12 middle managers down in front of networked PCs in the Hewitt VisionQuest conference room, and within an hour they had come up with "some very different answers than if we had simply talked about possible benefits programs," he recalls.

The tool helped "free up the thinking," Bruner says. Instead of talking about medical insurance carriers or retirement plans, "we heard things like, 'I'd like to be able to send my kids to college, buy a house, get my finances under control, improve my health.'" Once these ideas were on the table, Bruner's staff was able to guide the meeting participants to the next step—dividing company resources among benefits programs structured around those needs.

You could do this in the traditional way, says Bruner, but he believes that the anonymity allows for a more open-ended and creative discussion. He recalls doing this same sort of brainstorming exercise manually with another client: When it came time to vote on the ideas raised, no one was willing to commit, says Bruner. "*No one*," he reiterates. "I asked them what the problem was." It turned out that the manager of the group—a vice-president—had left the room for a moment, and no one wanted to vote before understanding how the manager felt about the issues. "It's really true: The anonymous format makes people feel freer to say what they think," says Bruner.

Hewitt has been so impressed with the results that it's put VisionQuest on the enterprise network that connects its IBM and Amdahl mainframes with LANs in a wide area network of 30-odd regional offices throughout the United States. The VisionQuest file server resides in Lincolnshire, and any regional office can log onto the server and use the software remotely.

Hewitt has used the technology in two virtual meetings to date—that is, meetings in which participants are sep-

arated by time, distance or both. One such virtual meeting was held by 16 members of the Hewitt consulting team to define contribution record-keeping. According to Larry Hebda, IS consultant for Hewitt, the participants logged onto VisionQuest from their individual PCs at 9 on a designated morning, and discussed and voted on the agenda items. He points out that although that meeting was considered highly successful, the group found it necessary to hold a traditional meeting later in the day to go over the results of the electronic discussion.

Hewitt had to learn the most effective way to use this technology. According to Hebda, it's easy to get overloaded with too many ideas. He remembers one early VisionQuest session—before he understood the importance of carefully directing brainstorming sessions—in which participants generated 100 ideas in less than 10 minutes. It was overkill, admits Hebda, "too much to digest."

Despite the usual learning glitches, the benefits of such systems far outnumber the drawbacks, says Bruner. He estimates that with VisionQuest, his staff can finish a consulting project in 60 percent of the time it would take them with traditional methods. "When you're on a per-hour basis, that means you can deliver more to your clients for less. And you can't argue that we're getting better results."

Case Study: How Westinghouse Uses Voting as a Discussion Stimulant

Jeff Jury remembers getting an urgent call from the head of a $150 million manufacturing division of Westinghouse Electric Corp. The division had reached a critical juncture in its 12-year history, but was deadlocked in its attempts to formulate a new strategic business plan.

Jury, a senior consultant at the Productivity and Quality Center, an internal management consulting group within Westinghouse, called a meeting of the division's top managers. He took his 386-based laptop out of his briefcase, along with a dozen small electronic voting keypads, and within

minutes had distributed one of the devices to every executive in the room. The keypads were linked via thin wire cables to his laptop, which was running a voting application called Option-Finder.

Jury began probing the group's attitudes by asking questions about the division's fundamental strategy. Participants answered his questions by pressing the keypads in front of them. Questions included: "Are you trying to be a low-priced competitor? Differentiate on value? Serve the entire market or just a niche?" Then he showed the executives the results, displayed in full-

color graphs on an overhead projector. The group was stunned to find that "answers were scattered across the board, with absolutely no agreement or consensus," says Jury. "Yet if I'd asked them this question vocally, we probably wouldn't have gotten any challenge."

Calculation is instantaneous. And results are displayed graphically—not just averages but distribution of votes as well. You immediately see not only which issues "won" but by how much—and whether the group is splintered. You can even calculate subgroups of agreement and disagreement according to preset demographics of attendees. And because the process is truly anonymous, people feel freer to vote their own minds.

Westinghouse spent just $15,000 to equip as many as 100 people with OptionFinder keypads and software. Usually, however, the device is used in much smaller meetings of between 15 and 25 people. "I'll put a list on a flip chart of 10 or 15 key issues, and we'll prioritize that list in just minutes," says Jury.

Alice LaPlante wrote about teleconferencing in the Sept. 13 Forbes ASAP.

Electronic Brainstorming Guide

Do use a meeting facilitator to manage the process.

Do decide upon a clear "deliverable," or goal, for the meeting.

Do make it clear who has ultimate decisionmaking power when all of the input has been collected.

Do vote early and often, and use the results to open further discussion.

Do be prepared to change gears if something isn't working.

Do be aware when things aren't working.

Do turn off the machines and talk for at least 50 percent of the meeting time.

Don't use GDSS for simple information-sharing.

Don't assume the results of voting activities are statistically valid. Instead, use them to probe conflicting attitudes and opinions.

Don't call a meeting unless you have a firm goal in mind.

Don't allow brainstorming sessions to spin out of control. Take charge of both the time allotted and the scope of the discussion.

Don't use GDSS with too few (less than four) or too many (more than 20) participants.

Don't impose GDSS on nontechnical employees without allowing adequate "familiarity" time and exercises.

THE NEW
POST-HEROIC
LEADERSHIP

"Ninety-five percent of American managers today say the right thing. Five percent actually do it." That's got to change.

John Huey

"Of the best leader, when he is gone, they will say: We did it ourselves."
—Chinese proverb

CORPORATE leadership used to be so simple. You had it, or you didn't. It was in the cut of your jib. And if you had it, you certainly didn't share it. The surest way to tell if you had it was to look behind you to see if anyone was following. If no one was, you fell back to flogging the chain of command. Because the buck stopped with you. Your ass was on the line. Your job was to kick ass and take names. These were the immutable truths of leadership that you learned as you progressed from the Boy Scouts to officer candidate school to the Harvard B-school, and they worked. God was in his heaven, and the ruling class . . . ruled.

Then, of course, the world turned upside down. Global competition wrecked stable markets and whole industries. Information technology created ad hoc networks of power within corporations. Lightning-fast, innovative entrepreneurs blew past snoozing corporate giants. Middle managers disappeared, along with corporate loyalty. And one day you noticed that many of your employees, co-workers, and customers weren't exactly like you anymore, not English-speaking white males—not even close.

REPORTER ASSOCIATE *Ricardo Sookdeo*

Some time after restructuring, but before reengineering and reinvention, you accepted the new dizzying truth: that the only constant in today's world is exponentially increasing change.

The few corporate chiefs who saw all this coming declared themselves "transformational" and embraced such concepts as "empowerment," "workout," "quality," and "excellence." What they didn't do—deep down inside—was actually give up much control or abandon their fundamental beliefs about leadership. As James O'Toole, a professor and leadership expert, puts it, "Ninety-five percent of American managers today say the right thing. Five percent actually do it."

The pressure is building to walk the talk. Call it whatever you like: post-heroic leadership, servant leadership, distributed leadership, or, to suggest a tag, virtual leadership. But don't dismiss it as just another touchy-feely flavor of the month. It's real, it's radical, and it's challenging the very definition of corporate leadership for the 21st century.

"People realize now that they really must do it to survive," says management guru Tom Peters. Just ask the fired ex-heads of such companies as GM, IBM, Kodak, Digital Equipment, Westinghouse, and American Express, where the time-honored method of ordering up transformation—maybe even stamping your foot for emphasis—proved laughably ineffective. When companies derive their competitive advantage from creating intellectual capital, from attracting and developing knowledge workers, explains Warren Bennis, a widely read author on leadership, "whips and chains are no longer an alternative. Leaders must learn to change the nature of power and how it's employed."

IF THEY DON'T, technology will. Business already is moving to organize itself into virtual corporations: fungible modules built around information networks, flexible work forces, outsourcing, and webs of strategic partnerships. Virtual leadership is about keeping everyone focused as old structures, including old hierarchies, crumble.

"The effect of information technology is just beginning to be felt," says Edward Lawler, director of the University of Southern California's Center for Effective Organizations. "It enables individuals to think of themselves as self-contained small businesses. So the challenge to corporate leadership becomes, 'Make me a case for why I should get excited about working for this company.'"

From *Fortune*, February 21, 1994, pp. 42-44, 48, 50. © 1994 by Time Inc. Magazine Company. All rights reserved. Reprinted by permission.

As the power of position continues to erode, corporate leaders are going to resemble not so much captains of ships as candidates running for office. They will face two fundamental tasks: first, to develop and articulate exactly what the company is trying to accomplish, and second, to create an environment in which employees can figure out what needs to be done and then do it well.

Executives who rose in traditional systems often have trouble with both. The quantitative skills that got them to the heights don't help them communicate. And if their high intelligence, energy, ambition, and self-confidence are perceived as arrogance, it cuts them off from information, which makes the challenge of empowering the work force even more vexing.

Post-heroic leaders don't expect to solve all the problems themselves. They realize no one person can deal with the emerging and colliding tyrannies of speed, quality, customer satisfaction, innovation, diversity, and technology. Virtual leaders just say no to their egos. They are confident enough in their vision to delegate true responsibility, both for the tedium of process and for the sweep of strategic planning. And they are careful to "model," or live by, the values they espouse. In a distinction that has been around for a while but is now taking on new meaning, they are leaders, not managers. What's the difference? Management, says the Harvard business school's John Kotter, comprises activities that keep an organization running, and it tends to work well through hierarchy. Leadership involves getting things started and facilitating change. In the past, most corporations groomed and promoted managers into so-called positions of leadership, while they discouraged or ran off leaders. Back in the era of mass production, when companies could succeed merely by doing more of what they were already doing, hierarchy substituted adequately for leadership. A company could be just about leaderless but still very well run—by middle managers, who operated by the numbers and by the book. When technology rendered them obsolete and competitive pressure made them an unaffordable luxury, corporations "flattened" their structures, pushing traditional management tasks down to the workers. Then upper management—often to its surprise—suddenly faced real leadership issues.

Virtual leadership requires courage, confidence, and, well, a leader, or a bunch of them. But it works to great effect in a variety of businesses. It's working right now at Ortho Biotech, a biopharmaceutical company with a diverse work force. It's working for W.L. Gore & Associates, the maker of Gore-Tex, which proudly calls itself unmanaged. And it's working in the traditionally rough-and-tumble 19th-century garment industry at Levi Strauss & Co.

If you don't believe it, come to the little Appalachian town of Murphy, North Carolina. Turn right just past the new Wal-Mart, and head up the hill over the Valley River to the old red brick Levi sewing plant. Here you'll meet Tommye Jo Daves, a 58-year-old mountain-bred grandmother—and the living incarnation of virtual management. She's responsible for the plant, which employs 385 workers and turns out some three million pairs of Levi's jeans a year.

Not that she's forgotten the old way. In 1959, Daves hired on at Levi's Blue Ridge, Georgia, plant for 80 cents an hour because she needed a new washing machine. It was so cold inside the place that she wore gloves, and it was so leaky that buckets sat everywhere to catch rainwater. Her job was to top-stitch back pockets. Period. She became a supervisor and eventually a plant manager. One part of traditional management she still remembers is the night somebody unloaded both barrels of a shotgun into her car during a nasty labor dispute.

But Daves prefers to talk about the personal invitation she received in the mail a few years ago from Levi CEO Robert Haas, great-great-grandnephew of Levi Strauss himself. Haas politely requested her presence in Santa Cruz, California, to attend something called Leadership Week. She accepted, having no idea what to expect.

"It was the most eye-opening experience of my life," she says. "I learned for the first time how I was perceived by others." What she recalls best was a videotaped exercise in which everyone was organized into teams, blindfolded, and asked to work as a group to shape some rope into a square. They failed, but two lessons stuck with Daves: "You can't lead a team by just barking orders, and you have to have a vision in your head of what you're trying to do." Many CEOs haven't learned either lesson yet.

She and her line supervisors have since been converting their plant, first to a gain-sharing system in which workers' pay is linked directly to the plant's performance. Then, later, from the old "check your brain at the door and sew pockets" system to team management, in which teams of workers are cross-trained for 36 tasks instead of one or two and thrust into running the plant, from organizing supplies to setting production goals to making personnel policy. Now Daves and her mostly female management crew get lots of direction from the ranks but much less from above: The Levi policy manual has shrunk to 50 pages from 700. In the language of deep thinkers on leadership, controls are "conceptual," not procedural.

LEVI, which is rolling out leadership training and team management worldwide, cites in its support significant improvements in quality, manufacturing costs, and quick response to customers' requests for product. At the Blue Ridge plant, "seconds," or flawed jeans, have been reduced by a third, time between an order and shipment has fallen by ten days, and the time a pair of jeans spends in process at a plant has shrunk to one day from five.

Even so, says Daves, "sometimes it's real hard for me not to push back and say, 'You do this, you do that, and you do this.' Now I have to say, 'How do you want to do this?' I have to realize that their ideas may not be the way to go, but I have to let them learn that for themselves."

The man behind the change, CEO Robert Haas, is an ideal candidate for corporate post-hero. His ticket punches include a White House Fellowship and an MBA from Harvard, as well as tours in the Peace Corps and as a McKinsey consultant. He led a family-driven LBO of the company in 1985. Skeptics of his radical changes have been quieted by five straight years of record profits.

"What we're trying to do around here is syndicate leadership throughout the organization," he says, exuding the soothing calm of some Bay Area therapist. "In a command and control organization, people protect knowledge because it's their claim to dis-

> "Sometimes it's real hard for me not to push back and say, 'You do this, you do that, and you do this.' Now I have to say, 'How do you want to do this?' "

tinction. But we share as much information as we possibly can throughout the company. Business literacy is a big issue in developing leadership. You cannot ask people to exercise broader judgment if their world is bounded by very narrow vision."

For all the post-heroic inspiration to be found in the conversion of old industrial models like Levi, the most fascinating, radical examples of virtual leadership tend to appear at companies built from the start on fresh leadership ideas. Perhaps the most advanced, or extreme, among these is W.L. Gore & Associates of Newark, Delaware, famous for the Gore-Tex waterproof fabric

found in spacesuits and expensive outdoor catalogues. In fact, the late Wilbert L. "Bill" Gore, who founded the company in 1958 at age 45, would be one of two leading candidates—neck and neck with Herman Miller Chairman Max De Pree—to be the first inductee into the post-heroic hall of fame.

Before founding his company, Gore spent 17 years at Du Pont, where his last assignment as an R&D chemist was to find new commercial uses for Teflon. Fiddling around in his basement one night, he discovered a method for making computer ribbon cable insulation. After failing to persuade Du Pont to enter that business, he founded his company—in the same basement.

Bill Gore had a number of funny ideas, not least of which was letting almost a dozen of his company's first employees live in his house in lieu of wages. And like a number of executives back then, Gore became interested in Douglas McGregor's classic management book, *The Human Side of Enterprise*, which expounded Theory Y, very similar to what we now call empowerment. Gore founded his company on Theory Y, and it hasn't wavered since.

Why should it? In 31 straight years of profitability it has grown into an enterprise with 5,600 associates (never "employees"), 35 plants worldwide, and annual revenue just shy of a billion dollars. The company won't disclose its profit margins but notes that it has been able to finance its growth while maintaining a "very strong cash position." In addition to Gore-Tex and cable insulation, the company's other Teflon products include vascular grafting material for surgical repair, industrial filters, and—a recent offering—a no-stick dental floss called Glide.

Privately held W.L. Gore is built, unabashedly, on what it calls un-management. Forget hierarchy; this company has no organizational structure. No one holds titles, except, as required for incorporation purposes, the president and secretary-treasurer, who happen to be Bill Gore's son and widow (he died in 1986, hiking in Wyoming's Wind River range). Nobody gets hired until a company associate agrees to "sponsor" the person, which includes finding work for him or her.

This is how Gore operates. A "product specialist" takes responsibility for developing a product. As it progresses, he or she creates a team, recruiting members from here or there until the team might become a whole plant. By that point the team has broken up into multiple teams, or manufacturing cells. Each member, who can perform most manufacturing processes, commits to performing certain tasks. Each cell has a leader, who evolves from within that cell. The leader is not appointed but

achieves the position by assuming leadership, which must be approved in a consensus reached through discussion—not a vote. All this reflects several of Bill Gore's leadership homilies, such as "Leadership is a verb, not a noun," or "Leadership is defined by what you do, not who you are," or "Leaders are those whom others follow."

No plant has more than 200 associates because Bill Gore thought people work best together when they know one another. Compensation is determined by a committee, which relies heavily on the evaluations of other associates. There are no budgets.

All post-heroic companies have a common trait: a clearly stated, oft-repeated set of core values that guide everyone's decisions. Gore's values number four:
▶ Fairness. A dedication to maintaining it.
▶ Commitment. If you make one, you keep it. Everyone makes his or her own.
▶ Freedom. The company allows individuals the freedom to grow beyond what they're doing, and they are expected to use it.
▶ Water line. A hole above a ship's water line won't sink it, but one below it will. Certain decisions, say, building a new plant, demand consultation and agreement. Other decisions, say, launching a new product, don't. This value substitutes for budgets.

LIKE ANY SYSTEM, Gore's has its downside—decentralization causes communications problems, exporting the Gore culture overseas is difficult, and not all workers like it. "You have to take a lot of responsibility to work here, and not everybody is willing to do that," says Bert Chase, an associate. "This place is for people with bound wings who want to fly."

Other corporations may love to study W.L. Gore, but hardly anyone is predicting a proliferation of its system. "The hierarchical organization isn't going to disappear like our academic friends think," argues Walter Ulmer Jr., a retired U.S. Army general and CEO of the Center for Creative Leadership in Greensboro, North Carolina. "We shouldn't waste too much intellectual energy on organizational structures that are never going to come about. We should work instead on making hierarchical organizations more humane, more productive, and more responsive to society's demands."

Bill Gore might not have disagreed. Associates say he always preached that it would be impossible to convert an existing organization to his kind of system. The larger point is this: Gore was a leader who created an organization under which other people's leadership blossomed, and in turn it achieved its mission—"To make money and have fun."

Hierarchy isn't always the issue anyway. Increasingly, the crucial challenge facing the would-be post-heroic leader is less about how to structure a company than about how to get people who are truly not like you, or even each other, to pull in the same direction.

Dennis Longstreet, the 48-year-old president of Ortho Biotech, faced just such a challenge in 1986 when Johnson & Johnson asked him to head up the biotech pharmaceutical division of its Ortho Pharmaceutical subsidiary. Says he: "The first thing you learn is that you can't start a biotechnology company by hiring a bunch of white males from New Jersey. If you want the best people in the field, you're hiring people from universities and small biotech companies—women, Asians, African Americans, very few of whom have ever worked in a corporate environment."

Like other post-heroic leaders, Longstreet warns of the risks: "You take a chance that employees may lead you someplace you don't want to go."

Longstreet, a 24-year veteran of J&J, felt that to succeed in this fast-moving field—marketing products to replace blood transfusions or seven-day treatments for hairy-cell leukemia—he needed a company unlike any he had seen, one with intense teamwork, commitment, and flexibility. But in 1990, while spinning the company off into a separate subsidiary, he learned from meetings with employees that many felt hindered by barriers tied to their differences. So Ortho made managing diversity a top priority.

"People walk around with prejudices, and you have to get past them if you want to build an effective team," says Andrea Zintz, Ortho's human resources vice president. Ortho tries to do that through intense, organized communication. Longstreet, for example, meets regularly with a number of so-called affinity groups—African American men; gay, lesbian, and bisexual men and women; white men; secretaries; single people.

Horrified by the idea of bowing to pressure from that many constituencies? Not to worry, says Longstreet: "This isn't about designing a customized approach for every group and every issue. It's about listening to people—their problems and their aspirations. It's amazing

how unaware you can be of the impact you have on people different from you. It's very easy for people to start feeling excluded because of artificial barriers."

Once he committed to listening, of course, Longstreet realized he had to change everything about the way he managed. "You start asking them to describe their ideal productive workplace, and you give up a lot of control," he says. "I was used to standing up on a stage behind a podium with slides and rehearsed scripts and saying, 'This is our policy. Thank you. Goodbye.' Now everything is done in a town-meeting fashion, with them doing most of the talking and me doing the listening."

Like other post-heroic leaders, Longstreet warns of the risks involved. "When you start something like this, you give up a lot of ability to make firm, hard decisions, and you take a chance that employees may lead you someplace you don't want to go. But then you learn that most of them want the same things you want. Everyone wants to succeed." That seems to be the focus at Ortho. The company has increased sales 50% but head count just 15% in each of the past two years. Employee turnover is down about 8%.

WHAT WORKS for Dennis Longstreet might well create total havoc at your company. Levi has a long tradition of company values stronger than those on which most organizations can fall back, as well as the support of an enlightened family owner. And almost nobody out there has the guts of a Wilbert Gore— and probably shouldn't. But none of these disclaimers negates the importance of understanding what post-heroic leadership is all about.

It still requires many of the attributes that have always distinguished the best leaders—intelligence, commitment, energy, courage of conviction, integrity. But here's the big difference: It expects those qualities of just about everyone in the organization. The time when a few rational managers could run everything with rational numbers, it seems, was just an anomaly, or part of an era very different from the fast-paced, continually shifting present. Now we're back to the real, self-reliant, democratic stuff of the kind envisioned by Jefferson and his friends when they were trying to craft a new reality out of chaos and change. As in that era, those who cling to the past are in danger of losing their way, while the pioneers who forge ahead are most likely to claim the future.

Index

Credits/Acknowledgments

Cover design by Charles Vitelli

1. Self and Personality
Facing overview—Superstock.

2. Social Perception
Facing overview—George Olson/Woodfin Camp.

3. Attitudes
Facing overview—Courtesy of Rebecca Holland.

4. Social Cognition
Facing overview—© 1943, 1971 Harvard University Press.

5. Social Influence
Facing overview—United Nations photo by L. Barns.

6. Social Relationships
Facing overview—Courtesy of Marcuss Oslnder

7. Prejudice, Discrimination, and Stereotyping
Facing overview—New York Convention and Visitors Bureau.

8. Aggression
Facing overview—Courtesy of Elaine M. Ward

9. Helping
Facing overview—© Bob Daemmrich, Stock Boston.

10. Group Processes
Facing overview—Blair Seitz/Photo Researchers.

*PHOTOCOPY THIS PAGE!!!**

ANNUAL EDITIONS ARTICLE REVIEW FORM

■ NAME: _____ DATE: _____

■ TITLE AND NUMBER OF ARTICLE: _____

■ BRIEFLY STATE THE MAIN IDEA OF THIS ARTICLE: _____

_____

■ LIST THREE IMPORTANT FACTS THAT THE AUTHOR USES TO SUPPORT THE MAIN IDEA:

_____

_____

_____

_____

_____

■ WHAT INFORMATION OR IDEAS DISCUSSED IN THIS ARTICLE ARE ALSO DISCUSSED IN YOUR
TEXTBOOK OR OTHER READINGS THAT YOU HAVE DONE? LIST THE TEXTBOOK CHAPTERS AND
PAGE NUMBERS:

_____

_____

_____

_____

_____

■ LIST ANY EXAMPLES OF BIAS OR FAULTY REASONING THAT YOU FOUND IN THE ARTICLE:

_____

_____

_____

_____

■ LIST ANY NEW TERMS/CONCEPTS THAT WERE DISCUSSED IN THE ARTICLE, AND WRITE A SHORT
DEFINITION:

_____

_____

_____

_____

*Your instructor may require you to use this ANNUAL EDITIONS Article Review Form in any
number of ways: for articles that are assigned, for extra credit, as a tool to assist in developing
assigned papers, or simply for your own reference. Even if it is not required, we encourage
you to photocopy and use this page; you will find that reflecting on the articles will greatly
enhance the information from your text.

We Want Your Advice

ANNUAL EDITIONS revisions depend on two major opinion sources: one is our Advisory Board, listed in the front of this volume, which works with us in scanning the thousands of articles published in the public press each year; the other is you—the person actually using the book. Please help us and the users of the next edition by completing the prepaid article rating form on this page and returning it to us. Thank you for your help!

ANNUAL EDITIONS: SOCIAL PSYCHOLOGY 97/98
Article Rating Form

Here is an opportunity for you to have direct input into the next revision of this volume. We would like you to rate each of the 50 articles listed below, using the following scale:

1. **Excellent: should definitely be retained**
2. **Above average: should probably be retained**
3. **Below average: should probably be deleted**
4. **Poor: should definitely be deleted**

Rating	Article	Rating	Article
	1. Body Mania		27. Laughs: Rhythmic Bursts of Social Glue
	2. Race and the Schooling of Black Americans		28. Up from Gorilla Land: The Hidden Logic of Love and Lust
	3. Who Is Happy?		29. The Lessons of Love
	4. At Last, a Rejection Detector!		30. What Makes Love Last?
	5. Is Self-Esteem Really All That Important?		31. Prejudice Is a Habit That Can Be Broken
	6. The Decline and Fall of Personality		32. Breaking the Prejudice Habit
	7. Are You Shy?		33. Psychologists Examine Attacks on Homosexuals
	8. Spotting Lies: Can Humans Learn to Do Better?		34. Crimes against Humanity
	9. The EQ Factor		35. Whites' Myths about Blacks
	10. EQ: What's Your Emotional Intelligence Quotient?		36. Gendered Media: The Influence of Media on Views of Gender
	11. Inferential Hopscotch: How People Draw Social Inferences from Behavior		37. The Biology of Violence
	12. Motivational Approaches to Expectancy Confirmation		38. A Violence in the Blood
	13. Attitude Affects Memory, Decisions, and Performance		39. Big. Bad. Bully.
	14. How Do You Persuade If Everyone Knows You Are Untrustworthy, Unbelievable, and Disliked?		40. In an Angry World, Lessons for Emotional Self-Control
	15. What's in a Brand?		41. Televised Violence and Kids: A Public Health Problem?
	16. Mindless Propaganda, Thoughtful Persuasion		42. Frankenstein Must Be Destroyed: Chasing the Monster of TV Violence
	17. Forbidden Thinking		43. The Roots of Good and Evil
	18. Road to Reward Is Rutted with Psychological Peril		44. Volunteerism and Society's Response to the HIV Epidemic
	19. Mindfulness and Mindlessness		45. Getting By with a Little Help from Some Friends
	20. Influences from the Mind's Inner Layers		46. Mobilization and Deterioration of Social Support Following Natural Disasters
	21. In Japan, Blood Type Can Be Key to Success—or Failure		47. Group Decision Fiascoes Continue: Space Shuttle Challenger and a Revised Groupthink Framework
	22. Making Sense of the Nonsensical: An Analysis of Jonestown		48. Blowup
	23. The Committed Heart		49. '90s Style Brainstorming
	24. What Is the Influence of One Flower Given?		50. The New Post-Heroic Leadership
	25. Suspect Confessions		
	26. A Nation of Hermits: The Loss of Community		

(Continued on next page)

ABOUT YOU

Name _____ Date _____
Are you a teacher? ❑ Or a student? ❑
Your school name _____
Department _____
Address _____
City _____ State _____ Zip _____
School telephone # _____

YOUR COMMENTS ARE IMPORTANT TO US!

Please fill in the following information:
For which course did you use this book? _____
Did you use a text with this *ANNUAL EDITION*? ❑ yes ❑ no
What was the title of the text? _____
What are your general reactions to the *Annual Editions* concept?

Have you read any particular articles recently that you think should be included in the next edition?

Are there any articles you feel should be replaced in the next edition? Why?

Are there other areas that you feel would utilize an ANNUAL EDITION?

May we contact you for editorial input?

May we quote you from above?

ANNUAL EDITIONS: SOCIAL PSYCHOLOGY 97/98

BUSINESS REPLY MAIL

First Class   Permit No. 84   Guilford, CT

Postage will be paid by addressee

Dushkin Publishing Group/
Brown & Benchmark Publishers
Sluice Dock
Guilford, Connecticut 06437

No Postage
Necessary
if Mailed
in the
United States